ASHGATE
**RESEARCH**
COMPANION

# THE ASHGATE RESEARCH COMPANION TO SECESSION

*Secessionist movements – often referred to by euphemisms such as "wars of national liberation", "remedial" responses to massive human rights violations, "unique" situations, or simply "dissolutions" of existing states – continue to disrupt the stability of the international order. This volume helps us to engage in an honest and necessary debate about ways of changing current borders, since demands for such changes will inevitably continue.*
Hurst Hannum, Tufts University, USA

*From Scotland to Puntland, and from South Ossetia to South Sudan, secession raises fundamental questions for national states and the international community. This uniquely comprehensive survey of current arguments and pressing prospects by political scientists, international lawyers, historians and political philosophers marks a major advance in an increasingly sophisticated field and will be the starting-point for future research.*
David Armitage, Harvard University, USA

ASHGATE
**RESEARCH**
COMPANION

The *Ashgate Research Companions* are designed to offer scholars and graduate students a comprehensive and authoritative state-of-the-art review of current research in a particular area. The companions' editors bring together a team of respected and experienced experts to write chapters on the key issues in their speciality, providing a comprehensive reference to the field.

Other Research Companions available in Politics and International Relations:

*The Ashgate Research Companion to Regionalisms*
Edited by Timothy M. Shaw, J. Andrew Grant and Scarlett Cornelissen
ISBN 978-0-7546-7762-8

*The Ashgate Research Companion to Non-State Actors*
Edited by Bob Reinalda
ISBN 978-0-7546-7906-6

*The Ashgate Research Companion to New Public Management*
Edited by Tom Christensen and Per Lægreid
ISBN 978-0-7546-7806-9

*The Ashgate Research Companion to Modern Warfare*
Edited by George Kassimeris and John Buckley
ISBN 978-0-7546-7410-8

*The Ashgate Research Companion to US Foreign Policy*
Edited by Robert J. Pauly, Jr.
ISBN 978-0-7546-4862-8

*The Ashgate Research Companion to Political Leadership*
Edited by Joseph Masciulli, Mikhail A. Molchanov and W. Andy Knight
ISBN 978-0-7546-7182-4

*The Ashgate Research Companion to Ethics and International Relations*
Edited by Patrick Hayden
ISBN 978-0-7546-7101-5

# The Ashgate Research Companion to Secession

*Edited by*
ALEKSANDAR PAVKOVIĆ
*Macquarie University, Australia and University of Macau, China*

PETER RADAN
*Macquarie University, Australia*

**ASHGATE**

© Aleksandar Pavković and Peter Radan 2011

All rights reserved. No part of this publication may be reproduced, stored in a retrieval system or transmitted in any form or by any means, electronic, mechanical, photocopying, recording or otherwise without the prior permission of the publisher.

Aleksandar Pavković and Peter Radan have asserted their right under the Copyright, Designs and Patents Act, 1988, to be identified as the editors of this work.

Published by
Ashgate Publishing Limited
Wey Court East
Union Road
Farnham
Surrey GU9 7PT
England

Ashgate Publishing Company
Suite 420
101 Cherry Street
Burlington,
VT 05401-4405
USA

www.ashgate.com

**British Library Cataloguing in Publication Data**
The Ashgate research companion to secession.
 1. Secession. 2. Secession--Case studies.
 3. Self-determination, National. 4. Self-determination,
 National--Case studies. 5. Separatist movements--History.
 6. Newly independent states--Foreign relations.
 7. Recognition (International law)
 I. Research companion to secession II. Pavković,
 Aleksandar. III. Radan, Peter.
 341.2'6-dc22

**Library of Congress Cataloging-in-Publication Data**
The Ashgate research companion to secession / [edited by] by Aleksandar Pavković and Peter Radan.
   p. cm.
  Includes bibliographical references and index.
  ISBN 978-0-7546-7702-4 (hardback) -- ISBN 978-0-7546-9403-8 (ebk.)
  1. Secession. 2. Separatist movements. 3. Self-determination, National. 4. Secession--History. 5. Separatist movements--History. 6. Self-determination, National--History. I. Pavković, Aleksandar. II. Radan, Peter.
  JC327.A76 2011
  321.09--dc23

2011021392

ISBN 9780754677024 (hbk)
ISBN 9780754694038 (ebk)

Printed and bound in Great Britain by
MPG Books Group, UK

# Contents

| | |
|---|---:|
| List of Figures | *xi* |
| List of Tables | *xiii* |
| Notes on Contributors | *xv* |
| Preface | *xxiii* |

Introduction: What Is Secession?     1
*Aleksandar Pavković and Peter Radan*

## PART I: INTRODUCTION TO SECESSION

1    Secession and International Order     11
     *James Mayall*

2    The History of Secession: An Overview     23
     *Bridget L. Coggins*

3    Explaining Secession     45
     *David S. Siroky*

4    Changing Borders by Secession: Normative Assessment of
     Territorial Claims     81
     *Frank Dietrich*

## PART II: SECESSIONS: PAST AND PRESENT

Introduction to Part II     99

5    An Attempt at Secession from an Early Nation-State:
     The Confederate States of America     103
     *Don H. Doyle*

| 6 | The UN Principle of Self-Determination and Secession from Decolonized States: Katanga and Biafra<br>*Joshua Castellino* | 117 |
|---|---|---|
| 7 | Constitutional Politics of Secession: Travelling from Quebec to Montenegro (and back?)<br>*Zoran Oklopčić* | 131 |
| 8 | Secession as a Way of Dissolving Federations: The USSR and Yugoslavia<br>*Richard Sakwa and Aleksandar Pavković* | 147 |
| 9 | Kosovo: Secession under UN Supervision<br>*Keiichi Kubo* | 171 |

## PART III: SECESSION IN CONTEXT

| | Introduction to Part III | 187 |
|---|---|---|
| 10 | Secession from an Economic Perspective: What Is Living and What Is Dead in Economic Interpretations of Secessionism?<br>*Lloyd Cox* | 191 |
| 11 | Secession and Ethnic Conflict<br>*Keiichi Kubo* | 207 |
| 12 | Secession and Political Violence<br>*Siniša Malešević and Niall Ó Dochartaigh* | 227 |
| 13 | International Involvement in Secessionist Conflict: From the 16th Century to the Present<br>*Mikulas Fabry* | 251 |
| 14 | The International Relations of Secession<br>*Stephen M. Saideman* | 267 |
| 15 | Secession and Contested States<br>*Deon Geldenhuys* | 285 |

## PART IV: SECESSION: LEGAL PERSPECTIVES

Introduction to Part IV                                                                 301

16    Secession and Territorial Borders: The Role of Law                                303
      Märta C. Johanson

17    International Law and the Right of Unilateral Secession                            321
      Peter Radan

18    Secession in Constitutional Law                                                    333
      Peter Radan

19    To Constitutionalize or Not? Secession as *Materiae Constitutionis*                345
      Miodrag A. Jovanović

20    Secession and State Succession                                                     365
      Tom Grant

## PART V: SECESSION: NORMATIVE APPROACHES

Introduction to Part V                                                                   381

21    Internal Self-Determination and Secession                                          385
      Michel Seymour

22    Remedial Theories of Secession                                                     399
      Reinold Schmücker

23    Choice Theories of Secession                                                       413
      David D. Speetzen and Christopher Heath Wellman

24    Secession and Domination                                                           427
      John McGarry and Margaret Moore

25    The Right to Secede: Do We Really Need It?                                         439
      Aleksandar Pavković

## PART VI: SECESSIONS AND SECESSIONIST MOVEMENTS IN THE WORLD

Introduction to Part VI     455

### ASIA

Case Study 1:    Aceh: The Secession That Never Was     459
*Edward Aspinall*

Case Study 2:    Bangladesh: Secession Aided by Military Intervention     463
*Peter Radan*

Case Study 3:    Kashmir: Separatism as Possible Trigger for Inter-State Conflict?     467
*Matthew J. Webb*

Case Study 4:    Separatism in Mindanao     471
*Damien Kingsbury*

Case Study 5:    Myanmar/Burma: Secession and the Ethnic Conundrum     475
*Renaud Egreteau*

Case Study 6:    Singapore: Expulsion or Negotiated Secession?     479
*Bill K.P. Chou*

Case Study 7:    Taiwan–China: A Case of Secession or a Divided Nation?     483
*Jean-Pierre Cabestan*

Case Study 8:    Tibet: Secession Based on the Collapse of an Imperial Overlord     487
*Robbie Barnett*

Case Study 9:    West Papua: Secessionism and/or Failed Decolonization?     491
*Damien Kingsbury*

### AFRICA

Case Study 10:    Eritrea: A Belated Post-Colonial Secession     497
*Kathryn Sturman*

Case Study 11:    Somaliland: An Escape from Endemic Violence     501
*Kathryn Sturman*

Case Study 12: Southern Sudan's Secession from the North 505
*Petrus de Kock*

# EUROPE

Case Study 13: Basque Secessionism: From Bullets to Ballots? 511
*Marc Sanjaume i Calvet*

Case Study 14: Peaceful Secessions: Norway, Iceland and Slovakia 515
*Aleksandar Pavković*

Case Study 15: Scotland's Independence 519
*Michael Keating*

Case Study 16: The Serb Krajina: An Unsuccessful Secession from Croatia 523
*Peter Radan*

# REST OF THE WORLD

Case Study 17: Abhkazia, South Ossetia and Transdniestria:
Secessions in the Post-Soviet Space 529
*Mikhail Ilyin*

Case Study 18: Chechnya: A Military Suppression of a Secession at a Cost 535
*Kristin M. Bakke*

Case Study 19: Kurdistan: A Suspended Secession from Iraq 539
*Peter Sluglett*

Case Study 20: Yemen: The Resurgent Secessionism in the South 543
*Iain Walker*

Index 547

# List of Figures

| | | |
|---|---|---|
| 2.1 | System members (1816–2008) | 27 |
| 2.2 | New states (1816–2008) | 28 |
| 2.3 | Secessionist movements (1931–2002) | 29 |
| 2.4 | Annual success rates (1931–2002) | 31 |
| 2.5 | Violent and non-violent secession (1931–2002) | 36 |
| 2.6 | Annual separatist violence (1946–2008) | 37 |

# List of Tables

| | | |
|---|---|---|
| 9.1 | Kosovo population by ethnic composition, 1921–2006 | 173 |
| 11.1 | Distribution of civil war onsets according to the two distinctions | 211 |
| 14.1 | Rare events logit analyses of the international relations of ethnic conflict | 274 |
| 14.2 | Relative impact of each independent variable | 276 |

# Notes on Contributors

Information about the contributors of the case studies in Part VI is found at the end of each study. The following are the contributors of chapters in Parts I–V.

**Joshua Castellino** is Professor of Law and Head of the Law Department at Middlesex University, London, UK and Adjunct Professor of Law at the Irish Centre for Human Rights at the National University of Ireland, Galway. He has been involved in programmes such as the *EU-China Diplomatic and Experts Dialogue*, and the *Programme of Support for Arab Lawyers*, and has engaged human rights and minority rights questions in a host of countries across the world. His scholarly work has focused on questions concerning self-determination, title to territory and indigenous and minority rights. His current research focuses on minority rights questions in the Middle East.

**Bridget L. Coggins** is Assistant Professor of Government at Dartmouth College. Her research lies at the intersection of domestic politics and international security. She has two book projects underway. The first, *States of Uncertainty*, examines global patterns of secessionism, the politics of recognition and the birth of new states. The second explores the external security consequences of internal weakness and state failure. Professor Coggins's work has appeared or is forthcoming in *International Organization*, *Foreign Policy*, and *Oxford Bibliographies Online*.

**Lloyd Cox** is a Lecturer in Politics and International Relations at Macquarie University, Sydney, Australia. His PhD research examined the relationship between nationalism and accelerated globalization, and he has since written widely on these themes. Some recent publications include: 'The Value of Australian Values?' in M. Mollering and C. Slade (eds), *From Migrant to Citizen: Testing Language, Testing Culture* (Houndmills, Basingstoke: Palgrave, 2010), pp. 77–98; 'Revisiting the Labor Question in the United States', *Thesis Eleven* 100 (February 2010), pp. 168–78; 'Globalization, Nationalism, and Changed "Conditions of Possibility" for Secessionist Mobilization', in A. Pavkovic and P. Radan (eds), *On the Way to Statehood* (Aldershot: Ashgate, 2008), pp. 33–50. He teaches undergraduate and post-graduate units on nationalism and Australian and American politics.

**Frank Dietrich** is Lecturer for Practical Philosophy at the University of Bielefeld Germany. His main areas of interest are political philosophy, philosophy of law, moral philosophy and medical ethics. He is the author of the *Dimensionen der Verteilungsgerechtigkeit* (Stuttgart: Lucius & Lucius, 2001), which deals with distributive justice, and of the *Sezession und Demokratie* (Berlin: deGruyter, 2010) which discusses the justification of secession of democratic states. With H. Kliemt and M. Imhoff he has edited two volumes on the rationing of health care: *Mikroallokation medizinischer Ressourcen* and *Standardisierung in der Medizin: Qualitätssicherung oder Rationierung?* (Stuttgart: Schattauer 2003 and 2004). His articles on political self-determination, nationalism, group rights and global justice have appeared in German and international journals. Most recent among them is 'The Status of Kosovo: Reflections on the Legitimacy of Secession', *Ethics and Global Politics* (February 2010).

**Don H. Doyle** is McCausland Professor of History at the University of South Carolina, USA and director of ARENA, the Association for Research on Ethnicity and Nationalism in the Americas, a network of scholars that sponsors collaborative work on nationalism. Among the books he has edited are: *Nationalism in the New World* (2006) (with Marco Pamplona), a collection of essays aimed at 'Americanizing the conversation on nationalism'; *Secession as an International Phenomenon: From America's Civil War to Contemporary Separatist Movements* (2010), which includes essays on the history and theory of secession; and *The South as an American Problem* (1995) (with Larry Griffin). He is the author of *Nations Divided: America, Italy, and the Southern Question* (2002), and several other books and essays dealing with the history of the United States and the American South. In 2010 he was the Public Policy Scholar at the Woodrow Wilson International Center for Scholars.

**Mikulas Fabry** is an Assistant Professor in the Sam Nunn School of International Affairs at the Georgia Institute of Technology and during the academic year 2011–12 a Fellow at the Woodrow Wilson Center for International Scholars. His research and teaching interests revolve around moral and legal dimensions of world politics, especially those pertaining to sovereignty, self-determination, democracy and territory. His research has focused mainly on questions of state and governmental legitimacy in international relations. He is the author of *Recognizing States: International Society and the Establishment of New States since 1776* (Oxford University Press, 2010). He has also published several chapters in edited volumes and articles in the journals *Millennium: Journal of International Studies*, *Diplomacy and Statecraft*, *Global Society* and *Nationalities Papers*. He is currently exploring the idea and historical practice of the norm of territorial integrity in international relations.

**Deon Geldenhuys** is attached to the Department of Politics at the University of Johannesburg, South Africa. He teaches International Relations and his research interests focus on non-conformist behaviour in international politics. His most recent books are *Contested States in World Politics* (2009) and *Deviant Conduct in World Politics* (2004).

NOTES ON CONTRIBUTORS

**Tom Grant** is a Fellow of Wolfson College, University of Cambridge, and a Research Fellow of the Lauterpacht Centre for International Law. His research interests include state immunity, treaty interpretation, international organizations, self-determination, and international dispute settlement. His books include *Admission to the United Nations* (Martinus Nijhoff, 2009) and *Recognition of States* (Praeger, 1999). He is co-founder and an associate editor of the *Journal of International Dispute Settlement* (Oxford University Press/University of Geneva) and a contributing writer in the *Max-Planck Encyclopedia of Public International Law*.

**Märta C. Johanson** is Senior Lecturer in International Law at the University of Örebro in Sweden. Her publications dealing with the area of territory and borders include *Self-determination and Borders: The Duty to Show Consideration for the Interests of Others* (Åbo: Åbo Akademi University, 2004) and 'Kosovo: Boundaries and the Liberal Dilemma', *Nordic Journal of International Law* 73 (2004). After working first in university administration and later on in human rights work abroad, she returned to legal research at the Örebro law department in 2008 and is presently engaged in a three-year project on human trafficking in Sweden and Europe.

**Miodrag A. Jovanović** is an Associate Professor of Jurisprudence at the Faculty of Law, University of Beograd, Serbia. He has research interests in the political theory of multiculturalism, federalism, the legal theory of collective rights, as well as in the problems of the European identity and the political and legal structure of the EU. He has published more than 40 articles on legal theory and political philosophy in Serbian scholarly journals as well as many articles in international journals and edited volumes. His books in English include *Constitutionalizing Secession in Federalized States: A Procedural Approach* (Utrecht: Eleven, 2007); (with Slobodan Samardzic), *Federalism and Decentralisation in Eastern Europe: Between Transition and Secession* (Zurich and Vienna: Institut du Fédéralisme, Fribourg/LIT Verlag, 2007). He has edited two books in English: with Kristin Henrard, *Sovereignty and Diversity* (Utrecht: Eleven, 2008) and with Ivana Krstic, *Human Rights Today: 60 Years of the Universal Declaration* (Utrecht: Eleven, 2010). His *Collective Rights: A Legal Theory* (Cambridge University Press) is due to appear in 2011.

**Keiichi Kubo** is an Associate Professor at the Department of Political Science and Economics, Waseda University, Tokyo, Japan. His research interests include ethnic conflict, post-conflict peace-building, post-communist democratization and emerging party system, with particular emphasis on the ex-Yugoslav region. He is the author of *The State Torn Apart: Democratization and Ethnic Problems in the Former Yugoslavia* (Tokyo: Yushindo-Kobunsya, 2003), written in Japanese. Among his recent publications are: 'Why Kosovar Albanians Took Up Arms Against the Serbian Regime: The Genesis and Expansion of the UÇK in Kosovo', *Europe-Asia Studies* 62:7 (2010); 'Elections and Government Changes in Slavic Eurasia', *Japanese Journal of Electoral Studies* 25:2 (2009) in Japanese; 'The Issue of Independence and Ethnic Identity in Montenegro', *Southeastern Europe* 31–2 (2007); 'The Radicalisation and Ethnicization of Elections: The 1990 Local Elections and the Ethnic Conflict in Croatia', *Ethnopolitics* 6:1 (2007).

**Siniša Malešević** is a Member of the Royal Irish Academy, Co-Director of the Centre for the Study of Nationalism and Organised Violence and Senior Lecturer in the School of Political Science and Sociology at the National University of Ireland, Galway. His research interests include comparative-historical and theoretical study of ethnicity and nationalism, ideology, war, violence as well as sociological theory. He has authored over 50 journal articles and book chapters and his work has appeared in the following international journals: *Ethnic and Racial Studies, Nations and Nationalism, European Journal of Social Theory, Critical Sociology, Government and Opposition, Nationalism and Ethnic Politics, International Political Sociology, Journal of Language and Politics, East European Quarterly, Journal of Power, Development in Practice* and *Europa Ethnica*. His recent books include *The Sociology of War and Violence* (Cambridge University Press, 2010), *Identity as Ideology: Understanding Ethnicity and Nationalism* (Palgrave, 2006), *The Sociology of Ethnicity* (Sage, 2004), *Ideology, Legitimacy and the New State* (Routledge, 2002; reprinted in 2008) and co-edited volumes *Ernest Gellner and Contemporary Social Thought* (Cambridge University Press, 2007), *Making Sense of Collectivity: Ethnicity, Nationalism and Globalisation* (Pluto Press, 2002) and *Ideology after Poststructuralism* (Pluto Press, 2002).

**James Mayall** is Emeritus Sir Patrick Sheehy Professor of International Relations and Fellow of Sidney Sussex College University of Cambridge, a Fellow of the British Academy and Academic Advisor to the Royal College of Defence Studies, London. His research interests include international theory, the impact of nationalism on international relations and humanitarian and other forms of intervention since the end of the Cold War. His publications include *Nationalism and International Society* (Cambridge University Press, 1990; Chinese edition, 2010), *World Politics: Progress and Its Limits* (Polity Press, 2000; Japanese edition with a new Introduction, 2009). He is the editor of *The Contemporary Commonwealth: An Assessment 1965–2009* (Routledge, 2009) and a co-editor with Ricardo Soares de Oliveira of *The New Protectorates: International Tutelage and the Making of Liberal States* (Hurst and Columbia University Press, 2011).

**John McGarry** is Professor and Canada Research Chair in Nationalism and Democracy in the Department of Political Studies at Queen's University (Kingston, Ontario), and a Fellow of the Royal Society of Canada. He has edited, co-edited and co-authored 11 books on ethnic conflict, nationalism and the politics of Northern Ireland, the latest of which are *European Integration and the Nationalities Question* (Routledge, 2006); *The Future of Kurdistan in Iraq* (University of Pennsylvania Press, 2005); and *The Northern Ireland Conflict: Consociational Engagements* (Oxford University Press, 2004). He is a member of the editorial board of *Ethnopolitics*, the *Journal of Conflict Studies, Irish Political Studies*, the *Journal on Ethnopolitics and Minority Issues in Europe (JEMIE)*, and *Peace and Conflict Studies*, and a member of the advisory board of the European Centre for Minority Issues. During 2008–09, he served as Senior Advisor on Power-Sharing to the United Nations (Mediation Support Unit).

**Margaret Moore** is Sir Edward Peacock Professor of Political Theory in the Political Studies department at Queen's University (Kingston, Canada). She has published a number of books and articles on issues of distributive justice, democratic theory, nationalism and multiculturalism. Most notable are *Foundations of Liberalism* and *Ethics of Nationalism*, both published by Oxford University Press, as well as two edited collections and numerous journal articles. She is currently working on issues of global justice and territorial right, that is, what is the basis for rights to territory/land and how the answer to this question fits in with a general theory of global justice.

**Niall Ó Dochartaigh** is College Lecturer at the School of Political Science and Sociology, National University of Ireland, Galway. His research is focused on the politics of conflict in Northern Ireland, conflict and new technologies and conflict and territory. He is the author of *Civil Rights to Armalites: Derry and the Birth of the Irish troubles* (Cork University Press, 1997; 2nd edn Palgrave, 2005) and two books on internet research (Sage, 2001; Sage, 2007). He has published in *Political Geography*, *Mobilization*, *Irish Political Studies* and *Identities*. Among his recent publications are 'Bloody Sunday: Error or Design?', *Contemporary British History* 24:1 (2010); 'Nation and Neighbourhood: Nationalist Mobilisation and Local Solidarities in the North of Ireland', in A. Guelke (ed.), *The Challenges of Ethno-nationalism* (Palgrave, 2010); 'Reframing Online: Ulster Loyalists Imagine an American Audience', *Identities: Global Studies in Culture and Power* 16:1 (2009).

**Zoran Oklopčić** is an Assistant Professor at the Department of Law, Carleton University, Canada. Previously he taught constitutional law at the University of Zagreb, Croatia. His current research focuses on the normative lenses used to justify state formation: self-determination of peoples in international law, constituent power and popular sovereignty in theory of constitutional law. Recently, he has written about the metamorphosis of self-determination in the post-Cold War context, the concept of territorial rights in the context of theories of secession, and the inadequacy of the concept of *pouvoir constituant* as means to justify the creation of new constitutional orders in non-First World countries. His recent publications include 'Constitutional (Re)Vision: Sovereign Peoples, New Constituent Powers, and the Formation of Constitutional Orders in the Balkans', *Constellations* (forthcoming); '*Populus Interruptus*: Self-Determination, Independence of Kosovo and the Vocabulary of Peoplehood', *Leiden Journal of International Law* 22:4 (2009).

**Aleksandar Pavković** is an Associate Professor of Politics at Macquarie University, Sydney, Australia and University of Macau, Macau, China. Previously he taught philosophy at the University of Beograd in Serbia. He is interested in theory and practice of secession as well as in political utopias such as that of the world state. His publications in English include: *Slobodan Jovanović: An Unsentimental Approach* to *Politics* (Boulder, CO: East European Monographs, 1993), *The Fragmentation of Yugoslavia: Nationalism and War in the Balkans* (London: Palgrave, 2nd edn 2000), *Creating New States: Theory and Practice of Secession* (with Peter Radan) (Aldershot: Ashgate, 2007). He is the editor of several volumes, including *Nationalism and Postcommunism* (with H. Koscharsky and A. Czarnota) (Aldershot: Dartmouth, 1995) and *On the Way to Statehood: Secession and Globalisation* (with Peter Radan) (Aldershot: Ashgate, 2008).

**Peter Radan** is a Professor in Law at Macquarie Law School at Macquarie University. Apart from the areas of self-determination and secession, his research includes the fields of contracts, law and religion, equity, and property. His publications include *The Break-up of Yugoslavia and International Law* (London: Routledge, 2002) and *Creating New States: Theory and Practice of Secession* (with Aleksandar Pavković) (Aldershot: Ashgate 2007). He has also edited *Law and Religion: God, the State and the Common Law* (with Denise Meyerson and Rosalind F. Croucher) (London: Routledge, 2005) and *On the Way to Statehood: Secession and Globalisation* (with Aleksandar Pavković) (Aldershot: Ashgate, 2008).

**Stephen M. Saideman** is Canada Research Chair in International Security and Ethnic Conflict, based in the Department of Political Science at McGill University. In 2001–02 Professor Saideman worked on the US Joint Staff working in the Strategic Planning and Policy Directorate in the Central and East European Division as part of a Council on Foreign Relations International Affairs Fellowship. Currently he is trying to understand the challenges of multilateral warfare and how different countries run their military operations in Afghanistan while also continuing his work on the international relations of ethnic conflict by focusing on the dynamics of diasporas. In addition to his books, *The Ties That Divide: Ethnic Politics, Foreign Policy and International Conflict* and *For Kin or Country: Xenophobia, Nationalism and War* (with R. William Ayres), he has co-edited *Intra-State Conflict, Governments and Security: Dilemmas of Deterrence and Assurance* and published articles on the international relations and comparative politics of ethnic conflict in *International Organization, International Studies Quarterly, Comparative Political Studies, Journal of Peace Research, Security Studies* and other journals.

**Richard Sakwa** is Professor of Russian and European Politics at the University of Kent at Canterbury and an Associate Fellow of the Russia and Eurasia Programme at the Royal Institute of International Affairs, Chatham House. He held lectureships at the Universities of Essex and California, Santa Cruz, before joining the University of Kent in 1987. He has published widely on Soviet, Russian and post-communist affairs. Books include: *Postcommunism* (Buckingham: Open University Press, 1999), *Contextualising Secession: Normative Aspects of Secession Struggles* (Oxford University Press, 2003), co-edited with Bruno Coppieters; the edited volume *Chechnya: From Past to Future* (London: Anthem Press; Sterling, VA: Stylus Publishers, 2005); *Russian Politics and Society* (London and New York: Routledge, 4th edn 2008), and *Putin: Russia's Choice* (Routledge, 2nd edn 2008). His recently published books are

*The Quality of Freedom: Khodorkovsky, Putin and the Yukos Affair* (Oxford University Press, 2009) and *Communism in Russia: An Interpretative Essay* (Palgrave Macmillan, 2010), *The Crisis of Russian Democracy: The Dual State, Factionalism and the Medvedev Succession* (Cambridge University Press, 2011).

**Reinold Schmücker** is a Professor of Philosophy at the Westfälische Wilhelms-Universität (WWU) Münster, Germany. He is a member of the Centre for Advanced Study in Bioethics in Münster focusing especially on ethical problems of incidental findings in bio-imaging and is currently working on a book on the ethics of international relations. He is the author of *Was ist Kunst? Eine Grundlegung* (Munich, 1998), which discusses the foundations of the philosophy of art, and has edited three volumes of the 'Hamburg Edition' of the works of Ernst Cassirer. He has also (co-)edited several books and published articles on a wide range of topics from the field of aesthetics and the philosophy of art to ethics and political philosophy.

**Michel Seymour** is full Professor of Philosophy at the University of Montreal. He teaches contemporary Anglo-American philosophy with a particular interest in philosophy of language and political philosophy. Among his books are *De la tolérance à la reconnaissance. Une théorie libérale des droits collectifs* (Boréal, 2008), *L'institution du langage* (Les Presses de l'Université de Montréal, 2005), *Le Pari de la démesure* (L'Hexagone, 2001). Among the books he has edited are: *The Plural States of Recognition* (Palgrave Macmillan, 2010) and *The Fate of the Nation-state* (McGill-Queen's, 2004). He also co-edited with Mathias Fritsch *Reason and Emancipation: Essays on the Philosophy of Kai Nielsen* (Humanities Books, 2007) and with Jocelyne Couture and Kai Nielsen, *Rethinking Nationalism*, Supplementary Volume XXII of the *Canadian Journal of Philosophy* (University of Calgary Press, 1996). His articles have been published in many international journals, including the *Journal of Philosophy*, *Philosophical Studies*, the *Canadian Journal of Philosophy*, *Dialectica*, *Nation and Nationalism*, and *The Monist*.

**David Siroky** is Assistant Professor of Political Science at Arizona State University (ASU). Previously he was a Henry Hart Rice Fellow at Yale University. His research interests include ethnic conflict processes, civil war dynamics, secessionist and irredentist insurgencies, and the interdependence of subnational and interstate conflict. He is also broadly interested in developments in methodology and formal theory. His work on statistical modelling has been published in *Statistics Surveys* (2009), and his work on state formation, nationalism and violent conflict recently appeared in the *Yale Journal of International Affairs* (2010). He is currently working on a book entitled *Secession and Survival: Nations, States and Violence*, which offers a theoretically rich, empirically rigorous and comparative treatment of violent secessionist conflict in the modern world. He has served as a consultant to the World Bank, the International Peace Institute and the International Rescue Committee. He has also written for *Kyiv Post* (Ukraine), *Gazeta Panorama* (Albania), *The Economist*,

*The Boston Globe* and the *News & Observer*. Additional information, including links to publications, is available online: http://sites.google.com/site/davidsiroky/.

**David Speetzen** recently received his PhD from Washington University in St. Louis, and is currently a Visiting Instructor there. His research focuses on international political theory, especially issues surrounding human rights, democracy, political self-determination and just war theory. His dissertation concerns the ethics of democratic regime change, and the moral and legal norms surrounding armed intervention, military occupation and political reconstruction.

**Christopher Heath Wellman** is Professor of Philosophy at Washington University in St. Louis and Professorial Fellow at the Centre for Public Philosophy and Ethics at Charles Sturt University in Canberra, Australia. He works in ethics, specializing in political and legal philosophy. He is the author of *A Theory of Secession: The Case for Political Self-Determination* (Cambridge University Press, 2005).

ASHGATE
**RESEARCH**
COMPANION

# Preface

Secession has been a subject of study of law and legal theory and to some extent in international relations for some time. Only in the past few decades did it become a separate subject of study of social science, applied ethics and political theory. As a result there have been very few attempts to approach secession from a multi-disciplinary point of view, combining a variety of scholarly disciplines that deal with this subject. This is one of such rare attempts. The Companion comprises chapters in social sciences, history, international relations, law and ethics/political theory – all of them dealing with secession or attempts at secession. It also contains a large number of short chapters outlining case studies of particular secessions and secessionist movements as well as a small number of detailed analyses of such cases. Our aim was to acquaint the reader with a variety of scholarly approaches to secession as well as a variety of present and past attempts at secession and secessionist movements.

Unfortunately, we were not in a position to offer a comprehensive account of all recent attempts at secession or secessionist movements. For example, the Companion has no study of the Tamil Tiger attempt to secede Tamil areas from Sri Lanka or of secessionist/irredentist movements in Xingjian province in China. Moreover, the Companion fails to explore in sufficient detail a very important aspect of secessionism: nationalist ideologies that provide both the mobilizational framework for most secessionist movements as well as ideological justification for their attempt to create a state of their own. We wanted to have a separate chapter exploring the role of nationalism and national ideologies but could not find a contributor who could undertake the task. Several social science theories of secession would have needed more detailed accounts as well. Finally, we hoped to include a world map which would locate the states and regions discussed in the Companion; this however proved technically impossible. Some of these deficiencies we can hope to remove in future – if any – editions of the Companion.

The Companion grew out of the work we did for our monograph *Creating New States: Theory and Practice of Secession* (Ashgate, 2007) and the collection of contributions which we edited in *On the Way to Statehood: Secession and Globalization* (Ashgate, 2008). Following the publication of these two, Ashgate commissioned us to prepare this Companion. We are grateful for the challenge that this task presented to us.

The Companion was initially prepared by both editors but once in 2009 we found that several contributors could not deliver their contributions, Aleksandar

Pavković took over the task of finding substitute contributors and of editing the final version of this volume.

We would like to thank all our colleagues who have contributed these chapters and who have also provided us with valuable advice and comments.

A major part of the editorial work was done while Aleksandar Pavković was working in the Faculty of Social Science and Humanities at the University of Macau, China. He would like to thank Quin Leong and his colleagues and students there for their friendship and support.

Aleksandar Pavković and Peter Radan,<br>Sydney

# Introduction:
# What Is Secession?

## Aleksandar Pavković and Peter Radan

Secession, like many other political phenomena, has been visiting us, via television and internet, in our homes. Thanks to television, we witnessed, in 1990–91, the secession of Lithuania, in 1991 the secession of Croatia and Slovenia, in 1992 the secession of Bosnia and Herzegovina and in 1999–2000 the secession of East Timor as well as many other attempts at secession (such as those of the Tamil Tigers in Sri Lanka). More accurately, through television broadcasts we witnessed the violent conflict associated with various attempts at secession, not all of which led to the creation of independent states. Television and, to some extent, the press often gives priority to the events which are characterized by violence and destruction. And most secessions during the past 20 years have been characterized by violent conflict.

Secession, as we shall explain in the next section, involves a process of withdrawal of a territory and its population from an existing state and the creation of a new state on that territory. In focusing on the violence and conflict associated with secession, the electronic and other media often ignore its wider – political, social and legal – aspects. In fact, when showing us, vividly and from close range, the violence and conflict, television broadcasts and press reports often fail even to use the word 'secession'. Thus, we have witnessed much secessionist conflict and violence, without being told that the violence and conflict are associated with attempts at secession, that is, with attempts to create new states out of existing ones. In a sense, we have witnessed a large number of attempts at secession without knowing what they are.

There are many reasons for this. As we note in the next section, 'secession' is often regarded as a 'dirty' word with negative or pejorative associations. For example, secession is widely viewed to be an act that is generally prohibited under international law, as a breach of the territorial integrity of a state, which is generally harmful to everyone concerned. In order to avoid such negative associations, the word 'secession' in media presentations and in secessionist rhetoric is replaced by a much more positive word, 'independence'. Those peoples or national groups who want to be independent from foreign rule, it is now generally assumed, deserve independence. Fighting for independence is thus a noble and praiseworthy act. As a consequence, in the media of the English-speaking world – as well as elsewhere – secessionist conflicts have, over the past two decades, often been presented as the brave fight by oppressed peoples for their independence from their oppressors. In a similar way, the fight for independence from colonial powers, during the period of decolonization, was, in at least some media, presented as a just struggle of the oppressed against colonial oppression. In the period from 1947 to 1980, around 90 colonial entities, mostly in Asia, Africa and the Pacific, gained independence from European colonial powers and became sovereign states. Among them, to mention only the largest, were India, Indonesia, Nigeria, Algeria, Angola and the Congo. In some cases – such as Indonesia, Algeria and Angola – independence was granted only after a protracted armed struggle against colonial military forces. The positive image of the fight for independence from colonial powers has found its parallel in the image of a secessionist conflict as a fight for independence from oppressive foreign rule. Yet colonies did not always gain their independence through an armed struggle against the colonial powers. In fact, in most cases of decolonization, in particular of the British colonies, there was no armed conflict with the colonial power. Likewise, a few recent secessions were peaceful: Latvia, Estonia, Macedonia (all in 1991) and Slovakia (in 1993) seceded without any armed conflict or violence (see Chapter 8 and Part VI). These peaceful secessions were not the subject of extended television or press coverage and thus one could hardly say that we have witnessed them in the same way as we did their violent counterparts.

Of course, secession is not quite the same thing as the liberation from colonial rule, usually called 'decolonization' – although in Chapter 2 some important similarities are noted. Decolonization involves the granting of independent statehood to a colony which was usually not part of the territory of the metropolitan state and was usually separated from that state by a sea or an ocean (which lead to 'the salt water test' of a colony). The race and culture of the majority populations of these colonies was different to that of the Europeans who ruled over them. European rule in those colonies was usually maintained by European military forces or by the forces commanded by Europeans. None of these elements were present in the secessions we have witnessed in the past 20 years – nor in most secessions in the past century. Yet the seceding populations in these cases of secession belonged to a national group different from the remaining population of the host state. Thus, to revert to the examples with which we started, Lithuanians, Croats, Slovenes, Bosnian Muslims (or Bosniaks) form national groups different from those which formed the majority of population in the former USSR and the former Yugoslavia. And in these two host states the commanding military officers who were in control of the territory of those national groups often belonged not to these but to other (usually majority) national groups.

Yet the outcome of secession and decolonization is of the same kind: both result in the creation of new states.[1] This raises the question of the definition of secession.

---

1   Secession and decolonization are not the only ways of creating new states. New states can also be created by the unification of previously independent states (or parts of

# Introduction: What Is Secession?

## The Definition of Secession

A sense of the meaning of secession flows from its roots in the Latin words 'se' meaning 'apart' and 'cedere' meaning 'to go'. Secession is thus associated with leaving or withdrawing from some place. Broadly speaking, secession can be viewed as withdrawing from an association or organization. Secession is thus a *process* (Kohen 2006: 14) which, in the present context, has the creation of a new state as its *outcome*. In general this process commences when representatives of a population settled on a territory proclaim a new state on that territory. In most cases they do so by means of a declaration of independence. In some, but not all, cases in which independence is so proclaimed, other states formally recognize the independence of the proclaimed state. When a sufficient degree of recognition has been achieved the proclaimed state becomes, at that time, a state in reality. The outcome of the process has been achieved and the process of secession is complete.

There is little consensus amongst scholars on the definition of secession. A consequence of this is that there is disagreement as to whether any particular instance of state creation did or did not arise as the result of secession.

A narrow definition of secession is provided by Crawford who defines it as:

> ... *the creation of a State by the use or threat of force without the consent of the former sovereign. (Crawford 2006: 375)*

By way of contrast Radan defines secession as follows:

> *Secession is the creation of a new State upon territory previously forming part of, or being a colonial entity of, an existing State. (Radan 2008: 18)*

The differences between Crawford's narrow definition and Radan's broad definition are that, for Crawford:

1. secession does not include all cases of state creation resulting from the process of decolonization;
2. secession requires the opposition of the host state;
3. secession requires the use or threat of force by the secessionist movement.

A consequence of Crawford's definition is that secession is a rare occurrence. Crawford argues that, outside the context of decolonization, Bangladesh constitutes the only case of secession since 1945 (Crawford 2006: 415). On the other hand, state creation as the result of secession is a much more frequent occurrence if one accepts Radan's definition of secession. For him secession occurs in a variety of contexts which include:

---

independent states) into a single political entity. The German Empire (*Reich*) (1871) and the Kingdom of Italy (1863) were created in this way.

1. cases where a colonial entity becomes a new state, which he labels *colonial secession*;
2. cases where, notwithstanding the continued opposition of the host state, part of that state becomes a new state and the host state continues its existence, which he labels *unilateral secession*;
3. cases where, irrespective of whether or not it initially opposed the creation of a new state, the host state consented to the creation of a new state at the time of the latter's creation and the host state continues its existence, which he labels *devolutionary secession*;
4. cases where, the demand for the creation of a new state leads to the host state being dissolved by consent, leading to the creation of a new state or states, which he labels *consensual secession*; and
5. cases where, the demand for the creation of a new state leads to the factual dissolution of the host state, leading to the creation of a new state or states, which he labels *dissolving secession* (Radan 2008: 30–31).

Whatever may be the parameters of secession it is undoubtedly the fact that recognition of the newly created state is of crucial importance. In international law the function of recognition is a controversial issue with two major schools of thought. According to the declaratory theory, recognition plays no role in the creation of a state. A territorial entity that meets the requirements of statehood is a state, irrespective of its recognition by other states, with recognition being simply the formal acknowledgment of that fact. According to the constitutive theory, recognition of a state creates that state, thereby constituting a further requirement of statehood (Crawford 2006: 19–28).

Whatever the merits of these competing theories, it is widely accepted that, in the context of secession at least, recognition of the seceded state by other states has at least some part to play in its creation (Dugard and Raič 2006: 99). That this is so is effectively conceded by secessionists themselves. Historically, international recognition of statehood has been the major foreign policy goal of any secessionist movement (Crawford 2006: 376). Thus, the recognition by India, a significant regional power, of Bangladesh in 1971 was crucial to the success of the latter's secession from Pakistan (see Part VI for a discussion of this case). Conversely, the failure to gain international recognition has been a major contributing factor to the failure of various attempts at secession. This is confirmed by a number of examples, including, the failure of the southern Confederacy to gain, in particular, British recognition of its attempted secession from the United States of America in the 1860s and the failure of Katanga to gain the recognition of any other state of its attempted secession from Congo in the 1960s. In cases where recognition is given by an insignificant number of states, notwithstanding such recognition, the attempted secession will fail. Illustrative examples here include the attempted secession of Biafra from Nigeria in the late 1960s and the, still unresolved, attempt at secession of the Turkish Republic of Northern Cyprus from Cyprus in 1983 (see also Chapters 5, 6 and 15).

# Introduction: What Is Secession?

A very effective means by which recognition can achieve its constitutive function in the context of secession is by admission of the proclaimed state to membership of the United Nations Organization (UN). Admission of a state to membership of the UN requires a recommendation by the UN Security Council which must be then accepted by a simple majority vote in the General Assembly. As membership to the UN is generally limited to states, admission to it is persuasive evidence of the new member being a state (Crawford 2006: 544–5). Alternatively, recognition by a significant collection of regional and/or other states will achieve the same result, as was evidenced by the widespread recognition of Bangladesh before its admission to the UN in 1974, and by the recognition of Slovenia and Croatia by the EC on 15 January 1992 and soon thereafter by various other states, all prior to their admission to the UN on 22 May 1992 (see also Chapters 13 and 15).

## What Is This Book About?

The definition of secession is important in relation to the varied legal issues raised by different types of secession. This book does not aspire to covering all of them, but rather focuses on the important legal issues that arise when a territorial entity secedes from an existing internationally recognized state. These issues, which are dealt with in Part IV, include those of the borders of the newly created state, the existence of a legal right of secession and the changes with respect to the international rights and obligations of the host state following secession.

Apart from the issues that secession raises for legal theory and legal practice of states, secession raises several issues in international relations, social science and applied ethics or political theory. Apart from a legal approach to attempts at secession, secession can be then approached as the subject of:

- the study of international relations and international systems;
- explanation within the framework social sciences (including history);
- normative assessment within ethics and political theory.

Essays in Part I of this Companion provide an introduction to the study of secession from the perspective of these three disciplines – international relations, social sciences and ethics/political theory.

In Chapter 1 James Mayall outlines, within a historical framework, the impact of secessions with the system of states and the responses that states have had to secessions. He also tentatively suggests that the current stance – discouraging secessions – is not likely to change in the near future.

In Chapter 2 Bridget Coggins outlines the history of secessions and identifies some of the factors that led to secessions and secessionist conflict in the past.

In Chapter 3 David Siroky lists a variety of questions that social scientists raise regarding secessions and attempts at secession. Siroky first identifies the principal actors – secessionists, host state governments, outside states or actors – in the secessionist process and then discusses a large variety of explanations which social scientists have recently offered as the role that each of the actors plays in attempts at secessions.

In Chapter 4 Frank Dietrich outlines and discusses four approaches to normative assessment of and territorial claim secessions: property, justice,[2] national and choice theories of secession. He also argues that choice theories have definite advantages over other approaches to normative assessment of secessions.

The discussions of past secessions, started in Chapter 2, are continued in Part II of the Companion in which detailed analyses are offered of attempts at secessions of the Southern Confederacy of America, Biafra, Katanga, Quebec, Montenegro and then secessions from the USSR and Yugoslavia as well as Kosovo from Serbia. In Part VI an even larger variety of secessions, attempts at secessions and secessionist movements is discussed in a series of case studies which are grouped on the basis of their geographical location.

The discussion of the place of secession in international order, started in Chapter 1, is continued in Part III, in particular Chapters 10, 13, 14 and 15.

Social science explanations of secessions, introduced in Chapter 3 are also further discussed in Part III in Chapters 10, 11, 12 and 14 as well as in Part V, Chapter 24.

Normative approaches to secession are further discussed in Part V. Chapter 21 develops a framework for a national or communitarian theory of secessions but primarily focuses on self-determination within an existing state. In Chapter 22 a justice or remedial theory of secession is developed while Chapter 23 develops a choice theory of secession. Chapters 24 and 25 discuss a variety of shortcomings of the contemporary theories of secession.

Part VI consists of short accounts of case studies of secession attempts and secessionist movements in Africa, Asia, Europe and the rest of the world.

Each part – except Part I – has its own brief introduction outlining the issues discussed in this part.

---

2   In Chapters 21, 22, 23 and 25 'justice theories' are called 'remedial theories' of secessions. In Chapter 24, these theories are called 'just cause' theories.

## References

Crawford, J. (2006), *The Creation of States in International Law*, 2nd edition (Oxford: Clarendon Press).
Dugard, J. and D. Raič (2006), 'The Role of Recognition in the Law and Practice of Secession', in M.G. Kohen (ed.), *Secession: International Law Perspectives* (Cambridge: Cambridge University Press), 94–137.
Kohen, M.G. (ed.), *Secession: International Law Perspectives* (Cambridge: Cambridge University Press).
Radan, P. (2008), 'Secession: A Word in Search of a Meaning', in A. Pavković and P. Radan (eds), *On the Way to Statehood: Secession and Globalisation* (Aldershot: Ashgate), 17–32.

# PART I
# INTRODUCTION TO SECESSION

# Secession and International Order

James Mayall

A glance at any historical atlas will reveal that the political map of the world has been transformed many times over the centuries. Even the most ancient states such as China or Morocco, whose core identity has been preserved for millennia, seldom if ever occupy exactly the same territory as when they were first established. In most parts of the world, and at most times, the main driver of territorial fusion has been conquest, often reinforced by dynastic marriage and/or commercial exchange. Conversely the main driver of territorial fission has been imperial decline, often accelerated by geopolitical opportunism. By this I simply mean that insurgencies have sometimes succeeded when the rebels against established authority were either supported by a powerful neighbour as a neutral buffer between themselves and a rival empire, or were able to play off two powerful neighbours against one another, or exploit their control over high mountain passes or strategic choke points, in order to preserve their independence. There was a time, for example, before it became a Japanese prefecture, when the island kingdom of Okinawa maintained at least quasi independence under the simultaneous protection of China and Japan.[1]

This prehistory has some relevance to the modern discussion of secession but not much. A successful secession is a very rare event but in the contemporary world it results in a change in the political and territorial map just as it did in the past following an imperial conquest or the disintegration of an established empire. But the similarity ceases at this point. The key distinction between the pre-modern world of imperial rivalry and the nationalist era that began with the American and French revolutions is that whereas in the former, territory was ceded, sometimes voluntarily, more often under duress, in the latter it is theoretically meant to reflect an act of self (se)cession, in other words of self-determination. It was only after the universal claims of the American Declaration of Independence and the French Declaration of the Rights of Man and the Citizen had spread throughout

---

1   From the 14th century the Ryuku kingdom in Okinawa and the neighbouring islands developed a tributary relationship with China. It was maintained even after the Satsuma clan from Kyoshu in Japan had invaded in 1609 and established Japanese hegemony over the kingdom. This did not prevent each of the three parties from maintaining the ostensible independence of the kingdom (Yokota 2010).

international society that the idea of a legally grounded international order based on self-determining nation-states gradually emerged. There are those who claim that in an age of globalization this idea is now an anachronism, but if so all that one can say is that it has proved an exceptionally tenacious idea, which shows few signs of loosening its hold on the popular imagination anywhere.

This tenacity – it should be said at the outset – is a mixed blessing. Once the national idea had taken hold, the tension – and sometimes open conflict – between different conceptions of justice and order, and power and law, became unavoidable. How was the national idea – and the invitation to secession that the principle of self-determination seemed to invoke – to be accommodated within international society?

I will attempt to answer this question by first looking briefly at how the principle of national self-determination has been accommodated within traditional international society, in theory and practice, before examining whether there have been any significant changes since the end of the Cold War. Since we are currently witnessing, however tentatively, the beginnings of a shift in world power from West to East, I will conclude by considering whether there are major regional, cultural and ideational variations in how separatism and secession are understood, which may lead to further changes in theory and practice in the years ahead.

## National Self-Determination and International Society

Traditional international society was largely composed of dynastic sovereign states. The patrimony of the rulers – and with it the borders of their states – could be changed as the result of the fortunes of war or the construction of dynastic alliances through marriage, and consequently by the acquisition of territory through inheritance. Think, for example, of the way in which the Normans swallowed England in the 11th century and so laid the basis for the subsequent claims of the English crown to large parts of what is modern day France. Or of the transfer of Quebec to the British crown under Article IV of the Treaty of Paris in 1763, transforming what these days we would be likely to think of as a wrong into a right, in other words a legal entitlement.

During the transition from the *ançien regime* to the nationalist era territory was sometimes also bought and sold, as in the American purchases of Louisiana from France in 1803, Florida from Spain in 1819 and Alaska from Russia in 1867. In November 2008, the President of the Maldives, Mohammed Nasheed, revived this idea by suggesting that he intended to build up a sovereign wealth fund to purchase land, elsewhere in the region, to resettle the population in the event of his country being submerged by rising sea levels. It is not impossible but seems unlikely that he will find a willing seller. Neither India nor Sri Lanka, the two countries to which he referred, have a tradition of ceding territory. A transaction of this kind would breach the modern norm, which emerged as a result of the elevation of the principle of national self-determination after 1919, namely the sacralization of national territory.

Some authors have argued that the quest for self-determination need not involve territory and therefore does not automatically have to lead to an attempt to secede.[2] On this view, their aspirations can be achieved either by affording them full citizenship rights or by granting them a special status under the host state's constitution. It is also true that in an era of globalization people have been widely dispersed around the world, so that large minority communities have grown up, which may identify as much if not more with their country of origin than with their host country. The issue of divided loyalties and the fears on the part of the majority population that they are harbouring a dangerous fifth column in their midst can have potentially serious international implications – think, for example, of the American and Canadian internment camps for Japanese during World War Two, or more recently the fears that Western countries may have provided a safe haven for jihadist terrorists from where they can plot their destruction. That the decentralized order of territorially defined sovereign states is coming under strain as a result of such developments is undeniable. But in a sense both the attempt to find non territorial definitions of self-determination, and the ability of opponents of the international order to operate away from their own homelands, provides evidence for the tenacity of the traditional system rather than its eclipse. In a world where national territory has been sacralized practical accommodations can be achieved, if the circumstances are propitious, but it remains virtually impossible to deal with these problems at the level of diplomatic theory or international law.

Why this should be so may become clearer if we briefly review the history of international society since the rise of nationalism in the 19th century. The traditional conception of international society as a society of sovereigns not peoples survived, dented but more or less intact, until World War One. Since 1919, international society has ostensibly been based on the principle of popular sovereignty. The collapse of the European dynastic empires and of the Ottoman Empire dealt a mortal blow to the dynastic principle. It was no longer possible to defend the state as a private possession of particular individuals or families. But if prescription was out, consent had to be in: ownership of the state, in other words, had to be transferred to the people. The difficulty in effecting this transfer arose because, in the last analysis, only individuals can give or withhold consent. Yet men and women are social creatures. Which, therefore, are the appropriate collective selves, whose right to self-determination must be recognized as the basis of the new political order?

The answer to this question would be straightforward if – as most nationalists believe – the identity of the nation was self evident. They almost invariably invoke particular historical myths and theories to justify their own claims and denigrate those of their secessionist opponents. Once in power they generally use the school curriculum – and their monopoly over the symbols of nationhood – to construct a national culture that will both justify and run congruently with state boundaries.

---

2  See, for example, Bishai (2007) and Guibernau (1999). For a discussion of a recent UN view of the problem see below.

Sometimes they succeed; sometimes they fail, and for reasons that ultimately remain mysterious. But either way, the reality is that while the doctrine of nationalism is clear – i.e. that the world is divided into nations and that consequently international society should be composed of nation-states – national identity itself is a deeply contested concept.

Two broad accounts of national identity are on offer. Primordialists maintain that the national map of the world was laid down a very long time ago, even if very few these days cling to the belief that it accurately reflects the natural world and remains essentially unchanged since the beginning of time (Smith 1983 and 1987). By contrast, except in a few anomalous or at least unexplained cases, modernists see the nation as only recently invented, imagined or constructed, dating only from the American and French revolutions (Gellner 1983 and 1997; Anderson 1983). Neither primordialists nor modernists generally pay much attention to the international implications of their theoretical accounts of the rise and spread of nationalism. To the extent that they consider the issue at all, they mostly adopt a realist approach to international relations. But while they pay little attention to legal or normative questions, implicit in their arguments is the recognition that political identity is a contingent matter. This is the crucial point. What is contingent cannot be settled by rational argument or a democratic vote. For political argument to take place, boundaries must be in place, but they lie behind or beyond such argument all the same.

Democrats, who generally still insist, as they did after 1919, that the recognition of any new state should be preceded by a plebiscite or popular vote, have difficulty in accepting this unpalatable truth. In the contemporary context it is not difficult to understand why. After 1945 strenuous efforts were made to outlaw the use of force as an instrument of foreign policy, let alone the right of conquest. So how were new states to come into existence? A plebiscite or referendum seemed an obvious prerequisite. But, as Ivor Jennings famously put it in 1956, 'on the surface it seemed reasonable: let the people decide. It was in practice ridiculous because the people cannot decide until someone decides who are the people' (Jennings 1956: 56).

In the intervening half century, very little progress has been made in finding a way out of this logical impasse. Nor do I believe that one is likely to be found in the near future. Indeed it seems likely that no general or theoretical solution to the problem is available at all, although the Australian political theorist, Harry Beran, would not agree with me. A major practical difficulty that arises in most secessionist conflicts concerns the presence of trapped minorities that prefer the *status quo ante* to the proposed new state. There are numerous examples of this phenomenon, but the refusal of Abkhazia and South Ossetia to accept that they should be incorporated in Georgia is a vivid and topical example. Beran maintains that a right of secessionist self-determination should be conceded if and only if the authorities of the new would-be state are prepared to grant a similar right to any subordinate group within their territory, and so on *ad infinitum*. Practical considerations would, he believes, call a halt to the process of fragmentation at a reasonably early stage (Beran 1984). It is an elegant solution but not one, I suspect, that is likely to appeal to any but the most enthusiastic advocates of permanent revolution.

So what to do? The answers to this question have been largely practical rather than theoretical. The extent to which the Wilsonian vision of a world made safe for democracy and self determination would challenge, rather than support the traditional Westphalian international order, became evident immediately after World War One. The gruesome consequences of the demands for ethnic and organic democracy in much of Europe, however, were eventually submerged by World War Two and the territorial stabilization imposed on Europe by the Cold War division. As a result, in the part of the world where both nationalism and the doctrine of national self-determination had their origins, the question was effectively ignored for a generation.

Beyond Europe this strategy was not available, partly because of the damage that the war had inflicted on both the reputation and the material power of the European imperial states; partly because of the strength of anti-colonial nationalism that increasingly challenged the attempt to restore the pre-war order; and partly because of the unholy alliance between the United States and the Soviet Union in support of the dismemberment of the European empires. The official position, to which all the major powers had signed up at San Francisco, was contained in Articles 1 and 55 of the UN Charter, which affirmed the right of all peoples to self-determination. But as we have already seen, this formula was notoriously question-begging. The practical answer that gradually emerged, was to equate the right of self-determination with decolonization, a once and for all event, tied in time and space to the withdrawal of European power.

Around the edges of their inheritance, some colonial successor states consolidated their territory without suffering serious international consequences: thus India swallowed Hyderabad and Goa, Indonesia, West Irian and then, in 1974, East Timor, and China, Tibet.[3] The Chinese absorption of Tibet was a decidedly pre-modern form of conquest, which the outside world was nonetheless able to digest, partly because no outside power was prepared to contemplate going to war over Tibet, but also because it had never been formally part of the British or any other empire. The British had exercised influence over Tibet but had not challenged Chinese claims of suzerainty, a position inherited in 1947 by the Government of India and endorsed, however reluctantly, by the United States (see also Part VI). But in general, throughout the Cold War, there was widespread antipathy to opening up the domestic political arrangements of sovereign states to outside scrutiny, and even more to any suggestion that the right of self-determination could be claimed by dissatisfied groups in existing states or colonies still awaiting independence.

Paradoxically, it was the expansion of international society to include most of sub-Saharan Africa in the 1960s that sealed the fate of all but the most persistent secessionists. Prior to independence, African nationalists had frequently denounced the 'Balkanization' of Africa by the European powers. At the Berlin Conference

---

3  I have discussed these cases of post-colonial consolidation, prior to the re-emergence of the principle of *uti possidetis juris*, in Mayall (2000).

in 1884 the Europeans had partitioned the continent amongst themselves without paying much attention to geographical, historical or ethnic considerations. The map of Africa, nationalists argued, needed to be redrawn to reflect these realities and African interests. But how? They were no more able to answer this regional question than international society as a whole was able to distinguish between legitimate and illegitimate national selves. With hindsight, it is completely unsurprising that African governments, once independent, quickly became the most ardent defenders of the territorial *status quo*. When Tom Mboya, Kenya's first Foreign Minister, was asked about the rights of the Somali, the majority population in Kenya's north-east province, he replied that they could exercise their right of self-determination any time they wanted – all they had to do was to walk across the border into Somalia (Castagno 1964).

The decision to restrict the right of self-determination to European colonies could not finally dispose of the secessionist challenge to international order, even from the point of view of a legal positivist. This was because in many parts of the world not only had populations been divided between different colonial jurisdictions but the borders themselves had often not been demarcated. In traditional societies where power was largely a personal attribute this had not mattered so much, but in ostensibly national societies of citizens it was fraught with danger. Since most African states were socially heterogeneous, their governments viewed the potential threat from secessionist and irredentist movements with particular alarm. Their solution, arrived at with the assistance of Latin American lawyers, was to underpin the *Pax Africana* with the legal principle of *uti possidetis juris*, which can be loosely translated by the maxim that you hang on to what you have got at the time of independence.

Some lawyers have followed Steven Ratner in arguing that this was essentially an external imposition designed to keep the process of decolonization orderly and therefore consistent with the dominant Cold War conception of Western international order (Ratner 1996: 610). It is certainly true that the major powers, like the authorities in most other states, welcomed it as a way of limiting international anarchy. But it was neither a Western nor a Cold War imposition. Indeed, in agreeing to pocket their differences over territory, most African leaders were reacting to what they often perceived as continued Western attempts to divide and rule. Katanga's secession in 1960 had been vigorously supported by Western mining interests, and President de Gaulle of France would almost certainly have followed the four African governments that had recognized Biafra, had the Federal Nigerian government not won the diplomatic battle within the OAU (see also Chapter 6).[4]

---

4   Biafra was recognized by Cote d'Ivoire, Gabon, Tanzania and Zambia. The argument for recognition was eloquently argued in a Memorandum submitted by President Julius Nyerere of Tanzania to his fellow African Heads of State in 1969. It failed, however, to win over any further states. For text see, Kirk-Greene (1971: 429–39). See Chapter 6.

## Secession after the Cold War

Once the principle of *uti possidetis* had been generalized throughout international society it successfully bottled up the aspirations for self-determination of many secessionist movements. The one Cold War exception to this statement – Bangladesh's successful bid for independence in 1972 – effectively proved the rule. Bangladesh succeeded not because of its own nationalist rebellion against the government in Islamabad, although no doubt this was an essential pre-requisite of success; it succeeded because India intervened on its behalf and defeated Pakistan's army. It was able to do this, moreover, because the Indian Prime Minister, Mrs Gandhi, had first neutralized the two super-powers – she signed a long-term treaty of cooperation with Moscow, which included a defence clause and ensured that the US Sixth Fleet could do nothing but sail into the Bay of Bengal and then sail out again (see also Part VI).

In these circumstances, it was perhaps not surprising that many nationalists and their mostly liberal supporters identified the injustices of the territorial map with the ideological divisions of the Cold War. In the early 1990s the then UN Secretary-General, Boutros Boutros-Ghali attempted to head off at the pass any optimism on this score. In *The Agenda for Peace* he argued that while the United Nations had not closed its doors to new members, 'if every ethnic, religious or linguistic group claimed statehood there would be no limit to fragmentation, and peace, security and economic wellbeing would become ever more difficult to achieve' (Boutros-Ghali 1993: #17 and 18). Instead he recommended that the way to resolve the rival claims of sovereignty and self determination was through respect for human rights, particularly the rights of minorities, on the one hand and democratization on the other. 'Respect for democratic rights at all levels of social existence is crucial: in communities, within states and within the community of states' (ibid.). The intimation that the old taboo against territorial change was weakening was sufficiently strong to urge the Canadian government into action. The two international experts they consulted on whether Quebec might have a unilateral right of secession provided some indication of how legal opinion on the subject was evolving. They were clear that Quebec did not have such a right, but nonetheless concluded that 'there may be developments in the principle of self-determination according to which not only colonialism but flagrant violations of human rights or undemocratic regimes could lead to a right of unilateral secession' (Department of Justice 1997).[5]

There are, so far as I know, no cases where such a right of unilateralist secessionist self determination has been unambiguously identified, although one might argue that the peace agreements between north and south Sudan (see Part VI) and between Papua New Guinea and Bougainville, both of which provided for referendums on independence after a transitional period of joint government,

---

5   The two experts were Professor James Crawford, Whewell Professor of International Law, University of Cambridge, and Professor Luzius Wildhaber of the University of Basel, who is also a judge on the European Court of Human Rights.

and the unilateral declaration of independence by the Kosovar majority Albanian government in February 2008, represent moves in this direction. In all three cases the final outcome is still to be decided. Moreover, the circumstances are so different in each case that it is doubtful whether any attempt to generalize from them will withstand close scrutiny.

In the first two cases – the Sudan and Papua New Guinea – where self-determination disputes were the subject of international mediation, there was a deliberate attempt to resolve the conflict by constitutional means. The Peace Agreement between the government of Papua New Guinea and the Bougainville secessionist movement in 2001 established a high level of autonomy for the province and envisaged a non-binding referendum on independence sometime between 10 and 15 years after the autonomy arrangements began in 2005. Whether the referendum will take place and if so whether the result will be respected are still unknowns. The relative weight of legal theory and international norms as against power political considerations has recently been tested in the Southern Sudan, which voted in January 2011 by over 98 percent to secede from the Republic of Sudan in July 2011, although several intractable issues remain unresolved, including the division of oil revenues and the status of the border. The Abyei region, which divides the grazing lands of both northern Arab pastoralists and the southern Dinka, is particularly troublesome. The rational solution would be to have a 'soft' border, with seasonal migration rights in both directions and cooperative arrangements to cover the shared management of water resources and the oil industry. There is little appetite for a return to civil war in either north or south, but with high levels of distrust between the two sides, negotiating a 'rational' solution will be difficult.

Kosovo's unilateral declaration of independence in February 2008 followed a period of international administration rather than mediation. The 74 states that had recognized Kosovo by March 2011 would also no doubt argue that the Kosovar government's independence was constitutional, although in this case the final outcome is similarly still unclear. In October 2008, a large majority of UN member states supported a Serbian resolution in the General Assembly, against the opposition of the United States and some of its allies, requesting an Advisory opinion on the legality of Kosovo's unilateral declaration of independence. Such opinions are not binding but a ruling that the declaration was illegal would nonetheless have been a major political set-back for the Kosovo government and its international supporters. In the event, the ICJ delivered an ambiguous verdict but one that was more favourable to Kosovo than many had anticipated. It did not rule on the substantive issue of whether Kosovo independence was legal, but on 22 July 2010, by ten votes to four, the Court found 'that the declaration of independence of Kosovo adopted on 17 February 2008 did not violate international law' (ICJ 2010) (for a further discussion see Chapter 17). Whether this opinion is strong enough to persuade a majority of UN member states to recognize Kosovo, remains to be seen; even if it does, Russia may use its veto to block admission.

So has anything really changed with the end of the Cold War? I am inclined to conclude that the answer is not much, particularly since the two successful cases of enforced secession – Eritrea's separation from Ethiopia in 1993 and East Timor's from Indonesia in 1999 – are better explained by reference to the conventional interpretation of self-determination as decolonization in accordance with *uti possidetis* than in terms of the evolution of the new democratic criteria.[6] If we discount the peaceful divorce between the Czech and Slovak Republics in 1992 and that between Serbia and Montenegro in 1996, on the grounds that there has never been any objection in either international law or state practice to separations of this kind, we are still left with the question as to how state-less communities are to register their claims and grievances at the international level?

By treating the disintegration of the Soviet Union and the collapse of Yugoslavia as analogous to decolonization, international society was able to maintain the fiction that the territorial map was still based on *uti possidetis*: the internal borders of the socialist republics in the first case and the national republics in the second, were accepted in the same way as colonial borders had been as the new international frontiers. But quite apart from the fact that in Yugoslavia the new dispensation was not accepted and therefore led to the anarchic blood-letting that *uti possidetis* was designed to prevent, there were some glaring anomalies. It is not obvious, for example, that in substantive terms the case for Chechnyan independence was any weaker than that of, say Azerbaijan, or for that matter Kosovo (for Chechnya see Part VI). But Chechnya was an autonomous Republic within the Russian Federation, and so lacked international legal personality, whereas Azerbaijan was a Soviet Socialist Republic and therefore a candidate for statehood under the decolonization formula. Kosovo – according to the majority in the UN General Assembly – is in the same situation as Chechnya despite having been under international administration.

Western manoeuvring over Kosovo was followed in 2008 by Russia's intervention in Georgia and recognition of South Ossetia and Abkhazia.[7] Both the West and Russia insist that the two cases are quite distinct, non comparable, and uniquely just or unjust as the case may be. But they would, wouldn't they. It is hard to avoid the conclusion that we have done little more than substitute confusion for a clear principle that may have sometimes been unjust in its application, but at least offered some constraining influence on the more blatant forms of power politics.

---

6    Eritrea had been unilaterally incorporated into Ethiopia by the government in Addis Ababa in 1952 without further reference to the UN, which had been agreed as part of the solution for the problem of arranging for the administration of former Italian colonies after 1945 (see Jacquin-Berdal 2002; Mayall and Simpson 1992) (see Part VI). Until the Indonesian army invaded East Timor in 1975, Indonesia had used civic and political rather than ethnic arguments to underpin Indonesia's national identity. State practice had by this time confirmed the principle of *uti possidetis juris* as the justification for post-colonial self-determination. As a former Portuguese colony in theory, therefore, the principle should have applied to East Timor after the withdrawal of the Portuguese authorities. See Mayall (2000).

7    For further discussion see Chapter 15 and Part VI.

## The Future of Secession

The values, institutions, operating conventions and laws of contemporary international society are Western in origin. They were spread around the world by the powerful forces of Western imperialism and the scientific and industrial revolutions. Nationalism, the doctrine that the state belongs to the people and not to a privileged class, blood-line or self-made potentate, also arose in the West and was incorporated in the already existing state-system. Inevitably, therefore, international society bears the cultural imprint of the Western great powers that dominated world politics from the end of the 17th century to the end of the 20th.[8] Even more than the other institutions of international society – law, diplomacy, the balance of power and even war itself – nationalist ideology became the instrument through which the hegemony of the West was first successfully challenged and may, in the end, be eclipsed.

We are still most probably a fair way off this denouement. But already we are witnessing the rise of a group of Asian powers – China most obviously, but also India – that will play an increasingly important role in shaping the evolution of international society. Great powers, whatever their leaders may say to the contrary, will always try to transform the international landscape in their own image. There is no logical reason that I can see why this should not be as true of China and India as it was of the European great powers and later the United States. So what might we conclude will be their likely attitude to the nationalist aspirations of minority groups within their own borders and in third countries?

Krishnan Srinivasan, a former Indian Foreign Secretary and Deputy Secretary-General of the Commonwealth, has concluded that we are heading back to the future and that the 21st-century world order will look more like the 19th than the 20th (Srinivasan 2009). He foresees a global system in which a few great powers tacitly agree to police their own neighbourhoods and will collectively refrain from pursuing a progressive multilateral agenda. On this view of the future the legacy of the European Enlightenment – and ideas such as self-determination and the protection of human rights that were central to it – will fade from view. His reasoning in coming to this conclusion is primarily based on empirical observation. Although India is a democracy and has often dealt with separatist pressures with the stratagem of creating new states to accommodate the linguistic and cultural demands of regional parties, it has been as ruthless as non-democratic China in resisting bids for outright secession whether in Kashmir, the Punjab or the north east. Indeed, its engineered incorporation of the formerly independent kingdom of Sikkim in 1975 was less brutal but possibly even more efficient than the Chinese take-over of Tibet following its invasion in 1951.

Srinivasan is an optimist in believing that the emerging multipolar system will pay dividends in delivering political stability, but a pessimist on the prospects for human emancipation. It is a plausible vision, particularly if we recall that both China and India face separatist challenges of their own, have a disputed borderland

---

8   The most influential study of international society and its institutions is Bull (1977).

between them, and are amongst the strongest supporters of the traditional pluralist conception of international society against solidarist arguments that the territorial map should be periodically redrawn in response to popular demand.

My own conclusions are more cautious, for two reasons. The first is that we still do not know whether the modernization of the new great powers – and it is this that has fuelled their rise – is dependent on their acceptance of values, which although Western in origin are universal in practice, even where these run counter to deeply held cultural beliefs. I am genuinely agnostic on this issue, but if there is a link between modernization and universalism, it may prove more difficult for rulers everywhere to row back from the idea that the modern state relies ultimately on consent. Secondly, and following on from my first doubt, I think Srinivasan probably underestimates the continuing power of nationalism. That power is crucially bound up with the plasticity of the concept – the fact that it can mean all things to all men – and therefore that so long as political identity remains contested, it will remain the most convenient vehicle for challenging the legitimacy of the state.

One of the most frequent criticisms of Thomas Hobbes's *Leviathan* is that he provided a blue print for tyranny. Critics sometimes overlook the fact that Hobbes allowed all human beings to retain one natural right – the right to life – and that he believed that sovereigns, who after all remain in a state of nature in relation to one another, would have an incentive to rule well since they might have to rely on the loyalty of their subjects in war against another sovereign. We know from experience that many rulers have preyed on their own people, but no ruler can sustain themselves over the long run on the basis of terror. I do not think it very likely that territorial secession will be any easier in the future than it has been in the past. But the new element – globalization and modern communications in particular – mean that it is now less likely that the problem will disappear over time as a result of assimilation. Whether one concludes that the prospects have improved at all in cases where a population is genuinely oppressed, depends, I suspect, on whether one is temperamentally inclined to see the glass as half full or half empty. I fear I side with the pessimists more often than with the optimists, but it is at least possible to hope that self-interest will persuade governments that they need to explore creative ways of meeting the desires of those who might otherwise be tempted to take up arms against the state.

# References

Anderson, B. (1983), *Imagined Communities: Reflections on the Rise and Spread of Nationalism* (London: Verso).
Beran, H. (1984), 'A Liberal Theory of Secession', *Political Studies* 32, 21–31.
Bishai, L.S. (2007), *Forgetting Ourselves: Secession and the (Im)possibility of Territorial Identity* (Plymouth, UK: Lexington Books).
Boutros-Ghali, B. (1993), 'Agenda for Peace', in A. Roberts and B. Kingsbury (eds), *United Nations, Divided World* (Oxford: Oxford University Press), 468–98.
Bull, H. (1977), *The Anarchical Society: A Study of Order in World Politics* (London: Macmillan).
Castagno, A.A. (1964), 'The Somali-Kenyan Controversy: Implications for the Future', *Journal of Modern African Studies* 2:2, 165–88.
Department of Justice, Ottawa, 1997.
Gellner, E. (1983), *Nations and Nationalism* (Oxford: Blackwell).
Gellner, E. (1997), *Nationalism* (London: Weidenfeld and Nicolson).
Guibernau, M. (1999), *Nations without States: Political Community in a Global Age* (London: Polity).
ICJ (2010), *Press Release*, International Court of Justice, No. 2010/25.
Jacquin-Berdal, D. (2002), *Nationalism and Ethnicity in the Horn of Africa: A Critique of the Ethnic Interpretation* (London: Edwin R. Mellen).
Jennings, I. (1956), *The Approach to Self Government* (Cambridge: Cambridge University Press).
Kirk-Greene, A.H.M. (1971), *Crisis and Conflict in Nigeria: A Documentary Sourcebook* (Oxford: Oxford University Press).
Mayall, J. (2000), 'Nationalism and International Order', in M. Leifer (ed.), *Asian Nationalism* (London: Routledge), 187–96.
Mayall, J. and M. Simpson (1992), 'Ethnicity Is Not Enough', *International Journal of Comparative Sociology* 33, 5–25.
Ratner, S. (1996), 'Drawing a Better Line: *Uti Possidetis* and the Borders of New States', *American Journal of International Law* 90:4, 590–624.
Smith, A.D. (1983), *Theories of Nationalism*, 2nd edition (New York: Holmes and Meir).
Smith, A.D. (1987), *The Ethnic Origins of Nations* (Oxford: Blackwell).
Srinivasan, K. (2009), 'Conflict and Cooperation in the 21st Century', in J. Mayall and K. Srinivasan, *Towards the New Horizon: World Order in the 21st Century* (New Delhi: Standard Publishers).
Yokota, R.M. *Okinawa is a State of Mind*. [Online] At http://www.uchinachu.org/uchinachu/history_early.htm [accessed 13 July 2010].

# The History of Secession: An Overview

Bridget L. Coggins

## Introduction

For as long as political communities have existed, discontented minorities within them have attempted to break away. Indeed, the Ionians enlisted Greece to help them escape the Persians as far back as 479 BC (Herodotus 1997: 719–20). They were certainly not the first, and far from the last to make such an attempt. Negative experiences with governance routinely cause people to see themselves as distinct from their rulers; as bound to a common fate with those who share the same ascriptive or socio-cultural traits; and as members of communities better served by self-government than alien domination. Self-determination demands can take various forms including calls for increased civil and cultural rights, local autonomy, condominium, suzerainty, or confederal arrangements. A small fraction of these movements will seek total independence, resolving that their governors can not—or more likely will not—accommodate their desire for self-determination. Since the rise of the modern state, these claims of complete territorial and political independence are manifest in secessionism, wherein a nationalist movement attempts to formally withdraw from an existing state in order to create a new one.[1]

---

1   The origins of the interstate system date back to the Peace of Westphalia (1648), comprised by the treaties of Osnabrück and Münster, which ended the Thirty Years and Eighty Years Wars in Europe. Contained in those documents are the foundational elements of the modern order: legal equality, domestic authority and non-intervention. However, the principles first glimpsed there were not fully embraced until the middle of the 19th century (Krasner 1999). Consequently, it is fair to say that secessionism, the modern phenomenon, only occurred from that point forward. Closely related though distinct from secessionism is irredentism, wherein a group demands independence from one state because it hopes to join another existing state. Had Ireland not revoked its claim to sovereignty over Northern Ireland, for example, we might argue that the conflict there was an irredentist, rather than a secessionist, conflict.

This chapter provides a brief introduction to the history of the multifaceted phenomenon of secession. Apart from some notable exceptions, existing work on the topic focuses on individual cases, like those of Tibet or Quebec (Bothwell 1998; Goldstein 1999; Shakya 1999; Young 1998), or on a particular historical moment, like the near simultaneous collapses of Yugoslavia and the Soviet Union (Bessinger 2002; Caplan 2005; Walker 2003).[2] Those studies have helped to identify secession's causes and consequences, its legal and normative characteristics, and potential strategies for conflict resolution. Unfortunately, isolated cases impede our ability to discern larger, long-term patterns or uncover meaningful similarities between seemingly disparate events. Rather than limiting its scope to a historically significant but non-representative sample, this chapter takes a macro-historical approach, tracking changes in secessionism across time. It begins by briefly describing the nature of secession. It then charts historical changes in secessionism and juxtaposes them against its more enduring characteristics. The chapter closes with a discussion of current secessionism and how it might shape world politics in the future.

## The Evolution of Nation-States

During the 17th and 18th centuries, the rise of the modern nation-state fundamentally transformed political authority. Sovereignty once held by emperors or legitimated by a divine unimpeachable right was gradually challenged from below. With the modern state's rise to ubiquity in Europe during the 19th century, sovereignty came to depend on the popular will of the citizenry. Or at least was legitimated on those grounds. Self-determination embodied the new idea that the people should determine the content and course of their government. Nationalism, the normative belief that governmental jurisdictions and the boundaries of national identity should align, also became a major political force. The growing threat of popular nationalist rebellion compelled governments to justify their continued rule and explain why their diverse populations should be governed together within a single polity. Rulers without a compelling national myth were more vulnerable to challenges at home and to predatory annexations along their borders.

By the middle of the 19th century, nationalist uprisings had spread across the continent. Many arose over the very definition of the nation. Opinions about the ideal basis for communal identity, be it history, language, religion or some combination of factors, and therefore about who rightfully belonged within the polity, were often at odds. Some populations believed they had a natural affinity with their neighbors and set about achieving self-government, but most did not. The nations championed by nationalists were rarely fully-formed. At times, a common

---

2  Exceptions include Armitage (2007), Hale (2008), Heraclides (1990), Pavković with Radan (2007), Premdas et al. (1990), Roeder (2007), Spencer (1998), Walter (2009) and a wealth of writings on normative or legal aspects of secession and secessionism.

identity had to be constructed wholesale. As d'Azeglio famously exclaimed, "We have made Italy, now we must make Italians!" (Emerson 1960: 95).

Nationalism took on two primary forms: civic and ethnic. Demands predicated upon civic, or liberal, nationalism, as enshrined in the American Declaration of Independence (1776), theoretically allowed individuals to become voluntary and equal members of the nation because the people were united by their ideals.[3] This type of nationalism was not inherently opposed to large multi-national states.[4] Ethnic nationalism though, was more restrictive. It prioritized a single ethnic group as the basis for the nation-state and relegated others to a lesser status. Most secessionist movements espoused this exclusionary, ethnic nationalism, which presented an inherently threatening possibility for any would-be minorities within the new state's borders. Even the most homogenous communities had some variation within them. As a result, ethnic nationalism fractured multinational empires and the tension between national self-determination and state integrity grew steadily throughout the 20th century.[5]

The ideology of nationalism spread globally in the late 19th and 20th centuries as colonial peoples adopted European beliefs about self-determination, particularly self-determination achieved via independence. Although the United Nations and imperial states did not condone it, the strong conviction that nations ought to be endowed with states, not merely granted rights within those that already existed, provoked opposition to various forms of "foreign" rule. Colonial borders became strong organizational focal points for nationalists, but rebellions also arose among traditional social groups that sometimes claimed territory within or across colonies, like the Kingdom of Buganda or the Pan-African movement.[6] In these cases, secessionists tried to undo the colonial borders that had been erected in the 19th century to disrupt traditional settlement patterns so that Europeans could assert control.

---

3   In practice, the Americans fell short of the civic ideal, restricting African Americans, Native Americans and women the full practice of citizenship.
4   It should also be noted, however, that civic nationalism is not always sufficient when it comes to deterring secessionist demands. The attempted secession of the Confederate States of America (CSA) (see Chapter 5 below) shows that no government is entirely immune.
5   Sensitive to the negative consequences of ethno-national secession, powerful external actors sometimes create legislative protections for minorities remaining within the newly independent state. At Versailles, statesmen attempted to ensure that recognition of any successor states would hinge on their protection of minorities (Fink 2000). More recently, the European Economic Community (now European Union) outlined requirements including minority protections for states emerging from the former Soviet Union and former Yugoslavia. Still, outsiders have found it difficult to enforce these protections once a new state is endowed with sovereignty because they have committed to non-intervention in its domestic affairs.
6   Not all Pan-Africanists aspired to unified independence, sometimes preferring a loose coalition of independent states.

By the middle of the 20th century, nationalists demanded that national identity be the presumptive basis for self-determination, sovereignty and membership in the international society of states. As with any ideology though, the nationalist vision is difficult to realize given the political reality. Jennings describes the crux of the problem well. "On the surface [self-determination] seemed reasonable: let the people decide. It was in fact ridiculous because the people cannot decide until somebody decides who the people are" (1956). Worldwide there is substantial disagreement over "who the people are." The boundaries of national identity and the borders of states have never perfectly aligned. And, in the few places where they have, they have often not remained that way for very long.

## Changes in Demands and Outcomes

In the latter half of the 18th century, the American colonies' declaration of independence was a harbinger of secessionist demands to come.[7] Both its spirit and the document itself served as templates for scores of movements to follow (Armitage 2007). But as pivotal as the American Revolution was to advancing ideals like the rights of man and self-determination, its influence was not instantaneous. Independence was a relatively uncommon demand and an infrequent source of new states until the turn of the century. Reliable records of secessionist demands during this period do not exist, however the pattern of state emergence during the 19th century provides some insight.

In 1816, there were 25 states in the international system (Correlates of War 2008).[8] One hundred years later, as World War One raged, there were still less than 50 states (see Figure 2.1).[9] Secession was rare over the course of the century, taking place principally in conjunction with anti-colonialism in the Americas. Even so, it was responsible for most new states and its cumulative effects sometimes proved significant enough to change even powerful states' fortunes. The Spanish case is illustrative. Early in the 19th century, Mexican Indians and mestizos, led by Miguel Hidalgo y Castilla, revolted against Spain (1810).

---

7   Many scholars reasonably argue that anti-colonial movements are not properly termed secessionist. Yet excluding anti-colonial movements from this project would be anachronous. Most imperial powers considered their own anti-colonial movements to be secessionist. Though it is certainly the case that anti-colonial secessions and non-colonial secessions had different inherent characteristics and conflict dynamics, both types ultimately sought to separate from an existing state in order to create a new one. Therefore, I consider them secessionist (see also the Introduction).

8   The most comprehensive and systematic data on system membership comes from the Correlates of War Project. Unfortunately, that data begins in 1816, not 1800.

9   Interestingly, the event that catalyzed World War One was Austrian Archduke Franz Ferdinand's assassination at the hands of the Bosnian Serb nationalist and irredentist group "Young Bosnia."

# THE HISTORY OF SECESSION: AN OVERVIEW

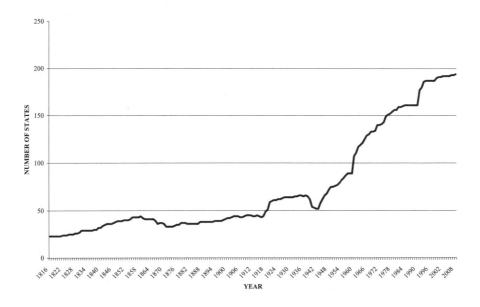

**Figure 2.1** System members (1816–2008)

The rebels were slaughtered at Guanajuato by loyalists at first, but their cause inspired a larger movement that ultimately led to a successful war of independence. The new state, the Mexican Empire, joined the interstate system in 1821.[10] Perhaps more important, Mexico's example provoked other secessionist demands as Spanish control in the hemisphere weakened. Argentina, New Granada (now Colombia), Chile, Peru and Upper Peru (now Bolivia), Paraguay, Uruguay and Venezuela were all among them. In total, Spain lost 18 of its colonies in less than 100 years and its international stature declined precipitously. Although the most notorious case of secessionism during that time was the Confederate States of America's (CSA) failed attempt to separate from the United States of America (1861–65), it was anomalous (see Chapter 5). Elsewhere, anti-colonial movements and their successes would be more influential to the future course of secessionism than the Confederacy's non-colonial defeat.

In contrast, the 20th century saw a dramatic rise in secession as a source of new states. Figure 2.2 shows that between 1816 and 1916, secession was responsible for approximately 63 percent (26) of the new states entering the system. The remaining 15 emerged due to other processes like state consolidation, unilateral decolonization, or the mutual dissolution of unions.[11]

---

10   The Mexican Empire was replaced by the Republic of Mexico in 1823.
11   Unilateral decolonization is distinct from secession. Unilateral decolonization occurred where there were not local aspirations to independence. Instead, the push toward independence was initiated by the colonial power.

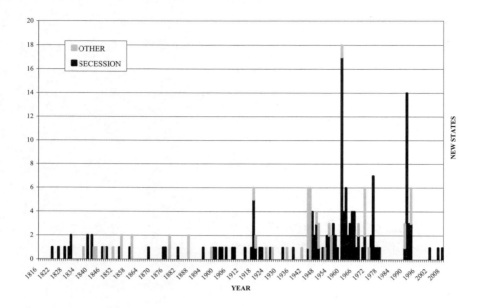

**Figure 2.2    New states (1816–2008)**

In the 20th century, far more members entered the interstate system and a greater percentage of those states emerged as a result of secession. The number of states nearly quadrupled, growing to 194 by 2008 (see Figure 2.1). During that time, the percentage born as a result of secession approached 70 percent. In the last 50 years it grew to 73 percent, making secession an increasingly common cause of state birth. Moreover, the 20th century saw secessionism transform from a sporadic, regional phenomenon into a common event worldwide.

Demands for secession in the 20th century came primarily from the second wave of anti-colonial movements in Africa and Asia. However, secessionism also saw a marked increase within the established states of Europe. In the colonies, exposure to ideas like self-determination and nationalism spurred rebellion against the imperial powers. Colonial peoples' widespread dissatisfaction with the order caught some of their host states by surprise, as did discontent among European minorities closer to home. Emerson explains, "[Early in the century] self-determination ... had been proclaimed as a dogma of universal application, but in practice it was not intended ... to reach significantly beyond the confines of Europe or, even there, to penetrate into the territory of the victors [of World War One]" (Emerson 1960: 3–4). President Woodrow Wilson's famous "Fourteen Points" speech and the later success of the UN's decolonization efforts catalyzed the striking increase in secessionism (see Figure 2.3).

# The History of Secession: An Overview

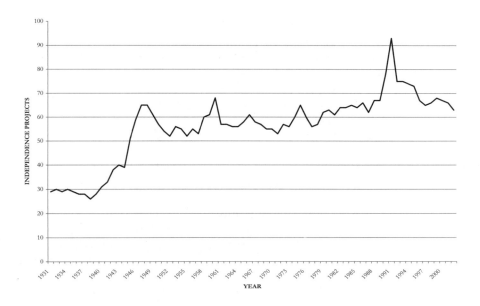

**Figure 2.3** Secessionist movements (1931–2002)

> What we demand ... is nothing peculiar to ourselves. It is that the world be made fit and safe to live in; and particularly that it be made safe for every peace-loving nation which, like our own, wishes to live its own life, determine its own institutions, be assured of justice and fair dealing by the other peoples of the world as against force and selfish aggression. All the peoples of the world are in effect partners in this interest, and for our own part we see very clearly that unless justice be done to others it will not be done to us. The programme of the world's peace, therefore, is our programme ... (Wilson 1918)

President Wilson's intention was not to foment nationalist rebellions, but to reinstate or create national independence for a limited number of peoples affected by World War One. And as planned, after the war, a number of states became independent within new borders including Austria, Hungary, and Poland. Some of Wilson's contemporaries were concerned about the long-term implications of what might be interpreted as unqualified support for self-determination, however. Robert Lansing, his Secretary of State, predicted that it would "raise hopes that can never be realized ... cost thousands of lives ... [and was] bound to be discredited, to be called the dream of an idealist who failed to realize the danger until [it was] too late to check those who attempt to put the principle in force" (1921: 97–8). Though perhaps a less unmitigated disaster than Lansing imagined, self-determination's appeal was also more potent than Wilson had anticipated (see also Chapter 13).

In Europe, the Irish raised demands for home rule beginning in the 1880s and waged a small war of independence against Britain, eventually securing control over 26 of its 32 counties on the heels of World War One.[12] Unfortunately, the peace resulting from the agreement granting Ireland a dominion status was short lived. Conflict reignited between Catholics and Protestants in the North and continued for decades before reaching a promising settlement in 2005.[13] A number of European secessionist movements emerged around the same time or a few years later. They included the Basque Country, Scotland, Flanders, and Alto Adige/South Tyrol. Further to the east, separatists had been or became active in Chechnya, Croatia, Cyprus, Kosovo, and Ukraine. Many have seen popular support wax and wane over the years, and have undergone ideological and strategic transformations. Still many remain active, and without independent states, to date.

It was not until World War Two that anti-colonial secessionism exploded. The movements were more successful at securing independence than their European peers. All the same, the imperial powers only grudgingly accepted the colonies' secessions. Spruyt (2005) observes that long-term, system-wide changes helped to secure the secessionists' success. By that time, control over land had significantly decreased in value and the global spread of nationalism had increased the costs of holding on to far flung territories. For the first time, the powers were also facing secessionism in many colonies at once. Moreover, at the end of the war, the allies had explicitly tasked the United Nations (UN) with decolonization (UN Charter 1945: Chapters XI–XII; UN 1960). The only remaining question was when—not whether—colonial secession would occur. Not all states acquiesced to the UN's new authority though, so the pace and shape of independence proved quite variable. For instance, Portugal insisted that it would not submit to the liquidation of its "overseas territories" including Angola, Mozambique, and Portuguese Guinea. And for many years its intransigence was rewarded because the United States and Britain consistently sided with the *status quo*. Even so, 67 successful anti-colonial secessions occurred between 1945 and 2002. In fact, the United Nations' Special Committee on Decolonization was so successful that today it has nearly run out of work.[14]

Unsurprisingly, the large number of successful anti-colonial secessions did not satisfy the global demand for independence. Instead, secessionism remained appealing for nations and nationalists without states; especially those who found themselves in exclusionary, newly independent states. Together, Figures 2.2 and 2.3 show that most anti-colonial movements began shortly after World War Two

---

12   Some suggest that Wilson's political failure at home after World War One was due, at least in part, to Irish-American disillusionment with his failure to support Ireland's independence and the nationalists' exclusion from Versailles.
13   Although the Belfast or "Good Friday" Agreement was signed in 1998, the Provisional Irish Republican Army (PIRA) did not end its campaign and decommission its weapons until summer 2005.
14   According to the UN, only 16 non-self-governing territories remain as of 2009. Only one, the Western Sahara, has an active anti-colonial secessionist movement (UN 2009).

and generally became independent by the mid-1960s. There was a noticeable dip in the number of secessionist projects shortly thereafter, but by 1976 the number was back up to 65 and remained relatively high through the end of the study period. The number of non-colonial secessionist demands was increasing. New post-colonial states that threatened their minorities prompted secessionist rebellions in Uganda, Nigeria, India, Burma, Indonesia, Ethiopia, and the Sudan (see Part VI), to name only a handful, replacing the movements that had recently secured the host states' independence. More new attempts at secession were made in China and Southeast Asia (see Part VI), which were framed within the ideological oppositions of the Cold War, and elsewhere among relatively small indigenous groups and island nations as in Bougainville, Puerto Rico, Anjouan, Corsica, and Vanuatu. These non-colonial secessionist demands were both less likely to be resolved quickly and less likely to result in statehood. Major international institutions and their member states were only willing to accept newcomers within a narrow set of parameters. Formal colonialism was often justification enough for independence, but anything else, typically, was not (see Chapters 13 and 15).

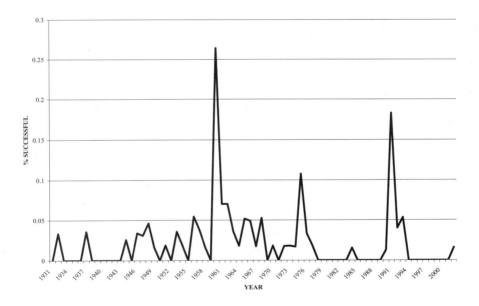

Figure 2.4  Annual success rates (1931–2002)

The dramatic rise in secessionism in the 20th century did not translate into a dramatic rise in the probability of success. The most comprehensive data (1931–2002) shows spikes in the likelihood of independence occurred as a result of decolonization in Africa in the early 1960s, the late independences of the Portuguese colonies and Bangladesh (formerly East Pakistan) in the 1970s, and the collapses of the Soviet Union and Yugoslavia beginning in 1991 (see Chapter 8 and Part VI) (see Figure 2.4). So while just over one out of every three secessionist movements (37 percent) ultimately secured an independent state, the deck was stacked in favor of anti-colonial movements and those emerging from a disintegrating host state. Anti-colonial movements' success rate was around 75 percent; the success rate for others was less than one in five (18.5 percent). In a given year, the chance of an average secessionist movement's securing independence was only about 2 percent (see also Chapter 15).

## Changes in Methods and Means

Most secessionist conflicts do not become full-scale wars, but the overwhelming majority of them do experience violence.[15] Of the 275 most recent cases of secessionism, 195 had incidents of mortal violence. In total, secessionist conflicts (including anti-colonial secessionism) killed more than 5 million combatants in the 20th century, and likely killed and displaced far more non-combatants. The conflict between the Sudanese government and secessionists in the South alone caused approximately 250,000 battle deaths (Lacina and Gleditsch 2005) and over a million civilian casualties (see also Part VI).

Secessionist conflicts are predisposed to violence. Secessionism can have disastrous consequences for host states. When formal separation occurs, the loss of people and territory means reduced manpower, tax revenue, natural resources, and infrastructure. In some cases, the deficit is so severe that it imperils the host state's continued viability. Secessionist conflicts themselves are also usually costly and violent because the parties do not bargain well. Statesmen tend to view their country's territory as an indivisible whole. And research suggests that this belief spurs and prolongs violence because leaders insist that a negotiated compromise cannot be reached with their secessionists. They refuse to even contemplate the destruction of what they believe to be inviolable. Therefore, the psychological stakes in secessionist conflicts may be high even where the objective value of the people and territory seceding appears low (Toft 2003). Furthermore, the government's refusal to negotiate means that secessionist conflicts are more

---

15   Only one party had to employ violence in order for a conflict to be characterized as violent, though both usually did so. Only in a small minority of cases did only the secessionists (6) or only the host state (13) use violence. Notably, in none of the conflicts where the government employed violence alone did the secessionists ultimately become independent (Coggins 2006).

destructive than they need to be. If bargaining is not a credible option, violent repression or total war are the only alternatives to remove the secessionist threat (Walter 1997).

It is easy to envision hypothetical circumstances where secession would leave a host state better-off. The region may be a net recipient of government funds, leaving the state more financially secure *ex post*. The territory might be difficult or expensive to control, leaving the state more geo-strategically secure. Or, the secessionist population might be seen as a liability, leaving the nation more homogenous and harmonious once it has departed.[16] But leaders of host states rarely see secession's potential benefits.

Even when they might otherwise be willing to permit a particular group's independence, host state leaders may oppose letting go for fear of setting a precedent that would encourage additional challengers to emerge (Walter 2006). For example, the USSR and Yugoslavia's collapses in the early 1990s stoked the longstanding fear that a single secession might initiate an irreversible, domino-like process of state dissolution (see Chapter 8). Governments with a number of discontented minorities may understandably fear this kind of demonstration effect (Horowitz 1985; Lake and Rothschild 1998). In short, once a movement for secession begins, host states almost universally believe they have much to lose and nothing to gain. As a consequence, they are often willing to take extraordinary steps to ensure that their state remains intact.

Secessionists face similarly high stakes but, unlike the host, they may ultimately secure gains. Secessionist demands rest upon the complaint that host states are impeding national self-determination. However, it is not usually groups' first or preferred strategy to demand independence. Before they seek secession, most have exhausted the potential domestic political remedies to their problems. In other words, they try to achieve sanctioned self-determination within the host state (see Chapter 21). For all of the aforementioned reasons though, statesmen generally crack down on the groups instead of conceding or compromising. This reaction, predictably, only intensifies the separatist nation's grievances against the host state. Further, the demands for self-determination brand the entire nation an internal enemy in the eyes of the state, so the whole population, including those not actively involved, is at risk. In sum, secessionists typically begin from a position of weakness and only become weaker as the conflict escalates; all the while their grievances against the host state become more acute. At the extreme end of the spectrum, secessionists may literally be fighting against their nation's extinction. Some groups have institutional leverage, like autonomous local governments, or have active diasporas abroad to provide monetary and ideological support.[17]

---

16   This kind of reasoning motivated apartheid era South Africa's failed attempt (at least insofar as external recognition and legitimacy was concerned) to unilaterally grant independence to the African Bantustans (see Chapter 15).
17   It is reasonable to believe that movements that choose to attempt secession do so, at least in part, because they are advantaged relative to other similarly aggrieved groups.

But, these advantages rarely make up for the significant economic and political repression visited upon separatist communities.

While potential loses accrue to the secessionist community as a whole, not all of the potential benefits of independence do. For a secessionist movement's leaders, independence holds the possibility of acquiring high-profile political positions in the new state. Those political positions often imply wealth, prestige, power, and lifestyle upgrades. Outside of domestic politics, statehood also carries valuable status for individuals including benefits like legal immunity, sovereign power, and control over the new state's diplomatic affairs (UN 1970). Some have observed that the individual incentives for power and prestige can corrupt the bargaining process on the secessionists' side as nationalist leaders become increasingly dedicated to independence at all costs rather than seeking a more optimal bargain that assures security and well-being for their nation.

Different benefits accrue to the national group in the seceded state. First, grievances against the host state are rectified. For example, civil and political rights are granted, access to education restored, natural resource wealth secured, and cultural life revived. Second, the national group's standing in international affairs is raised significantly. States are the only actors with legal personality, which grants them a right to self-defense, empowers them to make treaties and negotiate trade, and permits access to important international governmental organizations. Of course, the most significant prize is the nation's ability to determine its own political destiny. Still, secessionists often mistakenly believe independence is a panacea. Especially when success follows a costly war, material conditions in the new state may not be better than they were in the host state. Nor are new governments necessarily more participatory or less corrupt. Even within relatively wealthy, successful post-secessionist states, nostalgia for the old days is not uncommon (Standen 2006).

However, the intensity of violence varies substantially from case to case and some secessionist conflicts remain non-violent for their entirety. Concerning trends, secessionist violence has grown as a portion of global violence and greater numbers of secessions become violent, but the average level of violence in those conflicts has declined. The Correlates of War dataset, cataloguing all civil wars between 1816 and 1997, shows that a majority of the wars between states and non-state actors after 1900 were secessionist (2008). Before then, wars were mostly wars of conquest or rebellions unrelated to an independence demand. Data on civil violence since 1945 show that 113 of 275 major internal conflicts were caused by secession or separatism (Gates and Strand 2004).[18] Over the same time period, approximately 17 extra-territorial secessionist wars, between an imperial power and a non-contiguous non-state actor, were fought (Correlates of

---

18  According to the stated aims of the rebel organization identified by PRIO-CSCW. In cases where more than one rebel organization was named in a conflict, any individual organization making a demand for independence was coded as a demand for all of the organizations on that side of the conflict.

War 2008).[19] Altogether, secessionist conflicts constituted nearly half of the major violence between states and non-state actors in the 20th century. As compared to international wars, civil and extra-territorial wars do not kill as many people as quickly. But, ultimately, they kill more people because they are more frequent and tend to last much longer than interstate wars (Correlates of War 2008) (see also Chapter 12).

The balance of power between host states and secessionists means violence favors the host. Governments have a number of advantages relative to challengers including organized militaries, police forces and the ability to legally raise funds via increased taxation. That expectation is borne out historically. Secessionists are unlikely to win wars against their host states. Between 1931 and 2002, only 15 wars ended decisively in secessionists' favor whereas 26 wars favored host states or ended in a draw that favored the host. When secessionists succeeded militarily, the group usually went on to secure political independence (13/15), though far more often than not, the outcome favored the government.

Though host states have more material capacity, secessionists do have some strategic advantages. First, secessionist nations are geographically concentrated and often inhabit so-called hinterlands where the coercive reach of the state is weak and the secessionist population is indigenous to the area. As a result, secessionist combatants are more familiar with the terrain, geography, and population than are government troops. Second, guerrillas can literally blend into the civilian population to avoid capture or perpetrate surprise attacks. Finally, even when secessionist leaders do not believe they can prevail militarily, they often believe that their desire to achieve independence will outlast their host state's will to maintain control. Therefore, they pursue the host state's attrition rather than a conventional victory. In general, when secessionist wars take the form of guerrilla combat, it can expose governments' inflexibility and militaries' discomfort with unconventional war. Secessionists can occasionally exploit these seams and secure victory despite the odds against it. Still, these wars tend to be very long. For example, Eritrea's conflict with Ethiopia lasted 30 years (see Part VI) and Namibia's conflict with South Africa lasted 13.

Figure 2.5 shows that, over the course of the last seven decades, a majority of ongoing secessionist conflicts experienced violence. And that, as a proportion of ongoing secessions, violent conflicts have increased since the 1960s. In the 20th century, a number of major, very violent secessionist conflicts occurred in places like Vietnam, Algeria, the Sudan, Sri Lanka, Angola, Ethiopia, and the Philippines. Two periods witnessed particularly violent secessionism: the early 1950s during the Franco-Vietnamese and Korean Wars and the early 1960s through the middle 1970s due to anti-colonial wars.

---

19  The Extra-Systemic War Dataset only formally extends to 1997. The data were extended by surveying extra-systemic wars between 1997 and 2006.

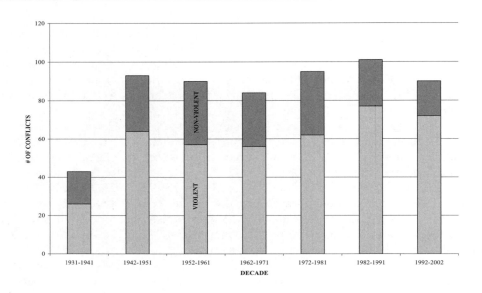

**Figure 2.5  Violent and non-violent secession (1931–2002)**

The rise in violence as a proportion of secessionist conflicts masks the notable downward trend in the intensity of violence within those conflicts (see Figure 2.6). Emblematically, in 1990 and 1992, there were 27 violent secessionist conflicts, but those conflicts averaged less than 1,000 battle deaths each year. In fact, in only one year since 1980 has an average of 1,000 battle deaths per conflict been exceeded. Between 2000 and 2009, the average secessionist conflict only caused around 300 battle deaths each year. In contrast, 50 years earlier (between 1950 and 1959), when there were approximately 13 ongoing secessions, the average was around 8,000 casualties per year.

The "frozen conflicts" in Moldova and the Caucasus (Abkhazia, South Ossetia, and Nagorno-Karabakh, and Transdniestria, see further Part VI) illustrate the general trend in violence. Each was a relatively small war that killed thousands, but not tens of thousands before reaching a stalemate.[20] The gradual decline in violence was also partially due to the decline in the great power rivalry between the United States and the Soviet Union (and the eventual dissolution of the latter), who funneled resources to the parties in Vietnam, Korea, Ethiopia, Angola, and Namibia. Lastly, some conflicts, particularly European attempts at secession involving terrorism, killed small numbers of people in most years. But many of these secessionists have shifted toward mainstream politics, and away from extra-political violence, as a means to self-determination.

---

20   According to Lacina and Gleditsch (2005), the most intense conflict of the four, in terms of battle deaths, was the Nagorno-Karabakh-Azerbaijan conflict. Between 1992 and 1994, the estimates for that war range from 4,200 deaths to approximately 13,500.

# The History of Secession: An Overview

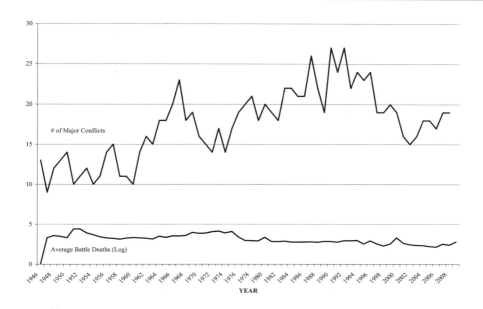

**Figure 2.6** Annual separatist violence (1946–2008)

So while the conflicts in Northern Ireland, the Basque Country, and Iraqi Kurdistan (see Part VI) were violent, they were significantly less so as the 21st century began.

Few states throughout history have included legal provisions for secession within their constitutions, and only a slightly larger number explicitly outlaw secession.[21] A large-scale survey of 89 historical and contemporary constitutions found only seven countries with explicit legal contingencies for secession (Monahan 1996). They are/were Austria, Ethiopia, France (for overseas territories only), Saint Christopher and Nevis, Singapore, the USSR, and Czechoslovakia. More recently, the State Union of Serbia and Montenegro, formed in 2003, contained a legal clause for secession, and dissolved peacefully following a referendum on Montenegro's independence in 2006 (see Chapter 7). Additionally, though the process and standards remain unclear, many legal scholars suggest that Canada now permits legal secession (see Chapters 7 and 18). Most states leave its legality ambiguous. Nevertheless, the absence of a prescribed, formal procedure does not mean that separation cannot sometimes occur without large scale violence. In fact, over 60 percent of non-violent secessionist conflicts ended in independence; a much higher success rate than violent conflicts.[22]

---

21 The People's Republic of China is a recent exception with its 2005 Anti-Secession Law (Xinhua 2005). Most laws do not expressly outlaw secession. Instead, governments extend existing laws against treason, subversion or terrorism.

22 This might be an effect rather than a cause. Host states might not respond violently to

In states without provisions for secession in place, nationalists have still found legal means of advocating for their independence. One common tactic is forming a political party with a secessionist platform. Independence parties have become common in Europe and North America. Some contemporary examples include the Parti Quebecois (PQ) in Canada, the Liga Nord in Italy, the Scottish National Party (SNP) in the UK, and Flemish Interest (VB: Vlaams Belang) in Belgium. Other parties, that have alternated between normal politics and insurrection, include Sinn Féin in Northern Ireland, Battasuna in Spain, the Front for the Liberation of the Enclave of Cabinda (FLEC) in Angola, and the Ogaden National Liberation Front (ONLF) in Ethiopia. These parties enjoy less domestic legitimacy, however, and are sometimes outlawed by the government as a result of their supposed or demonstrated support for terrorism and other forms of political violence.

Of course, not all states allow citizens to participate freely in politics, and this leaves groups with no options other than those outside the scope of permitted political action. In some cases, secessionists choose violence. In others, they form international campaigns for independence, advocating for change from the outside. And others still pursue some combination of the two. One example is the Tibetan Youth Congress, an international organization made up largely of the Tibetan diaspora, dedicated to Tibet's complete political independence from China (see Part VI). As Connelly observes in the Algerian case, international advocacy of this sort can have a pivotal effect on secessionist outcomes (2002). Though the Algerian National Liberation Front (FLN) could not defeat French forces on the battlefield, their diplomatic efforts persuaded foreign capitals to grant them formal recognition, which they successfully leveraged into independence in 1962.

## Enduring Characteristics of Secession

Despite rather dramatic changes in the frequency, character, and outcomes of secessionism over time, some features have remained relatively constant. First, although many scholars have foretold the fall of the nation-state and sovereignty's diminution (Rosecrance 1999; Kaplan 1994; Huntington 1993; Schreuer 1993), statehood remains a valuable commodity. The continuous stream of new secessions across time is a testament to the resilience of the state as an institution and the nation's centrality to it. No alternative has arisen as a credible challenge to its dominance.

Second, third-party states and international institutions have consistently played an influential role in secessionist conflicts. When a group demands an independent state of its own, self-government is only a part of what it seeks. Secessionists are also requesting recognition as rightful and legitimate members of the society of states, a highly exclusive and beneficent club. So while secessionist conflicts often

---

secessions that imply lower stakes or costs. And secessionists in this situation would not need to employ violence to achieve independence.

stay within the physical territory of a single state, they are rarely only domestic affairs. Statesmen sometimes defer to the host state as a sign of respect for its sovereignty. However, it is difficult for countries not to become involved when leaders believe their interests are at stake; either in support of or contrary to the *status quo*. For strong states with extensive interests and a global reach, intervention of some sort is the norm.

Foreign intervention in secession takes various forms. Governments sometimes intervene militarily in order to secure their preferred outcome, as when India fought Pakistan to secure the independence of Bangladesh (East Pakistan) in 1971. Or as India and Pakistan now fight over the future status of Kashmir. At other times they assist covertly as when the United States helped Croatia to retake Serb controlled territory in 1995's Operation Storm (for these cases see Part VI). More often, states provide material or diplomatic support to the parties. For instance, the United States and much of Europe unilaterally recognized Kosovo's independence early in 2008. For Kosovo, legitimacy within this powerful minority of states has already translated into membership in the International Monetary Fund (IMF) and World Bank, and has yielded significant financial and developmental resources. Russia disagreed with the Kosovo decision and, when given the opportunity, counter-recognized the independences of Abkhazia and South Ossetia (see Part VI). Since then, Russia has worked to secure legitimacy for its two new allies. In both cases, states lent their support to the parties to help make their independences a reality and to secure their international recognition.

Third, the tendency for international politics to seep into conflicts has stalled constructive normative or legal developments regarding secessionism. Despite a great deal of discussion, little has changed in the UN's approach to secessionism in the last 60 years. The UN has consistently maintained that the right to self-determination does not imply a right to secession. Apart from the United Nations, international law and the practice of states have each reaffirmed it.[23] However, the absence of a right of secession does not elucidate the conditions under which secession might be deemed acceptable or justified. It seems that just as statesmen are hesitant to outline the steps to legitimate secession within their constitutions, so the UN is hesitant to outline consistent standards for external legitimacy; or its members simply cannot agree. As a result, nations, host states and jurists are left to interpret precedents as ongoing secessionist conflicts continue to unfold (see Chapter 17).

---

23  This does not mean that strong arguments are not currently being made for a qualified right of secession or that practice has not occasionally appeared to support secession in cases of justified grievance. For discussions of normative approaches see Part V.

## Conclusion

Secessionism has transformed over the course of the last 200 years. In the 19th and early 20th centuries, anti-colonial secession was the most common source of new states, but remained relatively infrequent. By mid-century, secessionism rapidly spread to Africa and Asia as empires were replaced by sovereign states. Colonial independence did not create an enduring equilibrium or stability for the society of states though. Instead, the desire for independence and sovereignty rose to fill and surpass the vacuum left in the wake of the growth in membership. Violence accompanied secessionism far more often than not and became an increasingly common means of pursuing independence over time. Still, in the last 50 years, as violent secessionism proliferated, the level of violence within secessionist conflicts has been on a steady decline.

Though much has changed, some aspects of secession remain constant. The nation-state is still a powerful prize for those political communities without one. And, despite their significant influence over secessionist conflicts, outside states have not yet reached a consensus on norms or practice when it comes to non-colonial secession. Recent international responses to the secessions of Kosovo, Abkhazia, and South Ossetia seem to suggest states' positions on secession are diverging. Yet South Sudan's recent referendum on independence, if followed by widespread legitimacy and the successful implementation of the Comprehensive Peace Agreement (CPA), will demonstrate that the international community can serve as a guarantor to limit violence when acting in concert (see Part VI).

Together the dynamic and static characteristics outlined in this chapter suggest an uncertain future for secessionism. Historically, secessionist conflicts were resolved most quickly when there was broad agreement about the type of members interstate society was willing to accept. Notably, anti-colonial secessionism succeeded when powerful states colluded to pressure host states to concede. The contemporary politics of secession are less straightforward. Of late, secessionists that have created relatively stable and independent enclaves, including Abkhazia, Somaliland, and South Ossetia, have not been recognized as independent by their host states or the wider community of states and international institutions (see Part VI and Chapters 14 and 15). Conversely, secessionist movements that have not achieved stable authority or widespread domestic legitimacy, like Bosnia and Herzegovina, East Timor, and Kosovo, have nevertheless become states (see Chapters 8 and 9). Some that used terrorism and political violence were successful, some were not. Some that created participatory, democratic institutions were successful, some were not. There are victorious and failed exemplars of nearly every type. If the past is any indication of the future then, violent secessionism will continue to proliferate. But without an international consensus regarding secessionist norms, most conflicts will drag on or reach stalemates only to reignite because foreign capitals will not unanimously ratify battlefield outcomes or compel negotiated compromises between the parties.

# References

Armitage, David (2007), *The Declaration of Independence: A Global History* (Cambridge, MA: Harvard University Press).
Bessinger, Mark (2002), *Nationalist Mobilization and the Collapse of the Soviet State* (Cambridge: Cambridge University Press).
Bothwell, Robert (1998), *Canada and Quebec: One Country, Two Histories* (Vancouver: University of British Columbia Press).
Caplan, Richard (2005), *Europe and the Recognition of New States in Yugoslavia* (Cambridge: Cambridge University Press).
Coggins, Bridget (2006), "Secession, Recognition and the International Politics of Statehood," Doctoral Dissertation, Ohio State University.
Connelly, Matthew (2002), *A Diplomatic Revolution: Algeria's Fight for Independence and the Origins of the Post-Cold War Era* (Oxford: Oxford University Press).
Correlates of War Project (2008), "State System Membership List, v2008.1." [Online] At http://correlatesofwar.org [accessed December 2009].
Emerson, Rupert (1967[1960]), *From Empire to Nation* (Cambridge, MA: Harvard University Press).
Fink, Carole (2000), "Minority Rights as an International Question," *Contemporary European History* 9:3, 385–400.
Gates, Scott G. and Håvard Strand (2004), "Modeling the Duration of Civil Wars: Measurement and Estimation Issues." [Online] At http://www.prio.no/ [accessed August 2009].
Goldstein, Melvyn C. (1999), *The Snow Lion and the Dragon: China, Tibet and the Dalai Lama* (Berkeley, CA: University of California Press).
Hale, Henry (2008), *The Foundations of Ethnic Politics: Separatism of States and Nations in Eurasia and the World* (Cambridge: Cambridge University Press).
Heraclides, Alexis (1990), "Secessionist Minorities and External Involvement," *International Organization* 44:3, 341–78.
Herodotus (1997), *The Histories*. Trans. George Rawlinson (New York, NY: Alfred A. Knopf).
Horowitz, Donald L. (1985), *Ethnic Groups in Conflict* (Berkeley, CA: University of California Press).
Huntington, Samuel (1993), "The Clash of Civilizations?" *Foreign Affairs* 72:3, 22–49.
Jennings, W. Ivor (1956), *The Approach to Self-Government* (Cambridge: Cambridge University Press).
Kaplan, Robert D. (1994), "The Coming Anarchy," *Atlantic Monthly* 273:2 (February), 44–76.
Krasner, Stephen (1999), *Sovereignty: Organized Hypocrisy* (Princeton, NJ: Princeton University Press).
Lacina, Bethany and Nils Peter Gleditsch (2005), "Monitoring Trends in Global Combat: A New Dataset of Battle Deaths," *European Journal of Population* 21:2–3, 116–45.
Lake, David and David Rothschild (eds) (1998), *The International Spread of Ethnic Conflict: Fear, Diffusion and Escalation* (Princeton, NJ: Princeton University Press).

Lansing, Robert (1921), *The Peace Process: A Personal Narrative* (Boston, MA: Houghton Mifflin).
Monahan, Patrick J. (1996), "Coming to Terms with Plan B: Ten Principles Governing Secession," 83 (June) (Toronto: CD Howe Institute Commentary).
Pavković, Aleksandar with Peter Radan (2007), *Creating New States: Theory and Practice of Secession* (Aldershot: Ashgate).
Premdas, Ralph R. et al. (1990), *Secessionist Movements in Comparative Perspective* (London: Palgrave Macmillan).
Roeder, Philip (2007), *Where Nation-States Come From: Institutional Change in the Age of Nationalism* (Princeton, NJ: Princeton University Press).
Rosecrance, Richard (1999), *The Rise of the Virtual State: Wealth and Power in the Coming Century* (New York, NY: Basic Books).
Schreuer, Christoph (1993), "The Waning of the Sovereign State: Towards a New Paradigm for International Law?" *European Journal of International Law* 4: 447–71.
Shakya, Tsering (1999), *The Dragon in the Land of the Snows: A History of Modern Tibet* (New York, NY: Columbia University Press).
Spencer, Metta (ed.) (1998), *Separatism: Democracy and Disintegration* (Lanham, MD: Rowman and Littlefield).
Spruyt, Hendrik (2005), *Ending Empire: Contested Sovereignty and Territorial Partition* (Ithaca, NY: Cornell University Press).
Standen, Amy (2006), "'Yugonostalgia' Takes Hold in Slovenia," *All Things Considered*, 10/9/2006, National Public Radio.
Toft, Monica Duffy (2003), *The Geography of Ethnic Violence* (Princeton, NJ: Princeton University Press).
United Nations (1945), "Charter of the United Nations."
United Nations (1960), "Declaration on Granting Independence to Colonial Territories."
United Nations (1970), "Declaration on Principles of International Law Concerning Friendly Relations and Cooperation Among States in Accordance with the Charter of the United Nations."
United Nations (2009), "Non-Self Governing Territories Listed By General Assembly, 2002." [Online] At http://www.un.org/Depts/dpi/decolonization/trust3.htm [accessed 18 December 2009].
Walker, Edward W. (2003), *Dissolution: Sovereignty and the Breakup of the Soviet Union* (Oxford: Rowman and Littlefield).
Walter, Barbara F. (1997), "The Critical Barrier to Civil War Settlement," *International Organization* 51:3, 335–64.
Walter, Barbara F. (2006), "Building Reputation: Why Governments Fight Some Separatists but Not Others," *American Journal of Political Science* 50:2, 313–30.
Walter, Barbara F. (2009), *Reputation and Civil War: Why Separatist Conflicts Are So Violent* (Cambridge: Cambridge University Press).
Wilson, Woodrow (1918), "President Woodrow Wilson's Fourteen Points." [Online] At http://avalon.law.yale.edu/20th_century/wilson14.asp [accessed 6 October 2009].

Xinhua (2005), "Anti-Secession Law (Full Text)." [Online] At http://www.chinaview.cn [accessed 17 October 2009].

Young, Robert A. (1998), *The Secession of Quebec and the Future of Canada* (Montreal and Kingston, ON: McGill-Queen's University Press).

# Explaining Secession[1]

## David S. Siroky

Simultaneously destroying and creating order, secession is a watershed event marked by significant political change: the rise and fall of regional and global powers, new patterns of international and domestic alliances, and sudden opportunities for states and groups to improve or defend their relative positions. Secession stands solidly at the intersection of domestic and international politics. It is therefore hardly surprising that secession is a subject of interdisciplinary interest, and has been analyzed from the perspectives of political science, economics, sociology, philosophy, and law. Finally, secession is not simply of academic interest, but concerns policymakers and governments around the globe which must cope with it on a frustratingly frequent basis.

At one level, the problem of secession is philosophical—do groups have a right to self-determination that trumps states' rights to territory integrity, and if so under which conditions? At another level, it is an empirical question—why do ethnic groups attempt to secede in some places and not in others, at some times and not at others? Why do some secessions turn violent? Why do some secessions succeed in establishing states, while others fail, and still others settle into *de facto* sovereignty through territorial control? Why do some post-secessionist states establish the conditions for peace, while others only exacerbate ethnic tensions, and engender further violence? What role does state policy—whether it takes the form of repression or accommodation—play in propelling and subduing secession? What roles do external actors play—and why do some try to prevent ethnic violence while others do nothing, or even actively encourage it? In short, how do we explain secession?

When it occurs, secession is a practical, humanitarian issue, for it often entails considerable violence, destruction and tragedy. Violent secessionist conflicts

---

[1] I thank Davit Aphrasidze, Kristin Bakke, Lenka Bustikova, Ahsan Butt, Yon Ouk Cho, Mark Dietzen, Rachel Fabi, Michael Hechter, Donald Horowitz, Yukihiro Kumeno, Neil Moffatt, David Muchlinksi, Aleksandar Pavković, Stephen Saideman, Nicholas Sambanis, Jonah Schulhofer-Wohl, Ben Smith, and Paul Staniland for comments and suggestions on previous drafts, which significantly improved the quality of this chapter. All errors are my own.

account for the deaths of tens of millions, not to mention the brutal mistreatment of many more people (Isaacs 1975: 3; Horowitz 1985: xi; Gurr 2000; Brancati 2006). These conflicts are also widespread. According to one estimate, no more than 25 member states of the 196 member United Nations can claim to be free of such conflicts (Zarkovic-Bookman 1992: 7). The Stockholm International Peace Research Institute (SIPRI) data indicate that only five of the 23 major armed conflicts were non-ethnic in 1994, and only two of 26 in 1998 (Hechter 2000a, 2000b). Even these two exceptions—Ethiopia/Eritrea and India/Pakistan—were the direct result of earlier secessions. According to Fearon and Laitin's 2003 data, about half of the civil wars since the end of the Cold War have been driven by rebels aiming for secession or autonomy. Sambanis (2001) shows that roughly 70 percent of civil wars since 1945 have been ethno-nationalist wars. Whichever period or metric we choose, it is clear that a sizable portion of armed conflicts are related to secession.

The tremors from the disintegration of three federal republics—the Soviet Union, Yugoslavia, and Czechoslovakia—contributed to renewed interest in this profoundly political problem. All told, the last two centuries have seen the emergence of at least five to six dozen *de facto* and *de jure* independent secessionist states in Africa, Asia, the Americas, Europe, and Oceania, dozens more secessionist movements that failed and disappeared, and still more that remain engaged in efforts to break away from their host states (see Part II and Part VI).

Historically, even if only a small portion of declarations of secession or independence have come to fruition, their incidence is not diminishing over time (Armitage 2007). Indeed, since World War Two, the creation of new states through secession, including decolonization, has been on the rise (Fazal and Griffiths 2008). The threat of secession is not only a problem for developing countries (e.g., Georgia, Moldova, Nigeria, Russia, and Indonesia), but also for developed countries (e.g., Belgium, Spain, Switzerland, and the United Kingdom) (see Part VI). The fact that secession is at the core of political conflict in dozens of countries, afflicting both the developing and the developed world, provides solid ground for comparative analysis and theoretical synthesis. The events of the day also present the need for such an analysis. Although secession has long been a staple of the interstate system, only recently have social scientific efforts arisen to theorize and explain secessions in diverse places such as Abkhazia, East Timor, Eritrea, Kosovo, and Somaliland.

As with the study of any multidimensional phenomenon, the explanation of secession involves multiple issues, actors, and logics. Some of the core questions include:

1. Why do secessionist movements emerge among some groups, but not others?
2. What explains the timing of secession—why do ethnic groups pursue secession at certain times, but not others?
3. Why are some secessionist movements able to command extensive public support, while others only receive marginal or no support at all?
4. Why do some secessionist movements endure for many years, while others dissipate over time, ultimately disappearing altogether?

5. Why do some secessionist movements engage in violence against the government and other non-state actors, while others pursue non-violent strategies?
6. Why do some secessionist movements succeed in becoming independent states, while others fail, achieving only *de facto* independence or less?
7. Why do some host states pursue accommodation, while others opt for repression in responding to ethnic group claims?
8. What role do external actors, such as neighboring states, diasporas, international organizations, play in triggering secessionist violence, prolonging it, curbing it, and ending it?
9. Why do some states that emerged through secession establish peaceful internal and external relations, while others are almost immediately involved in intrastate and interstate conflicts?
10. What policy tools are available to governments, interested states and international organizations to tame secessionism?

Each question in this admittedly non-exhaustive list focuses on a distinct level of analysis and temporal phase within the political life-cycle of secession. A review of the relevant literature reveals that it can be fruitfully divided into three groups, according to the unit of analysis: the first set of studies focuses on the secessionist movement or ethnic group as the key actor; the second set concentrates on state behavior toward minorities; and the third set addresses the role of external actors or foreign powers. This tripartite structure provides a framework, or what Sartori (1970: 1039) called "data containers," into which our theories and empirical observations can be fitted (see also Horowitz 1985: 16).

In this review, the levels are separated for analysis, with a final section considering the aftermath of secession. The section on ethnic groups organizes the literature according to the main issues that drive grievances and facilitate collective action. This is followed by a discussion of state-centric approaches, which focuses on state capacity and state behavior towards ethno-nationalism within its borders. The third layer in the analysis is composed of international approaches to explaining secession, which includes a discussion of the main causes and consequences of external involvement in secession along with several conjectures. The final section is different, but represents an obvious and natural extension because it considers the crucial question of whether secession should be seen as a solution to ethnic conflict by analyzing secession's aftermath.

It will be useful for the reader to keep in mind that explaining secession requires integrating this triadic structure at the core of the secession generating process. Any coherent explanation for secession will need to account for the interactions, examining how groups and states bargain, fight, negotiate, and kill, along with how and why foreign powers—states, diasporas, international organizations— become involved, altering the domestic balance of power, and profoundly affecting the dynamics of secession.

## Ethnic Groups

The most natural level on which to begin thinking theoretically about secession is the group level, where secessionist sentiments are born, and sometimes take root. Two questions have driven the literature: one, where do secessionist sentiments come from and, two, how do they become politically mobilized, morphing into separatist movements? (see also Chapter 11). Three broad answers to these questions can be delineated: (1) political grievances, (2) economic inequality, and (3) ethnic demography/geography (Hewitt 1977; Levine 1996). While these answers can be usefully separated for the purpose of analysis, equally important in understanding their causal effects is to theorize their interactions, including but not limited to substitution and reinforcement effects.

Political grievances are generally understood as barriers to entry or obstacles to social mobility, accompanied typically by some disproportionality between "deserved" and "achieved" political power, where "deserved" is usually defined relative to ethno-demographic features such as relative ethnic group size and spatial concentration but may also be interpreted historically. "Achieved" is often understood relative to some metric of political influence, such as the proportion of legislative and administrative positions occupied by co-ethnics. As Wimmer (2002: 5) demonstrates, "modern institutions of inclusion are systematically tied to ethnic and national forms of exclusion. Correspondingly, ethnic conflicts … are integral parts of the modern order of nation-states."

However, sometimes political grievances are placated by a group's advantage or preponderance in other less political spheres, particularly in the economic realm, recognizing that there is often a division of labor among ethnic groups (Hechter 2000b; Horowitz 2000: 108–35). Other times, political and economic power go hand in hand, reinforcing minority political exclusion with economic inequality (Breton 1964). Once introduced, inequalities can be fortified through discriminatory legislation and language policy, which translates directly into educational disparities that reproduce political and economic inequality. Not surprisingly, this dynamic bodes poorly in the long run for the "out-group" and it begets resentment over perceived status inequalities, which bodes poorly in the long run for the "in-group" (Petersen 2002). In the Soviet context, this dynamic created demands from some regional minorities within union republics for an elevation of their status to autonomous provinces and republics, since autonomy implies power, prestige, and opportunities that are perceived as having been denied (Roeder 1991; Treisman 1997; Cornell 2002; Giuliano 2006).

Similar grievances can be identified in the economic realm, but with important differences. General inequality between groups in economic attainment, cost sharing, and redistribution benefits, arguably possess a curvilinear relationship with the disposition to secede. On the one hand, many theorists posit that relative economic deprivation increases the likelihood of secession, because opportunity costs are low when poverty is high, as in Bangladesh, Southern Sudan, and the case of Muslims in Thailand (e.g., Horowitz 2000). But others argue that impoverished groups stand the most to gain from remaining inside the state and the most to lose by exiting. Relatively wealthier groups also possess formidable grounds for complaint, because they often subsidize the less prosperous groups and therefore bear a disproportionate share of the economic cost of maintaining the state, as in Northern Italy, Slovenia, or Tatarstan (e.g., Hale 2008). This has led some to believe that both extremely impoverished and overly wealthy groups are most likely to secede, whereas those groups at relative parity with the average national income are the least likely to pursue secession (Stewart 2009; Cederman, Gleditsch, and Weidmann 2010).

Ethnicity and economics were already central in Horowitz (1985), who conceived of secession as a mix of economic calculation and fear. Analyzing secessionist movements in newly independent states in Africa and Asia, Horowitz focuses on the economic disparity between the secessionist group and the central government to explain the timing of secession, but recognizes and incorporates the role played by fears of political exclusion and cultural extinction, which he couches in terms of anxiety about relative worth. He writes: "separatism results from varying mixes of sheer economic interest and group apprehension" (Horowitz 1985: 259). Horowitz's theory conceives of groups and regions as either backward or advanced, relative to the mean levels of prosperity in the country as a whole. This produces four ideal types: backward groups in backward regions, advanced groups in backward regions, advanced groups in advanced regions, and backward groups in advanced regions. Each type follows a distinct causal logic that can be deduced from relative regional and group position (Horowitz 1985: 233ff). The relative weight attached to ethnic anxiety and economic calculation varies by group: backward groups in backward regions tend to give more weight to ethnic anxiety and less to economic costs and benefits, and it is precisely this type that is most likely to secede and to do so earliest after independence. The advanced groups in advanced regions are least likely to secede. When they do, secession is likely to be later rather than earlier. Since Horowitz also believes that there is likely to be less infighting (and more subgroup amalgamation) among advanced groups, secessionist movements among advanced groups are also likely to be more cohesive.

These background conditions, and many others that we could enumerate, require triggers to set secession in motion—to make it appear attractive relative to less extreme alternatives. The alternatives need to be credible, and often enough the potential secessionists see signals that they are not. Such signals can come in the form of unilateral actions from the central government, including legal changes that affect the region or group adversely, or culturally-oriented prohibitions on the legality of dress, language, and ritual. They may also emerge from signs that the central government is unstable, and may not even exist long enough to follow through on its promises. Ethnic riots, unpunished looting, and armed groups not under the government's control serve to indicate the government's inability to provide security to the region, and to suggest that alternatives to secession, which entail remaining in the state, are not truly viable (cf., Pavković with Radan 2007: 173ff).

Economic grievances between ethnic groups are pervasive, but when class is coterminous with ethnicity, the impetus to secede is more powerful, since there are fewer cross-cutting cleavages to undermine the impulse to exit and less fragmentation within groups to divide a secessionist movement. When ethno-economic discrimination is coterminous with minority status, solutions such as positive discrimination for minorities, which implies negative discrimination for the majority, are often proposed. Although these can minimize ethnic minority alienation, they can also exhaust majority tolerance, making the competition for resources between ethnic groups into a salient political issue. Such anti-discrimination measures may lead to the perception of disadvantage among the majority population, and even to status reversal in some sectors, augmenting animosity towards the "privileged" minority.

Economic wealth can of course come from greater productivity, but it may also result from exploiting the presence of raw materials, especially oil reserves and oil pipelines, as in Katanga, Bougainville, Chechnya, and Biafra. Mineral resources, as in northern Kosovo, Tatarstan, and Siberia, serve a similar function (see also Chapter 10). Grievances can result for both reasons, which boil down to a claim that the group is receiving less than "its fair share." This line of reasoning bears some similarity to work by scholars who believe internal rebellions, of which secession is one type, are driven by greedy motives. This literature implies that secession is likely driven by "atypical (economic) opportunities for building a rebel organization" (King 2001; Collier and Hoeffler 2004). These atypical opportunities include controlling, looting, and exploiting valuable resources, especially primary commodities (diamonds, timber, cocaine, minerals).

Some scholars have sought to apply this framework to explain the duration and persistence of separatist conflicts long after the major violence has ended in an effort to understanding the material benefits of ethnic wars (King 2001). King explains the duration of secessionist conflicts by focusing on the benefits that all sides reap from its duration. Since separatists become state-builders, "ending the conflict" is less about conflict resolution, he argues, and more about reintegration of "two functionally distinct administrations, militaries, and societies." Resolving secessionist conflict in these cases involves the unification of two states, one *de jure* and the other *de facto* (Coggins 2006).

Few actors possess an incentive to end the conflict. The rebel government and the official government exploit the territory's ambiguous legal status for economic gain, mainly through smuggling, laundering, and tax evasion. Eliminating this ambiguity would necessarily entail an economic loss for several key stake holders, whereas prolonging the *status quo* facilitates resource extraction, tax evasion, and enduring economic benefits, hence its duration.

In addition to such political and economic motives, ethnic demography and geography figure prominently into the decision to secede, since ethnic mobilization and collective action demand both the desire and the capacity, the willingness and the opportunity, to act. As a result, many theorists would agree that, when it comes to secession, "size matters" (Leff 1971; DeNardo 1985; Tarrow and Tilly 2006; cf. Horowitz 1972; Hechter and Okamoto 2001). One reason is that numbers are themselves arguments, buttressing group claims and counter-claims to power, status, and prestige (Siroky 2009). Though commonly treated as static, numbers can have a past, present, and future. Majorities that have become minorities remember the golden era, however distant, and majorities that can foresee the impermanence of their numerical superiority, provided that birth and death rates are forecasted correctly, have reasons for preemptive action to avert status reversal.

Demographics can also become politically relevant by more deliberate and sudden means, for example, through government-sponsored migration policies and settlement schemes that encourage members of one ethnic group (usually the majority) to settle areas occupied by large numbers of another ethnic group (usually a minority). The goal of such policies is clear—to dilute the power of a population pocket that is believed to possess dubious loyalty to the state. This strategy, whether performed through settlement policies or ethnic gerrymandering, is also intended to undermine any future claim to the territory or its infiltration by a foreign power using locals as a fifth column. China's efforts to dilute the populations in Tibet and Xinjiang fit this pattern, as do Georgia's redistricting of Javakheti, an Armenian province, to include a neighboring Georgian-majority district, Samtskhe, and attempts to dilute the Russian population in Crimea by encouraging the settlement of more loyal Tatars.

Demographic dynamics of this sort, when mixed with policies that favor the newcomers over current residents, can trigger secession because inaction begets adverse material consequences for the minority's employment, economic, and education opportunities. Besides the material consequences, which are significant, demographic changes have deleterious ideational effects, spreading fear, exacerbating security dilemmas, and ultimately radicalizing actors.

Wrapped in the garb of selective histories that include glorious battles lost, sacrifices made, and subsequent subordination, ethnic groups seek redemption. In its extreme form, this requires laying claim to a separate state; but lesser forms include obtaining credible commitments to increase ethno-regional power and prestige. Secessionist leaders and their separatist movements do not possess fixed demands, but rather adjust the extent of their demands on the central government along a spectrum all the way to independence (Horowitz 1985: 13). As Jenne (2007) has shown, this fluctuation in the extent of ethnic group demands over time and between groups is a form of bargaining leverage, the true extent of which is determined by previous autonomy, territorial concentration and access to resources, both internal and external.

Demographic factors are also important in more direct ways. Most scholars recognize, for instance, that a territorially concentrated minority is more likely than a spatially dispersed one to form a serious secessionist movement (Toft 2002, 2003; Collier and Hoeffler 2004). The mechanisms that have been suggested for the association between secession and spatial demography are sundry, and include the fact that concentration reinforces ethnic identity, facilitates collective action, minimizes internal opposition, and enables ethnic mobilization. The most appropriate means of measuring ethnic demography—in particular how to summarize it into a single index—remains the subject of considerable debate, however (Posner 2004; Siroky 2007; Chandra and Wilkinson 2008).

The vast majority of large-N studies that would be relevant to this debate employ the same measure of ethnic diversity—ethno-linguistic fractionalization or ELF—originally calculated in 1960 by Soviet researchers for 129 countries by summing the squared shares of "ethno-linguistic groups." According to a large body of theory on violent conflict, however, it is not ethnic "fractionalization" (a large number of small, splintered groups) that should be associated with conflict, but a small number of large, internally cohesive groups. There is a lot of evidence and theory suggesting that ELF is not the appropriate measure of the theoretical concept (Horowitz 1985; Esteban and Ray 1994, 2008; Collier 1998; Collier, Hoeffler, and Soderbom 2001; Ellingsen 2000; Reynal-Querol 2002; Sambanis 2002; Sambanis and Doyle 2006; Alesina et al. 2003; Fearon 2003; Cederman and Girardin 2007; Siroky 2007; Chandra and Wilkinson 2008). Although discontent with ELF is high, alternatives are still few and far between.

One noteworthy exception is proposed in Reynal-Querol (2002), which offers a measure of ethnic polarization to capture how far a country diverges from the case of two equally sized groups (e.g., split 50/50). One important limitation, however, is that not all countries look like Cyprus, Estonia, and Belgium; many have more than two relevant groups. Theoretically and empirically, we also expect more conflict for three large groups (e.g., Iraq, Gambia, Benin, or Bosnia) or four (e.g., Nigeria, Bolivia, Kenya, or the United Arab Emirates). This may be one reason that it has not been widely used. Until there is more work on the measurement—and new measures that match particular theories are created—progress on this front is likely to be slow. Missing from this discussion of size, however, is space—or any indication of where the region/group is located. Whether it is inland or on the periphery can be crucial for the viability of a secessionist movement. Most secessionist movements, but not all, occur in peripheral regions. Cederman et al. (2009) have demonstrated empirically that separatist conflict is significantly more likely in regions near the state border and at a distance from the capital than revolutionary conflicts, which tend to occur closer to the capital.

At the most basic level, geographic proximity is thought to influence the behavior of the central government, its military, and the insurgents (Sprout and Sprout 1956; Jackson 1958; Diehl 1991; Gleditsch and Ward 2001). The use of geography in the limited sense of distance is more a proxy of logistical interaction opportunities than an attempt to model the impact of geography on actors' behavior and strategies of conflict. Beyond distance, the most natural feature to think of in the context of secession is terrain. Terrain may influence strategy, and could affect the decision to continue fighting for secession rather than to negotiate, and therefore influences the duration of the secessionist conflict.

For example, Fearon and Laitin (2003) have argued that, since insurgencies thrive in weakly accessible areas such as dense forests or mountainous terrain, where offense advantages are minimized and defensive tactics have an edge, countries with these features are more likely to experience insurgent, often secessionist, civil wars (see also Fearon 2004a). Collier and Hoeffler (2004, 2009) find only marginal support for the mountainous component and no support for the forest component of the hypothesis. Current cross-sectional efforts to test this idea using the percentage of the country covered by mountain or dummy variables represent only crude approximations. Few studies, however, take full advantage of GIS and, as a result, geographic analysis tends to consider only very rough geographic measures of borders, proximity, and terrain. Efforts using GIS generated data will help to bridge the currently large gap between measurement and theory, here as in other areas, and will emphasize important interactions, such as those between geography, ethnicity, and conflict (Cederman, Buhaug, and Ketil Rod 2009).

In particular, more precise geo-coded data will enable us to examine theoretical propositions at their appropriate level. Often, the appropriate level of measurement is not the country *per se*, but the limited area in which the conflict occurs. Thus, slippage between measurement and theory is potentially considerable. For example, if mountains are hypothesized to influence the duration of secessionist and insurgent conflict, then it would make good sense to measure the terrain in the region of potential conflict rather than as a percentage of the entire country's territory for the simple reason that there is no obvious correspondence between the regional topography and the country's average topography.

The same goes for many other variables—including ethnic heterogeneity, geography, and inequality, which should be understood at the local level for regionally-based secessionist conflicts rather than solely at the national level. Sambanis and Milanović (2004) offer an insightful analysis using regional inequality data. But local data on ethnic heterogeneity are hard to come by for a large sample of states. Even such data at the national level are far from abundant and are often problematic (Siroky 2007). Despite data limitations, demographic and geographic features of the conflict deserve closer theoretical scrutiny and closer measurement than has been standard practice to date. It seems fair to presume that many characteristics of conflict zones are not necessarily well represented by features of the country as a whole. At the same time, characteristics of the region relative to the features of the country as a whole are most relevant to understanding some of the sources of secessionist conflict, especially economic and political grievances (Stewart 2009; Cederman, Gleditsch, and Weidmann 2010). Buhaug et al. (2009) have taken up this task in relation to the relative economic prosperity of regions, and have shown that, for civil wars, absolute poverty increases the probability of conflict in specific areas, but that relative wealth increases the probability of conflict only in poor states. An improved effort in this domain will also have payoffs for related questions, such as the causes and consequences of the spread, diffusion, and escalation of secessionist conflict within and across borders (see also Chapter 12).

This is why speaking of ethnic demography requires a parallel discussion of ethnic geography. Territorially dispersed ethnic groups, of whatever size, are less likely to engage in secessionist activity, because collective action is more difficult to achieve, ethnic ties are generally weaker, and internal opposition from other ethnic groups is likely to be greater. Ethnic groups that fit this pattern tend to pursue policies that redress the discrimination they face within the context of the existing state, seeking voice rather than exit (Hirschman 1970). Similarly, the discussion of ethnic demography and ethnic geography also must deal with the issue of ethnicity itself to show why it is ethnic groups, rather than some other collective identity, that seek secession. Hale (2008) has offered a creative psychological explanation for why ethnicity offers such a powerful strategy for mobilization, by separating ethnicity, which is viewed as an uncertainty-reduction technique and not necessarily a motive for behavior, from ethnic politics, which is about interests. This theoretical move places ethnicity on firmer ground, provides leverage in explaining why ethnicity is sometimes, but far from consistently, associated with conflict, and shows how ethnicity can resolve collective action problems faced by potential secessionist movements.

All of these explanations—political, economic, demographic, and geographic—focus on the ethnic group/region as the unit of analysis. They assume that the ethnic group is a more or less unitary actor, an assumption that should be relaxed to analyze particular settings (Kitschelt 1989; Stedman 1997; Gorenburg 2000; Cunningham 2006; Kalyvas 2008; Bueno de Mesquita 2008; Christia 2008; Pearlman 2008; Cunningham, Bakke, and Seymour 2010; Lawrence 2010; Staniland 2010) (see also Chapter 11). A direction for future research, then, involves examining how micro-level and intra-ethnic differences influence macro-level behavior, such as foreign policy. For example, how does the salience of differences between Gheg and Tosk Albanians influence the likelihood of a pan-Albanian movement aimed at uniting Albanian-inhabited lands in Kosovo, Macedonia, Montenegro, and Greece with Albania proper? Second, future research should exploit more vigorously the increasing precision of information available through GIS and geo-coded data of ethnic groups and conflicts. Third, ethnic group-level explanations often fail to take the state sufficiently seriously, ignoring the state's characteristics, behavior, and strategy. The next section redresses this omission by focusing squarely on the state.

## The State

Despite the centrality of the state, a good portion of the literature depicts secession in a seemingly stateless political space. Ironically, one way in which the state has been brought into the analysis is through its absence in studies of state weakness, state failure, and state capacity. In the case of state failure, the state cannot prevent secessionist sentiments from escalating into sustained movements—it is not what the state does, but what it does *not* do that matters. Fearon and Laitin (2003), among others, provide empirical evidence that poorer states are more prone to all forms of civil war, including separatist civil war, than are their wealthier counterparts (cf. Young 2009; Hechter, Quinn, and Wibbels 2004; Siroky 2007) (see Chapter 12). Theoretically, this correlation is sometimes interpreted as the effect of low state capacity—since weak states are unable to deter insurgencies, civil wars are more likely to erupt.

These indicators of state capacity—GDP per capita, mountainous terrain, oil revenue dependence—are all believed to make insurgency easier. We can theorize another mechanism, however. Secessionists gain popular support and are sustained by offering what weak states cannot—protection of property and provision of services—the basic elements of governance. Rebel rule, or guerilla governance as it is sometimes called, supplants the official government in some regions of the country (Wickham-Crowley 1987, 1992; Kasfir n.d.). In winning the battle to protect and serve, rebel groups succeed in establishing states, albeit inside other states.

In some cases, rebels are merely following the lead of the (host) state, which itself was formed through secession. The prior secession provides a convenient example and an obvious language in which to voice minority grievances (Beran 1984; Pavković 2007; Siroky 2009). When the size of the political unit shrinks, intra-group distinctions can become more politically salient, and ethnic competition at lower levels generally increases. Relations within groups that were once tempered by competition between groups in a larger polity are subject to reevaluation. Once other groups are out of the picture, smaller differences can assume greater importance, making ethnic co-existence less attractive and secession more so.

We have many examples of this phenomenon in Europe and Eurasia. Bosniak leaders, for example, were motivated in good measure to pursue secession after Croatia and Slovenia broke away, which left them in a smaller political unit in which the relative size of Bosniaks to other ethnic groups was much larger. Similarly, after Croatia and Bosnia and Herzegovina seceded from Yugoslavia, everything changed for Serb minorities in these new states, arguably for the worse, prompting recursive secessionist conflict to surface in Krajina and Republika Srpska (see Chapters 8 and 12 and Part VI). Georgia's secession from the Soviet Union, too, was soon followed by recursive secessionist violence in Abhkazia and South Ossetia. When Moldova broke away from the Soviet Union, Transdniestria claimed a right to remain part of the Soviet Union, ultimately producing a *de facto* independent statelet, sponsored by Russia, on the West Bank of the river Dnistr (see Part VI).

Likewise in Africa, once Somaliland broke away from Somalia, Puntland attempted to secede from Somaliland, leading yet another territory, Maakhir state, to proclaim independence in response to overlapping claims from Puntland and Somaliland (see Part VI). When Katanga declared its intent to leave Zaire, the Baluba in North Katanga saw that life was about to take a turn for the worse, and decided to get out while their window of opportunity remained open. And in South Asia, once Bangladesh left Pakistan, a Sindhi movement emerged for autonomy from both Punjabi and Muhajir dominance. Zulfi Bhutto's government then aided the Sindh in the 1970s, which facilitated Muhajir mobilization against Sindhi dominance. In short, when minorities exist in the new state, as they almost always do, reciprocal separatism can emerge even where such sentiments did not previously exist or were only latent. One scholar explains this phenomenon matter-of-factly: "one group's independence is another's servitude" (Horowitz 1985: 278).

The state is sometimes directly responsible for ethnic minority mobilization, as when the state initiates or prevents violence for political purposes (e.g., Wilkinson 2004). According to a domestic version of diversionary war theory, for example, governments militarily target disliked (and preferably defenseless) ethnic groups at home, blaming them for domestic shortcomings, creating an in-group, out-group distinction, and scapegoating to elicit public support (Coser 1956; Glaser

1958; Gagnon 1995; Tir and Jasinski 2008). Domestic diversion, it is argued, has many of the same benefits as international diversionary war, and some that it does not have, such as ethnic outbidding, but has far fewer costs and consequences (DeVotta 2005; Filippov 2009). It also has the benefit of being a strategy that is broadly available to most leaders, since most possess multiple ethnic groups, at least some of which offer low-cost opportunities for domestic diversionary conflict (Snyder and Ballentine 1996; Tir and Jasinski 2008).

State repression, more generally, can include non-violent policy, such as changing laws that adversely affect minorities, forbidding minority political parties, removing forms of positive discrimination that were in place, or it can be more aggressive, and involve jailing charismatic leaders, confiscating property, assassinating leaders (Davenport 1995; Poe, Tate, and Keith 1999; Moore 2000; Mylonas 2008). The risk associated with this form of repression is that it can backfire, causing latent, divided, and unorganized groups to mobilize, thus escalating tensions which were previously mild (Lichbach 1987). To avoid backlash, some have suggested that leaders seek defenseless (but despised) ethnic groups to achieve the effect without the attendant risk of escalation. Defenseless groups also tend to lack ethnic kin states that could intervene or support their brethren if threatened, but even groups with kin states may be targeted, provided that the kin states remain relatively uninterested in coming to their aid. The psychology of aggression literature, however, fairly thoroughly refutes the assumption that defenseless groups are more likely to be victimized by the states in which they reside than are strong groups (Horowitz 2001: 135–50) (see Chapter 12).

This relates to the more general question of whether repression works. Gurr, Tilly, and others sometimes identified with theories of "relative deprivation" tend to focus on state repression as the critical force driving group mobilization, so the answer is clearly no from the state's viewpoint (Gurr 1970; Tilly 1978; Eckstein 1965: 154; Lichbach 1987: 269). However, "resource mobilization" theorists argue that repression deters group mobilization by increasing the costs of organizing and decreasing the leader's capacity to do so (McCarthy and Zald 1977). Although it may exacerbate grievances, repression makes group violence against the state less likely. Lichbach attempts to resolve this "paradox" by suggesting that there is a key omitted variable—the consistency of the government's policy. Both consistent accommodation and consistent repression work to reduce violent ethnic group activity, whereas inconsistent policies generally increase ethnic group activity (Lichbach 1987).

The question of repression's effectiveness is also central to the closely related literature on the effectiveness of indiscriminate violence in counterinsurgencies. Downes (2007, 2008) questions the conventional wisdom that violence against noncombatants must be selective or risk alienating the population, and explores the conditions under which such violence can be effective. Downes finds that repression and indiscriminate violence are more effective when the geographic area and the size of the underlying population supporting the insurgents are smaller. Rather than alienating the local population, Downes argues, repression and indiscriminate force are sometimes needed to prevent the local population from supporting the separatists and insurgents. Downes and Cochrane (2010) present tentative evidence that repression and civilian victimization may help states win wars, especially against smaller targets, but also raise some important concerns about endogeneity and selection effects.

Lyall (2009) also questions the notion that indiscriminate violence and repression is necessarily counter-productive in terms of inciting insurgent attacks. Across matched pairs of similar shelled and non-shelled villages, Lyall shows that the shelled ones experienced a 24 percent reduction in post-treatment mean insurgent attacks relative to control villages. Lyall (2010) builds on this result and presents compelling evidence that ethnicity is also critical to understanding whether repression works to reduce violence in civil wars through its effect on the information available to co-ethnic pro-state counter-insurgents. Using evidence from the Second Chechen war, Lyall demonstrates that co-ethnics make more effective counterinsurgents, reducing subsequent insurgent attacks by about 40 percent after pro-Russian Chechen sweeps relative to similar Russian-only operations. Intra-ethnic networks and prior experience as an insurgent serve to reduce subsequent insurgent attacks by providing better information, which allows counterinsurgents to correctly identify the insurgents within the population, to issue more credible threats against civilians for noncooperation and to convert or, if necessary, to kill any fighters and their supporters.

The discussion of state behavior toward secessionists would be incomplete if it focused solely on repression and violence, and failed to consider the possibility of accommodation and the most common institutional solutions. There is a lively debate about which institutions work, what incentives they engender, and what effect they have on the propensity to mobilize and seek secession. Federal institutions, and decentralization more generally, are sometimes thought to be slippery slopes leading to secession (Roeder 1991; Bunce 1999; Cornell 2002). Others contend, however, that such institutions actually satisfy, rather than whet, separatist appetites (Diamond 1999; Stepan 1999; Bermeo 2002; Bermeo and Amoretti 2003). Scholars have made headway in unpacking this "paradox," and analyzing the conditions under which decentralization has one effect rather than the other, and the tradeoffs that stem from choosing between repressive and responsive policies (Hechter 2000a; Kohli 1997; Lustick, Miodownik, and Eidelson 2004; Bakke and Wibbels 2006; Brancati 2006, 2008).

Hechter (2000a: 10), for example, offers the following reconciliation of the two arguments in the literature, specifically with respect to federalism as one responsive policy with ambiguous effects: "Whereas decentralization may provide cultural minorities with greater resources to engage in collective action ... at the same time, it may also erode the demand for sovereignty." Kohli (1997) makes a related argument about accommodation from a strong state increasing instability in the short term, but decreasing it in the long term.

Lustick, Miodownik, and Eidelson (2004) provide an agent-based model of secessionism to explore these possibilities and find support for the views of Hechter and Kohli: "increasing representativeness," they write, "in fact decreased secessionist activity ... representative institutions, even if not fully autonomous, thus seem to inhibit secessionism." At the same time, the authors argue that rigorous repression can prevent mobilization, but only in the short term, "at great cost and without eliminating the threat of secessionism" (Lustick, Miodownik, and Eidelson 2004: 223). Power-sharing, they claim, can be more effective in the long term, yet it also tends to encourage larger minority "identitarian movements" and faces risks from spoilers (Stedman 1997; Sisk 2003). Northern Ireland, Fiji, and Papua New Guinea are often cited as power-sharing successes because they reduced the risk of spoilers by integrating and including them in decision-making (Horowitz 1985; Reilly 2001). Nigeria, Lebanon, and Cyprus, by contrast, are reminders that even carefully designed power-sharing institutions are far from a panacea, and can sometimes exacerbate problems in divided societies (Seaver 2000).

Bakke and Wibbels (2006) propose a different reconciliation of federalism's heterogeneous effects, contending that its ability to mitigate political and secessionist violence is contingent upon regional inequality and ethnic diversity. Specifically, they argue that fiscal decentralization increases the likelihood of ethnic rebellion when there are wide disparities in income across region. In addition, they find that when a strong national party excludes ethnic regions from national governance, ethnic conflict is more likely. Essentially, Bakke and Wibbels show that the effect of federalism is contingent on underlying societal features, especially ethnic group concentration and regional economic inequality.

Institutional arguments, such as those associated with federalism, also raise a number of important questions, including (1) why, despite decades of federal arrangements, secession happens at certain junctures, but not at others and (2) why secession occurs in the absence of federal arrangements, or how it helps to explain why secession happened in pre-federal times, say from the Habsburg and Ottoman Empires, where none possessed federal institutions and very few possessed any form of autonomy. In the post-Soviet context, it raises three key questions: (1) how to explain cases with autonomous status that did *not* experience violent conflict, (2) why cases with marginal levels of autonomy engaged in violent conflict *before* cases with actual autonomy, and (3) how to incorporate endogenous institutions, or the origins of autonomous arrangements, which often followed, rather than preceded, violent conflict (Saparov 2010).

These challenges aside, this literature pushes us to think harder about the heterogeneous effects of state policy on mobilization and separatism by specifying non-linear and dynamic relationships between rebel groups (dissidents, insurgents, and separatists) and the state (the central government, its armed forces) (Lichbach 1987; Rasler 1996; Gartner and Regan 1996). One conclusion that emerges clearly is that secessionists act and react to the state's actions, both present and past, and not only to the state's inaction and weakness. We therefore need to better understand the endogenous sources of variation in state minority policies and the conditions under which states pursue assimilation, inclusion, repression, cleansing, and killing (Mylonas 2008). Whether policy tends toward inclusion, the *status quo*, or exclusion is likely to sway minority leaders' calculus closer or farther from secession versus a less radical strategy (Bunce 2005). The state, its past and likely future behavior, must therefore be brought back into the analysis of secession to understand why and when some ethnic groups secede (see Chapters 11 and 12).

Walter (2006a) has done this in a framework that focuses on the government's past behavior toward ethnic groups and its likely future behavior. In particular, she shows that ethnic groups are considerably more likely to mobilize for self-determination, all else equal, when the government is unlikely to face additional ethnic challengers in the future and when it has a history of concessions to earlier ethnic separatist demands. Walter argues that understanding ethnic secession involves examining the past and future interactions between the state and its ethnic groups—in short, analyzing retrospective and prospective calculations—rather than merely focusing on the immediate structural conditions such as the state's capacity or topography. Incorporating this information into the analysis represents an advance on purely structural accounts, and adds a much needed dose of strategy and dynamism to explanations of separatist activism.

Walter (2006b) builds on this logic to explain why governments fight some separatists but not others. Drawing on a reputational mechanism, Walter shows that governments are less likely to pursue responsive policies and more likely to engage in repressive ones when the state faces multiple future ethnic challengers. She also shows that repression appears to work in the sense that governments which failed to accommodate one ethnic challenger were less likely to confront additional ones in the future, thus offering a causal link between the future and present behavior of strategic actors (see also Walter 2009; and, for a skeptical view, Evangelista 2002). Barktus (1999) explains this aspect of state behavior using a materialist logic and focusing on the strength of the disputants and the resources involved. Griffiths and Fazal (2008) focus on institutions, and argue that democracies are more likely to let secessionists leave peacefully, but that the administrative organization of the state determines who they can release without fear of setting a precedent, and who they must fight to maintain their reputation. Butt (2011) brings in an international angle, and argues that the government's response depends on its perception of whether the new state is likely to be a rival in the future, which is contingent on regional security dynamics.

This state-oriented secession literature usefully focuses our attention on how rebel ethnic groups and their host states interact strategically. Just as studies of secession focusing solely on ethnic group grievances, economic inequality, demographic and geographic factors will miss the crucial role of the state, so studies of state repression and accommodation must simultaneously account for the behavioral foundations of the ethnic group behavior (see Goodwin 2001, for a thorough treatment of state-centric approaches to revolutions). Incorporating the strategic interaction of states and groups enhances our ability to explain secession, but more must be done to capture the dynamics of secession. Hechter (1992), for example, advances a model of secession in this spirit in which four processes—some focused on the host state's decision, and others focused on the collective action problem faced by the population of the territorial sub-unit—work together to make secession unlikely among most regions.

Up to this point, the analysis at the group and the state level has bracketed out everything going on *outside* the state. If secession is a political phenomenon distinguished in part by being situated at the intersection of domestic and international politics, then a theoretical account of secession must also address the international dimensions of ethnic secessions, and the critical role played by foreign actors in escalating and suppressing secession.

## (Some Conjectures about) Foreign Powers

Even though secessions occur within states, which is where most of the literature has focused its attention, they cannot be understood fully without accounting for the actions and actors outside the state (see Chapters 13 and 14). Bracketing the international context and international actors from the analysis does not merely provide an "incomplete" picture. It is inferentially problematic in the sense that important aspects of secession elude explanation, including the onset, duration, and termination of secessionist conflict (see Chapter 12). A purely domestic story also risks falsely attributing to domestic politics what is driven by international affairs and world politics.

The existing literature at this level of analysis has focused on explaining the fundamental causes and consequences of external involvement. Indeed, external support for secessionists is one of the primary ways in which external actors influence the dynamics of secession and make it more likely to erupt into violence (Heraclides 1990; Jenne 2007; Saideman and Ayres 2008). External support can run the gamut from diplomatic and rhetorical support, to border lenience, or providing sanctuary for fighters, to explicit material support, which can include financial support, arms sales, military training, and even direct military involvement. How much support ensues will influence minority group–state bargaining dynamics, including whether secession even emerges as a serious possibility (see Chapter 14).

It is therefore not especially surprising that the actions of foreign powers have a direct bearing on the *success* of separatism. As the constitutive theory of statehood has long recognized, recognition by foreign powers is the *sine qua non* of secessionists' efforts to become new states (Crawford 2005) (see Chapter 13). Even when secessionist movements do not gain wider recognition, as in Northern Cyprus or Abkhazia, a minimum requirement for their success and sustenance seems to be that at least one state is willing to offer its support. Cetinyan (2002) shows that such external support, if and when it exists, can cast a long shadow over the domestic actors; some forms of support, Kuperman (2008) and Grigoryan (2010) argue, may even create moral hazards for insurgent groups, and increase the likelihood of escalation.

Drawing attention to the importance of international actors raises important and difficult questions that do not fit neatly into the group–state framework, including how to capture the heterogeneous effects of external actors on secession and how to explain third-party involvement in the first place. Introducing a third player alters the balance of power between the central government and the minority group and influences whether the group will remain silent, revolt and be crushed, receive some form of autonomy, or seek to exit the state altogether. As a result, bringing in a third player enables us to explain why, among diverse states with very similar endowments (i.e., structural conditions, ethnic composition, state capacity), some escalate into secessionist violence, while others do not. Since external involvement is highly variable and volatile, not only across cases but within them over time, it provides some leverage in explaining variation within cases over time (see Chapter 13).

To the extent that the presence of third parties shifts the balance of relative power toward one party and away from the other, any model that ignores this shift will inaccurately evaluate the game being played and will misjudge the outcome. This enables scholars to explain why some groups (possessing all or some of the above mentioned attributes) engage in secessionist violence, at certain times, and why these secessionist activities wax and wane over time.

Jenne (2004, 2007) shows that the inclusion of the external dimensions of secession can also potentially explain why the *same* group shifts its demands over time, sometimes advancing more moderate claims, such as language rights, and at other times making more radical demands, such as secession. The basic idea is that minority groups radicalize their demands when they enjoy significant external support, even when the central government has committed to protecting minority rights. Conversely, minority groups temper their demands, even if the central government pursues repression, when outside support is minimal or non-existent. This reasoning provides a compelling alternative to explanations based on credible commitments, security dilemmas, structural and historical factors, and casts some doubt on theories that focus on the host state's policy in explaining secession (see also Jenne, Saideman, and Lowe 2007 for a quantitative test; Saideman and Jenne 2009) (see also Chapter 14).

Closely related to the literature on the effects of external involvement is scholarship addressing its causes: why do some external actors involve themselves in the secessionist struggles of their neighbors, while others refrain, or even actively discourage separatism? If the involvement of external actors explains important aspects of secessionist dynamics, then what explains why external actors become involved in the first place?

Saideman (1997) takes this important question head on, challenging the prominent "vulnerability" argument, which has been used to explain the restraint of foreign powers in aiding secessionists in neighboring countries, and, most notably, in accounting for Africa's so-called "secessionist deficit" (see also Chapter 14). Vulnerability to secession at home has allegedly inhibited African states from supporting secessionists abroad (Herbst 1989, 1992; Englebert and Hummel 2005). As one scholar put it: "the greatest deterrent to territorial revision has been the fear of opening a Pandora's box. If any boundary is seriously questioned, why not [question] all the boundaries in Western Africa?" (Zartman 1966: 109; Jackson 1990, 1992; Saideman 1997: 722). Other scholars have sought to extend this logic to the European context (Nakarada 1991; Steinberg 1993; Woodward 1995).

Despite its plausibility, the theory has received relatively little empirical support, in part, perhaps because its predictions are indeterminate for states that are not "vulnerable" to secession. It is unclear how the theory can explain why states that are vulnerable to secession at home have engaged in overt and tacit support for insurgents in neighboring states through the horn of Africa, as well as in Central and West Africa (Saideman 1997: 724–6). Empirically, many states that intervene in their neighbors' secessionist conflicts have separatists in their own front yard (Heraclides 1990). Russia is a multiethnic state whose secessionist insurgency in Chechnya has done little to dampen its support for separatism in Transdniestria, Abkhazia, Crimea, and South Ossetia at various times.

The theory of ethnic ties, which stands as the main alternative, argues that ethnic affinity between external states and host state minority groups increases the likelihood of support. According to Saideman, in its extreme form, support stemming from ethnic ties can assume the form of irredentism, but lesser forms of support (diplomatic support, arms sales, subsidies, border lenience) can be critical to the success of a secessionist movement and are certainly also worthy of explanation. Unlike vulnerability, which merely explains the absence of interference, ethnic ties have the advantage of serving both to compel and to constrain states that may be considering involvement in other states' secessionist struggles. The theory of ethnic ties predicts that support for the secessionists will follow from states in which the ruling elite's constituency has ethnic ties to the secessionists. By contrast, states in which the ruling elite's constituency has ethnic ties to the state, support for *the host state* is predicted to follow. Cases in which the ruling elite's constituency has ethnic ties to both or neither, support is predicted for both sides or neither side (Carment 1994; Saideman 1997: 728; Saideman 2002, 2007) (see also Chapter 14).

Carment (1994: 577–8, n.130) argues that

> ... *defining transnational affinity is difficult, however, because there is more than one way to establish ethnic identity. Race, religion, tribal (kinship) and linguistic cleavages may not coincide, so affinity in one area (linguistic) may be at odds with another area (kinship). Moreover, elites can attempt to mobilize other transnational identities (pan-Arabism as opposed to Islam, for example) or cultural subsystems at the expense of transnational ethnic affinities. In sum, ethnic linkage with a group in another state does not guarantee mutual interest.*

It is therefore not surprising that the ethnic ties logic may over-predict foreign interference where ethnic ties exist, and under-predict it when such ties do not exist.

Many states have ethnic kin on the other side of their border with neighboring states—in Europe, in Asia, in Africa, and elsewhere—yet only *rarely* do these ethnic ties produce support for secessionists, or host states. Even less frequently do such ethnic ties lead to irredentism, which one scholar called "the prerogative of the few" (Horowitz 1985, 1991; Saideman and Ayres 2008). Sometimes states with strong ethnic ties to a minority on the other side of their border act with intense restraint, even actively detaining individuals promoting separatism, while strongly supporting its ethnic kin in other states (Siroky 2010). Cases like these, which abound in other parts of the world as well, are difficult to explain within the context of the ethnic ties framework. Finally, states *without* ethnic ties to either the secessionists or the host states sometimes become involved but the theory does not illuminate these cases.

It stands to reason that advancing this debate requires expanding the scope of vulnerability to include non-secessionist forms of vulnerability, including political and economic vulnerability at the interstate level, and also extending the idea of ethnic ties to incorporate non-ethnic ties, particularly "strategic ties." Strategic ties are those links between states — economic, political, and military — that determine the overall level of incentive-based cooperation between states. This feature of state-to-state relations subsumes vulnerabilities to secession at home and can supersede ethnic ties in some cases. In addition to interference in the presence of ethnic ties, it can also predict interference in the absence of ethnic ties, and can predict restraint even in the presence of ethnic ties. It can also explain cases that the logic of ethnic ties, which stands as the main alternative framework, may not be able to explain because either (1) ethnic ties exist but the external actor is inactive, or (2) there are no ethnic ties, but the external actor is nevertheless engaged.

The first prediction from this strategic perspective would be that a foreign state with strong strategic ties — which stems from economic dependence or geographic necessity — is highly unlikely to support secessionists in the host state, even if ethnic ties are present and domestic vulnerability is absent. The foreign power is likely to support the central government, provided that it becomes involved at all, when strategic ties (a form of interstate vulnerability) are significant. By contrast, strong strategic enmity — resulting from regional balance of power considerations, discrimination of ethnic kin, or the strategic value of territory — increases the probability that the foreign power supports secessionists in the host state over the central government. The extent and duration of support, and whether it assumes an ideational or material form, will depend not only on group characteristics but on the salience of these strategies ties with the host state.

This theoretical framework takes account of an important empirical fact — that external support for secessionists can come from all sorts of states, whether or not they possess ethnic ties, and regardless of their domestic vulnerability to secession (Byman et al. 2001; Siroky 2010). Support for Eritrean secessionists came from China, Kuwait, Libya, South Yemen, Saudi Arabia, Syria, Sudan, and the USSR. Explaining the interference of this motley crew requires a framework that extends beyond ethnic ties and vulnerability to include classic international relations considerations like strategic interest, supporting the enemies of one's enemy, spreading one's own ideology, and gaining an advantage in regional rivalries (for a further discussion of these issues see Chapter 14).

Ethnic ties seem to promote restraint as much if not more than they promote intervention, much to the dismay of the separatists with limited options of outside support. In instances in which irredentist states become involved in separatist conflicts, one might contend that these cases should be analyzed separately, since they possess distinct motives. Yet there is good reason to believe that irredentist states are similarly propelled and constrained by international political considerations, even when they are cloaked in the garb of redeeming ethnic kin (Saideman 2000; Saideman and Ayres 2008). States considering intervening or supporting separatists will frequently face multiple, often competing, considerations, domestic and international, ethnic and strategic. It is not my contention that strategic interests are the only consideration, but that they tend to trump others in the calculus of confrontation. It predicts that states with strong strategic ties to the host state will generally refrain from supporting separatists, at a minimum, and will support the central government, if needed, even in the face of ethnic ties.

In contrast to arguments that focus on the role of domestic ethnic politics, the strategic ties logic is explicitly an international theory, one that moves the focus away from group characteristics and host state behavior to include international relations and foreign policy objectives. This framework enables us to predict the full range of theoretically possible and empirically relevant outcomes, and is valid for all states, not only states which are vulnerable to secession, or states which possess ethnic ties. It allows us to explain the full array of external action, including behavior that is unexpected and cannot be derived from either domestic vulnerability or ethnic ties theories.

Take the South Caucasus region, a veritable laboratory of overlapping ethnic groups, separatist sentiments, and revisionist states. How can we explain Armenia's strong support of its ethnic kin in Azerbaijan, but its suppression of separatism by its ethnic kin in Georgia? The strategic ties perspective highlights Azerbaijan's interdependence with Georgia—mainly resulting from its geographic dependence on Georgia as a transit route to the sea and to its main trading partner, Russia. One reporter noted that "[the Georgian–Russian crisis] once again highlighted Armenia's economic and transit dependence on Georgia. Just a few days and weeks of internal instability in Georgia was enough to create a shortage of essential goods in our country" (Hakobyan 2008).

Armenian behavior is therefore restrained in Javakheti, because of its strategic ties to Georgia, but not in Karabakh, because strategic ties with Azerbaijan are fewer, and direct ties between Yerevan and Stepanakert in Karabakh are significant. The ethnic ties logic cannot explain this variation, since ethnicity is constant across the cases. Similarly, Russian involvement in Ossetia and Abkhazia cannot be explained by ethnic ties or by reference to the vulnerability argument, which would counsel against supporting more separatism in the Caucasus, especially in view of Chechnya and, to a lesser extent, Tatarstan (Frombgen 1999; Sharafutdinova 2000).

The above discussion of external forces and foreign powers is not intended to exhaust the range of approaches to the international dimensions of secession, which is a burgeoning area of research, but only to outline a few important arguments, explanations, and debates, and to suggest some promising avenues for current and future research. Some important issues associated with foreign powers and secession have been neglected due to space constraints, but represent other international approaches to understanding and explaining secession: some of these issues include the international politics of secessionist state recognition, the spread of secession and the issue of diasporas (Brubaker 1995; King and Melvin 1999; Fox 2001; Shain 2002; Saideman 2002, 2007; Belanger, Duchesne and Paquin 2005; Carment, James and Taydas 2006; Coggins 2006; Salehyan and Gleditsch 2006; Gleditsch 2007; Gleditsch, Salehyan and Schultz 2008).

Future theoretical and empirical work on secession should aim to further integrate the three levels of analysis highlighted in this essay, exploring the complex interaction of domestic and international politics that ultimately explain secession and its aftermath.

## After Secession

Explaining secession is not only about the struggle for separation and cohesion in a united polity, but also about what happens after secession achieves its target and creates two states where previously there was only one. This dimension of separatism has produced a vigorous debate in the literature that goes to the heart of what social science can contribute to policy toward secession, which oscillates between a belief that secession may be a solution to ethnic conflict, "when all else fails," and a conviction that secession is more likely to be the source of new conflicts, even if it "resolves" old ones. In this more skeptical view, secession, much like partition after civil war, does not resolve ethnic conflicts, but merely reorders them and creates new forms of violence (Siroky 2009).

There are numerous reasons why post-secessionist states may find themselves embroiled in violence, and there are several forms that the violence may assume. Some of the literature has focused on the problem of interstate conflict after separation, whether between the new state and the rump state, or with a new neighbor (Tir 2003, 2005). These studies show that ethnically based territorial disputes play a much greater role in conflict onset than do their economically or strategically based counterparts, and that peaceful secessions are, perhaps not surprisingly, more likely to lead to peaceful relations than violent secessions. Others have focused on the problem of civil war recurrence after partition (Sambanis 2000), finding that partition may reduce residual violence, but does not reduce civil war recurrence (Sambanis and Schulhofer-Wohl 2009).

Just as critical to evaluating the effects of separation on conflict reduction is the problem of recursive secessionist conflict, that is, the prospect of a new secessionist civil war (Beran 1984; Pavković 2000; Siroky 2010). More often than not, new states are heterogeneous—minorities are part of the package: some supported the movement for independence, others opposed it, but both must confront the prospect of living in the new state under new rules. If what may have appeared as a unified and more or less homogenous polity, may seem less so after independence is achieved. One reason is that the division of the spoils in the new state creates incentives for new groups to form and mobilize. Another is that individuals often possess more than one (sometimes overlapping) ethnic identity from which to choose, which is likely to be influenced by the new institutional setting (Posner 2005), and the aggregation of these choices may make a country look quite different than it did before independence.

The problem of accommodating ethnic groups, whether long established or newly constructed, is not to be taken for granted in new states. Indeed, it is usually little more than an after-thought and an unwelcome guest at the table of many new nation-states. "Nationalizing states," as Brubaker (1995) calls them, can make life for new minorities so unbearable that the risky struggle to fight their way out through secession becomes relatively attractive. In a sense, then, these recursive secessionists are merely following the example set for them by their host states, which recently seceded themselves. Needless to say, post-secessionist host states see the comparison differently.

Nonetheless, the pattern is a familiar one: oppressed nations pursue independent statehood to ensure their survival, and achieve independence only to oppress their own minorities. For this reason, recursive secessionist conflict presents one of the greatest threats to the emerging state's stability, security, and prosperity. Although recursive secession constitutes a persistent pattern worthy of explanation, discussions of secession have devoted surprisingly little attention to this specific form of violence (for an exception, see Pavković 2000). Investigating this violence can advance the current state of debate over secession's aftermath by identifying the conditions under which secession and partition reorder conflicts or are able to resolve them. It also speaks to the literature on democratic politics in divided societies and to debates on the effectiveness of repression, accommodation, and indiscriminate violence in counterinsurgency campaigns.

The debate on whether partition and secession represent peaceful solutions to ethnic conflict can be crudely divided into two camps. The first argues that, if the groups cannot get along, then the best way forward is to let them simply part ways, separating the warring parties into defensible enclaves (Mearsheimer and Pape 1993; Mearsheimer and Van Evera 1995; Kaufmann 1996, 1998; Tullberg and Tullberg 1997; Downes 2004; Johnson 2008). In this view, secession and partition are policy solutions to "intractable" domestic-level disputes.

Other scholars disagree (Kumar 1997; Sambanis 2000: 479ff; Horowitz 2003). Sambanis and Schulhofer-Wohl (2009) provide compelling large-N evidence that partition does not prevent civil war recurrence. Scholars also contest some of the assumptions on which the policy of redrawing borders is based—that secession can actually produce "homogeneous homelands." "Neither secessionist nor rump states are homogenous," writes one scholar, "… there is no clean break … what looks homogenous today in an undivided state in which large groups oppose each other can look quite different after a secessionist state establishes itself" (Horowitz 1998: 191). This is both because borders cannot be redrawn so as to include only one group and exclude all the others and also because even groups that look homogeneous before the break can look fractionalized, heterogeneous, or divided in the new political setting.

Conceding this critique, some proponents of secession have suggested "population transfers" to ensure a "clean cut" after secession: "facilitate the dismantling of war-torn multiethnic states and the transfer of populations into ethnic enclaves, or homogenous homelands" (Kaufmann 1996: 137). When secession seems to lead to further conflict, it is argued, this is only because the cut was not clean in the first place (Johnson 2008; Johnson, Horowitz and Weisiger 2009); and that is why it is sometimes necessary to move populations and not only borders. But, as others have noted, "population transfer only *sounds* hygienic" (Horowitz 1985: 592). The major historical example of it—the exchange of Greeks and Turks provided for in the "Convention Concerning the Exchange of Greek and Turkish Populations," signed in Lausanne (1923)—was an ugly affair and does not bode well as a general policy prescription.

Though there are clear limits to what can be learned from a single case, Lausanne demonstrates that moving populations, even if planned with cold precision, can be a bloody affair. The transfer of Indians in the early American Republic, or Sudeten Germans from Czechoslovakia after World War Two, are unlikely to be used as best practice templates any time soon.

It could be countered that future ethnic violence may ensue if populations are *not* moved; we can of course never know for certain whether there would have been more or less violence had those same groups stayed within that same state, but this line of reasoning is less of an argument for population transfers than it is an effort to trade in counterfactual futures of human suffering—exchanging the alleged elimination of uncertain bloodshed in the future for the certainty of (presumably less) suffering in the present. Trading off uncertain future suffering for certain present suffering is a tradeoff few would be willing to make. Phrased in this manner, moreover, the policy is unlikely to appeal either to the populations involved or to international organizations which would presumably have a large role in any international transfer of peoples.

Put differently, secession may not be the political analog of marital divorce, and a "clean cut" may be nothing more than a nice phrase (Buchanan 1991; Tullberg and Tullberg 1997: 4; Horowitz 1998: 191; Aronovitch 2000). There are also practical issues that make such an analogy flawed: the number of states is in the hundreds, but the number of current "nations" is in the thousands (Van Evera 1994; Laitin 1995). Some scholars have therefore suggested that efforts should be focused upon internal rearrangements, such as designing institutions to increase the satisfaction of minorities in existing states (Hechter 2000a), rather than breaking up states in a Sisyphean attempt to make nation and state tantamount (Horowitz 1998: 191; Horowitz 2003). Needless to say, incentives to implement accommodative policy options would be significantly diminished by supporting secession as a general solution to ethnic conflict, and could possibly create moral hazard problems that encourage rather than reduce violence by promising intervention to promote partition (Fearon 2004b; Kuperman 2008).

Proponents of partition and secession might retort that institutions rarely have any significant impact on reducing conflict, especially at the international level (Mearsheimer 1994/95). Secession or partition, however unpleasant, is really the only way to solve deep ethnic conflicts, and is therefore also the most humane (on recent attempts to apply this logic to Iraq, see Cockburn 2006; Kaufmann 2006; Galbraith 2006a, 2006b, 2006c; Gelb 2003, 2006). However contentious this argument remains at the interstate level, it has far fewer adherents at the sub-national level, where institutions are widely believed to influence the behavior of individuals and groups (Lijphart 1977, 1995, 2004; Lustick 1979; Horowitz 1990; Lustick, Miodownik, and Eidelson 2004; Posner 2005).

Of course, this debate would be moot if states could more or less peacefully agree to part ways, as did Norway–Sweden, Slovakia–Czech Republic, or Iceland–Denmark (see Part VI). But states willing to part peacefully with a portion of their territory are rare. More common is a violent struggle over separation that is unlikely to result in the creation of a new state. Even when a new state emerges through secession, as it has several dozen times over the past two centuries, the incidence of various forms of violence after secession—including ethnic riots and protests, center-seeking civil wars, recursive secessions, and interstate militarized disputes—is far from negligible (Siroky 2009). Secession rarely marks the end of ethnic politics or violence.

Recent research on secession has benefited from systematic studies of the reasons why, and the conditions under which, each variety of violence is likely to ensue in the aftermath of partition and secession. Additional work might profitably pursue comparisons between the fates of partitioned places, secessionist states, and decolonized countries, a task that is both called for by the apparent similarities and ridden with difficulties by the clear differences.

It is unlikely that we have seen the end of secession as a problem in world affairs, so additional work on this subject is not only needed to advance understanding of secession as an historical phenomenon but also to craft more effective strategies for confronting the challenge of separatism and related phenomena.

# Conclusions

Secession is a thorny political topic. As a subject of scholarly inquiry, it is filled with intense nuance, and therefore worthy of the sort of multidisciplinary attention that it has received in this volume. As a problem that is unlikely to disappear anytime soon, explaining secession is necessarily concerned with understanding historical data and with current political developments. Secession is also possible to evaluate out of humanitarian concern to reduce human suffering and tragedy where possible. As a complex problem, it is appropriate that it is being approached from the perspectives of philosophy, politics, economics, sociology, and psychology. To organize some of this sundry scholarship involves recognizing that explaining secession involves modeling the interaction of interest and passion among multiple strategic and interdependent actors (groups, states, and foreign powers).

The purpose of this chapter has been two-fold: first to take stock and examine what we know about secession, while providing the basis for an analytical and theoretical framework to explain secession, and second to highlight several important directions in recent research and to make some conjectures that might be helpful for future research. The framework offered in this chapter is a multilevel one, organized around the political actors most clearly involved in secession: ethnic groups, host states, and foreign powers. By dividing and organizing the literature in this way, we can more easily understand how scholars have framed the issues and drawn attention to different aspects of the problem, thus enabling us to see secession as the consequence of many actors' interactions.

The basic framework has three levels, according to the unit of analysis. The first level includes studies that focus on the secessionist movement or ethnic group as the key actor; the second concentrates on state behavior toward minorities and state-level characteristics; and the third set addresses the role of external actors and foreign powers. This tripartite framework provides a simple structure that is parsimonious but still able to arrange seemingly disparate studies and to underscore their similarities.

At the ethnic group level, the literature identifies political grievances, economic inequality, ethno-demography, and ethno-geography as key factors in explaining secession. Other studies at the host state level focus on the dynamics of repression, violence, dissent, and accommodation along with institutional characteristics of the state, including its relative strength and capacity. At the third level are studies that examine the behavior and effect of external powers on secession.

Although the levels are separated for analysis, each highlighting different dynamics, one cannot help but notice important interactions between levels. Explaining secession, I have suggested, requires understanding this triadic structure at the core of the secession data generating process, but a coherent explanation for secession must account for interactions. There is little doubt that much important work remains to be done to further our understanding of secession and to enhance our ability to explain, predict, and address it (see also Chapters 10–15).

While much of this chapter has taken the literature apart, it also has suggested several ways in which future work might judiciously put it back together. Progress on this front should be both theoretical—linking actions and incentives at different levels through causal mechanisms—and methodological, combining sub-national, spatio-temporal, and relational data, connecting micro-level data to macro-level events, matching measurement to theory, in order to explain secession's emergence, endurance and escalation.

# References

Alesina, A., A. Devleeschauwer, W. Easterly, S. Kurlat, and R. Wacziarg (2003), "Fractionalization," *Journal of Economic Growth* 8:2, 155–94.
Armitage, D. (2007), *The Declaration of Independence: A Global History* (Cambridge, MA: Harvard University Press).
Aronovitch, H. (2000), "Why Secession is Unlike Divorce," *Public Affairs Quarterly* 14:1, 27–39.
Bakke, K. and E. Wibbels (2006), "Diversity, Disparity and Civil Conflict in Federal States," *World Politics* 59, 1–50.
Bartkus, V. (1999), *Dynamic of Secession* (Cambridge: Cambridge University Press).
Belanger, L., E. Duchesne, and J. Paquin (2005), "Foreign Interventions and Secessionist Movements: The Democratic Factor," *Canadian Journal of Political Science* 38, 435–62.
Beran, H. (1984), "A Liberal Theory of Secession," *Political Studies* 32, 21–31.
Bermeo, N. (2002), "The Import of Institutions," *Journal of Democracy* 13:2, 96–110.
Bermeo, N. and U. Amoretti (eds) (2003), *Federalism and Territorial Cleavages* (Baltimore, MD: Johns Hopkins University Press).
Brancati, D. (2006), "Decentralization: Fueling the Fire or Dampening the Flames of Ethnic Conflict and Secessionism," *International Organization* 60:3, 651–85.
Brancati, D. (2008), *Peace by Design: Managing Intrastate Conflict through Decentralization* (Oxford: Oxford University Press).
Breton, A. (1964), "The Economics of Nationalism," *Journal of Political Economy* 72:4, 376–80.
Brubaker, R. (1995), "National Minorities, Nationalizing States and External National Homelands in the New Europe," *Daedalus* 124:2, 107–32.
Buchanan, A. (1991), *Secession: The Morality of Political Divorce from Fort Sumter to Lithuania and Quebec* (Boulder, CO: Westview Press).
Bueno de Mesquita, E. (2008), "Terrorist Factions," *Quarterly Journal of Political Science* 3:4, 399–418.
Buhaug, H., K.S. Gleditsch, H. Holtermann, G. Østby, and A. Forø Tollefsen (2009), "Revolt of the Paupers or the Aspiring? Geographic Wealth Dispersion and Conflict," Paper presented at the International Studies Association, New York, USA, February 15–18, 2009.
Bunce, V. (1999), *Subversive Institutions* (Cambridge: Cambridge University Press).
Bunce, V. (2005), "Status-Quo, Reformist and Secessionist Politics: Explaining Minority-State Bargaining in Multinational States," *NCEEER Working Paper*, 2005.
Butt, A. (2011), "Good-bye or See You Later?" Ph.D. Dissertation in Progress, University of Chicago.
Byman D. et al. (2001), *Trends in Outside Support Secession for Insurgent Movements* (Santa Monica, CA: RAND).
Carment, D. (1994), "The Ethnic Dimension in World Politics: Theory, Policy and Early Warning," *Third World Quarterly* 15:4, 551–82.

Carment, D., P. James, and Z. Taydas (2006), *Who Intervenes? Ethnic Conflict and Interstate Crisis* (Columbus, OH: Ohio State University Press).

Cederman, L.-E., H. Buhaug, and J. Ketil Rod (2009), "Ethno-Nationalist Dyads and Civil War: A GIS-Based Analysis," *Journal of Conflict Resolution* 53:4, 496–525.

Cederman, L.-E. and L. Girardin (2007), "Beyond Fractionalization: Mapping Ethnicity onto Nationalist Insurgencies," *American Political Science Review* 101:1, 173–85.

Cederman, L.-E., K.S. Gleditsch, and N.B. Weidmann (2010), "Horizontal Inequalities and Ethno-Nationalist Civil War: A Global Comparison," Typescript.

Cetinyan, R. (2002), "Ethnic Bargaining in the Shadow of Third-Party Intervention," *International Organization* 56:3, 645–77.

Chandra, K. and S. Wilkinson (2008), "Measuring the Effect of Ethnicity," *Comparative Political Studies* 41:4–5, 515–63.

Christia, F. (2008), "The Closest of Enemies: Alliance Formation in the Afghan and Bosnian Civil Wars," Ph.D. Thesis, Harvard University.

Cockburn, P. (2006), "Iraq Is Disintegrating as Ethnic Cleansing Takes Hold," *Independent*, May 20.

Coggins, B. (2006), "Secession, Recognition and the International Politics of Statehood," Ph.D. Thesis, Ohio State University.

Collier, P. (1998), "The Political Economy of Ethnicity," Working Papers Series 98-8, Centre for the Study of African Economies, University of Oxford.

Collier, P. and A. Hoeffler (2004), "Greed and Grievance in Civil War," *Oxford Economic Papers* 56:4, 563–95.

Collier, P. and A. Hoeffler (2009), "Beyond Greed and Grievance: Feasibility and Civil War," *Oxford Economic Papers* 61:1, 1–27.

Collier, P., A. Hoeffler, and M. Soderbom (2001), "On the Duration of Civil War," Policy Research Working Paper Series 2681, The World Bank.

Cornell, S. (2002), "Autonomy as a Source of Conflict: Caucasian Conflicts in Theoretical Perspective," *World Politics* 54:2, 245–76.

Coser, L. (1956), *The Functions of Social Conflict* (New York: Free Press).

Crawford, J. (2005), *The Creation of States in International Law* (Oxford: Oxford University Press).

Cunningham, D. (2006), "Veto Players and Civil War Duration," *American Journal of Political Science* 50:4, 875–92.

Cunningham, D., K. Bakke, and L. Seymour (2010), "Shirts Today, Skins Tomorrow: The Effects of Fragmentation on Conflict Processes in Self-Determination Disputes," Typescript, March.

Davenport, C. (1995), "Multidimensional Threat Perception and State Repression: An Inquiry into Why States Apply Negative Sanctions," *American Journal of Political Science* 39:3, 683–713.

DeNardo, J. (1985), *Power in Numbers* (Princeton, NJ: Princeton University Press).

DeVotta, N. (2005), "From Ethnic Outbidding to Ethnic Conflict," *Nations and Nationalism* 11:1, 141–59.

Diamond, L. (1999), *Developing Democracy* (Baltimore, MD: Johns Hopkins University Press).

Diehl, P. (1991), "Geography and War: A Review and Assessment of the Empirical Literature," *International Interactions* 17, 11–27.

Downes, A. (2004), "The Problem with Negotiated Settlements to Ethnic Civil Wars," *Security Studies* 13:4, 230–79.

Downes, A. (2007), "Draining the Sea by Filling the Graves: Investigating the Effectiveness of Indiscriminate Violence as a Counterinsurgency Strategy," *Civil Wars* 9:4 (December), 420–44.

Downes, A. (2008), *Targeting Civilians in War* (Ithaca, NY: Cornell University Press).

Downes, A. and K. McNabb Cochrane (2010), "Targeting Civilians to Win? Assessing the Military Effectiveness of Civilian Victimization in Interstate War," in A. Lawrence and E. Chenoweth (eds), *Rethinking Violence* (Cambridge, MA: MIT Press), 23–56.

Eckstein, H. (1965), "Theoretical Approaches to Explaining Collective Political Violence," in T.R. Gurr (ed.), *Handbook of Political Conflict: Theory and Research* (New York: Free Press), 135–66.

Ellingsen, T. (2000), "Colorful Community or Ethnic Witches' Brew? Multiethnicity and Domestic Conflict during and after the Cold War," *Journal of Conflict Resolution*, 44:2, 228–49.

Englebert, P. and R. Hummel (2005), "Let's Stick Together: Understanding Africa's Secessionist Deficit," *African Affairs* 104:416, 399–427.

Esteban, J. and D. Ray (1994), "On the Measurement of Polarization," *Econometrica* 62, 819–52.

Esteban, J. and D. Ray (2008), "Polarization, Fractionalization and Conflict", *Journal of Peace Research* 45:2, 163–82.

Evangelista, M. (2002), *The Chechen Wars: Will Russia Go the Way of the Soviet Union?* (Washington, DC: Brookings Institution Press).

Fazal, T. and R. Griffiths (2008), "A State of One's Own: The Rise of Secession Since World War II," *Brown Journal of World Affairs* 15:1 (Fall/Winter).

Fearon, J. (2003), "Ethnic and Cultural Diversity by Country," *Journal of Economic Growth* 8:2, 195–222.

Fearon, J. (2004a), "Separatist Wars, Partition, and World Order," *Security Studies* 13:4, 394–415.

Fearon, J. (2004b), "Why Do Some Civil Wars Last So Much Longer Than Others?" *Journal of Peace Research* 41:3, 275–302.

Fearon, J. and David Laitin (2003), "Ethnicity, Insurgency and Civil War," *American Political Science Review* 97:1, 75–90.

Filippov, M. (2009), "Diversionary Role of the Georgia-Russia Conflict: International Constraints and Domestic Appeal," *Europe-Asia Studies* 61:10, 1825–47.

Fox, J.J. (2001), "Religious Causes of International Intervention in Ethnic Conflicts," *International Politics* 38, 515–32.

Frombgen, E. (1999), "Secession, Ethnic Conflict and Violence in Tatarstan and Chechnya," *Nationalism and Ethnic Politics* 5:2, 91–117.

Gagnon, V.P. (1995), "Ethnic Nationalism and International Conflict: The Case of Serbia," *International Security* 19:3, 130–66.

Galbraith, P.W. (2006a), "The Case for Dividing Iraq," *Time*, November 5.

Galbraith, P.W. (2006b), "Iraq's Salvation Lies in Letting It Break Apart," *Sunday Times*, July 16.

Galbraith, P.W. (2006c), *The End of Iraq: How American Incompetence Created a War without End* (New York: Simon and Schuster).

Gartner, S. and P. Regan (1996), "Threat and Repression: The Non-linear Relationship between Government Repression and Opposition Violence," *Journal of Peace Research* 33, 273–87.

Gelb, L.H. (2003), "The Three-State Solution," *New York Times*, November 25.

Gelb, L.H. (2006), "Last Train from Baghdad," *Foreign Affairs* 85:4, 160–65.

Giuliano, E. (2006), "Secessionism from the Bottom Up: Democratization, Nationalism, and Local Accountability in the Russian Transition," *World Politics* 58:2, 276–310.

Glaser, D. (1958), "Dynamics of Ethnic Identification," *American Sociological Review* 23:1, 31–40.

Gleditsch, K. (2007), "Transnational Dimensions of Civil War," *Journal of Peace Research* 44:3, 293–309.

Gleditsch, K., I. Salehyan, and K. Schultz (2008), "Fighting at Home, Fighting Abroad: How Civil Wars Lead to International Disputes," *Journal of Conflict Resolution* 52:4, 479–506.

Gleditsch, K. and M.D. Ward (2001), "Measuring Space," *Journal of Peace Research* 38:6, 749–68.

Goodwin, J. (2001), *No Other Way Out: States and Revolutionary Movements, 1945–1999* (Cambridge: Cambridge University Press).

Gorenburg, D. (2000), "Not with One Voice: An Explanation of Intra-Group Variation in Nationalist Sentiment," *World Politics* 53:1, 115–42.

Griffiths, R. and T. Fazal (2008), "A State of One's Own: The Rise of Secession Since World War II," *The Brown Journal of World Affairs* 15:1 (Fall/Winter), 199–209.

Grigoryan, A. (2010), "Third-Party Intervention and the Escalation of State-Minority Conflicts," *International Studies Quarterly* 54:4, 1143–74.

Gurr, T.R. (1970), *Why Men Rebel* (Princeton, NJ: Princeton University Press).

Gurr, T.R. (2000), *Peoples Versus States: Minorities at Risk in the New Century* (Washington, DC: United States Institute of Peace Press).

Hakobyan, Tatul (2008), "Turkey Faces a Critical Decision," *The Armenian Reporter Online*, August 30, 2008, http://www.reporter.am/go/article/2008-08-30-turkey-faces-a-critical-decision.

Hale, H. (2008), *The Foundations of Ethnic Politics: Separatism of States and Nations in Eurasia and the World* (Cambridge: Cambridge University Press).

Hechter, M. (1992), "The Dynamics of Secession," *Acta Sociologica* 35:4, 267–83.

Hechter, M. (2000a), "Nationalism and Rationality," *Studies in Comparative International Development* 35:1, 3–19.

Hechter, M. (2000b), *Containing Nationalism* (Oxford: Oxford University Press).

Hechter, M. and D. Okamoto (2001), "Political Consequences of Minority Group Formation," *Annual Review of Political Science* 4, 189–215.

Hechter, M., K. Quinn, and E. Wibbels (2004), "Ethnicity, Insurgency and Civil War Revisited," Working Paper, University of Washington.

Heraclides, A. (1990), "Secessionist Minorities and External Involvement," *International Organization* 44:3, 341–78.
Herbst, J. (1989), "The Creation and Maintenance of National Boundaries in Africa," *International Organization* 43:4, 673–92.
Herbst, J. (1992), "Challenges to Africa's Boundaries in the New World Order," *Journal of International Affairs* 46:1, 17–30.
Hewitt, C. (1977), "Majorities and Minorities," *The Annals of the American Academy of Political and Social Science* 433, 150–60.
Hirschman, A.O. (1970), *Voice, Exit and Loyalty* (Cambridge, MA: Harvard University Press).
Horowitz, D.L. (1972), "Ethnic Secession and the Bigness Bias: A Dissent," Woodrow Wilson International Center for Scholars.
Horowitz, D.L. (1985), *Ethnic Groups in Conflict* (Berkeley and Los Angeles, CA: University of California Press).
Horowitz, D.L. (1990), "Ethnic Conflict Management for Policy-Makers," in J.V. Montville and H. Binnendijk (eds), *Conflict and Peace-Making in Multiethnic Societies* (Lexington, MA: Lexington Books), 115–30.
Horowitz, D.L. (1991), "Irredentas and Secessions: Adjacent Phenomena, Neglected Connections," in Naomi Chazan (ed.) *Irredentism and International Politics* (Boulder, CO: Lynne Rienner), 9–22.
Horowitz, D.L. (1998), "Self-Determination: Politics, Philosophy, and Law," in I. Shapiro and W. Kymlicka (eds), *NOMOS XXXIX: Ethnicity and Group Rights* (New York: New York University Press).
Horowitz, D.L. (2000), *Ethnic Groups in Conflict*, 2nd edition (Berkeley and Los Angeles, CA: University of California Press).
Horowitz, D.L. (2001), *The Deadly Ethnic Riot* (Berkeley, CA: University of California Press).
Horowitz, D.L. (2003), "The Cracked Foundations of the Right to Secede," *Journal of Democracy* 14:2, 5–17.
Isaacs, H.R. (1975), *Idols of the Tribe: Group Identity and Political Change* (New York: Harper and Row).
Jackson, R.H. (1990), *Quasi-States: Sovereignty, International Relations, and the Third World* (Cambridge: Cambridge University Press).
Jackson, R.H. (1992), "Juridical Statehood in Sub-Saharan Africa," *Journal of International Affairs* 46:1, 1–16.
Jackson, W.A.D. (1958), "Whither Political Geography?," *Annals of the Association of American Geographers* 48:2, 178–83.
Jenne, E. (2004), "A Bargaining Theory of Minority Demands: Explaining the Dog that Did Not Bite in 1990s Yugoslavia," *International Studies Quarterly* 48, 729–54.
Jenne, E. (2007), *Ethnic Bargaining* (Ithaca, NY: Cornell University Press).
Jenne, E., S.M. Saideman, and W. Lowe (2007), "Separatism as a Bargaining Posture: A Panel Data Analysis of Minority Demand," *Journal of Peace Research* 44:5, 537–56.
Johnson, C. (2008), "Partitioning to Peace: Sovereignty, Demography, and Ethnic Civil Wars," *International Security* 32:4, 140–70.

Johnson, C., M. Horowitz, and A. Weisiger (2009), "The Limits of Partition," *International Security* 33:4 (Spring), 203–10.

Kalyvas, S. (2008), "Ethnic Defection," *Comparative Political Studies* 41:8, 1043–68.

Kasfir, N. (n.d.), "When Guerrillas Govern," a dataset coding instances of government by all autonomous insurgent groups holding populated territory during civil war and active between 1945 and 2005.

Kaufmann, C. (1996), "Possible and Impossible Solutions to Ethnic Wars," *International Security* 20:4, 136–75.

Kaufmann, C. (1998), "When All Else Fails: Ethnic Population Transfers and Partitions in the Twentieth Century," *International Security* 23:2, 120–56.

Kaufmann, C. (2006), "Separating Iraqis, Saving Iraq," *Foreign Affairs* 85:4, 156–60.

King, C. (2001), "The Benefits of Ethnic War: Understanding Eurasia's Unrecognized States," *World Politics* 53:4, 524–52.

King, C. and N.J. Melvin (1999), "Diaspora Politics: Ethnic Linkages, Foreign Policy, and Security in Eurasia," *International Security* 24, 108–38.

Kitschelt, H. (1989), "The Internal Politics of Parties: The Law of Curvilinear Disparity Revisited," *Political Studies* 37:3, 400–421.

Kohli, A. (1997), "The Bell Curve of Ethnic Politics: The Rise and Decline of Self-Determination Movements in India," in Wolfgang Danspeckgruber (ed.), *Self-Determination and Self-Administration: A Sourcebook* (Boulder, CO: Lynne Rienner), 309–36.

Kumar, R. (1997), "The Troubled History of Partition," *Foreign Affairs* 76:1, 22–34.

Kuperman, A. (2008), "The Moral Hazard of Humanitarian Intervention: Lessons from the Balkans," *International Studies Quarterly* 52:1 (March), 49–80.

Laitin, D. (1995), "Ethnic Cleansing, Liberal Style," MacArthur Foundation, typescript.

Lawrence, A. (2010), "Triggering Nationalist Violence: Competition and Conflict in Uprisings against Colonial Rule," *International Security* 35:2, 88–122.

Leff, N. (1971), "Bengal, Biafra and the Bigness Bias," *Foreign Policy* 3 (Summer), 129–39.

Levine, A. (1996), "Political Accommodation and the Prevention of Secessionist Violence," in M. Brown (ed.), *International Dimensions of Internal Conflict* (Cambridge, MA: MIT Press), 311–40.

Lichbach, M. (1987), "Deterrence or Escalation," *Journal of Conflict Resolution* 31:2, 266–97.

Lijphart, A. (1977), *Democracy in Plural Societies* (New Haven, CT: Yale University Press).

Lijphart, A. (1995), "Self-Determination versus Pre-Determination of Ethnic Minorities in Power-Sharing Systems," in Will Kymlicka, *The Rights of Minority Cultures* (New York: Oxford University Press), 275–87.

Lijphart, A. (2004), "Constitutional Design for Divided Societies," *Journal of Democracy* 15:2, 96–109.

Lustick, I. (1979), "Stability in Deeply Divided Societies: Consociationalism versus Control," *World Politics* 31:3, 325–44.

Lustick, I., D. Miodownik, and R. Eidelson (2004), "Secessionism in Multicultural States: Does Power Sharing Prevent or Encourage It?" *American Political Science Review* 98:2, 209–29.

Lyall, J. (2009), "Does Indiscriminate Violence Incite Insurgent Attacks? Evidence from Chechnya," *Journal of Conflict Resolution* 53:3 (June), 331–62.

Lyall, J. (2010), "Are Co-Ethnics More Effective Counter-Insurgents? Evidence from the Second Chechen War," *American Political Science Review* 104:1 (February), 1–20.

McCarthy, J.D. and Mayer Zald (1977), "Resource Mobilization and Social Movements," *American Journal of Sociology* 82:6, 1212–41.

Mearsheimer, J. (1994/95), "The False Promise of International Institutions," *International Security* 19:3, 5–49.

Mearsheimer, J.J. and R.A. Pape (1993), "The Answer: A Partition Plan for Bosnia," *New Republic*, June 14, 22–8.

Mearsheimer, J.J. and Stephen Van Evera (1995), "When Peace Means War: The Partition That Dare Not Speak Its Name," *New Republic*, December 18, 16–21.

Moore, W. (2000), "The Repression of Dissent: A Substitution Model of Government Coercion," *Journal of Conflict Resolution* 44:1, 107–27.

Mylonas, H. (2008), "Making Nations: The International Politics of Assimilation, Accommodation, and Exclusion," Ph.D. Dissertation, Yale University.

Nakarada, R. (1991), "The Mystery of Nationalism: The Paramount Case of Yugoslavia," *Millennium* 20:3, 369–82.

Pavković, A. (2000), "Recursive Secessions in Former Yugoslavia: Too Hard a Case for Theories of Secession?," *Political Studies* 48:3, 485–502.

Pavković, A. (with P. Radan) (2007), *Creating New States: Theory and Practice of Secession* (Aldershot: Ashgate).

Pearlman, W. (2008), "Spoiling Inside and Out: Internal Political Contestation and the Middle East Peace Process," *International Security* 33:3, 79–109.

Petersen, R. (2002), *Understanding Ethnic Violence: Fear, Hatred, Resentment in Twentieth Century Eastern Europe* (Cambridge: Cambridge University Press).

Poe, S., C. Neal Tate and L.C. Keith (1999), "Repression of the Human Rights to Personal Integrity Revisited," *International Studies Quarterly* 43:2, 291–313.

Posner, D. (2004), "Measuring Ethnic Fractionalization in Africa," *American Journal of Political Science* 48:4, 849–63.

Posner, D. (2005), *Institutions and Ethnic Politics in Africa* (Cambridge: Cambridge University Press).

Rasler, K. (1996), "Concessions, Repression, and Political Protest in the Iranian Revolution," *American Sociological Review* 61:1, 132–52.

Reilly, B. (2001), *Democracy in Divided Societies: Electoral Engineering for Conflict Management* (Cambridge: Cambridge University Press).

Reynal-Querol, M. (2002), "Ethnicity, Political Systems, and Civil Wars," *Journal of Conflict Resolution* 46:1, 29–54.

Roeder, P. (1991), "Soviet Federalism and Ethnic Mobilization," *World Politics* 43:2, 202–22.

Saideman, S. (1997), "Explaining the International Relations of Secessionist Conflicts: Vulnerability versus Ethnic Ties," *International Organization* 51:4, 721–53.

Saideman, S. (2000), *The Ties that Divide: Ethnic Politics, Foreign Policy, and International Conflict* (New York: Columbia University Press).

Saideman, S. (2002), "Discrimination in International Relations: Examining Why Some Ethnic Groups Receive More External Support than Others," *Journal of Peace Research* 39, 27–50.

Saideman, S. (2007), "Ties versus Institutions: Revisiting Foreign Interventions and Secessionist Movements," *Canadian Journal of Political Science* 40:3, 733–47.

Saideman, S. and William R. Ayres (2008), *For Kin or Country* (New York: Columbia University Press).

Saideman, S. and E. Jenne (2009), "The International Relations of Ethnic Conflict," in Manus Midlarsky (ed.), *Handbook of War Studies III: The Intrastate Dimension* (Ann Arbor, MI: University of Michigan Press).

Salehyan, I. and K.S. Gleditsch (2006), "Refugees and the Spread of Civil War," *International Organization* 60:2, 335–66.

Sambanis, N. (2000), "Partition as a Solution to Ethnic War: An Empirical Critique of the Theoretical Literature," *World Politics* 52:4, 437–83.

Sambanis, N. (2001), "Do Ethnic and Non-Ethnic Civil Wars Have the Same Causes? A Theoretical and Empirical Inquiry (Part 1)," *Journal of Conflict Resolution* 45:3, 259–82.

Sambanis, N. (2002), "A Review of Recent Advances and Future Directions in the Literature on Civil War," *Defense and Peace Economics* 13:2, 215–43.

Sambanis, N. and M. Doyle (2006), *Making War and Building Peace: The United Nations Since the 1990s* (Princeton, NJ: Princeton University Press).

Sambanis, N. and B. Milanović (2004), "Explaining the Demand for Sovereignty," unpublished paper. [Online] At http://www.yale.edu/macmillan/globalization/Sambanis-Milanovic_May2004.pdf [accessed 27 July 2011].

Sambanis, N. and J. Schulhofer-Wohl (2009), "What's in a Line?" *International Security* 34:2, 82–118.

Saparov, A. (2010), "From Conflict to Autonomy: The Making of the South Ossetian Autonomous Regions 1918–1922," *Europe-Asia Studies* 62:1, 99–123.

Sartori, G. (1970), "Concept Misformation in Comparative Politics," *American Political Science Review* 64:4, 1033–53.

Seaver, B.M. (2000), "The Regional Sources of Power-Sharing Failure: The Case of Lebanon," *Political Science Quarterly* 115:2 (Summer), 247–72.

Shain, Y. (2002), "The Role of Diasporas in Conflict Perpetuation or Resolution," *SAIS Review* 22:2, 115–44.

Sharafutdinova, G. (2000), "Chechnya versus Tatarstan: Understanding Ethnopolitics in Post-Communist Russia," *Problems of Post-communism* 47:2, 13–22.

Siroky, D.S. (2007), "Ethnic Heterogeneity and Secessionist Conflict," Paper presented at the 40th Anniversary Conference of Comparative Political Studies, and the Association for the Study of Nationalities Convention.

Siroky, D.S. (2009), "Secession and Survival: Nations, States and Violent Conflict," Ph.D. Thesis, Duke University.
Siroky, D.S. (2010), "International Dimensions of Secessionist Conflict: Transcaucasian Conflicts in Theoretical Perspective," Paper presented at the Order, Conflict, and Violence Workshop, Yale University, March 2010.
Sisk, T.D. (2003), "Power Sharing," in Guy Burgess and Heidi Burgess (eds), *Beyond Intractability* (Boulder, CO: Conflict Research Consortium, University of Colorado).
Snyder, J. and K. Ballentine (1996), "Nationalism and the Marketplace of Ideas," *International Security* 21:2, 5–40.
Sprout, H. and M. Sprout (1956), *Man-Milieu Relationship Hypotheses in the Context of International Relations* (Princeton, NJ: Princeton University Press).
Staniland, P. (2010), "Explaining Cohesion, Fragmentation, and Control in Insurgent Groups," Ph.D. Thesis, MIT.
Stedman, S. (1997), "Spoiler Problems in Peace Processes," *International Security* 22:2, 5–53.
Steinberg, J.B. (1993), "International Involvement in the Yugoslavia Conflict," in L.F. Damrosch (ed.), *Enforcing Restraint: Collective Intervention in Internal Conflicts* (New York: Council on Foreign Relations Press), 27–75.
Stepan, A. (1999), "Federalism and Democracy," *Journal of Democracy* 10:4 (October), 19–34.
Stewart, F. (2009), *Horizontal Inequalities and Conflict: Understanding Group Violence in Multiethnic Societies* (Houndmills: Palgrave Macmillan).
Tarrow, S. and C. Tilly (2006), *Contentious Politics* (Cambridge: Cambridge University Press).
Tilly, C. (1978), *From Mobilization to Revolution* (Reading, MA: Addison-Wesley).
Tir, J. (2003), "Averting Armed International Conflicts through State-to-State Territorial Transfers," *Journal of Politics* 65:4, 1235–57.
Tir, J. (2005), "Keeping the Peace after Secessions: Territorial Conflict between Rump and Secessionist States," *Journal of Conflict Resolution* 49:5, 713–41.
Tir, J. and Michael Jasinski (2008), "Domestic-Level Diversionary Theory of War: Targeting Ethnic Minorities," *Journal of Conflict Resolution* 52:5, 641–66.
Toft, M. (2002), "Indivisible Territory, Geographic Concentration and Ethnic War," *Security Studies* 12:2, 1556–852.
Toft, M. (2003), *The Geography of Ethnic Violence* (Princeton, NJ: Princeton University Press).
Treisman, D. (1997), "Russia's 'Ethnic Revival': The Separatist Activism of Regional Leaders in a Postcommunist Order," *World Politics* 49:2, 212–49.
Tullberg, J. and B.S. Tullberg (1997), "Separation or Unity? A Model for Solving Ethnic Conflicts," *Politics and the Life Sciences* 16:2, 237–48.
Van Evera, S. (1994), "Hypotheses on Nationalism and War," *International Security* 18:4, 5–39.
Walter, B. (2006a), "Information, Uncertainty and the Decision to Secede," *International Organization* 60, 105–35.

Walter, B. (2006b), "Building Reputation: Why Governments Fight Some Separatists but Not Others," *American Journal of Political Science* 50:2, 313–30.

Walter, B. (2009), *Reputation and Civil War: Why Separatist Conflicts Are So Violent* (Cambridge: Cambridge University Press).

Wickham-Crowley, T. (1987), "The Rise (and Sometimes Fall) of Guerrilla Governments in Latin America," *Sociological Forum* 2:3, 473–99.

Wickham-Crowley, T. (1992), *Guerrillas and Revolution in Latin America: A Comparative Study of Insurgents and Regimes since 1956* (Princeton, NJ: Princeton University Press).

Wilkinson, S. (2004), *Votes and Violence: Electoral Competition and Ethnic Riots in India* (Cambridge: Cambridge University Press).

Wimmer, A. (2002), *Nationalist Exclusion and Ethnic Conflict: Shadows of Modernity* (Cambridge: Cambridge University Press).

Woodward, S. (1995), *Balkan Tragedy: Chaos and Dissolution after the Cold War* (Washington, DC: The Brookings Institution).

Young, J. (2009), "The Process of Civil War: State Strength, Dissident Behavior and the Production of Violence," Ph.D. Thesis, Florida State University.

Zarkovic-Bookman, M. (1992), *The Economics of Secession* (New York: Palgrave MacMillan).

Zartman, I.W. (1966), *International Relations in the New Africa* (Englewood Cliffs, NJ: Prentice-Hall).

# Changing Borders by Secession: Normative Assessment of Territorial Claims

## Frank Dietrich

## Introduction

Secession necessarily entails the redrawing of political borders. Separatist movements do not only desire to leave the existing state, but to assume control over parts of its territory. Therefore, any justification of a moral right to secede must address two closely connected questions. It must, firstly, explain how states or separatist groups may acquire (and lose) the right to govern a particular stretch of land. Secondly, it must provide criteria for the localization of borders and, thereby, for the precise scope of the territory claimed by both parties.

This chapter will survey the philosophical discussion on the justification of territorial rights which has developed during the last two decades. Territorial right will be understood as a moral entitlement to exert jurisdictional power, i.e. to enact and to enforce laws, within a certain area.[1] The theories of territorial rights which are currently debated in political philosophy can be broadly classified into four groups. The following will examine various forms of property theories, justice-based arguments, national accounts and choice theories. Justice-based (remedial) and choice arguments are discussed at greater length in Part V. Ultimately, this chapter will defend a plebiscitary version of choice theory which considers the will of the residents to be decisive for the assessment of territorial claims.

---

1   A more detailed account of the competences which a territorial right encompasses is to be found *inter alia* in Copp (1999: 21–6) and Simmons (2001: 305–8).

## Property Theories

Classical political philosophers largely neglected the question of the justification of territorial claims.[2] The contractual theory that John Locke developed in his *Two Treatises of Government* [1689] is an important exception. Hence, it is not surprising that his work is frequently referred to in the contemporary discussion on territorial rights. According to Locke, individuals in the state of nature can rightfully appropriate land and other natural resources by mixing it with their labour.[3] In his view, property rights are not created by the state; on the contrary, the state is created with the aim of protecting pre-existent property rights. By entering into the contract individuals submit themselves and their estates to the authority of the government. As Locke put it: 'It would be a direct contradiction, for any one, to enter into Society with others for securing and regulating of Property: And yet to suppose his Land, whose property is to be regulated by the Laws of the Society, should be exempt from the jurisdiction of that Government, to which he himself the Proprietor of the Land, is a Subject' (Locke 1689: II §120). Consequently, the state's territorial jurisdiction is coextensive with the land that the original contractors rightfully possess.

As regards the legitimacy of secession, the question of whether individuals are entitled to withdraw their land from the state is of crucial importance. Locke's argument is based on a distinction between the founders of the political society and members of successive generations. The original contractors, who consented explicitly (and irrevocably) to the creation of the state, cannot resign their membership (Locke 1689: II § 121). In Locke's view, they have neither the right to emigrate nor the right to secede from the political society. The descendants of the first generation are considered free persons who are not bound by the promises of their forefathers (Locke 1689: II §§95, 116). They can only tacitly agree to the government either by possessing land which is under the jurisdiction of the state or simply by residing within its borders (Locke 1689: II §119). But residence on the territory cannot be plausibly interpreted as a sign of consent, unless the individuals have the right to leave. Accordingly, they are allowed to incorporate themselves into another political society or to establish a new one in *vacuis locis* (Locke 1689: II §121). However, Locke grants the right to emigrate only to individuals who are prepared to renounce their property of land: 'Whenever the Owner, who has given

---

2   Only a few classical thinkers briefly mentioned secession as a form of justified resistance to tyrannical government. Johannes Althusius (1614: 187), for instance, stated that '... one part of the realm, can abandon the remaining body to which it belonged and choose for itself a separate ruler or a new form of commonwealth when the public and manifest welfare of this entire part altogether requires it, or when fundamental laws of the country are not observed by the magistrate ...' (see also Grotius 1625: 569–70). This view is discussed in the section 'Justice Theories' below.

3   Locke's account of appropriation presupposes that, although God has given the earth to mankind in common, every man has a property in his own person. Self-ownership of the labour of his body enables each person to add something to the fruits of nature which excludes the common rights of others (Locke 1689: II §§25, 27).

nothing but such a tacit Consent to the Government, will, by Donation, Sale, or otherwise, quit the said Possession, he is at liberty to go ...' (Locke 1689: II §121).

The restriction that Locke imposes on persons who are willing to dissociate from the political society needs, of course, a theoretical justification. Unfortunately, he provides no detailed explanation why landowners are not permitted to take their property with them. Perhaps the most persuasive interpretation of Locke's thoughts has been suggested by Charles Beitz (1980: 490–93).[4] According to Beitz, individuals in the state of nature who signed the original contract submitted their estates irrevocably to the authority of the government. Subsequent owners could only inherit or purchase the land on condition that it remains an integral part of the political society. Consequently, they have never enjoyed a fully unrestricted property right that would have authorized them to dismember the state. Thus neither the members of the first nor of any subsequent generation may reclaim their land from the political society. In Locke's view, individuals are not entitled to change the borders of legitimately constituted states by secession or unification with adjacent countries.

Locke's argument for the territorial integrity of political societies faces, however, serious problems. Most important, individuals in the state of nature appeared to have no rational reason for accepting such far-reaching restrictions on their land rights. According to Locke, the original contractors were prepared to confer rights on the state because they wished to gain protection for their property. Given this motive it is, however, difficult to see why these individuals should submit their land irrevocably to the political society. The capacity of the state to provide protection is normally not impaired if some citizens withdraw their land and gain political independence.[5] Moreover, it does not serve the interest of the original contractors to constrain the property rights of all subsequent generations (Beitz 1980: 499–500).

As regards Neo-Lockean theories of territorial rights, one can distinguish 'individualist' from 'collectivist' versions of the theory. Most proponents of individualist theories regard Locke's account as unpersuasive and accept a right to secede.[6] Hillel Steiner, for instance, wrote:

> *For, although Locke himself (for reasons which remain mysterious) balked at embracing this conclusion, it is very clearly implied by his principles. That is, precisely because a nation's territory is legitimately composed of the real estate of its members, the decision of any of them to resign that membership and, as it were, to take the real estate with them, is a decision which must be respected. (Steiner 1998: 66; Rothbard 1998)*

---

4 Further discussion of Locke's theory of territorial rights is to be found in Gale (1973); Grant (1987: 110–28); Baldwin (1992: 212–16); Franklin (1996); and Simmons (2001: 312–17).
5 Arguably individuals in the state of nature would have mutually agreed to less extensive restrictions, such as a prohibition to sell land to potential aggressors, in order to protect their property.
6 For a defence of Locke's views see Simmons (2001: 312–20).

One problem of individualist theories is that they cannot account for private possession of land in foreign countries. For instance, a considerable number of German pensioners have acquired real estate on the Spanish island of Mallorca. It is common understanding that the Spanish government has not lost jurisdictional authority over parts of the island. A theory which derives territorial rights of states from individual property rights fails to explain this finding (Brilmayer 1990: 14–15; Buchanan 1991: 104–14; Morris 1998: 262–5; Nine 2008b). Secondly, individualist Neo-Lockean theories, such as Steiner's, privilege landowners to other citizens. As outlined in the introduction, a territorial right entitles the state to enact and to enforce laws within a certain area. The laws apply to and protect the interests of all persons who live under the jurisdiction of the right holder. But individualist theories focus exclusively on the interests of a part, possibly a very small one, of the population. Although, all inhabitants are affected by the exercise of political power, only landowners have the capacity to confer territorial rights to the state. This does not accord well with a democratic understanding of political legitimacy and has puzzling consequences for any justification of secession. A single landowner who holds a strategically important piece of land may effectively veto a secession desired by a large majority of the people.

More recently, Cara Nine has proposed a collectivist account of territorial rights which does not run into the aforementioned difficulties. In contrast to individualist thinkers, she does not refer to property rights of the landowners who consent to the state's jurisdictional authority. Instead she argues as follows: 'The state is capable of changing the land, thereby creating a rights relation with it. States change the land in the same way as individuals, via labour. The state labours by creating, adjudicating and enforcing laws' (Nine 2008a: 155). Laws may change the land, insofar as they influence individual decisions on its cultivation and the exploitation of natural resources. In Nine's view, to create a territorial right the change must be morally valuable; in particular, it must promote individual liberties and encourage an efficient use of the land. To defeat a territorial claim of the state, a separatist group must prove that these requirements are not met. Most important, a secession can be justified if the state severely encroaches on the liberties of parts of its population (Nine 2008a: 158).[7]

One immediate problem for a collectivist theory is that the state's right to change the land needs to be explained. According to Nine (2008a: 160), the state must establish its relationship with the land over time before it acquires a territorial right. At the beginning of this process the state cannot yet claim jurisdictional authority over the land. Contrary to the individuals, who are vested with self-ownership rights, the state is initially not entitled to labour (to enact and to enforce laws) on the land. Hence, the analogy with Locke's account of individual appropriation of land is not as straightforward as Nine suggests. Moreover, the cultural practice of national groups within the state may as well influence the use of land. Thus not only states but also stateless nations may assert territorial rights by drawing an

---

7   Although arguing within the framework of a Lockean theory, Nine arrives at a similar conclusion as justice-based accounts of secession.

analogy with Locke's account (Meisels 2009: 105–9).[8] As regards the right to secede, Nine's restrictive interpretation appears debatable. Provided that the separatists are prepared to respect individual liberties, the creation of an independent state may be compatible with Lockean principles.

## Justice Theories

A justice-based account of territorial claims has been developed, most prominently, by Allen Buchanan within the framework of a remedial right theory of secession (see Chapter 22 for a further discussion of remedial theories). In his writings on the morality of secession he has from the very beginning emphasized the need to justify territorial demands (Buchanan 1991: 10–11). Buchanan regards the capacity to explain how states acquire and lose territorial claims as an important virtue of his remedial right theory. In his view, it is a major shortcoming of competing positions, such as property theories or choice theories, not to provide a plausible account of territorial rights (Buchanan 1991: 104–14 and 2004: 373–9).

Buchanan's basic idea is that only states which wield their political power in a just way can be morally entitled to the land which they control. To assert a right to a particular stretch of land, states must primarily meet two requirements of justice. Firstly, they must not have forcefully annexed the territory in the past and, secondly, they must respect the human rights of its inhabitants. If a state is guilty of an unlawful annexation, it has not established and, consequently, never possessed a right to govern the territory.[9] If a state engages in human rights violations, it thereby forfeits its right to rule over the areas where the victims of its persecution live. In Buchanan's words: 'A state's claim to territory can be voided by a persisting pattern of serious injustice, because it is the provision of justice that justifies state power in the first place' (Buchanan 2004: 370; see also Buchanan 2003: 199).[10]

If a state has never enjoyed or recently lost the right to govern parts of its territory, the way is clear for secession. In that case, a separatist group which seeks to gain political independence does not violate a valid claim of the host state to the territory. However, the fact that the host state cannot lay claim on parts of its territory does not necessarily mean that the secessionists are morally entitled to it. To acquire a territorial right, a separatist movement must meet the same requirements of justice as the host state. Evidently, a secession which is sought as a remedy against state injustice cannot be considered to be an unlawful annexation.

---

8   For a more detailed explanation of the 'cultural argument' which nationalist authors advance see the section 'National Theories' below.
9   As regards the forceful annexation of territory, Buchanan (2004: 355–7) has argued for a statute of limitations (see also Chapter 22).
10  At different stages of his writing Buchanan has referred to two other instances of injustice that deprive a state of its territorial rights, viz. discriminatory redistribution (1991: 38–45) and the violation of intrastate autonomy (2004: 357–9).

Hence, the key question is whether the newly created state is prepared to respect the human rights of all people who live under its jurisdiction. In Buchanan's view, the separatists can only establish a territorial right if they are determined to replace an unjust regime by a just one.

Buchanan's account has the advantage of giving host states and separatist states alike strong incentives to comply with human rights standards. His attempt to base territorial rights on considerations of justice faces, however, three closely related problems. To begin with, as far as just states are concerned, Buchanan's theory does not account for the localization of borders. The boundary lines between two states which meet the aforementioned requirements of justice can be drawn in many different ways. Buchanan's justice-based argument offers no normative guidance on how to choose between possible alternatives. From the perspective of his theory, any distribution of territorial authority between political units which respect human rights appears to be legitimate. Buchanan must presuppose that just states have already reached an agreement, e.g. on the basis of customary law or historical peace accords, on their borders. If the spatial scope of their jurisdiction has already been determined, states can acquire and maintain territorial rights by exerting a just rule. Their conformity to standards of justice, however, cannot determine how their borders with other just states must be drawn.

Secondly, states which meet the requirements of justice may lay competing claims on a particular stretch of land. If two or more states are willing and able to govern an area in accordance with human rights standards, the conflict must somehow be decided. Evidently, on the basis of Buchanan's argument it is impossible to assert which party is morally entitled to the territory. Two strategies for dealing with this problem can be imagined. On the one hand, the right could be assigned to the state which proves to be capable of imposing its rule on the territory. This, however, would come close to a 'might make right' principle which does not go well with a theory of justice. On the other hand, the right to control the territory could be assigned on the basis of an additional normative criterion, such as the will of the residents. Thereby, Buchanan's theory would, however, incorporate a plebiscitary element (see the section 'Choice Theories', below) and essentially change its character.[11]

This dilemma is evidently relevant to the normative assessment of secessionist demands. Most separatist movements which seek to gain independence from democratic states can be expected to meet the requirements of justice. For instance, in the case of Quebec or Scotland both parties, the host state and the separatists, are willing to respect human rights. To be sure, in Buchanan's view the host state is already vested with a territorial right which the separatists must not violate. If it is the aim of his theory to achieve justice for as many people as possible it is, however, not clear why the *status quo* enjoys a privilege. The creation of new states which are determined to comply with human rights standards means no setback in terms of justice. Hence, the territorial claims of separatists which sincerely intend to implement democratic institutions cannot easily be dismissed.

---

11   For attempts to refute this argument see Waldron (1993: 24–7) and Stilz (2009: 206–10).

Thirdly, the focus of Buchanan's argument is on basic human rights and other criteria of justice. He widely ignores that most people not only take an interest in the provision of just institutions, but also attach great importance to cultural ties and communal feelings. Usually individuals are not completely indifferent as to which (human rights respecting) state they are citizens of. The desire to live in a political community with which one identifies appears to be fully legitimate, unless it conflicts with the requirements of justice. There seems to be no reason why a justice-based account of secession should not take into account the people's sense of belonging.

## National Theories

In the last two decades, nationalist thought has enjoyed a remarkable revival within liberal political philosophy.[12] Not surprisingly, for many advocates of liberal nationalism the justification of territorial rights has been an important concern. In their view, the close connection with a particular geographic region constitutes a distinguishing feature of nations. National communities, unlike other types of communities, believe they have a historical homeland to which they are entitled.[13] Hence, stateless nations which aspire to gain political independence always lay claim to a specific territory. Basque nationalists, for instance, can only think of establishing a state of their own in the Basque Country; from their perspective it would be unacceptable to obtain political self-determination elsewhere. Other types of communities, such as families or religious groups, are not so intimately tied to a particular stretch of land. Although their members may attach great importance to ancestral homes or sacred sites, they usually do not deem it necessary to live there.[14]

For the justification of territorial rights it does, however, not suffice to demonstrate that the idea of a homeland is an important element of nationalist thought. One has to provide normative reasons as to why national communities are morally entitled to control a specific territory. Basically, the proponents of liberal nationalism have advanced three arguments. Firstly, they have referred to the historical fact that a previously uninhabited area was initially settled by the members of a national community. According to the *first occupancy argument*, the group which was the first to live in the place acquired the right to rule over it. Despite the prominence

---

[12] See Tamir (1993); Miller (1995, 2000 and 2007); Moore (2001); Gans (2003); and Meisels (2009). Kymlicka (1995) and Kolers (2009) hold a similar position, albeit they speak of cultural societies and ethnogeographic communities instead of nations.

[13] The territorial aspect of national identity is discussed in *inter alia* Knight (1982); Anderson (1988); Smith (1991: 8–15) and Miller (1995: 21–7).

[14] David Miller made this point very clearly: 'If you are a good Muslim you should make a pilgrimage to Mecca at least once, but you need not set up house there. A nation, in contrast, must have a homeland' (1995: 24).

of the 'we were first' claim in political conflicts, most liberal nationalists have come to see it rather critically. They largely agree that first occupancy as such, without prolonged settlement, fails to establish a territorial right (Khatchadourian 1989: 37–42; Gans 2003: 104–9; Meisels 2009: 35–9).

Secondly, and more important, nationalist authors have pointed to the formative influences that the cultural activities of a nation typically exert on a territory.[15] The members of a national community employ particular forms of agriculture, found towns and erect outstanding buildings, such as castles and cathedrals. Thereby they create a visible relationship between the nation and the territory which gives them, according to the *cultural argument*, a right to it. Some authors assert that the peculiarities of a territory frequently bear on the 'character' of a nation which has been settling on it over a long period of time. Thus not only the land is shaped by the national culture, the national culture is also shaped by the land (Gilbert 1998: 94–101; Kolers 2009: 86–93).

Thirdly, liberal nationalists have stressed the value that the members of national communities assign to a particular geographical region. Persons identifying with a nation usually have strong emotional bonds to the area which they regard as their homeland. The importance the individual members attach to the territory explains, according to the *identification argument*, why the nation is entitled to it. David Miller wrote: 'The case for having rights over the relevant territory is then straightforward: it gives members of the nation continuing access to places that are especially significant to them, and it allows choices to be made over how these sites are to be protected and managed' (2007: 219). Since individuals usually identify with an area because of its cultural characteristics the second and third arguments are closely connected (Miller 2000: 113–18; Moore 2001: 189–201; and Meisels 2009: 126–30).

The justification of territorial claims offered by nationalist authors faces a number of conceptual problems. To begin with, nationalist thought originated in the eighteenth and nineteenth centuries and thus is a relatively recent phenomenon. The achievements to which the cultural argument refers were mainly accomplished by groups who did not think of themselves as national communities. Hence, it may be difficult to establish whether the group which formed the territory many centuries ago is identical with the nation which presently lays claim on it. Furthermore, modern nations are rather heterogeneous communities whose members disagree on many questions. They can even hold different views on the size and borders of the territory which rightfully belongs to the nation. There is, for instance, an ongoing debate within the Zionist movement regarding the land to which the Israeli state is entitled (Gans 2008). If the members of a national community are split over territorial matters, the scope of their right cannot be readily determined. Since they have different conceptions of their homeland and accordingly different emotional ties, the identification argument yields no clear result.

---

15   In his discussion of historical rights Chaim Gans makes a distinction between 'first occupancy conceptions' and 'formative territory conceptions' (2001 and 2003: 97–123).

As regards the normative justification of territorial rights, a major weakness of the above arguments becomes apparent if nations lay claim on territories where they do not live anymore or are a minority.[16] In the course of history national communities sometimes leave the areas where they originally settled or they are outnumbered by other groups. Nevertheless the territory may play an important role for the nation's narrative and many of its members may feel a strong attachment to it. Claims to territories where for the most part other groups live are put forward by host states and separatist movements alike. The Serb government, for instance, strongly opposes the secession of Kosovo because it regards the province as the cradle of the Serb nation (see Chapter 9). Basque separatists aspire to establish an independent state on the historical homeland of the Basque nation which in their view includes parts of Navarre (Mansvelt Beck 2005: 76–80).

The cultural and the identification arguments, as stated above, suggest that national communities can be morally entitled to areas where predominantly other people live. Most obviously, the interests of the members of national communities that lay claim to a territory may conflict with the interests of its current inhabitants. Here it is important to recall that a territorial right has to be understood as a jurisdictional right. It authorizes the right holder to enact and to enforce laws on the people who live within the borders of the territory. Decisions by the territorial sovereign affect fundamental concerns of the inhabitants, such as their physical protection and social welfare. These concerns carry greater weight than any interest asserted by a national group whose members live elsewhere. Therefore, the justification of territorial rights must first and foremost take the interests of the residents into account. Giving the interests of the nation priority amounts to allowing a kind of alien domination over the actual inhabitants.[17]

Some nationalist authors accept this criticism and deny that nations can rightfully claim jurisdiction over areas where for the most part other people live. In their view, the above arguments should only be applied to territories where the national community is presently in the majority (Moore 2001: 193–7; Gans 2003: 109–15). Thereby they implicitly acknowledge, however, that a theory of territorial rights must primarily focus on the interests of the actual inhabitants. If the cultural formation of or the personal identification with a certain stretch of land conflict with residence, the latter criterion must be given priority. This suggests that neither cultural formation nor personal identification are sufficient to establish a jurisdictional right over a territory and thus to generate a right to secede.

---

16   The cultural argument and the identification argument, moreover, give rise to competing rights. Often more than one nation may claim that its culture has shaped the physical appearance of the territory and that its members identify with it.
17   Arguably, the interests of national communities may ground rights to the protection of cultural heritage and free access to important monuments.

## Choice Theories

In view of the preceding discussion, choice theories of territorial rights appear to be an attractive alternative (for an argument in support of a choice theory see Chapter 23). The adherents of choice theories propose to base decisions on territorial conflicts on the will of the inhabitants. If two parties, e.g. a host state and a separatist movement, lay competing claims on an area, a plebiscite must be held. The party which gains the majority of the votes is considered to be morally entitled to govern over the territory. The eligibility for the plebiscite is restricted to persons who meet two requirements: Firstly, they must have lived on the territory for a certain period of time and, secondly, they must not have taken home there by illegitimate means, such as the killing or expulsion of former inhabitants.[18]

Most prominently, Harry Beran has developed a choice theory of secession within a contractual framework (1987: 37–42). According to contract theory, a state is morally entitled to wield political power if its citizens consent to its rule. A state, in this view, clearly lacks the authority to control a territory if most of its inhabitants vote for secession. There is still another strategy for justifying choice theory in Beran's writings that should be distinguished from the *contractual argument*. Beran has repeatedly referred to central principles of liberal democracy, such as individual freedom, sovereignty and majority rule (1984: 24–9). According to the *coherentist argument*, the normative ideas that underlie modern democracies imply a right of secession. If one accepts the aforementioned principles, one cannot consistently oppose a plebiscitary right to secede.[19]

Perhaps the most important challenge a choice theory must meet is the justification of majority decisions. It must explain why the larger part of the inhabitants may establish a territorial right against the will of the minority. A choice theory that is based on a contractual argument does not succeed with justifying majority votes. Within a contractual framework, *each* person living on the territory must consent either directly to the jurisdictional authority of the state or indirectly to the decision procedure. Evidently, if the inhabitants of a territory are divided on the question of secession they will not reach a unanimous agreement. A coherentist argument appears to be capable of overcoming this problem by referring to established principles of liberal democracy. Within democratic societies majority decisions are deemed legitimate if fundamental individual liberties are not trespassed.[20] If one is prepared to accept the majority principle under this proviso the same must hold with regard to secessionist referenda. Provided that

---

18  In addition, persons who have suffered expulsion or fled from acts of violence must be admitted to the plebiscite.
19  A reference to contract theory is made by Gauthier (1994: 360); Philpott (1995: 355–62 and 1998: 81–4), Wellman (2005: 35–8) and Dietrich (2010: 242–51) base their argument on liberal democratic ideas.
20  Democratic societies determine the limits of legitimate majority decisions in different ways, but a core of individual liberties is throughout considered to be inviolable.

the separatists are willing to respect individual liberty rights, a majority vote on independence appears to be justified.

Now, it is of crucial importance to see how choice theories deal with separatist movements which are likely to oppress minorities. At first glance, the coherentist argument suggests that they cannot establish a moral title to the land by winning a majority vote. One can, however, make an analytical distinction between the right to rule over territory and the right to rule over people (Dietrich 2006: 590–93). A state's territorial jurisdiction as such cannot encroach on basic individual rights and thus cannot violate the principles of liberal democracy. Only a state's jurisdiction over persons may conflict with the provision under which a majority decision is considered to be legitimate. Hence, even a majority group that is not willing to respect minority rights may establish a territorial claim by plebiscite. Of course, jurisdiction over territory and over persons cannot be separated in practice – the former specifies the spatial scope of the latter. Permitting a majority which is determined to breach vital liberties of minority members to exercise its territorial right would not be acceptable. Hence, the majority must be prevented from making use of their territorial right until it is prepared to comply with human rights. The relevant group does, however, not lose its basic claim to the territory and any other party may only govern it on a provisional basis.

A further problem for choice theories is the specification of the area whose inhabitants are permitted to decide on political independence. In some cases the separatists and the representatives of the host state have conflicting views on the location of the plebiscite. Evidently, the chance of gaining a majority for or against secession depends very much on how the territory is defined. Thus it would be a serious weakness in a plebiscitary argument, if it had nothing to say on the question of border drawing (Schmücker 2006: 604–8). To solve this problem, Harry Beran (1984: 29–30) proposed to identify the area in which a plebiscite is to be held by making the use of the majority principle recursive.[21] According to Beran, the separatists may determine the size of the territory on condition that they grant an equal right to others. If they gain political independence as a result of the majority decision, any group within the newly created state must be allowed to organize a referendum on counter-secession. This time, the loyalists may establish the area in which the plebiscite is to be held on condition that they allow any group within it to organize further votes, etc. Thus the precise scope of the territorial rights the separatists and the host state possess emerges as the result of a reiterated majority procedure.[22]

Beran expects only one plebiscite to be necessary because he believes that the separatists can and will anticipate possible counter-secessions. In his view, the process of recursive secession must be understood as a thought experiment that helps to specify state borders. Given the fact that separatist movements usually

---

21  See also Beran (1987: 39–41, 1990: 154 and 1993: 485–6); Pavković (2000) and in a different context Pogge (1992: 69–72).
22  The process results in a situation where as many persons as possible live in the political association which they prefer (Gauthier 1994: 359–62).

know quite well in which areas they are likely to lose a majority vote, Beran's assumption is not over-optimistic. Beran's account has frequently been criticized for allowing the creation of very small states and enclaves. However, as the example of San Marino suggests, there is little evidence that these entities are economically not viable or not capable of guaranteeing individual liberties. Hence, a general restriction of the right to secede with regard to microstates and enclaves contradicts the principles of liberal democracy.[23]

In addition to specifying a territory, choice theories must stipulate who has a moral right to live there and thus to vote in a plebiscite. As indicated at the beginning of this section, some negative criteria readily come to mind. For instance, persons who have expelled the former inhabitants and occupied their homes clearly should not be permitted to vote. Choice theories, however, must positively state how a right to residence and thereby a right to participate in a referendum is established. According to Harry Beran, 'this right is acquired not simply by birth in a territory, let alone by some period of residence there, but by being a member of a group which traditionally occupies a territory or by being in a territory by permission of the traditional occupants' (1990: 158). As regards Beran's example, the dispute between Kanaks and French in New-Caledonia, this criterion may be sufficiently clear. Applied to other cases, such as the Israel–Palestine conflict, the meaning of 'traditional occupancy' has to be explained in more detail. Even more important, by referring to 'occupancy' and 'group membership' Beran comes close to nationalist theories. The proposed criterion does not match well with the principles of liberal democracy on which his overall argument is based. Thus a persuasive account of the entitlement to vote in a plebiscite has not yet been provided within the framework of choice theory.

## Conclusion

I have based my argument in this chapter on a view on political legitimacy which I hope to be widely acceptable. I have assumed throughout that the exercise of political power must be justified to all persons who are subjected to it. Territorial rights concern insofar an important aspect of political power as they authorize states to enact and to enforce laws within certain areas. Consequently, their justification must take the legitimate interests of all persons who permanently reside on a territory into consideration. The three theories which I have explored first appear for different reasons not to be capable of meeting this requirement. Individualist versions of property theory are systematically biased in favour of landowners and fail to consider the interests of other residents. Justice theories (and Nine's collectivist version of Locke's account) have a one-sided view of the relevant interests. They

---

23  Initially, Beran had considered to prohibit the creation of enclaves (1984: 30–31); later he changed his position (1998: 51–3). For an excellent discussion of the 'territorial unity demand' see Steiner (2008: 953–5).

only take account of the desire to live under just institutions, but largely ignore cultural attachments and communal feelings. Nationalist theories typically focus on the interests of persons who regard a territory as the nation's homeland, which may be not identical with the present inhabitants. As a consequence, each of the three theories may under certain circumstances accord territorial rights to states which the vast majority of the local population strongly reject.

Choice theories have the advantage of giving priority to the interests of those people who live under the territorial jurisdiction of the right holder. By deciding conflicting territorial claims on the basis of a majority procedure they effectively avoid the above stated problem. Beran's proposal to hold plebiscites recursively ensures that as many individuals as possible belong to the political community they identify with. His approach, moreover, provides a mechanism for the drawing of state borders which is missing in justice theories and national theories alike. However, as I have argued in the last section, the advocates of choice theory must explain more fully who counts as a legitimate resident. To develop a comprehensive account of the entitlement to vote in plebiscites they need to address a number of complex normative problems. *Inter alia* they have to consider possible restrictions on the right to return, e.g. for the descendants of Palestine refugees, and illiberal population policies, such as the Sinization of Tibet (for further discussion of normative approaches see Part V).

# References

Althusius, Johannes (1614) [1995], *Politica: Politics Methodically Set Forth, and Illustrated with Sacred and Profane Examples*, ed. Frederick S. Carney (Indianapolis, IN: Liberty Fund).

Anderson, James (1988), 'Nationalist Ideology and Territory', in R.J. Johnston, D.B. Knight and E. Kofman (eds), *Nationalism, Self-Determination and Political Geography* (London, New York and Sidney: Routledge), 18–39.

Baldwin, Thomas (1992), 'The Territorial State', in H. Gross and R. Harrison (eds), *Jurisprudence: Cambridge Essays* (Oxford: Oxford University Press), 207–30.

Beitz, Charles R. (1980), 'Tacit Consent and Property Rights', *Political Theory* 8, 487–502.

Beran, Harry (1984), 'A Liberal Theory of Secession', *Political Studies* 32, 21–31.

Beran, Harry (1987), *The Consent Theory of Political Obligation* (New York: Croom Helm).

Beran, Harry (1990), 'Who Should be Entitled to Vote in Self-determination Referenda?', in Martin Warner and Roger Crisp (eds), *Terrorism, Protest and Power* (Aldershot: Edward Elgar), 152–66.

Beran, Harry (1993), 'Border Disputes and the Right of National Self-Determination', *History of European Ideas* 16, 479–86.

Beran, Harry (1998), 'A Democratic Theory of Political Self-Determination for a New World Order', in Peter B. Lehning (ed.), *Theories of Secession* (London and New York: Routledge), 33–60.
Brilmayer, Lea (1990), 'Consent, Contract, and Territory', *Minnesota Law Review* 39, 1–35.
Buchanan, Allen (1991), *Secession: The Morality of Political Divorce from Fort Sumter to Lithuania and Quebec* (Boulder, CO, San Francisco, CA, Oxford: Westview Press).
Buchanan, Allen (2003), 'Secession, State Break Down, and Humanitarian Intervention', in D.K. Chatterjee and D.E. Scheid (eds), *Ethics and Foreign Intervention* (Cambridge: Cambridge University Press), 189–211.
Buchanan, Allen (2004), *Justice, Legitimacy, and Self-Determination: Moral Foundations for International Law* (Oxford: Oxford University Press).
Copp, David (1999), 'The Idea of a Legitimate State', *Philosophy and Public Affairs* 28, 3–45.
Dietrich, Frank (2006), 'Zur Legitimation territorialer Ansprüche', *Deutsche Zeitschrift für Philosophie* 54, 577–96.
Dietrich, Frank (2010), *Sezession und Demokratie. Eine philosophische Untersuchung* (Berlin: de Gruyter).
Franklin, Julian H. (1996), 'Allegiance and Jurisdiction in Locke's Doctrine of Tacit Consent', *Political Theory* 24, 407–22.
Gale, George (1973), 'John Locke on Territoriality: An Unnoticed Aspect of the Second Treatise', *Political Theory* 1, 472–85.
Gans, Chaim (2001), 'Historical Rights: The Evaluation of Nationalist Claims to Sovereignty', *Political Theory* 29, 58–79.
Gans, Chaim (2003), *The Limits of Nationalism* (Cambridge: Cambridge University Press).
Gans, Chaim (2008), *A Just Zionism: On the Morality of the Jewish State* (Oxford: Oxford University Press).
Gauthier, David (1994), 'Breaking Up: An Essay on Secession', *Canadian Journal of Philosophy* 24, 357–72.
Gilbert, Paul (1998), *The Philosophy of Nationalism* (Boulder, CO: Westview Press).
Grant, Ruth W. (1987), *John Locke's Liberalism* (Chicago, IL and London: University of Chicago Press).
Grotius, Hugo (1625) [2005], *The Rights of War and Peace*, ed. Richard Tuck (Indianapolis, IN: Liberty Fund).
Khatchadourian, Haig (1989), 'Criteria of Territorial Rights of Peoples and Nations', in John R. Jacobson (ed.), *The Territorial Rights of Nations and Peoples: Essays from the Basic Issue Forum* (Lewiston, NY and Queenstown, ON: Edwin Mellen Press), 29–51.
Knight, David B. (1982), 'Identity and Territory: Geographical Perspectives on Nationalism and Regionalism', *Annals of the Association of American Geographers* 72, 514–31.
Kolers, Avery (2009), *Land, Conflict, and Justice: A Political Theory of Territory* (Cambridge: Cambridge University Press).
Kymlicka, Will (1995), *Multicultural Citizenship* (Oxford: Oxford University Press).

Locke, John (1689) [1988], *Two Treatise of Government*, ed. Peter Laslett (Cambridge: Cambridge University Press).
Mansvelt Beck, Jan (2005), *Territory and Terror: Conflicting Nationalisms in the Basque Country* (London and New York: Routledge).
Meisels, Tamar (2009), *Territorial Rights*, 2nd edn (Dordrecht: Springer).
Miller, David (1995), *On Nationality* (Oxford: Oxford University Press).
Miller, David (2000), *Citizenship and National Identity* (Cambridge: Cambridge University Press).
Miller, David (2007), *National Responsibility and Global Justice* (Oxford: Oxford University Press).
Moore, Margaret (2001), *The Ethics of Nationalism* (Oxford: Oxford University Press).
Morris, Christopher W. (1998), *An Essay on the Modern State* (Cambridge: Cambridge University Press).
Nine, Cara (2008a), 'A Lockean Theory of Territory', *Political Studies* 56, 148–65.
Nine, Cara (2008b), 'Territory Is Not Derived from Property: A Response to Steiner', *Political Studies* 56, 957–63.
Pavković, Aleksandar (2000), 'Recursive Secessions in Former Yugoslavia: Too Hard a Case for Theories of Secession?', *Political Studies* 48, 485–502.
Philpott, Daniel (1995), 'In Defense of Self-Determination', *Ethics* 105, 352–85.
Philpott, Daniel (1998), 'Self-Determination in Practice', in M. Moore (ed.), *National Self-Determination and Secession* (Oxford: Oxford University Press), 79–102.
Pogge, Thomas (1992), 'Cosmopolitanism and Sovereignty', *Ethics* 103, 48–75.
Rothbard, Murray (1998), 'Nations by Consent: Decomposing the Nation-State', in D. Gordon (ed.), *Secession, State and Liberty* (New Brunswick, NJ and London: Transaction Publishers), 79–88.
Schmücker, Reinold (2006), 'Gerechtigkeit und Territorialität', *Deutsche Zeitschrift für Philosophie* 54, 597–621.
Simmons, A. John (2001), 'On the Territorial Rights of States', *Philosophical Issues* 11, 300–326.
Smith, Anthony D. (1991), *National Identity* (London: Penguin).
Steiner, Hillel (1998), 'Territorial Justice', in Peter B. Lehning (ed.), *Theories of Secession* (London and New York: Routledge), 61–70.
Steiner, Hillel (2008), 'May Lockean Doughnuts Have Holes? The Geometry of Territorial Jurisdiction: A Response to Nine', *Political Studies* 56, 949–56.
Stilz, Anna (2009), 'Why Do States Have Territorial Rights?', *International Theory* 1, 185–213.
Tamir, Yael (1993), *Liberal Nationalism* (Princeton, NJ: Princeton University Press).
Waldron, Jeremy (1993), 'Special Ties and Natural Duties', *Philosophy and Public Affairs* 22, 2–30.
Wellman, Christopher Heath (2005), *A Theory of Secession: The Case for Political Self-Determination* (Cambridge: Cambridge University Press).

# PART II
# SECESSIONS: PAST AND PRESENT

# Introduction to Part II

This part offers detailed analyses of a few selected attempts at secession. The aim of the chapters in this part is to explore the dynamics of secession attempts by identifying the grievances and motivations of the secessionists and the responses of central governments to their attempts at secession. In addition, these chapters explore how the involvement of other states and international organizations, including the United Nations, has influenced the dynamics and the outcome of the attempts. The basic model used in analysing the attempts at secession – which is mainly left implicit in these chapters – is based on the triadic relation among the secessionists (movements, parties, leaders), central government (its executive branch and various governmental agencies) and outside states and international organizations (such as the UN, EC, NATO). This basic model has been discussed in some detail in Chapter 3. The role of another important factor – the domestic and international media – is largely left unexplored. Broader issues, such as the meaning and scope of the UN principle of self-determination and the possibility of the further, exponential, fragmentation of the current states, are also briefly examined in Chapters 6 and 8.

These chapters do not attempt to identify all or even the major 'types' of secession. Further, much shorter accounts of attempts at secession and secessionist movements are found in Part VI. The attempts at secession in Part VI are grouped by the continent on which they took place.

Why then select these attempts at secession for a detailed analysis in Part II and why group them in this particular way? These cases are grouped by the particular political context in which they took place. The Southern Confederacy of America (Chapter 5) attempted to secede from a well-established liberal democratic (or republican) state which at the time faced a political crisis partly resulting from the southern states' loss of control over the central government. The cases of Biafra and Katanga, discussed in Chapter 6, were attempts at secession from newly decolonized states with ethnically diverse populations which lacked a unifying national identity. The secession attempts of Quebec and Montenegro (the latter being successful) – discussed in Chapter 7 – were attempts to secede in a legally acceptable way from federal states following a prolonged and peaceful public debate on the political and economic advantages and disadvantages of secession – a debate in which the population in each of those territories was almost evenly divided. Such a debate was lacking in almost all the other cases discussed in Part II and in most cases discussed in Part VI. The attempts at secession in the

USSR and Yugoslavia (Chapter 8) took place amidst a prolonged economic and political crisis centred around the question of the legitimacy of the monopolistic one-party Communist regime and the constitutional arrangements that it imposed on these two states. The second attempt at secession of Kosovo in 2008 (discussed in Chapter 9) came after the NATO bombing of the then host state, the Federal Republic of Yugoslavia, forced it to withdraw its armed forces from the province; its first attempt in 1990 failed in the face of the opposition from the anti-secessionist regime in the host federal unit, Serbia and the absence of support from other states and international organizations. As in the case of Bangladesh in 1970 – discussed in Part VI – outside military intervention was crucial for the success of the second attempt at secession of Kosovo.

The differences in the political context in which these attempts were made are also reflected in the following three poles of the triadic relation mentioned above:

1. the grievances and motivations of the secessionists;
2. the responses of the central government to secessionists' demands and to attempts at secession;
3. the involvement of outside states and international organizations and their impact on the dynamics of secession attempts.

(1) In the case of the Southern Confederacy (Chapter 5), the secessionists' grievances were primarily perceived threats of the (future) breach of the existing legal rights of the seceding states; its secession thus seem to be largely pre-emptive. In contrast, the grievances of Biafra included massacres and expulsions of the members of one ethnic group, the Ibo (and other Easterners) in the host state Nigeria; in Katanga grievances also included the host state government's almost exclusive control of natural resources mining in Katanga. The main interest of the secessionist parties in Quebec and Montenegro was not in redressing any particular wrongs or grievances but in gaining the sovereign powers which they lacked. Motivations of the secessionists in some federal units of the USSR and Yugoslavia appear to be similar to those of Quebec and Montenegro while in others – such as the Baltic republics of the USSR and Croatia in Yugoslavia – they centred on the grievances of past oppression and military conquest. The grievances in the second attempt at secession of Kosovo resembled the latter (in particular the forced displacement, in 1999, of many Kosovo Albanians); the grievances in the case of its first attempt in 1990 were, however, centred on the recent loss of wide legislative and political powers which the province enjoyed under the communist regime in its host state, Yugoslavia.

(2) In almost all cases under consideration (the exceptions being Kosovo and Katanga), the host states were ready to accommodate the demands of the secessionists stopping short of secession itself. Their responses to the declarations of independence or the intentions to declare independence, however, varied. The US government rejected the Southern Confederacy's declarations but was, at least initially, not prepared to use military force to suppress secession: the initial use of military force came from the secessionists. A similar situation arose in the former

## Introduction to Part II

Yugoslavia but not in the USSR. The USSR central government, under Gorbachev, proved to be unwilling to use military force against the secessionists, and, after the August 1991 coup in Moscow, lost command of the military force. In the case of Kosovo, the host state's use of military force against the secessionist armed forces was only stopped by NATO's military intervention. In contrast, in the cases of Quebec and Montenegro, the host states were not prepared to use military force and were ready to agree to the secession, provided that the agreed legal procedures and conditions were satisfied.

(3) The involvement of outside states in these attempts at secessions greatly varied too. The attempts of the Southern Confederacy to gain international (European) recognition as an independent state failed, primarily because slavery, which it was defending, was not acceptable to the public opinion and governments in Europe. The absence of formal recognition and military support probably contributed to the failure of that attempt at secession (see also Chapter 13). Likewise, the absence of formal recognition of Biafra by major powers and the relatively limited military aid that it received from outside also contributed to its defeat. In contrast to Biafra, where the UN and other international organizations did not intervene, in the case of Katanga the UN intervened with military force against the secessionist forces and thus ensured their eventual defeat. In contrast to these two cases, major powers – the USA and the EC member states – provided military support and formal recognition to the selected *secessionist* states in the former Yugoslavia (Slovenia, Croatia, Bosnia, and Herzegovina and Kosovo). This outside support appeared to be crucial to the success of these secessions and to the failure of the recursive secessions from some of the seceding states (the latter were suppressed by military force). In the case of the former Yugoslavia, the UN provided only peacekeeping and mediating services.

In contrast to the limited involvement of the UN, in 2006 the EC negotiated the constitutional framework, laid down some of the legal conditions for secession and supervised the secession referendum in Montenegro. In 1992 the EC member states, having failed to negotiate a constitutional settlement among the parties in the Yugoslav conflict, had only provided formal recognition to selected secessionist states in the former Yugoslavia. In contrast, outside states and international organizations were not involved in the secessions from the USSR and in the attempt at secession of Quebec.

The attempts of secession we have selected raise a variety of questions for both explanatory and normative approaches of secessions. For example, the attempts at secession discussed in Chapters 5 and 7, raise the following question:

- Do attempts at secession from liberal democratic federations such as the USA and Canada result from structural or from political failures to accommodate secessionist demands? Or, alternatively, do such federations, in devolving political power to federal units, encourage and facilitate attempts at secession?

The cases discussed in Chapters 5, 6, 7 and 9 raise the following issues:

- What are the factors that lead central governments to respond to attempts at secession by military suppression? Is the type of regime in place a key factor in this kind of response?
- In 1998 the Milosevic authoritarian regime responded by military force to the secessionist rebellion in Kosovo while a liberal democratic regime in 2006 in the same host state accepted the secession of Montenegro. Are liberal democratic regimes less likely to respond to attempts at secession by military force than authoritarian or mono-party regimes?

In Chapter 3 David Siroky has discussed a variety of theoretical approaches to these questions.

All of the cases examined in this Part raise the following normative questions:

- Does a group, not subject to oppression or systematic discrimination, have a right to secede – and if not, why not?
- Under what conditions, if any, should outside states and organizations support secessionist groups' demands for secession?

Some of these questions are discussed in Parts III, IV and V.

# An Attempt at Secession from an Early Nation-State: The Confederate States of America

Don H. Doyle

The United States of America became the first modern nation-state born of secession when it broke off from the British Empire in the 1770s, and it came near to being the first to die of secession nearly a century later. The example of the American Revolution was important, for it was a breakaway colonial rebellion led by people who shared with the 'mother country' common traditions of language, religion, law, and custom. It was essentially over conflicts of material interest, which originated in rather mundane disputes over the right to tax and the prerogatives of local government. All of this was, of course, justified by much broader Enlightenment principles of natural rights and the right of a people to govern itself and enjoy sovereignty as an independent nation-state. Though the specific list of grievances, the 'long train of abuses' in Jefferson's words, were particular to the American situation, the Declaration of Independence issued in 1776 became a template for hundreds of similar separatist movements ever since (Armitage 2007). It was essentially this formula that the southern states adapted to their rebellion in the 1860s.

Two historical experiences shaped the American view of the world and consequently its later foreign relations. The first is the simple fact of its birth in the modern world's first successful separatist revolution, one that would inspire hundreds of imitators around the world. The second is its history of secession and its survival as a nation and a state after four bloody years of internal rebellion. One experience made America a friend of revolutionary nationalism; the other its enemy.

If America's victorious independence movement inspired others, its Civil War should not have, for the American Civil War demonstrated the remarkable propensity of modern nation-states to maintain territory and resist fragmentation at almost any cost. More than 600,000 men died on both sides, approximately 2 percent of the entire national population at the time (equivalent to about six million deaths in today's US population). No other war over secession approached this death toll until the secessionist conflict between Nigeria and Biafra a century later.

What brought all this carnage? What divided the South from the rest of the Union? And, perhaps the most intriguing question, what compelled this still young, vast and rather inchoate new nation to hold onto the separatist South and maintain unity at such tremendous cost?

Terms such as 'union' or 'united' when used by nations or states very often disguise a troubled history of combination, which sometimes involved coercive annexation and subjugation. If this was not true of the United States at its inception, it certainly became true after its Civil War. The appellation 'The United States of America' derives from its origins as an alliance of 13 rather varied settler colonies which banded together to protest British rule, win independence and – as a means to that end – to forge a central government. Whether this 'perpetual union' was 'one nation indivisible', as the American Pledge of Allegiance would later proclaim, or a voluntary league of sovereign states bound to a federal government was precisely the issue at stake in the American Civil War – or the 'War of the Rebellion' as it was officially dubbed by the victors, or the 'War Between the States' as it has been labelled by diehard Confederates. Even the name of the war would be contested long after its military conclusion.

## Coming Together: The Origins of the Federal Union

In order to understand how this federal state came apart, it is essential that we understand how it came together in the first place. The seceding states would later claim that they were withdrawing as members from a confederacy they had voluntarily joined and, because certain conditions had not been met, they were voluntarily leaving. This historical interpretation of the origin of the federal union rested on a combination of undisputed facts and imaginative interpretation, all subject to debate – and, as it turned out, to armed conflict.

The founding of the United States of America is routinely identified with the Declaration of Independence issued 4 July 1776. However, a close reading of this document reveals it to be not the beginning of a united nation-state but the declaration of 13 'free and independent states'. A 'Continental Congress' acted as a *de facto* national government to organize the army, engage in diplomacy and in other ways represent the 13 states with one voice to the people and the world. Almost immediately the Continental Congress acted to replace itself with a more permanent national government supported by constitutional authority. 'The Articles of Confederation and Perpetual Union' were ratified early in 1781, just before the end of armed conflict with the British. For the first time we have the idea of a 'perpetual union' (the term was employed five times in the document) rather than a wartime alliance of states, and its first order of business was to name the new federal union: 'The Stile of this Confederacy shall be "The United States of America"'. It went on to guarantee that 'Each state retains its sovereignty, freedom, and independence' and described their confederation as 'a firm league of friendship'.

The Articles of Confederation were deemed unsuited to the needs of centralized government and nationalist minded political leaders soon called for their revision. The present US Constitution came about in 1787 in order to 'form a more perfect union'. In the name of 'We the People', rather than the member states, the new Constitution created a national government with broader powers over the states, but it retained a federal system by which states retained authority not granted to the central government. Each state had to ratify the Constitution before it was adopted, and it was the product of numerous compromises between large and small states and, notably, between southern and northern states.

Questions about how the slave population was to be represented in the lower house of Congress led to the 'three-fifths' compromise by which 60 percent of the slave population would count toward congressional representation. These compromises were necessary and sufficient to win ratification of the Constitution in the South. Whatever came before, ratification of the Constitution was the first act by which states joined the Union.

## Coming Apart: Economic and Demographic Origins of Sectional Conflict

From the beginning of the Union there were numerous conflicts among the different states and between eastern and western sections of the country, but the southern states eventually formed a section at odds with the rest of the Union only slowly over several decades. Even slavery, though it was heavily concentrated in the South since the colonial era, was not a distinguishing characteristic of the South in the early republic. Slavery could be found in all of the states and in the Middle Atlantic states, such as New York and Pennsylvania; enslaved domestic labour was commonly found, especially in the cities. Moreover, many northeastern merchants and financiers had been involved in the international trade that brought enslaved labour into the Americas.

Due largely to greatly increased immigration at the end of the Napoleonic wars and prolific natural increase, the population of the US had soared from 2.5 million at the time of the Revolution to over 31 million by 1860. A little more than 4 of the 31 million in 1860 were foreign born, and 90 percent of this group lived outside the South. An equal number of US inhabitants were African-American slaves, and virtually all of them lived in the South in 1860.

The future Confederate states in 1860 accounted for about 9 million of the population of 31 million people (under 30 percent), but among the non-slave population these states had only 5 million of 27 million total (under 20 percent).

The South's declining share of the national population meant a loss of power in the central government. It was the political implications of these demographic trends, not diverging economic development *per se*, nor deeply rooted cultural differences between the sections, that gave rise to southern separatism.

## Anti-slavery and Southern Defensiveness

The American South represented but one part of a vast New World slave economy that was centred in the Caribbean and extended north into the southern United States and south into central Brazil. During the first half of the 19th century the whole system of African enslavement, the transatlantic slave trade, and slave labour itself was rapidly being abolished throughout the Atlantic world. Since the time of the American Revolution, the northern states, one by one, had abolished slavery by legislation, typically through gradual programmes of emancipation. It was the moral condemnation of the commerce in human beings and the denial of freedom to slaves that compelled the movement against slavery. This new moral sensibility welled out of Enlightenment principles of natural rights as well as Christian morality, which together brought an end to a very lucrative enterprise with powerful support. In nearly every other state and colony the end of slavery came through legislation. The lone exception had been the French colony of Saint Domingue, where a bloody slave revolt in 1791 transformed into a revolution for the independence of what became Haiti in 1804. Independence was the path to emancipation for the slaves of Saint Domingue; for the planters of the American South independence came to be seen as the only path for the preservation of slavery.

Before the 1830s it was still possible for southern whites to debate how to contain and phase out slavery. After the Revolution many slave owners, granted freedom to their slaves in their wills. Nor was there any southern protest against the ban on the international slave trade in 1808; several southern states had already banned foreign imports of slaves. It seemed possible in post-Revolutionary America to imagine the eventual and complete end of slavery in the US.

The cotton boom that began in the 1790s gave the slave economy new life in the states of the Deep South, and by the 1820s the cotton frontier had swept rapidly westward, fuelled by the rise in prices of cotton and slaves. Across the South a debate that earlier had weighed the problems of slavery against the profits that it generated increasingly tilted toward the latter. Compared to the large slave rebellions of the Caribbean and Brazil, those in the US were infrequent and rarely very bloody affairs, but they were sufficient to create a climate of fear within a slave society. For some southern whites, the spectre of slave rebellion motivated plans to rid the land of slavery if only to protect whites from its dangers, but for others it strengthened their commitment to defend against any influence from those who wanted to abolish slavery (Ford 2009).

The increasingly defensive posture of southern slave holders coincided with the rise of radical abolitionism in the North. The main thrust of anti-slavery agitation from the 1830s forward came out of the North and went in two main directions: one, with a limited following, was immediate and uncompensated abolition of all slaves in the US. The other, far more dominant, strain of anti-slavery sentiment was the 'Free Soil' movement, which sought to limit the expansion of slavery outside those states where it already existed. Free Soilers all agreed that slavery was inimical to American values and ought to be contained in the South if not eradicated across America. Once blocked from expanding, they reasoned, slavery in America might be put on the road to eventual extinction.

Abolitionism, or anti-slavery of any stripe, had never been a successful issue, by itself, in national party politics because it alienated more southern voters than it attracted others. Politicians who won state elections running against the South's 'Slave Power' simply could not become viable candidates for president unless they moderated their views. But the expansion of slavery became politicized in the South and North and this issue, rather than the welfare of the slaves or their future in America, became the real wedge that divided North and South by the 1850s.

## Secession as a Political Threat

Threats of secession and nullification of federal law had been heard in the US before, but it was not until 1850 that the South began to threaten secession to protest federal policies they found obnoxious. There had been serious disagreement over the expansion of slavery into Missouri, which was admitted as a slave state in 1821, but the issue of slavery's expansion did not become a serious and permanent issue on the political stage until the 1840s with the Texas question and the territorial gains made in the US war against Mexico (1846–48).

Texas had seceded from Mexico in 1836, in large part because settlers, mostly American southerners, objected to Mexico's 1829 ban on slavery. After defeating Mexican forces and signing a treaty ending the conflict in 1836, the Republic of Texas immediately petitioned the US for admission as a state. Mexico, however, renounced the treaty and refused to recognize Texas's independence, insisting that it was a rebellious province they intended to bring under national control. Mexico warned the United States and other European powers that any intervention in Texas would be regarded as a hostile act toward Mexico. (This was very close to the policy President Lincoln would adopt when faced with rebellious states in the US 25 years later.)

President James K. Polk, a southern slave owner and ardent expansionist, was elected in 1844 in a bellicose campaign that threatened war against Britain, Mexico and any other power that might hamper US expansion. He proceeded to admit Texas into the Union (pro-slavery politicians wanted it to become four states) and then take over, by armed conquest, vast territory in northern Mexico, including California and its deep water Pacific Ocean ports. Many northern critics, including Free Soilers, saw Polk's bellicose strategy of conquest as a plot of the 'slave power' to expand their domain. Under Polk the US had expanded its territorial domain by nearly 70 percent but, despite Free Soilers' fears of this expansion, most of the new land acquired in the 'Mexican Cession' was sparsely populated and not suitable for slave plantation agriculture.

The territorial gains of the 1840s might have left the balance of power between slave and free states unchanged for a long time were it not for the discovery of gold in California in 1848. The California Gold Rush suddenly brought nearly 100,000 gold-seeking 'Forty-Niners' into what quickly became a lawless society; as a consequence, there was pressure to bring California immediately into the Union, bypassing the territorial stage to become a state.

The California question, which flared up in 1850, produced the most serious crisis in the balance of power between slave and free states. The US census would show population growth of almost 36 percent, much of it concentrated in the non-slave states, whose advantage in the House of Representatives would be strengthened. In the Senate where each state had two senators, the entry of California (as a free state) would put the slave states in the minority. Southern politicians understood that once the Senate tipped in favour of Free-Soil sympathizers, no more slave states would be admitted to the Union; the South would become a permanent minority power in Congress and very likely in the presidency as well. Radical proponents of 'southern rights' warned that this foreshadowed the end of slavery in America.

For the first time southern political leaders began to speak openly of secession as the only escape from their predicament. A vocal coterie of secessionists known as the 'Fire-Eaters' called for a convention to be held in Nashville in the summer of 1850. For their part, anti-slavery forces began to characterize the 'slave power conspiracy' acting not only to protect slavery in the states where it existed but to expand it throughout the republic and beyond to the Caribbean and Central America.

Meanwhile, a dedicated group of more moderate elder statesmen in Congress worked out a package of legislation aimed at appeasing both sides. The 'Compromise of 1850' consisted of a balanced set of concessions to each side which managed to postpone, not resolve, the impending crisis. Whatever its limitations, the Compromise of 1850 defused what might well have been a secession crisis, and for a time it appeared that the spirit of moderation and compromise had prevailed over that of extremism.

## The Rise of the Republican Party

Compromise was possible so long as southern political leaders felt they had leverage in national affairs. With the electoral victory of the Republican Party, based entirely on northern votes, the South faced a political regime they believed to be hostile to its interests. Secession, used as a threat *to influence* national policy now transformed into secession as a strategy *to escape* submission to national policy.

Stephen Douglas, a principal architect of the Compromise of 1850, had a bright future ahead as a Democratic Party presidential candidate. He wanted to bridge the sectional conflict between North and South and foster a spirit of nationalist support for westward expansion. He and other moderate-minded leaders in the

1850s considered the entire debate over the expansion of slavery to be irrationally inflamed by ideological and moral fanaticism. Slavery as a system of labour, Douglas and fellow moderates believed, was not adaptable to areas outside the South where a long growing season was conducive to the production of cotton and certain other crops, such as rice and sugar, suitable to slave labour. Nature, not ideology or legislation, would decide the limits of slavery as a practical system of labour.

What Douglas and the moderates failed to understand was that the expansion of slavery was no longer a matter of profit and loss; it was now part of a political struggle driven by southern conviction that any attempt to limit slavery's expansion was, in effect, an effort to destroy it altogether. Instead of a peaceful plebiscite to decide on the economic viability of slavery (as the Kansas-Nebraska Act envisaged), the new territory, particularly Kansas, became the scene of guerrilla warfare and massive political fraud. Pro-slavery 'border ruffians' led raids on anti-slavery opponents, destroyed their printing presses, and sacked their stronghold, the town of Lawrence, Kansas. To avenge the abolitionists John Brown and his sons massacred a group of southerners, using broad swords to mutilate their bodies.

As a result of the imbroglio in Kansas, the Democratic Party split into northern and southern wings and the opposition Whig Party vanished altogether from the political scene. The Republican Party, made up of Free-Soil Democrats, former northern Whigs, and a coterie of reformers, German immigrants, and other northern voters, emerged out of the turmoil of 1854 to become a major contender for national power.

The sudden rise of the Republican Party had the effect of strengthening, not moderating, southern secessionists. Their leaders, the Fire-Eaters, gained control of the southern wing of the Democratic Party and rejected compromise of any kind.

The Republican Party strategy was to hold onto anti-slavery northerners, avoid abolitionist extremism, and broaden their support among moderates through policies favouring economic development and westward expansion. Abraham Lincoln of Illinois offered distinct advantages to Republicans as a moderate presidential nominee. He had made several addresses staking out his moral disapproval of slavery, but he also made it clear he was not an abolitionist. He insisted on the right of the federal government to limit slavery's expansion in the territories but was equally emphatic that the Constitution did not permit interference with slavery in the states where it existed.

Lincoln won the presidential election of 1860 with less than 40 percent of all the votes cast, and in several southern states his name was not even on the ballot. According to the US Constitution the president is elected indirectly through an Electoral College, in which each state is allotted votes based on their representation in Congress. Lincoln's 40 percent of the popular electorate in populous northern states gave him a strong majority (180 of 303) of votes in the Electoral College. The unusual circumstances of 1860, combined with this constitutional provision for presidential elections, allowed a deeply divided electorate to elect a president with no support in the South.

The South, which until now had dominated the presidency and enjoyed great strength in Congress, saw itself forced into 'submission' to a party that emphasized its hostility to slavery and its disdain for the South as a slave society.

## Secession as a Political Strategy

Following Lincoln's election victory the southern secessionists denounced any mood of compromise or 'wait and see' as 'submission' to a hostile northern party whose intention it was to destroy slavery and unleash a racial holocaust. It was their interpretation of the implications of the election of 1860, rather than anything Lincoln and the Republicans did with their power, that led radical southerners to finally act on their long standing threats of secession during the 'secession winter' of 1860–61.

Southern secessionists took great pains to avoid any semblance of violent, unlawful rebellion against the existing authorities. This was a case of 11 different secessions from the Union which was followed by the formation of a new state, the Confederate States of America. Several, but not all, of the seceding states held popular plebiscites and conventions to give the legitimacy of democratic process to the decision.

Several states also issued formal declarations of the causes that led them to secede. One of the striking features of these declarations is their *anticipation* of tyrannical abuse yet to come at the hands of the Republicans and, indeed, well before the latter had even taken control of the government in March, 1861. The South Carolina declaration, the first and in many ways the model for others, was issued in December 1860. It laid out the case for secession in legalistic terms as a violation of a contract which they had voluntarily entered under certain terms in 1788 and then it outlined how those terms had not been upheld as promised by the federal government, thereby rendering the contract null and void. Every one of their grievances had to do with *perceived* threats to slavery. Northern states, South Carolina secessionists complained, had refused to enforce constitutional provisions for returning fugitive slaves to their rightful owners. Furthermore, these states had 'denounced as sinful the institution of slavery'. Now this hostility toward slavery had elected to the presidency a man 'whose opinions and purposes are hostile to slavery'. The declaration then shifted into the future tense with predications of 'a war on slavery' and the loss of self-government and self-protection. 'The slaveholding States will no longer have the power of self-government, or self-protection, and the Federal Government will have become their enemy.' 'All hope of remedy is rendered vain', it concluded. Other states followed similar lines of argument in justifying secession as a preemptive move to protect slavery and southern rights.

During the 'secession winter' of 1860–61 one state after another across the Deep South followed South Carolina by declaring their secession from the Union. Agents from the seceding states were sent out to persuade other states of the necessity of joining the new confederacy of seceded states. Sometimes behind closed doors, other times in open speeches and pamphlets, the arguments these agents made for secession centred almost entirely on the threat 'Black Republican' rule posed to slavery and to white racial supremacy (Dew 2001).

Abraham Lincoln did not assume office until 4 March 1861, at which point seven lower South states (South Carolina, Mississippi, Florida, Alabama, Georgia, Louisiana, Texas) had seceded and formed the Confederate States of America, which had already ratified a constitution and sworn in their own president, Jefferson Davis. Lincoln's inaugural address was a model of conciliatory but firm language appealing to a shared sense of nationhood and calming undue anxiety about his intentions as president. He forthrightly assured southern states that he would not interfere with slavery where it existed, and made it clear he had no lawful right, nor personal inclination, to do so. At the same time, Lincoln insisted the Constitution entailed a 'perpetual union', not a voluntary contract that states could enter and withdraw from lawfully, except with legitimate cause and agreement among all parties. He also confirmed that it was his sworn duty as president to defend the Constitution and see that its laws were upheld in all the states, and announced that he would use force to that end only if necessary.

## Denying Secession

Historians have often assumed that the secession of the Confederate states *necessarily* provoked the long and bloody war that followed, but this obscures the heated debate within the North and within the Lincoln administration over how to respond to secession. The main themes of nationalism in the nineteenth century had entailed narratives of the awakening of peoples and their unification and liberation from foreign rule. The language of nationalism typically stressed the natural rights of peoples to govern themselves and the abuse of those rights by foreign imperial powers. Southern secessionists employed the same rhetoric of liberal nationalism and cast Lincoln and the Union in the unsavoury role of the tyrannical foreign power imposing its will against self-rule of an alienated minority. The initial response by Lincoln was largely a legalistic denial of the right to secede and reassurance to the South that they would have no cause to secede under his administration.

There was vigorous debate in the North as to whether secession might not be a solution to the southern question. Many radical anti-slavery advocates initially welcomed secession as a means of ridding the 'model republic' of the moral stain of slavery. 'No union with slaveholders' had long been the abolitionist motto. Others argued that the southern radicals were bluffing and that the best policy was to issue guarantees of states' rights to preserve slavery and let time calm southern nerves. Many moderates rallied behind Kentucky Senator Crittenden and his compromise bill which would have guaranteed the expansion and perpetuation of slavery by Constitutional amendment and legislation. Secretary of State Seward urged Lincoln to launch a foreign war against Spain, France or Britain, which he predicted would unite all sections in a nationalistic war to defend America. There were a range of alternatives in play, one of which was forcible suppression of the rebellion and reunification of the United States. Instead of being understood as an 'irrepressible conflict', in Seward's words, the American Civil War was the product of deliberate choice on both sides.

Those most confident that secession would not lead to war, at least not such a long and indecisive one, were the radical Fire-Eaters leading the southern secessionist movement. They believed that a nation born in a Declaration of Independence from British rule and dedicated to the principle of self-government would find it difficult to sustain popular support for the forcible subjugation of the South just to keep it in the Union. They also doubted the northern public would be willing to sustain such a war, especially since the South had been so vilified by anti-slavery forces.

The immediate cause of the armed conflict was over the federal claim to its property within the seceding states, particularly military forts. One of the first acts of the new Confederate States of America had been to send a delegation to Washington to negotiate sale of the federal properties to the seceding states. Lincoln, of course, refused to negotiate with them or do anything to recognize their legitimacy.

Though careful to reassure the South that the Union would not incite war against the South, Lincoln also made it clear that he intended to maintain the presence of the federal government throughout the South, including federal military forts. One of them, Fort Sumter, located on a small island in the harbour of Charleston, South Carolina, was running short of supplies and would have to be abandoned if not resupplied. One supply ship had been turned back by hostile fire in January 1861; now Lincoln ordered a fleet of war ships to Fort Sumter in early April. As the fleet came south, Confederate forces opened fire on the fort and forced its surrender.

When Lincoln called on all states of the Union to supply volunteer troops for 90 days of service to put down the rebellion, slave states in the upper South were forced to choose their allegiance. To the seven Deep South states that had already declared secession, four more states (Virginia, Arkansas, North Carolina and Tennessee) now joined rather than comply with Lincoln's call to arms against their southern neighbours.

The Confederate initiation of armed conflict would prove an obstacle to Confederate diplomatic strategy, for it put the seceding party in the role of aggressor. Confederates had high hopes of winning international support, particularly from European powers Britain and France, who depended on southern cotton and might welcome an opportunity to weaken the rising power of the US. Confederate agents in England, along with pro-Confederate lobbyists from the British cotton industry and anti-republican aristocrats, pressured the British government to recognize the Confederacy or intervene and mediate a peace.

France appeared to be more sympathetic than Britain to pro-Confederate lobbying. Emperor Napoleon III saw America's disorder as an opportunity to launch a 'Grand Design for the Americas', a plan that included invading Mexico, ousting Benito Juarez and his liberal republican regime, installing a Habsburg monarch, Emperor Maximilian I, and expanding French commerce and influence throughout Latin America. Integral to Napoleon's plan was the recognition of the

Confederacy and an alliance with them to help fend off US interference in his new French empire in America.

## Union Nationalism and Emancipation

Amid contradictory advice from his cabinet members, the press and public, Lincoln alone was the most important person in the decision to maintain the Union and to go to war if necessary in order to suppress what he saw as an illegal insurrection. His motivation came largely out of his background as a lawyer and political leader with a strong sense of the federal government as a legally constituted entity forming a perpetual Union among the states. He understood the principle by which people, not least the American colonists of 1776, could overthrow tyrannical government when no other remedy was available. But he believed strongly that in the case of the South there simply was no valid evidence of past abuse or future menace, and therefore no legally or morally justifiable basis for revolution. What it was, he insisted, was an unlawful insurrection. This legalistic argument against secession was necessary, but never sufficient, to Lincoln's monumental task of summoning a nation to arms and defending America's claim to national (and territorial) integrity in the world of nations. Had he offered only this narrow legalistic defence of the Union, it is hard to imagine millions of young soldiers and their families sacrificing over four long years of war for such a cause.

Evolving in Lincoln's mind was a more ideological sense of nationhood, and of America as an experiment in democracy. This would be a cause that transcended the mere perpetuation of the United States and extended to holding out hope for people everywhere that 'government of the people, by the people, and for the people shall not perish from the earth', as he put it in the Gettysburg Address.

Historians today emphasize Lincoln's deliberate and ambivalent embrace of emancipation as a war aim as the main turning point in the drama of the Civil War, the point at which the legalistic goal of preserving the Union became coupled to the higher moral cause of freedom for slaves. However, most historians would agree that Lincoln's commitment to emancipating the slaves was tepid and to racial equality rather cool. The Emancipation Proclamation he issued in its final form in 1863 contained no moral condemnation of slavery and even promised its perpetuation to those states willing to desist in rebellion. He continued to entertain policies that would require or encourage the colonization of former slaves either within the United States (Florida was one possibility) or abroad in Central America or the Caribbean, as the best solution to the race question. The historians' interest in Lincoln's conflicted struggle with himself over slavery has obscured his more confident affirmation of America's historic mission as a nation. America must end slavery to preserve the nation, he reasoned, and it must preserve the nation in order to sustain hope for democracy everywhere. America, he told Congress by way of explaining the Emancipation Proclamation, is the 'last best hope of earth'.

Emancipation was not always popular among northern voters and soldiers, and Lincoln's political enemies used it against him effectively, questioning whether white soldiers were willing to fight and die to free black slaves, and making alarming predictions that freed slaves would stream north to take white jobs, or white women. The 1863 draft riots in New York City were inflamed by racial tensions, and several blacks were lynched by angry Irish immigrant mobs. But to the extent emancipation became nested within broader nationalist themes of America as a bulwark of democracy, it became embedded in a popular Union nationalism that was propagated in songs, sermons and political rhetoric of all kinds. Julia War Howe's 'Battle Hymn of the Republic' became a standard tune sung by soldiers and civilians during and after the war; its lyrics identify the Union army as God's 'terrible swift sword' and promised that 'As He died to make men holy, let us die to make men free'. Union soldiers recorded in their letters and diaries their approval of Lincoln's new policy of emancipation, some because they understood it as necessary to ending the war, others out of genuine compassion for the slaves, and still others out of enmity toward their masters (Manning 2007).

Lincoln's evocation of America's historic mission was also vitally important in the international arena where each side contended for support from the Great Powers of Europe in a massive battle of propaganda. Britain and France had immediately extended recognition as belligerents to each side and declared their own neutrality. According to the then prevailing principles of international law, the recognition of belligerents indicated that more was involved than an uprising or insurrection, which would have been a purely domestic affair for the US to resolve. The Confederacy met the criteria for belligerent status: they controlled distinct territory, had organized a government and had an organized military force operating according to the customs of war (Neff 2005) (see Chapter 13).

Recognition of the Confederacy and Union as belligerents at war seemed to undermine the Union claim that this was a treasonous rebellion and not a matter of international law. But status as a belligerent did not entail recognition of sovereignty for the Confederacy. Their diplomatic delegations were never officially received by any of the great powers. The closest the Confederates came to any international recognition was a letter of support from Pope Pius IX which was addressed to 'President' Jefferson Davis (Neff 2005; Doyle 2002).

The military struggle dragged on over four years without clear signs of victory for either side, which was due in large part to the peculiar nature of a civil war. The Union had to invade and subjugate areas in rebellion holding an olive branch to loyal citizens in one hand and a sword in the other. The Confederates did not need to conquer territory or subdue populations so much as defend itself against invasion and simply hold out until the Union gave up or European powers intervened. Meanwhile, much of the military effort in the eastern states focused on fruitless and costly campaigns to capture Richmond and Washington, the capitals of the Confederacy and Union, which lay but a few miles apart. Neither city offered any real strategic advantage to the other side but the psychological and diplomatic advantage of such a capture would undoubtedly have been powerful. It was late in the war, December 1864, before Union General William T. Sherman adopted a scorched earth policy aimed at undermining southern civilian morale and disrupting slavery and the economy that supported the army.

# An Attempt at Secession from an Early Nation-State

Casualty rates in the American Civil War were especially high, in part because of new deadly weaponry, such as the repeating rifle, but largely because of its very nature as a war over secession. The Union refused any form of negotiation that would suggest recognition of the Confederacy as a sovereign state. It also warned Britain and France not to mediate or intervene in any way, for that would be regarded as virtual recognition of the Confederacy and would invite war with the US.

The military struggle dragged on without firm resolution, even after the climactic Battle of Gettysburg and the fall of Vicksburg in July 1863, which were decisive Union victories. At one point in February 1865 a delegation of Confederate officials met with Lincoln and Seward at Hampton Roads, Virginia, to discuss terms of peace. But neither side was willing to concede its main goal: Lincoln insisted they cease all attempts to secede; the Confederates said they could not accept any offer that did not guarantee their national independence. The war continued for several months more before the surrender of Confederate forces at Appomattox, Virginia, in April 1865.

It was political and diplomatic events that decided the outcome in the end. First, the reelection of Lincoln in November 1864, in the face of strong anti-war and anti-emancipation opposition, proved to those at home and abroad that the Union cause could be sustained. Second, a sustained and effective propaganda campaign in Britain, France and across Europe swayed public opinion in favour of the Union and against what was depicted as a pro-slavery aristocratic regime in the Confederacy. Confederate propagandists tried to associate their bid for independence with the leading liberal nationalist movements of the day, and they strained to disassociate it from slavery as a motivation for independence. Once the Union embraced emancipation, Confederates found themselves having to defend slavery, white supremacy or consider their own programme of emancipation. There were last ditch efforts by Confederates in 1865 to win recognition from France and Britain by promising to abolish slavery, but this proved too little and too late to turn the tide of European opinion (Jones 1999; Levine 2005).

The Confederate determination to secede from the United States had astonished the public both in the US and in the world. Against tremendous odds, vastly outnumbered in population, much inferior in industrial capacity, largely deprived of foreign trade and constantly concerned with the danger of an uncontrolled slave population, the Confederates fought hard and sacrificed mightily for their independence during four years of war.

The North's resolve to deny secession and preserve the Union despite unprecedented sacrifice also surprised the world, as well as the secessionists. Lincoln and his administration had managed to mobilize a highly diverse population without strong bonds of national self-consciousness and unity to fight a war aimed at denying separation to a region they had little sympathy toward and to emancipate from slavery a population of whom most knew little and may have cared even less. Lincoln and his diplomatic corps also managed to impress the European powers that the Union would be sustained, that they must not recognize its enemies, and that the war was about more than cotton, territory and sovereignty, but also entailed a much loftier historic meaning for the survival of self-government. The war was a lesson to the world not just about American resolve, but also about the determination of nations to perpetuate themselves at any cost.

# References

Armitage, D. (2007), *The Declaration of Independence: A Global History* (Cambridge, MA: Harvard University Press).
Dew, C.B. (2001), *Apostles of Disunion: Southern Secession Commissioners and the Causes of the Civil War* (Charlottesville, VA: University of Virginia Press).
Doyle, D.H. (2002), *Nations Divided: America, Italy, and the Southern Question* (Athens, GA: University of Georgia Press).
Ford, L.K. (2009), *Deliver Us from Evil: The Slavery Question in the Old South* (New York: Oxford University Press).
Jones, H. (1999), *Abraham Lincoln and a New Birth of Freedom: The Union and Slavery in the Diplomacy of the Civil War* (Lincoln, NE: University of Nebraska Press).
Levine, B. (2005), *Confederate Emancipation: Southern Plans to Free and Arm the Slaves* (New York: Oxford University Press).
Manning, C. (2007), *What This Cruel War Was Over: Soldiers, Slavery, and the Civil War* (New York: Knopf).
Neff, S.C. (2005), *War and the Law of Nations: A General History* (Cambridge: Cambridge University Press).

# The UN Principle of Self-Determination and Secession from Decolonized States: Katanga and Biafra

Joshua Castellino

## Introduction

While the history of self-determination is rich and varied (Buchheit 1978; Casesse 1995; Hannum 1990) its practice in the context of the United Nations era has been beset with difficulties and inconsistencies (Sureda 1973). The attempted secessions of Katanga and Biafra, represent two of the instances where the emerging norm of self-determination came up for immediate challenge under evolving UN practice. If decolonization was a fundamental goal of the United Nations, self-determination was its conceptual framework and secession, its practical hand-maiden. The force of the evolving norm of self-determination had already created a dispute between Portugal and the United Nations, and questions had also been raised about the definition of 'colonial power' in the context of what came to be referred to as the Belgian Thesis (discussed below) (Van Langenhove 1954: 83–4). Both challenges had a material issue underpinning them: if secession in the specific context of decolonization could be considered justifiable, what constitutes colonization? In other words would it be possible for an entity that has already 'achieved' self-determination through decolonization, to be able to exercise its rights once again on the grounds that the original self-determination was not truly self-determination? This debate was also influenced by the reservation entered by India to join Article 1 of the 1966 human rights covenants, discussed below.

This chapter seeks to unpick these questions through an analysis of the situations in Katanga and Biafra. With this in mind the first section seeks to set the backdrop for the discussion of self-determination and secession that served as a context for the two events. As referred to above, an early challenge to the application of self-determination and secession to post-colonial situations that predated the events in Katanga and Biafra, occurred in the context of the Belgian Thesis. During the course of a debate in the General Assembly, the Belgian representative suggested that:

> *A number of States were administering within their own frontiers territories which were not governed by the ordinary law; territories with well defined limits, inhabited by homogenous peoples differing from the rest of the population in race, language and culture. These populations were disenfranchised; they took no part in national life; they did not enjoy self-government in any sense of the word. (UDOC A/Ac.67/2, 3–31)*

This addressed a question that remains fundamental to all post-colonial states: certain groups within current post-colonial 'self-determined' states are denied a right to democratic governance and self-determination. These groups, by virtue of existing within states, have no recourse to determine their own political future guaranteed by the UN Charter.[1] The delegate of Iraq questioned Belgium's motivation for raising this issue, suggesting that it was a mere tactic of '… anger at the criticism directed against conditions in the non-self-governing territories by less advanced States' (UNDOC A/C.4/SR.257, para. 11). The Belgians later admitted this (Van Langenhove 1954: 83–4) but the interpretation that surrounded the reaction built consensus on the restrictions that could be applied in the context of the exercise of the right of self-determination. Self-determination was thus viewed as the concept that exclusively freed people from 'salt-water' colonialism. This was borne by the appeal to geographic factors in the definition of a Metropolitan Colonial State that effectively ruled out broader interpretation of the principle (see also Chapter 17).

## The Three Options of Self-determination

To be able to analyse the attempted secessions in Katanga and Biafra it is important to reflect on the legal framework surrounding secession of that era. Decolonization had gained serious currency in the international climate, epitomized by the passage of the *Declaration on the Granting of Independence to Colonial Countries and Peoples* in 1960 which was contemporaneous to the evolving situation in Katanga. The declaration turned a political principle of uncertain value into a quasi-legal principle (Ratner 1996) (see also Chapters 13 and 17). At the time of its framing, the abhorrence of colonialism was acknowledged and the freedom of larger countries such as India from the colonial yoke helped in spurring this movement. The Resolution is linked to the UN Charter by the opening statement: '… Mindful of the

---

1   See the UN Charter preamble and Articles 1, 55 and 56.

determination proclaimed by the peoples of the world in the Charter of the United Nations to reaffirm faith in fundamental human rights ...' (UNGAOR 1514 (XV)).

However despite its optimistic tone, the 1960 Declaration unwittingly laid the basis for continued confusion around self-determination and secession. In reaffirming the principle of stability (UNGAOR 1514: para. 2) it prepared the ground for a collision between territorial integrity and self-determination especially in the context of secession (Brilmayer 1991). In colonial times of the 1960s, fears were that, with the exit of colonial powers, former territories rather than being able to constitute themselves into sovereign states, would fragment into anarchy and violence. The colonial powers had begun their land-grab towards the end of the 18th century and the Resolution was coming into force nearly 150 years after this event. By then, boundaries had been defined for a significant period. Besides, many of the regions annexed by the colonial powers and drawn together within a boundary had within them different peoples with strong antagonistic tendencies towards one another (Castellino and Allen 2005).

The 1960 Declaration recognizes that an increased number of conflicts are due to the denial to people of their freedoms and rights, labelling this as a menace that constitutes '... a serious threat to world peace'. Thereafter, it narrows the applicability of self-determination in the second half of the preamble, while specifying that the 'peoples of the world ardently desire the end of colonialism in all its manifestation'. There is no effort made to define colonialism, its attributes or 'manifestations' – a definitional lacuna that is particularly instructive in Katanga and Biafra.

In this regard, a question needs to be raised: What is 'colonialism' and how is it manifested? The document is largely silent on the issue save for recognition that colonialism 'prevents the development of international economic co-operation, impedes social, cultural and economic development of dependent peoples and militates against the United Nations ideal of universal peace'. The next paragraph suggests that colonization includes exploitation of resources endowed to a people by colonial powers that dominate them. The Resolution affirms that 'peoples may freely dispose of their natural wealth and resources without prejudice to any obligations arising out of international economic co-operation, based upon the principle of mutual benefit, and international law': a principle immediately challenged in the context of the Katanga. It also calls for an end to colonialism and 'all practices of segregation and discrimination' to avoid serious conflicts in the future. Finally, the emergence of new states is welcomed and the Resolution 'solemnly proclaims the necessity of bringing to a speedy and unconditional end colonialism in all its manifestations'.

As one of the powers targeted by decolonization, the Portuguese had grave problems in coming to terms with the new concept (Martelli 1964). Throughout decolonization Portugal had insisted that the 'overseas territories' it ruled were sovereign Portuguese territory and not colonies. It did not consider itself liable to make reports under Chapter XI of the Charter which dealt with non-self-governing territories and required the state overseeing them to progress them towards self-rule and report on that progress to the United Nations Trusteeship

Council. The Portuguese insisted that, by virtue of a domestic Act which made all overseas territories integral parts of Portugal, reporting on them would constitute a violation of sovereign Portuguese rights and a defeat of Article 2(7) of the UN Charter. The Portuguese had already fought one case in the ICJ in support of this right – The *Rights of Passage* Case (ICJ Reports 1960: 6) and were the focal point of discussions with regard to their duties under the UN Charter to report the progress made with respect to the independence of its non-self-governing territories (Pomerance 1982). Portugal continuously refused to report on overseas colonies, claiming that they did not come under the scope of this article. It was perhaps to bring situations such as these within the ambit of the resolution that the phrase 'colonialism in all its manifestations' was referred to in the Resolution (Castellino 2000a: 12–22). In *Rights of Passage* Portugal claimed the right to travel through India to gain access to their territory. The ICJ ruled that Portugal did not posses this right of passage, since the enclave concerned was colonial property (ICJ Reports 1960). However Portugal continued to insist that the territories under its control in various parts of the world were integral parts of their country. This prompted the formulation of General Assembly Resolution 1541 which reiterated that countries report on their overseas colonies. The first principle of the Resolution clearly indicates that '… an obligation exists to transmit information under Article 73(e) of the Charter in respect of such territories whose peoples have not yet attained a full measure of self government' (UNGAOR 1541 (XV) Principle II). The second principle suggests that the obligation to report on the situation exists as long as the territory concerned has not attained a 'full measure of self government' (UNGAOR 1541 (XV) Principle I). The Resolution confirms that this obligation is of an international legal nature. In response to Portugal's claim that its colonies were integral parts of the country, Principle IV states that an obligation exists to transmit information in respect of 'a territory which is geographically separate and is distinct ethically and/or culturally from the country administering it'. This is problematic since it privileges geography over other factors that could be of equal if not greater importance. The Resolution does admit that other elements such as administrative, political, juridical, economic and historic factors could be considered in determining the nature of relationship between a metropolitan state and its colony (UNGAOR 1541 (XV) Principle V). To safeguard the interests of self-determination, the Resolution defines what constitutes a 'full measure of self government' (Principle VI) stating that it must result in a decision where the people concerned vote in free and fair elections to decide whether to:

a. constitute themselves as a sovereign independent state;
b. associate freely with an independent state; or
c. integrate with an independent state already in existence.

Self-determination literature however, remains highly contradictory. On the one hand, it endorses that peoples should have the right to determine their own political future, while on the other hand suggesting that the sanctity of national boundaries requires to be respected and that breaking-down states is unacceptable in international law (Carrington 1962; Chowdhury 1977; Eagleton 1953; Sinha 1973; Suzuki 1976) (see also Chapter 25). Thus despite Resolution 1541 stating clearly the three available options of self-determination to a people, option (a) of secession, tends to be ruled out in the interests of international order. This seems a travesty: if a people is dominated by an alien regime and has the inherent right to self-govern it *may* be necessary to break-away from the government in power and form a new more representative regime (Castellino 2000b). However it becomes clearer if looked at in the post-war situations facing statesmen of the period: at this time the map of the world was shaded in the colours of the colonial powers. States such as Britain, France, Portugal, and the Netherlands and others 'owned' pieces of land and entities that were distant from their own borders. From that point of view self-determination meant allowing peoples under colonial regimes power to emancipate themselves of colonial oppressors. In that situation the need for breaking away from the main body of the state, or 'secession' as it is termed, was considered unnecessary since the act of colonized people choosing their own regimes ahead of the colonial powers fulfilled self-determination. There are few exceptions to this rule: notably the partition of colonial India into first, two and then, three smaller states: India, Pakistan and Bangladesh (for Bangladesh see also Part VI). Thus it can be asserted that colonized people emancipating themselves from foreign domination was an act of self-determination that rendered the option of secession redundant.

Allowing people to freely determine their political future without recourse to the *status quo* could destroy the international system of sovereign states and leave vulnerable populations open to influences of power mongers and anarchic forces. It is this rather justified fear that has been at the heart of the debate within self-determination literature of the conflict between territorial integrity and self-determination. Higgins (1982), for example, argues that the right to self-determination must always be secondary to the right to territorial integrity. She claims that this is the guarantee that keeps the international legal system in place. Brilmayer (1991) and Tomuschat (1994) on the other hand argue for a limited right that, in certain special circumstances, allows secession as an option of self-determination.

Principle VII of Resolution 1541 draws attention to options other than secession that may be more in keeping with the need for order. It emphasizes that free association should be the result of 'free and voluntary choice' gauged by a 'democratic process'. Further, the associated territory needs to be given a right to determine its own internal constitution, free from outside interference. Principle VIII lays down norms for equality of peoples in an erstwhile non-self-governing territory should it choose to integrate with a specific country; and attempts to safeguard the new entity from discrimination within the new state.

The 1960 Declaration remains an important but often neglected document in self-determination literature. It is one of the last documents in this area that attempts to define the terms it uses. Perhaps one of the reasons for this is that it concerns the specific dismantling of colonial oppression and has limited value outside this context. Since it deals with the situation surrounding the non-self-governing territories it cannot be used to draw general analogies. Nonetheless, there are aspects of it that merit closer examination. One of the best examples of the clarity of the document is the frequent reference to 'full measure of self government'. The Resolution defines the extent of the term, listing the three options mentioned above, as proof that a state has reached its full measure of self-government. In addition it deals with situations in which free association and/or integration is allowable as proof of a territory having fulfilled its right to self-government thus preventing colonial entities from hiding behind this garb. The Resolution is free from the contradiction present in later and earlier self-determination documents in that it does not mention territorial integrity in any of its Principles.

# Katanga and Biafra: The Challenge of Post-Colonial Secession

## The Secession of Katanga

In 1960 with the decolonization process in full swing, supported by countries such as Egypt and India, the situations in Katanga and Biafra posed practical questions that had already been engaged in a theoretical manner in the context of the so-called Belgian Thesis (Lemarchand 1962; Nayar 1975). In this process it also posed the fundamentally important question of the manner in which self-determination could be exercised in rich provinces within newly emerging post-colonial states. While international law clearly supported the territorial integrity of states, a pertinent question arose in the context of post-colonial states whose boundaries were often drawn through a process of colonial consultation between competing colonial powers, and as a result often had no bearing on the coherence of the population deemed within those boundaries. The issues with both Katanga and Biafra were less concerned with the legality of historic boundaries, but more with the issue of the extent to which 'the haves' within new states could secede from the 'have-nots'. This was most explicit in the context of Katanga where at the time of its independence Gerard-Libois (1966) estimated that the province contributed half of Congo's total revenue, while benefitting from only 20 percent of the government's expenditure. Of course, there were also significant ethnic and political cleavages between Katanga and the rest of Congo which were exploited by those political movements in Katanga which were advocating secession.

The Katangese situation offered a substantive challenge to the developing norm of self-determination. The Belgian withdrawal from the Congo had provided the opportunity for Congo to emerge as an independent state: however while this process was unfolding, the mineral rich province of Katanga made a declaration on independence on 17 July 1960, creating a serious crisis. The UN, concerned at the precedent that could be set, whereby well-endowed provinces could sever themselves from the rest of the state, acted swiftly (Lefever 1965). A Security

Council Resolution was passed a few days after the declaration, validating Congo as the territorial unit being decolonized, and the position was further reinforced by the Resolutions supporting Congolese territorial integrity later that year. Through Resolution 4741 the Security Council authorized then UN Secretary-General Hammarskjöld to negotiate the replacement of Belgian troops and mercenaries who were operational in that theatre, with UN troops. As Bartkus highlights, the assumption underlying this decision was that the secession would collapse as foreign forces withdrew. The subsequent death of Hammarskjöld on mission emboldened the Security Council to assert a clear position *vis-à-vis* the attempted secession. Resolution 5002 of 1961 re-stated the aim of the United Nations as maintaining the territorial integrity and political independence of Congo, and further:

> ... (b) to assist the central government of the Congo in the restoration and maintenance of law and order; (c) to prevent the occurrence of civil war in the Congo; (d) to secure immediate withdrawal and evacuation from the Congo of all foreign military, paramilitary and advisory personnel not under UN command, and all mercenaries; and (e) to render technical assistance; Deploring all armed action in opposition to the Government of the Republic of Congo specifically secessionist activities, and armed action now being carried on by the provincial administration of Katanga with the aid of external resources and foreign mercenaries, and completely rejecting the claim that Katanga is a sovereign independent nation. (UNSC Res 5002)

The commentary on the secession was made explicit, with the Security Council declaring:

> ... all secessionist activities against the Government of Congo are contrary to the Loi fundamentale and Security Council decisions and specifically demands that such activities which are now taking place in Katanga shall cease forthwith. (UNSC Res 5002: #2)

This clear statement was subsequently backed by the deployment of UN troops, who were directly responsible for quashing the secession movement. The intervention, which escalated into a full-blown war, included the capture of Moise Tshombe, the Katangan leader, who was compelled to negotiate with the President of Congo, Adoula, resulting in the signature of the *Kitona Agreement* which finally ended the secession. As Bartkus (1999: 75) highlights:

> *The UN troops defeated a secession movement which its 1960 Declaration on the Granting of Independence to Colonial Countries and Peoples would seemingly have validated.*

## The Secession of Biafra

Being particularly heterogeneous, Nigeria was faced with competing visions of the state among its three largest communities; the Hausa-Fulani, the Yoruba and the Ibo groups which dominate the North, the West and the East respectively (Bartkus 1999: 82).

Members of the Ibo group held a large number of government, military and academic positions and were often perceived as domineering and pushy. A military coup in the North in July 1966 in which senior Ibo officers were tortured and killed was followed by massacres and pogroms of the Ibo and other Easterners living in the north and west of Nigeria. These acts of violence led to a mass exodus of Easterners to the Eastern Region which was under the control of the Ibo authorities. Responding to the coup, the military governor of the Eastern Region, Colonel Ojukwu, called for a loose association or confederation of regions, rather than a federal state. The killing of Ibo officers and thousands of Easterners in the north was construed as an aspect of the physical threat that existed to the Ibos, that is, as a threat of genocide. Declaring the right to self-defence the Ibos began to advocate for self-rule: they argued that they had little option but secession from Nigeria since the state could no longer guarantee their security. After a period of negotiations and unsuccessful attempts to find a compromise between the central military government and the Eastern Region, in May 1967 the Eastern Region declared independence from Nigeria as the Republic of Biafra. Following this declaration the country plunged into a brutal civil war, with the Nigerian army invading Biafra where it met a well-organized and spirited resistance. In spite of the superior weapons, supplied by the USSR and the UK, and much greater numbers, the government forces took more than two years to defeat the secessionists. Thus the claims to peoplehood were relegated to being inconsequential and the moot point remains whether the Biafrans would have been a 'people' had they won the civil war against the Nigerian army.

Chastised by the lessons learnt in Katanga, the Security Council remained relatively silent in the Biafran context, leaving the then Organization of African Unity (OAU) as the primary international actor to condemn the secession attempt. In the Resolution on the Situation in Nigeria, passed in September 1967, the OAU stated its position by 'solemnly reaffirming ... adherence to the principle of respect for the sovereignty and territorial integrity of Member States' and condemning '... secession in any Member State'.

# Conclusion: Norm of Questionable Valence

When assessing the attempted secessions of Katanga and Biafra from this distance of time it is important to reflect upon two kinds of impacts. First the immediate impact of the two events on the unfolding discourse of decolonization and self-determination, and second on how it has contributed to the theory of secession as we are given to understand it in a contemporary context. The timeliness of the two events is striking: much of the debate *vis-à-vis* decolonization was effectively codified in the period between 1960 and 1970. This period reflected a growing belief in the UN for the independence of the world's colonized people, and is reflected not only in the two declarations of 1960 referred to above, but also by joint Article 1 of the International Covenants on Human Rights, and the 1970 Declaration on the Friendly Relations between States. Joint Article 1 of the *International Covenant on Civil and Political Rights*, and the *International Covenant on Economic, Social and Cultural Rights*, states:

1. All peoples have the right of self-determination. By virtue of that right they freely determine their political status and freely pursue their economic, social and cultural development.
2. All peoples may, for their own ends, freely dispose of their natural wealth and resources without prejudice to any obligations arising out of international economic co-operation, based upon the principle of mutual benefit, and international law. In no case may a people be deprived of its own means of subsistence.
3. The States Parties to the present Covenant, including those having responsibility for the administration of Non-Self-Governing and Trust Territories, shall promote the realization of the right of self-determination, and shall respect that right, in conformity with the provisions of the Charter of the United Nations.

With this article the right to self-determination could be said to have made the transition from a right in international law, to one that serves as the foundation for human rights law. The prevalent difficulty is age-old, namely 'who are the people?' This question dates back to Woodrow Wilson's articulation of self-determination in the context of his *Fourteen Point Address to the US Congress* on 8 January 1918, where he deliberately omitted the phrase 'self-determination' despite the fact that he was dealing with the specific territorial settlements of the remnants of the Austro-Hungarian and Ottoman empires. He did however, refer to it a month later suggesting that national aspirations must be respected and that 'peoples may now be dominated and governed by their own consent'. He warned statesmen that they would 'henceforth ignore [the principle of self-determination] at their peril' (Wilson 1918). However, despite the severity of the rhetoric a few sentences later Wilson immediately limited its scope. This has become a common phenomenon in all documents dealing with this issue ever since. While stating that 'all national aspirations shall be accorded the utmost satisfaction', Wilson still voiced concerns that it should be so 'without introducing new or perpetuating old elements of discord and antagonism' (Whelan 1994) that might disrupt Europe. It is clear that at the time that Wilson made his Fourteen Point Address, he was using 'self-determination' as a pseudonym for a right to democracy. This has, in modern self-determination literature, been classified as 'internal' self-determination which is language that drew upon the American Declaration and the concept of a 'democratic entitlement' (Thornberry 1994; Franck 1992).

Despite being framed in the aftermath of Katanga and just prior to the attempted secession of Biafra, the above article remains silent on important issues. In Article 1(2) it opens up the debate between the rights of the 'haves' and 'have-nots'. Yet any discussion about the meaning of those words needs to be placed in the context of the *travaux preparatoires* of the Covenants which makes it amply clear that the context envisaged is that of a classical 'salt-water' colonial situation coming to an end, with the emerging state having the full rights to its resources.

The other key document of the time that needs to be flagged to understand the immediate impact of the two secession attempts is the 1970 Declaration. Passed unanimously by the General Assembly, it is viewed as a clarification of the purposes and principles of the UN. While incorporating the 'principle of equal rights and self-determination' as one of its seven principles, it nonetheless falls short of shedding light on the treatment of the right to self-determination in international law. The text gives 'all peoples' the right to 'freely ... determine', without external influence, 'their political status and to pursue their economic, social and cultural development'. It also links the concept of the right to the duty that states have towards the respect and promotion of this right. This is interesting since it establishes two important points in the course of what the UN has come to view as self-determination. In the process, it also demonstrates the variation of the discourse from the original norm expounded by Wilson. Firstly, the Declaration clearly states that all peoples have the right to determine their future. This issue has of course, been discussed earlier since this statement is also echoed in the International Bill of Rights. However, the 1970 Declaration is one of the first documents to expand on the decision of these 'people'. It states that this determination is of 'political status' with the self-determination being the decision to choose a form of political governance. In this sense it is closer to the American Declaration, which enunciated the 'consent of the governed' as the basis for a legitimate government, and supports Franck's (1992: 56) analysis of the emergence of democracy within the system of sovereign states. The Declaration emphasizes that determination of political status should take place free of external interference. The second point established by the Declaration is the expansion of the role of the state in allowing/facilitating this process. This is extremely problematic and it is in light of these clauses that the Declaration begins to show its specific location within the context of decolonization. The requirement of states respecting the right in accordance with the Charter is logical: the state, either the colonizer itself, or a third party indirectly concerned with the entity seeking self-determination, is required to respect the Declaration and the ethos of self-determination expressed therein. Thus it has a duty to either isolate itself allowing the process to take place, or to engage pro-actively in helping the UN fulfil its goal of achieving self-determination. The latter could be achieved by facilitating the process indirectly, for instance in public support of the cause of the national liberation movement, or directly in providing arms to the national liberation movement. This view of options in support of self-determination is highly contentious since the Charter attempts to discourage the use of force in international relations, and provision of arms to national liberation movements remains dangerous to order. In assisting forces of self-determination, states may act collectively with other UN members, possibly through the mechanism of Chapter VII and the Security Council, in emancipating subjugated peoples. Despite the objection raised by some colonial states,[2] this was not problematic, since the process of decolonization was taking place with active involvement from colonial powers by the time of the 1970 Declaration (barring a few exceptions[3]). The 1970 Declaration clearly states that one of the purposes of the principle is to end colonialism. This, it is suggested, dates the international legal right of self-determination, since it presents us with a paradoxical argument in the context of the theory of secession. First we have a scenario where the norm of self-determination in the pre-UN era was interpreted as a right to be exercised by minorities to emancipate themselves and set them within their own sovereign states. This was broadened in the UN era to cover *all* people under colonial subjugation. However at the next step, when challenged in Katanga and Biafra, the realms of 'who' a colonial oppressor is was restricted to *salt-water* colonization (Keal 2003). This makes the self-determination aspect of the 1970 Declaration redundant today since the territories under subjugation of these forces have been emancipated.

In any case in the context of secession the message from the Declaration is clear and consistent with the response to Katanga and Biafra. On the one hand the Declaration states:

> *Every State has the duty to refrain from any forcible action which deprives peoples referred to above in the elaboration of the present principle of their right to self-determination and freedom and independence. In their actions against resistance to such forcible action in pursuit of the exercise of the right to self-determination, such peoples are entitled to seek and to receive support in accordance with the purposes and principles of the Charter of the UN. (UNGAOR 2625 XXV)*

This clause appears to endorse self-determination over territorial integrity by articulating duties of member states to seek and receive support. It remains a succinct expression of the right of a people to armed support in fighting a war of revolution. However this endorsement is negated by the next paragraph which plunges the discourse into the territorial integrity versus self-determination morass:

> *Nothing in the foregoing paragraphs shall be construed as authorising or encouraging any action which would dismember or impair, totally or in part, the territorial integrity or political unity of sovereign and independent States conducting themselves in compliance with the principle of equal rights*

---

2   The official Portuguese arguments are well captured in Nogueira (1963), who was then Foreign Minister of Portugal.
3   One notable exception is the Spanish withdrawal from the Western Sahara (Zoubir and Volman 1993).

> and self-determination of peoples as described above and thus possessed of a government representing the whole people belonging to the territory without distinction as to race, creed or colour. (UNGAOR 2625 XXV)

And, in addition, that:

> Every State shall refrain from any action aimed at the partial or total disruption of the national unity and territorial integrity of any other State or country.

Thus the endorsement of self-determination and the right of people to freely implement it towards achieving their desired status is subject to territorial integrity. This message was clearly reiterated in the articulation of Congolese and Nigerian sovereignty respectively. While this may seem contradictory to the spirit of the UN, it highlights the precedence of order within the international system (see also Chapter 1). A freely available process of self-determination, especially one potentially involving secession, would harm order, which is entrenched in the Charter. As a result, when the Declaration refers to not authorizing or encouraging action aimed at the dismemberment of an existing state, it locates the phenomenon of self-determination to its specific decolonization application. The incumbent metropolitan states were not considered as possessing rights over their 'overseas territories', and their achievement of independence was not considered disruptive to the state. In modern self-determination struggles, much like in Katanga and Biafra, this paragraph has been interpreted by states as negating the right to secession of an entity from the state. The Declaration thus contradicts itself by ruling out secession or the 'establishment of a sovereign and independent State' as an option; this is problematic as a general rule but it may have been appropriate in Katanga and Biafra (for further discussion see Chapter 17).

In terms of more general reflections on how Katanga and Biafra have influenced the discourse of secession, it could be argued that the cases reiterated the following key principles *vis-à-vis* secession in a post-colonial context:

a. that decolonization could occur only along the territorial dimensions of the colonial entity;[4]
b. that the whole post-colonial state would normally be deemed the unit seeking self-determination;
c. that the territorial integrity of the post-colonial state could defeat aspirations for secession among its constituents.

This hostility towards secession would dim in future years as entities such as Bangladesh, Eritrea and Timor Leste emerged (see Part VI), but the strength of

---

4   An issue already raised in the OAU's Cairo Resolution (1964), which in turn built upon the Roman law doctrine of *uti possidetis juris*. For more on this see Castellino and Allen (2005).

the norms above are still used by post-colonial states such as India to dismiss secessionist claims. In the two cases reviewed above, the actions for secession were defeated through military action: in Katanga through the use of UN troops and in Biafra through the deployment of the Nigerian army. In both cases the military action had the backing of international actors, and in both cases the heightened value given to territorial integrity effectively negated the principle of self-determination of the communities.

# References

Bartkus, V.O. (1999), *The Dynamic of Secession* (Cambridge: Cambridge University Press).
Brilmayer L. (1991), 'Secession and Self Determination', *Yale Journal of International Law* 16, 177–202.
Buchheit L.C. (1978), *Secession: The Legitimacy of Self-determination* (New Haven, CT: Yale University Press).
Carrington, C.E. (1962), 'Decolonisation: The Last Stages', *International Affairs* 38:1, 29–40.
Cassese, A. (1995), *Self-Determination of Peoples: A Legal Reappraisal* (Cambridge: Cambridge University Press).
Castellino, J. (2000a), *International Law and the Right to Self-Determination: International Law and Self-determination: The Interplay of the Politics of Territorial Possession with Formulations of Post-Colonial National Identity* (The Hague and Boston, MA, London: Martinus Nijhoff).
Castellino, J. (2000b), 'The Secession of Bangladesh in International Law', *Asian Yearbook of International Law* 7, 83–104.
Castellino, J. and S. Allen (2005), *Title to Territory in International Law: An Inter-Temporal Analysis* (Aldershot: Dartmouth/Ashgate).
Chowdhury, S. (1977), 'The Status and Norms of Self Determination in Contemporary International Law', *Netherlands International Law Review* 24, 72–84.
Eagleton, C. (1953), 'Self Determination in the United Nations', *American Journal of International Law* 47:1, 88–93.
Franck, T. (1992), 'The Emerging Right to Democratic Governance', *American Journal of International Law* 86, 1–46.
Gerard-Libois, J. (1966), *Katanga Secession*, translated by R. Young (Madison, WI: University of Wisconsin Press).
Hannum, H. (1990), *Autonomy, Sovereignty and Self-determination: The Accommodation of Conflicting Rights* (Philadelphia, PA: University of Pennsylvania Press).
Higgins, R. (1982), 'Judge Dillard and the Principle of Self-determination', *Virginia Journal of International Law* 23, 387–94.
Keal, P. (2003), *European Conquest and the Rights of Indigenous Peoples: The Moral Backwardness of International Society* (Cambridge: Cambridge University Press).

Lefever, E.W. (1965), *Crisis in the Congo: A United Nations Force in Action* (Washington, DC: Brookings Institution).
Lemarchand, R. (1962), 'Limits of Self Determination: Katanga', *American Political Science Review* 56, 404–16.
Martelli, G. (1964), 'Portugal and the United Nations', *International Affairs* 40.
Nayar, K. (1975), 'Self Determination beyond a Colonial Context: Biafra in Retrospect', *Texas International Law Journal* 10:2, 321–45.
Nogueira, F. (1963), *The United Nations and Portugal: A Study of Anti-Colonialism* (London: Sidgwick & Jackson).
Pomerance, M. (1982), *Self Determination in Law and Practice: The New Doctrine in the United Nations* (The Hague: Martinus Nijhoff).
Ratner, S. (1996), 'Drawing a Better Line: Uti Possidetis and the Borders of New States', *American Journal of International Law* 90:4, 590–624.
Sinha, S.P. (1973), 'Is Self Determination Passé?', *Columbia Journal of Transnational Law* 12, 249–60.
Sureda, Rigo (1973), *The Evolution of the Principle of Self-determination: A Study of UN Practice* (Leiden: A.W. Sijthoff).
Suzuki, E. (1976), 'Self Determination and World Political Order', *Virginia Journal of International Law* 16, 779–82.
Thornberry, P. (1994), 'The Democratic or Internal Aspect of Self-determination with Some Remarks on Federalism', in C. Tomuschat (ed.), *Modern Law of Self-Determination* (Leiden and Boston, MA: Martinus Nijhoff), 101–38.
Tomuschat, C. (1994), 'Self-determination in a Post Colonial World', in C. Tomuschat (ed.), *Modern Law of Self-Determination* (Leiden and Boston, MA: Martinus Nijhoff), 1–20.
Van Langenhove, F. (1954), *The Question of Aborigines Before the United Nations: The Belgian Thesis* (Brussels: Royal Colonial Institute of Belgium).
Whelan, A. (1994), 'Wilsonian Self-Determination and the Versailles Settlement', *International and Comparative Law Quarterly* 43, 99–115.
Wilson, W. (1918), 'Fourteen Point Address' (8 January 1918). [Online] At http://wwi.lib.byu.edu/index.php/President_Wilson's_Fourteen_Points [accessed 29 March 2010].
Zoubir, Y.H. and D. Volman (1993), *International Dimensions of the Western Sahara Conflict* (Westport, CT: Praeger).

# Constitutional Politics of Secession: Travelling from Quebec to Montenegro (and back?)

Zoran Oklopčić

## Introduction

The historical background, geopolitical context, legal environment, and their ultimate outcome preclude easy comparison between the successful secession of Montenegro from the State Union of Serbia and Montenegro, and the unsuccessful secession of Quebec from Canada. Montenegro is a small European polity that re-emerged as an independent state after decades of communist rule. Quebec remains a large province in a prosperous liberal-democratic federation. In the former, socialist, Yugoslavia, the right to secession was briefly mentioned, but never a subject of debate. In Canada, it was the other way around: secession was never far from the political and academic agenda, but its status in constitutional law, at least until the Supreme Court's judgment in the *Secession Reference*, was never certain.

Irrespective of different political contexts, which in both cases culminated in a referendum on independence, comparing Quebec and Montenegro is instructive for several reasons. First, the legal arguments employed in the struggle over the right of Quebec to secede unilaterally from Canada were later redeployed in the Montenegrin context. The requirements of a 'clear majority' and 'clear question' developed in the Canadian context were imposed on Montenegro by the European Union, as requirements with which to judge the legitimacy of the outcome of the referendum. In turn, the EU's endorsement of the Canadian constitutional experience in the case of Montenegro might serve to amplify the global attractiveness of the 'Canadian' approach to secession in the context of functioning liberal-democratic states. Second, the EU's gloss on the question of a 'clear majority' – requiring that independence be supported by at least 55 percent of those voting – may serve as a precedent, once again in Canada, with which to judge the legitimacy of a future attempt of secession by Quebec. Equally important, both cases raise the question of the contemporary meaning of the international legal norm of the 'self-determination of peoples'. While self-determination enjoyed a period of relative conceptual stability during the Cold War, its content, especially when it comes to the formation of territorial polities, remains heavily contested. Finally, both the Canadian and Serbian-Montenegrin experience with secession challenge the tacit premise of much of modern constitutionalism, which has often been conceived as an intellectual project invested in creating structures and justifications for the perpetuity of a political community.

# Different Historical Trajectories to Constitutionalized Secession

## Montenegro: From Independence to Independence

While Montenegro achieved independence in 2006, becoming the 192nd member state of the United Nations, it is actually one of the oldest independent European countries. Montenegro's tradition of political autonomy dates to its *de facto* independence from the Ottoman Empire in the 18th century, internationally and *de jure* recognized in 1878 at the Congress of Berlin. In 1918, Montenegro's Grand National Assembly unconditionally joined the Kingdom of Serbia, and through it became part of the new Kingdom of the Serbs, Croats and Slovenes (renamed, in 1929, Yugoslavia). The political elites of monarchical, interwar Yugoslavia, influenced by the political success of emancipatory movements of the Italian Risorgimento and German unification, emulated these nation-building efforts aiming to forge a single Yugoslav nation. Serbs, Croats and Slovenes were considered as three 'tribes' of a single 'three-name' Yugoslav nation. In this political equation 'Montenegrins' did not feature as an independent nation, but rather as a regional name for the Serbs living in Montenegro.

This changed after World War Two when Yugoslavia was reconstructed as a multinational federation under communist rule. Montenegro became one of Yugoslavia's six component 'people's republics', with Montenegrins as one of Yugoslavia's constituent nations. Following the Leninist doctrine regarding the national question, all constitutions of Yugoslavia – from 1945, 1963 and 1974 – assumed that the Yugoslav nations constituted Yugoslavia 'starting from' their right to self-determination, including the right of secession.[1] None of them, however, enshrined a constitutional mechanism for effectuating self-determination qua secession, and Yugoslavia's bloody collapse can, to a certain extent, be

---

1   For a discussion of self-determination and 'constitutional nationalism' in the context of the Yugoslav breakup see Hayden (1999).

attributed to a lack of a clear rule that would clearly designate the unit to which self-determination applies (see also Chapter 8).

When Yugoslavia broke apart, Montenegro remained united with Serbia in the newly reconstructed state, the Federal Republic of Yugoslavia (FRY), created in April of 1992. The Constitution of the now two-member Yugoslavia did not invoke a principle of self-determination in its preamble, referring instead to the 'tradition of statehood' of Serbia and Montenegro. In the same way, the 1992 Constitution did not provide the explicit mechanism for the dissolution of the FRY. However, one can infer from Art. 141 that the secession of either state was implicitly permitted, by means of a constitutional amendment to the provisions of the Constitution that define Yugoslavia as a 'sovereign federal state' (Art. 1), comprised of Serbia and Montenegro as its member-republics (Art. 2). According to Art. 141, such an amendment would have to be initiated by a resolution passed with a two-thirds majority in the Council of Citizens of the Federal Assembly. In order to be enacted, the proposed amendment would have to be adopted by the same Council by a two-thirds majority, and assented to by both Republics' assemblies.

Even though the Montenegrin ruling elite did not demand independence during the 1990s, it gradually distanced itself from the Milošević regime in Serbia. While one may have anticipated that deposing Milošević and the electoral victory of democratic parties in Serbia in 2000 would have led to a renewed commitment to the common federal framework, Montenegro's demands for wider autonomy continued, leading eventually to an outright demand for full independence. In 2002, fearing that the disintegration of the then-Federal Republic of Yugoslavia would bear negatively on the political process leading to the determination of Kosovo's status, EU officials became directly involved in the negotiations between Serbia and Montenegro concerning the transformation of the deadlocked federation (Mancini 2008: 576). An uneasy, never fully functional compromise emerged in 2002, under the stewardship of Javier Solana, the EU High Representative for Foreign and Security Policy. Serbia and Montenegro would continue to exist as a loose quasi-confederation, called the State Union of Serbia and Montenegro, but either member obtained the constitutional right to call a referendum on independence after three years. Towards the end of this waiting period, the Montenegrin government decided to act.

## Quebec: From Conquest, through Accommodation, to Failed Secession

While initially independent, Montenegrins – the general population and the elite alike – enthusiastically participated in the wider state-building projects of monarchist, communist and post-communist Yugoslavia. French Canadians, on the other hand, joined the Canadian confederation in 1867 against the backdrop of military conquest, assimilationist pressures and failed attempts at achieving political stability and national accommodation within the short-lived United Province of Canada. Even though the new Constitution of 1867 was formally an act of the British Imperial Parliament, many French Canadians understood it as a compact between two parties – the constituent nations of the Dominion of Canada. 'This constitution' – wrote George-Etienne Cartier at Confederation's inception – 'recognizes the French-Canadian nationality. As a distinct, separate nationality, we form a State within the State with the full use of our rights and the formal recognition of our national independence' (McRoberts 2001: 696). In its insistence on the compact theory of the federation, the Quebecois account of the nature of a federation resembled Croatian and Slovenian accounts of the Yugoslav state in the context of the former Yugoslavia. For Croatian constitutional scholars there is no doubt that 'the correct application of the federal principle entail[ed] an association based on voluntary participation in the union, as well as a right to peacefully leave the union' (Smerdel 2007: 29). In Quebec, this radical interpretation of the compact theory (and federalism) did not reach its apogee until the late 1970s. Following several failed attempts to accommodate Quebecois political demands within the Canadian constitutional order, the Parti Québécois assumed power in 1976, promising a referendum on the project of *sovereignty-association* with the rest of Canada. Even though sovereignty-association did not explicitly include internationally recognized sovereignty or independence as its goal, it suffered a defeat in the 1980 referendum by a wide margin; 59.56 percent of the Quebecois electorate voted against sovereignty-association advanced by the Parti Québécois (Russell 2004: 107).

Following the failure of the sovereigntist project, Canadian Prime Minister Pierre Elliott Trudeau moved to 'patriate' the Canadian constitution from the United Kingdom, and to complement it with the Charter of Rights and Freedoms. As a proponent of the essentially 'civic nationalist' project seeking to (re)construct Canadian identity around fundamental values entrenched in the Charter, Trudeau was hostile towards a unique constitutional status for Quebec. Responding to the federal government's initiative to accomplish patriation unilaterally, Quebec joined eight provinces (excluding New Brunswick and Ontario) in their demand for the patriation by 'proper means' – that is, with provincial participation (Oliver 1999: 543). The provinces signed the so-called April Accords, which guaranteed Quebec the complete right to opt out with compensation from any amendment derogating 'the legislative powers, the proprietary rights or any other rights or privileges of the legislature or government of a province'. In exchange, Quebec relinquished its earlier demand to preserve its alleged constitutional veto over future constitutional changes (Oliver 1999: 544).

In the aftermath of the Supreme Court's *Patriation Reference* (resulting from Trudeau's rejection of the Accords), the federal government reached a compromise with Anglophone provinces, making the April Accords a basis for the amending formula, but only with a limited right to opt out in matters relating to education and culture (Oliver 1999: 544). Quebec's government responded to this federal-provincial agreement with hostility and resentment; it withdrew its previous concessions, and challenged patriation in a subsequent reference. In the *Quebec Veto Reference*, the Court declared that Quebec's alleged right of veto doesn't exist. Since the new Constitution was patriated without its consent, Quebec rejected its legitimacy. The failure of the Meech Lake (1987) and Charlottetown Accords

(1992) that sought to accommodate Quebecois demands within the constitutional framework demonstrated the difficulty of reaching consensus on a 'single organizing vision' of the Canadian federation (Monahan 1997: 136). Riding the wave of popular resentment in Quebec following the failure of the Charlottetown Accords, Parti Québécois returned to power in 1994 promising to organize a referendum on the future status of Quebec.

## Constitutionalizing Secession in Canada

In the course of preparation for the referendum, the Parti Québécois introduced the *Draft Bill – An Act Respecting the Sovereignty of Quebec*, which described Quebec as 'a sovereign country', proclaiming that the sovereignty of Quebec would come into force one year after an affirmative vote in a referendum, irrespective of a lack of prior agreement with the rest of Canada.

During the 1995 referendum campaign, the Quebec Superior Court was asked to invalidate the *Draft Bill*, and to order an injunction to stop the referendum on sovereignty. According to the petitioner, Guy Bertrand, the *Draft Bill* violated his rights under the Canadian *Charter of Rights and Freedoms*. Although the Court held that the draft bill constituted a 'serious threat' to Bertrand's constitutional rights, it nonetheless held that issuing an injunction to prevent the referendum was inappropriate.

Echoing these developments in *Bertrand v. Quebec* and encouraged by strong popular support for the sovereigntist option, the Parti Québécois soon passed *Bill 1, An Act respecting the Future of Quebec*, the justification for which included the following:

> Quebec's accession to sovereignty is basically a fundamental democratic process that is sanctioned by public international law, and the superior Court has no jurisdiction over such matters ... [T]he judiciary should not intervene in Quebec's accession to sovereignty as the appropriateness of this process is not a matter for debate before the courts.

The referendum was held on 30 October 1995, with the citizens of Quebec answering the question: 'Do you agree that Quebec should become sovereign, after having made a formal offer to Canada for a new Economic and Political Partnership, within the scope of the Bill respecting the Future of Quebec and of the agreement signed on 12 June 1995?' (Hogg 1997: 19). Among those voting, 50.58 percent voted 'No' and 49.42 percent 'Yes' (Dawson 1999: 10). While the referendum failed by a very thin margin, some commentators argued that a significant number of voters were misled by an unclear question which led them to believe that voting for the sovereigntist side wouldn't entail the secession of Quebec from Canada (McRoberts 1997: 230).

Emboldened by the failure of the sovereigntist option, the Canadian government decided to initiate a reference before the Supreme Court on the legality of the unilateral secession of Quebec (see also Chapter 18). According to the federal government, 'all our provinces and the Canadian public have long agreed that the country will not be held together against the clear will of Quebecers [and t]his government agrees with that statement' (Bienvenu 2001: 203). Agreeing that secession is legitimate in principle was not a sign of political largesse on the part of the federal government. Rather, by conceding that secession is a legitimate political option, the government would make the Québécois wary of the significant political risks that would accompany secession rather than emphasizing the benefits of staying within Canada (Dodge 1999: 326).

In 1996, as a part of that strategy, the government asked the Supreme Court to clarify the legal framework of secession. Two years later, the Supreme Court of Canada delivered *Reference re Secession of Quebec* that would soon earn the reputation not only as one of the most important decisions in Canadian constitutional law, but also as a decision whose influence continues to be felt in comparativist and international legal circles (Walters 1999). The Court's judgment was framed by three questions posed by the federal government. The first question asked whether the unilateral secession of Quebec would be valid under Canadian constitutional law. The second asked whether international law gives Quebec a right to effectuate secession from Canada unilaterally – more specifically, is there a right to self-determination that would justify the unilateral secession of Quebec? And finally, in the event of a conflict between domestic and international law, which would take precedence in Canada?

Before answering the first question, the Court rejected the claim that its decision to answer the three questions 'usurp[s] any democratic decision that the people of Quebec may be called upon to make'. Instead, the Court maintained that its response would be 'strictly limited to *aspects of the legal framework* in which that democratic decision is to be taken' ([1998] 2 S.C.R. 217, para. 27). But 'interpreting the law' in relation to the first question was anything but obvious. Though the government stated in advance that it does not oppose constitutional secession, the amending formulas of the Canadian constitution do not provide any guidance on whether or not secession is admissible *in principle*. According to Jeremy Webber, this textual gap left the way open to different interpretations regarding the permissibility of Quebec's secession from Canada. The Court could have interpreted the constitution so as to conclude that either Canada is as a state indivisible; or, that secession is achievable through constitutional amendment; or, that unilateral secession is, in fact, warranted by the Canadian constitution (Webber 1997: 281).

The Court endorsed the second of these interpretations – secession through constitutional amendment – but went a critical step further. While the Court concluded that the unilateral secession of Quebec is unconstitutional, it stated that the positive result in a referendum on independence would not only confer democratic legitimacy on the government of Quebec to pursue demands for secession but would create binding constitutional effects. If a *clear majority* of the population of Quebec responded affirmatively to a *clearly formulated referendum question*, the federal government would be under a *legal* duty to negotiate in good faith the Quebecois' demand for secession.

This legal duty to negotiate in good faith cannot, however, be found in the text of the constitution. Therefore, in answering the first question, the Court resorted to using metaphors and concepts of Canadian constitutionalism that enabled it to remain faithful to the amending formula, but to also go further in legitimizing secession, and demanding that its proponents be taken seriously and with respect. In going beyond the text of the constitution, the Court invoked the 'living tree' metaphor, which denotes the capability of a constitution to grow and expand 'within its natural limits' (*Edwards v. Attorney-General for Canada*, 1930). The growth of such a living tree is animated by underlying unwritten principles. These unwritten principles are not only 'aids to the interpretation' of the ambiguous or possibly conflicting norms in the text of the constitution. More importantly, 'they are the vital unstated assumptions upon which the text is based' (*Secession Reference*, para. 49). As such, their invocation is critical in dealing with situations which are not 'expressly dealt with' by the written constitution alone (para. 32).

In the context of secession, the Court articulated four unwritten principles that together give rise to a duty to negotiate secession in good faith. In discussing the four principles – *federalism, democracy, rule of law and constitutionalism*, and *protection of minorities* – the Court rejected the proposition that the principle of popular sovereignty, or the compact theory of federation, could justify the unilateral secession of Quebec. Answering the hypothetical claim that

> [if] the notion of popular sovereignty underlies the legitimacy of our existing constitutional arrangements, ... the same popular sovereignty that originally led to the present Constitution must (it is argued) also permit 'the people' in their exercise of popular sovereignty to secede by majority vote alone,

the Court denied that there ought to be *symmetry* between (voluntary) entry into the federation and the equally voluntary exit from it. The Court implicitly rejected the compact theory of federation, stating that the political representatives of a province committed themselves, in the name of that province, to the rules of the game delineated in the constitution itself. These rules are 'binding' not in the sense of frustrating the will of a majority of a province, but as defining the majority which must be consulted in order to alter the fundamental balance of political power.

In the same way it rejected an absolutist interpretation of Quebecois popular sovereignty, the Court also rejected any straightforward application of the popular sovereignty of 'the Canadian people'. Even though the Court described the BNA Act 1867 as an 'act of nation-building', the will of the *Canadian* people could not trump the will of one of its sections – the people of Quebec. So, instead of positing a corporate agent – 'the people' – who would have an indisputable right to either prevent (as 'the people of Canada') or effectuate (as 'the people of Quebec') secession, the Court invoked popular sovereignty in the context of other values which give rise to a constitutional duty to negotiate secession in good faith. In the Court's reading, popular sovereignty emerges not as a principle that would unequivocally support 'the people's' political projects, but one that gives legitimacy to 'democratic expressions of a desire' for radical political change – which, by implication, demand that a constitutional order be responsive to those desires. Popular sovereignty is not a principle that can tell us what 'the people' – whoever it may be – deserves in a substantive sense, but is rather a principle that tells us what we can legitimately expect of a constitutional order. According to the Court, 'the continued existence and operation of the Canadian constitutional order could not be indifferent to a clear expression of a clear majority of Quebecers that they no longer wish to remain in Canada' (para. 92). Articulating clearly the need for a *good faith responsiveness to political radicalism* is the biggest theoretical contribution of the Secession Reference.

The Court declined to answer, however, what would be the end result of such responsiveness. On the one hand, the Court disagreed that a duty to negotiate would be relegated to sorting out the 'logistical details of secession' (para. 90). Equally, '[t]he rights of other provinces and the federal government cannot deny the right of the government of Quebec to pursue secession, should a clear majority of the people of Quebec choose that goal' (para. 91). Whatever the outcome, it would have to be achieved through a 'give and take of political negotiations', where the Court would have no supervisory role (para. 153).

Dovetailing its interpretation of popular sovereignty as incompatible with non-negotiable political demands, the Court's answer to the second question denied any role for self-determination as a legal principle in effectuating the secession of Quebec. The Court maintained that Quebec enjoys the full right of *internal* self-determination. Given that the citizens of Quebec 'occupy prominent positions' and 'have access to government', and that Quebec is 'equitably represented' in the Canadian government, it cannot be said that the internal self-determination of Quebec is violated (para. 136). According to the Court, however, the right to *external* self-determination is reserved only for colonized or oppressed peoples, that is, for peoples whose right to internal self-determination is being severely frustrated or impaired. Since this is not the situation in the case of Quebec, the Court declined to enter into discussion about the definition of the concept of 'the people' for the purposes of secession as irrelevant. Yet, in what can be read as an ominous warning to secessionists, the Court hinted that the 'give and take of political negotiations' may require the partition of the province. 'Nobody seriously suggests', the Court declared, 'that our national existence, seamless in so many aspects, could be effortlessly separated along what are now the provincial boundaries of Quebec' (para. 96).

Concluding its treatment of unilateral secession from the international point of view, the Court rebutted invocations of the effectivity principle as a basis for the legality of unilateral secession, claiming that its endorsement would mean that an 'initially illegal act retroactively creates a legal right to engage in the act in the first place'. The Court ultimately concluded that 'the broader contention is not supported by the international principle of effectivity or otherwise and must be rejected'. Finally, having given similar answers to the first two questions, the Court easily concluded that 'there is no conflict between domestic and international law to be addressed' (para. 147).

Before the judgment was delivered, the Quebecois Premier openly questioned the judges' impartiality, claiming that their 'federalist faith is not in doubt' (Des Rosiers 2000: 183). However, the delivered opinion of the Supreme Court was an indisputable success in terms of the broad support for its arguments from both sides. Both federalists and sovereigntists claimed that the Court vindicated their fundamental claim: the federalists, that any secession must be negotiated under the Canadian constitutional framework; the sovereigntists, that secession is a legitimate political option that should be approached in good faith.

Subsequent years, however, saw the retreat of the two camps to their initial positions. In 2000, the federal Parliament passed the *Clarity Act* which further sought to regulate the issues of a 'clear question' and a 'clear majority'. While mandating the House of Commons to solicit views on the clarity of the referendum question from a broad spectrum of political actors from within and outside of Quebec, the Act leaves the decision on clarity in the hands of the federal government (s. 1. ss. 1 and 3). This assertion of authority was immediately rejected by the Quebec National Assembly, which, in response, passed *Bill 99 – An Act Respecting the Exercise of the Fundamental Rights and Prerogatives of the Québec People and the Québec State* – reiterating the right of Quebec to leave the federation unilaterally, and to exercise its right to self-determination. (s. 1. ss. 1, 2 and 3) While these two Acts show that the possibility of political standoff hasn't been eliminated, the immediate political salience of these questions is currently small due to the modest support for secession among the Quebecois electorate.

## A 'Clear Majority' and a 'Clear Question' Travel East: The *Secession Reference* and the Secession of Montenegro

At home, the *Secession Reference* is widely held to be one of the most important decisions in Canadian constitutional history, with profound effect not only on the country's political life, but on subsequent jurisprudence as well. Already in 1999, Canadian constitutional scholars argued that the *Secession Reference* was destined to raise keen interest abroad, especially in federations or states containing substantial ethnic minorities (Gaudreault-Desbiens 1999: 793; see also Walters 1999). And indeed, the import of the Canadian experience with constitutionalizing secession was not lost on the political and academic elite in Serbia. Under the aegis of the Serbian Centre for Liberal Democratic Studies, Ronald Watts, Thomas Fleiner and Hans Peter Schneider published a study entitled 'Constitutional Recomposition of the Federal Republic of Yugoslavia' arguing that the 2001 Montenegrin *Referendum Act* can have only a consultative, but not a binding effect (Watts 2002: 55). In light of comparative experience, most notably *Secession Reference* and the *Clarity Act*, the constitutional experts concluded that Montenegro doesn't have a right to secede unilaterally from the existing Yugoslavia, and that the result of a referendum must satisfy the threshold of a 'clear majority' in order to trigger federal negotiations over secession (ibid.).

The suggestion of the constitutional experts to create a functional, if limited, federal state was ultimately rejected, and a right to secede *unilaterally* was enshrined in the Constitutional Charter of the short-lived State Union of Serbia and Montenegro. However, Canadian experience continued to be relevant for the secession of Montenegro as it became apparent that the Montenegrin government was not willing to abandon its goal to call a referendum on independence soon after the expiry of the stated three-year period.

In the interim, the influence of external, European political and quasi-legal bodies became crucial in shaping not only the political climate in Montenegro, but also the legal provisions of the referendum. In December 2005, following a request by the Parliamentary Assembly of the Council of Europe, the European Commission for Democracy through Law (the Venice Commission) published its opinion on the compatibility of Montenegro's legislation concerning the organization of referendums with international standards (Opinion no. 343/2005).

The Commission concentrated on the issues of the wording of the referendum question, the required turnout, majority and the eligibility criteria to vote. Discussing the wording of the referendum question, the Commission stated, without referring to Canadian experience, that any question submitted to the electorate must be clear, that it must not be misleading, and that it must not suggest an answer (para. 15). With respect to the issue of minimum voter turnout, the Commission concluded that even though there are no clear-cut international standards on what constitutes an acceptable minimum, it approved a provision in the Montenegrin *Law on Referendums* that requires that the minimum voter turnout be the majority of citizens with voting rights while stating that 'there are reasons for requiring a level higher than a simple majority of those voting'. In suggesting that Montenegro amend its *Law on Referendums*, the Commission critically relied on the *Secession Reference* and the *Clarity Act*. Selectively quoting the *Clarity Act*, the Commission stated that in making a decision on a clear majority, the views of all political parties represented in the legislature of the seceding entity should be considered. While quoting the first part of s.1 ss.5 of the *Clarity Act*, the Commission omitted the part referring to the inclusion of other political stakeholders outside of the province. In the Montenegrin context, faithful adoption of the approach of the *Clarity Act* would have required considering the opinion of the Serbian government on the definition of a clear majority as well.

The opinion of the Serbian government was disregarded about an equally, if not more significant question. Unlike in Quebec and Canada, in Serbia and Montenegro, citizens held both federal and member-state citizenship. For the purposes of the Montenegrin referendum this proved crucial. The question arose: are 'the people of Montenegro' the sum of its citizens, or only its residents? The people of Montenegro – as the body of its citizens – would extend across the boundaries of Montenegro. While Montenegro's population totalled approximately 600,000 inhabitants, over 260,000 residents of Serbia also held Montenegrin citizenship, representing a significant number that could have dramatically altered the results of the referendum. In June of 2005, in an attempt to alter the composition of the Montenegrin electorate, the Serbian government presented EU officials with evidence demonstrating that there are 264,802 citizens of Montenegro residing in Serbia, and that as a matter of respect for the principle of democracy, they should be included in the Montenegrin electorate. The Venice Commission Report rejected this claim. Drawing, in part, on the practice of federal countries with dual citizenship, such as Bosnia and Herzegovina and Switzerland, and the experience of referendums on devolution in the United Kingdom, the Commission concluded that the Serbian government's proposition was unfounded, arguing that altering the eligibility requirements to include non-resident citizens 'would be incompatible with the necessary stability of the voting rules and [would] jeopardise the legitimacy of the referendum' (para. 65).

While consensus on both issues – what constitutes a required majority and who counts as a member of the electorate – was ultimately reached by the Montenegrin government and the opposition, the role of the European Union in negotiations was critical. Following the suggestions of the Venice Commission, the EU envoy's proposal denied the franchise to Montenegrin citizens residing outside of Montenegro as a concession to the pro-independence side, but simultaneously demanded the display of a 'clear majority' in a referendum – 55 percent of those voting – going against the wishes of the government. Although Montenegrin President Đukanović initially called the EU's formula 'undemocratic' since it required voter turnout of over 50 percent, he ultimately gave in to political pressure from the EU (Ramušović 2006: 1).

The referendum was held in May 2006, and in keeping with the recommendations of the Venice Commission regarding 'clarity', the question read: 'Do you want the Republic of Montengro to be an independent state with full international and legal responsibility?' As in the Quebecois referendum 11 years earlier, the margin between the 'yes' and the 'no' camp was very small. In Montenegro, the pro-independence camp passed the threshold of 55 percent by a mere 2,300 votes. The legitimacy of the referendum, however, was not questioned due, in part, to the robust political involvement of the European Union. After the referendum, Miroslav Lajčák, the EU representative, didn't shirk from declaring that Montenegro 'has been a successful European project ... created with the active participation of the European Union' (Lajčák 2006: 1). In early June 2006, the Montenegrin parliament proclaimed the independence of Montenegro, and was speedily recognized by the countries of the European Union, United States and other countries as well as by Serbia. Less than two months after the referendum, Montenegro became a member of the United Nations.

# The Constitutionalization of Secession, the Role of Self-determination, and the (Absent) Vocabulary of Grievance

Constitutionalizing secession – treating it as a matter of domestic, and not international law – raises the question of the status of the norm that, arguably, governs secession in the international realm: the right of peoples to self-determination (for a further discussion see Chapter 19). Is secession by constitutional means still an exemplar of self-determination? Or, is self-determination as a justificatory tool for secession somehow undermined by the constitutional vocabulary which not only domesticates, but also legitimizes secessionist pursuits, *without* making use of the *legal* vocabulary of self-determination?

In the *Secession Reference*, the Supreme Court of Canada explicitly rejected the proposition that Quebec's unilateral secession could be justified by the right to self-determination of peoples. On the other hand, sovereigntists initially invoked self-determination, albeit implicitly, and not unequivocally, as one might expect. The preamble to *Bill 1* declared, for example, that '[w]e, the people of Québec, declare it is our will to be in full possession of all the powers of a State'. Conspicuously, the expression 'self-determination' appeared only in the title of s.1 of the Bill, declaring that 'the National Assembly is authorized, within the scope of this Act, to proclaim the sovereignty of Quebec'. While the National Assembly of Quebec sought to use the vocabulary of peoplehood to establish the legitimacy of Quebec's desire to secede unilaterally, it stopped short of *deriving* it from the international legal right to self-determination of peoples.

This rhetorical cautiousness is not surprising when understood in the context of previous efforts by Quebec's National Assembly to establish international law credentials for Quebec's unilateral independence. Only three years earlier, in 1992, the Assembly commissioned a report from five notable experts in international law who, drawing on the arguments of the Badinter Commission from the dissolution of Yugoslavia, *explicitly* stated that the independence of Quebec cannot be grounded in the right to self-determination of peoples.[2] While claiming that

---

2   Interestingly, the Badinter Commission Opinions are often considered as interpreting the right of self-determination as belonging not to ethnic nations but to the peoples of the component republics. However, the creation of states, for Badinter, was a matter not of self-determination, but rather of fact. When asked directly, the Commission declined to pronounce who had the right to self-determination, understood, in that context, as a right to create an independent state. Instead of using self-determination in a *positive* fashion to declare who is entitled to self-determination, Badinter used self-determination negatively: a minority population that ended up 'trapped' in the new states did not have the right to self-determination. Instead, self-determination entitled those minorities, Badinter argued, to ask for a robust minority protection regime without territorial connotations. Richard Caplan has rightly argued that 'the Commission did not invoke the principle in support of the republics' independence claims. ... *Badinter, in fact, invoked the principle of self-determination not to support but to*

Quebec's unilateral declaration of independence and territorial integrity would be sanctioned by international law, the experts reiterated that the principle of self-determination has 'limited relevance' for the creation of an independent state. According to the experts, Quebec enjoyed *internal* self-determination, understood merely as a right to participation in the expression of the will of a wider political community, and to recognition of its identity – within the Canadian federation. 'External' self-determination – in the form of secession – the experts maintained, is reserved for oppressed peoples, or those who do not have access to meaningful representation and participation in the organs of the wider state.

Following the adoption of the *Clarity Act* in 2000, however, the National Assembly seems to have retreated from the Five Expert Opinion. Unlike in 1995, when *Bill 1* only mentioned self-determination but stopped short of making it do any justificatory work, *Bill 99* now boldly asserted that 'the right of the Québec people to self-determination is founded in fact *and in law* [emphasis mine]. The Québec people is the holder of rights that are universally recognized under the principle of equal rights and self-determination of peoples' (Art. 1).

In the case of Montenegro, there was no need to invoke self-determination, neither as a legal right nor as a political principle. While Bills 1 and 99 solemnly invoked the 'will of the people', the Montenegrin *Declaration of Independence* merely recorded the 'will of the *citizens*' as the basis for independence. The invocation of the principle of self-determination in the Montenegrin context would have been not only unnecessary, but counterproductive. While the Yugoslav constitution of 1974 recognized a right to self-determination, it did not specify who is its bearer: the republic or the constituent people. The Constitutional Charter of the State Union of Serbia and Montenegro of 2003, on the other hand, recognized the right to unilateral secession of republics without grounding it in any overarching principle. Invoking self-determination in this constitutional context would not add anything to the independence cause, but would potentially enable sub-state national groups in Montenegro, such as the Serbs, to demand their own self-determination, in the form of recursive secession in order to join Serbia. Equally, the invocation of self-determination – as a general principle of international law – could have created rhetorical spillover in other multinational countries of the European Union, thus undermining the decision of the EU not to pressure Montenegrins to remain in the State Union. The secession of Montenegro, as a matter of internal constitutional arrangement between Serbia and Montenegro thus could not be invoked as a precedent to challenge the territorial integrity of a number of European states. But the secession of Montenegro, as a result of a universally applicable norm of international law, the right of peoples to self-determination, could.

Equally absent in the rhetoric surrounding self-determination in the case of Montenegro was the vocabulary of grievance, a usual component of secessionist projects. While the emotionally powerful Preamble of the Quebecois *Bill 1* heavily emphasized past political grievances, the Montenegrin *Declaration of Independence*

---

*restrict the emergence of new states in the region* (Caplan 2005: 69) [emphasis mine].

dryly invoked the legal basis for independence, describing only Montenegro's future political aspirations. In support of the claim that 'Quebec is a sovereign country' *Bill 1* recalled the act of initial conquest, the attempts of assimilation, being 'hoodwinked' in the process of patriation, and, generally, an overall trivialization of Québécois demands for autonomy. In contrast, the Montenegrin Declaration invokes the foreign policy projects to support Montenegro's credentials as an independent state. As an independent state, Montenegro would confirm its 'strategic priority of accelerated integration into the European Union' and its firm dedication to becoming a member of 'Euroatlantic-NATO security structures'. Later in 2007, when asked to justify the independence project, Montenegrin Prime Minister Đukanović responded that the chief purpose of independence was to enable Montenegro to 'assume responsibility for [its] European future' (Đukanović 2006).

## Concluding Remarks

Behind the difficulties of comparing Quebec and Montenegro, there are subtle links that connect the experiences of the two polities. The dissolution of Yugoslavia gave rise to international legal arguments that informed the Quebecois secessionist movement. In turn, the legal outcome of Quebec's unsuccessful attempt at secession provided the crucial elements of a constitutional package imposed on Montenegro by the European Union in its involvement with the secession Montenegro. Given that constitutional ideas, and international legal interpretation already travelled across such disparate contexts, the solutions adopted in the case of Montenegro are poised to 'travel' further. By way of conclusion let me speculate about what might happen if these constitutional ideas make their way back to Canada and Quebec, in the case of a new secessionist mobilization.

In light of the precedent set in Montenegro, will Quebec be impelled to adopt a qualified majority in a future referendum on secession? The *Clarity Act* did not address that question directly. While Quebecois secessionists will surely maintain the stance adopted in *Bill 99*, arguing that the differences in the context between Quebec and Montenegro are too large to allow for any further trans-constitutional fertilization, they will undoubtedly face the pressure from those who will argue that the suggestions of the European Union regarding a sufficient majority and its link to achieving international legitimacy should be taken into account (Choudhry 2007: 9).

If this aspect of Montenegro's secession potentially speaks against the approach pursued in *Bill 99*, the consensus on maintaining Montenegro's administrative boundaries may provide support for the claim that Quebec's territorial integrity is inviolable. An opposing argument will probably be made by the First Nations, such as James Bay Crees, or federalist politicians, such as Stéphane Dion, who early on argued that if Canada can be partitioned, so can Quebec (Dion 1996: 277). But the fact that the Serbs of Montenegro, concentrated in the north of the country, chose not to contest Montenegro's territorial integrity may provide support to those who would argue that upholding administrative boundaries is a 'new normal' in state reconstructions after the end of the Cold War, irrespective of its legally and morally questionable extension from the decolonization context.

Finally, both examples, for all their disparity, may be used as evidence that the constitution of a country can indeed be a 'suicide pact', a notion that many constitutional theorists continue to reject (Paulsen 2004: 1257) (see Chapter 19 for a further discussion). As a result, constitutionalism, as an intellectual project, ought to be perceived not as providing justification for the perpetuity of political communities, but rather as a discipline that contributes to our thinking about the orderly reconstruction of *territories*, and not only *institutions*, something that has so far been relegated to the disciplines of international law and normative political theory.

# References

Bienvenu, P. (2001), 'Secession by Constitutional Means: The Decision of the Supreme Court of Canada in the Quebec Secession Reference', *Hamline Journal of Public Law and Policy*, 185–253.

Caplan, R. (2005), *Europe and the Recognition of New States in Yugoslavia* (Cambridge: Cambridge University Press).

Choudhry, S. (2007), 'Referendum? What Referendum?', *Literary Review of Canada* 15:3, 7–9.

Dawson, M. (1999), 'Reflections on the Opinion of the Supreme Court of Canada in the Quebec Secession Reference', *National Journal of Constitutional Law* 11, 5–48.

Des Rosiers, N. (2000), 'From Quebec Veto to Quebec Secession: The Evolution of the Supreme Court of Canada on Quebec-Canada Disputes', *Canadian Journal of Law and Jurisprudence* 13, 171–83.

Dion, S. (1996), 'Why is Secession Difficult in Well-Established Democracies? Lessons from Quebec', *British Journal of Political Science* 26:2, 269–83.

Dodge, W.J. (1999), 'Succeeding in Seceding?: Internationalizing the Quebec Secession Reference', *Texas International Law Journal* 34, 287–326.

Đukanović, M. (2006), 'United towards the European Quality of Life', Democratic Party of Socialists website. [Online] At http://www.dpscg.org/index.php?option=com_content&task=view&id=107&Itemid=6 [accessed 25 October 2009].

European Commission for Democracy through Law (2005), 'On the Compatibility of the Existing Legislation in Montenegro Concerning the Organization of Referendums with Applicable International Standards', *Opinion no. 343 / 2005*.

Gaudreault-Desbiens, J.-F. (1999), 'The Quebec Secession Reference and the Judicial Arbitration of Conflicting Narratives about Law, Democracy, and Identity', *Vermont Law Review* 23: 793–843.

Hayden, R. (1999), *Blueprints for a House Divided: The Constitutional Logic of the Yugoslav Conflicts* (Ann Arbor, MI: University of Michigan Press).

Hogg, P.W. (1997), 'Principles Governing Secession of Quebec', *National Journal of Constitutional Law* 8, 19–76.
Lajčák, M. (2006), 'Serbia and Montenegro after the Referendum', *Südosteuropa Mitteilungen* 4, 6–11.
Mancini, S. (2008), 'Rethinking the Boundaries of Democratic Secession: Liberalism, Nationalism, and the Right of Minorities to Self-determination', *International Journal of Constitutional Law* 6, 553–84.
McRoberts, K. (1997), *Misconceiving Canada: The Struggle for National Unity* (Oxford and New York: Oxford University Press).
McRoberts, K. (2001), 'Canada and the Multinational State', *Canadian Journal of Political Science* 34:4, 683–713.
Monahan, P.J. (1997), 'The Canadian Constitution in the 21st Century', *National Journal of Constitutional Law* 8, 133–47.
National Assembly of Quebec (1995), Bill 1, 'An Act Respecting the Future of Québec'. [Online] At http://www.sfu.ca/~aheard/bill1.html [accessed 20 October 2009].
National Assembly of Quebec (2000), Bill 99, 'An Act Respecting the Exercise of the Fundamental Rights and Prerogatives of the Québec People and the Québec State'. [Online] At www2.publicationsduquebec.gouv.qc.ca, home site [accessed 23 October 2009].
Oliver, P. (1999), 'Canada, Quebec, and Constitutional Amendment', *University of Toronto Law Journal* 49, 519–610.
Paulsen, M. (2004), 'The Constitution of Necessity', *Notre Dame Law Review* 79, 1257–96.
Ramušović, A. (2006), 'Serbia and Montenegro: The Arithmetic of Secession', *Transitions Online*, 7 March, 1, www.tol.org (home page) [accessed 2 November 2009].
Reference re. Secession of Quebec, [1998] 2 S.C.R. 217.
Russell, P. (2004), *Constitutional Odyssey: Can Canadians Become a Sovereign People?* (Toronto, ON and Buffalo, NY, London: University of Toronto Press).
Smerdel, B. (2007), *Primjena federalno gnačela i pouke ustavne reforme 1971* (Zagreb: Centar Za Demokraciju i Pravo 'MikoTripalo').
Walters, M.D. (1999), 'Nationalism and the Pathology of Legal Systems: Considering the Quebec Secession Reference and Its Lessons for the United Kingdom', *The Modern Law Review* 62:3, 371–96.
Watts, R.E. et al. (2002), *Ustavno preuređenje Savezne Republike Jugoslavije* (Beograd: Centar za liberalno-demokratske studije).
Webber, J. (1997), 'The Legality of a Unilateral Declaration of Independence under Canadian Law', *McGill Law Journal* 42, 281–318.

# Secession as a Way of Dissolving Federations: The USSR and Yugoslavia

Richard Sakwa and Aleksandar Pavković[1]

## The USSR

All three communist federations disintegrated, but each did so in its own way. Czechoslovakia was peacefully divided in 1992 into its two constituent units (see Part VI), while Yugoslavia's dissolution was accompanied by war and bitter interethnic conflict (see below). The case of the disintegration of the Union of Soviet Socialist Republics (USSR) in 1991 falls somewhere in between, with some violence, notably in the Baltic republics and the south Caucasus, but overall the process was remarkably devoid of large-scale conflict. The secession process in the first instance took place cleanly along the lines of the already constituted sub-national sovereign legal entities, a process in which all the union republics participated with greater or lesser enthusiasm. In the long term, however, the formal dissolution of the USSR in December 1991 was the easy part. In the Caucasus and Moldova the disappearance of the USSR provoked a number of secessions within secessions in which what had been sub-sub-national territories (notably Abkhazia, South Ossetia, Nagorno-Karabakh and Transdniestria) sought to break away from the newly-established independent states (see Part VI). While the legal framework for the independence of union republics was relatively clear, the emergence of secessionist movements provoked entrenched conflicts that assumed a 'frozen' character until the recognition of the independence of Kosovo in February 2008, and following the Russo-Georgian war of August 2008, that of Abkhazia and South Ossetia (see Chapter 9). As with the peculiar status of the Turkish Republic of Northern Cyprus, whose declaration of independence on 15 November 1983 was recognized only by Turkey, this second wave of post-Soviet secessions entered uncharted legal and constitutional territory (see Chapter 15 and Part VI).

---

1   Richard Sakwa is the author of the section of this chapter on the USSR; Aleksandar Pavković is the author of the section on Yugoslavia.

## The Soviet Union and Its Progeny

The experience of secession in the Soviet case is distinctive in a number of respects. First, the nature of the host state from which secession was achieved remains a matter of considerable debate. The USSR was created in December 1922 as the apparently voluntary union of four original union republics: the Russian Soviet Federative Socialist Republic (RSFSR), Belorussia, Ukraine and the Transcaucasian Federation of Armenia, Azerbaijan and Georgia, which later became union republics in their own right. Union republics retained the constitutional right to secede, something once again recognized in the USSR's last constitution adopted in 1977 and formalized starkly in Article 69 of the Russian constitution: 'The RSFSR has the right freely to leave the USSR' (Konstitutsiya 1989). By the time the USSR disintegrated in 1991 there were 15 union republics, four of which represented territorial conquest during World War Two: the Baltic republics of Estonia, Latvia and Lithuania, and Moldavia (carved out of Bessarabia and North Bukovina). These four can be considered 'colonies' in some sense, but for the other 11 such a designation would be misleading. The characterization of the USSR as an empire, although appropriate in some abstract conceptual sense while recalling the overlapping sovereignties of medieval empires, would be at best partial if applied in the stronger colonial meaning of the term (Beissinger 1995). Even for the four republics seized by Soviet arms, their incorporation into the USSR did not entail the establishment of a simple exploitative model and instead membership in the USSR extended to them the communist developmental model, with all of its achievements and drawbacks.

Second, the political character of the host state is no less complex. The first Soviet constitution of January 1924 entrenched a type of ethno-federalism that guaranteed certain legal rights to a hierarchy of constituent entities, with union republics at the top that formally retained a degree of sovereignty, followed by autonomous republics, autonomous *oblasts*, and then ordinary units (*oblast* and *krai*). However, from the very first the governing and only party, the Communist Party of the Soviet Union (CPSU), was a firmly unitary entity, and thus was superimposed over the federal system as some sort of 'virtual' sixteenth republic, a whole apparatus of governance that lacked a territorial base. This was a distinctive type of governmentality that generated a whole pathology of double identities and deceptions, with power both alienated and distant while reaching into the very souls of its citizens. The supra-territorial aspect was pointedly emphasized by depriving the RSFSR, the largest republic by far, of its own communist party and certain other attributes of statehood, such as an academy of sciences and its own security services, established in the 14 other union republics.

The tension between the virtual 'communist' republic and the real physical entities became increasingly intolerable for all as Mikhail Gorbachev's *perestroika* (restructuring) of the Soviet system, launched in 1985, became increasingly radical, accompanied by the delegitimation of the communist system in its entirety. Thus the original dynamic of secession had more of a political than a national character, designed to achieve the dissolution of the communist order and not in the first instance the disintegration of the country. It is the mismanagement of this process by the Gorbachev leadership that from 1989 transformed a dissolution agenda, designed to destroy the powers of the communist virtual sixteenth republic, into a genuine territorial secessionist process. In the absence of the unitary glue of the CPSU, Gorbachev hoped to transform the USSR into a genuinely voluntary confederation of sovereign states through the negotiation of a new union treaty, but in the end these attempts failed and dissolution of the communist system was soon followed by the disintegration of the USSR.

The third feature focuses on the nature of the secessionist movements. Here we need to recognize that in each of the union republics the situation was different. In the Baltic republics the reformist communist leaderships elected from 1988 sought at first to participate in the renewal of the Soviet political system, but very soon their aspirations were radicalized as a result of the various blockages on reform at the federal level. With remarkable speed secessionist movements, encompassing the new communist leaderships all the way to extremist nationalist groups, advanced radical plans for separation from the USSR. Only Sweden and a few other states had formally recognized the annexation of the Baltic republics after World War Two, and thus their independence can be seen as the restoration of a prior legal order. In Moldova the issue was complicated by aspirations of some of the secessionists to unite with Romania, an idea that provoked the secession of Transdniestria, a territory strung along the left bank of the Dniester, from Moldova.

In the south Caucasus the three republics had enjoyed independence between 1918 and their reincorporation in 1920–21 into Soviet Russia, but now their renewed independence was accompanied by internal disintegration (with Adzharia, Abkhazia and South Ossetia effectively splitting away from the radical nationalist Georgian state), and inter-state conflict between Armenia and Azerbaijan over the Armenian-populated enclave of Nagorno-Karabakh. In the five Central Asian republics (Kazakhstan, Kyrgyzstan, Tajikistan, Turkmenistan and Uzbekistan) secessionist movements were lacking, in large part because of the subsidies and other sources of support from Moscow. This is not to deny the profound nation-building process that had taken place within the framework of Soviet nationality policy (Suny 2002). Out of a largely clan-based entity, for example, Turkmen leaders had exploited opportunities within the Soviet framework to forge a new nation that welcomed the chance to become a sovereign state in 1991 (Edgar 2004). Independence had not been sought, however, and in those chaotic months of 1991 the Soviet Union effectively left them: secession was achieved without the instrumentality of a secessionist movement. This also applies in large part to Belarus, where secessionist sentiments were minimal. However, in Ukraine secessionism, which in 1988 was limited to émigré intellectuals and Galicia (incorporated from Poland in 1945), swiftly gained traction following the attempted conservative coup in Moscow in August 1991. Ukrainian secession in 1991 reflected less a national narrative of statehood but was in large part a response to the immediate political needs of the political elite. The myth of the ineluctable necessity of Ukrainian statehood only came later (Beissinger 2002).

The relative weakness of secessionist sentiments, until stimulated by the crises of the regime and the state from August 1991, is reflected in the outcome of Gorbachev's appeal to the people over the heads of the fractious elites. The USSR referendum of 17 March 1991 confirmed that the majority of the electorate favoured the preservation of the Soviet Union 'as a renewed federation of equal sovereign republics', with an 80 percent turnout of the 184 million registered electors in which 76.4 percent voted in favour. Although the question was multifaceted, and modified in some republics, accompanied by additional questions in others, and blocked altogether in Armenia, Estonia, Georgia, Latvia, Lithuania and Moldova, the vote seemed to endorse Gorbachev's view that the USSR was a viable political community. In Russia 71 percent voted to preserve the union on a 75 percent turnout, although the vote in support was higher in the autonomous republics revealing greater fear of Russia than the union authorities. Even in Ukraine 70 percent voted in favour, but this was as nothing compared to the 98 percent in favour of the union in Turkmenistan (Walker 2003: 117–18).

The fourth and final feature concerns the response of the Soviet authorities. Gorbachev's initial reaction was bewilderment that the 'nationalities question' had re-emerged, since as late as 1986 the twenty-sixth party congress had asserted that the problem had, 'in the main', been resolved. This gave way to attempts to incorporate separatist aspirations, which initially, as we have seen, fell short of secession, into a revised union. However, once a new constituent treaty was mooted, the Baltic republics wanted out, and even the remaining 12 could find no adequate basis for agreement. Ultimately five drafts of a new union treaty were proposed, each granting more rights to the republics in what by the end was planned to be a confederal post-communist Union of Sovereign States (USS).[2] The final one, of 14 November 1991, conceded yet more powers to the union republics while retaining some central institutions such as a directly elected president and a bicameral legislature, but even this was too much for Ukraine. Without Ukraine the renewed union was considered pointless, and by this stage Russia had also lost faith in the renewal process. On 7–8 December 1991 the leaders of Russia, Ukraine and Belarus met to discuss the future of the union in a hunting lodge in the Belovezh Pushcha nature reserve in western Belarus. Since the three countries were original signatories in December 1922, they claimed the right to dissolve what they had previously formed, and in place of the USSR they created the Commonwealth of Independent States (CIS), joined two weeks later by all the other republics except Georgia and the Baltic republics. According to the Soviet constitution the only way that a republic could secede was by referendum, but this was ignored. Russia was impatient to free itself of Soviet tutelage in general and Gorbachev's leadership in particular, but this act of legal nihilism instituted a tradition that remains to this day.

While trying to renew the union, Gorbachev also pursued three other strategies. The first was to create a legal framework for secession. Although the right had

---

2   The five Union Treaties were published in *Izvestiya*: 24 November 1990; 9 March, 27 June, 15 August and 25 November 1991.

been granted by the constitution, no practical mechanism existed to manage the process. A new law of 3 April 1990 now provided a detailed and extremely onerous procedure, including the need for a referendum and some other detailed stipulations including a five-year transition period, that in effect rendered the legislation a 'law on non-secession'. The second was the attempt to define the precise powers of the federal centre and the republics, and thus to obviate the need for independence. The landmark law of 26 April 1990 sought in laborious detail to delineate the powers of the federal government and the union republics but its effect was only to exacerbate tensions between the union republics and the autonomous republics within them, while reinforcing the perception that secession would be prevented at almost any cost (Walker 2003: 74–5). To pre-empt the gate coming down on their aspirations, on 11 March 1990 Lithuania declared independence.

The third element was to raise the penalty threshold for major putative secessionist states. This Gorbachev did by diluting what had hitherto been the jealously guarded prerogative of union republics, and encouraged sub-sub-national separatism by suggesting that the autonomous republics could be granted the right to join the new union treaty as signatories in their own right. This stimulated a wave of separatism within Russia, against whom the measure was designed, and in particular in Tatarstan and Chechnya, in the vanguard of movements seeking greater sovereignty. Chechen separatists under Johar Dudaev continued to insist right up to his death in 1995 that Chechnya would be happy to remain a member of the redesigned Soviet Union but not of Russia, a possibility opened up by Gorbachev's constitutional innovations which, in political terms, turned out to be an impossibility. Gorbachev's attempt to outflank the Russian leadership would leave a terrible legacy as Russia tried to avoid going the way of the USSR. The struggle for Russian territorial integrity would be the dominant motif of its early years of independence, as it remains for Azerbaijan, Georgia and Moldova, and even in Uzbekistan the autonomous Karakalpak republic jealously defends its historical prerogatives.

## Secessionist Dynamics

Most third world federations remain intact because of the authoritarian practices of their central leaderships, but this is a highly inefficient mode of governance. Of the 44 federations created in the third world, 27 have broken apart or become fully centralized unitary states. Even in countries where federalism has sunk deep roots, as in Malaysia and Nigeria, it has assumed centralized forms (Mawhood 1984: 521). Democratizing federations find themselves in a particularly parlous situation, and in the Soviet case provoked the disintegration of the state (Hale 2004; Horowitz 1993).

Randall Collins' geopolitical theory offered a theoretical approach to the Soviet system that allowed him to predict the disintegration of the state. It focuses on three inter-related factors: size and resource advantage (size of the economy and the population); positional advantage (number and attitude of neighbours); and internal state fragmentation. Associated factors included stalemate between the great powers and imperial overextension. Collins argued that the 'Russian empire' (his term for the Soviet Union) suffered from critical structural weaknesses and predicted that 'in the long-term future Russia will fragment into successively smaller states' (Collins 1986: 196). By the 1980s the USSR was suffering declining economic growth rates, a growing burden of defence spending, and a general cultural and demographic malaise accompanied by the subjective appreciation, admitted by Gorbachev, that the political system was becoming increasingly dysfunctional.

What the country was not suffering from, however, was nationalist mobilization or any but very marginal separatist sentiments. Inter-ethnic tensions certainly existed, but on the whole in cultural terms a 'Soviet people' had been created; but the crucial point is that in political terms this was given weak representation and was fragmented. A 'Soviet' nation had not come into being, and the option of identifying oneself as 'Soviet', unlike the availability of a 'Yugoslav' identifier in that Balkan multinational federation, was not even offered in Soviet census returns. The notorious 'point 5' in the Soviet passport stated the holder's nationality, which perpetuated and indeed intensified national identification, and thus weakened the Soviet supranational identity. Nationalism as such, however, was a product rather than the cause of the Soviet disintegration.

The Soviet disintegration was a product of a triple process. The first could be labelled the 'decolonization' model, and this applies primarily to the Baltic republics, Moldova and to a degree to the south Caucasus (and the Galician part of Ukraine should certainly be included in this list). Here we have territories that were effectively forcibly reincorporated into the Soviet Union, although most have a long relationship with the Russian empire. Georgia, for example, joined the Russian empire in 1801 as a way of protecting itself from Ottoman and Persian threats, while the Baltic republics had been within the Russian sphere for several centuries. As part of the Russian and Soviet system these territories had maintained their own cultural identities, including their languages and festivals. Inevitably there had been a natural process of Russianization, although forced Russification was the exception rather than the rule.

The titular nations in Estonia and Latvia, however, felt increasingly threatened by the influx of Slavic workers employed in their burgeoning manufacturing industries and military establishments. The demographic balance had changed to the point that non-Latvians comprised nearly half the population by 1991. In political terms, however, the communist parties in these republics, although part of a unitary system, were able to give voice to republic concerns. The memory of the Soviet occupation in 1940 and the Stalinist deportations following 1945, however, continued to rankle, but during the long period of Brezhnevite stability from 1964 political repression was no more intense here than in any other Soviet republic. Neither was economic exploitation any different than throughout the Soviet union; and indeed standards of living in the Baltic republics were much higher than in Russia. This was a very peculiar 'empire', in which the peripheries (except in Central Asia) were more economically developed and prosperous than the alleged 'core' (Suny 1993). On 18 November 1988 the Estonian Supreme Soviet adopted a

Declaration affirming the sovereignty of the republic, and thus launched what in due course would become a 'parade of sovereignties' that in the end turned into a 'war of the laws' and the disintegration of the union.

The second process can be called the 'affirmation' model, which primarily concerns Russia. In effect, Russia seceded from the state that nationalists in non-Russian republics accused Russia of dominating. Since the 1960s there had been a growing Russian national awareness that the Soviet Union was not the best framework to advance Russia's specific national interests. Not only did it lack some of the political and social institutions present in the other republics, but there was also a sense that Russia was shouldering a disproportionate share of the burden of the Soviet enterprise, and was getting an unfair share in return (Brudny 1999). Russia felt that it was subsidising the other republics, and only gained opprobrium in return. Alexander Solzhenitsyn led the calls for Russia to shed the imperial burden and to focus on its own cultural and national development. On his election to chair the Russian Congress of People's Deputies (the new-style parliament) in May 1989 Boris Yeltsin gave expression to these sentiments, exacerbated by his personal conflict with Gorbachev. Russia issued its own declaration about state sovereignty on 12 June 1990, followed in rapid succession by Ukraine and other republics; and as we have seen it was Russia that declared the Soviet Union defunct in December 1991.

Ukraine is the second main case of the affirmation model. Here a number of specific grievances came together to fuel the explosive rise of a powerful secessionist movement, which the former communist leadership (embarrassed by its failure to condemn the 1991 August coup in time) came to head. The Ukrainian language had indeed been squeezed out by Russian, with few schools teaching the language and higher education entirely Russianized. The famine of 1932–33 (*golodomor*, in Ukrainian *holodomor*) was interpreted by nationalists as a deliberate Stalinist policy of anti-Ukrainian genocide, although Russian regions in the Kuban and lower Volga suffered as much. In economic terms there had long been a struggle between investment in Siberia and Ukraine, and in broad terms Ukraine had won out (the lack of a Russian communist party was a factor here), provoking Siberian regional separatism after 1991. Above all, the Cossack tradition and memories of Ukrainian statehood before unification with Russia in 1654 and during the Russian civil war of 1918–20 fostered a powerful sense of nationhood. Whether this required independent statehood is another issue: western Ukraine, with its distinctive religious tradition (the Uniates) certainly thought it did; whereas the Donbas to this day retains close cultural ties and economic affiliations with Russia.

The third model is 'secession by default'. This encompasses those countries which effectively had secession thrust upon them in the course of the Soviet disintegration. This includes Belarus, which shares a close cultural connection with Russia. The election of the anti-nationalist Alexander Lukashenko in 1994 reflected the ambivalence of Belarusan statehood; but once in power the entrenched national elites, despite much talk of creating a common state with Russia, were not willing to sacrifice their unexpected statehood. The Central Asian states had been latecomers to the Russian empire and resisted Bolshevik modernization plans, and had suffered terribly from Stalinist collectivization, but by the 1990s the Soviet

Union offered them a comfortable framework for modernization and membership of a world civilization. Corruption in the republics was tolerated in exchange for loyalty in the Brezhnev years, and Gorbachev's anti-corruption campaigns were an affront to national pride. There were no secessionist movements here, and instead communist leaders simply rebranded themselves as national elites and continued to rule as before, sans supervision from Moscow. Only in Kyrgyzstan was there some circulation of elites, but even here the newcomers soon succumbed to the clan politics and crony capitalism prevalent in the region.

## Post-Communist Secessionism

There is a large literature devoted to the question of whether Russia will disintegrate in a manner reminiscent of the Soviet collapse. One major difference is the demographic balance. Whereas ethnic Russians comprised just over half the population of the USSR, they now make up 80 percent of the Russian Federation. The nature of the state also differs. Whereas the USSR was a *treaty* federation, in which the contracting parties retained the right to secede, Russia is a *constitutional* federation, where its members are considered to be part of a pre-existing political entity and have no constitutional right to secede.

There are some similarities, however. Above all, the peculiar type of 'matrëshka federalism', formalized by the 1924 constitution, remains, based on a hierarchy of ethno-federal units. The American model of federalism, where ethnicity does not define any of the federal components, is an attractive model for many in Russia, where the ethnic republics act as a standing reproach to the view that ethnicity should be an individual attribute and not given political form in sub-national state construction. However, the logic of path dependency means that it would take a revolution to repudiate the federal representation of ethnicity, and despite attempts to foster a civic Russian nationalism, notably in the advocacy of the neutral term '*Rossiyanin*' (as opposed to the ethnic signifier *Russkii*) in the Yeltsin years, the political identity of titular ethnic groups remains as strong as ever.

This is particularly in evidence in the Caucasus. The attempt to push the boundaries of the 'Grotian moment', when state sovereignty is up for grabs, to encompass former autonomous (rather than union) entities to include Chechnya, South Ossetia and Abkhazia engendered prolonged confrontation that at times turned into outright war (see also Part VI). The logical problem of differentiating between peoples that the Soviet system decided had matured enough for statehood and those that had not (notably, Tatarstan and Abkhazia) in the early 1990s provoked a 'parade of sovereignties' that in the Chechen and Abkhaz cases turned into outright declarations of independence. It was clear that the Soviet Union had been far from a 'melting pot' of nations or even a historic union of peoples, but the post-Soviet states were no less challenged to define their national character and state identity (Sukhov 2007). In the Russian case a Federative Treaty in March 1992 stabilized the situation by granting extensive powers to what had become

21 sub-national republics and the other 'subject of the federation', in exchange for unity and loyalty (a deal refused by Chechnya and Tatarstan).

This principle was entrenched in the December 1993 constitution, although the sub-national units were deprived of even the formal entitlement to sovereignty. Different interpretations of sovereignty remained, however, with a type of relative sovereignty still prevalent in Russian debates whereas most other post-Soviet republics adopted the stronger Western definition focused on the pre-eminence of a single authoritative state (Deyermond 2007). In the 1990s Russian regionalism took a segmented form, where both the centre and the federal subjects engaged in mutually exclusive power accumulation strategies that rendered the system highly asymmetrical (Stepan 2000). The 'new federalism' under Vladimir Putin from 2000 sought to equalize federal imbalances and to overcome segmentation, but the centralization drive threatened federalism in its entirety. The abolition of gubernatorial elections in 2004 signified the consolidation of the 'power vertical' but the principle of federalism was not repudiated, although unitary practices increasingly jeopardized its operation.

The cases of post-Soviet separatism challenge existing practices of regulating sub-national conflicts but above all raise the question about whether secession really is the best option when peoples cannot or will not coexist within a single state. There is, moreover, no internationally-recognized mechanism to decide what would be the optimal option in any given case, and thus brute force and geopolitical expediency tends to govern the process of state formation (see Chapter 1). This certainly applies to Kosovan independence, as it does to Abkhazia and South Ossetia. The tension between the opposed UN principles of territorial integrity and national self-determination is endemic and there is no universal mechanism to reconcile the two (see Chapter 17). The vast majority of the 6,000-odd cultural-linguistic groups on the planet have no territorial recognition as states and thus no voice in international affairs, and yet decolonization and the disintegration of the Soviet Union and the Soviet bloc accelerated state formation in a process that is not yet over.

The differences between republics are significant, since Chechnya was formally part of a federal system and thus its claim to self-determination stopping short of independence could be encompassed by Russia's ethno-federal system. Following two terrible wars (1994–96, and 1999–2011) Chechnya under the leadership of Ramzan Kadyrov (in March 2007 he formally assumed the presidency) was granted extensive autonomy to manage its own affairs. This, however, was less an example of the asymmetrical federalism that has characterized Russian politics since independence in 1991 than a case of the extreme segmentation that in certain respects repudiates the fundamental federal principle of power-sharing. Nevertheless, by the time the 'counter-terrorist operation', as the second war was called, was formally ended on 16 April 2009 Chechnya had been brought back into the Russian political sphere, although its subordination to constitutionalism was rather more in doubt. While the secessionist *movement* had been defeated, this was at the cost of consolidating a potentially separatist *leadership* (on Chechnya see Part VI).

In Georgia matters had an opposed dynamic. The republic was proclaimed a unitary state in 1990, which immediately provoked the counter-mobilization of threatened minorities (Coppieters and Levgold 2005). Both Abkhazia and South Ossetia declared their independence and following various wars emerged as *de facto* independent states. They were recognized as such by Russia on 26 August 2008, although few other countries followed suit. The two republics appealed to a long history of separate political identity from Georgia as well as discrimination (just cause in the just war tradition) to bolster their claims to independence (Coppieters and Sakwa 2003).

At the heart of the post-Soviet secession struggles lies the question of just cause; that is, the prevention or remedying of injustices (see Chapters 4 and 23 for a discussion of the remedial theories). Whereas the normative framework of the Soviet disintegration lay in the sphere of constitutionalism, after 1991 sub-national separatist claims could only be justified by devising arguments based on political practices and mythologized national narratives. Even where elements of just cause could be demonstrated, moreover, separatist or secessionist movements are constrained by a set of other considerations, notably 'right intentions' (i.e. motives consistent with just cause), proportionality in methods, and the recourse to violence only as a last resort (Coppieters 2003). No less important are the dynamics of ethnic secession, with Horowitz's model of interest-based interactions inadequate in most dimensions when applied to post-Soviet cases (Laitin 2007).

The well-known claim about the 'artificiality' of the Soviet borders applies equally to the attempt by Nagorno-Karabakh to secede from Azerbaijan, to which it was given by Stalin's personal decision, and to join Armenia. It also applies to Transdniestria, a thin sliver of land on the west bank of the Dniester that was an autonomous republic of interwar Ukraine but which was attached to the new republic of Moldavia (carved out of Romanian territory) after World War Two. It could equally apply to the Crimea, which was transferred from Russian to Ukrainian jurisdiction in 1954, in large part based on economic considerations although the date was chosen to celebrate the three hundredth anniversary of the union of the two countries. Every post-Soviet republic (like most African states) could be accused of artificiality, and throughout the region populations remain mixed. The 1989 census, for example, revealed that of the 44.2 million Ukrainians in the USSR, only 37.4 million lived in Ukraine and Russia was host to 3.7 million. The figure would undoubtedly be higher if Stalin had not ordered that Ukrainian be replaced by Russian in the Kuban's schools in 1934, and the Ukrainian accent remains prevalent in south Russia.

As in the case of Kosovo, the language of the right of a nation to 'self-determination' is avoided in post-Soviet conflicts (Muharremi 2008). When discourse over the protection of national minorities is exhausted, historical and remedial arguments take precedence (Osipov 1997). The problem in the post-Soviet area as elsewhere is that there are endless problems of minorities within minorities, provoking a possible cascade of secessionist conflicts whose peaceful resolution is almost impossible. The former administrative borders of federal states were the primary line of division, representing three-quarters of all the borders in the region. For the minorities within the new republics, secession is only one possible form of self-determination. Federal solutions are usually posited as a way of combining minority rights with political representation; and in extreme cases, as in Georgia before 2008, the confederal option was probably the only way in which the integrity of the old union republic could have been maintained. In Estonia, however, talk in the early 1990s of the secession of the predominantly ethnic Russian Narva area has largely disappeared. The idea of the pre-emptive revision of borders holds little attraction; but delay sometimes leads to their forcible change, accompanied typically by ethnic cleansing. Cosmopolitan solutions that call for transparent borders as part of larger transnational communities are something yet to be achieved in the region.

# Yugoslavia

## Yugoslavia: A Departure from the Soviet Model

The Yugoslav federation was created in 1946, on the model of the USSR, following the Yugoslav Communist Party's victory in a multi-faceted civil war. Its first constitution of 1946 recognized five constituent nations (Serbs, Croats, Slovenes, Montenegrins and Macedonians), created six federal units (republics) to 'house' each of them and two sub-federal units – the province of Vojvodina (a plurality of Hungarians) and the region of Kosovo-Metohija (a majority of Albanians) both within the republic of Serbia. According to the constitution's preamble (retained verbatim in the last 1974 constitution of the Socialist Federal Republic of Yugoslavia, SFRY), these constituent nations ('peoples') created Yugoslavia as their common state, by exercising their right of self-determination ('including the right of secession'). Having thus exercised it, the preamble seemed to imply, they cannot exercise it again in some different way: unlike the USSR constitution, the SFRY constitution(s) provided no room for the exercise of the right of secession. Hence, the secessions of several republics and of the province of Kosovo in the 1990s followed no constitutional script of the communist federation (see also Chapter 7 and Radan 2001b).

Following the expulsion in 1948 of the Yugoslav Communist Party from the Soviet-controlled organization of Communist parties, the Yugoslav Communist party, in opposition to the Soviet Party and its ideology, developed its own ideology of socialist self-management as a Marxist project of the 'withering away of the state' (Jović 2008) and, accordingly, decentralized both the Party and the state to the level of the federal and sub-federal units. The constitution of 1974 established the collective presidency as the highest organ of the state in which a single representative of each republic and province had a veto (this could be overridden only by the president for life, Tito). The competencies of the federal state were limited to defence, foreign affairs, customs and monetary policy. Each republic (but not the provinces) had full control over its security service, its police forces as well as the second-tier territorial (reservist) defence units which, in their full mobilizational strength, were several times larger than the first-line defence force, the federal Yugoslav People's Army (YPA). In the early 1990s, the secessionist governments in several republics used this territorial armed force to gain military control over the territory contested, initially, by the YPA.

From 1945 until his death in 1980, Josip Broz,[3] nicknamed Tito, ruled the country through a network of personally loyal communist cadres who held top positions in federal and sub-federal units. From the 1960s onwards his hand-picked Party leaders were allowed to build-up their political power base within each federal unit by mobilizing the national group which they allegedly represented. By the early 1970s, elite politics in the SFRY increasingly took the form of bargaining among the leaders of the six constituent nations and the largest national minorities in which Tito was the final arbiter. After his death in 1980, the constitutional set-up prevented the emergence of any replacement for him. At that point this elite bargaining system became exposed to two complementary threats – a possible recentralization of the SFRY or secession of any federal unit(s). As we shall see, it was the threat of recentralization in the late 1980s, that triggered the secessions first from the Party in 1990 and then from the federation in 1991.

## Challenges to the Bargaining System

By the mid-1970s SFRY carried a relatively large debt to Western creditors which, due to a worsening economic situation in the West, it proved unable to repay on time. Partly as a result of this, the standard of living rapidly decreased while unemployment shot up to unprecedented heights, leading to an exponential increase in the number of industrial strikes as well as mass protests demanding the alleviation of economic hardship (Woodward 1995: 51–72). The issue of the macro-management of the economy, in particular foreign debt, split the collective leadership – leaders of Serbia and Montenegro called for a re-centralization of economic policy management while the leaders of Slovenia resisted any reform of the existing system. Faced with a prolonged crisis, Communist leaders of the federal units sought to broaden their support in the population beyond the existing Communist cadre patronage network. For this purpose the nationalist dissidents (see below) had already provided the most useful discourse: in each republic, except in the nationally divided Bosnia and Herzegovina, the Communist leaders appropriated the nationalist discourse while allowing for the creation of new political parties (Jović 2008).

---

3   Born in Croatia in 1882 (which was then a part of Austria-Hungary) of mixed Croat and Slovene background, Josip Broz trained as a turner-fitter and, as a corporal in the Austrian army, fought in World War One in Serbia and Russia; in captivity in Russia he was converted to the Communist cause.

## Nationalist Dissidents and Their Take-over of Power

The dismantling of the federal security apparatus in the mid-1960s was followed by a flourishing of dissident views which challenged the Communist ideology in Slovenia, Croatia and Serbia. Apart from liberalism and neo-Marxism, nationalism, dating from the 19th century, came to inspire this 'critical intelligentzia' (Dragović-Soso 2002). Serb nationalist dissidents sought the recentralization of the Yugoslav state as a remedy to the fragmentation of the Serb nation into four Yugoslav federal units (Dragović-Soso 2002). All nationalists contested the Communist-imposed federal boundaries; the Serb dissidents in particular advocated the unification of the Serb-populated territories in Croatia, Bosnia and Herzegovina and Montenegro with Serbia while the same territories were also claimed by the Croat, Bosnian Muslim and (later) Montenegrin nationalists as their own homelands. This contest of dissident nationalist blueprints of territorial borders anticipated the violent conflict over these territories which erupted in the 1990s (Pavković 1997).

In the late 1980s nationalist dissidents in all republics started to organize anti-communist political parties which in the early 1990s took power in most federal units of Yugoslavia. Thus within two decades nationalist intellectuals in all republics (except Montenegro) transformed themselves from dissidents into political leaders.[4] In Croatia, Slovenia and Bosnia and Herzegovina – but not in Serbia and Montenegro – former dissident nationalists succeeded in taking over power and seceding their federal units from the SFRY.

But before their take-over, the Communist party that created this federation had itself dissolved: in January 1990 its extraordinary Congress abruptly ended as the delegations of Slovenia and Croatia, refusing to accept the majority's decision to recentralize the party, walked out of the Congress (Jović 2008); thus ended the only mass party which at that time advocated a common Yugoslav state.

## An Early Attempt at Secession: Kosovo from Serbia

In addition to the economic crisis mentioned above, the SFRY collective presidency faced a prolonged secessionist crisis: in April 1981, a year after Tito's death, large scale demonstrations by Kosovo Albanians – amounting to a popular uprising – erupted in the capital of Kosovo and several other cities. A prominent demand of the demonstrators was 'Kosovo – republic', that is, the secession of Kosovo from the federal republic of Serbia and the establishment of Kosovo as a federal unit. But the systematic purge of the Kosovo Party organization, replacement of the veteran Kosovo Albanian leaders with a younger generation, and the jailing of thousands of secessionist supporters, did not stop sporadic demonstrations with the same demand and a continuing emigration of the non-Albanian, primarily

---

4   Former nationalist dissidents Dr Franjo Tudjman, Dobrica Ćosić and Alija Izetbegović became presidents, respectively, of Croatia, Serbia/Montenegro and Bosnia and Herzegovina.

Serb, population from Kosovo. In 1987 the Serbs in Kosovo started their own mass protests against the violence and intimidation perpetrated by Kosovo Albanians. Belgrade intellectual dissidents and a few media outlets took up their cause and, partly as a result, their initial demand for protection from violence was transformed to a demand for the re-integration of Kosovo into Serbia and curtailment of the powers of the Kosovo Albanian political elite.

The mass protest of a Serb minority offered an unprecedented opportunity for mass mobilization of the largest national group in Yugoslavia, the Serbs, not only in support of the centralization of Serbia but of the whole Yugoslavia. From October 1987 the then president of the collective presidency of the Communist Party of Serbia, Slobodan Milošević, launched a campaign of mass rallies and media saturation in support of his programme of recentralization of Serbia and Yugoslavia. For this purpose, he appropriated the discourse of the nationalist dissident tract, the leaked *Memorandum of the Serbian Academy of Sciences*, which only the year before he had denounced as a counter-revolutionary pamphlet (Dragović-Soso 2002). In response to this threat of recentralization of the federation, the Slovenian communist leaders embarked on mass mobilization in support of their programme of the 'disassociation' of Slovenia from the federation.

The cycle of secessionist and counter-secessionist mass mobilization started in the SFRY earlier than in the USSR and took a somewhat different path: it was the secessionist movement in a sub-federal unit (Kosovo) that from 1981 triggered repressive counter-secessionist policies in this unit and a demand for recentralization of the federation from the political leaders of the largest federal unit, Serbia. This in turn triggered a counter-recentralization mobilization in the economically most developed republic, Slovenia, which eventually grew into a broad-based secessionist movement. In contrast, the secessionist mobilization in the Baltic republics of the USSR did not result in any counter-secessionist mass mobilization in support of recentralization of the state (nor, of course, in any counter-recentralizing mobilization).

## Secessionist Movements[5]

As in other communist federations such as the USSR and Czechoslovakia, secessionist movements in Yugoslavia grew out of nationalist dissident groups which, following the introduction of the multi-party political system, formed political parties. But as in the USSR (see the first part of this chapter), mobilization for secession was highly uneven: in some federal and sub-federal units populations were mobilized earlier than others and in some support for secession was more widespread than in others.

*Kosovo*, the poorest region of SFR Yugoslavia, had a GDP per capita half of the most advanced republic, Slovenia, and an unemployment rate around 30 percent. Unlike the constituent nations of the SFRY, Albanians are not Slavs and most of

---

5   The following two sections are based on Pavković (2000b), chapters 4–10.

them are Muslim (in contrast to Serbs who are Eastern Orthodox). In medieval times it was the centre of the Serbian kingdom which was in 1389 incorporated into the Ottoman empire; the Ottoman empire ceded it to Serbia as a result of the first Balkan war in 1912. The Albanian population resisted the Serbian take-over and had periodically rebelled against the Serbian/Yugoslav state (in 1918, 1944 and 1998) (Pavković 2000b) (see also Chapter 9).

From 1981 to 1989 numerous clandestine Kosovo Albanian irredentist/ secessionist groups organized political demonstrations; however, in 1989 they were superseded by a mass secessionist political party, the League for Democratic Kosovo (LDK), formed by Kosovo Albanian ex-communist cadres and intelligentsia and led by an ex-communist academic, Dr Ibrahim Rugova who later became the first elected president of Kosovo. The LDK significantly differed from all other secessionist parties in the SFRY in that first, throughout the secessionist conflict it rejected (at least in its proclamations) the use of violence and attempted to achieve its political goals by non-violent means; second, it was an ideologically inclusive party, modelled on the Polish Solidarity movement and had, as a result, the overwhelming support of the Kosovo Albanians, relegating all other Kosovo Albanian parties to political insignificance.

*Slovenia* was economically the most developed region of SFRY whose population, speaking a distinct language, Slovenian, is overwhelmingly Roman Catholic. Already in 1988 the Communist Party of Slovenia joined the dissident groups and the Roman Catholic Church in organizing mass rallies against the perceived threat from Serbia and the Yugoslav state and army. After its walk-out from the Yugoslav Communist Party Congress in January 1990, with a changed name and a liberal-democratic programme this party committed itself to a 'separate' path of Slovenia to Europe under the slogan 'Europe, now'. While the renamed Communist Party stopped short of advocating immediate independence of Slovenia, a coalition of seven parties, DEMOS, formed by former dissidents, presented Communist Yugoslavia as an oppressor of the Slovenes and the immediate independence from Yugoslavia as national liberation. In April 1990 this coalition won the parliamentary majority with 55 percent of the vote and once in government started a rapid 'disassociation' from the SFRY.

*Croatia* was the second most developed region of SFRY with a strong Roman Catholic tradition among its majority Croat population. Unlike Slovenia, Croatia was a medieval kingdom which in the 11th century lost its independence to the Hungarian and later Habsburg crown. The main *topos* of Croat nationalist discourse has been the recovery of independence from foreign domination; Yugoslavia was, in this discourse, the latest foreign oppressor, following Hungary and Austria in 1918. Unlike Slovenia, Croatia had a significant Serb minority (around 12 percent of population) concentrated on the border areas with Bosnia and Serbia. During World War Two this minority in Croatia and Bosnia and Herzegovina was subject to gruesome massacres and expulsion by the pro-fascist Croat Ustasha regime. The memory of these massacres were used by local Croatian Serb leaders to mobilize the Serb population against the nationalist Croat parties which they likened to the Ustashas (see Part VI). The Croat Democratic Union (CDU), founded in 1989 by a leading Croat nationalist dissident, the former Communist general Tudjman, presented independence as the historical goal of the Croat nation and insisted that there was no place within Croatian borders for any one (including the Serbs) who did not accept Croatia as his/her only homeland. In April/May 1990 the four-party coalition led by the CDU won (with 44 percent of the vote) a majority in the Croatian parliament which elected its founder the president of Croatia. In coordination with the DEMOS government in Slovenia, it started its own 'disassociation' from Yugoslavia. But unlike the Slovenian government which had no minority opposition, it soon faced an armed rebellion of the Serbs which denied the new Croatian government control in the Serb-majority areas. YPA units, ostensibly deployed to prevent violent conflict, in effect supported the Serb rebels (see Part VI).

In both Slovenia and Croatia most political parties regarded Milošević's Serbian regime and its programme of recentralization as a threat of Serbian domination over their national groups; their mass mobilization against the Yugoslav state was a response to this threat. In addition, the protracted, tortuous and ultimately unsuccessful negotiations of the leaders of six republics over the constitutional reorganization of the SFRY (during 1990) showed to their electorates that Yugoslavia was not a viable state. Under these circumstances, no other political option apart from 'disassociation', that is, secession, appeared viable to most political parties in these two republics.

In *Bosnia and Herzegovina*, the issue of secession of this republic was closely tied to the success of the attempts at secession by Croatia and Slovenia. If the two republics seceded, the Bosnian Muslim (or Bosniak)[6] and Bosnian Croat population of this republic (constituting, respectively, 44 and 22 percent of its population) would become minority populations in the remaining state dominated by the Serbs and Serbia. Meanwhile, the multi-party elections in September 1990 reflected the results of nationalist mobilization: the parties which each separately mobilized Bosnian Muslims, Serbs and Croats gained the percentage of the vote roughly reflecting the census figures for these three major national groups. These three national parties formed a coalition government but once Croatia and Slovenia declared independence, in June 1991, the Bosnian Muslim and Bosnian Croat party, as expected, declared their support for the secession of their republic. The Bosnian Serb party opposed secession and proposed a division of Bosnia and Herzegovina, on the model of the division of the SFRY into three nation-states. From June 1991, each of the national parties mobilized their target population for their preferred political blueprint: the Bosnian Muslim and Croat parties for a unitary Bosnia and Herzegovina independent from the SFRY and the Bosnian Serb party for secession of the Serb-populated regions from this state (Burg and Shoup 2000) (see also Chapter 12). In a sense, both sides mobilized their population for secession – the

---

6   'Muslim' (Muslimani) was the official Communist appellation of the constituent nation in Bosnia and Herzegovina and elsewhere in Yugoslavia. In 1993, after the international recognition of the independence of this republic, the official appellation was changed to 'Bosniak' (Bošnjak).

first for secession from the SFRY and the second for secession from Bosnia and Herzegovina.

In *Macedonia*, one of the least developed republics, the support for secession was initially very limited among its Macedonian population. Only after the proclamation of the independence of Slovenia and Croatia did the ex-communist regime organize a referendum in September 1991 which resulted in a majority support for independence.

In *Montenegro* the ex-communist regime, which was installed in power in 1988 with the help of Milošević and his supporters, was opposed to secession, at least until 1996. In April 1992, following the secessions of all other republics from the SFRY, Serbia and Montenegro established the Federal Republic of Yugoslavia as a putative successor state of the SFRY. This two-unit federation (transformed in 2003 into a confederation) lasted until 2006, when, supported by the EU, Montenegro peacefully seceded, leaving Serbia an independent state for the first time since 1918 (see also Chapters 7 and 16).

## Secessions and Wars[7]

In contrast to the secessions from the USSR, all secessions from the SFRY and its 'successor' state – except those of Macedonia in 1991 and Montenegro in 2006 – were accompanied with violence – in some case amounting to conventional warfare – which was finally stopped only by the intervention of outside states and organizations. Unlike the secessionist movements in the USSR, the secessionist movements in Slovenia, Croatia and Bosnia and Herzegovina had, prior to the outbreak of fighting, mobilized and equipped large paramilitary forces which they deployed against the YPA and Serb secessionist forces. And unlike the central government of the USSR under President Gorbachev, the central government of the rump SFRY (from July 1991 controlled by the Serbian government) proved to be capable of using the remnants of the federal army, YPA, against the secessionist forces in these three republics.

The series of secessions in SFRY started in *Kosovo*: in June 1990 the Kosovo Albanian deputies of the Kosovo assembly (elected under the one-party Communist regime) proclaimed the independence of Kosovo from the federal republic of Serbia; this was followed in October 1991 (after the reiterated secessions of Croatia and Slovenia) by the proclamation of independence from SFRY; at the time only the neighbouring Albania recognized its independence. In 1998 the Kosovo Liberation Army (KLA) – a small armed group outside the mainstream secessionist movement led by the LDK – raised an armed rebellion in Kosovo against Serbian/Yugoslav authorities. The Serbian military suppression of the armed rebellion and expulsion of Albanian civilians triggered NATO's bombing of Serbia in March 1999. As the Serbian forces withdrew from the province in May 1999, under a UN Security

---

[7] For a discussion of these secessions from a normative (ethical) point of view see Detrez (2003) and Pavković (2000a).

Council Resolution, NATO-led forces and the UN took control over the province and the Albanian refugees (over 700 thousand of them) returned to the province while most non-Albanians left it. In 2008 the Kosovo assembly proclaimed independence from Serbia once again (see further Chapters 9, 13 and 17).

On 25 June 1991, the parliaments of *Croatia* and *Slovenia*, in a coordinated move, proclaimed independence ('disassociation') from the SFRY. This was preceded by plebiscites on independence in which the cause of independence was supported by overwhelming majorities. A day before the proclamation, the Slovenian defence forces blockaded the YPA's barracks in the republic and took over the international border crossing from SFRY officials. In response, YPA's units from Croatia were ordered into Slovenia, leading to a 12-day conflict in which around several dozen people lost their lives, most of whom were YPA conscripts. Responding to the call from the Slovenian government, the European Community (EC) intervened in the conflict and negotiated the lifting of the blockade of YPA barracks in Slovenia and a three-month moratorium on independence. In October 1991 both parliaments reiterated their proclamations of independence.

Large-scale fighting started in *Croatia* only in August 1991 with the blockade of the YPA's barracks in Croatia to which the YPA responded with a full-scale invasion of Croatia. In December 1991 the Serb-controlled areas of Croatia proclaimed independence as the Republic of Serb Krajina from Croatia; this was the first in the series of recursive secessions – secessions from seceding states – in the SFRY.[8] In January 1992 the UN negotiated a peace agreement under which the YPA's units in the Serb Krajina were replaced by the UN peacekeepers. The warfare led to large-scale destruction (caused mainly by the YPA artillery) and the death of around 10,000 Croats and an unknown number of Serbs and YPA soldiers. In 1995, the Croatian army, trained, equipped and supported by the US, conquered the Serb-controlled areas leading to the exodus of around 150 thousand Serbs (see also Part VI).

The reiteration of the declaration of independence of the above two republics led to the proclamation ('Memorandum of Sovereignty') of independence of Bosnia and Herzegovina in October 1991. The Serb members of the republic's assembly, opposing the independence, walked out of it and established a Serb assembly near the capital Sarajevo, which in April 1992 proclaimed the independence of the Serb Republic from Bosnia and Herzegovina; this was the second recursive secession in the SFRY. The sporadic fighting between the Bosnian Muslim and Serb militias started in February 1992 around the capital Sarajevo and the Serb artillery, inherited from the YPA, bombarded it regularly. In the warfare the Bosnian Serb forces, supported by the government of and volunteers from Serbia/Montenegro, conquered around 70 percent of the republic's territory and expelled non-Serb populations (see also Chapter 12). The Serbs were gradually expelled from the areas held by their opponents. In 1992 the Croat-held areas in the republic proclaimed independence as 'Herzeg-Bosna' which led to the war between erstwhile allies,

---

8   For a discussion of the term and its opposite 'sequential' see Pavković with Radan (2007) and Pavković (2000a).

the Bosnian Croat and Muslim forces; this was the third recursive secession.[9] This secession was ended by US diplomatic intervention and the creation in 1994 of a joint entity, the Federation of Bosnia and Herzegovina out of Croat and Bosniak held areas. In August 1995, following yet another bombing of civilians in Sarajevo, NATO air force and ground artillery attacked the Bosnian Serb military and communications position and the Croatian army from Croatia together with the Bosnian Muslim forces attacked their ground forces. This NATO-coordinated offensive reduced the territory held by the Bosnian Serbs to roughly 49 percent. The warfare was ended by the agreements negotiated by the US government in Dayton, Ohio which in 1996 re-constituted the state as a union of two separate 'entities', the Serb Republic and the Federation of Bosnia and Herzegovina, each with its own armed force and governmental structure, but both under the overall control of a UN administration and the NATO-led peace-enforcing force (Burg and Shoup 2000). Around 100 thousand citizens of all national groups lost their lives in this conflict and almost half of the population had been displaced by warfare and forced eviction (see also Chapter 12).

## International Intervention

In contrast to the dissolution of the USSR in which the involvement of outside states and international organizations was minimal, member states of the EC and the USA as well as international organizations such as the EC (later the EU), the UN and NATO all directly intervened in the secession processes and dissolution of the SFRY in various ways. Those can be classified into the following five major categories:

*(1) Diplomatic and military support for the secessionists*
Already in 1990 governments and political parties in Europe, particularly in Austria and Germany, offered support to the secessionist authorities of Croatia and Slovenia. The German government pressured the EC bodies to recognize the independence of these two states, finally recognizing their independence in advance of the EC. In addition, the military forces of the two republics gained weapons and equipment from West European states prior to the outbreak of violence in 1991. From 1993 on, the major supplier of military equipment and support became the US government. Using at times the cover of private companies, it provided weapons, training and logistic support to the Croatian, Bosnian Muslim and Kosovo Albanian forces. The governments of Turkey, Saudi Arabia and Pakistan, provided weapons and facilitated recruitment of Muslim volunteers to aid the Bosnian Muslim forces.

---

9  The fourth, in 1993, was the secession of a Bosnian Muslim-controlled statelet, the Republic of Western Bosnia (conquered by the Croatian army and Bosnian Muslim forces in August 1995).

Similar assistance was provided to the Serb forces by the Russian parties and government.

*(2) Recognition of independence, ceasefires and peace agreements*
In June 1991, immediately after the outbreak of fighting in Slovenia, the EC secured a ceasefire, the eventual withdrawal of the YPA units from Slovenia and a moratorium on their proclamation of independence. The EC also convened a conference on Yugoslavia, attempting, in vain, to find a peaceful resolution and political constitutional settlement to the crises caused by secessions of the two federal units.

In addition, the EC established an Arbitration Commission (called by the name of its chairman 'the Badinter commission'), which in November 1991, following the reiterated proclamations of independence in October 1991, proclaimed the SFRY to be a 'state in dissolution' and denied the right of independent statehood to any unit in it apart from the existing federal republics. Accordingly, in December 1991, the EC called on the federal units to submit, within five days, requests for recognition from the EC. Acting against the advice of its Arbitration Commission, in January 1991, the EC recognized the independence of Croatia and Slovenia but (initially) denied recognition to Bosnia and Herzegovina and Macedonia (Serbia and Montenegro, having been independent states before, declined to seek recognition from the EC) (see Radan 2001a).

Having failed to secure a lasting ceasefire in the war in Croatia, the EC abandoned its intervention in the SFRY and the UN took over. In January 1991 the UN negotiated a peace agreement which led to the withdrawal of the YPA units from Croatia and their replacement with UN peacekeepers (see the 'Serb Krajina' in Part VI). But the UN (and later the UN and EU jointly) failed to negotiate a similar peace agreement in Bosnia and Herzegovina. The 'Great Powers' Contact group (consisting of the USA, Russia, France, UK and Italy) which in 1994 took over the negotiating role did no better. Only after NATO's military intervention (see below) in 1995, was the US government able to negotiate a peace agreement re-constituting Bosnia and Herzegovina and placing it under UN administration (see the previous section).

The peace agreement ending the NATO military intervention against Serbia/Montenegro in 1999 was negotiated by the EU and Russian negotiators and confirmed by the UN Security Council resolution, establishing, in the province of Kosovo, yet another UN administration with a NATO-led military force. At the time of writing, the UN civilian administration in both Kosovo and Bosnia and Herzegovina has been replaced by EU administration (see also Chapter 13).

*(3) Peacekeeping*
The EC, together with the Organization for Security and Cooperation in Europe, was first to deploy peacekeepers in the SFRY: the unarmed, white-clad observers were deployed in July 1991 in Slovenia. The attempt to deploy such peacekeepers

in Croatia failed; in January 1992 the UN deployed an armed peacekeeping force there whose ostensible mission was to prevent conflict between the Serb militias and Croatian army in Serb-controlled areas. This force, however, had no mandate to prevent the US-supported invasion by the Croatian army in 1995 and was withdrawn once the Croatian forces took over the territory (see Part VI).

In the absence of any peace agreement in Bosnia and Herzegovina, the UN Protection Force, deployed there in 1993, was only to protect the provision of humanitarian aid mainly to Bosnian Muslims and the protection of 'safe (urban) areas' for this population. As the Bosnian Muslim military forces used the 'safe areas' to attack the surrounding Bosnian Serb forces, these safe areas came under Bosnian Serb attack. In 1994, the latter overran the 'safe area' of Srebrenica in West Bosnia and, in the aftermath, massacred several thousand Bosnian Muslim men and captured soldiers. The International Criminal Tribunal for Yugoslavia (see below) declared this an act of genocide.

In 1995, under the Dayton agreement, UN peacekeepers were replaced by a much larger NATO-led force of 35 countries whose aim was to enforce the peace agreement in the newly reconstituted Bosnia and Herzegovina and to demobilize the military forces of both sides in the conflict. A similarly large NATO-led force, deployed in Kosovo in 1999, provided protection both to the remaining non-Albanian population in Kosovo and to the new Kosovo Albanian authorities. At the time of writing each of the two forces are still in place but greatly reduced in strength.

*(4) Military intervention*
In its first engagement ever, in August 1995, NATO's air force and artillery joined the Croatian government and Bosnian Muslim forces in their major offensive against the Bosnian Serb forces in the Serb-controlled territory of Bosnia and Herzegovina which reduced the Serb-controlled territory in that region to less than 50 percent and ended with a peace agreement in Dayton, Ohio.

In its second engagement, from March to May 1999 the NATO air force and cruise missiles attacked military, communication and industrial targets primarily in Serbia. The aim was to force the Serbian regime to withdraw its forces and civilian administration from Kosovo and to support the KLA forces in it. As in Bosnia and Herzegovina, the withdrawal of Serb armed forces was accompanied by a mass exodus of non-Albanian, primarily Serb, civilians to Serbia.

*(5) International justice*
In September 1993 the UN Security Council established the International Criminal Tribunal for the former Yugoslavia (ICTY) to try those responsible for war crimes and crimes against humanity. The Tribunal, while convicting members of all the parties to these conflicts, did not indict the Croat and Bosnian Muslim political leaders and acquitted the top Kosovo Albanian ones. However, the political and

military leaders of Serb secessionist movements as well as of Serbia's government supporting these movements were all indicted and, when tried, convicted.

## The Outcome

Similarly to the USSR, the SFRY was dissolved as a result of a series of secessions of its federal units, starting in the latter case with the secession of a sub-federal unit in 1990. In contrast to the USSR, the SFRY's initial dissolution into five states also involved armed rebellion of minority populations in three of them – Croatia, Bosnia and Herzegovina, and Serbia.[10] In the case of the SFRY – but not the USSR – outside states and international organizations attempted to regulate the process of secession/dissolution, to stop the warfare and to determine its outcome by military intervention. At first the EC and the US ruled out recognizing independence of any sub-federal unit of the SFRY and, accordingly, assisted the military suppression of recursive secessions from Croatia and Bosnia and Herzegovina. But in 1998 the US and its NATO allies reversed this policy and provided military assistance to the Kosovo Albanian armed rebellion in the sub-federal region of Kosovo whose independence they recognized in 2008.[11]

At the time of writing (2011), the SFRY has been divided into seven states, two of which, Kosovo and Bosnia and Herzegovina, are still under EU administration and continue to receive substantial aid from the EU and the US. These two states also face further secessionist threats: the Serb-controlled northern part of Kosovo and the Serb-controlled Serb Republic in Bosnia and Herzegovina would probably secede, if the EU administrators were to allow secession plebiscites to be held in Serb-populated areas (for evidence of secessionist sentiment see Chapter 12). Serbia also faces potential secessionist threats of the Hungarian minority in the northern province of Vojvodina and of the Muslim minority in the southern region of Sandžak. Macedonia (a former republic of SFRY, not the northern province of Greece) faces a potential secessionist threat of its Albanian minority, which forms a substantial majority in the western parts of the state. Montenegro's large Serb minority at the moment show no signs of a secessionist inclination nor are there any Serb secessionist parties in Montenegro (see Chapter 7). Out of the seven new states, only Slovenia and Croatia are at present nationally homogenous and hence face no secessionist threat. The dissolution of the Yugoslav federation had obviously not put an end to secessionist threats in this part of Europe.

---

10    The armed conflict in Kosovo has its parallel in the conflict in Chechnya (see Part VI) and the recursive secessions from Croatia and Bosnia and Herzegovina have parallels in the secessions of South Ossetia and Abkhazia (see Chapter 15 and Part VI).
11    One could only speculate whether an alternative policy aiming to accommodate the demands for self-determination of the 'trapped' minorities in Croatia, Bosnia and Herzegovina, and Kosovo would have reduced the likelihood of violent conflict and the concomitant large-scale displacement of populations.

# References

Beissinger, M. (1995), 'The Persisting Ambiguity of Empire', *Post-Soviet Affairs* 11:2, 149–84.

Beissinger, M. (2002), *Nationalist Mobilization and the Collapse of the Soviet State* (Cambridge: Cambridge University Press).

Brudny, Y.M. (1999), *Reinventing Russia: Russian Nationalism and the Soviet State, 1953–1991* (Cambridge, MA: Harvard University Press).

Burg, S.L and P.S. Shoup (2000), *War in Bosnia and Herzegovina: Ethnic Conflict and International Intervention* (Boulder, CO: M.E. Sharpe).

Collins, R. (1986), *Weberian Sociological Theory* (Cambridge: Cambridge University Press).

Coppieters, B. (2003), 'Secession and War: A Moral Analysis of the Russian-Chechen Conflict', *Central Asian Survey* 22:4, 377–404.

Coppieters, B. and R. Levgold (eds) (2005), *Revolution Statehood and Security: Georgia after the Rose* (Cambridge, MA: MIT Press).

Coppieters, B. and R. Sakwa (eds) (2003), *Contextualising Secession: Normative Studies in a Comparative Perspective* (Oxford: Oxford University Press).

Detrez, R. (2003), 'The Right to Self-Determination and Secession in Yugoslavia: A Hornets' Nest of Inconsistencies', in B. Coppieters and R. Sakwa (eds), *Contextualising Secession: Normative Studies in a Comparative Perspective* (Oxford: Oxford University Press), 112–32.

Deyermond, R. (2007), *Security and Sovereignty in the Former Soviet Union* (Boulder, CO: Lynne Rienner).

Dragović-Soso, J. (2002), *'Saviours of the Nation': Serbia's Intellectual Opposition and the Revival of Nationalism* (London: Hurst and Montreal: McGill-Queen's University Press).

Edgar, A.L. (2004), *Tribal Nation: The Making of Soviet Turkmenistan* (Princeton, NJ: Princeton University Press).

Hale, H. (2004), 'Divided We Stand: Institutional Sources of Ethnofederal State Survival and Collapse', *World Politics* 56:2, 165–93.

Horowitz, D. (1993), 'Democracy in Divided Societies', *Journal of Democracy* 4:4, 18–38.

Jović, D. (2008), *Yugoslavia: The State That Withered Away* (West Lafayette, IN: Purdue University Press).

Konstitutsiya (1989), *Konstitutsiya (osnovnoi zakon) Rossiiskoi Sovetskoi Federativnoi Sotsialisticheskoi Respubliki* (first adopted in 1978, with changes of 27 October 1989) (Moscow: Sovetskaya Rossiya).

Laitin, D.D. (2007), *Nations, States and Violence* (Oxford: Oxford University Press).

Mawhood, P. (1984), 'The Politics of Survival: Federal States in the Third World', *International Political Science Review* 5:4, 521–31.

Muharremi, R. (2008), 'Kosovo's Declaration of Independence: Self-Determination and Sovereignty Revisited', *Review of Central and East European Law* 33, 401–35.

Osipov, A.G. (ed.) (1997), *Pravo narodov na samoopredelenie: ideya i voploshchenie* (Moscow: Zven'ya).

Pavković, A. (1997), 'Anticipations of the Disintegration: Nationalisms in Former Yugoslavia 1980–1990', *The Nationalities Papers* 25:3, 427–42.
Pavković, A. (2000a), 'Recursive Secessions in Former Yugoslavia: Too Hard a Case for Theories of Secession?', *Political Studies* 48, 485–502.
Pavković, A. (2000b), *The Fragmentation of Yugoslavia: Nationalism and War in the Balkans*, 2nd edn (London: Macmillan).
Pavković, A. with P. Radan (2007), *Creating New States: Theory and Practice of Secession* (Aldershot: Ashgate).
Radan, P. (2001a), *The Break-up of Yugoslavia and the International Law* (London: Routledge).
Radan, P. (2001b), 'Secession and Constitutional Law in the Former Yugoslavia', *University of Tasmania Law Review* 20, 181–204.
Stepan, A. (2000), 'Russian Federalism in Comparative Perspective', *Post-Soviet Affairs* 16:2, 133–76.
Sukhov, I. (2007), 'Russian Federalism and Evolution of Self-Determination', *Russia in Global Affairs* 5:2. [Online] At http://eng.globalaffairs.ru/numbers/20/ [accessed 21 October 2010].
Suny, R.G. (1993), *The Revenge of the Past: Nationalism, Revolution and the Collapse of the Soviet Union* (Stanford, CA: Stanford University Press).
Suny, R.G. (2002), *A State of Nations: Empire and Nation-Making in the Age of Lenin and Stalin* (Oxford: Oxford University Press).
Walker, E.W. (2003), *Dissolution: Sovereignty and the Breakup of the Soviet Union* (Lanham, MD: Rowman & Littlefield).
Woodward, S.L. (1995), *Balkan Tragedy: Chaos and Dissolution after the Cold War* (Washington, DC: Brookings Institution Press).

# Kosovo:
# Secession under UN Supervision

## Keiichi Kubo

## Introduction

On 17 February 2008 the declaration of independence of Kosovo was adopted by the members of the Assembly of Kosovo. Major Western countries, such as the US, France, the UK and Germany, immediately recognized the Republic of Kosovo. By the end of November 2010 Kosovo had been recognized by 72 UN member states, and in June 2009 Kosovo became a member of the World Bank group and the IMF. Although the international community is still divided on the issue of Kosovo, it is obvious that Kosovo Albanians are one of the most successful among the secessionist groups or nations.

This chapter examines the evolution of the secessionist demands and movements among the Albanian population in Kosovo. The chapter is divided into four sections: the first briefly reviews the background of the conflict in Kosovo; the second presents the rise of Milošević and his repressive policies as a direct cause of the secessionist conflict in Kosovo; the third analyses the evolution of the secessionist movement in Kosovo; and the fourth examines the involvement of the international community and the path to Kosovo's independence.

## The Background of the Conflict in Kosovo

### Historical Background

Kosovo has been regarded as a sacred place in Serbia, because the area of Kosovo was the religious centre of the medieval Serbian Kingdom. The seat of the Patriarchy of the Serbian Orthodox Church was located in Peć in the western part of Kosovo and many historically important monasteries were constructed in the area of Kosovo in the 13th and 14th centuries, such as Dečani and Gračanica. In Serbia, the area of Kosovo is called 'Kosovo and Metohija' (or 'Kosmet' as its shortened version), and the name of the western part of the area 'Metohija' originates from the Greek word *metókhia*, meaning 'monastic estates', which demonstrates the deep historical linkage between Kosovo and the Serbian Orthodox Church. The Albanians do not use the term 'Metohija' and refer to the whole territory as 'Kosova'.

Kosovo is of further historical and symbolic importance to the Serbs, as the battle of Kosovo in 1389 between the army of the Christian alliance, led by a Serbian prince, and the army of the Ottoman Empire resulted in the collapse of the Serbian medieval state. During the era of the Ottoman Empire, the myths and legends related to the battle of Kosovo evolved into epic poems and were passed down orally among the Serbs. These epic poems were collected and published by Serbian scholars in the 19th century and constituted an important source for a programme of 'national revival' among the Serbs. These myths associated with the battle of Kosovo were repeatedly used by Serbian leaders to mobilize the Serbian people.

Kosovo is of historical and symbolic importance to Albanians as well. During the Ottoman era, which lasted nearly four centuries, the number of Albanians grew to become a majority in the area. Moreover, Kosovo played an important role in the 'national awakening' of and the movement for independence among Albanians. For example, the League of Prizren, formed in the southern part of Kosovo in 1878, was the first expression of Albanian demands for rights and autonomy. Furthermore, it is widely believed that the area of the current Kosovo constituted a central part of the kingdom of the Illyrians, the 'ancestors' of the Albanians. Thus, Kosovo is regarded by Albanians as a historical homeland.

After the Balkan wars in 1912–13, the area of the current Kosovo became a disputed area in negotiations on the borders between the Balkan states. Austria-Hungary supported Albania and claimed that the area of the present-day Kosovo should be incorporated into Albania, while Russia supported Serbia and its territorial expansion. As a result of the compromise between the two camps, the current border between Albania and Serbia/Kosovo was drawn, and the area of Kosovo was incorporated into Serbia. After World War Two, under Communist rule, in 1946 Kosovo became an 'autonomous region' within the federal republic of Serbia when the current borders of Kosovo were drawn for the first time (in 1963 Kosovo was upgraded to an 'autonomous province' on a par with Vojvodina) (see Chapter 8).

## Socio-economic Background

Kosovo was the poorest region in the former Yugoslavia, and regional disparity continued to grow under the socialist regime. For example, the income per capita in Kosovo was 48 percent of the national average of Yugoslavia in 1954, but decreased to 27 percent in 1980. The illiteracy rate was also the highest in the region, 31.5 percent in 1979, while the national average was 15.1 percent. The unemployment rate was 18.6 percent in Kosovo in 1971, which increased to 27.5 percent in 1981, while that in Slovenia in 1981 was only 2 percent. Despite being an area rich in natural resources – such as coal, lead, zinc, chromium, silver, nickel and iron – these resources did not bring about Kosovo's economic development.

Kosovo has experienced a significant demographic change since the beginning of the 20th century. The key factor is the high birth-rate of Albanians compared to other ethnic groups. Thus, the population of Kosovo grew rapidly, as did the proportion of Albanians in Kosovo (see Table 9.1). Poverty in Kosovo also played an important role as more and more Serbs left Kosovo for other parts of the former Yugoslavia, seeking better education and employment opportunities. Serbian and Yugoslav authorities have repeatedly attempted to change this trend. For example, in the interwar era, authorities of the government of the Kingdom of Yugoslavia attempted to increase the number of Serbs in Kosovo through colonial settlement, which allegedly led to the settlement of 60,000 Serbs in Kosovo. Further, this government attempted to decrease the number of Albanians by making an agreement with Turkey to 'emigrate' 200,000 people from Kosovo to Turkey. However, these policies could not change the demographic trend in Kosovo.

Table 9.1    Kosovo population by ethnic composition, 1921–2006

| Years of census | Total | Albanians | Serbs | Turks | Romas | Others |
|---|---|---|---|---|---|---|
| 1921 | 439,010 | – | – | – | – | – |
| 1931 | 552,064 | – | – | – | – | – |
| 1948 | 733,034 | 498,244 | 176,718 | 1,320 | 11,230 | 45,522 |
| % | 100 | 68.0 | 24.1 | 0.2 | 1.5 | 6.2 |
| 1953 | 815,908 | 524,562 | 189,869 | 34,590 | 11,904 | 54,983 |
| % | 100 | 64.3 | 23.3 | 4.2 | 1.5 | 6.7 |
| 1961 | 963,988 | 646,605 | 227,016 | 25,764 | 3,202 | 61,401 |
| % | 100 | 67.1 | 23.5 | 2.7 | 0.3 | 6.4 |
| 1971 | 1,243,693 | 916,168 | 228,264 | 12,244 | 14,593 | 72,424 |
| % | 100 | 73.7 | 18.4 | 1.0 | 1.2 | 5.8 |
| 1981 | 1,584,440 | 1,226,736 | 209,798 | 12,513 | 34,126 | 101,267 |
| % | 100 | 77.4 | 13.2 | 0.8 | 2.2 | 6.4 |
| 1991 | 1,956,196 | 1,596,072 | 194,190 | 10,445 | 45,745 | 109,744 |
| % | 100 | 81.6 | 9.9 | 0.5 | 2.3 | 5.6 |
| 2006 | 2,100,000 | 1,932,000 | 111,300 | 8,400 | 23,512 | 24,788 |
| % | 100% | 92.0 | 5.3 | 0.4 | 1.1 | 1.2 |

*Notes*:    For the years of 1948, 1953, 1961 and 1981, data were obtained from the publication of the population censuses.

For 1991, data were assessments of I EFS.

For 2006, data were assessments of SOK.

*Source*:    SOK 2008.

# The Rise of Milošević and His Policies: The Direct Cause of the Conflict

## Kosovo before the Rise of Milošević

While Kosovo became an 'autonomous region' within Serbia, the institutions of Kosovo were dominated by Serbs and Montenegrins under the control of Aleksandar Ranković, a Serb communist leader who controlled the Yugoslav security service; hence its 'autonomy' existed only on paper. After the downfall of Ranković in 1966, in 1968 large demonstrations by Kosovo Albanians took place, following which Yugoslav federal authorities started to make a series of concessions to Kosovo Albanians, including, among others, increasing the number of Kosovo Albanian officials in the provincial authorities, the right to raise the Albanian flag, and the establishment of a university with instruction in Albanian. Under the 1974 Yugoslav Constitution republics and autonomous provinces became almost fully equal, and the two autonomous provinces in Serbia gained full autonomy over their parliaments, budgets and judicial systems. These measures benefited many Albanians in Kosovo, in particular Communist party cadres, and made them into loyal supporters of the Yugoslav communist regime. The 1970s are now seen by many Kosovo Albanians as a 'golden age' (Judah 2008: 55–63). Following the death in 1980 of the Yugoslav communist leader Tito, in 1981 Kosovo Albanian demonstrations erupted again, calling for Kosovo's elevation to the status of republic, fully equal to (and independent from) Serbia and other republics. After the 1981 demonstrations, Kosovo Albanians suspected of supporting this programme were branded as 'chauvinists' and 'counterrevolutionaries' and were purged from the Communist party or arrested by the authorities.

Serbian nationalist intellectuals and Serb activists in Kosovo were increasingly frustrated by the 1974 constitutional regime, which, in their eyes, gave too many concessions to the Albanians and did not protect the Serbs in Kosovo. In 1986, Serbs from Kosovo staged demonstrations and called for the Yugoslav authorities to revise the autonomy of Kosovo. In the same year, the 'Memorandum' intended for the Yugoslav communist leadership and drafted by the members of the Serbian Academy of Arts and Science pointed out that Serbs were divided by the different republics within the Yugoslav federation and called for the re-unification of the Serbs. However, the Serbian authorities, led by Ivan Stambolić and loyal to the Titoist ideology of brotherhood and unity, criticized the 'nationalist' tendency of these moves and rejected the demands made by Serbian nationalist intellectuals and activists.

## Rise of Milošević and His Policy of Repression

The rise of Slobodan Milošević changed the situation completely. Milošević, a protégé of Stambolić and then the president of Serbia's Party Presidency, confronted with Serb demonstrators in Kosovo, declared: 'No one should dare to beat you.' This public statement, repeatedly broadcasted by the mass media in Serbia, instantly made Milošević a hero in the minds of many Serbs. Milošević thus won an internal power struggle against Stambolić within the party, and by the end of 1987 took control of Serbia's party and government (Vladisavljević 2008). From then on, Kosovo became the rallying cry at a series of large public rallies, organized by his supporters ostensibly to show 'solidarity' with the Serbs in Kosovo. In June 1989, at the large public celebration of the 600th anniversary of the Battle of Kosovo, held at the site of the battle in Kosovo, Milošević praised the fighting spirit of the Serbs throughout the ages, appealing to them to ready to fight for their land again and presented himself and his government as protectors of the Serbs.

On the seizure of power in 1987, Milošević started implementing various repressive policies against Albanians in Kosovo. Opponents of his policies were purged from the workplace, and in November 1988 Azem Vllasi and Kaqusha Jashari, the Kosovo Albanian leaders of the Communist Party of Kosovo, were forced to resign. In March 1989, Milošević severely restricted the autonomy of Kosovo through an amendment of the Serbian constitution, allowing the laws passed in the Serbian assembly to be directly implemented in Kosovo. The Serbian assembly then passed laws that led to the exclusion of Albanians from the institutions and public life of Kosovo. Albanian workers were fired *en masse*; primary education in Albanian was abolished and education in the Serbian language was forced on Albanian teachers and pupils; the media in the Albanian language were closed. Finally, the new Serbian constitution in September 1990 reverted Kosovo (and Vojvodina) to the level of fake autonomy that the provinces had held from 1946 until the 1960s.

In protest against these policies Kosovo Albanians staged a series of large demonstrations. After the resignation of Vllasi and Jashari, for example, workers from the Trepca mining complex led a demonstration march to the capital Prishtina. In November 1988, Kosovo was placed under a state of emergency. When the constitutional amendments of March 1989 were approved by the Provincial Assembly of Kosovo, surrounded by tanks to secure the building (thus the amended constitution became known as the 'Constitution of the Tanks'), Kosovo Albanians organized protest demonstrations throughout Kosovo. The Serbian authorities responded by imposing a curfew and by mobilizing security forces to repress demonstrations, which led to the death of more than 20 Albanians. Clashes between the security forces and demonstrators continued from 1989 until early 1990.

It should be noted that demonstrations by Kosovo Albanians at this stage mostly demanded the end of repressive policies and the reinstallation of the 1974 constitutional regime. Many demonstrators and workers often raised the photo of Tito during the demonstrations. In other words, most of them were reacting to the repressive policies introduced by Milošević, and not demanding secession from Yugoslavia or Serbia. When it became clear that Milošević would never change his repressive policies, their demands changed into secessionist ones.

# From Peaceful Protest to Violence: Secessionist Conflict in Kosovo, 1990–99

Facing the repressive measures taken by the Serbian authorities, the Albanian elite started making secessionist demands too. In July 1990, the Kosovo Albanian members of the Provincial Assembly of Kosovo unilaterally declared that Kosovo become a republic and independent from Serbia, even though it still remained a part of the Yugoslav federation. In September 1990, they gathered secretly in Kaçanik and adopted the 'Constitution of the Republic of Kosovo' (the so-called Kaçanik constitution). In September 1991, a referendum on the 'sovereignty and independence of Kosovo' was organized, in which, according to the organizers, the voter turnout was 87 percent and 99.87 percent of those who voted supported it. Thus, by the end of 1991, a vast majority of Albanians were supporting the demand that Kosovo should secede from Serbia/Yugoslavia and become independent. Not only Milošević's repressive policies but also the overall political context within which Slovenia and Croatia were seceding from Yugoslavia contributed to the widespread support for this demand. From 1988, Slovenian and Croatian political leaders and media had also lent support to the Albanian demonstrations against Milošević's policies.

## The Rise of Rugova and the Strategy of Non-violent Resistance

While consensus among Albanians for the secessionist cause had emerged by the end of 1991, this did not lead immediately to violent conflict in Kosovo, because Kosovo Albanian political leaders had chosen a strategy of non-violent resistance rather than violent rebellion. Even when Croat and later Bosnian Muslim politicians encouraged Albanians to take up arms and open the 'southern front' against Serbia, Kosovo Albanian leaders rejected their request (Judah 2000: 113–15). The Kosovo Albanians organized their own presidential and parliamentary elections in which the Democratic League of Kosovo (Lidhja demokratike e Kosovës, LDK) won the overwhelming majority (76.44 percent) and its leader, Ibrahim Rugova, became president of Kosovo. Rugova and the LDK started to construct a 'parallel system' of government in Kosovo. They also organized their own educational system, with teaching in the Albanian language, using ordinary houses as temporary schools (Kostovicova 2005). In order to sustain their parallel system, the Albanian elite established their own 'tax' system, into which not only local Albanians but also diaspora communities in Europe and Northern America paid money to finance the parallel system.

Why did the Kosovo Albanian leaders choose peaceful resistance rather than violent rebellion? Several factors affected their decision. First, the idea of a parallel system was influenced by the notions of autonomy and self-organization developed among Central European intellectuals, particularly Polish Solidarity (IICK 2000: 44–5). Secondly, taking into account a pragmatic assessment of their situation, the

Serbian armed forces were simply too strong to fight against. In 1992, for example, Rugova stated: 'we would have no chance of successfully resisting the army ... in fact the Serbs only wait for a pretext to attack the Albanian population and wipe it out. We believe it is better to do nothing and stay alive than be massacred' (Vickers 1998: 264). Finally, the government of Albania (which was the only government to recognize formally the independence of Kosovo at the time) did not support an openly violent course because it would jeopardize the economic assistance it was receiving from outside as well the security of Albania by inviting Serbian reprisals (Judah 2000: 115).

Rugova and the LDK attempted to achieve Kosovo's independence with the support of the international community. They frequently visited major Western countries to meet their leaders and to lobby for the Albanians' secessionist cause. Their efforts, however, did not yield results. For example, their persistent attempts to put the issue of Kosovo's independence on the agenda of international conferences aiming at the solution of the Yugoslav crisis were consistently ignored. Albanian leaders lobbied the US government to address the issue of Kosovo's independence in 1995 at the US-led negotiations in Dayton, Ohio (which reconstituted Bosnia and Herzegovina, see Chapter 8), but their efforts failed again. For Albanians in Kosovo, the Dayton peace agreement marked a serious failure, as it recognized the existence of 'The Serb Republic' (*Republika srpska*) as an entity within Bosnia and Herzegovina, thus apparently rewarding the violent actions taken by Serbs in Bosnia. After the agreement in Dayton, the situation for Kosovo Albanians did not improve in any way: the UN embargo imposed on the Federal Republic of Yugoslavia was lifted; the EU states officially recognized this state and Germany and Yugoslavia agreed for Germany to repatriate 100,000 Kosovo Albanian refugees to Yugoslavia.

## The Emergence of the UÇK (KLA)

The successive failures of Rugova and the LDK to achieve independence peacefully led to increasing disillusionment with his pacifist strategy. This disillusionment among Albanians was perceived as an opportunity by those who advocated more radical and violent action. In Kosovo, such action was begun by a small guerrilla organization called the Kosovo Liberation Army (Ushtria çlirimtare e Kosovës, UÇK).

The UÇK was founded in 1993 and grew out of the Popular Movement for Kosovo (Lëvizja popullore për Kosovës, LPK), an underground Marxist organization formed in the early 1980s as a result of the unification of various small anti-Yugoslav illegal organizations founded by Albanian dissidents in Western Europe (Kubo 2010). The UÇK was organized by Kosovo Albanian activists or students who left Kosovo after having been imprisoned or otherwise punished by the Serbian authorities. When they commenced their violent actions, resources at their disposal were very limited. For example, up to 1997, the UÇK had only about 150 active members (Judah 2000: 118). Albanian diaspora communities in

Western countries provided financial support to the mainline organization LDK and, consequently, the UÇK or LPK members could not obtain much financial support from them. This severely limited their financial resources at the time.

The first violent action allegedly undertaken by the UÇK was the killing of a Serbian policeman in 1995, but it was not until 1996 that an organization calling itself the UÇK claimed responsibility for the attacks (IICK 2000: 51). The first 'planned' assaults took place in April 1996, when four almost simultaneous attacks were launched in separate locations that killed two Serbian policemen. From then on UÇK launched sporadic attacks on Serbian policemen, but the intensity of rebellion remained quite low. While the number of attacks increased (31 in 1996, 55 in 1997, and 66 in January and February 1998 alone), the death toll remained relatively low in this period. According to the Serbian authorities, these attacks from 1996 to February 1998 led to the death of ten Serbian policemen and 24 civilians.

The UÇK, however, presented a serious challenge to the Albanian leadership. Until then, Rugova and the LDK had enjoyed broad support from the overwhelming majority of Albanians in Kosovo and abroad, and few challenged their leadership. However, the emergence of the UÇK meant that an *intra-ethnic* division emerged among the Kosovo Albanians. At the beginning, Rugova denied the authenticity of the UÇK and suggested it was a fabricated organization set up by the Serbian secret service to justify Serbian military actions against Albanians.

Development of the conflict from then on depended in part on whether Kosovo Albanians would support the LDK (pacifists) or the UÇK (radicals). In this regard, until 1998 the UÇK remained fairly marginal among Kosovo Albanians. Even after the UÇK started their violent actions and their existence became known to many Kosovo Albanians, few people joined the UÇK, even though they had an enormous number of small arms at their disposal following the collapse of the pyramid scheme in neighbouring Albania in the spring of 1997. In order to explain why a vast majority of Albanians did not join the rebellion immediately after the appearance of the UÇK, one should take into account not only the fact that the Serbian regime was still powerful and ruthless but also that Rugova rejected violence and that he kept the LDK under tight control. Despite Rugova's international image as a pacifist leader, he governed the LDK in an authoritarian manner, allowing no opposition to his decisions (Clark 2000: 84, 123). His strong rejection of violence and his tight, even authoritarian, control of the LDK structure prevented most Albanians from joining the UÇK.

## Serbian Police Operations and the Expansion of the UÇK

While Serbian authorities tolerated UÇK activities until 1998, thereafter police operations against them began. Heavily armed Serbian police forces attacked several villages in the Drenica region, located in central Kosovo, leading to the killing of many civilians. In Prekaz, the Serbian police killed almost every member of the clan (a total of 59 people) of Adem Jashari, a local strongman who had allegedly killed Serbian policemen several years earlier and was believed to be involved in the UÇK. These killings were reported as the 'massacre' in Drenica.

These operations led to a significant change in the balance between the pacifists and the radicals. Following the deaths of the Jasharis, resulting in a huge influx of volunteers, the UÇK began to expand rapidly. As various clan elders decreed that now was the time to fight the Serbs, local militia units were rapidly organized. Consequently the UÇK membership skyrocketed. It seems that the UÇK themselves were surprised by the course of events: their plan was to start the war in 1999, but due to the large influx of volunteers they were forced to speed things up (Judah 2000: 141). Serbian scholars claim that in May 1998 the UÇK had about 1,200 members, but that by July 1998 it had grown to 25,000 (Mijalkovski and Damjanov 2002: 128).

The expansion of the UÇK was rather chaotic in manner. Besides the original UÇK which started the rebellion, a new structure under LDK leader Bukoshi, called the 'Armed Forces of the Republic of Kosova (FARK)', appeared on the ground, as well as local armed fighters organized by youths on a village-by-village basis, calling themselves 'Rugova's UÇK', who fought till the end of the war under the impression that the UÇK was under Rugova's control (Kola 2003: 336–7). The UÇK had a de-centralized and localized structure with a non-functioning 'general headquarter'. Indeed, Ramush Haradinaj, zone commander of the Dukagjini area during the conflict, testified that 'there was no general commander' until the selection of Sylejman Selimi in 1999 (Hamzaj 2000: 128).

The expansion of the UÇK naturally led to the escalation of conflict in Kosovo. By the summer of 1998 the UÇK had taken control of three major routes in Kosovo. In order to deal with the expansion of the UÇK, in July 1998 the Serbian authorities began counterinsurgency operations against the organization, using Yugoslav military forces and heavy armaments in the operations. As a result, tens of thousands of Albanians fled to hide in the hills and the woods, houses were looted and burned, and crops and cattle were destroyed. By the beginning of August 1998, reports estimated that between 200,000 and 300,000 Albanians had been displaced from their homes.

# Involvement of the International Community and the Path to Independence

## From Mediation to the NATO Bombardment

As the conflict in Kosovo escalated and more and more people fled their homes, the situation there became more extensively covered by the international media. As a consequence international pressure on Milošević to halt military operations mounted, and the US and European countries began to become involved in the conflict. On 23 September 1998, the UN Security Council (UNSC) adopted Resolution

1199 calling for a ceasefire, the withdrawal of security forces and cooperation with international monitoring efforts. The US special envoy Richard Holbrooke was dispatched to negotiate with Milošević. Threatened with the prospect of NATO air strikes, Milošević made an agreement with Holbrooke on 13 October 1998. By the end of October, some 4,000 Serbian special police forces had been withdrawn and the OSCE Kosovo Verification Mission (KVM), a team of 2,000 observers who would monitor enforcement of the agreement, was deployed.

This agreement, however, did not lead to peace in Kosovo: the UÇK took advantage of the withdrawal of the Serbian forces and renewed its military actions. During the period of reduced fighting, UÇK members returned without difficulty to burnt-out villages, and the organization found 'the time to train seriously and to consolidate a rather chaotic command structure' (Judah 2000: 24). The UN, NATO and OSCE called on the UÇK to cease provocative actions, but to no avail. The Serbian police and army again moved into Kosovo, with tanks and heavy weapons, leading to the resumption of violent conflict. Hockenos observes that the provocative actions of the UÇK were conducted in order to draw international actors into the conflict: he argues that 'part of the UÇK strategy entailed provoking the Serbs, getting them to lash back with predictable ferocity and thus forcing a Western military response,' because 'the more cruel the repression, the more vivid the message that Albanians could not live under Serb domination' (Hockenos 2003: 250).

In January 1999, Serbian forces assaulted Raçak village and killed 45 Kosovo Albanians. The next day, the OSCE-KVM investigated the site and concluded that they found evidence of arbitrary detentions, extra-judicial killings and mutilation of unarmed civilians, while the Serbian authorities argued that they were not civilians but fighters. The Contact Group composed of the US, Russia and major European states organized peace negotiations between the Yugoslav government and the Albanian delegates (UÇK and LDK leaders) in Rambouillet, France. As the Yugoslav representatives refused to sign the proposed agreements, these peace talks failed. In consequence, on 24 March 1999 the NATO air force started bombing Serbia, an operation that lasted 78 days. This 'humanitarian intervention', ostensibly conducted to halt the Serbian authorities' ethnic cleansing and massacres of Kosovo Albanians, was conducted without the authorization of the UNSC (since Russia and China were expected to veto any such attempt). The perceived lack of legality of this military intervention has provoked serious debate among diplomats and scholars. When in June 1999 Milošević finally accepted the G8 principles and signed an agreement with the EU and Russian negotiators, Serbian forces withdrew from Kosovo.

## From the Deployment of the UNMIK and KFOR to Kosovo's Independence

After the NATO bombardment, an international force led by NATO (KFOR) and the UN Mission in Kosovo (UNMIK) was deployed in Kosovo, based on UNSC

Resolution 1244 adopted in June 1999. The purpose of the UNMIK presence was to 'provide an interim administration for Kosovo under which the people of Kosovo can enjoy substantial autonomy within the Federal Republic of Yugoslavia', and in order to achieve this, UNMIK was to exercise executive, legislative and judicial powers in Kosovo. Following the deployment of UNMIK, various activities were conducted under the auspices of the international community, including the return of refugees and internally displaced persons, the improvement of the security environment, the reconstruction of the infrastructure, the development of the state and local administrative organizations, and the organization of elections.

In May 2001, in order to develop 'provisional democratic self-governing institutions' as set forth in the UNSC Resolution, UNMIK adopted the 'Constitutional Framework for Provisional Self-Government', which determined the basic political structure of Kosovo, creating the President, the Assembly, the Prime Minister, and the Court and the office of Public Prosecutor in Kosovo. While UNMIK retained the power to override the decisions made by these institutions, the executive, legislative and judicial powers were gradually transferred to these Provisional Institutions of Self-Government (PISG) dominated by Kosovo Albanians. The first elections for the Assembly of Kosovo were conducted in November 2001.

UNSC Resolution 1244 also stipulated that UNMIK had a responsibility to facilitate 'a political process designed to determine Kosovo's future status'. However, such a political process did not start after UNMIK's deployment, and frustrations towards the maintenance of the *status quo* grew among Albanians. Some Albanians thus started to consider UNMIK an obstacle to the achievement of Kosovo's independence, and UNMIK became a target of attacks by radical Albanians. For example, when massive riots by Albanians broke out throughout Kosovo in March 2004, the Albanian rioters attacked not only Serbs and their properties but also the UNMIK facilities.

In November 2003 the US announced the Contact Group initiative, which promised the revision of the status of Kosovo if Kosovo met certain standards regarding its government and the protection of minorities. In December 2003, UNMIK and the PISG agreed on the 'Standards for Kosovo', a set of eight targets that Kosovo had to meet in order for talks about its future political status to begin, including functioning democratic institutions, rule of law, freedom of movement, a well-functioning economy and so on.

In the summer of 2005, 'the comprehensive review of the situation in Kosovo' was conducted by Kai Eide, Special Envoy of the UN Secretary-General, who recognized that progress in standards implementation had been made and recommended that a process should begin to determine Kosovo's final status. As a result, in October 2005, the UNSC agreed to start a political process to determine Kosovo's future status, and the UN Secretary-General appointed Martti Ahtisaari, a former President of Finland, his Special Envoy in November 2005. Ahtisaari initiated negotiations between the Serbian government and the Kosovo government (PISG). However, the two sides were not able to reach an agreement, with the former insisting that Kosovo must remain under the sovereignty of Serbia given 'the commitment to the sovereignty and territorial integrity of Federal Republic of

Yugoslavia' expressed in UNSC resolution 1244, and with the latter claiming that the independence of Kosovo was not negotiable. In March 2007 Ahtisaari made his recommendations without the two parties reaching an agreement, proposing that Kosovo's independence be supervised by the international community based on a detailed plan of Kosovo's political system and the role of the international community after independence (the so-called 'Ahtisaari plan'). Most Western countries and the PISG of Kosovo supported this plan while the Serbian government rejected it and strongly criticized Ahtisaari for his alleged bias.

Since Russia rejected acceptance of the Ahtisaari proposal without Serbian agreement, UNSC deliberations on the plan were halted in July 2007, and negotiations on the status of Kosovo were resumed with mediation by the US, Russia and the EU, but to no avail. On 17 February 2008, the declaration of independence of Kosovo was finally adopted by the members of the Assembly of Kosovo elected under UNMIK auspices. While major Western countries, most notably the US, have recognized Kosovo's independence, at the time of writing (November 2010), Serbia, supported by Russia and China, continues to deny the statehood of Kosovo and regards its 'unilateral' declaration of independence as an illegal act (see also Chapters 13 and 17).

## Conclusion

In his article on ethnic separatism, Horowitz (1981: 167) observed:

> *Whether a secessionist movement will emerge at all is determined by domestic politics, by the relations of groups and regions within the state. Whether a secessionist movement will achieve its aims, however, is determined largely by international politics, by the balance of interests and forces that extend beyond the state.*

This observation summarizes well the evolution of the secessionist conflict in Kosovo. The emergence of the secessionist movement among Albanians was primarily determined by the rise of Milošević and his repressive policies. The pacifist movement for secession led by Rugova, however, failed largely due to international politics, as Western countries ignored secessionist demands. Failure to achieve independence led to increasing disillusionment with the pacifist strategy, which led to the commencement of the low-intensity rebellion by the radicals. Expansion of the guerrilla army then became the response to the violent repression conducted by the Serbian authorities. Here again domestic politics appears to be the key factor for the emergence of a large-scale, violent secessionist movement. The eventual achievement of its secessionist aspirations, however, became possible primarily thanks to international politics, most notably thanks to strong support from major Western countries, including the US, the UK and Germany.

The current lack of mutual recognition between Serbia and Kosovo poses a serious challenge for regional cooperation within the Western Balkans and for the EU in promoting it. Furthermore, while most Serbs left Kosovo following withdrawal of the Yugoslav forces in 1999, some still reside in Kosovo; however, a vast majority of them do not accept Kosovo's independence and deny the legitimacy of its political institutions. While at the moment Serbs in Kosovo are not demanding a secession of the territory on which they live, they may well begin making secessionist demands in the future (see also Chapter 8). The disputes over Kosovo are, as it seems, far from over.

# References

Clark, Howard (2000), *Civil Resistance in Kosovo* (London: Pluto).
Hamzaj, Bardh (2000), *A Narrative about War and Freedom (Dialog with the Commander Ramush Haradinaj)* (Prishtina: Zëri).
Hockenos, Paul (2003), *Homeland Calling: Exile Patriotism and the Balkan Wars* (Ithaca, NY: Cornell University Press).
Horowitz, Donald (1981), 'Patterns of Ethnic Separatism', *Comparative Studies in Society and History* 23:1, 165–95.
Independent International Commission on Kosovo (IICK) (2000), *Kosovo Report: Conflict, International Response, Lessons Learned* (Oxford: Oxford University Press).
Judah, Tim (2000), *Kosovo: War and Revenge* (New Haven, CT: Yale University Press).
Judah, Tim (2008), *Kosovo: What Everyone Needs to Know* (Oxford: Oxford University Press).
Kola, Paulin (2003), *The Search for Greater Albania* (London: Hurst).
Kostovicova, Denisa (2005), *Kosovo: The Politics of Identity and Space* (London: Routledge).
Kubo, Keiichi (2010), 'Why Kosovar Albanians Took Up Arms against the Serbian Regime: The Genesis and Expansion of the UÇK in Kosovo', *Europe-Asia Studies* 62:7, 1135–52.
Mijalkovski, Milan and Petar Damjanov (2002), *Terorizam Albanskih Ekstremista* (Beograd: Vojska).
Statistical Office of Kosovo (SOK) (2008), *Demographic Changes of the Kosovo Population 1948–2006* (Pristine: K.G.T.).
Vickers, Miranda (1998), *Between Serb and Albanian: A History of Kosovo* (London: Hurst).
Vladisavljević, Nebojša (2008), *Serbia's Antibureaucratic Revolution: Milošević, the Fall of Communism and Nationalist Mobilization* (Basingstoke and New York: Palgrave Macmillan).

# PART III
# SECESSION IN CONTEXT

# Introduction to Part III

The chapters in this part explore a variety of contexts in which secessions take place and causal factors that influence the secessionist populations and their political leaders. In this sense, these chapters explore some variables which are used in various attempts to *explain* secessionist processes or responses of external actors to attempts at secession.

In Chapter 10 Lloyd Cox explores the impact of economic factors both as causes of secessionist endeavours and as motivations or incentives of secessionist groups. Cox primarily explores the theories and arguments that attempt to prove that economic factors are the sole or primary cause of secessions. The first set of theories he discusses attempts to show that uneven economic development and consequent economic deprivation of certain national groups causes them to put forward secessionist demands in order to remedy the economic inequalities to which they are subjected. The second set of theories attempts to show that economic self-interest is the primary motivation of individuals and groups that put forward such demands. Both, Cox argues, fail for a variety of reasons; therefore, he concludes economic factors are not sufficient to cause secessions nor do they constitute primary motivations of secessionists. But in spite of that a variety of economic factors – both relative deprivation and relative wealth – are important causal factors in any attempt to explain secession.

In Chapter 11 Keiichi Kubo explores the role of ethnicity – defined as group identity based on cultural and/or physical traits – in attempts at secessions. Many scholars, Kubo notes, wrongly equate secessionist with ethnic conflict and many assume that attempts at secession are made by ethnic groups alone. Not all ethnic conflict arises in response to secessionist demands and not all secessions are attempted by ethnic groups distinct from those of the majority host state. In view of this, the chapter addresses two general and distinct questions:

- How is an ethnic group mobilized for secession (whether violent or not)?
- Is secession an effective solution to ethnic conflict?

In answer to the first question, Kubo argues that in order for an ethnic group to seek secession, it needs to be radicalized in terms of its political goals (in the spectrum of political goals, secession is a radical one); and for a secessionist process to turn violent, it is often necessary that the secessionist group becomes radicalized in terms of the means for the achievement of that political goal. But in both of these processes, there is a differentiation within the ethnic group and its political leadership into those who support and those who oppose such a radicalization; in this sense, ethnic groups are not unitary actors. Further, violence that accompanies attempts at secession need not be only a product of radicalization (of both the ethnic group and the host government) but in fact may be an independent factor which enhances radicalization of both goals and means.

Kubo also discusses the current debate on the question of whether secession (in the form of state partition) is or is not an effective solution to ethnic conflict. He notes that the debate is complicated by the normative aspects of the question – some scholars reject, on normative grounds, partition as a solution– and that at the time of writing the debate is still unresolved.

In Chapter 12 Siniša Malešević and Niall Ó Dochartaigh address the question:

- Why and when do organized attempts to promote the establishment of an independent polity become violent?

The authors note first that most secessionist activity is *not* violent and that only in some circumstances secessionists resort to violence. But they argue that three dominant social science paradigms – the economic, culturalist and political – that have been used to answer the above question are all wanting: each of them identifies a possible causal factor or a set of conditions that may lead to the use of violence but fail to show that the preferred conditions/factors are necessary and sufficient for the rise of violence. Instead, Malešević and Ó Dochartaigh argue that in order to explain the slide to violence one needs to take into account two general factors that have been often ignored: first, a wider geopolitical context within which a secessionist movement operates and, second, the ideology or ideologies which the actors in the conflict espouse and use to justify their actions. Variables of those two kinds, of course, interact with the already identified conditions – economic self-interest, cultural affinities and political structures.

To illustrate how the evolving ideologies and changing geopolitical dynamic influence the rise of violence, the authors discuss the rise of violent secessionism/irredentism among the Serbs in Bosnia and Herzegovina in the 1990s and in the Catholic Irish community in Northern Ireland in the 1960s. Although in both cases the goals of secessionist organizations/groups were articulated in the form of irredentism – a political union with the kin-group state – the kin-group state's response significantly differed: Ireland did not support the Catholic Northern Irish secessionists while Serbia supported the Bosnian Serb secessionist authorities and its military. The rise of violent secessionism in each case is, however, explicable by an interaction of a different set of geopolitical, ideological and local political factors. 'As a strategy aimed at repositioning a particular space within the international system', the authors conclude 'secessionist violence is decisively shaped by wider geopolitical changes.'

In most post-1945 secessionist conflicts – but not in all secessions – outside states have often had a crucial role to play by supporting either secessionists or host states. In Chapter 13, Mikulas Fabry outlines and discusses these changing norms of legitimate involvement in secessionist conflicts by outside states ('external' actors) in view of illuminating the nature of the external involvement itself. In the post-Westphalian era the external involvement in secessionist conflict was in general not considered acceptable on the grounds of dynastic legitimism: the monarchs had, on this view, inalienable rights over their domain and no external actor had the right to breach them by supporting opposition to the monarch's rule. This non-intervention norm was first severely tested by the French monarchy in its military and diplomatic support for the secessionist British colonists in North America. Another test came with the revolutions in Latin America against Spanish and Portuguese rule in the early 19th century: the Holy Alliance (of the European monarchies – France, Austria and Russia) wanted to breach the non-intervention rule by supporting, with military force, the re-establishment of the Iberian rule while the UK and USA strongly opposed any intervention in the conflicts in Latin America. The non-intervention norm was, at the time, thought to guarantee that 'people can become free by their own efforts' – not to be thwarted by alien powers. The corollary of the non-intervention norm in this form was the requirement of the recognition of the outcomes of these attempts to 'become free' from foreign rule: if the secessionists succeed in establishing their own state and in removing the former ruler, other states are obliged to recognize this outcome and to recognize the independence. This norm of international recognition of *de facto* statehood has, Fabry argues, fundamentally changed with the 1960 UN *Declaration on Granting Independence of Colonial Peoples* (for a further discussion of the Declaration and the principle enunciated see Chapters 6 and 17). This declaration singled out colonized people as holders of the right to statehood *prior* to any *de facto* establishment of their state. As a result, the recognition of *de facto* states was abandoned, and Fabry argues, self-determination of *non-colonial peoples* has been ruled out. This change in the approach to recognition of the right to statehood, has in effect made unilateral secession illegitimate. This prohibition of unilateral secession has been maintained, Fabry argues, in the post-Cold War era in which the secessions from the USSR and SFR Yugoslavia were regarded as consensual or near-consensual dissolutions of states. The norm, rejecting unilateral secession, provided a motivation for NATO military intervention to maintain the territorial integrity of Bosnia and Herzegovina as well as the *sui generis* argument justifying the recognition of secession of Kosovo. In conclusion, in spite of the human costs and political instability resulting from adherence to this norm, Fabry suggests that there is no likelihood that it will be abandoned or changed any time soon. As we have seen, James Mayall in Chapter 1 offered a similar if somewhat more cautious prediction. In contrast, Peter Radan in Chapter 17, in his review of the dissenting judgments in the International Court of Justice (ICJ) *Kosovo Declaration of Independence* case, appears to suggest that some form of remedial *justification* of unilateral secession may be emerging in international law. For further discussion of the issues of justification of secession see also Part V.

In contrast to Fabry's exploration of the norms of states' involvement in secessionist conflict, in Chapter 14 Stephen M. Saideman explores a variety of explanations of the (outside) states' responses to secessionist conflict in other states.

He focuses on three types of explanation: '1) the vulnerability of states to secession inhibits their foreign policies; 2) the domestic politics of states influence their foreign policies; and 3) that security and power shape foreign policy towards ethnic conflicts elsewhere.' For purposes of testing these explanations and the resulting hypotheses, Saideman has constructed a new dataset – Minorities and Potential Supporters Dataset, or MAPS – combining the ethnic groups in the Minorities at Risk Dataset [MAR] (Gurr 1999, 2000) with the countries in the Correlates of War dataset. In Chapter 14 he explains in detail the coding of a variety of variables used in testing as well as the logit and Relogit tools that he has used in his analysis. The results of his analyses contravene the explanations which have been accepted so far. First, vulnerability of states to secession *does not* prevent or stop their support of secessionist movements; on the contrary, countries facing separatism at home are more likely to support separatism elsewhere. This may be explicable in terms of reciprocity – countries respond to cooperation with cooperation and to conflict with conflict – as well as in terms of the realist hypothesis of state competition. States in competition with each other may be seeking to make use of every advantage, including the secessionist conflict in another state. Further, proximity (being a neighbour of the group or the state) and linguistic, religious and racial ties to the secessionist group – in this order – appear also to increase the likelihood in supporting the secessionist groups in another state. Thus ethnic politics do matter: states are more likely to support ethnically related secessionist groups in other states. Perhaps unexpectedly, the relative power of a particular state also raises the probability of its supporting secessionist groups: more powerful states are more likely to intervene in weaker states. Saideman suggests that greater power allows more powerful states to do what they want and that other factors, such as ethnic ties or strategic considerations, may then influence or determine what they want. These results appear to confirm the offensive realists' view of international relations: in cases of secessionist conflict states appear to be predatory.

In Chapter 15, Deon Geldenhuys explores another consequence of unilateral secession mentioned in Chapter 13, the absence of international *de jure* recognition of states created by unilateral secession. The states which lack collective *de jure* recognition due to the internationally disputed nature of their purported statehood are, in Geldenhuys nomenclature, 'contested states'. Such states arise in various ways, including military conquest, unilateral imposition of minority (usually white) regimes as well as by unilateral secession. Geldenhuys discusses a large number of such cases in the 20th century and explores some of the reasons why these states did not gain any or only limited recognition. As Fabry has already noted in Chapter 13, the adherence to the principle of territorial integrity of established or recognized states appears to be the main reason why many states created by unilateral secession from the already recognized states fail to gain widespread recognition of other states: unilateral secession breaches the territorial integrity principle (see also Chapters 6 and 17). As Geldenhuys notes, the current United Nations system, in upholding the territorial integrity of its members against attempts at unilateral secession, functions as a protection club for its members.

# Secession from an Economic Perspective: What Is Living and What Is Dead in Economic Interpretations of Secessionism?

Lloyd Cox

Economic interpretations of secessionism have fallen from intellectual favour in recent years.[1] Many contemporary texts on secessions either neglect economic interpretations altogether, or subsume them within broader discussions of 'instrumentalism'. Where economic theories are dealt with, they are frequently castigated for a variety of intellectual sins, including a failure to address the affective dimensions of secessionist sentiment, a tendency to elevate abstract theorizing at the expense of empirical realities, and an over-reliance on reductionist and functionalist forms of reasoning.

But such curt dismissals have not always been widely accepted. Although never occupying a dominant position in the literature, some major contributions from the 1970s through to the early 2000s had placed economic developments at the forefront of analyses that sought to explain how and why national minorities mobilized to win independence. Most obviously, neo-Marxist authors developed theories that claimed to address the widely acknowledged short-comings of Marxist approaches to 'the national question', while preserving key Marxian assumptions about the centrality of capitalism for explaining ideational and political phenomena such as nationalism. Tom Nairn, for example, could concede that 'nationalism represents Marxism's great historical failure', but then argue that it could nonetheless 'be understood in essentially materialist terms'. It was 'the machinery of world political

---

1   For a survey of some key economic theories of secession see the relevant section of chapter 6 of Pavković with Radan (2007).

economy' that allegedly provided the key to unlocking 'the most notoriously subjective and ideal of historical phenomena' (Nairn 1975: 3, 8).

Some influential Marxist sociological and historical accounts of sub-national challenges to existing states were more focused on intra-societal dynamics than global political economy. Michael Hechter's important book *Internal Colonialism* (1975) provided a template for a host of imitators to explore the ways in which capitalist industrialization, far from dissolving minority identities within states, exacerbated ethnic differentiation through the establishment of a cultural division of labour. This could and frequently did become the basis for demands for greater autonomy or even outright secession from the central state. Similarly, historian Miroslav Hroch's (2000 [1985]) celebrated account of the emergence of patriotic groups and small nations in 19th-century Central and Eastern Europe – originally published as two monographs in 1969 and 1971 (the first in German, the second in Czech) but only translated into English as a single book in 1985 – made much of the spread of capitalist exchange relations. The basic proposition was that expansion of the capitalist market drove political centralization, linguistic standardization and social mobility, while sharpening material conflicts of interest. The latter often had, or could be portrayed as having, a national dimension, which became the basis for agitation amongst 'patriots' drawn from the intelligentsia, the petit bourgeoisie and the peasantry in the non-dominant ethnic groups. Such resistance could, in circumstances where a cross-class, mass movement was mobilized, be transformed into a fully-fledged struggle for national independence.

Economic interpretations of secessionism and of nationalism more generally have not been limited to Marxists. Even a thinker as resolutely anti-Marxist as Ernest Gellner (1983; 1994; 1997) placed a heavy emphasis on economic development in both the origins and spread of state-led and state-challenging nationalism. If one substitutes Gellner's 'industrialism' for Hroch's 'capitalism', the commonalities between their respective works are obvious. Gellner viewed economic development, as manifested in industrialization, as entailing a culturally homogenizing logic that could give rise to oppositional nationalist movements within existing states and/or empires. As with the central states that they were resisting, such oppositional movements sought to bring political boundaries into alignment with cultural boundaries, and hence to build a 'political roof' of their own.

Whatever their differences, and they are considerable, all of these approaches share an emphasis on the *economic preconditions* contributing to the origins and spread of (state-challenging) nationalism. They do not so much provide causal accounts of the relationship between economy and nationalism, as thick descriptions of the general economic conditions under which secessionist politics is likely to emerge and flourish. Moreover, they often subsume secessionism – understood as the ideology justifying 'the creation of a new state upon territory previously forming part of, or being a colonial entity of, an existing state' (Radan 2008: 18) – within broader discussions of nationalism. Hence, to the extent that they develop intellectual resources for helping to understand secessionist politics at all, these often have to be excavated from their more general analyses of nationalism.

Other approaches emphasizing the importance of economic factors for explaining the emergence of secessionist politics develop more straightforwardly causal accounts. Many of these theories concentrate less on the structural linkages between the economy and secessionist movements, and more on the pattern of economic costs and benefits influencing nationalist entrepreneurs and the target populations at which they direct their mobilizing efforts. Such causal accounts are exemplified in a more recent contribution by Collier and Hoeffler (2002), who argued that it is economic self-interest that best explains why particular populations adopt a secessionist political posture. In a nutshell, ethnically distinct minorities pursue their own state when they perceive that such an outcome would benefit them economically. Michael Hechter (1992; 2000) developed a similar account, though premised on a more rigid rational choice methodology, after having shifted from his earlier Marxist-inspired position. Minority nationalist entrepreneurs choose secessionist politics, and minority populations choose to follow them, when they rationally calculate that doing so will be advantageous to them as individuals. These private interests are calculated mainly, though not exclusively, in economic terms.

It would be misleading to assimilate all of these contributions to a single approach. As we shall see, many of the key propositions of the scholars mentioned are incompatible with those of the others. That said, they all share an emphasis on the centrality of economic phenomena for understanding secessionism. As such, they can legitimately be said to exemplify economic interpretations of secessionism, albeit with differing inflections on the precise nature of the relationship between economy and secessionist politics. In particular, the cleavage between those who focus on the *economic preconditions* contributing to secessionist politics, and those providing *causal accounts*, is a useful way of demarcating these different economic approaches. In what follows, I deploy this classificatory schema to discuss the merits and demerits of various economic interpretations, with a view to answering the question posed in the title of the chapter. I begin with non-causal approaches that focus on economic preconditions, dividing these into two distinct types – transnational and intra-societal – and continue with an appraisal of causal accounts. In the concluding section, I end by trying to crystallize what is living and what is dead in economic interpretations of secessionism.

## Economic Structures as Preconditions 1: Transnational Economic Forms

In considering economic structures and processes that might contribute to the emergence of secessionist politics, two distinct approaches can be discerned. In the first, transnational economic forms are emphasized as crucial preconditions out of which more localized secessionist politics arise. In the second, it is intra-societal economic structures and dynamics that are the main focus for interpretations purporting to explain why some national minorities coalesce into independence movements while others do not.

Historically, the first of these broad approaches emerged at that intellectual juncture where society-centred forms of theorizing in general, and modernization theory in particular, were being widely criticized. The latter had typically viewed sub-national challenges to existing state power as being a type of social pathology. This could be mitigated by economic modernization along a unitary path to Walt Rostow's (1960) much-vaunted 'age of high mass consumption'. Radical theorists retorted that far from being a social pathology, minority movements for independence were a necessary consequence of a capitalist world system divided by deep structural inequalities (Frank 1969; Wallestein 1984). Setting aside the arcane debates and fine-grained distinctions that differentiated the protagonists of these radical theories, what they shared was an emphasis on the necessary connection between global economic unity and political dis-unity, driven by the political economy of a global capitalist system that developed between the 16th and 20th centuries. The latter had created artificial political boundaries that cut across pre-existing cultural space, thereby establishing the fault-lines along which future secessionist demands might emerge. When this was coupled with economic deprivation, exploitation and the establishment of a cultural division of labour within post-colonial states, the stage was set for secessionist conflicts to occur. For Immanuel Wallerstein, one of the most articulate defenders of such a position, this expressed the contradictory tendencies between economic integration and political fragmentation that is said to define the world system (1991: 185–93). It is a dialectic that gave rise to states and an inter-state system, but also to sub-national movements for political independence within states. The latter are, in the final instance, determined by the structure of the world capitalist economy.

In his seminal essay, *The Modern Janus*, Tom Nairn developed a similar account to Wallerstein's, which is worth sketching in more detail. The original argument was focused specifically on national liberation struggles – as opposed to secessions within existing sovereign states – though he would later attend to the fissiparous tendencies to which such struggles subsequently gave rise. In the first instance, Nairn argued that uneven capitalist development generates relations of political and economic domination and subordination between core and peripheral regions in the world economy. In the periphery, this uneven development is expressed as a discrepancy between the emerging middle classes' expectations on the one hand, and their material reality on the other. The exclusion of the periphery from the fruits of modernity led their elites to mobilize against external domination. To do so effectively, they needed to invite the masses into history, and 'the invitation card had to be written in a language they understood' (Nairn 1975: 12). This metaphorical 'language' encompasses the ethnic particularities of the peoples being invited into history – peoples being mobilized to resist foreign domination while also preserving its vital, modernizing force. In short, elite groups in the periphery employed 'nationality' as a basis for mobilizing against foreign domination. Where the substantive dimensions of nationality did not exist they had to be invented, drawing upon whatever common cultural, linguistic and historical elements were at hand. It is from this passage to modernity that nationalism derives its Janus-faced character: 'As human kind is forced through its straight doorway, it must look desperately back into the past, to gather strength wherever it can be found for the ordeal of development' (Nairn 1975: 18).

In his original essay, Nairn's focus is on accounting for nationalism in the periphery of the capitalist world economy. The object of and impetus for his essay was the struggle of national liberation movements in the Third World against European colonialism. Yet implicit in his account of the *'Modern Janus'* is also an explanation of secessonist tendencies within new *and* old states. Uneven capitalist development is no less important at a state and regional level than at the level of global political economy. Peripheries form within the periphery, as well as within the core. Their *relative* economic deprivation and subordination can become the basis for sub-national, secessionist mobilizations against the central state. For Nairn, this is perhaps best exemplified in the struggles of people's in Britain's Celtic fringe for greater autonomy and even independence *vis-à-vis* the English-dominated central state, which are analysed at length in his collection of essays on *The Break-up of Britain* (1977). These secessionist tendencies, Nairn declares, are more correctly labelled as manifestations of 'neo-nationalism' rather than nationalism plain and simple, as they are distinguishable from their anti-colonial counterparts by the higher level of economic development in the regions out of which they arise. Nonetheless, they are comparable to anti-colonial nationalist struggles in so far as they, also, are 'a forced by-product of the grotesquely uneven nature of capitalist development' (Nairn 1977: 127–8).[2]

Approaches such as Nairn's and Wallerstein's that emphasize the centrality of global political economy for establishing the conditions in which secessionism thrives are vulnerable to two related criticisms. On the one hand, they are most often premised on an economically reductionist logic. This is overt in Wallerstein (1991), who continues to use the metaphor of base and superstructure, arguing that secessionism and nationalism more generally – as parts of a political and ideological superstructure – are derivative of the capitalist world-economy, which constitutes an economic base. By contrast, Nairn explicitly rejects economic reductionism, but periodically smuggles it back into his analysis.[3] Thus, when he says that the

---

2 In his book published two decades after the *Break-up of Britain*, Nairn suggested that, '[i]n retrospect "uneven development" seems a pathetically inadequate way of trying to cover such varied and occasionally cataclysmic shifts [as those associated with the rise and spread of nationalism]' (1997: 16). Nevertheless, elsewhere in the book he more or less repeats his earlier arguments word-for-word, asserting that development 'could only be uneven; the unevenness could only generate a continuing reaction, the politically driven mobilisation of those excluded, "left behind", colonized or sentenced to become heritage trails' (1997: 50).

3 In his original essay, Nairn forcefully rebuts the charge of economic reductionism: '[his conception of nationalism] … does not wish or think away the phenomena in question (political romanticism, the idealism of under-development, subjectivism, the need to "belong", etc.) by asserting that these are merely manifestations of economic trends. It does exactly the opposite. It awards them real force and weight in modern historical

'subjective' and 'ideal' phenomenon of nationalism is 'a by-product of the most brutally and hopelessly material aide of the history of the last two centuries' (1975: 8), he strongly implies that it *is* epiphenomenal, and that the direction of the causal arrows run from the 'machinery of world political economy' to modern nationalism and secessionism. By treating these phenomena as 'by-products', Nairn implies that the 'original product' is the world political economy, which, presumably, is the lens through which any investigation of secessionism must proceed and should properly focus.

On the other hand, these approaches are often criticized for not adequately identifying the mediating linkages that tie global political economy to more localized political processes such as secessionism. In other words, they are pitched at such a high level of abstraction that in seeking to explain everything they end up explaining very little. The abstraction 'uneven economic development' turns out to be an exceedingly blunt analytical instrument in the absence of knowing how it manifests itself empirically and how it interacts with other cultural and political variables within states. It is these that determine if and when uneven economic development expresses itself as secessionist tendencies, demands for greater autonomy, or closer integration into an existing state. After all, all politics is, as the saying goes, local, even if influenced by remote structures and processes like global political economy.

## Economic Structures as Preconditions 2: Intra-Societal Economic Structures

In contrast to those perspectives emphasizing the importance of transnational political economy, other scholars have focused more on intra-societal economic structures and dynamics as decisive preconditions to secessionism. Here some general themes emerge that one finds widely repeated in the literature, although they are not always substantiated with empirical evidence.

To begin with, the capitalist market and industrialization are frequently said to entail an economic logic that demands both political centralization and cultural and linguistic homogenization. The needs of a modern industrial economy are such, so the argument runs, that the central state must attend to what Ernest Gellner once referred to as the 'cultural branding of its flock' (1983: 35). But such state-led cultural homogenization, driven by economic imperatives, can and often does intensify the political alienation of geographically concentrated, cultural minorities, who are materially disadvantaged by the centralization of economic

---

development … by explaining the material reasons for this newly-acquired leverage …. To show they are the other face of capitalism's invasion of our world does not entail their demotion to mere appearance or epiphenomenon' (1975: 25).

and political power in the hands of a culturally distinct majority.[4] Historically, this has often manifested itself in the development of what Michael Hechter (1975) termed a 'cultural division of labour', whereby the organization of the labour market and hence the distribution of a society's scarce resources is largely shaped by ethnicity. The unequal distribution of resources frequently becomes a source of ongoing grievance for the group that perceives itself as being, rightly or wrongly, materially disadvantaged by the existing economic and political order.[5] When a cultural division of labour is mapped onto the territorial concentration of particular identity groups, demands for greater autonomy or even independence can emerge. They are most likely to emerge, most scholars of this persuasion would argue, in periods of heightened economic stress, which, Miroslav Hroch suggests, sharpens 'nationally relevant conflicts of interest' between competing identity groups within the boundaries of the existing state (1996: 88). His views nicely exemplify some key ideas of approaches that emphasize intra-societal economic structures.

Hroch's (2000 [1985]) comparative work on national revivals in 19th-century Europe (including those of the Norwegians, Czechs, Finns, Estonians, Lithuanians, Slovaks, Flemish, Croatians and Danes) discerned three structural phases in the growth of secessionist movements, all premised on the emergence and subsequent extension of capitalist exchange relations. In phase A, 'learned researchers' cultivate awareness of the historic, cultural and linguistic distinctiveness of the subordinated ethnic group. In phase B, 'patriots' strive to win a majority of their compatriots to the secessionist cause. In phase C, a cross-class mass movement mobilizes on the basis of the national identity cultivated and widely disseminated in phases A and B, and struggles to free itself from what is now widely understood as alien rule. This 'phase' account enables Hroch to systematically compare conditions that facilitated or impeded the transition from one phase to another. With respect to the transition between phases A and B, three facilitating processes are identified: (1) a crisis of the old order, as manifested in (2) broad-based disillusionment and discontent throughout the subordinate ethnic population, and (3) a loss of faith in traditional belief systems, including religion. For a transition to phase C to occur, however, there also has to exist relatively high levels of social mobility and social communication, along with 'nationally relevant conflicts of interest'. During phase C, such conflicts were and are exhibited in political demands, including the demand for national independence.[6] The circumstances outlined do not guarantee

---

4    I use the terms 'minority' and 'majority' in their sociological rather than numerical sense. A distinct, named population may constitute a numerical majority in a given state, but still be a minority in the sense that it is economically and culturally marginalized and politically disenfranchised.

5    It is important to note that economic grievances and the perception of disadvantage are not the exclusive preserve of identity groups who occupy lower rungs on the socio-economic ladder. Economically privileged groups within a state can also harbour a sense of grievance and perceive themselves as being disadvantaged by existing political-economic arrangements; for example, some northern Italians resent the disproportionate transfer of revenue and resources to the south of the country.

6    The relevance of this account is not limited to the struggles for national independence

that an actual attempt at secession will occur or be successful, but they do present conditions that are conducive for such an occurrence.

Ernest Gellner advanced arguments similar to Hroch's while rejecting their underlying Marxian assumptions. Gellner's starting point is the functional requirements of a modern industrial economy:

> *So the economy needs both the new type of central culture and the central state; the culture needs the state; and the state probably needs the homogenous cultural branding of its flock ... In brief, the mutual relationship of a modern culture and state is something quite new, and springs, inevitably, from the requirements of a modern economy. (Gellner 1983: 140)*

And yet such state-imposed homogenization in the service of economic necessity may in turn engender counter-nationalisms (secessionist movements) from below, which are an effect of uneven industrial development. It is here that Gellner's account is relevant for understanding secessionist politics. He crystallized the substance of his argument in an extended fable about the relationship between the fictional entities of 'Ruritania' and 'Megalomania' (1983: 58–62). His main point was that Ruritanians only came to see themselves as Ruritanians, and to politically organize as Ruritanians, when they experienced material and cultural disadvantages arising from actions by the Megalomanian-controlled central state to culturally homogenize its population in the service of economic ends. Indeed, Ruritanian identity is defined by its contrast with Megalomania. The tensions between the two, Gellner suggests, can only be resolved if Ruritanians assimilate to the dominant Megalomanian culture, or if they are successful in making the territorial boundaries of their culture congruent with its political boundaries. In other words, if they do not assimilate they must secede and achieve their own 'political roof' (1983: 66). The functional requirements of an industrial economic order, then, find expression in both state-promoting *and* state-opposing (secessionist) nationalism.

A variety of criticisms have been made of views that focus on intra-societal economic structures as pre-conditions to secessionism. First, it is not at all clear that capitalism and/or industrialism (and they are not, of course, the same thing) have in fact been important factors in *all* cases of secessionism. Indeed, a strong *prima facie* case can be made that both have often been absent, or only very weakly present, in

---

in 19th-century Europe. In fact, Hroch himself deploys this framework to compare these with more recent secessionist movements in the post-communist world. He argues that there are arresting parallels between the two sets of cases. These are revealed in the contemporary, post-communist efflorescence of linguistic and cultural demands, not to mention political demands for greater autonomy if not outright secession. Moreover, the emergence of new capitalist ruling classes in the lands where 'already existing socialism' once stood, and their struggles to consolidate their rule as hegemonic 'national' classes, closely parallels their 19th-century predecessors. Finally, sharpening economic, social and political crises, which can plausibly be interpreted within a nationalist frame, are shared by secessionist nationalisms of both periods. See Hroch (1996: 88–90).

situations where secessionism has emerged. Eritrea's secession from Ethiopia, East Timor's from Indonesia, and Bangladesh's from Pakistan are but three examples where the emphasis on capitalism and industrialism seems somewhat misplaced, to say the least (see Part VI). Second, and closely related to the previous point, some scholars suggest that in focusing on economics these approaches neglect political not to mention social and psychological preconditions. In particular, they neglect the ways in which political institutions can either be an irritant to or a salve for secessionist sentiment, irrespective of economic considerations (see O'Leary 1998: 61–3). Various forms of political accommodation, for example, ranging from cultural autonomy and arbitration, to federalism and consociation, can work to dampen down secessionist politics, even where uneven economic development creates conditions for its aggravation. Third and finally, the identification of economic preconditions or 'elective affinities' between economic circumstances and secessionist politics is no substitute for developing *causal* accounts about the nature of that relationship. It is to several such accounts which I now turn.

## Causal Economic Accounts of Secessionism

Many scholars have recognized the empirically verifiable fact that some secessionist political parties have won support on the basis of a platform promising economic benefits for their target constituents. Milica Zarkovic Bookman (1992), John Wood (1981) and Russell Hardin (1995) for example, are three scholars who recognized the importance of economic factors (such as relative income, levels of economic development, trade dependency, the nature of tax transfers and the connection between economic self-interest and group identification) in attracting support to secessionist causes. As Wood observes, often '[s]ecessionists believe that they have been denied their rightful share of material benefits and that they will gain through secession' (1981: 118). For Malica Zarkovic Bookman, demands for outright independence typically find their most fertile political soil in regions with relatively high incomes as compared to the host state overall, or in regions with a relatively low level of economic development. Similarly, Russell Hardin (1995) provides a sophisticated argument for the ways in which national and ethnic group identification is shaped by material self-interest, with the latter frequently being a basis for mobilizing or at least reinforcing other non-material, nationalist motivations (1995: 14). For Hardin and for Wood and Zarkovic Bookman, however, it is important to point out that they do not accept that all secessionist politics can be explained in straightforward economic terms, abstracted from the broader cultural and political fields in which economic phenomena is necessarily embedded. As Hardin notes, 'the way economic issues matter is not merely through a linear causal effect'. Rather, economic issues 'construct the range of possibility of conflict', which is only then activated by what he refers to as 'tipping phenomena' that may or may not be principally economic (1995: 145–6). By contrast, some theorists have inflated the relatively un-contentious observation that economic factors are important in *some* secessionist cases, into full-blown theories that posit economic motives as the *principal* causes of secessionist politics in general.

Paul Collier and Anke Hoeffler, for example, argue that the political identities on which secessionist movements are premised are 'typically a recent contrivance designed to support perceived economic advantage ...' (2002: 2). This is particularly the case where the population in a relatively wealthy, geographically contiguous part of a given state 'perceives secession to be economically advantageous' (2002: 3). Here Collier and Hoeffler emphasize the importance of natural resource endowment. Secessionist politicians, even if genuinely motivated by other ends, have a powerful propaganda weapon where their region has a disproportionate share in natural resources, on which the host state is disproportionately dependent for tax revenues. The argument that 'we would be economically better off if we politically divorced the host state' has an obvious, self-evident quality that is more likely to resonate with the target population than simple appeals to what the authors refer to as 'romantic nationalism'. In the absence of an economic catalyst, they argue, the latter is likely to remain a marginal political movement.

To illustrate these arguments, Collier and Hoeffler enlist the support of several well-known case studies. The case of Scottish nationalism is particularly instructive. The Scottish National Party (SNP), founded on an explicitly secessionist platform, had been largely irrelevant until its electoral breakthrough in 1974, where it leaped from political obscurity to capture 30 percent of the popular vote. The explanation for its success, Collier and Heoffler contend, is obvious. After the discovery of North Sea oil in 1966, and the subsequent oil crisis of 1973/74 that quadrupled the price of oil and greatly enhanced the flow of tax revenues to Westminster, the SNP had a ready-made issue on which to campaign. Indeed, they ran on the slogan 'Its Scotland's oil' and vociferously argued that Scotland's five million people would greatly benefit if the oil taxes were not being shared with Britain's other 45 million inhabitants. As Collier and Hoeffler summarize, '[t]he fragile and recent cause of romantic nationalism could thus be allied to the robust and ancient cause of economic self-interest' (2002: 7).

Collier and Hoeffler go on to outline additional cases where natural resources were allegedly crucial to secessionist politics (Biafra, Katanga, East Timor and Aceh), and cases where economically-inspired secessions were not linked to natural resources (Eritrea, Slovenia, Croatia, Bangladesh and the Southern Confederacy in the United States). Without discussing the detail of all these cases, their main point is that in each case it is economic motives that trump other considerations, and hence economic factors that constitute the primary causal variable in explanations of secessionism. This interpretation, which I scrutinize more fully below, is largely shared by Michael Hechter, the last theorist to be discussed here.

As I have previously intimated, Michael Hechter's (1992; 2000) position has shifted from one that was broadly informed by Marxian assumptions, to one firmly premised on a rational choice paradigm. The latter views collective action, such as attempts at secession, as being reducible to rationally calculated individual preferences. Individuals choose particular courses of action based on considerations of what will benefit them as individuals, with such benefits being measured largely in terms of economic gain. Individuals choose to support secessionist entrepreneurs and political parties, therefore, where they rationally calculate that separation from the existing state will be in their private economic interests:

> *For a group to attempt to secede, it is causally necessary (but not sufficient) that its members believe that the secession will bring them more private benefits than remaining in the host state. (Hechter 1992: 268)*

Viewed from the standpoint of the politician advocating secession, they must be able to offer their target constituents the promise of some personal economic benefit should the secession be successfully concluded. Hechter suggests that the key economic benefit that secessionists can hold out to potential followers is the promise of jobs and therefore economic security in the future state (1992: 275). It is for this reason that secessionism tends to draw its strongest support from layers of the middle classes.[7] Interestingly, in his book-length elaboration of these ideas, *Containing Nationalism*, Hechter suggests that in the contemporary age of accelerated economic and military globalization, the incentive structure favouring secessionism has been greatly enhanced. In general, the economic and military benefits of remaining within a larger political-economic unit are not what they once were. The expansion of both free trade and regional military alliances have reduced two of the main burdens of being a small state – economic viability and national defence – thereby improving the structure of political opportunities that secessionist politicians confront (Hechter 2000: 117, 124).

Causal economic accounts such as those developed by Collier and Hoeffler and by Hechter offer inadequate explanations of secessionism for several reasons. To begin with, their underlying assumption that human agents are actuated mainly by economic gain, and that 'rationality' ought be assessed against an economic measure of value, does not stand up to scrutiny. While it can be accepted that human agents are *often* motivated by economic considerations, and that they *often* rationally choose means that can effectively realize those motivations, the historical and anthropological record, not to mention the history of secessionism itself, clearly demonstrates that many other non-economic preferences enter into the choices that human beings make about where and in whom to place their political allegiances.

The problematic nature of the economistic assumption is brought into sharp relief when considering Collier and Hoeffler's and Hechter's responses to cases of secession that apparently contradict their central thesis. With Collier and Hoeffler, for example, the choice of Slovakians to secede from a political federation in which they clearly derived economic benefits is dismissed as a 'serious mistake', without any further elaboration (2002: 23). Non-economic alternatives that might possibly

---

7   For additional critical commentary on Hechter – especially his rather curious definition of secession that limits the concept to those cases where the host state freely acceded to secessionist demands (Sweden accepting the secession of Norway in 1905 and the UK accepting the secession of the Irish Free State in 1922) – see Pavkovic and Radan (2007: 186–8).

have motivated Slovaks and their political leaders are not even considered. Similarly, the difficult-to-identify economic benefits that Kosovo Albanians might derive from seceding from Yugoslavia are glossed over by invoking the instrumental role of the Albanian diaspora, who are said to have funded and energized the secessionist movement. The required economic benefits come from outside rather than from the material promise of secession itself. To sum up, the anomalies to Collier and Hoeffler's theory are either dismissed as mistakes of calculation by separatists, or additional *explanada* are invoked but packaged in economic terms to preserve a theory found wanting in the face of reality.

Michael Hechter's reading of Southern Ireland's secession from the United Kingdom in 1922 has similar problems. It neglects both the economic difficulties into which the new Irish Free State was predictably plunged, and the economic (and non-economic) costs that the Irish population had to bear in their struggle for independence. A strong *prima facie* case can be made that an Irish individual's cost-benefit calculation would suggest that they should not support secession, as doing so would imperil their property, their individual liberty and even their lives for very uncertain economic benefits. Consequently, if we take Hechter's theory seriously, they were either being irrational or making a monumental mis-calculation. He does not consider the more obvious and historically informed explanation that the Irish population, and their nationalist leaders, were prepared to forsake immediate economic benefits in the interests of securing non-economic goods (Pavkovic and Radan 2007: 188). Casting off the ritual, quotidian humiliations of British rule, securing a privileged political position for one's own religion, avenging the lost lives of past patriots, and having an Irishman as Head of State, were all non-economic benefits that were at least if not more important than crude economic gain in persuading Irish men and women that they needed their own state.

Other empirical cases that contradict the main thesis of Collier and Heoffler and of Hechter could no doubt be multiplied. But that is neither necessary nor possible in this chapter. The key point is that their accounts simplify complexity and over-generalize the obvious importance of economic factors in *some* (perhaps much) secessionist politics to *all* secessionist politics. As the positions of Zarkovic Bookman (1992) and John Wood (1981) cited at the beginning of this section make clear, while economics is important for secessionism, not all secessionist politics can be explained in such straightforward economic terms.

## What Is Living and What Is Dead?

As we have seen, accounts of secessionism that emphasize transnational and intra-societal economic preconditions, as well as more strictly causal economic accounts, have both strengths and weaknesses.

At the outset, one can say that mono-causal economic interpretations of secessionism are dead. That is, interpretations that view economy, however construed, as being the prime mover of all secessionist politics are subject to the usual problems associated with mono-causal explanations, plus some additional ones that relate specifically to the issue of secessionism.

Mono-causal reductionist explanations have been widely discredited in the social sciences for mechanistically simplifying social complexity, and for failing to appreciate the *relational* nature of social reality. Different elements of that reality draw their meaning from, and can only be understood in the context of, other elements with which they interact. Consequently, effects in the social world never have singular causes but are the outcomes of complex processes involving multiple causes. Those outcomes in turn react back on the phenomena that helped produce them, which belies the mono-causalist's assumption that causal arrows always run in one direction, from the prime-moving, independent variable (in this case, economy) to the affected, dependent variable (in this case, secessionism).

These problems are particularly acute when it comes to analysing secessions. Every attempt to explain the latter in terms of the primacy of one particular cause – such as the needs of an industrial economy, uneven economic development, the economic disadvantage or advantage of a particular group, or the perceived economic benefits that will accrue to rational human agents should a secession be successful – invariably encounter instances of secessionism that clearly contradict such explanations. We saw this with Ernest Gellner's erroneous emphasis on the alleged connection between industrialism and national secessions, and with Collier and Heoffler's and Hechter's view that secessions are always actuated by the perception of economic gain. The empirically verifiable exceptions to these explanations are just too numerous and too contradictory to be explained away in the ways that these theorists attempt. Simply dismissing them as mistakes is a declaration of explanatory bankruptcy, while repackaging non-economic variables in economic terms highlights the inadequacy of such theories in the first place. And there is the rub. Mono-causal explanations can assert the primacy of a particular cause in the abstract, but invariably have to invoke additional causes when confronting the complexity of the real world.

But this should in no way be construed as implying that all economic interpretations of secessionism are necessarily mono-causal, or that economics is unimportant for understanding secessionism. Economic considerations *are* demonstrably important in many manifestations of secessionist politics, though their causal efficacy has to be established empirically in individual cases, and cannot be assumed *a priori*. That said, there are some recurring economic phenomena that many instances of secessionism seem to manifest, and to which contemporary theorists of secession should be sensitive.

As we have seen, several scholars – Nairn, Wallerstein, Hroch, Gellner, Hechter – emphasize the importance of uneven economic development in the generation of secessionist sentiment and political mobilization. They are right to do so, but I would want to add some qualifications to the way in which uneven development is conceptualized.

As I argued in the discussion of Nairn, uneven capitalist development is a necessary but not a sufficient condition for the emergence of secessionist politics. Uneven economic development distributes material rewards and thus economic grievances unequally across the surface of the planet, both within and between states. These are frequently, perhaps always, overlaid with cultural differences that can take on a nationalist cast. But whether they do or not, and if they do whether this manifests itself in secessionist politics, cannot be determined *a priori* by the mere presence of economic unevenness and inequality. Some economically disadvantaged (or advantaged) groups sharing a common territory and identity that can be plausibly portrayed in nationalist terms will opt for secession, but many will not. The task of the theorist of secession, therefore, is to identify those conditions under which economic disparities and material grievances (of economically dominant and subordinate groups) are most readily translated into secessionist demands and mass mobilizations for separatist objectives.

The other key economic pre-condition with which secessionist politics is often entwined is, as Miroslav Hroch argued, economic crisis and dislocation. Certainly the secessions of the latter part of the 20th century – in the Balkans, the Post-Soviet successor states, Africa and Asia – were frequently bound up with economic crises that contributed to, but that were also exacerbated by, separatist conflicts (see Chapter 8). Yet whether or not economic crises led to *actual* attempts to secede had as much to do with the actions and organization of the state against which separatists agitated, as it did with economic conditions.

And herein lays the key qualification that is necessary for preserving the relevance of economic interpretations of secessionism. Economic conditions and processes, including those that impact on secessionist tendencies, should be understood in relation to, rather than abstractions from, the state and the inter-state system. While states are certainly constrained by the logic of capital accumulation on a global scale, they remain the key institutions for ordering, regulating and controlling the political spaces within which state-promoting *and* state-seeking nationalists fight it out. The great diversity of institutional arrangements that have developed within these political spaces have no lesser material effect than do economic conditions. Indeed, the latter are often consequences, both intended and unintended, of a state's institutional arrangements. As such, economic interpretations of secessionism must embrace *political*-economy if they are to remain relevant and avoid becoming the intellectual corpse that many have already taken them to be. Hopefully, I have shown in this chapter that the works of at least some of the theorists encountered, when suitably trimmed and qualified, are economic interpretations that still have something useful to contribute to our understanding of secessionist politics (see also Chapter 3).

# References

Collier, A. and A. Hoeffler (2002), 'The Political Economy of Secession'. [Online] At http://users.ox.ac.uk/-ball0144/self-det.pdf [accessed 19 October 2009].
Frank, A.G. (1969), *Capitalism and Underdevelopment in Latin America: Historical Studies of Chile and Brazil* (New York: Monthly Review Press).
Gellner, E. (1983), *Nations and Nationalism* (Oxford: Basil Blackwell).
Gellner, E. (1994), *Encounters with Nationalism* (Oxford: Basil Blackwell).
Gellner, E. (1997), *Nationalism* (London: Weidenfield and Nicolson).
Hardin, R. (1995), *One for All: The Logic of Group Conflict* (Princeton NJ: Princeton University Press).
Hechter, M. (1975), *Internal Colonialism: The Celtic Fringe in British National Development, 1536–1966* (Berkeley, CA: University of California Press).
Hechter, M. (1992), 'The Dynamics of Secession', *Acta Sociologica* 35, 267–83.
Hechter, M. (2000), *Containing Nationalism* (Oxford: Oxford University Press).
Hroch, M. (1996), 'From National Movement to the Fully-Formed Nation: The Nation-Building Process in Europe', in G. Balakrishnan and B. Anderson (eds), *Mapping the Nation* (London: Verso), 78–97.
Hroch, M. (2000 [1985]), *Social Preconditions of National Revival in Europe: A Comparative Analysis of the Social Composition of Patriotic Groups among the Smaller European Nations* (New York: Columbia University Press).
Nairn, T. (1975), 'The Modern Janus', *New Left Review* 94, 3–29.
Nairn, T. (1977), *The Break-Up of Britain: Crisis and Neo-Nationalism* (London: New Left Books).
Nairn, T. (1997), *Faces of Nationalism: Janus Revisited* (London: Verso).
O'Leary, B. (1998), 'Ernest Gellner's Diagnosis of Nationalism: A Critical Overview, or, What Is Living and What Is Dead in Ernest Gellner's Philosophy of Nationalism', in J. Hall (ed.), *The State of the Nation: Ernest Gellner and the Theory of Nationalism* (Cambridge: Cambridge University Press), 40–88.
Pavković, A. with P. Radan (2007), *Creating New States: Theory and Practice of Secession* (Aldershot: Ashgate).
Radan, P. (2008), 'Secession: A Word in Search of a Meaning', in A. Pavkovic and P. Radan (eds), *On the Way to Statehood: Secession and Globalisation* (Aldershot: Ashgate), 17–32.
Rostow, W. (1960), *The Stages of Economic Growth: A Non-Communist Manifesto* (Cambridge: Cambridge University Press).
Wallerstein, I. (1984), *The Politics of the World-Economy* (Cambridge: Cambridge University Press).
Wallerstein, I. (1991), *Geopolitics and Geoculture* (Cambridge: Cambridge University Press).
Wood, J.R. (1981), 'Secession: A Comparative Analytical Framework', *Canadian Journal of Political Science* 14, 109–35.
Zarkovic Bookman, M. (1992), *The Economics of Secession* (New York: St Martin's Press).

# 11

# Secession and Ethnic Conflict

Keiichi Kubo

## Introduction

Secession and ethnic conflict are both close and distant at the same time. On the one hand, secession and ethnic conflict are viewed as largely overlapping, and in extreme cases are treated as synonyms, often without rigorous theoretical or empirical foundation. On the other hand, the academic literature on secession and that on ethnic conflict have developed relatively independently of each other, without much mutual referencing. Many fundamental works in the literature on ethnic conflict are virtually ignored in the literature on secession, and vice versa. This chapter thus attempts to clarify the conceptual differences between the two, and, at the same time, to bridge the gap between the study of these two by integrating important findings and arguments in the literature on both issues.

In order to do so, this chapter attempts to address a number of questions, namely:

- Is secession connected to ethnic conflict? If so, how, and to what extent?
- What is the relationship between ethnic identity and secession? Can we assume that ethnic identities always exist before secession takes place?
- Why does secessionist ethnic conflict occur? What are the causes and dynamics of ethnic conflict that matter for the understanding of secession?
- Can secession be an effective solution to ethnic conflict?

Before addressing these questions, however, the definition of ethnic conflict needs to be discussed.[1] The questions presented above will then be addressed in each of the sections that follow. The chapter concludes with a brief recapitulation of the main arguments.

---

1   As for the definition of secession, this chapter follows the definition presented in the Introduction.

## Definition of Ethnic Conflict

For a definition of *ethnic conflict*, a natural starting point is to define *ethnicity*. Generally speaking, scholars agree that ethnicity is a type of identity shared by a group of people, normally based on some kind of cultural and/or physical traits, such as language, religion, customs and so on. For example, the 'inclusive conception' of ethnicity proposed by Horowitz (1985: 17–18) defines ethnic groups 'by ascriptive differences, whether the indicum is color, appearance, language, religion, some other indicator of common origin, or some combination thereof'. This inclusive conception is needed because what is important is not whether objective differences *per se* are present but whether they are used to mark one group off from another: different attributes may be invoked for different contexts of group interactions (Horowitz 1985: 41–51). This characteristic makes it difficult to formulate a precise definition of ethnicity, and scholars cannot always agree on what ethnicity should and should not include. For example, while Horowitz (1985: 53) views ethnicity as something that covers tribes, races, nationalities and castes, Smith (1991: 21–2) argues that ethnicity and race should be clearly distinguished.

As Smith (1991) points out, ethnic identity has both objective and subjective elements. Objective elements – language, customs, physical traits and so on – make it difficult for people to freely choose or change their ethnic identity. Thus, for some, ethnicity is a form of extended kinship, with ethnic identity being established at birth for most group members (Horowitz 1985: 52, 57). Fearon (2006: 853) points out that the key constitutive feature of ethnicity is 'membership reckoned primarily by descent'. Indeed, ordinary people often believe that ethnic identities are fixed by human nature – a belief termed *everyday primordialism* by Fearon and Laitin (2000). On the other hand, subjective elements of ethnicity are often based on certain myths, such as myths about common ancestry (Smith 1991: 22). As Horowitz (1985: 52–3, 64–74) notes, individual membership can be recognized by criteria other than birth, such as conversion, intermarriage and 'forgetting' origins, and group boundaries can change over time by amalgamation, incorporation, division or proliferation. This 'interplay of givens and chosens in ethnicity' (Horowitz 1985: 64) has significant implications for our understanding of the relationship between ethnicity and secession, as discussed below.

What, then, is *ethnic conflict*? For some, this question does not cause much difficulty. For example, Wolff (2004: 1) defines ethnic conflict as 'a form of group conflict in which at least one of the parties involved interprets the conflict, its causes, and potential remedies, along an actually existing or perceived discriminating ethnic divide', and states that it is empirically 'relatively easy to determine which conflict is an ethnic one: one knows them when one sees them'. For others, however, things are not that simple. For example, Sambanis (2001: 261–2) argues that 'not all wars that involve ethnic groups as combatants should be classified as ethnic wars' and the 'issues at the core of the conflict must be integral to the concept of ethnicity'. This definition, however, requires that one should make a judgment whether issues at the core are 'integral to the concept of ethnicity', which is by no means an easy task. Furthermore, as discussed above, the precise definition of 'ethnicity' is also difficult, which makes it all the more difficult to judge whether a conflict is 'ethnic' or not. Some even argue that the label 'ethnic' conflict or 'ethnic' war is misleading and inappropriate, because the motivations of the participants in a conflict are fairly diverse (Kalyvas 2003) and violence is often 'carried out chiefly by small, ill-disciplined, and essentially cowardly bands of thugs and bullies' (Mueller 2000: 43). A further confusion is caused by the term 'conflict'. Some believe that this term implicates violence, as it is far less common to describe peaceful manifestations of dynamic interactions between ethnic groups as 'ethnic conflicts', for which terms such as 'tension', 'dispute' and 'unease' are more often used (Wolff 2006: 2–3). Others criticize this confusion of 'conflict' and 'violence', arguing that it is important to distinguish these two terms (Varshney 2001).

Even when one focuses solely on violence, *ethnic conflict* still remains broad and vague, including various types of violence, such as rebellion, pogroms, genocide, riots, anti-immigrant violence and state violence. Thus, some scholars think that treating ethnic conflict as a single and homogeneous category holds little promise; they tend to focus instead on a specific type of violence in their theoretical analyses. For example, Brubaker and Laitin (1998: 446) argue that different types of ethnic violence seem to involve 'sharply opposed mechanisms and dynamics'. As for secessionist conflict, the most relevant category is *ethnic rebellion*, which implies that there is an organized group or movement (*'rebels'*) behind the violence and that the target of the violence is the state authorities, because secessionist conflicts almost invariably involve the state authorities as a party to the conflict, challenged by a secessionist movement. Thus, for example, Gurr (2000: chapter 6) examined the patterns and outcomes of *secessionist* wars in his analysis of ethnic rebellion against the state.

This tendency among some scholars to focus on a specific type of violence is understandable, and may even be inevitable if one attempts to achieve theoretical rigour. It also has some drawbacks, however, because this tendency distracts scholarly attention from the relations and dynamism *between different types of violence*. As for secession, while many scholars treat *rebellion* as a relevant category of ethnic violence, other kinds of violence also matter. For example, in some cases, *pogroms* against ethnic groups have played a significant catalytic role in pushing minority ethnic groups towards secessionist demands, for example in Nigeria (Biafra) and Sri Lanka. According to Pape (2003), 82 percent of the total 188 *suicide bomb attacks* between 1980 and 2001 were associated with campaigns to achieve the independence of Palestine, a Kurdish state, a Tamil state or Chechnya, or to separate Kashmir from India. The dynamic relationship between various types of violence has been largely neglected both theoretically and empirically and seems to require much more attention than it attracts now.

## Secession and Ethnic Conflict: How to Link the Two?

Secession and ethnic conflict, as we have seen, are often associated with each other. For Fearon (2004), 'separatist wars' are synonymous with 'ethnonationalist wars'. In a similar vein, 'secessionist conflicts' and 'ethnic civil wars' are used almost synonymously by Downes, who points out that 'many ethnic wars are secessionist' (2004: 234). For Hale (2008), the terms 'secessionism' and 'separatism' are assumed to have ethnic content, while he admits that 'separatism' pure and simple need not involve distinct nations. In an analysis on the effect of decentralization by Brancati (2006), 'ethnic conflict and secessionism' are used as a single category of conflict in his causal model: while he defines these two as distinct from each other, practically no distinction is made between the two in the actual analysis.

There are two key factors behind this association. The first factor is *nationalism*. On the one hand, almost all secessions (including attempted ones) in the 20th and 21st centuries were justified by reference to nationalism (Pavković with Radan 2007: 17). Due to the strength of the nationalist world view, which regards nations or national groups as the fundamental/natural sources of political sovereignty, secessionist movements often promote a nationalist ideology to mobilize the target population and gain international support for their cause. Thus, almost all secessionist conflicts are presented or interpreted as nationalist conflicts. On the other hand, nationalism is closely related to the concept of ethnicity. For example, Smith (1986) argues that modern nations formed around what he calls *ethnie*, i.e. pre-modern 'ethnic cores'. For Connor (1994), nation means a self-differentiating ethnic group, and nationalism, defined as 'identification with and loyalty to one's nation', is synonymous with *ethnonationalism*. Hale (2008: 3) simply defines nation as 'an ethnic group associated with a particular territory'.

The second factor is territory. As the definition of secession in this volume shows, secessionist conflict invariably entails a territorial dimension. Ethnic conflict very often, though not always, involves territory as an important issue, because for 'ethnic groups, territory is invariably tied to the group's identity' and 'control over territory means a secure identity' (Toft 2002: 84). As Moore (1998) points out, ethnicity also provides an ideological basis for the secessionists to adopt the 'ethnic principle' to ground their rights to land, because ethnic nationalisms often attach symbolic and historical importance to territory.

Indeed, this association between secession and ethnic conflict does have a certain empirical foundation. Table 11.1 shows the distribution of cases of civil war onset from 1945 to 1999 analysed by Fearon and Laitin (2003) according to the types of civil war – whether they are 'ethnic civil wars' or not,[2] and whether the rebels aimed primarily at (1) the seizure of central authority or (2) exit (secession) or autonomy, or (3) their aims were mixed/ambiguous.

---

2   Here, 'ethnic civil wars' are defined as civil wars in which fighters were mobilized primarily along ethnic lines. See Fearon and Laitin (2003: 79).

## Table 11.1 Distribution of civil war onsets according to the two distinctions*

|  |  | Ethnic or non-ethnic: | | | Total |
|---|---|---|---|---|---|
|  |  | Non-ethnic | Ambig./mixed | Ethnic |  |
| Rebels aim at: | Centre | 33 | 12 | 16 | 61 |
|  | Mixed/ambig. | 3 | 4 | 7 | 14 |
|  | Exit or autonomy | 0 | 3 | 32 | 35 |
| Total |  | 36 | 19 | 55 | 110 |

Note: * Excluding colonial wars. Based on the replication dataset of Fearon and Laitin (2003). This table is reproduced from Kubo (2005).

This table demonstrates that there is indeed a significant overlap between secessionist (autonomist) conflict and ethnic conflict: out of a total of 35 secessionist/autonomist civil wars, the vast majority of cases (32 cases) were ethnic conflicts, and none was a clearly non-ethnic civil war. One can conclude, therefore, that almost all secessionist conflicts were ethnic conflicts, at least in the period after the end of World War Two.

However plausible the association may be, however, one should also note that secession and ethnic conflict are *not* the same and that the overlap or association between the two is neither automatic nor necessary. On the one hand, secession does not necessarily involve ethnic groups, ethnic politics or ethnic conflict. Some territorial unit within a state may attempt to secede even without a distinct national or ethnic identity among the population. A clear example here is the attempt of West Australia to secede from the Commonwealth of Australia in the 1930s (Musgrave 2003). Similarly, the American Civil War, in which the 11 southern states attempted to secede from the US to form the Confederate States of America, did not involve race or ethnicity as a basis for division and secession; rather, it was caused by differences over the issue of slavery and the conflicting economic interests of the two sides (Thornton and Ekelund 2004; McPherson 1988) (see also Chapter 5). A more recent example of (attempted) secession without ethnicity is the case of Western Bosnia in the 1990s: the Autonomous Province of Western Bosnia, which attempted to secede from Bosnia-Herzegovina, was dominated by the same ethnic group, i.e. Bosnian Muslims, which dominated the rump state at the time (O'Shea 1998) (see Part VI).

On the other hand, ethnic conflict covers a wide range of phenomena, as discussed above, and secessionist conflict is only a subset thereof. Some ethnic conflicts – even the largest – have been fought over issues other than secession, such as control of central government and recognition of cultural rights. One of the worst genocides in ethnic conflict, that which took place in Rwanda in the 1990s, was not related to the issue of secession or autonomy (see, for example, Straus 2006). Table 11.1 clearly supports this observation: a significant number of ethnic civil wars (16 out of 55 cases) were fought *not* over the issue of secession or autonomy but rather over the control of central state power. Therefore, it would certainly be excessive to equate ethnic conflict with secessionist conflict. In order to avoid such an equation, a secessionist conflict in which an ethnic group seeks secession from a given country will hereafter in this chapter be referred to as *secessionist ethnic conflict*.

## Ethnic Identity and Secession

Scholars have been sharply divided over the nature and origins of ethnicity. Typically the debate has been described as one between 'primordialism' and 'constructivism', the former emphasizing the essential, stable, and enduring nature of ethnicity and the latter emphasizing its constructed and changeable nature (see Chapter 1). Recently, Hale (2008) has criticized this kind of characterization of the debate, arguing that the most fundamental cleavage in the field is between what he calls 'ethnicity-as-conflictual theories' and 'ethnicity-as-epiphenomenal theories', the former built on the assumption that ethnicity inherently reflects motivations that tend to put groups in conflict, and the latter rejecting the notion that ethnicity contains its own intrinsic value and seeing both ethnicity and ethnic politics as means by which people struggle for more mundane goods like power, material resources, security or status.

This debate is important when one attempts to understand the relationship between ethnicity and secession, because it has significant implications for the causal relations between the two. On the one hand, the primordialist view tends to lead to the assumption that ethnic identities are 'given', treating ethnicity as an *independent* variable. Similarly, 'ethnicity-as-conflictual theories' assume that ethnicity itself is one of the causes of secessionist ethnic conflict and, thus, a part of the problem. On the other hand, the constructivist view emphasizes the constructed nature of ethnicity, thereby treating ethnicity as a *dependent* variable. For example, as Hale (2008: 15) has pointed out, the 'ethnicity-as-epiphenomenal theories' often stress the role of elites who manipulate ethnic identity and draw people into conflict. Here, ethnicity itself is the object of manipulation, i.e. a dependent variable in the dynamism of conflict, or at least as an intermediate variable which causes conflict and secession but is affected by elite manipulation, and does not function as a truly independent variable.

Even though primordialism itself is not particularly popular in the literature on ethnic conflict and secession, many scholars, implicitly or explicitly, have treated ethnicity as 'given', as one of the causes of secession. For example, Gurr (2000) declares that he treats ethnic identity as given in his analysis of ethnic conflict, even though he rejects primordialism. Almost all game-theoretic accounts of ethnic conflict and secession, such as those by Lake and Rothchild (1998), Fearon (1998), Weingast (1998), Posen (1993), Öberg (2002) and Jenne (2007), explain the occurrence of ethnic conflict and secession as an outcome of strategic interactions between ethnic groups (or between an ethnic group and the state), and thus assume that ethnic groups already exist and act as a unitary actor. Even when scholars emphasize the role of elite manipulation, as 'ethnicity-as-epiphenomenal theories' do, ethnicity is still often assumed to be pre-existing and waiting to be manipulated by the elite, rather than created by the elite from scratch.

This would seem only natural and justifiable, because in many cases the presence of ethnic identities seems indeed to precede escalation of conflict and occurrence of secession. As Bartkus (1999: 10–15) argues, in order for secession (a secession crisis or a secessionist conflict) to happen, secessionist demands must be presented by a pre-existing identifiable unit, or 'distinct community', which is smaller than the state and threatens to withdraw from it, be it nation, national group, ethnic group, tribe, minority group or something else. As Pavković with Radan (2007: 16–17) point out, all groups which were mobilized in support of secession in the past possessed a common set of markers by which members of the group were able to distinguish themselves from other groups in the state, and in the great majority of attempts at secession, these markers were cultural, including common language and customs. It seems undeniable that ethnicity can provide a basis for such a 'distinct community' or 'common set of markers' for the secessionist mobilization, and thus functions as an independent variable.

Yet, it is necessary to emphasize here the importance of the implications of the constructivist view, namely the possibility that ethnicity is affected by conflict and secession.[3] For example, based on the 'segmental institutions thesis', Roeder (2007: 31) challenges the common view that nationalism represents the politicization of ethnicity and argues that 'often ethnicity is the product of a nation-state project, not the other way round', referring to the fact that governments of the nation-state often attempt to 'ethnify' the nation, i.e. to propagate a myth of common origin, in order to privilege the nation-state project that favours the *status quo*. Indeed, in the area which would later become Greece and Serbia, 'nationalism' was virtually absent among the local population when uprisings were first organized in the 19th century: rather, nationalism was promoted by the state authorities *after* the establishment of autonomous government (Roudometof 1998; Stokes 1976). In the case of Montenegro, the issue of secession led to a massive shift of ethnic identity: almost one third of those who declared themselves as 'Montenegrins' in 1991 changed their ethnic identity and declared themselves as 'Serbs' only 12 years later, due to their support for continued unity with Serbia (Kubo 2007). Therefore, it is indeed possible that ethnicity is affected by secession – not the other way round.

# Causes and Dynamics of Ethnic Conflict and Secession

As ethnic conflict and civil war has become an important phenomenon requiring explanation in political science, various scholars have attempted to analyse the causes of ethnic conflict. Drawing on some of their major findings, this section attempts briefly to analyse why and how secessionist ethnic conflict occurs. It is

---

3   For a more detailed discussion of the implications of the constructivist view for the understanding of ethnic conflict, see Fearon and Laitin (2000).

divided into two parts. The first reviews the possible causes of secessionist ethnic conflict, thereby treating it as a dependent variable, as most scholars do. The second part focuses on the role of violence in the process of ethnic conflict and secession, pointing out that treating violence simply as a dependent variable has certain drawbacks, as violence plays an important role in the process of ethnic conflict and secession (see also Chapter 3).

## Occurrence of Secessionist Ethnic Conflict as a Dependent Variable

In order to understand why a secessionist ethnic conflict occurs, one should answer two separate questions. First, why do some ethnic groups (mostly ethnic minorities) seek secession while others do not? This question is important because there are a huge number of ethnic minorities in the world (for example, Fearon's list [2003] contains 709 minority ethnic groups) but by no means all of them seek secession: we observe a much smaller number of secessionist ethnic conflicts. Second, why do some secessionist demands lead to violent 'conflict' while others do not? This question is also of significance because there are cases where secessionist demands are met peacefully, such as in Norway and Slovakia (see Pavković with Radan 2007: 65–94).

As ethnic conflict is fairly complex, involving a variety of actors, it is difficult to answer these two questions in a concise manner. However, most of the existing works on ethnic conflict focus mainly on three key aspects of ethnic conflict, namely (1) radicalization of an ethnic minority, (2) radicalization of the government, and (3) involvement of external actors. Let us examine each of these below.

### *Radicalization of an ethnic minority*

In order to answer the first question, one must analyse the actions of an ethnic minority. As Horowitz (1991: 13) notes, ethnic groups 'are not born irredentist or secessionist'. Among the demands made or goals held by ethnic minorities, secession constitutes one of the most extreme ones, more extreme than other demands, such as regional autonomy, cultural autonomy, affirmative action, proportional representation and so on. Because secession challenges the territorial integrity of the state, it is normally much more difficult to persuade the state authorities to accept their demands than to accept other, more moderate demands. This fact leads many scholars to ask why some ethnic groups decide to seek and attempt secession (whether they succeed or not) while others do not. Various scholars have pointed to such factors as the distinctiveness of the ethnic identity (Hale 2008), various kinds of discrimination or economic disparity (Horowitz 1985), economic exploitation (Hechter 1975), external support (Laitin 1998), level of support from the domestic public (Giuliano 2006) and various kinds of strategic interactions between the minority and the government (e.g. Fearon 1998; Jenne 2007). Whether ethnic groups seek secession or not is related to the political goals of the ethnic group. Thus, when ethnic groups do seek secession, this can be regarded as the radicalization of an ethnic minority *in terms of political goals*.

Equally important is the radicalization of an ethnic minority *in terms of the means to achieve their goals*. Some secessionist groups remain peaceful in terms of the means to achieve their objective, as shown by the cases of Quebec and Montenegro, while other secessionist groups choose violent means, ranging from sporadic bomb attacks to highly organized armed rebellion, as shown by the cases of the Serbs in Croatia and Bosnia and the Biafrans in Nigeria. In analysing why some ethnic groups take up arms or why civil war occurs, scholars have pointed to various factors like the salience of ethnic identity, high levels of grievance, opportunity structures such as domestic political institutions and international factors (Gurr 2000), factors associated with 'economic greed' like poverty, low levels of education and the abundance of natural resources in the host state (Collier and Hoeffler 1998), territorial concentration of the ethnic group (Toft 2002), factors associated with the 'right conditions for insurgency' like the political instability and rough terrain of the host state (Fearon and Laitin 2003), and so on. These arguments are more related to the second question presented above than to the first.

These two kinds of radicalization are sometimes confused and assumed to occur simultaneously, but this is not necessarily the case. Some ethnic minorities may be fully radicalized in terms of goals but remain moderate in terms of the means. The Albanians in Kosovo, for example, almost unanimously supported the secession of Kosovo from Serbia but were united under the leadership of Ibrahim Rugova, who advocated a strategy of peaceful resistance, not violent rebellion (Clark 2000) (see also Chapters 8 and 9). Also, some rebel groups may resort to violent means while their goals remain relatively moderate. For instance, the armed rebel organization of the Albanians in Macedonia – the National Liberation Army – resorted to violent means, such as bombing and ambush attacks, but it only demanded the improvement of the status of the Albanians in Macedonia, such as the protection of language rights and more access to public jobs, and not outright secession from Macedonia (Phillips 2004). Thus, these two kinds of radicalization must be conceptually distinguished.

In both kinds of the radicalization processes discussed above, one should note that there is often an *intra-ethnic division*: there are moderates and radicals *within the ethnic group*, who compete with and confront each other. While many scholars assume that ethnic groups act as unitary actors and take the decision to seek secession and/or to take up arms, this is 'rarely a plausible assumption' (Fearon 2004: 407) regarding the ethnic group (see also Laitin 1998: 331; Brubaker and Laitin 1998: 438). In reality, the radicalization of an ethnic minority, in terms of both goals and means, reflects not only the deliberate decision made by some leaders of the ethnic group but also a shift of the balance of power within the ethnic group. How and why this shift of balance takes place has attracted the attention of certain analysts, who point to such factors as democratic elections (democratization) and inter-ethnic as well as intra-ethnic electoral competition (Rabushka and Shepsle 1972; Aklaev 1999; Hislope 1996), support of the kin-state (Caspersen 2003), excessive military repression by the state authorities (Bose 2003) and so on.

## Radicalization of the government

In order to answer the second question presented above, explaining the actions of an ethnic minority is not sufficient. The other key actor in a secessionist conflict is the government of the host state, which often draws its support from the ethnic majority. In order for a secessionist ethnic conflict to take place, the government must be equally radicalized and resort to organized violence such as military operations. Also, central state policies can affect and alter the perceptions of regional leaders and of the masses and thus have an important influence on secessionism (Hale 2008). Therefore, as Premdas (1990: 24) notes, just as a separatist/secessionist movement is analysed organizationally, 'so must a ruling regime be analysed for its leadership, ideology, resources, and tactics'. Some governments take a tough stance against a minority group or rebels and resort to military repression, while others are more accommodating and make concessions in order to resolve the conflict peacefully. This variance has attracted much less attention compared to the variance across ethnic minorities, but scholars have pointed to such factors as the nature of the political regime (Gurr 2000; King 2000) and the official ideology of the state (Kirişci and Winrow 1997).

Here again, an intra-ethnic dynamic *within the ethnic majority* can be an important factor for moderation or radicalization of the government. For example, as Horowitz (1985: 132–3) points out, the Sri Lankan government was forced to abandon its policy of seeking an agreement or a pact with the minority Tamils because of the fierce opposition of Sinhalese mass opinion led by politically active Buddhist monks; in this case, 'the elite interests were overridden by mass concerns that ran counter to them'. Although scholars generally argue that the democratic regime is more likely to lead to more moderate actions by the government (Gurr 2000; King 2000), it is thus possible that pressure from the electorate can lead to the radicalization of the government in a democratic setting. As Kaufmann (1996: 157) argues, 'under conditions of hypernationalist mobilization and real security threats, group leaders are unlikely to be receptive to compromise, and even if they are, they cannot act without being discredited and replaced by harder-line rivals'.

## Involvement of external actors

Finally, various types of external actors play a significant role in a secessionist ethnic conflict (see also Chapter 14). First, a kin-state of the ethnic minority often plays an important role, providing political, economic, military, logistic, diplomatic and other kinds of support to the ethnic minority. Thus, Brubaker (1996) proposes a 'triadic nexus' model linking national minorities, the nationalizing states where they live, and their external homelands. A kin group in a neighbouring country can play a similar role, as the Tamils in India did for the Tamil rebellion in Sri Lanka (Bose 1994), and so can a diaspora community worldwide, especially in developed countries such as the US and in Western Europe, as the Albanian diaspora community did in the case of Kosovo (Hockenos 2003). Second, internationally powerful states such as the US and Russia may take sides either with the government of the host state or with the ethnic minority, and their support can be extremely important for the course of conflict. Thus, support from Russia was crucial for the secessionist ethnic conflicts in the post-Soviet region (Moldova, Georgia, Azerbaijan and so on), support from the US was crucial for the success of the Albanian rebellion in Kosovo, and support from India was crucial for securing independence for Bangladesh. Third, international organizations such as the UN, NATO and the OSCE sometimes intervene in an ethnic conflict and thus influence the course of events. Fourth, various types of non-state actors including international NGOs, transnational religious movements and global terrorist networks also play an increasingly important role in secessionist ethnic conflict. How and why these external actors become involved in such conflicts has been examined in depth by scholars such as Esman and Tehlami (1995) and Saideman (2001). The involvement of external actors is often behind the radicalization of both an ethnic minority and the government and constitutes part of the answer to both of the two questions presented above.

The configuration of the external supporters for the host state and an ethnic minority, shaped during the course of ethnic conflict, is particularly important for secessionist ethnic conflict because of the significance of international recognition for secessionist aspirations. As Horowitz (1985: 272) notes, international relations play a prominent role in explaining the *outcome* of secessionist movements: if (almost) no country recognizes the seceding state, it only achieves *de facto* independence, not *de jure*, leading to a situation sometimes called 'frozen conflict', as in the case of Moldova and Georgia as of 2009. External supporters for secessionists tend to be among the first to offer recognition once secessionists declare independence and sovereignty, as India did for Bangladesh and the US did for Kosovo (see also Chapters 14 and 15 for a detailed discussion of external actors).

These three aspects – the radicalization of an ethnic minority, that of the government, and the involvement of external actors – are mutually connected to each other, as some scholars have already noted. For example, in formulating his triadic nexus model, Brubaker (1996) argues that the emergence of a radical stance in one of the three fields – national minority, nationalizing state or external homeland – leads to the emergence of a radical stance in the other two fields, and *vice versa*. In addition, as Horowitz (1985: 574) has argued that 'a principal limitation on interethnic co-operation is the configuration of intra-ethnic competition', intra-ethnic relations and inter-ethnic relations also affect each other. This mutually reinforcing and interacting relationship among different actors and between inter-ethnic and intra-ethnic processes makes the overall dynamics of ethnic conflict quite complex.

## The Role of Violence in Ethnic Conflict and Secession

What makes the dynamics of ethnic conflict even more complex is the *role of violence*. Scholars quite often treat the occurrence of (a certain type of) violence, especially that which is large-scale, as a dependent variable, and thus a result of the radicalization processes (see also Chapter 12). This tendency is most visible among the large-N analyses and game-theoretic accounts of ethnic conflict, in which the 'occurrence' of violence is assumed to be a one-shot event, operationalized by a dichotomous dependent variable in the statistical analysis, and assumed to happen when minority groups decide to take up arms after strategic interaction with the state. In reality, however, things are not that simple, and what is often observed in real cases is a *cycle of violence and radicalization*, in which an occurrence of a certain type of violence triggers a radicalization process of some kind, which in turn leads to an occurrence of another type of violence. For example, in Sri Lanka, pogroms against Tamils led to the radicalization of the Tamils, who had peacefully accepted the statehood of Sri Lanka, leading to the emergence of a small rebel organization, the LTTE (Bose 1994). Low-intensity violence conducted by the LTTE, in turn, led to the radicalization of the Sri Lankan government, which started 'counter-insurgency' military operations not only against the LTTE but against the Tamil population at large, inflicting serious civilian casualties among the Tamils. This military repression played a 'vital catalytic role' (Bose 1994: 91) in the further radicalization of the Tamils and contributed to the ascendancy of the LTTE, whose membership increased from only 30-odd individuals as late as in 1983 to 4,000 in 1987, leading to large-scale ethnic conflict.

As the case of Sri Lanka shows, an act of violence taken by one side tends to trigger the radicalization of the other side in the interaction between an ethnic minority and the state. When members of an ethnic minority resort to violence, it tends to radicalize a government that attempts to take a tough stance, and to radicalize the ethnic majority group and fuel their anger against the ethnic minority. On the other hand, when a government or members of the ethnic majority resort to violence against an ethnic minority, it tends to radicalize the minority group either in terms of goals or means. This happens, for example, when pogroms or massacres against the minority are conducted by members of the majority group (e.g. Sri Lanka, Nigeria), when the police and military violently repress peaceful demonstrations (e.g. Northern Ireland, Kosovo) and when the government use excessive military force against the ethnic minority as 'counter-insurgency' operations against the rebels (e.g. Sri Lanka, Kosovo, Turkey, Chechnya). This tendency of the violence by one side to incite the radicalization of the other seems to explain why a *cycle of violence* is often observed in ethnic conflict.

The violence also plays an important role in the intra-ethnic dynamics (Fearon and Laitin 2000: 864–8). When violence is chosen by a radical elite, it often serves their interests because it can silence opposition against them within the ethnic group. Thus, Gagnon (2004) argues that the war in Croatia, Bosnia and Kosovo occurred not because of ethnic hatred among the local population but because the authoritarian leadership in Croatia and Serbia faced a serious challenge from the reformists *within the country* and resorted to a war policy as a strategy of 'demobilization', i.e. to suppress the challenge by the opposition and silence opposing voices. On the other hand, when violence is chosen by a rather marginal segment within a minority group, it often constitutes a serious challenge against the dominant leadership within the minority group, i.e. an attempt by marginalized radicals to discredit the incumbent leadership and replace them.

Finally, violence can also play a significant role in drawing external actors into a conflict. In some cases, the occurrence of violence was a critical trigger for external actors to increase their level of involvement in the conflict, either in favour of the government or of the rebels. For example, the escalation of violence in Sri Lanka led to the increased involvement of India in the conflict in favour of the Sri Lankan government. The escalation of conflict in Croatia in 1991, especially the bombardment of Vukovar and Dubrovnik, which was broadcast by the international media, led to a change in public opinion in favour of Croatia in many Western European countries (Cohen 1993). When an armed conflict occurred in Georgia in the summer of 2008, Russia quickly responded with military involvement in favour of South Ossetia. One of the most striking cases in this regard is Kosovo, where the Albanian rebels 'succeeded beyond what must have been their wildest dreams, with NATO intervening on their behalf in 1999' by deliberately provoking Serbian attacks, as Fearon (2004: 406) has observed[4] (see Chapter 9). Needless to say, the connection between the occurrence of violence on the ground and the change of attitudes of external actors is far from automatic, as many instances of violence are simply neglected by countries like the US, even when the level of violence is extremely high (e.g. the case of civil war in Sudan). Here, international media coverage and the 'public relations' strategy of the parties to the conflict sometimes play a crucial role, as shown by the cases of ex-Yugoslav conflicts, including Kosovo.

Given the extent of influence that violence can have in the course of ethnic conflict, therefore, one should not simply treat the occurrence of violence as a 'dependent' variable, caused by the processes of radicalization. Rather, the violence can have a significant impact on the processes of radicalization. Violence may even be used intentionally in order to cause radicalization, for example to silence moderates within an ethnic group, to discredit a pacifist leadership within an ethnic group, to incite an excessive response from the other side to increase the level of grievances within the group, and to draw external actors into a conflict (see Chapter 12 for further discussion of the role of violence).

## Secession and Ethnic Conflict Settlement

As the severity of ethnic conflict has attracted growing attention from the media, scholars and policymakers, ethnic conflict settlement has become an important topic for scholarly debate. This debate is relevant here, because secession constitutes one of the options for ethnic conflict settlement. For example, in classifying various methods of ethnic conflict settlement, Wolff (2006: 140) makes a distinction between methods that aim at eliminating differences between conflict parties and methods that try to manage them, and secession is listed as one way to achieve the elimination of differences, together with genocide, ethnic cleansing, and integration or assimilation (the latter methods include control regimes, federalism and autonomy, and various forms of power-sharing).

Can secession be an effective solution to ethnic conflict? Scholars are divided on the answer to this question. Some view secession or partition positively. The

---

4   For a similar observation, see Hockenos (2003: 250).

most well-known proponent of partition is Kaufmann, who emphasizes the usefulness of partition as a solution to an ethnic civil war, arguing that stable resolutions of ethnic civil wars become possible 'only when the opposing groups are demographically separated into defensible enclaves' (Kaufmann 1996: 137). While his argument is about partition and not about secession (indeed, he argues that sovereignty is secondary and defensible ethnic enclaves reduce violence with or without independent sovereignty), secession can undoubtedly be an effective solution to ethnic conflict according to his theory, as long as it achieves the demographic separation of ethnic groups. Downes (2004) also argues that ending ethnic civil wars through partition (or military victory) may be more stable than negotiated agreements to share or diffuse power within the confines of a single state. More recently, based on their statistical analysis, Chapman and Roeder (2007) argue that, after nationalist conflicts, partition is more effective than alternative institutions at reducing the likelihood of a recurrence of violence among the parties to a dispute and increasing the prospects that all will live under democratic rule. Unlike Kaufmann, they put emphasis on sovereignty: according to them, partition is effective 'only when partition is implemented fully through creation of separate sovereign states. Half-measures short of full partition and independence, which seek to keep these lands and peoples together, are less likely to result in peace and democracy' (Chapman and Roeder 2007: 677).

Others disagree, claiming that partition is not a solution to ethnic and communal conflict (Kumar 1997; Schaeffer 1999). Sambanis (2000) argues that there is no systematic empirical evidence that supports the 'partition theory' proposed by scholars like Kaufmann, and that partitions do not help prevent recurrence of ethnic war and fare no better than other outcomes of ethnic civil war, based on the results of his empirical tests. Based on the cases of Indo-Pakistani conflict and Bosnia, Bose (2002: 177–80) argues that the causal relationship runs in the opposite direction: it is the prospect of partition which caused violence, not the other way round. One may also question the effectiveness of partition as a solution to ethnic conflict because domestic conflict may simply be transformed into its international counterpart, as shown by the cases of Indo-Pakistani conflict after partition (see e.g., Bose 2002: 183–4).

In Kaufmann's argument, the effectiveness of partition is conditional on the clear demographic separation of ethnic groups. Critics to partition theory often argue that this condition is unrealistic because it is extremely difficult to create ethnically pure successor states through secession or partition (see e.g., Sambanis 2000: 441) (see also Chapter 8). Indeed, in some cases, secession seems to exacerbate ethnic conflict because of the ethnic composition of the host state and seceding state. For example, when seceding states are multi-ethnic, ethnic minorities in the seceding states may seek *secession from the seceding states* – a phenomenon called 'recursive secession' by Pavković with Radan (2007: 129) – as in the cases of the Serbs in Croatia and Bosnia, and Abkhazia and South Ossetia in Georgia. One should note, however, that this phenomenon does not directly challenge the logic of Kaufmann's argument: indeed, he argues that partitions that do not unmix hostile populations actually increase, rather than decrease, conflict (Kaufmann 1999: 248–9).

This debate on secession or partition as a solution to ethnic conflict is further complicated by normative judgments. One may oppose the proposal of Kaufmann by arguing that population transfers cause serious human suffering and thus are morally unacceptable as a solution, whether they are effective or not. For example, Schneckener (2004) argues that strategies of elimination of ethnic difference, such as genocide, forced population transfer/expulsion and forced assimilation, are hardly justified from a normative perspective (though, unlike Wolff, he does not treat secession as a strategy of elimination). As Sisk (1996: 2) has pointed out, the bias against secession in international law and practice remains fairly strong, due to the emphasis on the virtues of the territorial integrity of sovereign states, as witnessed in the determination of the international community to maintain the territorial integrity of Bosnia-Herzegovina (see Chapters 13 and 18). On the other hand, some scholars develop normative theories to justify secession, arguing that people have the liberty to choose the state in which they prefer to live, or that people have the right to live in a functioning and protective state (see Pavković with Radan 2007: 199–219, for a good review of normative theories of secession). Those who support secession often refer to the principle of / right to self-determination, enshrined in the UN Charter and two human rights treaties adopted by the UN General Assembly in 1966 (see also Chapter 4 and Part IV).

This debate is unresolved, and secession or partition has both advantages and disadvantages. One may thus be tempted to conclude that one should simply decide whether secession or partition can (should) be a solution or not on a case-by-case basis, considering various domestic and international conditions. Indeed, 'international responses to wars of separatist nationalism have been ad hoc' (Fearon 2004: 396), but this policy of *ad hoc* partition that treats each case in isolation is exactly what Fearon argues against. According to him, such a policy has 'two incentive problems': first, if violence is the implicit criterion for major power intervention, this will encourage separatist movements to resort to violence; second, if the major powers forcibly intervene to carve up sovereign states, it would be to abandon the standard of no border changes by force, a valuable agreement that has helped structure international relations since 1945 (Fearon 2004). The fact that the recognition of the unilaterally declared independence of Kosovo by the US and European states led to Russia's military intervention in the Georgian conflict in 2008 and her recognition of Abkhazia and South Ossetia seems to support his argument (see also Chapter 13).

## Concluding Remarks

This chapter has analysed the relationship between secession and ethnic conflict. Secession and ethnic conflict should be conceptually distinguished, but they certainly overlap and are related to each other. While many assume ethnic identity to be a 'given' in secessionist ethnic conflict, the implications of the constructivist view should be taken seriously, as ethnic identity is sometimes significantly affected by the course of conflict and secession. Secessionist ethnic conflict involves a variety of actors that influence each other and diverse dynamics that are mutually reinforcing. Secession and partition may be an effective solution to ethnic conflict in some cases, but not in others. All of these arguments demonstrate that secession and ethnic conflict are connected in a number of different ways. And yet, as suggested at the outset, the academic literature on these two topics has not been sufficiently integrated. Future research should perhaps further the integration of the currently separate scholarly approaches to secession and ethnic conflict.

# References

Aklaev, Airat R. (1999), *Democratization and Ethnic Peace: Patterns of Ethnopolitical Crisis Management in Post-Soviet Settings* (Aldershot: Ashgate).
Bartkus, Viva Ona (1999), *The Dynamic of Secession* (Cambridge: Cambridge University Press).
Bose, Sumantra (1994), *States, Nations, Sovereignty: Sri Lanka, India and the Tamil Eelam Movement* (Thousand Oaks, CA: Sage).
Bose, Sumantra (2002), *Bosnia after Dayton: Nationalist Partition and International Intervention* (London: Hurst).
Bose, Sumantra (2003), *Kashmir: Roots of Conflict, Paths to Peace* (Cambridge, MA: Harvard University Press).
Brancati, Dawn (2006), 'Decentralization: Fueling the Fire or Dampening the Flames of Ethnic Conflict and Secessionism?', *International Organization* 60, 651–85.
Brubaker, Rogers (1996), *Nationalism Reframed: Nationhood and the National Question in the New Europe* (Cambridge: Cambridge University Press).
Brubaker, Rogers and David D. Laitin (1998), 'Ethnic and Nationalist Violence', *Annual Review of Sociology* 24, 423–52.
Caspersen, Nina (2003), 'The Thorny Issue of Ethnic Autonomy in Croatia: Serb Leaders and Proposals for Autonomy', *Journal on Ethnopolitics and Minority Issues in Europe* 3, 1–26.
Chapman, Thomas and Philip G. Roeder (2007), 'Partition as a Solution to Wars of Nationalism: The Importance of Institutions', *American Political Science Review* 101, 677–91.
Clark, Howard (2000), *Civil Resistance in Kosovo* (London: Pluto).
Cohen, Lenard J. (1993), *Broken Bonds: The Disintegration of Yugoslavia* (Boulder, CO: Westview).
Collier, Paul and Anke Hoeffler (1998), 'On Economic Causes of Civil War', *Oxford Economic Papers* 50, 563–73.
Connor, Walker (1994), *Ethnonationalism: The Quest for Understanding* (Princeton, NJ: Princeton University Press).
Downes, Alexander B. (2004), 'The Problem with Negotiated Settlements to Ethnic Civil War', *Security Studies* 13, 230–79.
Esman, Milton J. and Shibley Telhami (eds) (1995), *International Organizations and Ethnic Conflict* (Ithaca, NY: Cornell University Press).

Fearon, James D. (1998), 'Commitment Problems and the Spread of Ethnic Conflict', in David A. Lake and Donald Rothchild (eds), *The International Spread of Ethnic Conflict: Fear, Diffusion and Escalation* (Princeton, NJ: Princeton University Press), 107–26.

Fearon, James D. (2003), 'Ethnic and Cultural Diversity by Country', *Journal of Economic Growth* 8, 195–222.

Fearon, James D. (2004), 'Separatist Wars, Partition, and World Order', *Security Studies* 13, 394–415.

Fearon, James D. (2006), 'Ethnic Mobilization and Ethnic Violence', in Barry R. Weingast and Donald A. Wittman (eds), *Oxford Handbook of Political Economy* (Oxford: Oxford University Press), 852–68.

Fearon, James D. and David D. Laitin (2000), 'Violence and the Social Construction of Ethnic Identity', *International Organization* 54, 845–77.

Fearon, James D. and David D. Laitin (2003), 'Ethnicity, Insurgency, and Civil War', *American Political Science Review* 97, 75–90.

Gagnon, Valère P. Jr (2004), *The Myth of Ethnic War: Serbia and Croatia in the 1990s*, (Ithaca, NY: Cornell University Press).

Giuliano, Elise (2006), 'Democratization, Nationalism, and Local Accountability in the Russian Transition', *World Politics* 58, 276–310.

Gurr, Ted Robert (2000), *Peoples versus States: Minorities at Risk in the New Century* (Washington, DC: United States Institute of Peace Press).

Hale, Henry E. (2008), *The Foundations of Ethnic Politics: Separatism of States and Nations in Eurasia and the World* (Cambridge: Cambridge University Press).

Hechter, Michael (1975), *Internal Colonialism* (Berkeley, CA: University of California Press).

Hislope, Robert (1996), 'Intra-Ethnic Conflict in Croatia and Serbia: Flanking and the Consequences for Democracy', *East European Quarterly* 30, 471–94.

Hockenos, Paul (2003), *Homeland Calling: Exile Patriotism and the Balkan Wars* (Ithaca, NY: Cornell University Press).

Horowitz, Donald L. (1985), *Ethnic Groups in Conflict* (Berkeley, CA: University of California Press).

Horowitz, Donald L. (1991), 'Irredentas and Secessions: Neglected Connections', in Naomi Chazan (ed.), *Irredentism and International Politics* (Boulder, CO: Lynne Rienner), 9–22.

Jenne, Erin K. (2007), *Ethnic Bargaining: The Paradox of Minority Empowerment* (Ithaca, NY: Cornell University Press).

Kalyvas, Stathis N. (2003), 'The Ontology of "Political Violence": Action and Identity in Civil Wars', *Perspectives on Politics* 1, 475–94.

Kaufmann, Chaim (1996), 'Possible and Impossible Solutions to Ethnic Wars', *International Security* 20, 136–75.

Kaufmann, Chaim (1999), 'When All Else Fails: Evaluating Population Transfers and Partition as Solutions to Ethnic Conflict', in Barbara F. Walter and Jack Snyder (eds), *Civil Wars, Insecurity, and Intervention* (New York: Columbia University Press), 221–60.

King, John C. (2000), 'Exploring the Ameliorating Effects of Democracy on Political Repression: Cross-National Evidence', in Christian Davenport (ed.), *Paths to State Repression: Human Rights Violations and Contentious Politics* (Lanham, MD: Rowman & Littlefield), 217–39.

Kirişci, Kemal and Gareth M. Winrow (1997), *The Kurdish Question and Turkey: An Example of a Trans-state Ethnic Conflict* (London: Frank Cass).

Kubo, Keiichi (2005), 'Do Men Rebel because the State Is Weak?: A Critique of the Fearon-Laitin Model', *The Waseda Journal of Political Science and Economics* 359, 93–104.

Kubo, Keiichi (2007), 'The Radicalisation and Ethnicization of Elections: The 1990 Local Elections and the Ethnic Conflict in Croatia', *Ethnopolitics* 6, 21–41.

Kumar, Radha (1997), 'The Troubled History of Partition', *Foreign Affairs* 76, 22–34.

Laitin, David D. (1998), *Identity in Formation: The Russian-Speaking Populations in the Near Abroad* (Ithaca, NY: Cornell University Press).

Lake, David A. and Donald Rothchild (eds) (1998), *The International Spread of Ethnic Conflict: Fear, Diffusion and Escalation* (Princeton, NJ: Princeton University Press).

McPherson, James M. (1988), *Battle Cry of Freedom: The Civil War Era* (New York: Oxford University Press).

Moore, Margaret (1998), 'The Territorial Dimension of Self-Determination', in Margaret Moore (ed.), *National Self-Determination and Secession* (Oxford: Oxford University Press), 134–57.

Mueller, John (2000), 'The Banality of "Ethnic War"', *International Security* 25, 42–70.

Musgrave, Thomas (2003), 'The Western Australian Secessionist Movement', *Macquarie Law Journal* 3, 95–129.

O'Shea, Brendan (1998), *Crisis at Bihac: Bosnia's Bloody Battlefield* (Phoenix Mill: Sutton Publishing).

Öberg, Magnus (2002), *The Onset of Ethnic War as a Bargaining Process: Testing a Costly Signaling Model* (Uppsala: Department of Peace and Conflict Research, Uppsala University).

Pape, Robert (2003), 'The Strategic Logic of Suicide Terrorism', *American Political Science Review* 97, 343–61.

Pavković, Aleksandar with Peter Radan (2007), *Creating New States: Theory and Practice of Secession* (Aldershot: Ashgate).

Phillips, John (2004), *Macedonia: Warlords and Rebels in the Balkans* (London: I.B. Tauris).

Posen, Barry R. (1993), 'The Security Dilemma and Ethnic Conflict', in Michael E. Brown (ed.), *Ethnic Conflict and International Security* (Princeton, NJ: Princeton University Press), 103–24.

Premdas, Ralph R. (1990), 'Secessionist Movements in Comparative Perspective', in Ralph R. Premdas, S.W.R. de A. Samarasinghe and Alan B. Anderson (eds), *Secessionist Movements in Comparative Perspective* (London: Pinter Publishers), 12–29.

Rabushka, Alvin and Kenneth A. Shepsle (1972), *Politics in Plural Societies: A Theory of Democratic Instability* (Columbus, OH: Charles E. Merrill).

Roeder, Philip G. (2007), *Where Nation-States Come From: Institutional Change in the Age of Nationalism* (Princeton, NJ: Princeton University Press).

Roudometof, Victor (1998), 'Invented Traditions, Symbolic Boundaries, and National Identity in Southeasten Europe: Greece and Serbia in Comparative Historical Perspective', *East European Quarterly* 32, 429–68.

Saideman, Stephen M. (2001), *The Ties That Divide: Ethnic Politics, Foreign Policy and International Conflict* (New York: Columbia University Press).

Sambanis, Nicholas (2000), 'Partition as a Solution to Ethnic War: An Empirical Critique of the Theoretical Literature', *World Politics* 52, 437–83.

Sambanis, Nicholas (2001), 'Do Ethnic and Nonethnic Civil Wars Have the Same Causes? A Theoretical and Empirical Inquiry (Part 1)', *Journal of Conflict Resolution* 45, 259–82.

Schaeffer, Robert K. (1999), *Severed States: Dilemmas of Democracy in a Divided World* (Lanham, MD: Rowman and Littlefield).

Schneckener, Ulrich (2004), 'Models of Ethnic Conflict Regulation: The Politics of Recognition', in Ulrich Schneckener and Stefan Wolff (eds), *Managing and Settling Ethnic Conflicts: Perspectives on Successes and Failures in Europe, Africa and Asia* (London: Hurst), 18–39.

Sisk, Timothy D. (1996), *Power Sharing and International Mediation in Ethnic Conflicts* (Washington, DC: US Institute of Peace).

Smith, Anthony D. (1986), *The Ethnic Origins of Nations* (Oxford: Blackwell).

Smith, Anthony D. (1991), *National Identity* (London: Penguin).

Stokes, Gale (1976), 'The Absence of Nationalism in Serbian Politics before 1840', *Canadian Review of Studies in Nationalism* 4, 77–90.

Straus, Scott (2006), *The Order of Genocide: Race, Power, and War in Rwanda* (Ithaca, NY: Cornell University Press).

Thornton, Mark and Robert B. Ekelund, Jr (2004), *Tariffs, Blockades, and Inflation: The Economics of the Civil War* (Wilmington, DE: SR Books).

Toft, Monica Duffy (2002), 'Indivisible Territory, Geographic Concentration, and Ethnic War', *Security Studies* 12, 82–119.

Varshney, Ashutosh (2001), 'Ethnic Conflict and Civil Society: India and Beyond', *World Politics* 53, 362–98.

Weingast, Barry R. (1998), 'Constructing Trust: The Political and Economic Roots of Ethnic and Regional Conflicts', in Karol Soltan, Eric M. Uslaner and Virginia Haufler (eds), *Institutions and Social Order* (Ann Arbor, MI: University of Michigan Press), 163–200.

Wolff, Stefan (2004), 'Managing and Settling Ethnic Conflicts', in Ulrich Schneckener and Stefan Wolff (eds), *Managing and Settling Ethnic Conflicts: Perspectives on Successes and Failures in Europe, Africa and Asia* (London: Hurst), 1–17.

Wolff, Stefan (2006), *Ethnic Conflict: A Global Perspective* (Oxford: Oxford University Press).

# 12

**ASHGATE RESEARCH COMPANION**

# Secession and Political Violence

Siniša Malešević and Niall Ó Dochartaigh

## Violent Secessionism: The Origins and Causes

Whenever an existing state implodes or finds itself in a process of slow disintegration along ethno-national lines there is a high expectation that this process will involve violence. And indeed for much of modern human history secessionism was regularly identified with mass bloodshed: many attempts to set up an independent sovereign polity or to unite one ethno-national collectivity under a single political roof were accompanied by wars, revolutions, terrorism or insurgency. From the American Civil War, Biafra, Katanga and Kurdistan to the Yugoslav wars of succession, Chechnya and Sri Lanka, the 19th and 20th centuries were marked by the hostile and aggressive actions of separatist movements, the host state governments or both (see Chapters 5, 6 and 8 and Part VI). This historical experience might suggest that there is an inherent link between secession and violence and that an increase in separatist demands will automatically translate into coercive behaviour. However, this is rarely the case. Not only is most secessionist activity resolutely non-violent but in addition, instances of separatist violence are statistically quite rare despite journalistic clichés that suggest the ubiquity of such violence (Fearon and Laitin 2000; Brubaker 2004; Laitin 2007) and the two processes can be inversely proportional. For example, the Québecois and Catalan separatist movements have acquired large-scale popular support in a distinctly non-violent context: rare instances of violent insurgency (mostly in the early 1960s and 1970s) were instantly denounced and the decrease in violent activity was followed by a widening increase in support for the separatist cause (Conversi 1997; Rocher 2002). Hence the central questions are: why and when do organized attempts to promote the establishment of an independent polity become violent? More specifically, why and under which circumstances do some secessionist movements adopt violent tactics while others never do? Why do some governments respond violently to secessionist activities while other state authorities do not?

The existing answers to these questions focus either on economic, cultural or political reasons. The three dominant, and in most respects mutually exclusive, explanatory paradigms emphasize either the instrumental rationality of individual actors, asymmetric positions in class structure, incommensurable cultural values or the differing character of political regimes.

For the economically oriented approaches such as rational choice theory or neo-Marxism, both separatism and the adoption of violent tactics are rooted in economic motives. For neo-Marxists (Hechter 1974, 1999; Bonacich 1972; Stone 1979) secessionist demands originate in the social inequality whereby culturally distinct periphery reacts against exploitation of the economically and politically dominant metropolitan centre. For Hechter (1999) this unequal relationship between the centre and periphery is a form of internal colonialism where the separatist mobilization emerges as the most rational response to the structural inequalities generated by the capitalist induced cultural division of labour. The reliance on violence is interpreted as a last resort against the coercive and oppressive capitalist state (see also Chapter 10). For the rational choice theorists violent separatism stems from the calculation of individual self-interests (Laitin 2000; Fearon 1994; Wintrobe 2006). As Laitin (2007: 22) argues: 'Civil war is profitable for potential insurgents, in that they can both survive and enjoy some probability of winning the state. If there is an economic motive for civil war in the past half-century, it is in the expectation of collecting the revenues that ownership of the state avails.' Since the use of violence is a costly strategy for an individual actor, its deployment is linked to the coordinated collective cooperation and economic gains that result from such a collective action. In other words the adoption of violent action either by the host state authorities or the separatist movements hinges on its profitability: if there is a perception that one's security and economic well being can be attained with less cost through coercive actions and secession then it is more likely that social actors will follow this course of action.

Although economic interpretations are often useful in pinpointing social inequalities and individual motives for joining or supporting secessionist movements they are largely ineffective in explaining the inherent structural complexities of this phenomenon. While profit maximization and class interests can play a significant part in one's decision to support or oppose violent secessionism, these motives by themselves can explain neither the origins nor the principal structural causes of separatist violence. Not only are the social actions of human beings regularly more complex, messier and richer than the pure instrumentalism of *homo economicus* suggests, but most utilitarian explanations operate with tautological arguments that generate weak, unfalsifiable, *ex post facto* interpretations of social reality (Smelser 1992; Malešević 2004). Furthermore, whereas the voluntarist and formalist models of rational choice remain overly ahistorical and hence unable to explain the changing character of secessionism over long historical periods of time, the neo-Marxist accounts find limited application in social orders where there is little private ownership or the economy has little or no autonomy (i.e. most communist and theocratic systems as well as some military dictatorships) (for a similar criticism see Chapter 10). Most of all, economistic accounts can not properly explain the non-instrumental, non-rational and structural sources of secessionism and in particular violent forms of secessionist activity.

In contrast to the economic models, culturalist explanations stress precisely these non-utilitarian, emotional and normative aspects of human behaviour. The early symbolists such as Shils (1957), Geertz (1973) and Parsons (1975) understood ethnic and national identities as primordial, that is, *a priori* given, objective and overpowering identities acquired at birth and reinforced through primary socialization. In this context the inherent strength of ethno-national attachments by itself is understood to be an obstacle to the existence of multiethnic states. In other words, violent forms of secessionism are seen as inevitably emanating from the incommensurability of different cultural values and distinct life styles.

Nevertheless contemporary culturalism is more interested in identifying and exploring the normative foundations of ethno-national cohesion and the historical embeddedness of separatist claims. For neo-Durkhemians such as Smith (1981, 2003, 2009), Hutchinson (2005, 2007), and Hastings (1997) both ethnic groups and nations are tangible, corporeal and historically durable entities that gradually become politicized and eventually opt for sovereign statehood. In this view poli-ethnicity is synonymous with instability as modern nation-states usually entail a coherent, and preferably a singular, myth of common ethnic origin. In other words neo-Durkhemians argue that with the arrival of modernity ethnicities have 'to move towards nationhood' (Smith 1986: 57) or even that they 'turn naturally' into independent nationhood (Hastings 1997: 13). Consequently secessionism is viewed as directly originating in the mutually incompatible ethnic origins of modern nations. For Smith (1986, 2009) both *ethnies* and nations are essentially moral communities developed around common myths and memories many of which reproduce cultural meanings associated with violent sacrifices. For culturalists all modern states require coherent narratives of common origin which are usually historically built around the ethnic cores (i.e. dominant *ethnies*), the mythology of blood sacrifice, the commemorations of the 'glorious dead' and ethno-national martyrdom. In this view successful secessionist activity often entails historical memories of violence: the commemoration of war heroism establishes ethical parameters that determine future actions as they bind posterity in moral obligation to dead heroes.

The culturalist interpretations of violent secessionism have proved valuable in accounting for the strength and intensity of emotional appeal that permeates separatist rhetoric and the ever present search for authenticity that characterizes most secessionist claims. However, culturalism is oblivious to the arbitrary, *ad hoc* and manipulative nature of such claims to uniqueness. Moreover, both primordialists and neo-Durkhemians operate with an extremely hard and nonflexible concept of culture that reifies and essentializes collective action (Brubaker 1996, 2004; Malešević 2006, 2010, 2011a). Nevertheless since Weber (1978) and Barth (1969), social scientists know well that cultural similarity does not necessarily translate into joint collective action and particularly not in violent collective action. Rather than being an automatic reaction, ethno-national mobilization requires intensive and long-term work involving cultural elites, political entrepreneurs, social organizations, mass media, education systems and so on (Fenton 2003; Brubaker 2004; Jenkins 2008). In other words, since there is a large repertoire of cultural symbols, myths of origin and collective memories to draw upon, the process through which a mere ethno-national category is transformed into a self-aware ethno-national group that supports (and is willing to use) violence in the establishment of an independent sovereign state is a historically contingent process that is always based on arbitrary actions. Since culturalists understand groups as intrinsically homogeneous and bounded entities that possess collective will and other personality traits they are unable to see the full complexity and fluidity that are a hallmark of group formation: rather than studying the actual mechanisms of ethnic group socialization they operate with virtually untestable notions of ineffability, apriority and simple affectivity (Eller and Coughlan 1993). There is no one-way relationship between cultural difference and violent separatism: if this was the case we would live in a world where state break up would be a daily routine. Simply put, despite the rhetoric of cultural authenticity the roots of secessionism are not, for the most part, cultural. Furthermore, even if there was a strong link between cultural difference and political independence this in itself does not explain why some secessionist movements adopt violent tactics and most do not.

Finally, the most popular explanatory models of secessionism emphasize the political nature of this phenomenon.[1] For one group of scholars the central issue is the character of the political regime (Buchanan 1991, 1998; Meadwell 1999; Belanger et al. 2005). They draw on the long tradition of the so-called democratic peace literature (Doyle 1997; Moaz and Russett 1993; Lake 1992) which argues that unlike their authoritarian counterparts democratic states rarely if ever engage in violent conflicts against each other. In a similar vein they counterpoise democratic and authoritarian political orders and argue not only that democracy in a host state delegitimizes secessionism (Buchanan 1998) but also, since democratic regimes are able and willing to accommodate group rights including self-determination within existing state structures as the process of democratization intensifies, it is likely to impede secessionist claims (Belanger et al. 2005; Meadwell 1999; Rummel 1994). Moreover they argue that since democracy provides voice and freedom of organization for all collective actors it fosters the peaceful resolution of conflicts.

Other authors shift attention to the institutional design of state organizations. In particular they explore the levels of state centralization, federal, regional and other organizational arrangements, the form and operation of electoral systems and the structure of coercive apparatuses such as the military and police (Horowitz 1985; Herbst 1989; Linz and Stepan 1996; Lijphart 2002). While many of these authors share the view that democratic political orders are better equipped to deal with and less likely to experience secessionism, the focal point of their view is the role of internal state organization. More specifically they argue that both violence and separatist movements are products of ineffective state organization. For example, whereas Horowitz (1985), and Linz and Stepan (1996) argue that secessionism stems

---

[1] Although much of the literature that focuses on secessionism as a political phenomenon is normative in character (i.e. addresses the issue of legitimacy of one's claim for independent statehood) we deal here only with the explanatory models that identify the primary role of politics in secessionism.

from weak electoral systems that foster ethno-national divisions, Lijphart (2002) insists on the necessity of accommodating ethno-national differences through elite centred consociational arrangements.

There is no doubt that political factors play a very important role in the development, organization and activities of violent secessionist movements as well as those of the host state governments. Secessionism is first and foremost a political phenomenon. However, much of the work on the political determinants of secessionism is overly preoccupied with the internal dynamics which averts attention from the greater, external, picture. By focusing so much on the electoral laws and practices and the character of a political regime one can lose sight of the fact that democratic social orders are immune neither to separatism nor to violent secessionism. In fact if one is to look at the European continent in the 1970s it would become apparent that virulent secessionism was much more prevalent in the democratic half of the continent than in its Communist, authoritarian part, with violent confrontations spread out from Northern Ireland, the Basque country, Catalonia and Corsica to Cyprus.

In addition, as a number of recent influential studies demonstrate (Snyder 2000; Chua 2004; Mann 2005) the intensive democratization of authoritarian states is in fact more likely to foster a proliferation of secessionism, and especially violent secessionism, than to prevent it. Both Mann and Snyder provide empirical evidence that authoritarian regimes are 'better at damping down ethnic tensions than democracies unless democracies are already securely institutionalized' (Mann 2005: 22). Similarly, the institutional design of states does not necessarily foster or impede secessionist claims: secessionism emerges in a variety of electoral systems and under diverse levels of state centralization. The historical and contemporary experience shows that neither consociational arrangements nor increased centralization are able to stop the proliferation of separatist demands.

Hence we argue that to understand properly the relationship between secessionism and violence the focus of one's analysis should shift from stringent economism, inflexible culturalism and formal institutionalism towards more reflective theoretical models. In particular there is a need to explore the influence of external political actors and the role ideologies play in mobilizing public support for both secession and violence. Thus our analysis attempts to integrate the standard cultural, economic and political factors with the broader impact that geo-politics and ideological mobilization play in fostering violent secessionism.

Since the focal point of geopolitics are the relationships between political power and geographic space (Osterud 1988; Agnew 2003) the hub of our attention is the changing nature of territorial claims. That is, to understand fully the origins and development of secessionist movements, their trajectories towards violence as well as the coercive response of the host states it is paramount to go beyond the legalistic concept of sovereignty and look at the processes through which space becomes politicized and politics territorialized. By exploring the geopolitical correlates of power we will be able to demonstrate how and why secessionism emerges, operates and changes. Most of all, by looking at the social actions of various political actors and social organizations beyond and below the borders of existing nation-states it will become apparent how interdependent these actors and organizations are and how this interdependence influences the intensity and character of secessionism. Simply put, secessionist claims do not emerge nor do they function in a geopolitical vacuum. Although claims for cultural authenticity, economic interest and state organization are all relevant ingredients of secessionist processes none of them in itself is sufficient to generate these processes or to make them virulent. All separatist movements operate, expand or shrink in a given and changing geopolitical context. One has to look at geopolitics to understand why some political entities become independent states while others of the same size and importance do not. It is geopolitics that helps us to explain why some secessionist movements are tolerated and others are violently crushed; why some irredentist organizations embrace militancy and others never do.

Nevertheless, since the entire process through which a particular stretch of territory becomes politicized is dependent on the articulation of specific meanings and perceptions, there is no secessionism without ideology. By ideology we do not mean unquestioned adherence to a system of rigid and closed ideas but adherence to fairly flexible and adaptable beliefs and practices that infuse daily life and motivate social action. Ideology is a form of 'thought-action' that projects transcendent grand vistas of an envisaged social and political order that surpass experience by invoking advanced ethical norms, superior knowledge claims and collective interests (Malešević 2002, 2006, 2010). In this sense all human beings are ideological creatures as social facts and political events that surround us never speak for themselves but require decoding and political understanding. Hence we all need and use available ideological maps to contextualize and comprehend these events and facts (Freeden 1996). Ideologies are complex social processes that impose coherence and provide structure and organization to contingent actions, events and images. Ideologies are cognitive apparatuses through which social agents articulate their beliefs and actions. Not only is there no viable secessionist movement without ideology, but ideologies are essential in the process of legitimizing violent action.

Hence we argue that the changing character of secessionism and in particular its periodic and unpredictable metamorphosis from being mostly a benign phenomenon towards acquiring distinctly malign features and vice versa requires prioritizing the role of geopolitics and ideology. To illustrate the heuristic value of this approach in the study of secessionist movements we provide a brief comparative analysis of two diverse secessionist experiences: Serb separatism in Bosnia and Herzegovina and Irish republican secessionism in Northern Ireland.

# Serb Secessionism in Bosnia and Herzegovina: From Violence to Institutional Separatism

As with most secessionisms the Serb separatist movement in Bosnia has historically oscillated: it gained momentum with the Austro-Hungarian annexation of Bosnia and Herzegovina (1908) culminating in Gavrilo Princip's assassination of Archduke Franz Ferdinand, was subdued and almost nonexistent for much of the 20th century, only to re-emerge and dramatically expand since the early 1990s. However, notwithstanding a few obvious exceptions, much of this secessionism was to remain non-violent until the war of 1992–95. In contrast to the democratic peace and electoral organization models Serb secessionism was weak and invisible under authoritarian systems and proliferated in the circumstances of democratization and liberalization. Whereas the autocratic context of monarchist and communist Yugoslavia did not yield any visible separatist movements among the Bosnian Serbs,[2] the accelerated democratization of the late 1980s and early 1990s proved auspicious for the emergence and expansion of violent secessionism. In addition, although the attempts to change the electoral systems in post-Dayton Bosnia did not generate violent responses, they were still unable to soothe secessionist sentiments.

Similarly, despite the profound economic inequalities of monarchist Yugoslavia, the lack of political voice under Communist rule and the position of living in 'an internal colony', most Bosnian Serbs channelled their dissatisfaction in socio-economic rather than ethno-national terms. The situation was similar under state socialism where Bosnian society had a fairly egalitarian social structure with no ethnic group dominating in any major sector of economy, politics or culture[3] (Katunarić 1991). Paradoxically, and contrary to the expectations of most economistic theories, the significant rise of living standards in 1989–90, brought about by the economic reforms of the last Yugoslav government, did not lead towards greater economic rationality of individual utility maximizers. Instead these economic gains had little impact on the upsurge of secessionist demands that would eventually end up in full-blown warfare.

Finally although the Serb secessionist movement invokes the preservation of cultural difference as one of the principal reasons for establishing the autonomous Republika Srpska, most of its official symbolism and ethno-national mythology were created during or after the 1992–95 war. Rather than building on the well

---

2  It is worth noting that in the last free pre-World War Two Yugoslav elections in 1928 most Bosnian Serbs favoured the anti-centralist policies of the Peasant-Democratic Coalition (see Goldstein 1999).

3  As Katunarić's (1991) large-scale research indicates, unlike Croatia where Serbs were over-represented in the police and the military forces, Bosnia's three main ethnic groups were nearly equally represented in top echelons of power and the economy (i.e. communist party central committee, high ranking posts in state-run enterprises, among higher professionals, top military and police positions).

established narrative of common descent, unique myths and memories specific to the territory inhabited by the Bosnian Serbs, much of its key symbolic signifiers were either directly imported from Serbia's ethno-national imagery or were simply invented[4] (Torsti 2004; Bartulovic 2006). Even the very name and the territorial borders of this entity have no historical precedent, both being a war time creation. The fact that the foundation of a distinct and almost fully autonomous entity did not end separatist demands but has in fact fostered their proliferation is a poignant indicator that secessionism is not cultural but first and foremost a political phenomenon.

While there is no doubt that in this case as in many others culture, economics and political institutions play an important part in generating secessionist demands, it is geopolitics and ideology that have proved decisive for the expansion of Serb secessionism in Bosnia and particularly for its transformation into a virulent phenomenon (see also Chapter 10).

For much of its history Bosnia was part of the various large-scale empires and multiethnic states where Bosnian Serbs were just one among many ethnic collectivities, a group relatively small and with little authentic political organization. The origin and development of secessionist movements among the Bosnian Serbs over the last two centuries are deeply rooted in regional and European geopolitics. It is these geopolitical changes together with the gradual spread of ideological blueprints of self-determination that were decisive for the emergence of secessionism and its violent articulations. Although the period of Ottoman rule (1463–1878) saw some popular resistance and dissatisfaction with the existing colonial status most rebellions involving Bosnian Serbs were essentially peasant uprisings which even when couched in the religious discourse (Christian peasantry against Muslim aristocracy) were expressions of social not ethno-national discontent (Mazower 2003; Gerolymatos 2004; Malešević 2011b).

The Austro-Hungarian occupation (1878–1918) coupled with the rise of modern nationalist ideologies in neighbouring Serbia and Croatia provided more incentive for secessionism. Most of Bosnia and Herzegovina's population was illiterate and rural. Because, as Gellner (1983) rightly argues, peasants do not make good nationalists, the Bosnian Serb secessionist movement rarely spread beyond a small circle of intellectuals, Orthodox clergy and middle-class professionals. Nonetheless regardless of its diminutive size this movement would have a decisive impact on world history: the gunshots of one of its members proved to be a catalyst for the start of Wold War One. Among the several secessionist organizations that emerged in this period Young Bosnia (Mlada Bosna) was most prominent.[5] Even though this movement was not composed exclusively of Bosnian Serbs and was

---

4   For example the flag, national anthem, coat of arms and most national holidays and religious celebrations were all directly copied from the repertoire of Serbia's ethno-national imagery.

5   Another highly influential organization was a Serb movement for freedom of religious education (1893–1903) but their ambitions were rather modest with little or no inclination towards secessionism (Lovrenović 2001: 150).

advocating unification of all south Slavs, rather than all Serbs, into a single state, its organization and development was spearheaded by the several secretive Serb nationalist organizations based in Serbia (the People's Defence, Black Hand/ Unification or Death) (Malcolm 1994; Hoare 2007). In other words the principal ideological ambitions of the movement were heavily dependent on the external, geopolitical, conditions and in particular on the growing territorial competition between Austro-Hungary and the rising power of the Serbian state. Serbia's military success in the Balkan wars (1912–13) provided even stronger impetus for the further rise of Serb nationalism throughout the region. This development coincided with gradual democratization and modernization in Bosnia and Herzegovina that also included the organization of the first parliamentary elections (1910). Hence, rather than preventing secessionist tendencies democratization has helped advance such claims. Under external ideological influences and changing geo-political contexts this early secessionism become radicalized and ultimately violent, relying on sporadic assassination attempts and small-scale terrorist actions.[6]

The geopolitical and (relative) ideological stability of the interwar and post-World War Two years was a principal reason that there were very few if any secessionist demands among the Bosnian Serbs living in monarchist and communist Yugoslavia. Although Bosnia remained one of the most undeveloped regions in both periods, any organized political opposition towards regional or state authorities came mostly in social rather than ethno-national form (Ramet 2006). While the authoritarian state, in both its royalist and communist guises, has proved able to contain even the mildest form of secessionism, the hasty democratization of the late 1980s and early 1990s galvanized an explosion of secessionist movements throughout the former Yugoslav federation (see Chapter 8). Nevertheless, even in this situation Bosnian movements lagged behind events developing in Slovenia, Serbia and Croatia. As the Yugoslav federation started to unravel it generated a new and highly unstable geopolitical situation. The rampant secessionist activities in other republics created a domino effect in Bosnia too with the three principal ethnic collectivities mobilizing around mutually exclusive ideological projects: the unification of all ethnic Serbs in a single state, the creation of an independent Croatian state incorporating large parts of Bosnia, and a multi-ethnic sovereign state with a Bosniak majority. The escalation of violence in Slovenia and Croatia created a new geopolitical and ideological environment with the radical groups utilizing the politics of fear and violence to mobilize individuals along ethno-national lines. It is important to emphasize that before the atrocities of 1992–95 there was little if any animosity between the ethnic groups living in communist Bosnia and no popular support for secessionism. As all available data demonstrate, together with Vojvodina, Bosnia had the highest proportion of inter-ethnic marriages and among the lowest rates of social distance

---

6    It is important to emphasize that resistance to Habsburg rule was in great part fuelled by the agrarian question. The Austro-Hungarian rulers preserved the Ottoman feudal order in which four-fifths of peasants were still awaiting land reform and emancipation from the shackles of feudal bondage (Mazower 2003: 107).

among the three main ethnic collectivities (Dyker 1979; Katunarić 1987; Botev 1994). The last large-scale survey conducted before the war (in 1989) indicated that 90 percent of respondents described inter-ethnic relations in their region as good or very good while 63 percent agreed with the statement that 'one's ethnicity should be of no importance in choosing a life partner' (Pešić 1995).

Nevertheless as the geopolitical and ideological context changed so too did the attitudes of the population: with the proliferation of paramilitary groups and the virtual disintegration of the communist Yugoslav People's Army as a multi-ethnic force, the general population became more radicalized providing support to the political movements advocating mutually incompatible secessionist projects. The implosion of the federal state brought rampant volatility and instability while the presence of armed groups coupled with the ethno-nationalist mobilization of what Brubaker (1996) terms 'nationalizing homeland states' of Serbia and Croatia further fuelled Bosnian Serb (and Croat) secessionism. The swift transformation of Bosnian Serb secessionism from being a relatively benign political movement into a brutal violent force is rooted in the increasing militarization and ideologization of the entire region. Although the movement was autonomous it was ideologically, economically and militarily dependent on the external support base – the Serbian state apparatus, remnants of the Yugoslav military machine and militant civil society groups in Serbia and the diaspora (Ron 2003; Mann 2005).

Since the war in Croatia was propagandistically depicted in the Serbian mainstream media as an attempt to resurrect the pro-fascist Ustasha's 'Independent State of Croatia', an entity responsible for mass killings of Serbs during World War Two, the Bosnian Serb population became receptive to similar depictions of the emerging independent Bosnian state. Hence, as the war in Croatia reached a stalemate in 1992 much of the military and ideological apparatus shifted to Bosnia which further galvanized violent secessionism. By depicting ethno-national sovereignty and the establishment of an independent state as a question of the physical survival of the entire group, the Serb secessionist movement was able to mobilize wide support and to legitimize its use of violence. By combining geopolitical military might with a self-righteous sense of ideological right the secessionist movement was able to portray its reliance on violence as a mere defensive strategy. Hence both secessionism and violence were products of the changing regional geopolitical and ideological conditions. Violent secessionism emerged as a chain reaction in the turbulent political environment: it developed and was justified as the only available option in the context of a disintegrating federal state.

Although the unusual and highly complex territorial organization of the Bosnian state created in Dayton proved useful in ending inter-group slaughter, it did not prevent secessionism. On the contrary, by institutionalizing cultural difference and territorializing ethnicity the Dayton agreement has fostered separatist demands. Not only has the war experience increased social distance, animosity and polarization among the three dominant ethnic groups but it has also spurred popular support for secessionism among Serbs and Croats (Zunec 1998) (see Chapter 8). Rather that stifling secessionist claims, post-war democratization has helped foster separatism: the highly decentralized state structure with two almost fully independent ethno-nationally organized entities inhibits the development of successful all state civic parties and impels political moderates to embrace ethno-national discourse. Although ethnic differences are not mobilized as a source of direct and violent conflict as they were in early 1990, ethnicity is now institutionally so entrenched that it penetrates most of political life. Inter-ethnic relations are in a better state now but this is mostly in part due to the virtual disappearance of ethnically mixed areas.

The transformation of the Serb secessionist movement from violence towards institutional separatism is again a result of changing geopolitical and ideological conditions. External military and political involvement (UN, EU and NATO) was crucial in stopping the war and in monopolizing the legitimate use of coercion on the entire territory thus preventing the emergence of insurgency. Furthermore, by disarming the warring factions and integrating them into a single all Bosnian military the external arbiters were instrumental in removing the principal means of violence from everyday life. This process was accompanied by regional ideological and geopolitical shifts: the weakening of 'organic' nationalist movements in the neighbouring Serbia and Croatia, whose new reformist governments were less supportive of secessionism; the rising expectations of eventual EU membership; ICTY pressure to arrest and deport war crime indictees; and the EU demands for building joint all-state institutions. In other words, the relatively swift transformation of violent secessionism into institutional separatism is rooted in the changed geopolitical and ideological environment: the strong presence of external organizations and softening of aggressive ethno-nationalist discourses in the 'nationalizing homeland states' has hindered further development of violent secessionism. However, the decrease in violence did not translate into diminished popular support for an independent Republika Srpska (the Serb Republic). As recent surveys show, more than 63 percent of its population supported the idea of breaking away and joining Serbia in 2006 whereas in 2007 77 percent agreed with the view that following Kosovo's independence Republika Srpska should secede from Bosnia (Reuters 2006; Stanić 2007). Instead the new secessionism now thrives on local geopolitics as competing political elites have a strong institutional basis to pursue separatist claims through electoral means.

## Irish Republicanism in Northern Ireland: Violent Secessionism in a Western Democracy

As a 'hot' nationalism in the cold north-west of Europe violent secessionism in Ireland presents a challenge to the proposition that well-established liberal Western democratic norms and institutions inoculate against large-scale political violence. It provides an example, from within the broader Anglo-American cultural sphere, that illustrates the intertwined development of democratization and secessionist violence.

As an 'island behind an island' the geopolitical context has powerfully shaped the rhythm of secessionist violence in Ireland, from the first modern rebellion in 1798, inspired by the American and French Revolutions and directly supported by the revolutionary French Republic (Gough and Dickson 1990), to the 25-year campaign of the Provisional IRA, originating in the local manifestations of an international wave of street protest in 1968, and drawing some strength from the locked-in power relations of the Cold War (Purdie 1990; Cox 1997).

Modern secessionist politics in Ireland first emerged in the late 18th century, directly inspired by the United States' 1776 Declaration of Independence from Britain. The United Irishmen organization was dominated by the republican and democratic nationalism of a growing Protestant artisan class and middle class in Ireland that invoked the experience of the American colonists to argue that Ireland too should be freed from British rule, that Ireland's weak and subordinate parliament, elected by a tiny number of members of the established Anglican church, should become the democratic parliament of an independent republic (Dickson et al. 1993). From the beginning, secessionism in Ireland was bound up with republicanism and demands for increased democracy, and nested in international ideological networks.

This avowedly secular republican nationalism was complicated by older lines of division in Ireland. Much of the popular support for the United Irishmen, and the mobilization for the large-scale rebellion of 1798, came from marginal and impoverished sections of the Catholic majority, from peasant communities where long-standing resentment at the legal exclusion of Catholics, the confiscation of land and the influx of Protestant settlers from England and Scotland over the previous two centuries drove the rejection of British rule (Dickson et al. 1993; Whelan 1996). Ambitions to overturn the political *status quo* had been manifested throughout the 18th century in support for the restoration of a Catholic monarch to the English throne rather than on separation from England however (Foster 1989; Ó Ciardha 2004) As in Bosnia and Herzegovina, pre-modern forms of resistance that were later assimilated to nationalist analyses did not have a clear nationalist or secessionist colouration at the time. Massacres of Protestants in parts of Ireland during the 1798 rebellion eroded liberal Protestant support for secessionist republicanism. The tension between secular and progressive republican ideology, and sectarian divisions overlaid with social class divisions remain central problematics for Irish secessionist politics. While chauvinist ethnic sentiments were strong among many secessionists and sectarianism of varying degrees was evident at various stages, Irish secessionist ideologists regularly rejected the identification of the movement with ethnic or sectarian particularism. Irish republicans characterized it as a movement for Irish freedom, analogous to the American war against British rule and, later, the anti-colonial struggles in the developing world, and strongly rejected the characterization of conflict in Ireland as 'ethnic'.

In the wake of the rebellion, Britain abolished the Irish parliament and the bulk of Irish Protestants became firm opponents of restoring any form of autonomy for

Ireland, fearful that it would place them under a hostile government dominated by Irish Catholics. The extension of the franchise during the 19th century revealed the depth and persistence of political divisions along religious lines in Ireland. In the course of the 19th century a parliamentary movement for Irish autonomy within the UK (Home Rule) gained the support of a large majority of the Irish population. The leadership of the Home Rule movement included strong Protestant representation but at grassroots level the vast majority of supporters were Catholic. Meanwhile, the great majority of the Protestant population coalesced around support for Union with Britain (Bew 2007).

Violent secessionism was poorly supported for much of the 19th century. Brief and hopeless localized rebellions rich in dramatic gesture but mobilizing tiny numbers of people and easily crushed, were led by Robert Emmett in Dublin in 1803 and by the Young Ireland movement in 1848, the latter in emulation of the liberal and nationalist revolutions across Europe in that year. Violent secessionism did not re-emerge as a serious force in Irish politics until the founding in 1858 of the Irish Republican Brotherhood (IRB), a secret movement committed to plotting armed rebellion, the direct forerunner of the IRA. Significantly, it was founded simultaneously as the Fenian Brotherhood in the USA where huge numbers of Irish emigrants had gone during and after the Great Famine of 1848. Like the Young Irelanders, influenced by European currents of romantic nationalism, the Fenians invoked an ancient Irish nation, emphasizing cultural distance from Britain (Hoppen 1984; Townshend 1983). As with earlier secessionist movements, Irish Protestants were strongly represented at leadership level but grassroots support came overwhelmingly from the Catholic community. Very much a minority, militant separatists maintained an uneasy relationship with parliamentary nationalists and the political mainstream regarded this tradition with a certain ambiguity. 'Violence is the only way of ensuring a hearing for moderation' as one 19th-century Irish parliamentary nationalist put it (O'Brien 1978). Despite this ambiguity, the sporadic and very localized Fenian rebellion of 1867 seemed to illustrate once again the futility of armed challenges to British rule, and the lack of popular support.

When the next violent uprising took place, led by IRB members in Easter 1916, it came after three decades of intense parliamentary activity aimed at securing autonomy had been seen to fail. Once again, the geopolitical context was crucial to the timing and organization of the rebellion, the rebels invoking 'our gallant allies in Europe' as a German ship laden with arms unsuccessfully attempted to land on the southwest coast in support of the rebels (Townshend 2006).

Far from riding on a wave of primordialist sentiment, secessionists found it extremely difficult to mobilize mass support for violent challenges to British rule. When sustained mass mobilization finally did take place, in the guerrilla warfare of the Anglo-Irish war from 1919 to 1921 that culminated in the establishment of an independent Irish state, it was generated to a great degree by the harsh repressive response to the failed rebellion of 1916. It was not until British rule took the form of direct military repression in the spaces of everyday life that involvement in secessionist violence began to move beyond a small minority. And even then that mobilization was extraordinarily uneven, heavily concentrated in the south-west and the capital. The unevenness of this violent mobilization, not correlated with social class or levels of nationalist cultural activity, or even with electoral support for secession, indicates that secessionist violence is not mechanically generated by broader national patterns, but decisively influenced by local cycles of repression and atrocity, territorially uneven historical experiences of violent repertoires of action and the intensity of localized events (Hart 1997, 1998).

With the signing of the Anglo-Irish treaty and the establishment of an independent Irish State in 1921 Irish secessionists achieved their aim of independence at the cost of partition. 'Northern Ireland', composed of six northern counties in the province of Ulster, remained within the United Kingdom although one third of its population was nationalist.

By contrast with the crucial role played by 'nationalizing homeland states' in Bosnia in the 1990s, the Irish government eschewed the use of force and supported northern nationalists in a minimalist fashion (despite incorporating a formal irredentist claim to the northern counties in the Irish constitution of 1937). An Irish government policy of rapprochement with the Unionist government in the mid-1960s marked what seemed to be a final acceptance of stable Unionist domination in the North, and acquiescence in the ongoing exclusion of the nationalist minority. By contrast with Bosnia, social distance between Protestant unionist and Catholic nationalist in Northern Ireland was large. Despite this social distance, inter-communal violence was intermittent and limited (Barrit and Carter 1972; Harris 1972; Rose 1971). And the outbreak of extensive violent rioting in Belfast provoked by economic distress during the depths of the depression in the mid-1930s, illustrated once again that violence directly driven by economic discontent had no inevitable or necessary relationship with separatist violence.

The secessionist tradition remained a tiny and marginal current in northern nationalist politics, dominated by a small number of key families. When the IRA launched a rural guerrilla campaign in 1956 in imitation of the successes of 1919–21, it was a disastrous failure, failing to mobilize any significant popular support. When it was finally called off in 1962 it seemed to sound the death-knell for the violent secessionist tradition in Ireland. The new leadership of the IRA and Sinn Féin, excited by the growth of popular left-wing protest internationally and characterizing 'militarism' as a key flaw of the movement, began to transform the movement into a Marxist political party that would ultimately build strong institutional links with the Communist Party of the USSR. Its 'army' would turn to social activism and plans for military activity were reserved for a far-distant social revolution throughout Ireland (Bell 1980). When violence began in Northern Ireland in 1968, it was not instigated by the IRA leadership but emerged from escalating street confrontations associated with that very 1960s phenomenon, protest marches (Ó Dochartaigh 2005). Rhetoric, repertoires of contention and political frames generated in the civil rights campaign in the US, in the May 1968 protests in Paris and in student protests elsewhere combined with the influence of television (a new medium at the time) to provide in the 1960s novel ways to challenge Unionist domination in Northern Ireland (Purdie 1990; Ó Dochartaigh 2008). When violent secessionism re-emerged, it was generated in the first place by the experience of confrontation between state security forces and the nationalist minority that accompanied civil rights protests. When British troops were deployed to restore order and became the day-to-day policing agency in nationalist urban working-class areas, this fitted well with Irish republican interpretations of Britain's historical role as an oppressive external force. As in 1919–21, the direct experience of repression in everyday life was crucial in generating strong local networks prepared to use violence in pursuit of a broader nationalist goal (Ó Dochartaigh 2010).

The Marxist-dominated IRA leadership was reluctant to respond violently to the escalating street violence; as a result, a breakaway faction established the 'Provisional IRA', ready to encourage and intensify the conflict on the streets with the British army. But even this new leadership found itself under intense pressure from new recruits radicalized by violent confrontation on the ground to act more aggressively (Ó Dochartaigh 2005). Increasing repression generated increasing violence and a widespread radicalization of large sections of the nationalist population. By the early 1970s a once marginal tradition of violent secessionism had become a powerful mainstream force in northern nationalist politics, powerful enough to sustain a 20-year 'long war' by the Provisional IRA.

Invoking the legacy of the civil rights movement, secessionists claimed that an independent united Ireland would provide the only 'permanent guarantee of civil rights' (Ó Dochartaigh 2005: 172). Seccesionists argued that acceptable political arrangements and, in particular, freedom from repression in everyday life could only be achieved through completing the Irish secessionist project. When the Provisional IRA ultimately accepted a political settlement in 1998 that left Northern Ireland radically reformed but within the United Kingdom, the settlement was endorsed by over 90 percent of the nationalist minority (and by barely half of the unionist majority). Subsequent electoral challenges to the Provisional IRA by purist secessionists indicated that uncompromising ideologically-driven secessionists represented a miniscule proportion of the population. Ultimately a reformist internal settlement that softened the border between the two parts of Ireland and guaranteed that 'disloyal' secessionists who retained their ultimate aim of leaving the United Kingdom were entitled to participate in government, proved acceptable to virtually all of those who had previously supported secessionist violence. The agreement offered the prospect of peacefully pursuing secessionist aims without being disadvantaged or politically excluded on the basis of 'disloyalty'. The fact that the Irish border was an internal EU border at a time when those internal borders were being progressively softened was crucial to the peace settlement and central to the argument that the Irish border would effectively disappear after a peace settlement. 'This island will be as one ... The historical train – Europe – determines that' as one British government negotiator put it in secret contact with the Provisionals in 1993 (Sinn Féin 1994).

By contrast with the role of 'nationalizing homeland states' in Bosnia, secessionists in Northern Ireland enjoyed the active and often intense hostility of the Irish government and, after a brief surge of popular sympathy south of the Irish border at the outset of conflict, limited popular support throughout most of the island. Nonetheless, despite the opposition to violence, the Irish state and population took a quite different view of the violence in the North to that of the British government, appealing in 1969 (with the full awareness that their call would be unsuccessful) for the deployment of UN peacekeepers in Northern Ireland and the consequent internationalization of the conflict (O'Kane 2002). But the imbalance of power between the British and Irish states, long-established international recognition of British sovereignty in Northern Ireland, not to mention the fact that the UK was one of the five permanent members of the UN Security Council, ensured that Britain was easily able to insulate the conflict from international intervention and treat it as an essentially internal affair. Crucial to the peace settlement of the 1990s was the gradual internationalization of the problem with the increased acceptance of Irish government involvement in a search for a solution and the direct intervention and support of the United States and the EU (Mallie and McKittrick 2001; Powell 2008).

For most of the modern period secessionism was a minority taste in Ireland, viewed with varying degrees of disfavour by mainstream nationalists seeking autonomy. Only with the war of independence of 1919 did the majority of the Irish population come to support secessionist politics at the polls, and even then there was strong ambiguity towards the armed campaign of the IRA in support of the elected secessionist representatives (Garvin 1981). The peace settlement in Northern Ireland did not mark the end of secessionist politics, but demonstrated that support for violent secessionism could be drastically eroded by reform, by the acceptance of secessionists in the business of government and by the softening of borders rather than by their redrawing. Crucial to this was a limited 'internationalization' of the conflict through the involvement of the USA and the EU.

## Violence and Secession between Ideology and Geopolitics

Far from being the inevitable consequence of cultural diversity and ethnic mixing, secessionist violence is extremely difficult to generate and sustain and is relatively rare and intermittent. In both Bosnia and Herzegovina and Northern Ireland, outbreaks of secessionist violence followed long periods when secessionist sentiments were weak and violence was minimal. The failure of zealous minorities to spark off popular mobilization by launching violent campaigns, as the IRA did in the 1950s, illustrates that it takes far more than elite manipulation and a fanatical leadership to set alight what culturalist theorists see as the dry tinder of ancient hatreds. What then are the circumstances in which mass support for secessionist violence grows and secessionists can mobilize widespread direct involvement in, support for and acquiescence in the use of violence? How do we explain secessionist violence?

Rational choice explanations and economistic Marxist analyses are important in correcting culturalist emphases on primordial hatreds and indissoluble differences, but the impoverished simplicity and rigidity of their analytical concepts constitute serious flaws and limit their usefulness. Approaches that treat complex entities such as states, militant organizations or even ethnic groups as though they were unified actors with a single interest and rationality, are insufficient. If hunger-strikers, suicide-bombers and teenagers who join a hopeless cause with the almost certain prospect of death or imprisonment can be said to be rationally pursuing their interests, the concept of rationality becomes so thinly stretched that it ceases to add much to the concept of human action. Ideology, the sets of ideas and practices with which we interpret the world, that suggest goals and the methods of achieving them, is crucial to understanding the circumstances in which individuals should act so directly against their 'objective' interests, even to the point of self-destruction.

Rational choice explanations fail too to explain why nationalist struggles that are set to disproportionately benefit new 'clerical' classes and the middle class, should so often be disproportionately supported by marginalized working-class and rural communities who can expect little direct personal economic benefit from the new nationalist dispensation (*pace* Laitin 2007). In both Bosnia and Herzegovina and Northern Ireland the rank and file of violent separatist movements could not reasonably expect that the success of secessionist violence would significantly improve their personal economic status at a lower price than alternative paths (see also Chapter 10).

Marxist explanations are useful in understanding the social and political consequences of economic marginalization and the economic dimension to alienation from authority. But Marxist theories emphasizing uneven development and economic exploitation can not fully explain why secessionist violence occurs only at certain times, only in certain exploited regions and why it is not at all limited to economically peripheral regions but takes place too in core industrial regions such as the Basque Country. Violence directly driven by economic marginalization can remain quite distinct from secessionist violence, as with the Irish 'Land War' of the late 19th century, while at other times it can constitute a powerful current within violent secessionist campaigns as in Bosnia and Herzegovina during the period of Austro-Hungarian rule. There is no direct mechanical relationship between these two forms of violence and even in regions with strong secessionist traditions, there is no inevitability that campaigns of violence associated with economic grievances will generate secessionist violence.

Political and institutionalist explanations similarly contribute to our understanding of the sources of conflict but fail to explain the timing of secessionist violence and the patterns of mobilization. Institutions can fail to secure legitimacy, generate resentment and exclude minorities and yet survive for long periods of time without experiencing secessionist violence.

While much academic analysis deals with secessionist violence as an essentially internal matter and treats the sovereign states that face secessionist violence as natural territorial units, secessionism is predicated precisely on contesting existing demarcations between the internal and the external, aiming to externalize the internal thus creating a space free of the direct coercive capacities of their opponents. To analyse secessionist movements entirely within the politics of the states that they seek to secede from is to naturalize existing state boundaries and to foreclose on an understanding of the dynamics of secessionist violence. As a form of violence aimed at altering the existing global system, albeit at localized locations in that system, all secessionist violence, whether externally supported or not, can only be understood and explained in a geopolitical context (see also Chapter 1). By challenging the state's monopoly of violence it challenges state sovereignty in the most direct way and calls into question the state's place within the international system. It is an internationalizing strategy that can only be explained by reference to wider geopolitical conditions. Defining, explaining and interpreting it as an internal challenge to states, comparable to other endogenous sources of social discord, forecloses on the very debates that surround secessionism. As a strategy aimed at repositioning a particular space within the international system, secessionist violence is decisively shaped by wider geopolitical changes. The growth of secessionist politics worldwide, the spread of nationalist ideology and the shifting balance between great powers was crucial to creating the space for secessionist politics in both Ireland and Bosnia and Herzegovina from the very beginning, while the ending of the Cold War had a crucial influence on the use of secessionist violence in both Bosnia and Northern Ireland, albeit in directly opposing directions.

A crucial dimension to this geopolitical context is ideological. New currents of thought, providing new interpretations, new visions of the future, and new prescriptions for attaining that future, provided frameworks for understanding local conditions, economic inequalities, inter-ethnic relations and relations to authority and the state in new ways. Similarly important is the spread of new repertoires of action; popular violent rebellion in the name of democracy, guerrilla warfare, militia organizations, terror tactics. Ideologies provide new frameworks for understanding old divisions, new prescriptions for resolving discontents. But they don't operate in a mechanical way to produce outcomes. The 19th-century nationalism that generated rebellions in much of Europe, had little purchase in a mainly rural Bosnia and was manifested in Ireland in a moderate democratic mass movement for autonomy, leaving violent secessionists marginalized. The rhetoric of self-determination in the early 20th century, providing an apparent answer to the decline of large multi-national empires, strengthened the hand of secessionists and of small-state irredentist nationalism in Bosnia as in Ireland.

In the case of Northern Ireland a global ideological current of change in the 1960s, in the context of a world ideologically polarized and politically balanced between two great powers, was crucial to generating a new kind of challenge to the state. The new challenge led to the breakdown of a stable system of domination which in turn gave renewed resonance to secessionist ideologies that had been weak and marginal for decades previously. In Bosnia and Herzegovina it was a later shift in the global system, and the collapse of the established ideological framework in 1989/90 that created the space for the growth of secessionist violence. That same shift in global power relations and ideological frameworks had a quite different impact in Northern Ireland. While Irish secessionists in Northern Ireland had rejected alignment with the Soviet bloc, they had a leftist orientation and the shift in the global system at the time isolated some states such as Libya (whose supply of arms in the 1980s had significantly boosted the IRA's capacity to sustain its campaign).

The Irish and Bosnian cases illustrate not only that intense secessionist violence and democracy are compatible but that democratization is, in certain important senses, a key driver of secessionist politics and violence. And the experience of Northern Ireland shows that one of the longest-established democratic systems and deeply-embedded democratic norms provide no obstacle whatsoever to the open-ended exclusion of an ethno-national minority and the associated growth of violent secessionism (see also Chapter 24). An international order built on the combined principles of democratic majority rule and relatively untrammelled state sovereignty provides a powerful incentive for minority groups to seek the security of majority control in a sovereign state of their own, to ask the question 'Why should we be a minority in your state, when you can be a minority in our state?' (Gligorov 1994: 158).

If democratization does not inoculate against large-scale secessionist violence how then can secessionist violence be ended or reduced? Recent solutions include permitting levels of internal autonomy that come close to granting sovereignty and statehood without formal secession, as in Iraqi Kurdistan and in Bosnia and Herzegovina (see Part VI). This solution has the advantage of removing many of the motivations for secession but at the cost of territorializing and institutionally embedding internal ethno-national diversity, fixing it in the rigid configurations established during violent conflict. On the other hand, the territorial institutionalization of ethno-national identity could be said to be the fundamental organizing principle of the international system. An alternative is to weaken the inhibitions surrounding secession, to have a new openness in relation to boundary changes, what O'Leary et al. refer to as 'Right-Sizing the state' (2001), to resolve secessionist violence through a new readiness to consider and address secessionist claims on their merits. But the United Nations is not a 'suicide club' for its sovereign state members and it is difficult to imagine states approving a new system that radically transformed and eroded the concept of sovereignty and the principle of territorial integrity. A third approach, evident in the Northern Irish peace settlement and made possible by the framework of the EU, is to soften contested international boundaries, to weaken or abolish the border controls and restrictions on movement that provide one major source of discontent with existing international boundaries.

Mechanical and uni-dimensional explanations of secessionist violence that reify ethno-national categories, exaggerate the economic drivers of social action and treat the messy, arbitrary and uneven progress of social change and of human motivation and mobilization as if it might follow the predictable patterns of a chemical reaction, are insufficient to explain the radically uneven incidence of secessionist violence. Explanations of secessionist violence must incorporate the complexity and contingency of events and the relationship of patterns of secessionist violence to wider geopolitical changes. Ideology and geopolitics are crucial to understanding the uneven, intermittent and ultimately extremely rare incidence of secessionist violence.

## References

Agnew J. (2003), *Geopolitics: Revisioning World Politics* (London: Routledge).
Barritt, D. and C. Carter (1972), *The Northern Ireland Problem: A Study in Group Relations* (Oxford: Oxford University Press).
Barth, F. (1969), 'Introduction', in F. Barth (ed.), *Ethnic Groups and Boundaries* (Bergen: Universitetsforlaget), 9–38.
Bartulovic, A. (2006), 'Nationalism in the Classroom: Narratives of the War in Bosnia-Herzegovina (1992–1995) in the History Textbooks of the Republic of Srpska', *Studies in Ethnicity and Nationalism* 6:3, 51–72.
Belanger, L., E. Duchesne and J. Paquin (2005), 'Foreign Interventions and Secessionist Movements: The Democratic Factor', *Canadian Journal of Political Science* 38:2, 435–62.
Bell, J.B. (1980), *The Secret Army: The IRA, 1916–1979* (Cambridge, MA: MIT Press).
Bew, P. (2007), *Ireland: The Politics of Enmity 1789–2006. Oxford History of Modern Europe* (Oxford and New York: Oxford University Press).
Bonacich, E. (1972), 'A Theory of Ethnic Antagonism: The Split Labor Market', *American Sociological Review* 37, 547–59.
Botev, N. (1994), 'Where East Meets West: Ethnic Intermarriage in the former Yugoslavia 1962 to 1989', *American Sociological Review* 59, 461–80.
Brubaker, R. (1996), *Nationalism Reframed: Nationhood and the National Question in the New Europe* (Cambridge: Cambridge University Press).
Brubaker, R. (2004), *Ethnicity without Groups* (Cambridge, MA: Harvard University Press).
Buchanan, A. (1991), *Secession: The Morality of Political Divorce from Fort Sumter to Lithuania and Quebec* (Boulder, CO: Westview Press).
Buchanan, A. (1998), 'Democracy and Secession', in M. Moore (ed.), *National Self-Determination and Secession* (Oxford: Oxford University Press), 14–33.
Chua, A. (2004), *World on Fire: How Exporting Free Market Democracy Breeds Ethnic Hatred and Global Instability* (New York: Anchor Books).
Conversi, D. (1997), *The Basques, the Catalans and Spain: Alternative Routes to Nationalist Mobilisation* (London: Hurst).
Cox, M. (1997), 'Bringing in the "International": The IRA Ceasefire and the End of the Cold War', *International Affairs* 73, 671–93.
Dickson, D., D. Keogh and K. Whelan (1993), *The United Irishmen: Republicanism, Radicalism, and Rebellion* (Dublin: Lilliput Press).
Doyle, M. (1997), *The Ways of Peace and War* (New York: Norton).
Dyker, D. (1979), 'Yugoslavia: Unity out of Diversity?', in A. Brown and J. Gray (eds), *Political Culture and Political Change in Communist States* (London: Macmillan), 66–100.

Eller, J. and R. Coughlan (1993), 'The Poverty of Primordialism: The Demystification of Ethnic Attachments', *Ethnic and Racial Studies* 16:2, 183–202.

Fearon, J. (1994), 'Signaling versus the Balance of Power and Interests: An Empirical Test of a Crisis Bargaining Model', *Journal of Conflict Resolution* 38, 236–69.

Fearon, J. and D. Laitin (2000), 'Violence and the Social Construction of Ethnic Identity', *International Organization* 54:4, 845–77.

Fenton, S. (2003), *Ethnicity* (Cambridge: Polity).

Foster, R.F. (1989), *Modern Ireland, 1600–1972* (London: Penguin Books).

Freeden, M. (1996), *Ideologies and Political Theory: A Conceptual Approach* (Oxford: Clarendon Press).

Garvin, T. (1981), *The Evolution of Irish Nationalist Politics* (Dublin: Gill and Macmillan).

Geertz, C. (1973), *The Interpretation of Cultures* (London: Fontana).

Gellner, E. (1983), *Nations and Nationalism* (Oxford: Basil Blackwell).

Gerolymatos, A. (2004), *The Balkan Wars* (New York: Basic Books).

Gligorov, V. (1994), 'Is What Is Left Right? The Yugoslav Heritage', in J.M. Kovacs (ed.), *Transition to Capitalism?* (New Brunswick, NJ: Transaction), 147–72.

Goldstein, I. (1999), *Croatia: A History* (London: Hurst).

Gough, H. and D. Dickson (1990), *Ireland and the French Revolution* (Dublin: Irish Academic Press).

Harris, R. (1972), *Prejudice and Tolerance in Ulster* (Manchester: Manchester University Press; Totowa, NJ: Rowman and Littlefield).

Hart, P. (1997), 'The Geography of Revolution in Ireland 1917–1923', *Past and Present* 155, 142–76.

Hart, P. (1998), *The IRA and Its Enemies: Violence and Community in Cork, 1916–1923* (Oxford: Clarendon Press).

Hastings, A. (1997), *The Construction of Nationhood* (Cambridge: Cambridge University Press).

Hechter, M. (1974), 'The Political Economy of Ethnic Change', *American Journal of Sociology* 79:5, 1151–78.

Hechter, M. (1999), *Internal Colonialism: The Celtic Fringe in British National Development, 1536–1966* (New Brunswick, NJ: Transaction).

Herbst, J. (1989), 'Creation and Maintenance of National Boundaries in Africa', *International Organization* 43:40, 673–92.

Hoare, M.A. (2007), *The History of Bosnia: From the Middle Ages to the Present Day* (London: Saqi).

Hoppen, K.T. (1984), *Elections, Politics, and Society in Ireland, 1832–1885* (Oxford and New York: Oxford University Press).

Horowitz, D. (1985), *Ethnic Groups in Conflict* (Berkeley, CA: University of California Press).

Hutchinson, J. (2005), *Nations as Zones of Conflict* (London: Sage).

Hutchinson, J. (2007), 'Warfare, Remembrance and National Identity', in A. Leoussi and S. Grosby, *Nationalism and Ethnosymbolism: History, Culture and Ethnicity in the Formation of Nations* (Edinburgh: Edinburgh University Press), 42–52.

Jenkins, R. (2008), *Rethinking Ethnicity* (London: Sage).

Katunarić, V. (1987), 'Autoritarnost – Etnocentrizam – Seksizam i drustvene grupe', *Revija za Sociologiju* 29:1, 603–10.

Katunarić, V. (1991), 'Uoči novih etno-političkih raskola – Hrvatska i Bosna i Hercegovina', *Sociologija* 33:3, 373–85.

Laitin, D. (2000), 'Language Conflict and Violence: The Straw that Strengthens the Camel's Back', *European Journal of Sociology* 41:1, 97–137.

Laitin, D. (2007), *Nations, States, and Violence* (Oxford: Oxford University Press).

Lake, D. (1992), 'Powerful Pacifists: Democratic States and War', *American Political Science Review* 86:1, 4–37.

Lijphart, A. (2002), 'The Wave of Power-Sharing Democracy', in A. Reynolds (ed.), *Architecture of Democracy: Constitutional Design, Conflict Management, and Democracy* (Oxford: Oxford University Press), 37–54.

Linz, J. and A. Stepan (1996), *Problems of Democratic Transition and Consolidation* (Baltimore, MD: Johns Hopkins University Press).

Lovrenović, I. (2001), *Bosnia: A Cultural History* (London: Saqi Books).

Malcolm, N. (1994), *Bosnia: A Short History* (New York: New York University Press).

Malešević, S. (2002), *Ideology, Legitimacy and the New State: Yugoslavia, Serbia and Croatia* (London: Routledge).

Malešević, S. (2004), *The Sociology of Ethnicity* (London: Sage).

Malešević, S. (2006), *Identity as Ideology: Understanding Ethnicity and Nationalism* (New York: Palgrave Macmillan).

Malešević, S. (2010), *The Sociology of War and Violence* (Cambridge: Cambridge University Press).

Malešević, S. (2011a), 'Ethnicity in Time and Space: A Conceptual Analysis', *Critical Sociology* 37:1, 67–82.

Malešević, S. (2011b), 'Did Wars Make Nation-states in the Balkans? Nationalisms, Wars and States in 19th and early 20th Century South East Europe', *Journal of Historical Sociology* 24:4, 1–32.

Mallie, E. and D. McKittrick (2001), *Endgame in Ireland* (London: Hodder & Stoughton).

Mann, M. (2005), *The Dark Side of Democracy: Explaining Ethnic Cleansing* (Cambridge: Cambridge University Press).

Mazower, M. (2003), *The Balkans* (London: Phoenix Press).

Meadwell, H. (1999), 'Secession, States and International Society', *Review of International Studies* 25, 371–87.

Moaz, Z. and B. Russett (1993), 'Normative and Structural Causes of Democratic Peace, 1946–1986', *American Political Science Review* 87:3, 624–38.

O'Brien, C.C. (1978), *Herod: Reflections on Political Violence* (London: Hutchinson Radius).

Ó Ciardha, E. (2004), *Ireland and the Jacobite Cause, 1685–1766: A Fatal Attachment* (Dublin: Four Courts Press).

Ó Dochartaigh, N. (2005), *From Civil Rights to Armalites: Derry and the Birth of Irish Troubles* (New York: Palgrave Macmillan).

Ó Dochartaigh, N. (2008), 'Northern Ireland', in M. Klimke and J. Scharloth (eds), *1968 in Europe: A History of Protest and Activism, 1956–77* (New York: Palgrave), 137–52.

Ó Dochartaigh, N. (2010), 'Nation and Neighbourhood: Nationalist Mobilisation and Local Solidarities in the North of Ireland', in Adrian Guelke (ed.), *The Challenges of Ethno-nationalism* (Basingstoke: Palgrave), 161–76.

O'Kane, E. (2002), 'The Republic of Ireland's Policy Towards Northern Ireland: The International Dimension as a Policy Tool', *Irish Studies in International Affairs* 13:1, 121–33.

O'Leary, B., I. Lustick and T. Callaghy (2001), *Right-sizing the State: The Politics of Moving Borders* (New York: Oxford University Press).

Osterud, O. (1988), 'The Uses and Abuses of Geopolitics', *Journal of Peace Research* 25:2, 191–9.

Parsons, T. (1975), 'Some Theoretical Considerations on the Nature and Trends of Change of Ethnicity', in N. Glazer and D.P. Moynihan (eds), *Ethnicity: Theory and Experience* (Cambridge, MA: Harvard University Press), 53–83.

Pešić, V. (1995), 'Drustveni i drzavni aspekt multikulturalnosti u Bosni i Hercegovini', in B. Jakšić (ed.), *Interkulturalnost* (Belgrade: IFDT).

Powell, J. (2008), *Great Hatred, Little Room: Making Peace in Northern Ireland* (London: Bodley Head).

Purdie, B. (1990), *Politics in the Streets* (Belfast: Blackstaff Press).

Ramet, S. (2006), *The Three Yugoslavias: State-Building and Legitimation, 1918–2005* (Bloomington, IN: Indiana University Press).

Reuters (2006), 'Majority of Serbs Back Secession from Bosnia, Says Opinion Poll', *Reuters News Agency*, 6 July.

Rocher, F. (2002), 'The Evolving Parameters of Quebec Nationalism', *International Journal on Multicultural Societies* 4:1, 74–96.

Ron, J. (2003), *Frontiers and Ghettos: State Violence in Serbia and Israel* (Berkeley, CA: University of California Press).

Rose, R. (1971), *Governing without Consensus: An Irish Perspective* (Boston, MA: Beacon Press).

Rummel, R. (1994), *Death by Government* (New Brunswick, NJ: Transaction).

Shils, E. (1957), 'Primordial, Personal, Sacred and Civil Ties', *British Journal of Sociology* 8:2, 130–45.

Sinn Féin (1994), *Setting the Record Straight* (Dublin: Sinn Féin).

Smelser, N. (1992), 'The Rational Choice Perspective: A Theoretical Assessment', *Rationality and Society* 4:3, 381–410.

Smith, A. (1981), 'War and Ethnicity: The Role of Warfare in the Formation, Self-Images, and Cohesion of Ethnic Communities', *Ethnic and Racial Studies* 4, 375–97.

Smith, A. (1986), *Ethnic Origins of Nations* (Oxford: Blackwell).

Smith, A. (2003), *Chosen Peoples: Sacred Sources of National Identity* (Oxford: Oxford University Press).

Smith, A. (2009), *Ethnosymbolism and Nationalism: A Cultural Approach* (London: Routledge).

Snyder, J. (2000), *From Voting to Violence: Democratization and Nationalist Conflict* (New York: Norton).

Stanić, O. (2007), 'Bosnian Serbs Want Secession if Kosovo Goes', *Reuters News Agency*, 21 November.

Stone, J. (1979), 'Internal Colonialism', *Ethnic and Racial Studies* 2:3.

Torsti, P. (2004), 'History Culture and Banal Nationalism in Post-War Bosnia', *Southeast European Politics* 5:2–3, 142–57.

Townshend, C. (1983), *Political Violence in Ireland: Government and Resistance since 1848* (Oxford: Oxford University Press).

Townshend, C. (2006), *Easter 1916: The Irish Rebellion* (London [u.a.]: Penguin Books).

Weber, M. (1978), *Economy and Society* (New York: Bedminster Press).

Whelan, K. (1996), *The Tree of Liberty: Radicalism, Catholicism, and the Construction of Irish Identity, 1760–1830. Critical Conditions, 1* (Notre Dame, IN: University of Notre Dame Press, in association with Field Day).

Wintrobe, R. (2006), *Rational Extremism* (Cambridge: Cambridge University Press).

Zunec, O. (1998), *Rat i društvo* (Zagreb: Jesenski i Turk).

# 13

**ASHGATE RESEARCH COMPANION**

# International Involvement in Secessionist Conflict: From the 16th Century to the Present

## Mikulas Fabry

Cases of secession, or a process of withdrawal of a territory and its population from an existing state and the creation of a new state in that territory (Pavković with Radan 2007: 1), nearly always elicit some type of outside involvement. This is because such withdrawal is organically linked to the external environment of the existing or host state. While secession originates within the domestic jurisdiction of the host state, its goal is to establish a new sovereign, independent state not only *vis-à-vis* the host state but also *vis-à-vis* other states. A secessionist entity cannot hope to be treated as a state internationally without a prior determination by external, third party states that it is in fact a new sovereign, independent entity as opposed to a continuing part of the host state. Thus, at minimum, an attempt at secession requires third party states to make judgments with respect to the status of the secessionist entity. Even when the attempt is not contested by the host state – and the overwhelming majority of secessions since the 16th century has been launched unilaterally against the will of the host government – a mere public intimation of this judgment constitutes external involvement capable of carrying material consequences for the outcome of the breakaway bid. Still, many cases of unilateral secession have led to a variety of additional forms of external involvement, including good offices, intercession, conciliation and mediation efforts to cease or to resolve the confrontation between the secessionists and the host state, humanitarian aid, cease-fire monitoring, peacekeeping, economic, diplomatic and military assistance to one of the parties, full-scale use of armed force, and international territorial administration. Secessionist conflicts involving multiple forms of external involvement over the course of their duration have been quite common (see also Chapters 1, 2, 8, 9, 11 and 14).

Given that outside involvement in secessionist conflicts can encompass, and has as a matter of historical record encompassed, a whole range of actions, how can we make sense of this phenomenon? The prevailing scholarly approach is to investigate why foreign states involve themselves in secessionist conflict. The question animating this approach is: what causes that involvement and what determines its varying degrees? (for an answer see Chapter 14). The debate on this question has generated a burgeoning literature (for an overview, see Paquin and Saideman 2010), but the answers have so far proved decidedly inconclusive. This chapter proposes a different approach. Rather than asking what causes external involvement in secessionist conflicts, it seeks to examine the moral and legal norms that delineate the appropriateness of that involvement, regardless of possible causes behind it in any particular case. This approach has at least two analytical advantages. First, when states involve themselves in foreign civil, including secessionist, conflicts, their governments almost invariably justify their acts by reference to these norms. As an empirical matter, then, governments believe both in the existence of the prevailing norms of legitimate external involvement and in the importance of convincing their fellow members of international society[1] that they act within them. Second, these norms help us understand external involvement in secessionist conflict by focusing our attention on a crucial factor that constrains and shapes that involvement. Regardless of their actual motivations, if governments cannot provide satisfactory explanations of their actions, then they can expect negative repercussions internationally. This is not to suggest that the norms of legitimate external involvement operate in simple and straightforward fashion. Their character resembles that of most other norms that demarcate standards of appropriate conduct in a states system without central government: they lack firm procedures for adjudication of interpretive differences as well as for enforcement. More specifically, during periods of international change, states sometimes disagree on the content of norms; agreement on their content does not guarantee agreement on their application in particular situations; and even their broadly perceived infringement may not lead to significant adverse consequences for the violators, especially if these happen to be major powers. Despite these limitations, this chapter believes that the study of norms framing an activity gives us a powerful window to the understanding of the activity itself.

What have been the main contours of legitimate external involvement in secessionist conflicts? Since the early 19th century they have revolved around the norm of non-intervention. The modern norm had its origins in British and American policies outlining acceptable external response to unilateral secessions of Latin American territories from Spain and Portugal. Its essence was the prohibition of coercive, dictatorial interference in the domestic affairs of states, whether in military, economic or diplomatic form. Its normative underpinning was the

---

1  By 'international society' I mean an association where 'states, conscious of certain common interests and common values, form a society in the sense that they conceive themselves to be bound by a common set of rules in their relations with one another, and share in the working of common institutions' (Bull 1995: 13).

classical liberal right of people to live under a government of their choosing, which included a change of the governing state no less than that of the governing regime. While outsiders were free to offer non-forcible assistance in the form of conciliation or meditation proposals to the parties to a secessionist conflict, they were not free to side coercively with either party because that would interfere with the right of the people of a state to determine their own future. The only major exception to this prohibition of intervention was a situation in which individual or collective rights of third parties suffered actual and direct harm from the contest. From the perspective of British and US leaders, the foreign secessionist conflict ended either with domestic accommodation or defeat of secessionists, which did not alter membership in the family of states, or with the triumph of secessionists, which did. The 'triumph' of secessionists was taken to be their effective establishment of a stable and functioning independent state in which the population displayed habitual compliance with the rule of the new authorities. The emergence of such a *de facto* polity was deemed to furnish the most convincing vindication of the right of people to determine their government and, as such, the source of the claim to foreign recognition as a new state. This accomplishment transformed the situation from one of domestic affairs of the host state, which prohibited unwarranted external intervention, to one in which the very condition of domestic affairs, as far as the territory of the seceded state was concerned, ceased to exist.

The norm of non-intervention into civil, including secessionist, conflicts, as well as the corollary norm of recognizing *de facto* statehood, were gradually adopted by other countries and became an entrenched part of 19th-century international law, and the practice of external involvement in secessionist conflicts took place largely within its parameters. The non-intervention norm has survived to this day, but with important changes that have occurred since the early 1960s, not least in regards to secessionist conflicts. Perhaps most importantly, it became increasingly accepted that third parties may justifiably intervene to assist host states to suppress separatist challengers. This development mirrored a new consensus on who qualifies as a legitimate candidate for sovereign statehood. Starting with decolonization, foreign recognition was extended to the candidates who were deemed to have a pre-existing international entitlement to, rather than who achieved *de facto*, independence. By the same token, acknowledgment was denied to those not possessing such a right, even if they did achieve *de facto* independence (for a discussion of these cases see Chapter 15). Most significantly, the post-1950s practice delegitimized the hitherto legitimate unilateral secession. As such, coercive forms of external intervention on behalf of host governments and against secessionists became commonly accepted. This picture has become more complicated with the increasing post-Cold War emphasis on international human rights protection in internal conflicts. Military intervention against the host government rather than the secessionists in the Kosovo conflict generated marked, though by no means universal, support in international society. As with other types of civil conflicts, it is the developments in international human rights that will likely contribute most to the changing patterns of outside interventionism in secessionist conflict. However, neither these nor any other developments have so far led to the emergence of new generally accepted norms of legitimate external involvement in secessionist conflict which would replace those established at the time of decolonization (see also Chapters 1, 6 and 17).

## Sovereignty and Non-Intervention in Internal Affairs

External involvement in the internal affairs of states gives frequent rise to international controversy because such involvement *prima facie* encroaches upon the foundational principle of modern international society, state sovereignty. Sovereignty embodies the idea of a governing authority that is supreme in relation to all other authorities in the same territorial jurisdiction, and that is constitutionally independent of all foreign authorities (Jackson 2007: 10). The principle of non-intervention can be said to be implied by this foundational principle: if a state is to have its right to sovereignty respected, other states have a duty to abstain from intervening in its domestic jurisdiction (Vincent 1974: 14, 20). This would include a duty not to intervene in internal acts challenging the very boundary of that jurisdiction.

Whereas in the course of the 18th century it became widely accepted that sovereignty and non-intervention were two sides of the same coin, both commentators on and practitioners of international relations accepted that there were valid exceptions to the principle of non-intervention. Early modern publicists such as Christian Wolff and Emmerich de Vattel argued that outside intervention into the internal affairs of a state is justified if those affairs lead to a breach of obligations towards, or to a direct harm of, outsiders (Vincent 1974: 28–30). In addition, Vattel, in an argument espoused earlier by Hugo Grotius, contended that external intervention in civil wars is justified if it is undertaken on behalf of oppressed populations suffering in the hands of tyrants. Many later writers endorsed these general exceptions and sought to specify the precise conditions of their application. Although coercive intervention against tyrants oppressing their population, and more broadly humanitarian intervention, did not command unified endorsement, it was generally accepted that counter-intervention against unjustified intervention was a legal and legitimate means by which to uphold and reinforce the non-intervention norm (see Oppenheim 1905: 181–91; Winfield 1924: 154–5, 161–2).

## External Involvement in Secessionist Conflict, 1776–1960

Prior to the 19th century the question of external involvement in secessionist conflict arose only rarely in international relations. Considerable outside assistance, including in the form of formal alliances, was provided to the belligerents in the secessions of the Netherlands from Spain (1581–1648) and Portugal from Spain (1640–68), but that assistance occurred prior to the full emergence of state sovereignty as the normative basis of international relations. In contrast, Corsica's secession from Genoa (1755–70) garnered relatively little attention of foreign states. The first notable case of external involvement was the French intervention in the unilateral secession of the 13 British colonies, initially by providing them with secret material assistance and, then, by recognizing US independence and joining the struggle against Britain. The reaction of other countries to France's actions was not supportive and revealed that sovereign rights in a states system composed mostly of hereditary monarchies were understood as dynastic rights. Dynastic rights were taken to imply that the dominion of a legitimate monarchy was in principle inalienable. The only valid change of title to sovereignty or territory was through freely given consent of the affected monarch, which meant that open siding by a third party with a unilateral secessionist attempt was not considered legitimate. The overwhelming majority of existing states refused to have normal relations with the United States prior to the British acknowledgment of its independence in the preliminary peace treaty of 1782.

Dynastic legitimism was fatally undermined in Latin America as Spanish and Portuguese American territories, beginning with Venezuela in 1811, followed in the footsteps of the 13 colonies and unilaterally broke away from their host states. When the major legitimist powers collectively assembled in the Holy Alliance espoused not only the non-recognition of the secessionist rebels but some also considered coercive intervention to help restore Iberian rule, they ran into strong opposition from Britain and the United States. At the core of the dispute were two different interpretations of the valid exception to the Westphalian principle of non-intervention. Contending that it sought to prevent a repeat of the French Revolutionary Wars, the Holy Alliance held that whereas states generally had no right to intervene coercively in the domestic affairs of other states, they had a right to do so with respect to 'revolutions' against legitimate monarchs, as these could threaten, even if only potentially and indirectly, other states. In contrast, early 19th-century British and American statespersons held that unless they were actually and directly injured, states had an obligation to stay neutral and not to interfere coercively in foreign civil conflicts. They believed that people have a natural right to determine their political destiny, which included a 'revolutionary' right to renounce the sovereignty under which they live. Conscious of their respective legacies of the Glorious and American Revolutions, they understood this right of self-determination as 'the right of a people "to become free by their own efforts" if they can, and non-intervention [was] the principle guaranteeing that their success will not be impeded or their failure prevented by the intrusion of an alien power' (Walzer 2006: 88). This is how classical liberal thinkers such as Immanuel Kant (1991: 96) and J.S. Mill (1962: 410–11) thought about self-determination and secession as well.

According to British and US foreign policymakers, third parties could offer non-forcible, impartial diplomatic involvement designed to end the secessionist conflict. Britain repeatedly offered to mediate the war between Spain and its territories and was actually successful in mediating the resolution of Portugal's confrontation with Brazil in 1825. Third parties could not, however, use armed force or economic sanctions to compel one or both parties to accept a settlement. While the contest was in progress, they had a duty to continue to respect Spain's and Portugal's sovereignty and territorial integrity in the Americas. But this duty was not limitless: the requirement that third parties abstain from intervening in the self-determination process also demanded that they respect self-determination outcomes. If the host state country was displaced on a part of its territory by an indigenously established *de facto* state, this 'self-determined' fact extinguished external obligations towards the host state and gave rise to a new right of sovereignty. A collectivity that had attained independent statehood in demonstrable fact was entitled to acknowledgment of that statehood in law due to the decisive normative meaning of the achievement: the formation of a stable entity in which the population habitually obeyed the new rulers was taken as an authoritative expression of the will of the people to constitute an independent state as neither the *de facto* state's founding nor its continued existence could come to pass without at least tacit approval by its inhabitants. In the absence of international agreement as to what constitutes a valid method of verifying popular will, any foreign assessment thereof was necessarily presumptive (Roth 1999: 38–9, 413–14): the *de facto* secessionist state was taken to embody, in Thomas Jefferson's words, 'the will of the nation substantially declared'.[2] It was this presumption of popular consent – and its normative trumping of the idea of dynastic consent – that in American and British eyes converted the fact of new independent states into the right to independence and external recognition.

Proclaimed to the world by the United States most famously in the Monroe Doctrine[3] and by Britain in the now much lesser known Polignac Memorandum[4] – both warned the Holy Alliance against coercive intervention on behalf of the Spanish crown in the firmly established independent states – the twin norms demarcating non-intervention and recognition of *de facto* seceded states were gradually adopted by other powers. They became the undisputed standards of external involvement and state recognition in the Americas, and with the decline of the Holy Alliance they displaced the anti-revolutionary interventionist interpretation of dynastic rights in Europe (see Fabry 2010: chs 2–4).[5] They were evoked in response to

---

2   Thomas Jefferson to Gouverneur Morris, 7 November 1792, in Wharton (1887: 521).
3   In the famous address on the Western Hemispheric affairs that later became known as the Monroe Doctrine, President James Monroe declared: 'With the existing colonies or dependencies of any European power we have not interfered and shall not interfere. But with the governments who have declared their independence and maintain it, and whose independence we have, on great consideration and on just principles, acknowledged, we could not view any interposition for the purpose of oppressing them, or controlling in any other manner their destiny, by any European power in any other light than as the manifestation of an unfriendly disposition toward the United States.' The American government, he explained, considered 'the government *de facto* as the legitimate government' (see Message of President James Monroe to Congress, 2 December 1823, in Manning 1925: 217).
4   George Canning to the Prince de Polignac, 22 September 1823, in Webster (1938: 114–15).
5   Prior to this displacement, in 1848 Russia sent its troops, at the invitation of Austria, to

unilateral secessionist bids such as Texas (1836), the Confederate States of America (1861–65) and the Baltic republics (1917–22) and applied in a wide range of contexts, including those that saw external military interventions (see Chapter 5 and 8). These interventions, whether in the case of Greece (1827), Belgium (1831–32), Serbia, Montenegro and Romania (1877–78), Cuba (1898) or Panama (1903), had multiple justifications, several of them also humanitarian ones, but each was carried out principally in defence of third party rights and elicited support or at least acceptance of major powers as well as numerous other countries (see Fabry 2010: chs 2–4).

## External Involvement in Secessionist Conflict, 1960–90

The post-World War Two international order reaffirmed the basic norm of non-intervention into the internal affairs of states, whether in Article 2 (7) of the Charter of the United Nations (UN), a number of important UN General Assembly resolutions, the founding treaties of a number of regional organizations, or the *Nicaragua* decision (1986) of the International Court of Justice (ICJ). However, the legitimate exceptions to this norm did undergo certain changes, including those related to secessionist conflict. Most of the changes had to do with decolonization's abandonment of *de facto* statehood as the standard for recognizing indigenously founded new states. Since the late 1950s the decisive factor in admission of new members into the society of states has been whether an entity has a prior right to independence rather than whether it actually is independent. Reflecting the global normative consensus that developed in the course of the 1950s that colonial domination was no longer tolerable, international society, in the landmark UN General Assembly Resolution 1514 (1960), defined, for the first time, specific peoples who were deemed to be entitled to state sovereignty: the populations of non-self-governing and trust territories. The key to their foreign recognition was not their attainment of *de facto* statehood but rather prior acceptance of their asserted right to self-determination and independence in positive international law. This right required colonial powers to withdraw and third parties to facilitate the emergence of a new state in their place as soon as colonial peoples voiced their desire for independence (see also Chapters 6 and 17).

The identification of the peoples eligible for independence inevitably entailed some corresponding notion of ineligibility. While evident in the past, the grounds for limiting recognition of claims of statehood was not immediately clear now as the main decolonization texts which began with a proclamation that 'all peoples have the right to self-determination' did not define the 'peoples' bearing the

---

help crush the secession of Hungary. While British and US governments resented this course of events, neither had, in contrast to the Americas, sufficient interest in counter-intervention against the most powerful member of the Holy Alliance, and Hungary was defeated in 1849.

right beyond the populations of colonial territories. The decolonization and post-decolonization recognition practice clarified what the documents left obscure. The legitimate candidates for recognition were restricted to colonial territories whose right to independence was blocked, violated or otherwise not realized,[6] to constituent units of dissolved states, and to seceding entities that received the consent of their host states (see also Chapters 6, 17 and 25). Unilateral secession from sovereign states, which gave rise to recognition of *de facto* statehood in the 19th century, became for all practical purposes illegitimate, if not outright illegal.

This practice has been the result of conscious and deliberate subordination of all non-colonial notions of self-determination to the principle of territorial integrity. One of the most critical sections in Resolution 1514 is the sixth paragraph postulating that 'any attempt aimed at the partial or total disruption of the national unity and the territorial integrity of a country is incompatible with the purposes and principles of the Charter of the United Nations'. That an ex-colony cannot lose territory against its will – not just from outside, by way of conquest, outlawed since the adoption of the League of Nations Covenant in 1919, but also from inside, by way of unilateral secession – was later broadened to encompass all UN member states in another important UN General Assembly Resolution 2625 (1970) (see Shaw 1997: 481–2, 501). Whatever the right to self-determination meant outside the colonial context – it has been typically interpreted as an internal right consisting of the right to political participation and minority rights – it excluded the right to unilateral secession.[7]

Beginning with the watershed UN SC Resolution 169 (1961), which affirmed Congo's territorial integrity and rejected 'completely' Katanga's unilateral declaration of 1960 (see Chapter 5) that it was a 'a sovereign independent nation'

---

6    This category included Southern Rhodesia, Namibia, Angola, Mozambique, Cape Verde, Guinea-Bissau and East Timor. It still includes Western Sahara. That the group shrank is to a significant extent thanks to international society, which applied various degrees of pressure on the deniers or violators of the right to self-determination to leave.

7    According to a number of international lawyers, UN GA Resolution 2625 and later the Vienna Declaration of the UN World Conference on Human Rights (1993) contain a 'safeguard clause' which entitles peoples oppressed on the basis of race, creed or colour to remedial secession (see, for instance, Cassese 1995: 109–25). Nevertheless, international practice suggests that no more than a handful of states have accepted that groups within sovereign states have a right to remedial secession. Some countries which recognized the unilateral secession of Kosovo, including Germany, Switzerland, Ireland, Poland, Estonia, Finland and the Netherlands, argued that such a right exists and that it applies to Kosovo, but they did so not at the time of their recognition but only months later during the proceedings before the ICJ in the advisory opinion case of *Accordance with International Law of the Unilateral Declaration of Independence in respect of Kosovo*. In the same proceedings Russia made ambiguous references to the 'safeguard clause', perhaps to provide another layer of justification of its earlier recognition of South Ossetia and Abkhazia. It asserted, however, that Kosovo did not meet the clause's criteria (for a discussion of the clause and the ICJ opinion see Chapter 17).

(see Chapter 6) each change in the international status of a territory had to be blessed by the sovereign government in question. Withholding state consent has meant almost certain non-recognition and international illegitimacy. Aside from Bangladesh in 1971, no post-colonial sub-state entity has been able to create a new state without such consent,[8] regardless of the reason given for the secession or the degree of effective control it might have attained. Under the old rules, entities such as the 'Republic of Eritrea',[9] 'Tamil Eelam', 'Free South Sudan', the 'Republic of Bougainville' or the 'Republic of Somaliland' would have at a certain point in their existence likely qualified for foreign recognition, but under the new ones they were condemned to languish for years in an international legal and political limbo (for some of those cases see Part VI). External non-recognition legally maintained them as part of the states they had broken way from, leaving them continuously liable to being re-absorbed by the central government, as indeed 'Tamil Eelam' was in 2009.

With the privileging of the territorial integrity of states, international society went beyond non-forcible tools of outside involvement, which presuppose consent of and neutrality towards the parties to a secessionist conflict, and also came to accept more forcible forms of intervention on behalf of host governments (see Weller 2005: 3–28; Nolte 2006: 76–83). After declaring Katanga's secession illegitimate, the UN abandoned its earlier mediation efforts as well as initial neutrality in regards to the substance of the Congolese contest, and its peacekeeping forces joined the fight to defeat Katanga's armed forces. Their intervention was crucial to ending Katanga's secessionist bid in 1963. Biafra's unilateral secession from Nigeria in 1966 was roundly condemned by the Organization of African Unity (OAU) and many individual countries (see also Chapter 6). While the organs of the UN took no formal position on the matter, its Secretary-General U Thant (1970a: 36) declared that his institution 'spent over $500 million in the Congo primarily to prevent the secession of Katanga … The United Nations' attitude is unequivocal. As an international organization, the UN has never accepted and does not accept and I do not believe it will ever accept the principle of secession of a part of its member state.'[10] In addition to the verbal disapprovals of Biafra's action, Nigeria's federal government was being supplied with large amounts of weaponry from the Soviet Union and Great Britain, to no widespread global opposition. Biafra received only minimal open diplomatic and material support from abroad. Its claim to statehood was recognized, on the grounds that its people had suffered gross human rights

---

8   As in the past, such consent was extremely hard to come by. Between 1945 and 1993 Singapore was the only sub-state unit of a post-colonial country that managed to obtain it when the central government asked that it leave Malaysia in 1965 (regarding Singapore see Part VI).

9   Eritrea did eventually garner recognition, but this occurred only after Ethiopia's assent to let the Eritreans choose independence in a 1993 referendum. It was this consent that accomplished what the three-decades-long control of large swaths of Ethiopian territory could not (see Part VI). The same scenario was recently replayed in South Sudan.

10  On another occasion, U Thant (1970b: 39) was emphatic that 'self-determination of peoples does not imply self-determination of a section of population of a particular member state'.

abuses at the hands of the Nigerian military before and after Biafra's declaration of independence, by no more than five small countries: Tanzania, Gabon, Zambia, the Ivory Coast and Haiti (see Chapter 6).[11]

There can be little doubt that the overwhelming international siding with Congo's and Nigeria's claims of territorial integrity contributed to the demise of the secessionist attempts they faced. Although the 1971 unilateral secession of Bangladesh (East Pakistan) from Pakistan ultimately materialized due to India's military intervention, this does not mean that the normative framework disclosed in the two earlier African cases was somehow irrelevant. International society affirmed Pakistan's right to sovereignty and territorial integrity notwithstanding brutal Pakistani army violence against Bangladeshis before and after Bangladesh's declaration of independence. When its government launched an attack against Pakistan eight months into the secessionist conflict, India was condemned by the majority of UN members outside the Soviet bloc, despite its primary justification of self-defence against Islamabad's military and 'refugee aggression'. Ultimately, Bangladesh owed its independence to the eventual international acquiescence to India's victory over the Pakistani army which disabled Pakistani authority in East Pakistan (for Bangladesh see Part VI). However, this outcome of Cold War power politics in South Asia did not change the basic normative understandings concerning unilateral secession, self-determination and coercive intervention developed during decolonization, including in the case of India and countries that supported its use of force in East Pakistan.[12] These understandings privileged host governments facing secessionist challenges, legitimized intervention on their behalf, and disfavoured intervention on behalf of the secessionists.[13]

## External Involvement in Secessionist Conflict since 1990

The developments of the last two decades have on the whole solidified the self-determination and recognition norms settled in the wake of the largest wave of decolonization in the 1960s. Rather than transforming the previously established recognition practice, the end of the Cold War in fact extended it beyond the ex-

---

11  Biafra was, however, the first major case in which large-scale humanitarian aid was provided by both states and non-governmental organizations. Ever since then, impartial humanitarian aid to those suffering from fighting has been accepted as a legitimate, even necessary, form of external involvement in internal, including secessionist, conflict.

12  In fact, in 1987–90 the Indian military found itself fighting the Tamil secessionists who rejected India's mission to assist the Sri Lankan government with the implementation of an India–Sri Lanka accord designed to resolve the Sri Lankan conflict.

13  A wide-ranging survey of the 1960–90 period found that incumbent governments have tended to attract more support than secessionists, that involvement on behalf of the latter was often secretive or was denied, and that global and regional organizations almost never sympathized with secessionists (Heraclides 1990: 353–78).

colonial world. Grounded in regional documents such as the Helsinki Final Act (1975), the Charter of Paris (1990) and the Copenhagen Document (1990)[14] in addition to the previous global documents, that practice has continued to inhibit secession without the consent of the sovereign government in question as a legitimate way of acquiring statehood. The break-ups of the Soviet Union in 1991 and Czechoslovakia in 1992 might have commenced as secessionist bids by some of their constituent units, but foreign recognition of the successor republics came only once the respective central governments had agreed to the dissolution of the unions.[15] Western and other countries waited for prior agreement of the centre even in the case of the Baltic republics, despite the fact that most considered them to be restoring their sovereignty after illegal occupation by a foreign power rather than seceding from a country of which they had been an integral part. Unilateral separatist drives from the newly independent states, whether it was the 'Nagorno-Karabakh Republic' (Azerbaijan), the 'Republic of Abkhazia', the 'Republic of South Ossetia' (both Georgia), the 'Transdnester Republic', the 'Republic of Gagauzia' (both Moldova), the 'Republic of Crimea' (Ukraine) or the 'Republic of Chechnya' (Russia), met with general foreign non-recognition (see also Part VI). In addition, those providing open diplomatic and material assistance to the secessionists, in particular Armenia in regards to Nagorno-Karabakh and Russia in regards to the two breakaway Georgian territories, have found themselves internationally isolated in their activities.

The foreign response to the claims arising out of the complex and violent break-up of the Socialist Federal Republic of Yugoslavia (SFRY) was consistent with this 'neo-decolonization territorial approach' (Hannum 1993: 38). During the initial phase of the Yugoslav collapse, which also started as a series of secessionist undertakings by its constituent republics, external authorities espoused the territorial integrity of the SFRY. That position changed only after a majority of Yugoslav republics had ceased to be represented in the highest federal institution, the presidency, under contentious circumstances in early October 1991. The withdrawal of the majority of the population and territory from a federal state was a historically unprecedented occurrence, but one to which third party states as well as relevant international organizations found a speedy solution that no public authority besides the governments of Serbia and Montenegro opposed: they came

---

14  All three are documents of the Conference for Security and Cooperation in Europe (CSCE) which in 1994 changed its name to the Organization for Security and Cooperation in Europe (OSCE). While the Helsinki Final Act affirms the principles of inviolability of frontiers and territorial integrity of states only in the context of interstate relations, the Charter of Paris extends it to intrastate relations, reaffirming 'the equal rights of peoples and their right to self-determination in conformity with the Charter of the United Nations and with the relevant norms of international law, including those relating to territorial integrity of states'. The Copenhagen Document goes even further: it stipulates that persons belonging to national minorities do not have 'any right to engage in any activity or perform any action in contravention of ... the principle of territorial integrity of states'.

15  The 2006 dissolution of the Union of Serbia and Montenegro also falls into this category.

to regard what was occurring in the SFRY as a case of dissolution legally equivalent to the consensual dissolutions of the USSR and Czechoslovakia.[16] Only after this judgment did the individual republics become eligible for foreign recognition.

As during decolonization, the successor states became safeguarded, as a matter of international right, against external territorial designs as well as against unilateral secessions even prior to recognition. This was made evident in non-recognition policies towards those who challenged the territorial integrity of Croatia, Bosnia and Herzegovina and later the Federal Republic of Yugoslavia (FRY). The 1991–92 independence claims of the 'Republic of Serbian Krajina', the 'Croat Community of Herzeg-Bosna', the 'Republika Srpska' and the 'Republic of Kosova' were rebuffed by individual countries as well as regional and global organizations (see Chapter 8 and Part VI). Furthermore, the UN, the European Community (EC, from 1994 the European Union, EU), the Organization for Security and Cooperation in Europe (OSCE), and a number of powers sought to stop, diplomatically and by way of economic sanctions, the various forms of material aid provided by Serbia and Croatia to their secessionist ethnic kin across the newly created international boundaries, and the EU tried to restrain the political support of Albania for the Kosovo Albanian cause.

In contrast to the Cold War era, international society began to respond much more actively and forcefully to the violations of international humanitarian and human rights law in civil, including secessionist, conflict. In several instances the UN Security Council went so far as to authorize military force under its legally binding Chapter VII authority to 'maintain or restore international peace and security'. In Bosnia and Herzegovina the Council, under its Chapter VII powers, declared a no-fly zone for military aircraft (Resolution 781 [1992]), established an International Criminal Tribunal for the former Yugoslavia (Resolution 827 [1993]), and authorized the UN peacekeepers and member states to take all necessary measures to protect the six UN-declared 'safe areas' (Resolution 836 [1993]). It was under Resolution 836 that the Western countries associated in the North Atlantic Treaty Organization (NATO) bombed various targets in that country in 1994–95.

In Bosnia and Herzegovina NATO employed military force, on the grounds of violating humanitarian 'safe areas', against the Bosnian Serb army who were secessionists. In Kosovo, where a conflict between the Kosovo Liberation Army and Serbia's authorities flared up in 1998, the alliance used military force, on humanitarian grounds, against the Yugoslav army and Serb police who acted on behalf of the host state (see Chapters 8 and 9). This intervention of 1999 was controversial because while the UN Security Council determined that the Kosovo situation constituted a threat to international peace and security, it did not authorize the use of force because of persistent opposition of two of its permanent members, Russia and China. NATO's bombing campaign without UN SC endorsement split

---

16 This position was consistent with the findings of the Badinter Commission, an advisory panel of jurists created by the European Community to consider legal questions arising from SFRY disintegration (see its Opinion No. 1 of 20 November 1991 and Opinion No. 8 of 4 July 1992 in Trifunovska 1994: 417, 635).

international society, which suggested at minimum that there was no consensus among states on the right of unilateral humanitarian intervention. There was no divide, however, on the territorial integrity of the FRY, which was explicitly affirmed not only in UN SC Resolution 1244 (1999) passed in the aftermath of the hostilities, but also in numerous statements of leaders of NATO and its member countries before, during and after the campaign (see, for instance, North Atlantic Treaty Organization 1999).

In Bosnia and Herzegovina in 1995 and in the FRY in 1999, the main external actors went so far as to insist on interim international administration within their territories rather than to sanction separation of their respective secessionist entities. These arrangements generated considerable challenges, especially in Kosovo. Whereas members of NATO assumed that it was possible to act on human rights abuses while disregarding the underlying cause of the political conflict that led to them, this logic was not accepted by the very beneficiaries of the intervention. There was an inescapable tension between NATO's intervention on behalf of the Kosovo Albanians and its continued opposition to Kosovo's unilateral secession. Bent on independence since its declaration by the representatives of the 'Republic of Kosova' in October 1991, the Kosovo Albanians were even more encouraged to pursue their ambition by the bombing campaign against the FRY; yet Kosovo was consistently proclaimed to be an integral part of the FRY and its government was adamant that it would not assent to such an option under any circumstances (see also Chapter 9).

The major Western powers' way out of this self-made quandary was eventually to abandon their opposition to Kosovo's unilateral secession on account of its unique circumstances, all the while insisting on their continued general support for the post-decolonization norm of territorial integrity. After almost eight years of UN administration and a year of abortive talks between Serbia and the Kosovo Albanian authorities on the final settlement of the conflict, the UN Special Envoy overseeing the negotiations, Martti Ahtisaari, recommended to the UN Security Council in 2007 that the UN administration of Kosovo end, and the province gain 'independence, supervised by the international community' (UN Security Council 2007). This proposal was supported by the Kosovo Albanians and most Western powers as the only viable future option for Kosovo, but rejected by Serbia and Russia as a breach of Serbia's right of territorial integrity and Resolution 1244. After several more months of fruitless talks co-mediated by the EU, the United States and Russia, the Kosovo Albanian authorities declared unilateral independence for the second time in February 2008. Despite resistance from Serbia as well as Russia, China, India and other powers, this time the Kosovo Albanians gained recognition from all the major Western powers and dozens of other countries. Still, the United States and European powers went to great lengths to emphasize that recognition of Kosovo's unilateral secession constitutes a *sui generis*, one-time exception to, rather than any kind of departure from, the norm of territorial integrity. The US statement explained it thus:

> *The unusual combination of factors found in the Kosovo situation – including the context of Yugoslavia's breakup, the history of ethnic cleansing and crimes against civilians in Kosovo, and the extended period of UN administration – are not found elsewhere and therefore make Kosovo a special case. Kosovo cannot be seen as a precedent for any other situation in the world today. (US Department of State 2008)*[17]

The Kosovo exception argument did not convince most countries: at the time of this writing the territory's independence has not been acknowledged by roughly two thirds of UN members. The status of Kosovo, which is still a host to foreign troops and civilian administrators rather than a fully self-governing entity, remains unsettled.[18] Resorting to the norm exception argument as well as the widespread non-acceptance of it would suggest that greater post-Cold War interventionism for human rights, even when directed against the host state in secessionist conflict, has not altered the post-decolonization norm of territorial integrity (see Chapter 17). Events since then appear to confirm this judgment. When Russia, in the wake of its armed intervention against Georgia's 'aggression and genocide' in August 2008, replicated the exception argument to acknowledge Abkhazia and South Ossetia on account of their special circumstances (Medvedev 2008), it was roundly condemned by many individual countries as well as the EU, OSCE, NATO and Group of Eight (G8) as violating Georgia's territorial integrity. Its recognition has so far been emulated only by Nicaragua, Venezuela, Nauru and Hamas, which is not a state (see Chapter 15 and Part VI). And when the Sri Lankan government came under international criticism for the treatment of Tamil civilians in its military campaign against the Tamil secessionists in 2009, this censure did not extend, just as it did not in Kosovo in 1999, into questioning the sovereignty of Sri Lanka over Tamil-majority territories. In conclusion, neither individual states nor international organizations seem ready to abandon: (a) the normative protection of territorial integrity of states against disruptions from inside as well as outside, and (b) the post-decolonization understanding of the right of self-determination as not including the right to independence via unilateral secession.

---

17   The EU saw the Kosovo situation as *sui generis* too, and this was reflected in the decisions of those member countries opting for recognition (Council of the European Union 2007).

18   In its advisory opinion of 22 July 2010 the ICJ did not much clarify the question of the legality of Kosovo's independence submitted by the UN General Assembly on Serbia's request in October 2008. The ICJ found merely that the unilateral declaration of independence of Kosovo, as a public act, was not a violation of general international law or specific legal instruments dealing with Kosovo. It did not rule on the consequences of this proclamation – whether Kosovo is a state in the sense of international law, or whether its foreign recognition was legal. The ICJ did not address the question of the 'remedial' right of secession either (see Chapter 17).

# References

Bull, H. (1995), *The Anarchical Society: A Study of Order in World Politics*, 2nd edn (New York: Columbia University Press).

Cassese, A. (1995), *Self-Determination of Peoples: A Legal Reappraisal* (Cambridge: Cambridge University Press).

Council of the European Union (2007), *Presidency Conclusions*, 14 December 2007. [Online] At http://www.consilium.europa.eu/ueDocs/cms_Data/docs/pressData/en/ec/97669.pdf [accessed 6 December 2009].

Fabry, M. (2010), *Recognizing States: International Society and the Establishment of New States since 1776* (Oxford: Oxford University Press).

Hannum, H. (1993), 'Rethinking Self-Determination', *Virginia Journal of International Law* 34:1, 1–69.

Heraclides, A. (1990), 'Secessionist Minorities and External Involvement', *International Organization* 44:3, 341–78.

Jackson, R. (2007), *Sovereignty: The Evolution of an Idea* (Cambridge: Polity).

Kant, I. (1991), 'Perpetual Peace', in H. Reiss (ed.), *Immanuel Kant: Political Writings*, 2nd edn (Cambridge: Cambridge University Press), 93–130.

Manning, W.R. (ed.) (1925), *Diplomatic Correspondence of the United States Concerning the Independence of the Latin American Nations, Vol. 1* (New York: Oxford University Press).

Medvedev, D. (2008), *Interview of President Medvedev with BBC Television*, 26 August 2008. [Online] At http://www.kremlin.ru/eng/speeches/2008/08/26/2131_type82915type82916_205790.shtml [accessed 6 December 2009].

Mill, J.S. (1962), 'A Few Words on Non-Intervention', in G. Himmelfarb (ed.), *John Stuart Mill: Essays on Politics and Culture* (Garden City, NY: Doubleday and Company).

Nolte, G. (2006), 'Secession and External Intervention', in M. Kohen (ed.), *Secession: International Law Perspectives* (Cambridge: Cambridge University Press), 65–93.

North Atlantic Treaty Organization (1999), *Statement on Kosovo Issued by the Heads of State and Government Participating in the Meeting of the North Atlantic Council*, 23 April 1999. [Online] At http://www.nato.int/docu/pr/1999/p99-062e.htm [accessed 6 December 2009].

Oppenheim, L. (1905), 'Intervention', in *International Law: A Treatise*, Vol. 1 (London: Longmans).

Paquin, J. and S.M. Saideman (2010), 'Foreign Intervention in Ethnic Conflict', in *Encyclopedia of Ethnicity, Nationalism and Migration*, ISA Compendium Project (Oxford: Blackwell).

Pavković, A. with P. Radan (2007), *Creating New States: Theory and Practice of Secession* (Aldershot: Ashgate).

Roth, B.R. (1999), *Governmental Legitimacy in International Law* (Oxford: Oxford University Press).

Shaw, M.N. (1997), 'Peoples, Territorialism and Boundaries', *European Journal of International Law* 8:3, 478–507.

Thant, U. (1970a), 'Secretary-General's Press Conference in Dakar, Senegal, 4 January 1970', *UN Monthly Chronicle* 7:2, 36.
Thant, U. (1970b), 'Secretary-General's Press Conference in Accra, Ghana, 9 January 1970', *UN Monthly Chronicle* 7:2, 39.
Trifunovska, S. (ed.) (1994), *Yugoslavia through Documents: From Its Creation to Its Dissolution* (Dordrecht: Martinus Nijhoff).
UN Security Council (2007), *Letter Dated 26 March 2007 from the Secretary-General Addressed to the President of the Security Council (Report of the Special Envoy of the Secretary-General on Kosovo's Future Status)*, S/2007/168. [Online] At http://daccess-dds-ny.un.org/doc/UNDOC/GEN/N07/272/23/PDF/N0727223.pdf?OpenElement [accessed 6 December 2009].
US Department of State (2008), *U.S. Recognizes Kosovo as Independent State*, 18 February 2008. [Online] At http://2001-2009.state.gov/secretary/rm/2008/02/100973.htm [accessed 6 December 2009].
Vincent, R.J. (1974), *Nonintervention and International Order* (Princeton, NJ: Princeton University Press).
Walzer, M. (2006), *Just and Unjust Wars*, 4th edn (New York: Basic Books).
Webster, C.K. (ed.) (1938), *Britain and the Independence of Latin America*, Vol. 2 (London: Oxford University Press).
Weller, M. (2005), 'The Self-Determination Trap', *Ethnopolitics* 4:1, 3–28.
Wharton, F. (ed.) (1887), *A Digest of the International Law of the United States*, Vol. 1 (Washington, DC: Government Printing Office).
Winfield, P.H. (1924), 'The Grounds of Intervention in International Law', in *The British Year Book of International Law*, Vol. 5 (London: Oxford University Press).

# The International Relations of Secession[1]

## Stephen M. Saideman

When the United States and many allies decided to recognize Kosovo's independence in 2008, old arguments about fears of precedents and their deterrent effect were deployed once again. In Canada, for instance, a delayed response was seen as a result of concerns about the impact upon Quebec separatism.[2] Indeed, many of the countries refusing to recognize Kosovo are those that face serious secessionist movements, including Georgia, India, Pakistan and Russia. However, many countries recognizing Kosovo also face their own separatist threats, including Belgium, Croatia, France, Macedonia and Turkey. We can always find anecdotes one way or the other, but a systematic analysis of the international relations of ethnic conflict should reveal whether vulnerability to separatism is the deterrent that it is often averred to be, or whether other factors, such as ethnic ties or relative power, matter more.

This is an important question because outside support has always been seen as critical to the chances that a secessionist movement will succeed (Horowitz 1985). While the material resources of arms, funding and bases are critical as secessionists fight to become independent, recognition matters as well. Secessionist movements that gain recognition can join international organizations, get finances from regional and world financial institutions, and generally join the club of countries. Those that do not get recognized dwell in an ambiguous situation where informal

---

1 Acknowledgements: first, the Carnegie Corporation of New York funded the creation of the dataset. Of course, the statements made and views expressed are solely the responsibility of the author and not of the Carnegie Corporation. Second, I owe a debt to Ted Gurr, Anne Pitsch, Amy Pate and the rest of the Minorities at Risk project for providing me with their dataset and raw data, and for helping me in using it. Third, I am grateful to Douglas Van Belle and James Fearon for help with some of the additional data. Finally, I am very thankful for the research assistance provided by Cari MacDonald, Young Choul-Kim and J.W. Justice.
2 'Harper Defends Kosovo Recognition as Unique Case', CBC News, 19 March 2008, http://www.cbc.ca/canada/story/2008/03/19/harper-kosovo.html, accessed 12 July 2010.

economic exchanges tend to predominate (King 2001). Thus, international support and recognition matter a great deal for any secessionist effort.

This chapter addresses what countries actually did in the early 1990s in the aftermath of the Cold War, when fears of precedents should have been at their highest level. To address this question, I consider the conventional wisdom about vulnerability and the international relations of ethnic conflict and then consider counter-arguments. Next, I present a set of quantitative analyses that test competing arguments. I conclude with implications for policy and future research.[3]

## Understanding the International Relations of Secession

While we can imagine many explanations of why states react to ethnic conflicts in other states, three stand out: 1) the vulnerability of states to secession inhibits their foreign policies; 2) the domestic politics of states influences their foreign policies; and 3) that security and power shape foreign policy towards ethnic conflicts elsewhere.

### Vulnerability

The first approach focuses on the vulnerability of states to secession – if states face their own ethnic strife, they are less likely to support ethnic groups in conflict elsewhere (see Chapter 11). Robert Jackson and Carl Rosberg (1982) and Jeffrey Herbst (1989) argue that African states refrained from challenging the boundaries of other African states because of their vulnerability to separatism.[4] States are deterred by their vulnerability because of fears of retaliation and because they fear that efforts to challenge one boundary would upset the existing regime, leading to the collapse of all boundaries. Herbst suggests that the fear of reciprocity gone awry, the harmful potential of the 'echo effects' of a feud, deters states from supporting boundary-changing efforts, including secessionist movements.

Studies have shown that vulnerability does not deter as much as argued. Saideman (1997, 2001) examined cases of secessionist crises and found that vulnerable states frequently support the secessionists. Further, quantitative analyses have shown both that states fighting their own separatist movements are more likely to support ethnic groups in conflict and that separatist groups are more likely to receive external assistance than ethnic groups pursuing other objectives (Saideman 2001, 2002). However, these findings do not directly undermine the vulnerability argument. In the quantitative analyses, it could be the case that

---

[3] Due to space constraints here, the dataset is largely explained online at http://profs-polisci.mcgill.ca/saideman/Current%20Research.htm.
[4] For related work, see Zacher (2001), Englebert, Tarango and Carter (2002), and Hensel, Allison and Khanani (2009).

states facing separatist groups are careful to support only non-separatist groups, and, therefore, do not directly challenge the boundary regime. Similarly, perhaps relatively invulnerable states may have been the countries supporting the separatist movements. We would have to question seriously the conventional wisdom if states facing separatism domestically support separatism in other countries. As a result, the vulnerability approach provides us with a testable hypothesis: *states confronting separatism at home are less likely to be supporters of separatist groups.*

Given that a fear of retaliation is part of the core vulnerability argument, we should also expect that countries are unlikely to support ethnic groups in neighbouring states. Neighbouring states are best equipped to retaliate, so this should deter vulnerable countries from supporting groups in adjacent countries. Also, fear of contagion is another fundamental focus for vulnerability theorists.[5] The states most likely to pay the price of a conflict spilling over are the neighbours. Thus, *states are less likely to support groups in neighbouring countries.*

## Ethnic Politics and Foreign Policy

This approach focuses on how the need for political support provides incentives to politicians to assist groups elsewhere having ties to their constituents. It assumes that politicians care most about gaining and retaining political office (Mayhew 1974, Ames 1987). To do so, they must appeal to domestic audiences, particularly those whose support is required to stay in office. For understanding the international relations of ethnic conflict, this approach assumes that what matters most to voters and other constituents are their ethnic ties to the rest of the world. If ethnic identity influences individuals' preferences towards domestic policies, these same identities should influence preferences towards foreign policies. Ethnic identity, by its nature, creates feelings of loyalty, interest, and fears of extinction (Horowitz 1985), and these feelings need not stop at international boundaries. Further, ethnic groups can use foreign policy as a litmus test for the sincerity of leaders' attitudes towards their group. Moreover, politicians can use foreign policy to highlight certain identities at home, diverting domestic audiences from other issues (Gagnon 1994/95).[6] Because politically relevant supporters, by definition, are a crucial concern for policy-makers, if ethnic ties shape the foreign policy preferences of constituents, then such ties also influence the politician's foreign policy choices.[7]

---

5    For whether ethnic conflict might be contagious, see Lake and Rothchild (1998) and Buhaug and Gleditsch (2008).

6    For diversionary theories of war literature, see Levy (1989) Smith (1996) and Pickering and Kisangani (2010).

7    This discussion and the subsequent analyses assume that ethnic groups can influence politicians, ignoring the problems of lobbying and of collective action. Obviously, some ethnic groups will be more effective in influencing politicians than others (Cuban-Americans versus Serb-Americans).

Previous studies have had a difficult time assessing the impact of ethnic ties. Because ethnic ties are inherently relational, it has been hard to develop monadic studies that test such claims. Performing monadic analyses, Saideman (2001) finds that groups with kin dominating nearby states are more likely to receive support. However, these quantitative analyses do a better job of casting doubt on competing approaches than saying much about the impact of ethnic ties.

Recent efforts to use dyadic datasets have suggested that ethnic ties do matter. Cederman, Girardin and Gleditsch (Cederman et al. 2009) develop a dyadic dataset, determining that ethnic ties do matter, as transnational ties are associated with more conflict.[8] However, they do not consider some of the other hypotheses considered here, especially those focused on vulnerability.

The evidence thus far suggests that ethnic politics matters. We should expect that: *states with closer ethnic ties with a group than to its host state are more likely to give assistance to that group.*

## Power

If vulnerability fails to explain why states take sides, then we ought to consider another approach – that states make decisions based on calculations of relative power as they maximize their security. While realism, surprisingly, has rarely been applied to the international relations of ethnic conflict,[9] we ought to consider this approach, as it is still the dominant approach to understanding international conflict. One study suggests that security concerns matter, asserting that the most important factors driving decisions to assist one side are: 'the existing constellation of states for and against the secessionists, strategic gains, the positions of allies, great and middle powers and friends, and relations with the state (government) threatened by secession' (Heraclides 1990). However, while Heraclides asserted that various realist concerns mattered, but he did not develop testable hypotheses.

As realism has split into two camps, offensive and defensive, we can develop competing realist expectations about how states are likely to behave as they react to ethnic conflicts elsewhere. Defensive realism argues that states are 'defensive positionalists' (Grieco 1988), seeking at least to maintain their security by preserving their relative position and by seeking stability (Paquin 2008). Balance of threat theory fits into this camp as states will balance against those states that pose the greatest threats, with threat operationalized as a composite of relative power, offensive capability, proximity and perceived intentions (Walt 1987). States balance threat by aligning with the enemies of the most threatening states, including ethnic

---

8   See also Davis and Moore (1997). I engaged in a debate with Belanger and his co-authors (Saideman 2007; Belanger, Duchesne and Paquin 2005, 2007) over whether ethnic ties or democracy better account for the patterns of support for secessionists. Some of the data presented in this article is also presented in my 2007 piece.

9   Instead, realists have focused on applying concepts from international relations to the domestic politics of ethnic conflict. For instance, see Posen (1993) and Kaufmann (1998).

groups within them (Hager and Lake 2000). If defensive realism is correct, we should expect that: *states are more likely to support groups in relatively stronger states* (holding constant the other components of threat). Further, because proximity is an important determinant of threat, defensive realism leads us to expect that: *states are more likely to support groups in neighbouring states*.

However, offensive realism suggests a different conclusion. Offensive realists suggest that predation is a constant threat in international relations (Mearsheimer 2001). The strong do what they want (to get stronger), and the weak do what they can. In the realm of ethnic conflict, stronger states will prey upon weaker ones, supporting groups within, to manipulate them, to control them, and to weaken them further. The clearest example is India's support for the secession of Bangladesh from Pakistan. Already stronger than Pakistan, India significantly increased its power relative to Pakistan. Thus, according to offensive realists, we should expect that: *states are more likely to support groups in relatively weaker states*.

## The Minorities and Potential Supporters Dataset

To consider the question at hand, I have used existing datasets, along with other sources of data, to create a new dataset – the Minorities and Potential Supporters Dataset, or MAPS. Essentially, MAPS combines the ethnic groups in the Minorities at Risk Dataset [MAR] (Gurr 1999, 2000) with the countries in the Correlates of War dataset (Singer and Small 1995). The MAPS dataset consists of 39,663 dyads of ethnic groups and potential supporters for 1994–95. I chose the most recent year for which all of the necessary data were available. Saideman (2001) shows that patterns of international support for ethnic groups were quite stable throughout the 1990s.[10] However, we need to be modest about the analyses' implications here since they address behaviour in only a two-year period.

### Dependent Variable: What Is International Support?

The puzzle is why do states assist some groups and not others, so the dependent variable is 'support'.[11] The Minorities at Risk project coded various forms of international support. Assistance can vary from very modes to quite intense. However, because the existence of any support is quite rare (only 0.5 percent), we need to focus more on what causes a state to give any support to a group rather than which forms it may take. Therefore, I code the dependent variable as 0 for no

---

10 Groups received similar levels of support, states gave similar levels of support, and multivariate monadic analyses produce consistent results throughout the decade.
11 This study does not address support given to the state resisting the ethnic group, a.k.a. the host state, due to the difficulties of separating normal forms of assistance from those aimed against a group.

support and 1 for any support. Consequently, I perform logit analyses to answer the question of why states would give any support to particular groups.

## Independent Variables

First, a dyad is coded as *vulnerable* if the group is considered to be actively separatist in the 1980s and/or 1990s, and if the potential supporter (the term used to describe the external actor in each dyad) has one or more actively separatist ethnic groups within its territory.[12] For instance, the dyad of India and the Serbs of Croatia would be coded as vulnerable.

Second, I develop an indicator of relative power, using a composite index from Correlates of War data (Singer and Small 1995). The numbers produce a ranking similar to what common intuitions are of the great powers, middle powers, and the rest of the world.[13] I use 1992 data for this study. Since this is a dyadic analysis, I divide the potential supporter's power relative to the world by the host country's power relative to world totals. This ratio is greater than one if the potential supporter is more powerful than the host state and less than one if the host is more powerful.

Third, I use the standard measure of contiguity – if the potential supporter and the group's host country border each other or are separated by less than 150 miles of water. That is, Cuba and the United States are considered contiguous.

Fourth, I develop separate measures of ethnic ties. I code each group and each country as having a dominant race, religion and language. For states (both potential supporters and host states), I code the ethnic characteristics shared by a plurality of the most politically important group(s) in 1994–95. I choose race, religion and language as these three markers of ethnic identity are frequently salient politically, and to gather data on other ethnic characteristics, such as kinship or custom, would have been quite burdensome.[14]

A potential supporting country is coded as having racial ties with a group if the state's elites are coded as having the same race as the group. Likewise, a country is coded as having racial ties with a host state if both the potential supporter and the host state have been coded as the same race. A dyad is coded as 1 if the potential supporter has racial ties only to the ethnic group, as 0 if it has racial ties to both the host state and ethnic group or to neither, and as -1 if it has racial ties to the host state. Thus, we should expect a positive relationship between this variable and the level of support – states should be more likely to support ethnic groups with which they have racial ties, and less likely to help ethnic groups when they have racial ties with only the host state.

How do we code religious ties? I developed two measures: religious ties, narrowly defined; and religious ties, broadly defined. In the former, religious ties

---

12 MAR variables are used to generate the coding here unless otherwise specified.
13 See the online discussion of the dataset.
14 Again, see my website for a discussion of how these ethnic ties were coded. Also, see Saideman (2007).

are coded as 1 if the ethnic group and the potential supporter largely shared the same religion – if the ethnic group was largely Sunni and the potential supporter was mostly Sunni.[15] The dyad is coded as zero if the group is mostly Sunni and the potential supporter is mostly Shi'ite. For broadly defined religious ties, I collapsed the Protestant, Catholic, Other Christian categories into one category, and the Sunni, Shi'ite, and Other Islamic into a second category. This helps us to address arguments about Christians versus Muslims, and so on. Further, it also might help us address the reality of Shi'ites (Iran) supporting Sunnis (Bosnian Muslims). In the analyses, I consider both definitions of religious ties.

For linguistic ties, I use the language family index from *Ethnologue* (Grimes and Grimes 2000) that codes groups by common supersets.[16] This ultimately produces an indicator of linguistic ties ranging from -4 (linguistic ties to host) to 4 (linguistic ties to ethnic group).

Finally, I have included variables to control for other potentially relevant factors: the level of violence between the host state and the ethnic group and whether the host and potential supporter reside in the same region. Violence between the group and the host may matter for many reasons.[17] Outsiders may be more likely to respond when there is a humanitarian crisis, when the potential to spill across boundaries is greater, when the media cover the conflict more intensely, and when the ethnic ties become that much more salient. I use violence data from the previous period, so that support during 1994–95 cannot be influencing the level of violence in the analyses, although this solution is hardly perfect.

The second variable controls for region. I code this variable as 1 if the host state and the potential supporter are in the same region,[18] and 0 if they are not. As an indicator, it may stand in for a variety of factors, including economic ties, joint membership in international organizations, similarly secure or dangerous neighbourhoods, and the like.

## Reading the MAPS: Vulnerability, Relative Power and Ethnic Ties

With a dataset of this size focusing on a relatively rare event, the first question to consider is what should the scope of the analyses be (King and Zeng 2001). First, I focus on all possible combinations of ethnic groups and potential supporters.

---

15  This discussion, for the sake of simplicity, does not consider ties to the host state. The indicators here, like the racial ones, vary from -1 to 1.
16  Again, the online supplement.
17  Regan (1998, 2000) suggests that intervention is least likely in very violent conflicts, as these situations are harder to manage, so outsiders looking for success will intervene elsewhere.
18  I use region as coded by the Correlates of War project.

Table 14.1 Rare events logit analyses of the international relations of ethnic conflict

| | All dyads | | | Same region | | | Politically relevant dyads | | |
|---|---|---|---|---|---|---|---|---|---|
| | 1 | 2 | 3 | 4 | 5 | 6 | 7 | 8 | 9 |
| Contiguity | 3.340*** | 3.300*** | 3.330*** | 3.370*** | 3.370*** | 3.390*** | | | |
| Relative power | 0.003*** | 0.003*** | 0.003*** | 0.002** | 0.002** | 0.002** | 0.001** | 0.001*** | 0.001** |
| Vulnerable | 0.550** | 0.530** | 0.560** | 0.500* | 0.450* | 0.540** | 0.370* | 0.390* | 0.310 |
| Racial ties | 0.390** | 0.460** | | 0.160 | 0.230 | | 0.450** | 0.500** | |
| Broad religious ties | 1.000*** | | | 1.000*** | | | 0.530** | | |
| Narrow religious ties | | 0.950*** | | | 0.960*** | | | 0.640** | |
| Linguistic ties | 0.470*** | 0.470*** | | 0.450*** | 0.450*** | | 0.670*** | 0.650*** | |
| All ties | | | 0.730*** | | | 0.700*** | | | 0.720*** |
| States in same region | 0.580** | 0.590** | 0.600** | | | | | | |
| Violence in 1993 | 0.120** | 0.120*** | 0.440*** | 0.180*** | 0.180*** | 0.180*** | 0.270*** | 0.270*** | 0.260*** |
| Constant | -6.600*** | -6.530*** | -6.560*** | -6.100*** | -6.050*** | -6.090 | -4.360*** | -4.390*** | -4.310*** |
| N | 36,046 | 36,046 | 36,046 | 6,002 | 6,002 | 6,002 | 6,245 | 6,245 | 6,245 |

*Note:* * 0.1, ** 0.05, *** 0.001.

This reduces selection bias, but will tend to underestimate the probability that states give assistance to ethnic groups. Second, I perform a set of tests on dyads where both the host and potential supporting states reside within the same region. Finally, I adopt a standard used for dyadic study – politically relevant dyads, which include all contiguous dyads and dyads including at least one great power (Lemke and Reed 2001). By doing three different sets of analyses, we can consider whether proximity (defined by region or by contiguity) matters and how it interacts with the other variables.

The size of the dataset and its skewed dependent variable raise important questions about which tools one should use. King and Zeng (2001) argue that standard logit techniques can underestimate the likelihood of rare phenomena. They develop an alternative procedure, called ReLogit. I performed analyses using both logit and ReLogit, finding similar results. I display only the ReLogit results here.[19]

Table 14.1 indicates that most of the findings are consistent regardless of specification. We find that most variables have a positive relationship with support given to ethnic groups elsewhere. Ethnic ties, contiguity, being relatively more powerful, vulnerability to separatism all increase the likelihood that a state will give assistance to an ethnic group.

Before moving on, I consider the relative impact of each factor on the international relations of ethnic conflict. The use of ReLogit and other tools written by King and his collaborators[20] allow us to determine the first differences associated with each variable.[21] The result reported represents the change in probability of a country giving support to an ethnic group as we manipulate the value of the particular independent variable.

Table 14.2 displays the first differences of each variable and the 95 percent confidence interval.[22] This information is useful for assessing the relative impact of each variable.

---

19  Weak correlations among the variables suggest that multicollinearity is not a problem.
20  The programs, written for STATA, run simulations to determine the impact of each variable on the dependent variable. See King, Tomz and Wittenberg (2001); Tomz, Wittenberg and King (2000) and King and Zeng (2001).
21  See online for more explanation.
22  The latter refers the likely range of possible first differences. When zero falls between the lower bound and the upper bound, we cannot have much confidence that the variable has a consistent impact on the outcome.

Table 14.2  Relative impact of each independent variable

| | All | | Same region | | Politically relevant dyads | |
|---|---|---|---|---|---|---|
| | FD | 95% CI | FD | 95% CI | FD | 95% CI |
| Change from linguistic ties with host only to ties with ethnic group | 73% | 52% – 86% | 70% | 43% – 84% | 80% | 63% – 90% |
| Change to host and potential supporter being neighbors? | 66% | 55% – 73% | 66% | 53% – 74% | | |
| Change from religious ties* with host only to ties with ethnic group | 38% | 21% – 54% | 37% | 17% – 56% | 20% | 3% – 41% |
| Change from no linguistic ties to ties with ethnic group | 35% | 23% – 48% | 32% | 18% – 46% | 57% | 43% – 70% |
| Change from no violence in 1993 to protracted civil war | 12% | 5% – 23% | 20% | 9% – 34% | 40% | 27% – 52% |
| Dyadic power relationship, least to most power of potential supporter relative to host state | 12% | 5% – 25% | 10% | 2% – 21% | 12% | 2% – 27% |
| Change from racial ties with host only to ties with ethnic group | 10% | 0.1% – 0.2% | 4% | -5 – 16% | 17% | -0.2% – 40% |
| Change from a dyad not characterized by joint vulnerable to joint vulnerability | 7% | 2% – 15% | 6% | -0.2% – 16% | 6% | -0.1% – 14% |
| Change from potential support and host in different regions to same region | 7% | 2% – 17% | | | | |
| Dyadic power relationship, from 25th percentile to 75th percentile | 0.1% | 0.1% – 0.2% | 0.04% | 0.003% – 0.1% | 0.05% | 0.0001% – 0.01% |

*Notes:* FD: first difference; 95% CI refers to the 95% confidence interval.

\* The indicator for broadly defined religious ties was used.

# Findings

Below, I first examine the surprising finding (from the standpoint of vulnerability theorists) that in 1994–95, states facing separatist movements at home may actually be *more likely* to give assistance to separatists abroad. I then consider how realist arguments fared. I move on to assess how ethnic politics matters, and then review the impact of the controls.

## Examining the Dark Side of Vulnerability

Countries facing separatism at home are more likely to assist separatists. Despite providing the smallest impact on the dependent variable (Table 14.2), the direction of its influence is directly opposite to what the conventional wisdom predicts. How can we make sense of it? At least two potential explanations come to mind: the logic of reciprocity suggests that feuds might develop and realism suggests that, rather than mutual deterrence, we ought to expect conflict spirals.

Reciprocity is when a country will respond to cooperation with more cooperation and to conflict with more conflict (Axelrod 1984). Thus, when country A supports an ethnic group in country B, then country B is likely to retaliate by supporting an ethnic group in country A. There is plenty of evidence to suggest that mutual vulnerability leads to mutual interference. In 1994–95, some examples are: India and Bangladesh; India and Pakistan; and Croatia and Serbia. These cases and the statistical findings suggest that the fear of retaliation is not sufficient for deterring support. In the end, reciprocity, by itself, does not help us very much as it fails to account for why feuds or cooperation develop. 'Reciprocal destablilization' may be quite normal (McGinnis 2001).

Realists would suggest that this finding is not surprising, as spirals of conflict are common in international relations.[23] The logic flows from anarchy and the security dilemma (Jervis 1976, 1978; Waltz 1979). If states must compete with each other in a system of self-help, then they will be reluctant to forgo any advantage over their adversaries. If a country limits itself, either it puts itself at a disadvantage as the other state refuses to be constrained, or it fails to give itself an advantage. Thus, states are likely to engage in arms races and other behaviour that spirals – ultimately leaving all worse off. Supporting groups within adversaries is likely to be counter-productive as well (which vulnerability theorists assert), as efforts to weaken an adversary via support of ethnic rebels are likely to provoke retaliation. This will reinforce the first country's policy of supporting the rebels. One example of this dynamic would be Iraq's support for Iran's Kurds and Iran's assistance to Iraq's Kurds.

Both dynamics seem to play out in reality. Further research is necessary to disentangle the competing arguments. What is abundantly clear is that *vulnerability does not deter*. Additionally, as Table 14.2 indicates, states were about two-thirds

---

23   I am grateful to Jack Snyder for raising this possibility.

more likely to support groups in neighbours, which runs contrary to fears about direct retaliation or spillover. Contiguity is discussed more directly in the next section, but it matters here as it provides further evidence that the vulnerability logic apparently does not apply, at least in these analyses. Fear does not inhibit, that much is certain.

## Realism and the International Relations of Ethnic Conflict

The analyses included two realist variables: proximity and relative power. A state was 66 percent more likely to support a neighbouring ethnic group than a distant one. The strongest state in the most dominant dyad (US and Botswana) was between 12 percent and 20 percent more likely to give support than the weakest state in the most dominated dyad (Gambia and the US). The proximity results make sense, but lend support to other arguments as well as realism. The relative power results suggest that offensive realists are correct about the predatory nature of international relations.

First, neighbours are more likely to get involved in each other's ethnic conflicts. Part of this story might be that proximity breeds suspicion and fear. Proximity greatly facilitates most of the means of supporting ethnic groups, making them greater threats. As a result, state A may be likely to support ethnic groups in its neighbour, state B, not only because it can, but also because B can do it to A.

Second, relative power matters. Throughout the analyses, relative power produced consistently significant and positive coefficients. However, the direction of the coefficient is different than a defensive realist would expect – relatively more powerful states tend to support ethnic groups in weaker countries. This suggests that offensive realist arguments may be correct, at least in this issue area.[24] Given that several of the stronger countries seem to be motivated by ethnic politics (Russia tends to support Russians in the Near Abroad), this finding suggests that stronger countries do what they want, but something else may determine what they want (which ethnic groups they prefer). Further work may reveal whether it is simply opportunity (Siverson and Starr 1991) that motivates great powers, or other factors, such as ethnic politics, or both.

## Ethnic Politics

We find that ethnic ties powerfully condition the international relations of ethnic conflict. Religious, racial and linguistic ties matter consistently. According to

---

24   Indeed, when I used a composite of contiguity and weakness to test whether states were more or less likely to support groups in more powerful countries close by, I found a negative relationship – weaker states were less likely to support groups in stronger neighbours. The converse is also true – stronger states were more likely to support groups in weaker neighbours.

Table 14.2, religious ties increase the probability of international support by 38 percent among all dyads. Regardless of how we define religious ties, narrowly or broadly, states with populations having religious ties to an ethnic group are more likely to give assistance than those without such ties or those with ties to the host state. Religious ties consistently had the third greatest impact, behind only proximity and, surprisingly, linguistic ties. That the existence of religious ties is not the most powerful 'ethnic' factor contradicts the conventional wisdom (Huntington 1993, 1996).

Potential supporters speaking identical or nearly identical languages as an ethnic group were at least 70 percent more likely to give support than those sharing a language with a host state. Language may be playing a larger role than expected as linguistic affinities may coincide with kinship ties. This variable may play a larger role as shared language facilitates communication between the ethnic kin in trouble and those in the potential supporter. This allows the ethnic group to make their case more clearly, as the media will not have to translate their pleas for assistance. Also, with growing transnational communications networks, sharing the same language may also mean watching the same network or listening to the same broadcast.

Race plays a smaller, yet still significant role in the analyses. However, it is not significant in the same region tests, suggesting that race is more likely to draw in distant outsiders rather than folks in the same region. Given how difficult it is to code race, we must consider these findings cautiously.

I constructed a variable that combines the ethnic ties variables – total ties. Instead of determining the relative influence of each ethnic tie compared to the other ethnic bonds and to the other variables, this allows us to consider what happens when a state has multiple ties to an ethnic group (ranging from -3 for all ties with the host state to +3 for all ties to the group). The total ties variable has an impact similar to proximity – raising the probability of support by *more than two-thirds*. These results, particularly that race, religion and language all matter, not only suggest that ethnic ties matter and matter quite strongly, but they also suggest that more simplistic arguments, like the 'clash of civilizations', focusing solely on one kind of identity are misguided.[25] Clearly, ethnic ties shape how states respond to ethnic conflicts elsewhere, nearly as strongly as proximity and more so than the other variables (see also Chapter 11).

## Other Factors

Violence and co-existing in the same region also shape how states react. States are more likely to support an ethnic group if the group was fighting its host state. This was consistent across the analyses, although violence played a lesser role than most of the other variables. This finding contradicts Regan (1998, 2000), who suggests that violence is likely to deter intervention.

---

25  See Huntington (1993, 1996); Henderson (1997, 1998) and Henderson and Tucker (2001).

Sharing the same region matters, as countries were more likely to give assistance to a group in the same region. This finding could undermine neo-liberal institutional arguments, as regions tend to have organizations that develop norms of cooperation and patterns of positive reciprocity. The OAU was explicitly said to do exactly this (Jackson and Rosberg 1982; Herbst 1989). These arguments may have been right in what countries should fear – spillover; yet fears of spillover did not deter states.

## Conclusion

We now know more about why states take sides as they support some ethnic groups but not others. States do not avoid supporting separatist groups, even when they, themselves, are fighting separatists domestically. Instead, such states are *more likely* to support separatists. Proximity matters, but why it matters is not yet clear. Relative power plays an important role, significantly influencing which states support which groups. States are opportunistic, taking advantage of weaker countries by supporting ethnically defined rebel movements within them. Finally, ethnic politics strongly influences how states respond to ethnic conflict, as states are much more likely to give support to those groups with which constituents have ethnic ties.

We found that the focus on vulnerability is misplaced. Thus, it is not surprising that the conventional wisdom could not account for the international relations of Yugoslavia's demise. Instead, it is remarkable that the conventional wisdom has held up as long as it has, given its inability to account for behaviour in the past (Saideman 1997, 2001) or more recently. The findings suggest, again, that power matters, though we now have evidence to suggest that the offensive realists may be right, at least here, that the predatory environment of international relations causes the strong to dominate the weak, rather than the weak to balance against the strong.

While the ethnic politics argument cannot explain every outcome, it can account for some of the behaviour we see in international relations in this issue area since the end of the Cold War. Constituents care about those who are like themselves, and pressure their government to give assistance. Or, politicians can create foreign policies to appeal to ethnic constituencies at home to gain domestic political support.

How can we advise future policy-makers? First, we cannot depend on states restraining themselves due to their own vulnerability. Second, unless all relevant states have ties to only one side of an ethnic conflict (which is very unlikely), states are likely to disagree about whom to support and, thus, what to do. Outsiders can try to engage in agenda setting so that identities producing favourable coalitions come to the fore. However, countries with competing interests will do the same, making such efforts quite difficult at best. Third, since states are likely to disagree, policy-makers ought to engage in mini-lateralism (Kahler 1993) – cooperating with those with common interests and excluding those who are likely to disagree. For instance, the United States seemed to learn this, as it kept the Kosovo conflict as a NATO matter, rather than an issue for the United Nations to handle, thus keeping Russia and China out of the decision-making process.

This study is likely to produce more pessimism for those who study secessionist conflict or international relations. Rather than re-affirming the optimistic view that common interests will breed cooperation, we find support for those who argue that ethnocentrism, power, and parochial interests govern foreign policy. Countries seem to support only those groups that have ties to their politically relevant constituencies or those in weaker states who can be exploited. To manage secessionist conflict, we cannot gloss over the likely difficulties.

# References

Ames, B. (1987), *Political Survival: Politicians and Public Policy in Latin America* (Berkeley, CA: University of California Press).
Axelrod, Robert M. (1984), *The Evolution of Cooperation* (New York: Basic Books).
Belanger, L., E. Duchesne and J. Paquin (2005), 'Foreign Interventions and Secessionist Movements: The Democratic Factor', *Canadian Journal of Political Science – Revue Canadienne De Science Politique* 38, 435–62.
Belanger, L., E. Duchesne and J. Paquin (2007), 'Democratic Norms Remain Stronger Than Ethnic Ties: Defending "Foreign Interventions and Secessionist Movements"', *Canadian Journal of Political Science – Revue Canadienne De Science Politique* 40, 749–57.
Buhaug, H. and K.S. Gleditsch (2008), 'Contagion or Confusion? Why Conflicts Cluster in Space', *International Studies Quarterly* 52, 215–33.
Cederman, L.E., L. Girardin and K.S. Gleditsch (2009), 'Ethnonationalist Triads Assessing the Influence of Kin Groups on Civil Wars', *World Politics* 61, 403–14.
Davis, D. and W. Moore (1997), 'Ethnicity Matters: Transnational Ethnic Alliances and Foreign Policy Behavior', *International Studies Quarterly* 41, 171–84.
Englebert, P., Stacy Tarango and Matthew Carter (2002), 'Dismemberment and Suffocation', *Comparative Political Studies* 35:10, 1093–18.
Gagnon, V. Jr (1994/95), 'Ethnic Nationalism and International Conflict: The Case of Serbia', *International Security* 19, 135–7.
Grieco, Joseph M. (1988), 'Anarchy and the Limits of Cooperation: A Realist Critique of the Newest Liberal Institutionalism', *International Organization* 42, 485–507.
Grimes, B. and J. Grimes (eds) (2000), *Ethnologue*, CD-Rom (Dallas, TX: SIL International).
Gurr, T. (1999), *Minorities at Risk Dataset* (College Park, MD: Center for International Development and Conflict Management). [Online] At http://www.bsos.umd.edu/cidcm/mar/.
Gurr, T. (2000), *Peoples Versus States: Ethnopolitical Conflict and Accommodation at the End of the 20th Century* (Washington, DC: US Institute of Peace Press).

Hager, R. Jr and D. Lake (2000), 'Balancing Empires: Competitive Decolonization in International Politics', *Security Studies* 9, 108–48.

Henderson, E. (1997), 'Culture or Contiguity: Ethnic Conflict, the Similarity of States and the Onset of Interstate War, 1820–1989', *Journal of Conflict Resolution* 41, 649–68.

Henderson, E. (1998), 'The Democratic Peace through the Lens of Culture, 1820–1989', *International Studies Quarterly* 42, 461–84.

Henderson, E. and R. Tucker (2001), 'Clear and Present Strangers: The Clash of Civilizations and International Conflict', *International Studies Quarterly* 45, 317–38.

Hensel, P.R., M.E. Allison and A. Khanani (2009), 'Territorial Integrity Treaties and Armed Conflict over Territory', *Conflict Management and Peace Science* 26:2, 120–43.

Heraclides, A. (1990), 'Secessionist Minorities and External Involvement', *International Organization* 44, 341–78.

Herbst, Jeffrey (1989), 'The Creation and Maintenance of National Boundaries in Africa', *International Organizations* 43, 673–92.

Horowitz, D. (1985), *Ethnic Groups in Conflict* (Berkeley, CA: University of California).

Huntington, S. (1993), 'The Clash of Civilizations?', *Foreign Affairs* 72: 22–49.

Huntington, S. (1996), *The Clash of Civilizations and the Remaking of World Order* (New York: Simon & Schuster).

Jackson, R. and C. Rosberg (1982), 'Why Africa's Weak States Persist: The Empirical and the Juridical in Statehood', *World Politics* 35: 1–24.

Jervis, R. (1976), *Perception and Misperception in International Politics* (Princeton, NJ: Princeton University Press).

Jervis, R. (1978), 'Cooperation under the Security Dilemma', *World Politics* 30, 167–214.

Kahler, M. (1993), 'Multilateralism with Small and Large Numbers', in J. Ruggie (ed.), *Multilateralism Matters: The Theory and Praxis of an Institutional Form* (New York: Columbia University Press), 681–708.

Kaufmann, C. (1998), 'Where All Else Fails: Ethnic Population Transfers and Partitions in the Twentieth Century', *International Security* 23, 120–56.

King, C. (2001), 'The Benefits of Ethnic War: Understanding Eurasia's Unrecognized States', *World Politics* 53, 524–52.

King, G., M. Tomz and J. Wittenberg (2000), 'Making the Most of Statistical Analyses: Improving Interpretation and Presentation', *American Journal of Political Science* 44, 347–61.

King, G. and L. Zeng (2001), 'Explaining Rare Events in International Relations', *International Organization* 55, 693–716.

Lake, D. and D. Rothchild (1998), *The International Spread of Ethnic Conflict: Fear, Diffusion, Escalation* (Princeton, NJ: Princeton University Press).

Lemke, D. and W. Reed (2001), 'The Relevance of Politically Relevant Dyads', *Journal of Conflict Resolution* 45, 126–44.

Levy, J. (1989), 'The Diversionary Theory of War: A Critique', in Manus I. Midlarsky (ed.), *Handbook of War Studies* (Boston, MA: Unwin Hyman), 259–88.

Mayhew, D. (1974), *Congress: The Electoral Connection* (New Haven, CT: Yale University Press).

McGinnis, M. (2001), 'Reciprocal Destabilization: A Two-Level Security Dilemma Involving Rebellion, Refugees, and Regional Conflict', Paper presented at the Annual Meeting of the International Studies Association, 21–24 February, Chicago, IL.

Mearsheimer, John J. (2001), *The Tragedy of Great Power Politics* (New York: Norton).

Paquin, J. (2008), 'Managing Controversy: U.S. Stability Seeking and the Birth of the Macedonian State', *Foreign Policy Analysis* 4, 437–58.

Pickering, J. and E.F. Kisangani (2010), 'Diversionary Despots? Comparing Autocracies' Propensities to Use and to Benefit from Military Force', *American Journal of Political Science* 54, 477–93.

Posen, B. (1993), 'The Security Dilemma and Ethnic Conflict', *Survival* 35, 27–47.

Regan, P. (1998), 'Choosing to Intervene: Outside Intervention in Internal Conflicts', *Journal of Politics* 60, 754–79.

Regan, P. (2000), *Civil Wars and Foreign Powers: Outside Intervention in Intrastate Conflict* (Ann Arbor, MI: University of Michigan Press).

Saideman, S. (1997), 'Explaining the International Relations of Secessionist Conflicts: Vulnerability vs. Ethnic Ties', *International Organization* 51, 721–53.

Saideman, S. (2001), *The Ties That Divide: Ethnic Politics, Foreign Policy, and International Conflict* (New York: Columbia University Press).

Saideman, S.M. (2002), 'Discrimination in International Relations: Analyzing External Support for Ethnic Groups', *Journal of Peace Research* 39, 27–50.

Saideman, S.M. (2007), 'Ties Versus Institutions: Revisiting Foreign Interventions and Secessionist Movements', *Canadian Journal of Political Science – Revue Canadienne De Science Politique* 40, 733–47.

Singer, J.D. and M. Small (1995), 'National Military Capabilities Data: Modified', *Correlates of War Project* (Ann Arbor, MI: University of Michigan).

Siverson, R. and H. Starr (1991), *The Diffusion of War: A Study of Opportunity and Willingness* (Ann Arbor, MI: University of Michigan Press).

Smith, A. (1996), 'Diversionary Foreign Policy in Democratic Systems', *International Studies Quarterly* 40, 133–54.

Tomz, M., J. Wittenberg and G. King (2000), *CLARIFY: Software for Interpreting and Presenting Statistical Results*. Version 1.2.2. (Cambridge, MA: Harvard University).

Walt, S. (1987), *The Origins of Alliances* (Ithaca, NY: Cornell University Press).

Waltz, K. (1979), *Theory of International Politics* (New York: Random House).

Zacher, M.W. (2001), 'The Territorial Integrity Norm: International Boundaries and the Use of Force', *International Organization* 55, 215–22.

# Secession and Contested States[1]

## Deon Geldenhuys

The enormous proliferation of states in the 20th century revealed a variety of origins. War was of course a major factor in the creation of new states. The break-up of the defeated Ottoman, Austro-Hungarian and German empires in the wake of World War One produced the century's first wave of state formation. Six new European states emerged from the disintegration of the Austro-Hungarian Empire, including Austria, Czechoslovakia and Yugoslavia. Germany in turn ceded territory to a reconstituted independent Poland, while the liquidation of the Ottoman empire paved the way for the later emergence of a host of independent states like Albania, Iraq, Jordan, Lebanon and Syria. The second wave followed World War Two, when European empires in Africa, Asia and the Pacific were dismantled. Thanks mainly to decolonization, the United Nations' founding membership of 51 had doubled by 1961 and reached 127 in 1970. Ten years later, when decolonization had largely run its course, UN membership stood at 154 (Biersteker 2000: 159). The dissolution of the Soviet Union (1991), Yugoslavia (1991–92) and Czechoslovakia (1993) constituted the third wave. Primarily because of the new states emerging from these three multinational federations, UN membership increased to 184 in 1993. Some small island states, Switzerland, Timor-Leste and Montenegro subsequently joined, bringing the UN's membership at the time of writing to 192. In the vast majority of cases, the new entities' admission to the League of Nations and later the UN was virtually automatic. Being granted membership of the international organizations was tantamount to collective *de jure* recognition of the new countries' statehood.

Given the vast increase in the number of states since World War One, it is easy to overlook the fact that over two dozen purported states failed to obtain collective recognition of their proclaimed independence. Ten of these entities still experience what will be called contested statehood. It is instructive that several of the contested states had attempted the secessionist route to statehood, meaning they unilaterally broke away from existing states.

---

1    The contribution draws on the author's book, *Contested States in World Politics* (Geldenhuys 2009a).

This chapter defines contested statehood and traces the emergence of contested states over the course of the 20th century to establish the precise incidence of secessionist origins among them. The link between secession and contested statehood is then examined more closely in terms of the formal requirements of internationally recognized (or confirmed) statehood. Do contested states, especially those born of secession, carry 'birth defects' that condemn them to a life on the margins of world society? Or do contested states, based on their different roots, experience varying levels on non-recognition and hence isolation?

## Definition and Roll-call

The defining feature of contested states is their lack of collective *de jure* recognition due to the internationally disputed nature of their purported statehood. In most cases their very right to statehood is challenged widely, resulting in no formal recognition at all or recognition by only a limited number of established (or confirmed) states. In a few instances contested states' right to statehood found wide acceptance and even endorsement by the UN, but the realization of the right was disputed or obstructed by some influential foreign states. Whatever the differences in status, all contested states experienced collective non-recognition in the sense of being excluded from membership of the UN (and previously the League of Nations). Lacking the 'birth certificate' of confirmed states, these entities were relegated to life in international limbo. For some of the aspirant states life on the margins was not merely solitary but also short, before being reabsorbed into their original states. Others, by contrast, have lived with contested statehood for decades. Virtually all contested states aspired to confirmed statehood that would flow from collective *de jure* recognition. They regarded contested statehood as an unnatural and harmful and hopefully only a transient status.

The 20th century's first batch of contested states were the products of aggressive powers' territorial aggrandizement. In 1932 imperial Japan proclaimed the State of Manchukuo on the occupied Chinese territory of Manchuria. The archetypal puppet state, Manchuria received *de jure* recognition from only five states, including Germany and Italy. In the wake of Japan's surrender to Allied forces in 1945, China reclaimed Manchuria and so ended Manchukuo's purported statehood (Jones 1949: 223–5; Crawford 1979: 107, 122). During World War Two Japan created another puppet state in occupied Burma, giving the former British colony nominal independence (Selth 1986: 492–5). The Independent State of Croatia was proclaimed in 1941 by the German and Italian forces occupying Yugoslavia. Apart from four Axis powers, only Spain and Switzerland accorded Croatia *de jure* recognition. Croatia's brief existence as an Axis puppet state ended in 1944 (Darby et al. 1966: 209, 233). Slovakia was another wartime puppet-*cum*-contested state (1939–45) set up by the German occupiers.

The origins of Taiwan's contested statehood date back to 1949, when communist forces conquered the entire mainland of China and proclaimed the People's Republic of China (PRC) as successor to the Republic of China. The latter's Kuomintang government fled to the island of Taiwan. As more and more countries recognized the PRC as the sole Chinese state and its government as the legitimate ruler of all China, the Republic of China on Taiwan suffered a severe loss of *de jure* recognition. Presently Taiwan is recognized by about two dozen mostly small states (see Part VI).

Two unsuccessful secessions in the 1960s produced Africa's first contested states of the post-colonial era. Barely a week after the former Belgian Congo achieved independence in mid-1960, the province of Katanga broke away. Not a single country recognized Katanga's self-proclaimed independent statehood, which ended in January 1963 with its military defeat. Four years later Nigeria's Eastern Region seceded. The self-styled Republic of Biafra obtained formal recognition from four African states and Haiti, but that could not save the entity. Biafra succumbed on the battlefield in early 1970 and was reabsorbed into Nigeria (see Chapter 6).

The first contested state in southern Africa came into being with white-ruled Rhodesia's unilateral declaration of independence from the United Kingdom in 1965. The UN held that the so-called Rhodesian rebellion violated two peremptory norms of international law relating to the prohibition of systematic racial discrimination and the right to self-determination; Rhodesia was subjected to comprehensive sanctions by the UN and not a single state granted it *de jure* recognition. Following the installation of a democratically elected black government in 1980, the state, renamed Zimbabwe, was given full international recognition.

In March 1971 East Pakistan broke away from Pakistan to found the new state of Bangladesh. Pakistan's military leadership responded to this unilateral move with a military assault. Shortly after recognizing the besieged Bangladesh's statehood in December 1971, India staged a massive military intervention on behalf of the fledgling state. The Pakistani forces were routed and Bangladesh's survival was ensured. Scores of other countries thereafter recognized its statehood and in 1974 Bangladesh attained confirmed statehood with its admission to the UN (see Part VI).

The next contested state to emerge was East Timor. In 1975 the Portuguese colonial administration abandoned East Timor to its own fate. Anarchy prevailed as local factions fought a civil war and neighbouring Indonesia staked its claim to the former Portuguese colony. In November 1975 the Fretilin nationalist movement issued a unilateral declaration of independence, hoping that statehood would offer East Timor some international protection against Indonesia's territorial designs. According to Fretilin, 15 states granted the Democratic Republic of East Timor formal recognition, including China and several former Portuguese colonies (Machover 1995: 210). Barely a week after Fretilin's declaration of independence, Indonesian troops invaded East Timor, snuffing out its purported statehood and forcing its incorporation into Indonesia in 1976. It was only in 2002 that the territory finally gained internationally recognized statehood – as the Democratic Republic of Timor-Leste – following a UN-supervised transition to independence.

White-ruled South Africa gave birth to no less than four contested states, when it conferred independence on the black homelands or Bantustans of Transkei (1976), Bophuthatswana (1977), Venda (1979) and Ciskei (1981). The origins of the four entities condemned them to contested statehood and severe international isolation:

they were products of the policy of apartheid, which the UN had previously declared a crime against humanity. The abolition of apartheid and the installation of a non-racial democracy in 1994 spelled the end of the Bantustans.

In the same year that Transkei became independent under South African law, the former Spanish colony of Western Sahara proclaimed itself independent as the Sahrawi Arab Democratic Republic (SADR). This desperate act of self-decolonization by the Polisario independence movement was designed to prevent the territory being dismembered and the parts incorporated into neighbouring Morocco and Mauritania upon Spain's departure from Western Sahara. Polisario's preventive move failed, causing it to set up an SADR government-in-exile and to take up arms against the occupying states. In 1979 Mauritania relinquished its portion of Western Sahara, which Morocco promptly annexed. While Western Sahara remains under Moroccan control and the SADR's writ is confined to pockets of 'liberated' territory, the entity's right to statehood is supported by the African Union (previously the Organization of African Unity) and the SADR is a member of this body.

The European Union has to contend with a contested state in its midst in the shape of the Turkish Republic of Northern Cyprus (TRNC). Turkish Cypriot leaders founded the TRNC in 1983, nearly ten years after the island had been effectively partitioned between the Greek South and Turkish North following inter-communal war and the intervention of troops from Turkey to support their kinsfolk. Turkey remains the TRNC's patron and protector state and the only one to have given it *de jure* recognition. While Northern Cyprus is still subjected to extensive isolation as its right to separate statehood is widely rejected, the Greek-controlled South joined the EU as the Republic of Cyprus, formally representing the entire island.

In 1988 Palestine joined the ranks of contested states when the Palestine National Council (the territory's parliament-in-exile) issued the Palestinian Declaration of Independence. 'The State of Palestine is an Arab state', it read, with Jerusalem as its capital. This should be regarded as a symbolic proclamation of the establishment of an independent Palestine on the basis of the UN's partition plan of 1947, rather than as a declaration intended to create the legal effects of conventional statehood (Kalidi 2006: 194–5). The UN General Assembly acknowledged the proclamation of a Palestinian state, without recognizing the state. Palestine was formally recognized by over 100 states. In 1994 the exiled leadership of the Palestine Liberation Organization returned to Palestine and formed a Palestinian government on home soil. Four years later the General Assembly upgraded the PLO's existing observer status by allowing the movement to participate in general debates, but stopped short of granting it full UN membership as a state.

The Chechen part of the Chechen-Ingush Republic opted for a unilateral declaration of independence only weeks before the Soviet Union imploded in 1991, making the Chechen Republic of Ichkeria the first contested state to emerge from the dissolution of the Soviet state (see Part VI). The new Russian Federation rejected Chechnya's claims to sovereign statehood and at first used limited military action and economic sanctions to bring its rebellious region to heel. When that failed, Russia resorted to full-blown military intervention in 1994. Against huge odds, the Chechen forces prevailed. Peace accords concluded between Russia and Chechnya in 1996 and 1997 left the question of Chechnya's final status deliberately vague. While the nationalist rulers of Chechnya took the agreements as implicit Russian acceptance of the putative state's independence, Moscow continued to regard Chechnya as a subject of the Russian Federation with no right to separate statehood. That was also the view of member-states of major international organizations; Taliban-ruled Afghanistan was the sole state to recognize Chechnya's independence. Russia's victory in the second war against Chechnya, which broke out in 1999, brought the territory's contested statehood to an end. Chechnya was integrated into Russia as one of the Federation's 21 ethnically defined republics (Graney 2004: 119–32).

In 1991 Africa produced another contested state when the Northern Region broke away from the Somali Republic and proclaimed itself the independent Republic of Somaliland (see Part VI). Arguing that their 30-year union with the dominant South had subjected the North to deprivation and repression, the leaders of Somaliland insisted that theirs was not an act of secession but a dissolution of the North–South union and a reversion to the territory's former (albeit brief) independent status based on the same internationally accepted borders. Despite its legal and historical claims to statehood and the remarkable measure of peace, order and freedom prevailing in Somaliland – in contrast to anarchic Somalia – the purported state has not managed to gain any formal recognition.

The chronology next takes us back to Europe, where Kosovo experienced two rounds of contested statehood. The first began in 1991, when the largely Albanian populated territory seceded from the disintegrating Yugoslavia and declared itself independent. Only Albania recognized its self-proclaimed statehood. In 1999, after NATO's war against Yugoslavia, Kosovo became a ward of the UN and NATO. This heralded a new period of international contestation over Kosovo's political fate as its final status was being negotiated by interested parties. While the process was still underway, Kosovo in 2008 issued its second unilateral declaration of independence. This time a host of countries immediately extended *de jure* recognition. In July 2010 Kosovo's claims to statehood received a major boost when the International Court of Justice in an advisory opinion ruled that the entity's 2008 declaration of independence did not violate general international law. By then 69 states had formally recognized Kosovo's independence. Admission to the UN, however, still eludes the new state (see also Chapters 9 and 17).

The dismemberment of Yugoslavia produced two more contested states, twin Serbian entities founded under comparable conditions and meeting similar fates (see Chapter 8 and Part VI). Both the Serb community in Croatia and that in Bosnia and Herzegovina (BiH) flatly rejected the two constituent republics' bids for independence from Yugoslavia. When Croatia proclaimed its independence from Yugoslavia in June 1991, the Serb areas of Croatia promptly declared their independence as the Republic of Serb Krajina. The Serb state comprised roughly one-third of Croatian territory, while Serbs constituted only about 12 percent of Croatia's total population. In like fashion the Serb community of BiH, comprising roughly 40 percent of the territory's total population, proclaimed the independence of the Republika Srpska (separate from Bosnia and Herzegovina) in response to the latter's declaration of independence from Yugoslavia in April 1992. Both Croatia and Bosnia and Herzegovina immediately received *de jure* recognition from existing states, whereas the two Serb entities' unilateral acts gained no international acceptance and instead caused vicious inter-ethnic wars in the two former Yugoslav republics. The pair of Serb contested states had the trappings of statehood (such as their own constitutions, flags, legislatures, executives, judiciaries and armed forces), but their domestic autonomy was curtailed by the deployment of UN peacekeeping forces. In 1995 Croatian forces finally conquered the bulk of Krajina, which was reincorporated into Croatia. The war in Bosnia and Herzegovina was also brought to an end in 1995, but under the Dayton Agreement brokered by the US. Republika Srpska (the Serb Republic) lost its independent statehood, becoming one of the two main territorial-*cum*-ethnic constituent 'entities' of BiH and occupying nearly half the entire state's surface area; the other entity is the Bosniak-Croat Federation (Pavković 2000: 490–93; GlobalSecurity.org; wordiQ; *The World Factbook*).

The last four contested states were the products of the dissolution of the Soviet Union. Abkhazia, South Ossetia, Transdniestria and Nagorno Karabagh are all located in the territorial space of the former Soviet state (see Part VI). In the early 1990s they took up arms individually to break free from successor states and proclaimed themselves independent. Abkhazia and South Ossetia seceded from Georgia, Transdniestria hived off from Moldova and Nagorno Karabagh broke away from Azerbaijan. Moscow's hand has been all too evident in the founding and survival of the quartet of Eurasian entities. Russia even extended *de jure* recognition to South Ossetia and Abkhazia, with Nicaragua, Venezuela and Nauru following suit. Nagorno Karabagh and Transdniestria, by contrast, remain wholly unrecognized by confirmed states.

## The Criteria of Statehood

In trying to explain the causes and consequences of contested states' lack of recognition, it is necessary to look into the familiar criteria of statehood in international law. These represent the minimum formal preconditions for an entity's acceptance into the community of sovereign states. Are contested states refused recognition because they failed to meet the basic requirements of statehood? More specifically, do secessionist states carry a birth defect that seals their fate?

The 1933 Montevideo Convention on Rights and Duties of States embodies customary international law on what constitutes a state. Such an entity has to meet four qualifications: a permanent population, a defined territory, a government, and a capacity to enter into relations with other states (Castellino 2000: 77–89; Dixon 2000: 105). Contested states typically met these criteria. They all had populations, whether settled or nomadic. They likewise possessed territories, although the borders were not internationally recognized as legal and legitimate frontiers separating them from other states. The governments of most contested states exercised effective control over their territories and populations, even though these governments' right to govern independent states was generally disputed. Contested states furthermore had the ability and desire to enter into the standard array of inter-state relations, but confirmed states denied them this opportunity.

A fifth commonly accepted standard of statehood, sovereignty, is highly problematic in the case of contested states. True, as a rule they possessed internal sovereignty in that they detached themselves from any larger (foreign) constitutional arrangement and formalized their independent status by adopting their own constitutions. Their independence was also formally proclaimed, whether unilaterally or in conjunction with a patron or creator state or directly by an external creator. However, as mentioned, confirmed states challenged the self-declared states' exclusive right to create and operate their own institutions of government independent from their original states. Where the latter insisted on the right to continue ruling the break-away territories, this derogated – under international law – from the purported states' formal independence.

What further detracted from several contested states' independence in terms of international law, was their substantially illegal origins. These were pretender states whose creation violated peremptory international norms such as those prohibiting aggression and occupation (Manchukuo and Northern Cyprus) and racial discrimination (Rhodesia and South Africa's homeland states). The universal commitment to maintaining the territorial integrity of states – a hallowed principle of international law enshrined in, among others, the UN Charter and the Declaration on Principles of International Law Concerning Friendly Relations, adopted by the UN General Assembly in 1970 – has been a further powerful argument against recognizing the products of territorial fragmentation, especially if they originated *via* non-consensual secession (Shaw 2008: 1123) (see Chapter 17).

Recognition, a final criterion commonly associated with statehood, can take one of two forms. *De facto* recognition may be extended when the recognizing state judges that an aspirant complies with some but not all the formal requirements of statehood. Such recognition is provisional and may be withdrawn if the remaining criteria are not satisfied. Should these conditions be met, *de jure* recognition may follow, indicating that reservations have been sufficiently addressed to extend full acceptance. *De jure* recognition can have major legal, political and material benefits for a state, such as becoming a party to international agreements, making its voice heard in multilateral forums, opening diplomatic representation, and gaining access to the public goods distributed by the likes of the World Bank and International Monetary Fund (Crawford 1979: 23; Shaw 2008: 459–60). The ultimate form of acceptance, a candidate state's 'baptism', is collective recognition extended by inter-governmental organizations, above all the UN. Collective non-recognition, conversely, indicates existing states' refusal to legitimize an entity's claim to statehood (Grant 2000: 221).

The brief introductory survey of contested states revealed that they were all excluded from the UN (and previously the League of Nations), but in other respects displayed varying recognition deficits. Based on state practice, several levels of formal recognition can be distinguished; a pretender state could fall into more than one category or move from one to another. *De facto* recognition is omitted from the classification because all contested states experienced some degree of factual recognition.

1. *Titular recognition* refers to the wide formal acceptance of an entity's right or title to statehood, as with Western Sahara and Palestine. The two are, however, severely constrained in translating this conceded right into political reality (and so exercising the domestic rights and duties of fully-fledged states) because of external occupation.
2. *Partial recognition* means that a contested state receives *de jure* recognition from a minority of existing states. Kosovo and Taiwan are current examples.
3. *Paltry recognition* occurs when a contested state is recognized by only a handful of existing states. Manchukuo and Biafra were in this category previously and South Ossetia and Abkhazia are today. The lowest form of paltry recognition is where a contested state gains formal recognition from a single confirmed state that is not its creator or patron state, as happened to the Chechen Republic of Ichkeria.
4. *Patron recognition* indicates that the only confirmed state willing to recognize a contested state is its patron or creator, as in the cases of Northern Cyprus and South Africa's homeland states.
5. *Peer recognition* involves contested states recognizing each other, as did South Africa's four Bantustans (also recognized by South Africa) and the contested states of the former USSR.
6. *Zero recognition* simply means that a contested state is not formally recognized by either confirmed or contested states. This previously applied to Katanga and Rhodesia, more recently to the two Serb republics in Croatia and Bosnia and Herzegovina respectively, and it is the present status of Somaliland.

Despite the inequalities in recognition, it is fitting that the subjects of this investigation are called 'states' because virtually all of them satisfied the four Montevideo requirements. Moreover, they aspired to confirmed statehood and in many ways acted like typical states. It is equally appropriate that their statehood is qualified with the designation 'contested' because of its highly disputed nature and their consequent consignment to the periphery of the world community. As Bull noted, a polity that claims sovereign statehood 'but cannot assert this right in practice, is not a state properly so called' (Bull 1977: 8–9). The term 'contested' state is preferable to two other familiar designations. Non- or unrecognized states imply that the entities concerned received no recognition whatsoever. In practice all the aspirant states mentioned enjoyed *de facto* recognition and several of them even obtained *de jure* recognition. The term *de facto* states is likewise problematic because it does not allow for instances of *de jure* recognition.

## 'Birth Defects' of Contested States

Among the different origins of contested states, it has been established, unilateral secession was the single most common one; 14 of the 26 contested states had secessionist roots. Non-consensual secession is therefore a highly risky road to statehood. In both international law and the practices of states there is, as suggested, a strong presumption against (non-consensual) secession because of its unilateral, state-shattering nature. The original state's role was also critical. Since secession by definition occurred against the wishes of the central state, the move was usually accompanied by violence between the two sides. Hence Crawford's definition of secession as 'the creation of a State by the use or threat of force and without the consent of the former sovereign' (Crawford 1979: 247) (see also the Introduction, 'Definition of Secession'). Even if the break-away attempt could not be stopped, the original state as a rule tried to prevent its illegitimate offspring gaining international recognition and joining the community of confirmed states. In this capacity the original state exercised veto power over the aspirant's status ambitions. Whenever the precursor state persisted in its opposition to the secession of one or more of its regions, Crawford found, break-away bids attracted virtually no foreign support or recognition. Indeed, no new state created since 1945 outside the colonial context has gained membership of the UN in the face of the predecessor state's opposition, with the qualified exception of the former Yugoslav republics. This experience led Crawford to conclude that state practice since World War Two revealed clearly 'the extreme reluctance of states to recognise or accept unilateral secession outside the colonial context' – a practice that has been 'powerfully reinforced' in the post-Cold War era (Crawford 1997: 5, 17–21).

Examples of successful secession – with the separatists eventually prevailing in hostilities (or the national government abandoning its forcible repression of the break-away bid) and receiving *de jure* international recognition of their statehood – are scarce. Over the last 40 years Eritrea and constituent units of the former Yugoslavia managed to do so, while Bangladesh went through a period of contested statehood before advancing to confirmed statehood. Among the numerous unsuccessful attempts at secession are Tibet (China), Kashmir (India), Katanga/Shaba (Congo), Biafra (Nigeria), Karen and Shan States (Burma), Bougainville (Papua New Guinea), Chechnya (Russia), Anjouan (Comoros) (Crawford 1997: 15–16), the Republic of Serb Krajina and Republika Srpska (see Part VI). None of these entities still claim to be independent states.

Up to now we have dealt exclusively with the non-consensual or unilateral form of political secession, the latter defined as 'the formal withdrawal from an established, internationally recognized state by a constituent unit to create a new sovereign state' (Bartkus 1999: 3). There is also a consensual type of secession, where the government and separatists agree to the break-up of the existing state and its replacement with two or more sovereign entities. Because the parties involved consent to partition, international recognition of the new states should be unproblematic. Twentieth-century examples of partition include Norway's detachment from Sweden in 1905, Iceland's separation from Denmark in 1944,

Senegal's departure from the Mali Federation in 1960, Singapore's withdrawal from the Federation of Malaysia in 1965, the so-called velvet divorce between the two former component units of Czechoslovakia in 1993, and Montenegro's withdrawal from the Union of Serbia and Montenegro in 2006 (see Chapters 7, 18 and Part VI). While international law acknowledges both forms of secession (Wheatley 2005: 85–6), their implications for emerging states are profoundly different: one has typically led to contested states and the other usually produced confirmed states. True, international law allows for the recognition of political realities once the independence of a seceding entity is firmly established and in relation to the territory under its effective control (Crawford 1997: 5, 17–21). This is *de facto* recognition, which all contested states enjoyed, but the first prize of collective *de jure* recognition eluded them.

There are several entities whose unilateral proclamations of independent statehood are still being contested internationally: Abkhazia, South Ossetia, Nagorno Karabagh, Transdniestria, Somaliland, Northern Cyprus and Kosovo (see Chapter 9 and Part VI). The last three cases are somewhat unconventional: Somaliland owed its existence to a combination of secession and reversion (to its former status of sovereign statehood); the TRNC seceded from the Republic of Cyprus while the north of the island was under Turkish military occupation; and Kosovo declared itself independent while under *de facto* international trusteeship.

Not all of today's contested states ended up in their status predicament because of unilateral secession from parent states. Taiwan's ongoing contested status flows from it being the last remnant of a Chinese regime that had been overthrown in a communist revolution 60 years ago (see Part VI). While the PRC regards Taiwan as a rebellious province destined to be reunified with the mainland, the island sees itself as the embodiment of the Republic of China and tries to act the part of a fully-fledged state on the world stage. The unilateral declaration of independence that brought the SADR into being was tantamount to an act of self-decolonization. Although Western Sahara's right to statehood is recognized by a large number of states, especially in Africa, its territory is occupied by and integrated into Morocco and the SADR government remains in exile. The self-proclaimed state of Palestine's right to statehood enjoys virtually universal recognition, but the translation of the right into practice is in large measure obstructed by Israel's policies and the support they receive from Israel's allies.

## Conclusion

It is no coincidence that non-consensual secession has been a major source of contested statehood over the last 80 years or so. Confirmed states virtually automatically rejected secession as an illegal and illegitimate act and consequently denied the self-declared states collective recognition. Existing states feared that a permissive approach to unilateral secession could trigger an unstoppable series of violent state fragmentations that will destroy scores of confirmed states and undermine international order. Far from declaring open season on themselves, the existing members of the community of states – operating above all through the UN – have functioned like a mutual protection society.

Whereas earlier secessionist-*cum*-contested states like Katanga and Biafra had short life-spans, most of those presently in this league have been in existence for many more years; consider Nagorno Karabagh, South Ossetia and Transdniestria, as well as Somaliland and Northern Cyprus. As with their predecessors, very few of today's contested states are likely to graduate to confirmed statehood; Kosovo may be the exception that proves the rule. On the whole, then, contested statehood is not an antechamber to confirmed statehood or a finishing school for states-in-waiting.

Despite the risks attached to contested statehood, the current clutch of pretender states will probably not be the last. The repression that scores of ethnic minorities continue to suffer (Hewitt et al. 2007: 14) may 'push' them out of their existing states, while the protection promised by states of their own serve as a powerful 'pull' factor towards separate statehood. In addition to security, the allure of the state as the highest form of political organization also rests on the freedom *à la* self-determination it offers, the socio-economic benefits it can bestow, the psychological sanctuary it promises (a sense of belonging or affiliation), and the opportunity it gives for full participation in world politics (Geldenhuys 2009b: 41–59).

Should a central government wish to prevent state dismemberment through unilateral secession or entice a contested state back into the fold, the key may well lie in undercutting the allure of own statehood for a restive community. This means offering the alienated group the substance of the benefits it seeks in a state of its own – i.e. meaningful autonomy at home and a visible presence abroad – in return for its renunciation of secession and separate statehood. In exceptional cases, where this formula cannot be used for preventive or remedial purposes, international organizations may need to consider guiding the putative state to fully-fledged internationally recognized statehood under the kinds of conditions the UN had applied to Kosovo and the European Community had earlier done with regard to other successor states of former Yugoslavia.

# References

Bartkus, V. (1999), *The Dynamic of Secession* (Cambridge: Cambridge University Press).

Biersteker, T. (2000), 'State, Sovereignty and Territory', in W. Carlsnaes, T. Risse and B.A. Simmons (eds) (2000), *Handbook of International Relations* (London: Sage), 157–76.

Bull, H. (1977), *The Anarchical Society: A Study of Order in World Politics* (London: Macmillan).

Castellino, J. (2000), *International Law and Self-Determination: The Interplay of the Politics of Territorial Possession with Formulations of Post-Colonial 'National' Identity* (The Hague: Martinus Nijhoff).

Crawford, J. (1979), *The Creation of States in International Law* (Oxford: Clarendon Press).

Crawford, J. (1997), 'State Practice and International Law in Relation to Unilateral Secession', *Report to Government of Canada Concerning Unilateral Secession by Quebec*, 19 February 1997, Tamilnation.org. [Online] At http://www.tamilnation.org/selfdetermination/97crawford.htm [accessed 20 July 2007].

Darby, H. et al. (1966), *A Short History of Yugoslavia: From Early Times to 1966* (London: Cambridge University Press).

Dixon, M. (2000), *Textbook on International Law*, 4th edn (London: Blackstone).

Geldenhuys, D. (2009a), *Contested States in World Politics* (Basingstoke: Palgrave Macmillan).

Geldenhuys, D. (2009b), 'The Continuing Allure of Statehood', *Politeia* 28:2, 41–59.

GlobalSecurity.org, 'War and Ethnic Cleansing in Yugoslavia'. [Online] At http://www.globalsecurity.org/milatray/world/war/yugo-hist4.htm [accessed 18 July 2010].

Graney, K. (2004), 'Chechnya', in T. Bahcheli, B. Bartmann and H. Srebnik (eds), *De Facto States: The Quest for Sovereignty* (London: Routledge), 118–42.

Grant, T. (2000), 'Hallstein Revisited: Unilateral Enforcement of Regimes of Nonrecognition since the two Germanies', *Stanford Journal of International Law* 36:2, 221–51.

Hewitt, J. et al. (2007), *Peace and Conflict 2008* (Baltimore, MD: Center for International Development and Conflict Management, University of Maryland).

Jones, F. (1949), *Manchuria since 1931* (London: Royal Institute of International Affairs).

Kalidi, R. (2006), *The Iron Cage: The Story of the Palestinian Struggle for Statehood* (Boston, MA: Beacon Press).

Machover, D. (1995), 'International Humanitarian Law and the Indonesian Occupation of East Timor', in *International Law and the Question of East Timor* (London: Catholic Institute for International Relations).

Pavković, A. (2000), 'Recursive Secessions in Former Yugoslavia: Too Hard a Case for Theories of Secession?', *Political Studies* 48, 485–502.

Selth, A. (1986), 'Race and Resistance in Burma, 1942–1945', *Modern Asian Studies* 20:3, 483–507.

Shaw, M. (2008), *International Law*, 6th edn (Cambridge: Cambridge University Press).

*The World Factbook*, CIA, 'Bosnia and Herzegovina'. [Online] At https://www.cia.gov/library/publications/the-world-factbook/geos/bk.html [accessed 11 August 2010].

Wheatley, S. (2005), *Democracy, Minorities and International Law* (Cambridge: Cambridge University Press).

wordiQ, 'History of Bosnia and Herzegovina – Definition'. [Online] At http://www.wordiq.com/definition/History_of_Bosnia_and_Herzegovina' [accessed 11 August 2010].

# PART IV

# SECESSION: LEGAL PERSPECTIVES

# Introduction to Part IV

The chapters in this part explore a number of important legal issues that arise in the context of the secession of a territorial entity from an existing internationally recognized state.

In Chapter 16 Märta Johanson explores the vexed question of the international borders of the state created as a result of secession. Johanson examines the different functions and effects of internal borders of a state as opposed to its international borders and calls into question the approach of the international community to insisting that the internal borders of a territorial unit become international borders if that unit secedes and becomes a new state. This approach of the international community has been justified as a legitimate adaptation of the principle of *uti possidetis juris* which holds that in the case of decolonization existing colonial borders become international borders. Johanson questions whether this adaptation has evolved into a customary norm of international law and suggests that the question of international borders following secession would best be determined on a case-by-case basis in which negotiations, involving groups affected by the location of borders, be the means of resolving the issue rather than the application of any fixed international law rules.

In Chapter 17 Peter Radan explores the question of whether international law grants any right of secession. Although there is no explicit recognition of any such right in international law, it has been argued by many that an implicit, but limited, right of unilateral secession exists pursuant to the right of peoples to self-determination. Such a right is said to arise if a territorial community within a state is systematically discriminated against. In such circumstances the territorial integrity of the state is no longer protected by international law and the territorial community is entitled to secede. Although the opinion of the International Court of Justice in its 2010 decision relating to the secession of Kosovo did not address the issue, two of the three judges who did so in separate opinions suggested that such a right of secession did and should exist in international law. Such a right, if established, is generally consistent with remedial theories of secession discussed in Chapter 22.

In Chapter 18 Peter Radan examines the jurisprudence of various courts in relation to the existence of a right of secession under a state's constitutional law. Radan's analysis of decisions in the United States of America, the former Yugoslavia and, in particular, Canada, point to a right of secession provided that it is consented to by, first, the population of the territorial entity that seeks to secede and, second, the host state as a whole. In relation to the first, consent is generally established by means of a referendum of the territorial entity. In relation to the second, consent is usually determined by means of the adoption of an appropriate constitutional amendment. However, as Radan points out, even an illegal secession by a territorial entity may be successful if it is recognized by the community of international states.

In Chapter 19 Miodrag Jovanović explores the question of whether a state's constitution should or should not include a provision regulating secession. Jovanović argues that such clauses are consistent with contemporary constitutionalism. He critiques the arguments against such constitutional provisions presented by, in particular, Cass Sunstein and suggests that a constitutional secession clause is justified, not so much on grounds of normative necessity, but rather on grounds of political prudence. He furthermore suggest that the constitutionalization of secession promotes core liberal-democratic values associated with the rule of law, democracy and peaceful co-existence between different groups in multi-cultural states.

In Chapter 20 Tom Grant discusses the issue of state succession in relation to secession. The creation of a new state as the result of secession raises issues of the international rights and obligations of both the new state and of the host state. These include issues of vital concern such as the continuity or dissolution of the host state, succession with respect to treaties entered into by the host state, admission to international and regional organizations, the nationality of the residents of the new state, and currency. As Grant observes, the resolution of many of these issues is as likely to be determined by *ad hoc* agreements, sometimes supervised by international institutions, as opposed to the application of customary rules or law-making treaties of general application.

# Secession and Territorial Borders: The Role of Law

Märta C. Johanson

## The Importance of Borders

Territorial boundaries affect our lives on most levels.[1] We are territorially limited and always within territory where we have varying rights and obligations that follow with the territory, stemming from our physical presence there, for example as visitors, or our legal status, for example as citizens. Territorial boundaries are the markers of division between one territory and another, for example international ones between states, or internal ones between federal or other lower-level internal units. Internal borders vary: some states are divided into federal units with further sub-divisions; other states use varying types of division where the units may be delimited for multiple purposes. Most maps depicting territorial boundaries, whether international or internal, nevertheless fail to reflect the different functions that borders have and risk leaving the casual observer with the impression that borders function more or less similarly – merely delimiting one territory from another. In the same vein, within public international law attention has primarily been given to the issue of the location of borders, rather than to their function and effect on different interests and groups.[2] Regarding territory generally, international law has primarily focused on questions of statehood, title to territory and its delimitation – less on borders *per se*.[3] International boundaries are commonly negotiated, and there are few norms about boundaries binding on states.[4] As it is for states to freely determine the organization and administration of their territory,

---

1   Distinctions are often made between frontiers, borders and boundaries, and the definitions vary. The terms boundary and border will here be applied interchangeably. See e.g. van Houtum (2005).
2   See e.g. Verzijl (1970: 513–621).
3   Some standard international law works on territory are: Jennings (1963); Verzijl (1970); Brownlie (2008: chs 6–8) and Crawford (2006).
4   One of the few norms, the principle of the stability and finality of boundaries, is discussed later in the chapter.

internal borders have been understood to fall within the domestic affairs of states. Secession, however, brings the issue of internal borders onto the international stage, and lawyers have grappled with the change from internal to international borders when groups or units attempt to break away from the larger state and new borders are sought. This chapter aims to discuss the role of law in relation to secession and territorial borders. It will attempt to give an introduction to the purpose, function and effect of borders in order to show why the shift from an internal border to an international one can be destabilizing, even when a pre-existing internal border is transformed into a new international boundary. The assumption that the most stable solution at secession is transforming an existing internal boundary into an international one is examined, and the role of law is discussed.

## Borders, Territory and Law

States are the primary creators, actors and enforcers of international law, and territory has historically been seen by states as a primary interest to be sought after and guarded. The international legal system has little interest in self-destruction, and will necessarily be protective of what it perceives as stability. An example of this is the role that the principle of effectiveness has played in relation to territorial claims, as contested claims of title to territory had to be consolidated by effective territorial jurisdiction. There is understandable reticence among states, and, formerly among empires, to their break-up, and a reasonable inclination towards solutions that seem to be the least territorially destabilizing. Territorial changes have often been the product of violent conflict, or the reason behind it. With regard to retaining most of the prior colonial boundaries at decolonization, the ICJ stated in a well-known dictum:

> *The maintenance of the territorial status quo in Africa is seen as the wisest course, to preserve what has been achieved by peoples who have struggled for their independence, and to avoid a disruption which would deprive the continent of the gains achieved by much sacrifice.*[5]

Though the present borders of most states were different or non-existent only a century ago, there exists a common perception that the extent and borders of states' territory has generally been stable and changed little, as though territorial changes are an aberration rather than a common experience for the majority of present-day states (O'Leary et al. 2001). In the desire to avoid conflict, and territorial changes being associated with high levels of violence, reference is often made to international law in efforts to prohibit undesired occurrences. But while some norms are clearly established, others are less so. Certain norms are simply misunderstood. Under

---

5   *Case Concerning the Frontier Dispute (Burkina Faso and Mali)* [1986] ICJ Rep. 554 at (para. 25).

the UN Charter it was agreed that attacks against other states and annexing their territory was prohibited (UN Charter 1945: Art. 2[4]). The inter-state character of the prohibition against use of force against the territorial integrity of a state has, nonetheless, often gone unnoted; the prohibition has commonly been referred to in support of also keeping a state's internal boundaries unchanged by forces that break up a state.[6]

The area that international law regulates has expanded greatly over the last 60 years, and many issues that were previously considered internal affairs, such as the state's treatment of those within its jurisdiction, are now internationally regulated. The subjects who are bound by international law have also expanded. For example, indigenous peoples are understood to constitute subjects with specific rights often connected to the use of territory, and individuals can be tried under international law for certain crimes. The duty to maintain international peace and security, and the expansion of what are considered threats to such peace and security, have also meant that international involvement in internal conflict – not only inter-state conflict – is based on law. These developments have altered and sometimes muddied vital distinctions: the ambit of international law and the internal affairs of states; why and how the system of international law functions effectively and is upheld, and areas where international regulation will be less useful in gaining compliance; who is bound by international law and what areas of law these subjects are bound by; and, how the norms of international law are created, as distinct from what is political consensus.

If a position or decision by political leaders can be made with reference to supporting law, this is understandably preferable, and lawyers generally support the expansion of law as a stabilizing agent. There has thus been a predisposition towards arguing for more law in a growing number of areas with less attention given to some of the disadvantages and problems this may cause and sometimes little effort in examining whether a rule actually has developed. The motivation for complying with international norms generally seems to be the benefits that states assume that they gain by avoiding conflict and participating in various forms of co-operation. If they recognize their subjection to international law and their duties under the system, they also have access to the rights, such as the right not to be attacked and dismembered by other states. The system of international law thus relies on the self-interest of states – that there is mutual advantage in complying with international norms – and the system would not function in its present form if the threat of force were the primary motivator for compliance. There has been traditional caution in arguing for the existence of rules of international law that states would not wish to follow consistently, as it leads to problems of both compliance and enforcement. This partly explains the heterogenous appearance of international law: areas of immediate mutual benefit and inter-dependence, such as trade and commerce, are often closely regulated and international supervision is accepted, while issues closer to the identity and perceived survival of states, such

---

6    See statements by several states as part of the proceedings of the case concerning the recognition of Kosovo, at http//www.icj-cij.org.

as the scope of use of force and self-defence, are highly contested and there is less consensus on clear rules. Agreement and uniform practice exists to a high degree in the first area, but not in the second.

How is this relevant to territory and secession? If the critical interests of a state are perceived to be at stake, the desire to conform to norms that undermine its existence will very likely be low, and norms may then have less impact on behaviour. If there is no 'inner' willingness to comply because no benefit at all is evident to a state, external force would necessarily have to be used to ensure its compliance. Compliance is thus a challenge because of the nature of the issue. States will understandably not develop a consistent practice that threatens their possibilities to take action in issues that are understood to be of crucial importance to their continuation. They desire flexibility and several options. So in arguing for the existence of a rule of international law in relation to territory, it is of the essence to ascertain whether state practice is consistent and if states uniformly believe they must comply. If not, they will be unlikely to act in accordance with the rule when they are under threat, and the international community would need to be willing to use force to ensure compliance. It should also be remembered that groups within states are not bound by all the norms that bind states; they are primarily bound by humanitarian and criminal law norms. Arguing for the application of rules that ignore their concerns, especially groups who perceive themselves to be under threat, will likely result in low compliance with the norms, the risk that they resort to violence to protect their interests, and the consequent need for international enforcement. If the legitimacy behind a rule is argued to be peace-maintaining character, then its actual history of stabilizing or destabilizing situations would need to be examined. There are thus many reasons for urging caution and thorough research when approaching the existence of rules on territory and borders.

The territorial changes that historically have been of concern and regulated by international law have been between states, where there previously was the highest risk of conflict. The norms concerning territory were developed and applied between entities with similar external characteristics. It is interesting to note, however, that most disputes concerning territory, for example of title and boundary location, have been settled diplomatically by states through negotiations. In cases where disputes have been submitted to courts or arbitration, contextual factors such as geography, ethnicity and economy have been considered when applying the law in the form of agreements, customary law norms and general principles. Context is thus necessarily taken into account. States have thus opted for a variety of tools and considerations in order to reach conclusion. Either agreement to the result has been reached through direct negotiations or the issue has been submitted to adjudication or arbitration.

Contrast this with secession, which concerns other relationships and types of territorial change: between a group or groups, or a territorial unit or units, and the state. While international law has traditionally generated norms for states, the internal structures of states, and relationships between groups within them, are more dissimilar; the internal differences between states are enormous. Understanding the internal workings of a state, for example the impact of its federal structure and the location of these borders on relations between groups, would prove vital when attempting to reduce internal conflict. This should make obvious the difficulty inherent in constructing uniform and inflexible rules appropriate for fulfilling the aim of peace and stability in issues as sensitive as territory, identity and possibly a group's survival. Is it possible or advisable to develop such rules? Different contexts often require a variety of available tools and solutions depending on the actual problem. If states have not restricted themselves to this in their direct relations, it becomes doubtful why it would succeed in even more complex situations involving parties not formally bound by the rules.

In keeping with the desire for the least territorial alterations, and the maintenance of the *status quo* in attempting to avoid violence, it has sometimes been suggested that where the break-up of a state seems inevitable, the best option to promote stability is to use a pre-existing internal boundary as the new international border between the entities. This means retaining the boundary's location, but changing its status from national to international – thus altering its function and effect. To examine whether this could be understood as preserving the *status quo*, the purpose, function and effect of borders, and general characteristics of international and internal borders will be outlined, and the interrelationship between boundary location and functionality will be addressed.

## An Introduction to Borders

Though borders have been studied within several disciplines, perhaps the most in-depth studies of borders have been conducted within political geography (Minghi 1963; Power and Campbell 2010). Borders have also been analysed from other than geographical perspectives, such as their effects on identity and order (Albert, Jacobson and Lapid 2001) and the philosophical and political assumptions underlying their existence and application (Miller and Hashmi 2001).

The characteristics of territorial borders can usefully be analysed from the dimensions of purpose, function and effect. This may help to indicate what the consequences might be of changing a boundary – when changing either its location or its function. Such changes lie at the very heart of secession and are integral to it, as the desire of the group attempting to break away from the larger state is to introduce an international boundary between itself and the host state.

*Purpose* concerns the aim for which a boundary was first delimited. Understanding why a boundary was constructed in the mode and location it was can explain its characteristics, how the boundary might differ from other boundaries, and the impact of developments and change on how it is perceived. African colonial boundaries were agreed upon by European states in order to prevent conflicts between them over African territory. The common 19th-century practice of not requiring actual administration and effective control of the entire claimed territory as evidence for colonial territorial possessions had led to overlapping claims between the European powers and mounting risk of conflict. The colonial borders were therefore constructed to delimit European states' zones of interest for purposes of trade, and were generally not intended to be supervised on the ground or to restrict the movement of the inhabitants. It was never anticipated that the borders would later be used to delimit independent states. Therefore careful delimitation of the borders was commonly considered less important, and little was done to avoid the division of groups, as the borders were thought to have low impact on the local population (Griffiths 1986).

*Function* concerns how the border functions in practice, and how it restricts or permits certain activities. With a few exceptions the African colonial borders were to function on paper between the European parties and, for example, keep foreign traders away. On the ground they were often not demarcated or supervised, and thus easy to pass over physically. This can be contrasted with today entering a foreign country that requires a prior visa, identification documents and restrictions such as transporting currency and addictive substances.

*Effect* is studied from one or several groups' perspectives of how the boundary's function and location practically affects their lives and interests. This will go beyond examining the purpose for which the boundary was constructed, to how the boundary actually affects various groups: these may be impacted differently depending on what the border's function is. Examining a border from the perspective of dissimilar groups may reveal how changing a boundary's location or function may affect groups differently and thus provide a mechanism for reducing tensions between groups within a state.

At the end of World War One political geographers began studying the relation between boundary changes and conflict, suggesting *inter alia* that reducing the function of a boundary might correspondingly reduce tensions (Minghi 1963). The only available solution was thus not changing a border's location, but instead making it more responsive to the needs of those divided, such as by reducing restrictions to movement, thereby facilitating passage and trade (Prescott 1987: 74–5). The most beneficial approach for stable and lasting solutions will depend on what the problems and needs are in a specific situation and context. The decision to retain African colonial boundaries at independence was generally unproblematic because the boundaries, which had generally not been restrictive during colonial times, were kept open to passage and avoided adding hardship to the lives of those they divided.

## International Borders

The purposes of international borders are to separate states and delimit the territorial extent of each state's rights and duties. One of the criteria for statehood is in fact that the entity has a delimited territory (Montevideo 1933: Art. 1). In its own territory each state has the full extent of the rights and duties laid down by international law, and the location of a boundary between states is therefore highly important. Resources are either on one or the other side of the boundary, or may be divided by it, thus providing or denying states access to them. Border location is important for groups and individuals because they are either on one side or the other with attending rights and duties. If the boundary is 'hard' and close to impenetrable, then which side one is on can become vital, as crossing is difficult. Examples are the boundaries between South Korea, North Korea and China. If the boundary is 'soft' or permeable, one's location can more easily be changed and therefore perceived as less problematic, as in the case of the Finnish/Norwegian/Swedish borders, and inner EU borders. International borders can function differently and the effects can vary over time depending on how the boundary is used. Common functions are: delimiting the extent of a state's territory, as the border between Norway/Sweden, and the US/Canadian border; to exclude or protect, as in the case of outer EU borders and the US/Mexican border; to contain, as the North Korean/Chinese border; or to allow for free movement of goods and people, as in the case of inner EU borders. The location of international boundaries is not always the result of a peaceful negotiation: a delimitation may have been the result of war, of colonial administration, or of an imposed decision by other states, as in the borders determined at the Paris Peace Conference 1919–20, and the border between North and South Korea. Borders that have not been freely agreed upon may constitute a source of friction between states because of their location or because their restricted function hinders certain groups' or states' wishes, for example a desire for further trade.

## Internal Borders: Federal and Other

Internal borders involve additional purposes. Sometimes a distinction is made between federal and other internal borders, as federal borders often are the result of negotiations between groups within the state (Prescott 1987: 167 n.26). This is, nonetheless, not always the case: the federal borders of the Socialist Federal Republic of Yugoslavia (SFRY) were not constructed on the basis of negotiations (Johanson 2004). Internal boundaries are less likely to have been negotiated or clearly delimited, thus often lacking clarity (Prescott 1987: 70 n.26). Internal borders have more varied purposes than international borders. They rarely aim to restrict passage, and their actual location is often not physically apparent on the ground, apart from on maps. Internal borders or divisions are often used for diverse administrative and political purposes. The administrative divisions within a state may affect the impact and effect of citizens' votes, their taxation rates, their access to health care, schooling, garbage collection, their vehicle registration and so on. The more decentralized a state is, the greater the impact is also of lower-level administrative borders on individuals.

Federal borders have often been constructed for certain specific purposes. Some federal states are constructed from existing entities using established boundaries, while others are federalized after having been unitary states.[7] The federal borders may serve to unite minority groups into a unit in which they might gain greater

---

7   Some federal states have a mix of these two: prior and newly established borders.

influence. Their inclusion in a federal unit may also strengthen their influence in the greater state through power-sharing and voting rights, serving to satisfy the minority's need for protection or influence against the larger majority. Federal borders may serve to disperse majorities into several units in which they become minorities, and thus are reduced as a threat or as the majority they would constitute in a single constituency. Post-World War Two Yugoslavia illustrated this. Federal borders may serve to separate groups so that the federal units may develop more autonomously, for example in culture and economy, or to allow for projects of nation-building, such as within the Union Republics of the USSR (Carriere d'Encausse 1992). Federal borders are thus often set up in order to allow the greater state to function with less friction in light of different interests within the state: either the interests of various groups, or of individuals. In other words, the purpose with the borders is often to *unite* the state by certain administrative and political divisions in order for it to function better. The object is not to create easily separable units.

## The Interplay between Location and Function

The interplay between the factors of location and functionality has important implications for stability: the functionality that a boundary has can add to or subtract from the perceived importance of its location. The location of an internal border gains greater importance the more functions the boundary has, for example with regard to taxation, local legislation, or political influence for groups. The fewer functions a boundary has the less importance its location is correspondingly perceived to have. Determining therefore what the function of a specific boundary is, and what the effects are on a specific group because of its location (function + location in relation to a/several group/s = its effect) is important in order to understand possible consequences of changing the boundary's location or function. Changing a boundary's function can be as destabilizing as changing its location. Transforming an internal boundary into an international one changes its status, and thereby its function, as it will now perform a different task and thereby have a changed effect on those who are included, excluded or divided, than the former internal boundary previously had. The effect on groups and individuals is changed even though the border remains in the same location. Passage may for example be restricted, visas required and taxes imposed on transported goods.

The implications of transforming an internal boundary into an international one will differ depending on the context. A boundary's function has sometimes been explained as not necessarily deriving from the nature of the line, but from the characteristics of the communities it separates (Minghi 1963: 413). If the boundary forms the delimitation between two friendly states with relatively free passage and few restrictions, the transformation carries with it less implications for those thus divided, apart from citizenship and connected rights and duties. The boundary's primary impact may only be on the relations between states, for example in determining each state's jurisdiction and access to certain attractive resources. If the boundary instead forms the delimitation between two hostile states, which is not uncommon in the aftermath of secession, the boundary may become a barrier to passage, family relations or trade. It may have even more sinister implications: it may be perceived as a boundary that divides or confines groups who feel more affiliated to the state they are now separated from, and who might find it difficult to leave, or perceive themselves to be without future or protection in the new state. Thus, the context surrounding the boundary, and the function and effect that the new boundary is predicted to have, is important for determining how stabilizing or destabilizing retaining the location of a boundary will be in a case of secession. Transforming an internal boundary into an international one should not be understood as retaining the *status quo* in a situation, as the function and, thereby, the effect of the boundary is changed. If searching for a stable solution in a concrete situation, the first question should be what the challenges and perceived problems are in the specific context, and how these can most constructively be responded to. One solution may be to reduce the boundary functions and, thereby, its effects on specific groups. Another may be to negotiate about the location of the boundary in order to try to avoid problematic effects that would arise if its status is changed. The latter option may actually involve less change for groups in issues that are vitally important to them. An example is the claims of First Nations with regard to Quebec's possible secession from Canada: some of them have declared that if Quebec secedes, they would not accept to be part of it but wish to remain in larger Canada (Dallas 1998) (see also Chapter 7). As borders have different roles and impact in varying contexts, the search for stability necessarily involves studying what would benefit stability most in specific contexts.

## The Continuing Relevance of Borders for Stability

One of the reasons why little attention has been paid to border differences is that after the Berlin Wall fell many suggested that globalization would spell the end to territorial borders as an obstacle to movement and exchange. The spread and growth of democracy was expected to reduce the differences between states, and thus the impact of the borders separating them would lessen for groups and individuals. There was also an expectation that ethnic identity would reduce in importance as it was replaced by more cosmopolitan belonging, for example, as 'citizens of the EU'. This lent support to the vision that citizenship and which side of an international border one lived on would no longer make a vital difference and provide the spark that set off violent conflict (Buchanan 2003: 231–2).

When a group attempts to secede from the host state it has been suggested that using the federal boundary as the new international boundary is the option most conducive to long-term stability (Shaw 1996: 388). It has even been understood as a way of retaining the *status quo*, making renegotiations of boundaries unnecessary. When the international community was faced with the tensions within the SFRY and the expressed desire of some of the federal units to secede without the consent of the other republics, the European Community (EC) made a declaration on

Yugoslavia and on guidelines for the recognition of new states arising from its breakup. The EC and its member states agreed to recognize the republics that fulfilled the requirements of the Declaration, which included reference to the requirements for recognition of new states in Eastern Europe and the Soviet Union. One of the requirements listed for recognition was 'respect for the inviolability of all frontiers which can only be changed by peaceful means and by common agreement' (EC Declaration 1992). The frontiers referred to included the federal borders of the USSR and the SFRY (see also Chapters 8 and 17). The 'change' referred to the requirement that common agreement was only of location – not of status or function. The federal republics that desired to leave were given the possibility of recognition as independent states, turning their federal boundaries into international ones, if they fulfilled the requirements listed. There was no requirement upon them to negotiate about the location of the borders with the SFRY or the other republics prior to their acceptance by the international community.[8] Thus the use of the federal borders as new international borders was not a default option if negotiations were unsuccessful; instead, any negotiations about boundary alterations by the entities wishing to become independent states were optional. As the seceding units retained more territory by not entering into boundary negotiations, none of them did. The assumption was that if the guarantees of the rights of ethnic, national and minority groups were upheld and democracy strengthened in the new states, as required by the EC declarations, the location of the new international borders would matter little (Owen 1995: 32–4) (see also Chapter 17).

The question is whether this holds true in all contexts. As described earlier, federal borders have rarely been constructed for the purpose of creating easily separable units. The opposite is often true – that federal borders were delimited for the purpose of functioning within the larger state. Therefore, an important question to ask when boundaries are discussed at secession is how the location of the boundary matters: what was the purpose of a specific federal boundary, how did it function, and what was its effect on different groups within the state? The next question concerns what the effects would be of a change from a specific national to an international border.

There are several examples of the implications of changing internal or federal borders into international ones. When the international border between the Republic of Ireland and the United Kingdom of Great Britain and Northern Ireland was established in 1921 the former Protestant Irish minority became the majority in the province of Northern Ireland (Fraser 1984: 1–67). The division between India and Pakistan, and later, between Pakistan and present Bangladesh, are

---

8   The terminology for the break-up of the SFRY was not secession of republics, but dissolution of the state. This is understandable from the point of view of the few remaining federal republics not continuing as the SFRY, but being required to reapply for membership, e.g. to the UN. From the perspective of what actually took place, the events were clearly secessionist: federal units wished to separate from the larger state and there was not consent by all the republics to their leaving (see Chapter 8).

further examples of shifts from minorities into majorities when internal borders are internationalized.

At the dissolution of the USSR the leaders of its federal units – union republics – (except for those of the Baltic republics, Armenia and Azerbaijan) agreed that the federal borders should constitute the new international borders of independent states (see Chapter 8). The Russian majority of the USSR, who had been minorities in most of the federal units, now became minorities with little protection within newly independent states. They emigrated *en masse*, one of the reasons being nation-building policies of the new states which were often perceived to be discriminatory (Smith et al. 1998). However, the history of relations between the groups, the context of vulnerability and options available for the groups were different than in the SFRY, and the borders were still generally easy to cross.

When post-World War Two Yugoslavia was constructed as a federal state the backdrop was one of fear between ethnic groups, especially between Serbs and Croats. The state was divided into six federal units where Croatians, Slovenians, Macedonians, Montenegrins and Serbs each were a majority in only one of the units (see Chapter 8). In Bosnia and Herzegovina no ethnic group was in majority; the entity instead contained three large ethnic groups: Bosniak Muslims, Croats and Serbs. The largest ethnic group in Yugoslavia, the Serbs, were a majority in one federal unit only, Serbia, and were dispersed as minorities in the other federal units: most importantly, in the Croatian federal unit, and in Bosnia and Herzegovina. This division of the Serbian population allowed the Croats to be part of the state without fearing domination; the division was acceptable to Serb minorities in the units because these groups were still part of the larger state in which their ethnic group constituted a majority (Radan 1999: 144). Decisions on the national level were taken in the Federal Assembly where republics and provinces were represented; in this way ethnic groups were to have equal decision-making. The relations between the ethnic groups were thus stabilized by the organization of the state into federal units with the balance of majority–minority that this entailed.[9] Using the federal borders as the new international ones at the break-up of the SFRY then meant that the majority–minority relations that had existed were transformed. When the Croatian entity declared its independence in 1991, and Bosnia and Herzegovina followed suit in 1992, the Serbian minorities in those two federal units were turned into minorities not in a federal unit with protection within the larger state, but into minorities isolated from their 'mother state'. They were thus vulnerable to the perception that they were enclosed and without protection in newly independent states that they sensed were hostile (see Chapter 8 and Part VI).

---

9   It should also be noted that force was used if there was opposition; a factor that played an important role. However, it also needs to be taken into account that once the unifying force disappeared (Tito died) and nationalist rhetoric was voiced (Serb domination through Milošević, illustrated clearly in 1989 with the removal of Kosovo's autonomous status) the military was no longer loyal to the state but dispersed into ethnic groups (see Chapter 8).

As illustrated, retaining federal boundaries has in some cases provided a stable solution when territorial units gain independence. However, there are important differences between the cases where the application of the boundaries was peaceful and where it was not. There are contextual differences regarding the boundaries' construction, purpose, function and effect on the communities they separate. The communities affected and the relations between them were markedly different; for example the sense of vulnerability of groups differed. There are also differences regarding the procedure leading up to the borders' retention: whether based on the consent of all the parties involved, or lacking such consent. It is thus far from clear that applying federal boundaries as new international borders in cases of secession will provide a stable and peaceful solution in all cases.

## The Background to Retaining Internal Boundaries at Secession

Some have suggested that international law requires the retention of federal boundaries at secession with reference to 'the principle of respect for the territorial *status quo* and, in particular, from the principle of *uti possidetis*'.[10] It has been argued above that the retention of federal boundaries does not seem to bring stability in all cases, but the question here is whether such a rule has nonetheless developed in international law. Rules of international law are created by the will of states, either in express form by treaties or by their practice. The practice involves two requirements: uniformity (*usus*); and that it results from the perception that states have a legal obligation to comply with it (*opinio iuris*). How norms are created has developed with changes in the international community, and is hotly contested. Suffice to say that norms are not created by academic consensus or the practice of courts – these are subsidiary sources (Statute of the ICJ 1945: Art. 38[1][d]).

The point that deserves to be made here is that although the requirement of state practice for the formation of international law norms may seem old-fashioned, positivistic and unresponsive to human needs, in the case of territory it plays a vital role. Substituting negotiations for a rule may involve a huge cost in lives when the stakes and risk of conflict are high. *Usus* and *opinio iuris* constitute evidence of the clear will of states to abide by certain rules. If they are lacking it is perhaps because states desire that a certain practice remain optional and non-binding. In international law it is important to distinguish between the creation of a binding rule and a practice that states often use because they find it beneficial or because they have agreed to do it. This is one of the important points that scholars differ

---

10 Conference on Yugoslavia [Badinter] Arbitration Commission Opinion No. 3, *International Legal Materials* 31, 1499 (1992).

on when it comes to *uti possidetis*: is it an option and useful tool, or is it a rule of international law?[11]

Practically, if retaining the next level internal border is accepted to be an international rule, in a case of secession there will in all likelihood be no negotiation between the parties regarding the location of the new border. Any adjustment would be subject to the good will of the seceding entity, and minority groups contained within would simply be brought along with the secessionists. On the other hand, if there is no rule, then the parties would have to negotiate until they came to an acceptable solution for all groups. Retaining an internal border would be an option requiring the consent of the negotiating parties, which would provide evidence of its general acceptability.

The roots of advocating the use of internal borders as new international borders go back to the independence of the Latin American states from Spain in the early 1800s. In order to avoid foreign and indigenous claims to territory a majority of the leaders of Spanish descent of the various internal colonial units agreed to disregard the traditional requirement of effective control to consolidate claims of title, as they generally could not fulfil this criterion. Instead, they agreed amongst themselves to use the former Spanish administrative divisions as the new divisions of independent states, pending final resolution of the issue. By this they hoped to avoid foreign claims and the risk of costly conflict and have time to prepare for final resolution of the claims (Alvarez 1909: 259–353).

In the wave of decolonization beginning in the 1950s, most leaders of the African independence movements had originally advocated redrawing the African borders, as the colonial borders were generally perceived to be arbitrary and unjust. However, due to the territorial claims of certain states, such as Morocco, and the attempted secession of Katanga from the Congo, in 1964 a majority of the leaders voted in an Organization of African States (OAU) resolution to use the former colonial divisions as the borders of their newly independent states. Most of the colonial divisions had been agreed between European states on the basis of the 1884–85 Berlin Conference, and were thus internationally negotiated. A smaller number of borders adopted had formed internal borders of a colonial territory, and were thus the result of a unilateral decision. All internationally agreed borders were nevertheless not retained at decolonization: units were divided (Ruanda-Urundi); united (French and Spanish Marocco, British and Italian Somaliland, Ethiopia and Eritera); and certain enclaves were integrated in the surrounding state.

The cases of Latin America and Africa concern the birth of new states where units successfully break away. They also concern units separating from a geographically distant colonial state. The adoption of existing internal borders in the case of the units formerly under Spanish administration, and internal and international ones in the case of Africa, was, in both cases, based on agreement of the representatives

---

11  Prof. Brownlie wrote that '[i]t must be emphasized that the principle is by no means mandatory', but found it to be 'good policy', after more than a decade earlier having declared it to be an established principle of general international law (Brownlie 2008: 130).

of the units concerned – not on the basis of complying with an existing legal obligation.

The above cases also need to be distinguished from non-colonial secession, such as in the case of the SFRY, and Serbia and Kosovo, when a group or a smaller entity wishes to leave the larger state without its consent and is located within the larger state.[12] If the secession is successful the new state will be directly adjacent to the 'old' state. Those who agreed amongst themselves in the Latin American and African cases were all leaders of entities who were separating and who were in similar situations – in no case was the geographically separate colonial state involved in the discussions of the borders. Agreements to use existing internal borders were thus based on the agreement of the neighbour. The above cases thus do not provide clear evidence for the development of rules on the continuation of all 'next level' internal borders. As neither the Latin American nor the African cases concerned federal borders, they provide examples of a very different context. The USSR and the Czech and Slovak Republic are two recent cases where federal borders were more or less successfully transformed into international ones, but the implications of the transformation were very different for groups, and the basis in those cases was agreement between the leaders of the federal republics.

The International Court of Justice's (ICJ) decisions in several delimitation cases are unclear enough to be read as supporting the development of international norms despite not fulfilling the traditional requirements of international law. In the 1986 *Frontier Dispute Case* the ICJ stated:

> *The elements of* uti possidetis *were latent in the many declarations made by African leaders in the dawn of independence. These declarations confirmed the maintenance of the territorial status quo at the time of independence, and stated the principle of respect both for the frontiers deriving from international agreements, and for those resulting from mere internal administrative divisions.*[13]

This is equating two inherently different state actions: useful solutions that were adopted in many cases based on agreement, and uniform state practice deriving from an understanding that there is a legal obligation to act thus. In many areas of law the implications of this conflation might not be as grave as with regard to territory. Arguing that *uti possidetis* is a rule of law was intended to defuse conflict, on the assumption that disgruntled parties would accept a negative outcome on the basis of complying with international law. But compliance is often less forthcoming when there is fear for one's survival or core interests. To make the option of negotiations dependent on the willingness of a seceding entity – who

---

12  Perhaps it should be noted that the borders between Serbia and Kosovo were not federal, and the position that federal borders are useful at secession thus is not applicable in the case of Kosovo.

13  *Case Concerning the Frontier Dispute (Burkina Faso and Mali)* [1986] ICJ Rep. 554 at (para. 22).

retains more territory by *not* negotiating – may undermine the possibility of a peaceful resolution.

## International Principles of Stability and Boundaries

The principle of the stability and finality of boundaries should be mentioned in this context as it may be understood to imply that federal borders should not be renegotiated and altered in cases of secession. The principle has nevertheless so far only been applied to boundaries that have been delimited by international treaty and which at least one party claims is correct. It functions to transform a boundary agreed to by treaty into an independent 'fact' that continues to exist even after the treaty has ceased to be binding, unless both states separated by the boundary agree to change it. If neither party desires the continuation of a boundary, the principle of the stability of boundaries has not formed the basis for the continuation of the boundary. The principle thus functions as a kind of estoppel and a method of interpretation with regard to boundary treaties, and does not apply to internal borders within states that have not been the object of international agreement.[14] Thus the principle is silent on whether or not internal borders, especially federal ones, should continue as international ones in cases of secession.

In some cases there has also been made use of something simply called the principle of stability. This should probably not be understood as a clear legal principle, but an articulation of the general aim to preserve international order and stability. The interest of stability was prioritized in the Rann of Kutch case and in the case of several African enclaves during decolonization, where the internationally agreed boundaries were not retained, but the enclaves were instead included in the surrounding independent state (Kaikobad 1996: 20–21, 31–2, 44–7). The 'principle of stability' cannot therefore be used to buttress the retention of borders; on the contrary, it provides the opportunity to ignore them in light of peace and security concerns.

Stability is one of the primary aims of the international legal system and the motivation behind the norms. What promotes stability is nevertheless contested and perhaps the expectations have shifted towards law providing the best solution. The ambit of international law has expanded and more and clearer norms have developed. In this process, the importance of taking context into account for appropriate solutions in complex situations concerning territory should nevertheless not be underestimated, nor the necessity of negotiations.

---

14   Case Concerning the Territorial Dispute (Libya/Chad), ICJ Rep. (1994) 6 at 37; Art. 62 (2) (a) of the Vienna Convention on the Law of Treaties (1969), 1155 *UNTS* 331; The Aegean Sea Continental Shelf case (Greece v. Turkey), ICJ Rep. (1978) 3 at 35–6.

# End Note

Is it in the interest of stability to develop rules that regulate the borders to be adopted in cases of secession? This might not be the best approach to actually reducing internal tensions, as border contexts vary to such a high degree. An absence of uniform state practice may indicate that rules are not seen by states as necessary or desirable; they may prefer negotiations and having several options with regard to borders available. If states have not adopted uniform rules in their own boundary disputes, it is doubtful whether such rules would be constructive in more complex disputes. The basis for retaining internal borders has most often been agreement, there is not convincing evidence of *opinio iuris*, and state practice has not been uniform. This should caution against arguing for the existence of a rule that prior internal borders must be used at independence. When states break up and groups or units attempt secession, contexts will differ to such a high degree that static rules may not respond beneficially to the diverse needs that arise. At secession the *status quo* is changed, and the implications of a boundary change or retention in the specific case needs to be examined. Historical responses have included reducing boundary functions for partitioned groups, or redrawing boundaries in order not to separate groups feeling threatened by partition. The consent of all affected groups needs to be sought for acceptable solutions. This does not mean that international law is silent in cases of attempted or successful secession. Where international rules on the substance matter of borders may be of less utility, rules about negotiations and the involvement of groups in decisions that affect them, as well as general human rights norms, may provide the approach best suited to reduce friction and use of violence.[15]

# References

Albert, M., D. Jacobson and Y. Lapid (eds) (2001), *Identities, Borders, Orders: Rethinking International Relations Theory* (Minneapolis, MN: University of Minnesota Press).

Alvarez, A. (1909), 'Latin America and International Law', *American Journal of International Law* 3:2, 269–353.

Brownlie, I. (2008), *Principles of Public International Law* (Oxford: Oxford University Press).

Buchanan, A. (2003), 'The Making and Unmaking of Boundaries: What Liberalism Has to Say', in A. Buchanan and M. Moore (eds), *States, Nations, and Borders: The Ethics of Making Boundaries* (Cambridge: Cambridge University Press), 231–61.

Carrère d'Encausse, Hélène (1992), *The Great Challenge: Nationalities and the Bolshevik State 1917–1930* (New York: Holmes & Meier).

---

15  Reference re: Secession of Quebec [1998] 2 SCR 217.

Crawford, J. (2006), *The Creation of States in International Law* (Oxford: Clarendon Press).
Dallas, S. (1998), 'Free Quebec? Not If You Ask the Cree', *Business Week*, 9 March, 24–5.
EC Declaration (1992), European Community Declaration on the 'Guidelines on the Recognition of New States in Eastern Europe and in the Soviet Union', *International Legal Materials* 31, 1487.
Fraser, T.G. (1984), *Partition in Ireland, India and Palestine* (London: Macmillan).
Griffiths, I. (1986), 'The Scramble for Africa: Inherited Political Boundaries', *Geographical Journal* 152:2, 204–16.
Jennings, R. (1963), *The Acquisition of Territory in International Law* (Manchester: Manchester University Press).
Johanson, M.C. (2004), 'Self-Determination and Borders: The Obligation to Show Consideration for the Interests of Others', PhD thesis, Åbo Akademi, Åbo.
Kaikobad, K.H. (1996), 'Self-Determination, Territorial Disputes and International Law: An Analysis of UN and State Practice', *Geopolitics and International Boundaries* 1:1, 15–54.
Miller, D. and S. Hashmi (eds) (2001), *Boundaries and Justice: Diverse Ethical Perspectives* (Princeton, NJ: Princeton University Press).
Minghi, J. (1963), 'Boundary Studies in Political Geography', *Annals of the Association of American Geographers (AAAG)* 53:3, 407–28.
Montevideo (1933), *Montevideo Convention on the Rights and Duties of States*, 165 LNTS 19.
O'Leary, B., I. Lustick and T. Callaghy (eds) (2001), *Right-Sizing the State: The Politics of Moving Borders* (Oxford: Oxford University Press).
Owen, D. (1995), *Balkan Odyssey* (London: Harcourt Brace).
Power, M. and D. Campbell (2010), 'The State of Critical Geopolitics', *Political Geography* 29, 243–6.
Prescott, J.R.V. (1987), *Political Frontiers and Boundaries* (London: Unwin Hyman).
Radan, P. (1999), 'Yugoslavia's Internal Borders as International Borders: A Question of Appropriateness', *East European Quarterly* 33:2, 137–55.
Shaw, M. (1996), 'The Heritage of States: The Principle of *Uti Possidetis Juris* Today', *British Year Book of International Law* 66, 333–413.
Smith, G., V. Law, A. Wilson, A. Bohr and E. Allworth (1998), *Nation-building in the Post-Soviet Borderlands: The Politics of National Identities* (Cambridge: Cambridge University Press).
Statute of the ICJ (1945), *Statute of the ICJ*, 59 Stat. 1055, T.S. No. 993.
UN Charter (1945), 59 Stat. 1031, T.S. No. 933.
van Houtum, Henk (2005), 'The Geopolitics of Borders and Boundaries', *Geopolitics* 10:4, 672–9.
Verzijl, J.H.W. (1970), *International Law in Historical Perspective. Part III: State Territory* (Leyden: A.W. Sijthoff).

# International Law and the Right of Unilateral Secession

## Peter Radan

The existence of a legal right to unilateral secession from an existing independent state in international law is a question that has generated considerable debate and disagreement. James Crawford asserts that 'secession is neither legal nor illegal in international law, but a legally neutral act the consequences of which are, or may be regulated internationally' (Crawford 2006: 390). According to his claim 'unilateral secession [does] not involve the exercise of any right conferred by international law' (Crawford 2006: 388). One of the principal bases for denying a right of secession from an independent state lies in the principle of the territorial integrity of states that is embedded in Article 2(4) of the United Nations (UN) Charter. However, other scholars argue that the principle of territorial integrity is not absolute and that a qualified right of secession does exist in international law. Furthermore, such a right is said to stem from the right of peoples to self-determination.

## The Right of Peoples to Self-Determination

The right of peoples to self-determination is recognized as one of the few peremptory and non-derogable norms of international law (*jus cogens*) that applies in favour of all members of the international community (*erga omnes*) (Cassese 1995: 133–40). Thus, common Article 1(1) of the two human rights treaties adopted by the UN General Assembly in December 1966, the International Covenant on Economic, Social, and Cultural Rights and the International Covenant on Civil and Political Rights states:

> *All peoples have the right of self-determination. By virtue of that right they freely determine their political status and freely pursue their economic, social and cultural development.*

Article 1(1) is important for two reasons. First, the reference to the 'right' of self-determination means that the provision deals with a *legal* right, rather than a political principle. Whether self-determination was a legal right or a political principle was somewhat in doubt until 1966 because the UN Charter, in its references to self-determination in Articles 1(2) and 55, refers to a 'principle' of self-determination. Second, Article 1(1) is unambiguously clear to the effect that the right of self-determination of peoples is universal and not confined to colonial peoples.

The two crucial elements of the right to self-determination relate to first, the meaning of 'peoples' and second, how that right can be implemented.

## The Meaning of 'Peoples' in Relation to Self-Determination

The right of self-determination vests in a 'people'. The meaning of 'people' has been a controversial issue ever since the principle of self-determination was set out in the UN Charter. For much of the UN era the prevailing view was that 'people' referred to the population of an independent state or colonial entity. This was of important practical significance in the early post-World War Two decades when the process of decolonization was at its height, in that it helped underpin the principle of *uti possidetis juris* by which former colonial boundaries were generally transformed into international borders of the new states that resulted from decolonization. The principle of *uti possidetis juris* would have been severely tested if the word 'people' included groups defined according to their ethnic or cultural origins, as such groups would have been entitled to seek independent statehood for the territories they occupied irrespective of existing colonial boundaries. The territorial-based definition of peoples also underpinned the widespread opposition of the UN to secession from independent states, because a part of a state's population was not a 'people' and therefore had no right to self-determination (Higgins 1994: 124).

However, the definition of 'people' according to territorial criteria was not universally accepted. Some argued that a textual analysis of the key UN instruments dealing with self-determination led to a definition of 'people' that included groups determined by common ethnic or cultural origins (Radan 2002: 24–68), with the consequence that a state could consist of a number of 'peoples'. Support for this view is also found in the *Quebec Case*, where the Canadian Supreme Court ruled that a 'people' may be constituted by only a portion of the population of an existing state (Quebec Case 1998: 281).

In more recent times, with the process of decolonization almost complete, it appears that a modified form of the territorial-based definition of criteria has been accepted by the international community. This is best exemplified by the secession of republics from the Socialist Federal Republic of Yugoslavia (see Chapter 8). Decisions of the Badinter Commission relating to the secessionist claims of various republics of Yugoslavia clearly rejected the notion that a 'people' was the population of an independent state, but went on to hold that the population of a federal unit of an independent state was a 'people' (Radan 2002:

221). Although this was still a definition based upon territorial criteria, in practical terms it amounted to a definition based upon national, ethnic or cultural origins of the population of Yugoslavia's federal units, as these units were established largely to accommodate the desires of Yugoslavia's multinational or multiethnic population (see also Chapter 16). Thus, although the international community insisted upon self-determination occurring within the boundaries of its federal units, 'Yugoslavia was in reality an act of self-determination by a particular ethnic group' (Musgrave 1997: 124).

## Implementation of the Right to Self-Determination

In various resolutions and declarations the UN General Assembly has consistently stated the manner in which the right to self-determination can be implemented. The first major such statement was its Resolution 1541(XV) adopted in December 1960. This resolution was applicable to the context of decolonization and, in Principle VI, stipulated that non-self-governing territories could reach 'a full measure of self-government by: (a) Emergence as a sovereign independent State; (b) Free association with an independent State; or (c) Integration with an independent State'.

This formulation of the implementation of the right to self-determination was repeated in the important UN General Assembly's Declaration on Principles of International Law Concerning Friendly Relations and Co-operation Among States in Accordance With the Charter of the United Nations (Declaration on Friendly Relations) adopted in October 1970. As its title indicates, the Declaration on Friendly Relations expounds a number of principles relating to friendly relations and co-operation among states, and is thus of universal scope and not confined to the context of decolonization. In relation to 'the principle of equal rights and self-determination of peoples' (Principle 5),[1] the Declaration on Friendly Relations stipulates, in Paragraph 4:

> *The establishment of a sovereign and independent State, the free association or integration with an independent State or the emergence into any other political status freely determined by a people constitute modes of implementing the right of self-determination by that people.*

In referring to the emergence or establishment of sovereign and independent states, it is clear that secession is a means of state creation envisaged by the right of peoples to self-determination. Although the UN and its member states have been generally reluctant to recognize independence through unilateral secession, it has done so on occasion, the most notable example being the case of recognition of the secession of Bangladesh from Pakistan in 1971 (see Part VI and Chapter 13).

---

1 The numbering of Principles and of their paragraphs do not appear in the original text and are inserted here for convenience in relation to the discussion of the Declaration on Friendly Relations.

## Self-Determination and Unilateral Secession

The most important and authoritative international law document that is relevant to self-determination and the existence of a right to unilateral secession is the Declaration on Friendly Relations. In relation to the right of self-determination, the key parts of Principle 5 of the Declaration read as follows:

> *[1] By virtue of the principle of equal rights and self-determination of peoples enshrined in the Charter of the United Nations, all peoples have the right freely to determine, without external interference, their political status and to pursue their economic, social and cultural development, and every State has the duty to respect this right in accordance with the provisions of the Charter ...*
>
> *[5] Every State has a duty to refrain from any forcible action which deprives peoples referred to above in the elaboration of the present principle of their right to self-determination and freedom and independence ...*
>
> *[7] Nothing in the foregoing Paragraphs shall be construed as authorizing or encouraging any action which would dismember or impair, totally or in part, the territorial integrity or political unity of sovereign and independent States conducting themselves in compliance with the principle of equal rights and self-determination of peoples as described above and thus possessed of a government representing the whole people belonging to the territory without distinction as to race, creed or colour.*

In interpreting the wording of Paragraph 7 of Principle 5, it is clear that the territorial integrity of a state is guaranteed if that state conducts itself 'in compliance with the principle of equal rights and self-determination of peoples'. Pursuant to Paragraph 1 of Principle 5, a state's conduct is governed by a principle that requires it to allow 'all peoples' the right to determine freely their political status and pursue their economic, social and cultural development, or what Antonio Cassese refers to as 'equal access to government' (Cassese 1995: 114). Thus, in requiring a state to conduct itself in accordance with the principle of equal rights and self-determination of peoples, Paragraph 7 obliges that state to guarantee equal access to government for all of its peoples, or what is often referred to as internal self-determination (see also Chapter 21). If a state does not so conduct itself, its territorial integrity is not protected by Paragraph 7. By not absolutely assuring a state's territorial integrity, Paragraph 7 implicitly envisages the emergence of a new state or states from an existing state. In other words, Paragraph 7 implicitly sanctions secession in certain circumstances.

The potential impact of Paragraph 7 was confirmed soon after its adoption with the secession of Bangladesh from Pakistan in 1971. An International Commission of Jurists observed, in its 1972 study entitled *The Events in East Pakistan, 1971*, that the right to self-determination and the principle of territorial integrity were conflicting principles, and that Paragraph 7 gave primacy to the principle of territorial integrity. However, the Commission also noted:

> *It is submitted, however, that this principle is subject to the requirement that the government does comply with the principle of equal rights and does represent the whole people without distinction. If one of the constituent peoples of a state is denied equal rights and is discriminated against, it is submitted that their full right of self-determination will revive.* (International Commission of Jurists 1972: 46)

Thus, according to the Commission, if the circumstances are present, as indeed they were in the case of Bangladesh, secession, as the exercise of a people's right to self-determination, is permissible.

The limitation on the scope of the right of secession set out in Paragraph 7 stems from the fact that a state will be seen as honouring its equal access to government obligations if it is 'possessed of a government representing the whole population belonging to the territory *without distinction as to race, creed or colour*' (emphasis added). The only inference that can be drawn from the 'without distinction' provision is that the right to secede is open only to groups defined in terms of 'race, creed or colour'. If that is so, it is critical to determine the meaning of 'race, creed or colour' in order to determine who comes within the range of groups that could possibly have the right to secede pursuant to Paragraph 7.

Cassese gives a very narrow definition of the words 'race, creed or colour'. He claims that 'race' and 'colour' are identical expressions of the concept of race. He also confines 'creed' to 'religious beliefs', and gives a narrow interpretation to 'religious beliefs'. The effect of such a narrow interpretation is that Cassese excludes from the range of groups that are entitled to secede pursuant to Paragraph 7 those that he refers to as '*linguistic* or *national* groups' (Cassese 1995: 112–14).

Whatever one may make of the meaning of the words 'race, creed or colour' in Paragraph 7, it is now likely that the issue is merely academic because of the adoption, in October 1995, by the UN General Assembly, of the Declaration on the Occasion of the Fiftieth Anniversary of the United Nations (Fiftieth Anniversary Declaration). By Article 1, the UN declared that it would, *inter alia*:

> *Continue to reaffirm the right of self-determination of all peoples, taking into account the particular situation of peoples under colonial or other forms of alien domination or foreign occupation, and recognize the right of peoples to take legitimate action in accordance with the Charter of the United Nations to realize their inalienable right of self-determination. This shall not be construed as authorizing or encouraging any action that would dismember or impair, totally or in part, the territorial integrity or political unity of sovereign and independent States conducting themselves in compliance with the principle of equal rights and self-determination of peoples and thus possessed of a Government representing the whole people belonging to the territory without distinction of any kind.*

As can be seen from its wording, Article 1 has similarities to Principle 5, and in particular Paragraph 7, of the Declaration on Friendly Relations. The standard of conduct of states required by Article 1 is expressed in identical terms to that found in Paragraph 7.

The critical difference between Article 1 and Paragraph 7 is the qualification at the end of both provisions. Paragraph 7 speaks in terms of representative government 'without distinction as to race, creed or colour', whereas Article 1 is unlimited in scope, speaking of representative government 'without distinction of any kind'. Whatever the limitations that may have existed by virtue of the last few words of Paragraph 7 on the range of groups entitled to exercise their right of secession, they have now been removed by the terms of Article 1. A group within a state that is the victim of that state's unrepresentative or discriminatory policies has a legal right of secession from that state, provided that such a group is territorially concentrated and can therefore be defined as a 'people' in accordance with the meaning of 'people' discussed above. If a particular state denies equal access to government for any such territorially concentrated group, it is not conducting itself 'in compliance with the principle of equal rights and self-determination of peoples', and thus, its territorial integrity is not absolutely protected by Article 1. In such circumstances such a territorially concentrated group is entitled, pursuant to the right of self-determination of peoples, to secede from that state.

The argument for a legal right of secession set out above, whilst noted by some commentators, has more often than not been downplayed (Radan 2002: 54–5). However, the significance of Paragraph 7 of the Declaration on Friendly Relations and Article of the Fiftieth Anniversary Declaration cannot be denied. In this respect, Antonio Cassese notes as follows:

> [S]ecession is implicitly authorized by the Declaration ... when the central authorities of a sovereign State persistently refuse to grant participatory rights to a religious or racial group, grossly and systematically trample upon their fundamental rights, and deny the possibility of reaching a peaceful settlement within the framework of the State structure ... A racial or religious group may secede – thus exercising the most radical form of external self-determination – once it is clear that all attempts to achieve internal self-determination have failed or are destined to fail. (Cassese 1995: 119–20)

The existence of the implied, but limited, right of secession referred to by writers such as Cassese has been recognized and commented upon in a number of judicial decisions. Thus, in 1998, the Canadian Supreme Court in the *Quebec Case* said:

> [T]he international law right to self-determination only generates, at best, a right to external self-determination in situations of former colonies; where a people is oppressed, as for example under foreign military occupation; or where a definable group is denied meaningful access to government to pursue their political, economic, social and cultural development. In all three situations, the people in question are entitled to a right to external

> *self-determination because they have been denied the ability to exert internally their right to self-determination. (Quebec Case 1998: 287 [emphasis added])*

This right to secession, or external self-determination as the Canadian Supreme Court put it in the *Quebec Case*, is one that can be exercised unilaterally, in the sense that the secessionist group does not need to have the consent of the state from which it seeks to secede. That secession is unilateral is a by-product of the circumstances in which is arises, namely, the discrimination by the state against the relevant group. Such discrimination disqualifies that state from its right to territorial integrity and from any say in whether the secession is permitted.

## Establishing the Right to Secede

If a right to unilateral secession is claimed by a group within a state, the question arises of establishing that such a right exists. At present there is no judicial forum in which such claims can be evaluated and determined, leaving claims to be determined by political and other means, especially the use of force. It has been suggested that an international tribunal – possibly the International Court of Justice – be established or given jurisdiction to determine secession claims. An international tribunal is seen as preferable to the host state's domestic courts having jurisdiction, on the ground that the latter would likely be biased against the group seeking to secede (Buchanan 2004: 359–60; Groarke 2004: 169–71).

## The *Kosovo Advisory Opinion* Case

More recently, the International Court of Justice (ICJ) in its *Kosovo Advisory Opinion* had the opportunity to examine the existence of a right of unilateral secession in international law. Although the ICJ's majority opinion refrained from making a ruling on this question (Kosovo Advisory Opinion 2010: 1432), a number of judges did so in separate opinions.

In the *Kosovo Advisory Opinion* the UN General Assembly sought an advisory opinion from the ICJ on the question of whether 'the unilateral declaration of independence by the Provisional Institutions of Self-Government of Kosovo [proclaimed on 17 February 2008 was] in accordance with international law?'

The ICJ's majority opinion looked at this question in two parts: (i) whether the declaration of independence was in accordance with general principles of international law, and (ii) whether it was in accordance with the special law applying to Kosovo (*lex specialis*) that flowed from Security Council Resolution 1244 in 1999 (SCR 1244) and the institutional and constitutional framework for the administration of Kosovo pursuant to that resolution.

In relation to the first of these two parts the ICJ said that it was asked to decide 'whether or not the applicable international law prohibited the declaration of independence'. In construing the question the ICJ's majority opinion took a technical and legalistic approach, ruling that the question was narrow and specific. It made a distinction between, on the one hand, the proclamation of a declaration of independence and, on the other hand, whether such a proclamation constituted the exercise of a right conferred by international law. In determining that the question put to it by the UN General Assembly raised only the first point and not the second, the majority opinion said:

> [T]he task which the Court is called upon to perform is to determine whether or not the declaration of independence was adopted in violation of international law. The Court is not required by the question ... to take a position on whether international law conferred a positive entitlement on Kosovo unilaterally to declare its independence or, a fortiori, on whether international law generally confers an entitlement on entities situated within a State unilaterally to break away from it. (Kosovo Advisory Opinion 2010: 1425)

It thus logically followed that the Court's ruling was that the question demanded no decision on 'whether or not Kosovo has achieved statehood' nor on the 'legal effects of the recognition of Kosovo by those States which have recognized it as an independent State' nor as to 'whether or not the declaration has led to the creation of a State' (Kosovo Advisory Opinion 2010: 1424). Indeed, the Court repeated on a number of occasions that such issues were not the subject of the Advisory Opinion and that it made no comment on them.

Furthermore, the majority opinion rejected arguments that Kosovo's declaration of independence was illegal on the basis of previous Security Council resolutions relating to Southern Rhodesia, Turkish Northern Cyprus and Republika Srpska that had condemned the declarations of independence by these entities. In this respect the Court's majority said:

> In all of those instances the Security Council was making a determination as regards the concrete situation existing at the time that those declarations of independence were made; the illegality attached to the declarations of independence thus stemmed not from the unilateral character of these declarations as such, but from the fact that they were, or would have been, connected with the unlawful use of force or other egregious violations of norms of general international law, in particular those of a peremptory character (jus cogens). In the context of Kosovo, the Security Council has never taken this position. The exceptional character of the resolutions enumerated above appears to the Court to confirm that no general prohibition against unilateral declarations of independence may be inferred from the practice of the Security Council. (Kosovo Advisory Opinion 2010: 1431)

As to whether the Kosovo Declaration of Independence breached the 'local law' created by and pursuant to SCR 1244, the majority opinion avoided the issue by ruling that the declaration was not made by any of the Provisional Institutions of Self-Government of Kosovo set up pursuant to SCR 1244. Rather, the majority opinion ruled that the declaration was made by the individuals who signed the Declaration and not the Kosovo Assembly (one of the Provisional Institutions of Self-Government of Kosovo) and that, as such, these individuals were not bound by the institutional framework established by SCR 1244. Had it been a declaration proclaimed by the Kosovo Assembly there would have been a violation of the international law set up pursuant to SCR 1244.

Although the majority opinion of the ICJ did not discuss the substantive question of the right of secession in international law, some of its judges did so in separate opinions. Thus, Judge Yusuf, (paragraphs 11–12 and 16 of his separate opinion), observed that there was no right of unilateral secession simply because a racially or ethnically distinct group within a state wished to secede. However, His Excellency went on to say:

> [W]here the State not only denies [such a group] the exercise of their internal right of self-determination (as described above), but also subjects them to discrimination, persecution and egregious violations of human rights or humanitarian law ... the right of peoples to self-determination may support a claim to separate statehood provided it meets the conditions prescribed by international law, in a specific situation, taking into account the historical context. Such conditions may be gleaned from various instruments, including the Declaration on [Friendly Relations] ... [Paragraph 7 of this Declaration] implies that if a State fails to comport itself in accordance with the principle of equal rights and self-determination of peoples, an exceptional situation may arise whereby the ethnically or racially distinct group denied internal self-determination may claim a right of external self-determination or separation from the State which could effectively put into question the State's territorial unity and sovereignty ... All possible remedies for the realization of internal self-determination must be exhausted before the issue is removed from the domestic jurisdiction of the State which had hitherto exercised sovereignty over the territory inhabited by the people making the claim. In this context, the role of the international community, and in particular of the Security Council and the General Assembly, is of paramount importance.

Judge Cancado-Trindade (paragraphs 177–81 of his separate opinion), on the basis of similar reasoning, reached the same conclusion.

On the other hand, in his dissenting opinion, Judge Koroma ruled that there was no right of secession in international law. In support of his contention Judge Koroma (paragraph 22 of his separate opinion) cited that part of Paragraph 7 of the Declaration on Friendly Relations which stipulates:

> Nothing in the foregoing Paragraphs shall be construed as authorizing or encouraging any action which would dismember or impair, totally or in part, the territorial integrity or political unity of sovereign and independent States ...

However, His Excellency omitted the crucial remaining words of Paragraph 7 which stipulate:

> ... conducting themselves in compliance with the principle of equal rights and self-determination of peoples as described above and thus possessed of a government representing the whole people belonging to the territory without distinction as to race, creed or colour.

The failure to take into account the latter part of Paragraph 7 highlights the difference in approaches taken by, on the one hand, Judge Koroma, and on the other hand, Judges Yusuf and Cancado-Trindade, as it was this very part of Paragraph 7 upon which the latter based the existence of a qualified right of unilateral secession.

## Conclusion

Whether the right of peoples to self-determination grants a right of unilateral secession from an existing independent state is still an unresolved issue. It may be that international law is moving slowly towards the recognition of a 'remedial' right of secession along the lines suggested by Judges Yusuf and Cancado-Trindade in *Kosovo Advisory Opinion*.

The current position is perhaps best summarized by Brad Roth who, in the light of analysing Paragraph 7 of the Declaration on Friendly Relation, writes:

> Where a government manifestly fails to 'represent the whole people belonging to a territory without distinction', as by the conduct of ethnic cleansing, the imperatives of 'territorial integrity' and 'political unity' lose their rationale. Arguably, being subject to gross and systematic discrimination reveals a minority group (whether marked by ethnic or other characteristics) to be a 'people' with its own right of self-determination – though no minority group in the non-colonial context has ever been authoritatively declared to be a 'people'. More likely, patterns of extreme discrimination are now seen as justifying the international community – especially collectively, through Security Council action under Chapter VII of the Charter – in derogating from the system's ordinary respect for territorial integrity and political unity. (Roth 2008: 136–7)

# References

Buchanan, A. (2004), *Justice, Legitimacy, and Self-Determination: Moral Foundations for International Law* (New York: Oxford University Press).

Cassese, A. (1995), *Self-Determination of Peoples: A Legal Appraisal* (Cambridge: Cambridge University Press).

Crawford, J. (2006), *The Creation of States in International Law*, 2nd edn (Oxford: Clarendon Press).

Groarke, P. (2004), *Dividing the State: Legitimacy, Secession and the Doctrine of Oppression* (Aldershot: Ashgate).

Higgins, R. (1994), *Problems and Process: International Law and How We Use It* (Oxford: Clarendon Press).

International Commission of Jurists (1972), 'East Pakistan Staff Study', *The Review* 8, 23–62.

Kosovo Advisory Opinion (2010), 'Advisory Opinion, Accordance With International Law of the Unilateral Declaration of Independence in Respect of Kosovo', *International Legal Materials* 49, 1410.

Musgrave, T.D. (1997), *Self-Determination and National Minorities* (Oxford: Clarendon Press).

Quebec Case (1998), *Reference re: Secession of Quebec* [1998] 2 SCR 217.

Radan, P. (2002), *The Break-up of Yugoslavia in International Law* (London: Routledge).

Roth, B.R. (2008), 'State Sovereignty, International Legality and Moral Disagreement', in T. Broude and Y. Shany (eds), *The Shifting Allocation of Authority in International Law* (Oxford: Hart), 123–61.

# Secession in Constitutional Law

## Peter Radan

In 1998 the Canadian Supreme Court observed that the issue of secession raises 'momentous questions that go to the heart of [any] system of constitutional government' (Quebec Secession Reference 1998: 292). However, few state constitutions have explicit provisions governing the issue. Ethiopia in Article 39, Saint Kitts and Nevis in Articles 113–14, and Liechtenstein in Article 4(2) are the only current states that explicitly allow for secession in their constitutions. The constitutions of some states do contain provisions implicitly permitting secession. Thus, Article 3 of Austria's constitution states that changes to the federal territory of Austria can be 'effected by corresponding constitutional laws of the Federation and the State whose territory undergoes change'. Article 6 of Singapore's constitution stipulates that the sovereignty of Singapore can only be surrendered if approved by a two-thirds vote at nationally organized referendum. Notwithstanding that the issue of secession is, according to Sanford Levinson, 'the most fundamental' of constitutional questions (Levinson 2004: 461), it has only occasionally been the subject of judicial analysis, with decisions by the supreme judicial bodies in the United States of America (Radan 2006), Canada (Quebec Secession Reference 1998) and the former Yugoslavia (Radan 2001) being the most important.

An analysis of constitutional texts and judicial pronouncements on secession reveals that consent is the fundamental legitimizing principle that informs the constitutional law rules regulating the process of secession. Secession cannot be legitimate unless there is a manifested willingness on the part of the relevant territorial community of its desire to secede. But such consent is, of itself, insufficient to legitimize secession. The host state must also be willing to allow that territorial community to secede. The necessity of host state consent means that unilateral secession is unconstitutional, a point made by Abraham Lincoln in his address to the American people on 4 February 1861 on the occasion of his inauguration as President of the United States, when he said:

> *It follows from these views that no State upon its own mere motion can lawfully get out of the Union; that resolves and ordinances to that effect are legally void. (Lincoln 1992: 287)*

The judicial decisions, referred to above, of the courts in the United States of America, Canada and the former Yugoslavia have all made rulings consistent with the sentiments expressed by Lincoln.

Constitutional rules regulating the process of secession all reflect the underlying principle of consent. In cases where secession is explicitly provided for in a constitution these rules are set out in the relevant constitution. In cases where there is no explicit constitutional stipulation relating to secession, judicial decisions in a number of states clearly indicate that constitutional amendment procedures are central to its regulation. Invariably constitutional amendment rules and procedures reflect the principle of consent. Although there are variations from state to state in the details of the relevant rules, such variations do not undermine the fact that they all embody the legitimizing principle of consent. On the other hand it must be recognized that many state constitutions contain provisions that explicitly or implicitly prohibit secession. In analysing the topic of constitutional law and secession, this chapter will first, briefly assess the efficacy of constitutional law provisions that prohibit secession. It will then explore the rules and principles upon which secession can be effected in a constitutionally legal manner. This will involve an analysis of principle of consent as it applies to both the territorial entity seeking to secede as well as that of the host state. The final part of the chapter will look at the possibility of an effective, but constitutionally illegal, secession.

## Constitutional Prohibitions on Secession

Before exploring the rules that determine whether the principle of consent has been complied with, there is an important preliminary point that must be dealt with. In many cases the constitutional law of a given state will stipulate that the state cannot be dismembered, thereby prohibiting secession. Such stipulations are found in express provisions that affirm one or more of the concepts of the indivisibility,[1] national unity[2] or territorial integrity[3] of the state. Provisions that impose duties upon a state's citizens, officials or institutions to protect the territorial integrity or unity of the state[4] also impliedly prohibit secession. Furthermore, even in the absence

---

1   Albania, Article 3; Australia, Preamble; Azerbaijan, Articles 5(2) and 11(1); Croatia, Article 1(1); Cyprus, Article 185(1); Estonia, Article 2(1); France, Article 2(1); Italy, Article 5; Laos, Article 1; Nigeria, Preamble and Article 2(1); Russia, Article 4(3); South Africa, Section 41(1)(a); Spain, Article 2; Thailand, Ch. I, Sect. 1; Turkey, Article 3(1); Ukraine, Article 2.
2   Azerbaijan, Article 5(2); India, Preamble; Russia, Articles 4(3), 5(3); South Africa, Section 41(1)(a); Turkey, Article 3(1); Vietnam, Articles 1 and 13(2).
3   Iran, Article 9; Mongolia, Article 4(i); Uganda, Article IV(i); Vietnam, Articles 1 and 13(2).
4   China, Articles 52 and 55(1); Greece, Article 33(2); India, Article 51A(c); Russia, Articles 5(10), 80(2) and 82(1).

of such provisions, the United States Supreme Court has held that the United States is 'an indestructible Union, composed of indestructible States' (Radan 2006).

However, such constitutional stipulations ultimately do not stand in the way of any constitutionally processed secession, simply because such stipulations themselves can be deleted or rendered inoperative by the relevant state's constitutional amendment procedures, thereby clearing the path for a constitutionally legal secession to take place (see also Chapter 19).

## Determining the Will of a Territorial Community to Secede

In cases where secession is to be achieved through a constitutionally legal process, the first step is to determine whether the relevant territorial community wishes to secede. The key mechanism for doing so is that of the referendum, which was described by the Supreme Court of Canada as 'a democratic method of ascertaining the views of the electorate on important political questions' (Quebec Secession Reference 1998: 265).

Express constitutional provisions permitting secession in Ethiopia, Saint Kitts and Nevis, and Liechtenstein all stipulate the referendum as the institutional means to determine the will of the relevant territorial community to secede. Furthermore, the Canadian Supreme Court has referred to the referendum as one way of assessing the will of a Canadian province to secede (Quebec Secession Reference 1998: 264–5). Finally, in the context of the break-up of the Yugoslavia in the early 1990s, the so-called Badinter Arbitration Commission, when offering its opinions as to whether four Yugoslav republics should be recognized as independent states, specifically noted that Slovenia, Croatia and Macedonia all referred to the referendum votes in favour of secession as part of their cases for recognition (Radan 2002: 174, 187, 194). However, in the case of Bosnia and Herzegovina such a referendum had not been held at the time the application for recognition was made. The Badinter Commission's recommendation was against recognition of Bosnia and Herzegovina's independence on the ground that 'the will of the peoples of Bosnia and Herzegovina' on the question of secession and independence had not been established. It was only after a successful referendum vote in favour of independence from Yugoslavia was held that international recognition was extended to Bosnia and Herzegovina (Radan 2002: 186–7). Although writing in the context of the Badinter Commission's recommendation in relation to Bosnia and Herzegovina, Antonio Cassese is undoubtedly correct when he notes that the holding of a referendum has been 'elevated ... to the status of a basic requirement for the legitimation of secession' (Cassese 1995: 272).

In the holding of a referendum a variety of issues arise, the most important of which are:

1. who calls for the referendum to be held;
2. who is entitled to vote;

3. the wording of the referendum question; and,
4. what majority vote must be reached for the referendum to be passed.

## Who Calls for the Referendum to be Held?

In most cases of attempts at secession, the territorial entity seeking independence is a federal unit within a federal state. Less frequently the territorial entity will be constituted by one or more local government units within the host state. In either case there are governmental structures in place which are controlled by secessionist politicians who will use their control over the instruments of power to call for, organize and run what is often referred to as a 'legislative referendum'. In cases where secessionist leaders do not hold political power of this kind, the ability to call for a referendum on secession depends upon whether the relevant political unit enables citizens to initiate what is often referred to as a 'popular referendum'.

In the United States, although a legislative referendum is possible in all of its states, only 24 states allow for the holding of a popular referendum. In relation to the latter relevant state laws set the rules to be complied with for such a referendum to be held. For example, under Alaskan law a popular referendum cannot take place if it proposes something that is clearly unconstitutional. It was on the basis of this rule that, in late 2006, the Supreme Court of Alaska ruled that a popular referendum on the question of whether Alaska should seek a legal path to independence could not proceed (Kohlhaas v Alaska 2006). In coming to its decision the Court relied on the 1869 decision of the Supreme Court of the United States in *Texas v White* which it mistakenly interpreted as authority for the proposition that secession is clearly unconstitutional. The decision in *Texas v White* only renders unilateral secession illegal and leaves it open for constitutionally legal secession to take place (Radan 2006). Thus, the decision in *Texas v White*, was not a basis to conclude that secession was unconstitutional and therefore not a basis upon which the Alaskan Supreme Court could properly rule against the holding of a popular referendum on a possible secession of Alaska from the United States of America.

## Who Is Entitled to Vote?

The overwhelming practice in cases of referendums on secession has been that entitlement to vote in the referendum is based upon residence within the territorial unit seeking independence from the host state. In Liechtenstein, this is explicitly stated in Article 4(2) of its constitution. Such a practice excludes the right to vote to persons born in the territorial unit but living elsewhere in the host state. For example, in Montenegro's referendum on secession in 2006, some 260,000 Montenegrin citizens living in Serbia were not entitled to vote. Montenegro's Law on Referendum, 2001, in Article 8, stipulated that only those citizens who enjoyed voting rights were entitled to vote in the referendum. To enjoy voting rights, a Montenegrin citizen had to be a permanent resident of Montenegro for two years prior to the relevant voting date (Jovanović 2007: 132). This was a matter of significance, for it is likely that the referendum proposal would have failed had the non-resident Montenegrin citizens been allowed to vote (see also Chapter 7). In supporting the residency test on this issue Stephen Tierney has written:

> Through the inclusive liberal nationalist concept of the nation, any process towards the constitutional accommodation of sub-state national society should fully reflect the cultural and ethnic heterogeneity of the territory ... This seems to be a preferable model in terms of a civic vision of nationhood since it is based entirely upon residence and hence upon a notion of political citizenship which does not give credence to any extraneous and highly dubious birthplace or other ethnic criteria. (Tierney 2004: 308)

The problem with Tierney's argument is that, although the residence criterion reflects a civic notion of statehood, the secessionist impulse is, more often than not, driven by a nationalist vision of statehood. This contradiction has been recognized in the case of Ethiopia's constitution where, in Article 39, the right to secession is granted to a 'Nation, Nationality or People' and eligibility to vote depends upon membership of the particular 'Nation, Nationality or People'. Article 39(5) of Ethiopia's constitution defines a 'Nation, Nationality or People' as 'a group of people who have or share large measure of a common culture or similar customs, mutual intelligibility of language, belief in a common or related identities, a common psychological make-up, and who inhabit an identifiable, predominantly contiguous territory'.

## The Wording of the Referendum Question

There is general consensus that the referendum question on secession must, in the words of the Canadian Supreme Court in Quebec Secession Reference, be 'free of ambiguity' (Quebec Secession Reference 1998: 265). This sentiment was echoed by the Russian Constitutional Court in 1995 when it rejected the constitutionality of a secession referendum in Tatarstan, *inter alia*, on the ground that the question was confusing and did not meet 'the requirement of clarity and unambiguousness' (Summers 2007: 276). As argued by Margaret Moore, this requirement of clarity 'is justifiable both in terms of democratic accountability and as a requirement of fairness' (Moore 2000: 247).

Where there are doubts as to whether voters understand that they are being asked to vote on whether the territorial unit on which they live is to become a separate state, the referendum should be viewed as illegitimate. The referendum on secession in Quebec, held in 1995, is an example of a question not clearly worded. In that referendum voters were asked the following question: 'Do you agree that Quebec should become sovereign, after having made a formal offer to Canada for a new Economic and Political Partnership, within the scope of the Bill respecting the Future of Quebec and of the agreement signed on 12 June 1995? YES or NO?'

(Young 1999: 26). It has been shown that a 'Yes' vote in response to this question was not always understood as a vote for independent statehood. This flowed from the confusion over what was meant by the word 'sovereignty' in the referendum question. Between one-quarter and one-third of Quebec voters favouring sovereignty for Quebec believed that it meant that Quebec would remain a province of Canada (McRoberts 1997: 230). The October 1995 question put to Quebec voters is in stark contrast to the question put to the voters of Nevis in August 1998 who were asked: 'Do you approve of the Nevis secession bill and Nevis becoming an independent state separate from St Kitts?' (Stewart 1998). Similarly so in relation to the question put to Montenegro's voters in 2006 when they were asked: 'Do you want the Republic of Montenegro to be an independent state with full international and legal personality?' (Jovanović 2007: 134) (see also Chapter 7).

## The Required Majority for a Successful Referendum

There is a preponderance of opinion that more than a simple majority of votes cast at a referendum on secession is sufficient for the will of the territorial community to be viewed as in favour of creating a new state. This is reflected in the statement of the Canadian Supreme Court in Quebec Secession Reference to the effect that there must be a 'clear expression' of support for independence at the referendum (Quebec Secession Reference 1998: 265). As argued by Margaret Moore, the requirement of more than a simple majority is 'justifiable in terms of establishing procedural barriers against too easy a right to exit that may undermine the very basis of democratic politics' (Moore 2000: 247). Similarly, Paul Groarke notes that 'the idea that the constitutional structure of a state can be changed by a simple majority divests the concept of a constitution of its primary purpose' (Groarke 2004: 183).

In Quebec Secession Reference the Supreme Court expressly declined to define what was meant by a 'clear expression' by the people in the context of a secession referendum in Quebec, on the ground that this was a matter to be determined by the political process (Quebec Secession Reference 1998: 294). In the 1980 and 1995 referendums on Quebec's proposed secession, the Quebec government claimed that a bare majority of votes cast would have been sufficient, a position that was expressly reaffirmed by legislation enacted two years after the Supreme Court's decision. However, such an approach cannot be reconciled with the decision in Quebec Secession Reference. On the other hand, the Canadian federal government has repeatedly rejected the Quebec government's contention. By virtue of the Clarity Act, passed in 2000, the federal government has asserted that unless the federal House of Commons is satisfied that a clear majority of Quebec's eligible voters, and not merely a clear majority of those who actually vote, supports independence, it will not participate in any constitutional negotiations on secession (Radan 2003: 635–6).

In seeking guidance on what sort of majority vote would be needed to amount to a 'clear expression' in favour of secession, it can be noted that in Liechtenstein there is an explicit constitutional provision set out in Article 4(2) that requires a simple majority, not of votes cast, but of the total number citizens who are eligible to vote in the referendum. In Saint Kitts and Nevis, Article 113(2) of its constitution requires a referendum vote in favour of secession of 'not less than two-thirds of all the votes cast on that referendum'. In the failed 1998 secession referendum in Nevis only 61.7 percent of votes cast supported secession from St Kitts and Nevis (Jovanović 2007: 138). In Ethiopia, Article 39(4)(a) of its constitution permits secession in accordance with procedures that require, *inter alia*, a referendum on secession supported by a majority vote. However, both of the above constitutional provisions have a significant hurdle to overcome before a secession referendum can be held. In the case of Nevis, the Nevis Island legislature must vote in favour of secession with a majority of at least two-thirds of all the elected members of its Assembly. Similarly, in the case of Ethiopia a two-thirds vote is required by the relevant legislative council in support of secession. More recently, in the context of Montenegro's secession from Serbia and Montenegro in 2006, Montenegro's referendum legislation required a turnout of at least 50 percent of registered voters and a majority of at least 55 percent of those who voted in favour of independence for the referendum to be successful (Jovanović 2007: 130–32).

Notwithstanding that some form of super-majority in favour of secession is required, the legitimacy of the referendum vote can still be questioned in some cases where a minority group within the territorial unit opposes secession. The problem of these minorities can be illustrated by the following possible scenario involving a future secession referendum in Quebec. On the basis that a super-majority vote in favour of secession is achieved and is thus indicative of a 'clear expression' in favour of secession, would such a result be viewed as legitimate if it were achieved in circumstances in which significant majorities of Quebec's minority populations voted against secession? In other words, what would be the status of a referendum vote in favour of secession achieved on the strength of significant support by the French-speaking population of Quebec, but strongly opposed by the English-speaking and indigenous populations? It could be argued that, having achieved the required super-majority as required by the terms of the Clarity Act, there is a 'clear expression' in favour of secession. The independence referendum held in Bosnia and Herzegovina in 1992 would support this view. As a federal republic within Yugoslavia, Bosnia and Herzegovina's constitution recognized its Muslims, Serbs and Croats as its three constituent peoples. In the independence referendum the Bosnian Muslim and Croat populations overwhelmingly voted in favour of independence. Of the 63.4 percent of the population that voted, 99.4 percent voted in favour of independence. The Serb population's boycott of the referendum was in effect a vote against independence. The referendum result meant that the vote of 62.7 percent of the total electorate of Bosnia and Herzegovina in favour of independence legitimated the secession of that republic notwithstanding the opposition to secession from its significant Serb minority population (Radan 2002: 187).

A possible solution to this problem was proffered during the course of the Yugoslav secessions. In the year preceding the outbreak of war in Yugoslavia in mid-1991, federal authorities attempted to initiate a process of constitutional reform in a desperate effort to preserve the federation. On 17 October 1990, the Yugoslav Presidency submitted to the Federal Assembly a document entitled 'Concept for the Constitutional Structure of Yugoslavia on a Federal Basis'. This document was a draft set of principles for further constitutional reform. Principle 11 of the draft stipulated that, on the basis of a successful referendum, each republic was entitled to leave the federation in accordance with procedures to be set out in the federal constitution. Details of the Presidency's thinking on the actual implementation of a right of secession are found in documents considered, but not adopted, by the Presidency in early March 1991. These documents noted that a successful referendum in any republic required a simple majority of voters to cast their votes in favour of secession. An important qualification on the referendum procedure related to republics with more than one constituent people. In such republics the majority of each people had to vote for secession. If any constituent people did not vote for secession, then areas in which that people was the majority population would remain in Yugoslavia, provided such areas bordered on the remaining part of Yugoslavia. In effect this provided for the possible partition of republics following a secession referendum. Where such partition was to occur, the Federal Assembly was to determine the appropriate territorial division as a precondition to formal legislation validating the secession and partition (Radan 2001: 200–201).

Although these proposals for constitutional reform failed to proceed to implementation, their essence was echoed in Quebec Secession Reference, where the Canadian Supreme Court recognized that Quebec's borders could be an issue for negotiations to be settled following a successful referendum vote (Quebec Secession Reference 1998: 269). Prior to the Court's decision the issue of borders had generated major differences of opinion between the central government, Quebec's aboriginal peoples and Quebec's government. The Canadian government and the James Bay Crees argued that Quebec's present provincial borders would not automatically become international borders following secession. The Quebec government, relying heavily on the break-up of Yugoslavia as a precedent, took the opposite view. However, in the wake of the Supreme Court's decision there is greater recognition in Quebec that its current provincial borders are not sacrosanct and could change in the event of secession taking place. Experts advising the Quebec government in March 2002, suggested that Quebec's borders would be negotiable. Indeed, it is arguable that Quebec's aboriginal communities living in northern Quebec have a right to veto any proposal for a constitutional amendment that allows Quebec to secede within its current provincial borders (Radan 2003). Thus, in relation to the hypothetical scenario involving Quebec, it could be argued that the referendum would be legitimate, but only to the extent that it legitimated the creation of an independent Quebec covering only those regions of the province that voted for independence (see also Chapter 7).

## Granting of Consent by the Host State to Secession

If a territorial entity within the host state has held a successful and legitimate referendum on secession, that will not usually mean that the process of secession has effectively been completed. Such a result could only arise in cases where there is a specific constitutional law provision to that effect, as is the case, for example, in St Kitts and Nevis. The fact that such a provision exists in a state's constitution is also tantamount to the host state consenting to the secession.

In cases where there is no such provision in a state's constitution, the holding of a secession referendum will not of itself bring about secession. However, in the words of the Canadian Supreme Court in Quebec Secession Reference, a clear referendum vote in favour of secession is important because it 'would confer legitimacy on the efforts of the Quebec government to initiate the Constitution's amendment process in order to secede by constitutional means' (Quebec Secession Reference 1998: 265). The political legitimacy that would flow from a referendum that showed a clear desire on the part of the population of a Canadian province to secede would place an obligation on the other provinces and the federal government 'to negotiate constitutional changes to respond to that desire'. These negotiations would need to be conducted in a manner consistent with the principles of federalism, democracy, constitutionalism and the rule of law, and respect for minorities. A refusal by any party to so act would undermine the legitimacy of that party's position and could jeopardize the negotiations as a whole. The negotiations could reach an impasse, in which case, provided they had been conducted in good faith, it would mean, from the perspective of Canada's constitutional law, that the secession of the province would not be permitted because of the absence of a constitutional amendment (Quebec Secession Reference 1998: 265–70).

However, secession facilitated through a host state's constitutional amendment procedures may not be the only way in which the consent of the host state could be achieved. The case of the United States of America can be used to illustrate the point. Although Article V of its constitution would require three-quarters of its states to approve the secession of one of its states by means of a constitutional amendment, it has been argued by Akhil Reed Amar that a national referendum on the matter would also constitute consent of the United States of America as the host state, on the basis that the its constitutional regime is based upon the people's ultimate sovereignty. According to Amar, '[c]onceivably, both Article V amendments and national referenda might ... authorize a wholly lawful and peaceful secession' (Amar 2001: 1115).

## Unconstitutional Secession

In light of the above analysis, if the host state does not consent to the secession of a territorial unit within it, there cannot be a constitutional legal secession. However, this does not necessarily mean that the secession cannot be successful.

In Quebec Secession Reference, the Supreme Court opined that in the event that a Canadian province's attempt to secede was thwarted by a failure of any of the other parties to the negotiations to negotiate in good faith, independence of the province in defiance of the constitutionally ordained process could succeed if the province gained 'effective control of [its] territory and recognition by the international community' (Quebec Secession Reference 1998: 274–5). In such a case secession is not constitutional, but rather, revolutionary.

A similar sentiment was expressed by the Supreme Court of the United States of America in its 1877 decision of *Williams v Bruffy*. In that case, the court discussed the validity of acts 'where a portion of the inhabitants of a country have separated themselves from the parent State and established an independent government'. Speaking for a unanimous court, Field J said:

> *The validity of its acts, both against the parent State and its citizens or subjects, depends entirely upon its ultimate success. If it fail to establish itself permanently, all such acts perish with it. If it succeed, and become recognized, its acts from the commencement of its existence are upheld as those of an independent nation.* (Williams v Bruffy 1877: 186)

## Conclusion

Although the constitutions of states rarely make express provision enabling secession, there is nevertheless a recognition that secession from a state can take place in a constitutionally legal manner. The fundamental principle underpinning a constitutional right of secession is that of consent. The consent of the population of the territorial entity wishing to secede must be established and a referendum with some form of super-majority in favour of secession is the accepted manner of determining that consent. However, such a referendum, in the absence of express provisions in the host state's constitution to the contrary, does not of itself result in a constitutionally legal secession. What is also needed is the consent of the host state. This consent can be achieved if the secession is processed in accordance with the provisions for the amendment of the host state's constitution, or, it can be argued, through a national referendum of the host state's population. If an attempt at secession does not meet these requirements of consent the secession cannot be constitutionally legal. However, such an attempt may be eventually successful if recognized by the international community.

# References

Amar, A.R. (2001), 'Abraham Lincoln and the American Union', *University of Illinois Law Review* (October), 1109–33.

Cassese, A. (1995), *Self-Determination of Peoples: A Legal Appraisal* (Cambridge: Cambridge University Press).

Groarke, P. (2004), *Dividing the State: Legitimacy, Secession and the Doctrine of Oppression* (Aldershot: Ashgate).

Jovanović, M. (2007), *Constitutionalizing Secession in Federalized States: A Procedural Approach* (Utrecht: Eleven).

Kohlhaas v Alaska (2006), *Kohlhaas v Alaska* 147 P 3d 714 (2006).

Levinson, S. (2004), '"Perpetual Union," "Free Love," and Secession: On the Limits of the "Consent of the Governed"', *Tulsa Law Review* 39, 457–83.

Lincoln, A. (1992), *Lincoln Selected Speeches and Writings* (New York: Vintage Books/Library of America).

McRoberts, K. (1997), *Misconceiving Canada: The Struggle for National Unity* (Toronto: Oxford University Press).

Moore, M. (2000), 'The Ethics of Secession and a Normative Theory of Nationalism', *Canadian Journal of Law and Jurisprudence* 13, 225–50.

Quebec Secession Reference (1998), *Reference re: Secession of Quebec* [1998] 2 SCR 217.

Radan, P. (2001), 'Secession and Constitutional Law in the Former Yugoslavia', *University of Tasmania Law Review* 20, 181–204.

Radan, P. (2002), *The Breakup of Yugoslavia and International Law* (London: Routledge).

Radan, P. (2003), 'You Can't Always Get What You Want: The Territorial Scope of an Independent Quebec', *Osgoode Hall Law Journal* 41, 629–63.

Radan, P. (2006), '"An Indestructible Union ... of Indestructible States": The Supreme Court of the United States and Secession', *Legal History* 10, 187–205.

Stewart, E. (1998), 'Nevis Vote Pleases Edgy Ottawa', *The Toronto Star*, 12 August.

Summers, J. (2007), *Peoples and International Law: How Nationalism and Self-Determination Shape a Contemporary Law of Nations* (Leiden: Martinus Nijhoff).

Tierney, S. (2004), *Constitutional Law and National Pluralism* (Oxford: Oxford University Press).

Williams v Bruffy (1877), *Williams v Bruffy*, 96 US 176 (1877).

Young, R.A. (1999), *The Struggle for Quebec: From Referendum to Referendum?* (Montreal and Kingston, ON: McGill-Queen's University Press).

# To Constitutionalize or Not? Secession as *Materiae Constitutionis*

Miodrag A. Jovanović

## Introduction

Secession can be brought up in a conceptual connection with each of the three different themes from constitutional theory and practice – constitutionalism, constitutional law and constitutionalization. In the first case, the emphasis would be on the question whether placing a right to secession in the supreme law of the state would be in line with constitutionalism, as a set of specific liberal and democratic principles and practices. In the second case, the focus would be on the historical cases of constitutionally entrenched secession clauses and/or on the *de lege lata* analysis of the current comparative constitutional law of secession. This survey would not cover only explicit constitutional clauses on secession (for example, Constitution of Ethiopia), but also relevant judicial decisions, which interpret constitutional documents as, in principle, not excluding the possibility of entrenching an exit option (for example, *Secession Reference* of the Supreme Court of Canada). Finally, in the third case, the principal question would be: what is the most appropriate constitutional design of the secession clause (*de lege ferenda*)? This inquiry, first, would have to answer which of the two basic models – substantive or procedural constitutional right to secession – is more preferable. In the next step, it would be necessary to determine a series of practical issues, that is, the definition of a potential holder of a right to secession, the appropriate territorial unit for the exercise of such a right, the problem of the 'recursive secession' of dissenting minorities in a seceding area, the clarity of the referendum question, the eligibility to vote, the majority threshold and so on.

These three research routes are intertwined though. For instance, no *de lege ferenda* inquiry is possible without the reference to the design and operation of the past or already existing constitutional rules on the exit option. On the other hand, constitutionalism itself is not a static concept and its meaning is susceptible to changes with every new wave of constitution drafting (for example in the post-communist European countries) or with certain important decisions of influential constitutional tribunals. Finally, normative arguments advanced in favour of constitutionalization of secession usually largely influence our understanding of the preferable design of the constitutional clause on secession.

This chapter will discuss only the normative problem of under which circumstances, if any, constitutions should adopt the secession clause. This task, however, implies addressing several interrelated issues. The first part of the chapter will briefly tackle the question of whether the substance of the concept of constitutionalism has been modified so as to cope with some new challenges, such as ethno-cultural diversity, self-determination and minority nationalism. In arguing so, the chapter will try to demonstrate that these emerging precepts of constitutionalism open the room for the possible constitutionalization of secession. Nevertheless, even if such a move would not principally contradict the concept of constitutionalism, it still makes sense to ask why any state, let alone a liberal-democratic one,[1] would ever constitutionally consent to the exit option of its constituent part. The second part of the chapter will argue that in exceptional circumstances of a credible secessionist threat, liberal-democratic states would presumably have good reasons to constitutionalize secession. These reasons would stem not so much from *normative necessity* (for example, justice), but rather from *political prudence*. Finally, the third part of the chapter will try to determine which values of liberal-democratic constitutionalism, if any, might be protected in the case of the constitutionalization of secession.

## Constitutionalism and Secession: The Question of Compatibility

In a recent article, Marmor (2007: 69) argues that '[l]iberalism may not have won the global victory that some commentators predicted, but constitutionalism certainly has'. It is noticeable that constitutionalism as a concept is nowadays 'burgeoning and spreading to parts of the world where it was previously unimaginable' (Henkin 1994: 51), which leads some authors to speak of 'the rise of world constitutionalism' (Ackerman 1997: 771). Nevertheless, one should take cautiously these optimistic assertions, because a brief look at comparative constitutional history shows us that it is very hard to conceive of 'a clear cut, unambiguous and undisputed idea of constitutionalism' (Preuss 1996: 24).

However, what the traditional doctrine teaches us is, at least, that not every constitution abides by the *telos* of constitutionalism. In a seminal article from 1962,

---

1  I argue that the constitutionalization of secession would be adequate primarily in countries that can be said to meet the 'minimal liberal-democratic setting' requirement, because a *necessary prerequisite* of this strategy is that in a given polity constitution is not treated as 'a dead letter'. For a fuller account, see Jovanović (2007: 2–10).

Sartori distinguishes between the constitution proper (*garantiste* constitution), nominal and façade (fake) constitution. He says that with the fall of the era of Absolutism 'people began to cast about for a word which would denote the techniques to be used for controlling the exercise of State power', and eventually 'this term turned out to be ... "constitution"' (Sartori 1962: 860). Concerning this specific, historically rooted, ultimate purpose of a constitution, either the very term is used in its *garantiste* meaning, or, as is the case with nominal and fake constitutions, 'it is meaningless (and deceiving) duplicate of terms such as organization, structure, form, pattern, political system, and the like' (Sartori 1962: 863). The question, thus, arises whether constitutionalism, taken this way, is necessarily embedded in the liberal ethos, understood to encompass the following elements:

> ... the atomistic rational agent whose existence and interests are ontologically prior to society; the belief that the ultimate worth of the individual is expressed in terms of political egalitarianism, conceived as negative liberties and formal rights; the separation of public and private spheres and the location of the political within the public; the transcendence of particularity and difference in the name of equality and universality; the endorsement of priority of the right over the good and so on. (Squires 1996: 621)

Even though the birth of the modern concept of constitution has steadily led to the conflation of concepts of liberalism and constitutionalism[2] it seems to me that the answer to this question is rather negative. I subscribe to Graham Walker's argument that '[c]onstitutionalism in its essence is not individual rights but fettered power' (Walker 1997: 164).[3] But, to my mind, it still very much makes sense to call this constitutionalism 'liberal', or more precisely 'liberal-democratic', because the very idea of constraining absolute governmental power is one of fundamental principles of liberal political philosophy. Consequently, Squires's schematic presentation of liberal-democratic constitutionalism remains intact, even when separated from the aforesaid liberal ethos. She argues that this concept comprises two basic elements: rights provisions (safeguarding various rights and liberties) and structural provisions (installing the representative system, separation of powers and so on). While the letter provisions 'limit potential threats *to* democracy through the political process itself', the former 'limit the dangers *of* democracy by expelling certain issues from the political agenda altogether' (Squires 1996: 621 n. 10).

---

2   Walker (1997: 164) points out that '[t]o a remarkable degree, constitutionalism has become an American synonym for *liberal* constitutionalism; the adjective is understood even when omitted'.

3   The different historical routes of Europe and the USA have largely triggered present indeterminacies with respect to the meaning of the concept in the political sphere. Hence, whereas political 'liberalism' in nowadays America has more to do with the European-style social democracy and is as such contrasted to libertarianism or conservativism, the 'liberal' label in Europe is more often used to denote a political ideology that is exactly in stark opposition to social-democratic ideas. See *Economist* (1996: 19).

Initially, the concept of constitutionalism was theoretically formulated as to match the liberal normative ideal of state, created of rational individuals, 'of human beings as Homo sapiens which, independent of culture, religion and tradition are essentially the same and therefore equal'. Put differently, '[t]he idea of a *multi-cultural state is* ... foreign to the basic philosophy of the state of modernity' (Fleiner and Basta Fleiner 2009: 16). In contrast, a number of contemporary scholars argue that it is exactly the 'multicultural'[4] or 'plurinational'[5] character of current states that represents the real challenge to both the general theory of state and constitutional theory.[6] What we have been witnessing in the last several decades around the globe was 'a politics of identity: being true to one's nature or heritage and seeking with others of the same kind public recognition for one's collectivity' (Modood 2007: 2). Consequently, 'the politics of recognition' (Thompson 2006) has gradually entered the realm of constitutionalism, not only in the emerging constitutional democracies (for example, in Eastern Europe), but in well established liberal-democratic orders as well (for example, Canada, Belgium, Great Britain) (see also Chapter 20).

These political developments on the ground are readily recognized in constitutional theory. Tierney argues that, at a deeper level, the constitutional agenda of sub-state nationalism 'represents a theoretical challenge to those conceptual and normative assumptions which underpin a monistic approach to liberalism and to liberal constitutionalism – assumptions which presuppose the existence of only one people or demos within the state'. Furthermore, this form of nationalism within liberal democracies not only 'asks whether a particular state can accommodate constitutionally the sociological reality of its plurinationality', but 'it also queries whether liberalism as an ideology can make the necessary adjustments to account for such deep territorial diversity within the state' (Tierney 2004: 9).

Tully is of the opinion that a contemporary constitution is in need of reconceptualization if it is to recognize cultural diversity. He says that the supreme law of the state 'should be seen as a form of activity, an intercultural dialogue in which the culturally diverse sovereign citizens of contemporary societies negotiate agreements on their forms of association over time in accordance with the three conventions of mutual recognition, consent and cultural continuity' (Tully 1995: 30 n. 21). Proceeding from Taylor's and Walzer's well-known distinction between 'liberalism 1' (classical) and 'liberalism 2' (endorsing 'the politics of difference'), Requejo argues that the second variant adds to traditional elements 'those of the protection and development, in the public and constitutional spheres, of specific

---

4   According to Kymlicka (1995: 1) most countries today, with the possible exemptions of Iceland and the Koreas, 'are culturally diverse'.
5   According to Keating (2001: 26–7) 'plurinationalism' describes 'the coexistence within a political order of more than one national identity, with all the normative claims and implications that this entails'.
6   Tully, for instance, questions whether a modern constitution is able to recognize and accommodate cultural diversity. In his opinion, 'this is one of the most difficult and pressing questions of the political era we are entering at the dawn of the twenty-first century' (Tully 1995: 1).

cultural and political "differences" for distinct national groups living within the same democracy' (Requejo 2001: 161) (see also Chapter 21).

German scholar Denninger suggests that the traditional values of constitutionalism, emanating from the French revolutionary slogans – *liberté, égalité, fraternité* – are today to be supplemented with new, post-modern constitutional paradigms – *security, diversity* and *solidarity* (*Sicherheit, Vielfalt* und *Solidarität*) (Bitzer and Koch 1997; Denninger 2000: 519).[7]

Finally, Fleiner and Basta Fleiner further emphasize the collectivist dimension of the contemporary cultural diversity of states. They argue that different collective entities 'have been united by emotions, culture and history and feel themselves at least subjectively as a community bound together by a common destiny'. What these groups frequently demand is 'their own collective rights and autonomy, and may go so far – invoking natural law right of self-determination – as to strive for secession'. Consequently, 'there is an almost irresolvable tension, with the inherent potential for explosive conflicts, between the state as the rationally chosen and constructed community on the one hand, and other natural communities based on emotional ties on the other' (Fleiner and Basta Fleiner 2009: 20–21).

Does all this imply that the far-reaching request of the politics of recognition – that of a group (collective) right to secede[8] – can also be said to be compatible with this newly emerged concept of constitutionalism? If the new precepts of constitutionalism are indeed multiculturalism, respect for diversity and self-determination,[9] it seems, then, that there is no principal reason why the institutionalized exit option would also not be compatible with this version of constitutionalism. In fact, Keating (2001: 107) notices that, somewhat paradoxically, 'most states have found it easier to countenance secession than to recognize internal pluralism'. Tierney (2004: 96) similarly argues 'that the search for sophisticated models of accommodation within the state may in fact pose a more radical challenge to the state and its constitutional arrangements than secession'. Be that as it may, the question still remains: why would a state, in particular a liberal-democratic one, actually consent to the constitutionalization of secession? This problem is addressed next.

---

7   For a critical examination see Habermas (2000: 522).
8   Buchanan (1991: 75) says that right to secession is 'a right, ascribed to a group, to engage in collective action whose purpose is independence from the existing state, where the coming to be independent includes the taking of territory'.
9   Henkin (1994: 42) also points out that constitutionalism nowadays 'may also imply respect for "self-determination" – the right of "peoples" to choose, change, or *terminate* their political affiliation'.

## Why Constitutionalize Secession?

The issue before us can be approached in a completely reversed way. Then, the question would rather be whether a state, *especially* a liberal-democratic one, would be *morally obliged* to let go a group which presumably does not consider the state 'common' political community anymore? The answer to this question would decisively depend on normative considerations about the ultimate source of political authority. In political philosophy, one may come across several conflicting theories about political obligations, such as *consent, political benefits, fairness* and *natural duty* theories, as well as certain hybrid ones. However, irrespective of the normative standpoint taken, the final answer would at best establish a *moral duty* of the state to allow secession.[10] Still, even if such moral duty is acknowledged, it is highly doubtful whether this in any sense would affect the institutionalization of the corresponding *legal right* of a seceding group through means of constitutional law. In that respect, my inquiry is concentrated on a somewhat different question: would it be *politically prudent* for a liberal-democratic state, faced with the *credible possibility* of secession,[11] to constitutionalize the exit option?[12]

In the debate about the constitutionalization of secession, which was instigated at the beginning of the 1990s, Cass Sunstein was the scholar who most vehemently opposed this strategy.[13] He proceeds from the normative concept of constitution as a specific *precommitment strategy* to a certain course of action, where the central goal of a constitution is 'to ensure the conditions for the peaceful, long-term operation of democracy in the face of often persistent social differences and plurality along religious, ethnic, cultural, and other lines' (Sunstein 2001a: 96). He admits that '[i]t is not clear whether most constitutions ... were originally intended as precommitment strategies' but it is nonetheless 'clear that most good constitutions *function* as such'. More precisely, they 'operate as pragmatic instruments, helping to solve problems that would otherwise be quite serious in the particular nation for which they were designed' (Sunstein 2001b: 350). Despite the fact that secession is one such problem and that it might sometimes be justified as a matter of politics or morality, Sunstein argues that 'constitutions ought not to include a right to secede' (Sunstein 1991: 634). This stance is supported by several arguments why it would not be politically

---

10  For a consent model of political obligation which might imply such a *prima facie* moral duty see Beran (1977: 266). For an argument questioning the existence of any such duty or right see Chapter 25.

11  What may count as 'credible possibility' is a completely contextually bounded, empirical question, which in the last instance should be recognized as such by the political leadership of the state in question.

12  At this point, it is important to stress that, while the very decision of a minimally liberal-democratic state to open the room for secession should be primarily driven by reasons of political prudence, once the exit option has to be institutionalized, both the content and the form of a corresponding instrument need to be designed so as to match the basic principles of liberal-democracy.

13  The most active participants in this debate on the pro-constitutionalization side are Daniel Weinstock (2000, 2001) and Wayne Norman (1998, 2001, 2003, 2006).

prudent to assign the task of coping with secessionist conflict to the supreme law of the state even in the exceptional circumstances of credible secessionist threat.[14] In this part of this chapter, Sunstein's most important arguments are briefly outlined before I attempt to refute them. In this way I will make my own case in favour of the constitutionalization of secession (Jovanović 2007: ch. 1).

## Sunstein: Constitution as Marriage

Sunstein (1991: 649) says that the role of a constitution might be compared to that of marriage, insofar as the political community ought not to be divisible for the simple reason 'of current dissatisfaction, but only in extraordinary circumstances'. Providing an exit option only in exceptional cases, in turn, can 'serve to promote compromise, to encourage people to live together, to lower the stakes during disagreements, and to prevent any particular person from achieving an excessively strong bargaining position.

### *A response: avoiding the impasse of ungovernability*

The analogy that Sunstein draws with family law works directly against his case. More precisely, it works in favour of the argument that constitutionalization of secession might be a politically prudent strategy exactly in 'extraordinary circumstances' of a credible secessionist threat. In the absence of such a right, '[t]he great *dis*analogy between divorce and secession is that the former is within a legal framework … while the latter remains outside of both international law, and the domestic constitutional law of the great majority of states today' (Norman 2001: 91).

The argument I am advancing here is that systematic neglect of the possible rise of secessionist sentiment, particularly amongst a population that is territorially concentrated, might lead the central government into an *impasse of ungovernability*. Although this scenario is less likely in liberal democracies, it is not altogether excluded. Canada, for instance, came to the verge of experiencing such a situation while passively waiting for the 1995 referendum results in Quebec. Had the provincial referendum succeeded, the secessionists would have exactly achieved 'an excessively strong bargaining position'. As Young dramatically reports, '[i]f fewer than 30,000 people had switched to the Yes side, Canada would have been thrown into the deepest political turmoil of its history'. He says that the affirmative referendum vote,

> would have produced an unprecedented level of uncertainty about the future: right across the country, while dollar's value plummeted and interest rates

---

14   'Where strong nationalist passions persist and threaten to infect daily politics if given an explicit constitutional home, a right to secede would be especially damaging to the prospects for democratic government' (Sunstein 2001a: 105).

*rose sharply, Canadians would not have known whether trade with Quebec would continue, whether the North American Free Trade Agreement would still apply to Canada, what currency they would be using in twelve months, or even whether Canada would continue to exist. (Young 1998: 11)*

After the tight referendum result, and before the Canadian Supreme Court issued its famous opinion on secession in 1998, a number of scholars repeated that the Government of Canada had to attempt to cope with the consequences of possible secession simply because 'failing to do so would be morally and politically irresponsible. Governments may wish for the best, but they have an obligation to prepare themselves for the worst' (Monahan and Bryant 1996: 4). Put differently, 'like homeowners who purchase fire insurance even though they believe the risk of fire may be remote, prudent Canadians should contemplate the possibility of the dismemberment of their country in the hope of containing the calamity and rebuilding a new country if the worst should come to pass' (Monahan and Bryant 1996: 6).

Liberal-democratic states might utilize various means, even coercive ones, before reaching the 'terminal phase' of the governing process. However, at some point in time it becomes prudent to try to control the eruptive secessionist politics by providing a legal path for the exercise of the exit option. Take, for example, the case of the United Kingdom and Northern Ireland. After decades of relying on repressive measures to suppress the secessionist (irredentist) movement, the UK government eventually enabled the Secretary of State for Northern Ireland, under the *Northern Ireland Act 1998*, to issue an order directing the holding of a referendum if 'it appears likely to him that a majority of those voting would express a wish that Northern Ireland should cease to be part of the United Kingdom and form part of a united Ireland' (*Northern Ireland Act 1998*). I believe that avoiding the impasse of ungovernability was precisely the major incentive for this move.

## Sunstein: Constitutionalizing Secession Leads to an Undesirable Strategic Behaviour

Sunstein says that '[a] decision to stigmatize divorce or to make it available only under certain conditions ... may lead to happier as well as more stable marriages' (Sunstein 2001a: 102). A constitutional right to secession would, on the other hand, produce just the opposite effects, insofar as it would

> *increase the risks of ethnic and factional struggle; reduce the prospects of compromise and deliberation in government; raise dramatically the stakes of day-to-day political decisions; introduce irrelevant and illegitimate considerations into those decisions; create dangers of blackmail, strategic behavior, and exploitation; and, most generally, endanger the prospects for long-term self-governance. (Sunstein 1991: 634)*

## A response: enhancing political stability

When summarized, Sunstein's argument implies that potential secessionists would be tempted to use the threat of secession as a strategic tool of their everyday politics (blackmail threat), while the state, that is, the majority population, faced with the possibility of disintegration, would, in response, thwart every request for a territorially-based self-government unit (threat of oppression) (Weinstock 2001: 195). However, it is precisely the unregulated state of affairs, common for the vast majority of present constitutions, which makes the costs of raising secessionist threats quite low. Since no sanction is attached to the making of such threats, they could be freely used in everyday politics, even for gaining advantages on some unrelated policy debates. Dion notices that in Canada, in the recent past, politicians in various provinces 'have brandished the threat of secession' in relation to such issues 'as a budget deficit, a budget surplus, a scholarship program, health care funding, dwindling salmon stocks, ratification of the Kyoto Protocol, and so on' (Dion 2003). In such a situation, Weinstock argues, 'there are no limits on the frequency with which the threats are made' (Weinstock 2001: 188).

Furthermore, those who hold that the mere introduction of a constitutional right to secession would promptly endanger the stability of the state tend to exaggerate the power that legal norms might have 'in generating motivation *de novo*'. This argument rests on the assumption that 'once we have decided that there are reasons for a legal system to grant a right, it will simply state, without further qualification, that the right exists'. Naturally, 'such a coarse instrument as the simple recognition of a right can have quite disastrous consequences'. This is why Weinstock eventually calls for the 'judicious formulation of the procedure which must be followed to avail oneself to the right' (Weinstock 2001: 196). Such a procedure might eventually 'remove some of the incentives which are presented to political actors in an unregulated state' (Weinstock 2001: 188).

It might have been expected that, after the close referendum loss in 1995, and the subsequent recognition of 'a quasi-constitutional right to secession' (Weinstock 2001), the secessionist movement in Quebec would accelerate its activities towards independence. However, judging from the present point in time, things have gone in the opposite direction, and one can conclude that the secession issue does not dominate the everyday politics of this province. It turned out that 'a significant percentage of people who would prefer to live in an independent Quebec would rather not have the province go through another bruising referendum' (Norman 2003: 233 n. 34). Consequently, even a half-institutionalized exit option, such as the one provided in the Supreme Court's *Secession Reference* and the subsequent contradicting legislation of the central state and the province (see Chapters 7 and 18), can help normalize the political situation and take the issue off the agenda of everyday politics.[15] On the other hand, when a secession clause is there and it is not

---

15   Naturally, one such clause might eventually trigger actual secession, if it was unwillingly constitutionalized in the last minute, after a dragging period of political conflicts over the future design of the common state. This was exactly the outcome in the case of Serbia and Montenegro. See Jovanović (2008: 133) and Chapter 7.

used, then this 'can come to be seen as evidence that the state is united by consent and not force' (Norman 2001: 90).

## Sunstein: Negotiated Agreement Is Preferred to a Constitutional Right to Secession

Sunstein argues that if the right to secede is justified as a remedy for historical wrongdoings suffered by a sub-state group, then the same objective might be promoted through other means, such as federalism, checks and balances, entrenchment of civil rights and liberties, and judicial review. If the ultimate goal of a sub-state group's protection is unattainable through the mentioned measures, then the preferred solution is again not the constitutionalization of secession, but a negotiated agreement or even a right of revolution (Sunstein 1991: 635).

*A response: excluding decisive interference of international actors*
It is clear that there can be two types of negotiated agreements between the central state and secessionists.[16] The first one would concern the agreement negotiated by local actors only, whereas the second one would imply the substantial involvement of international actors as well. As for the first type, if a constitutional clause on secession is understood, as it should be, as an *agreeing*, on the part of a state, to the possibility that some territorially concentrated group can constitute itself in the future as a separate state, provided that certain constitutionally stipulated conditions are met, it is unclear how this sort of constitutional agreement would be any different and/or less desirable than the one proposed by Sunstein. In other words, it is unclear in what way would the *content* of Sunstein's 'negotiated agreement' be distinctive and different from a constitutional right to secession, for it would certainly have to contain the very same issues as a putative constitutional clause, such as the bearer of the right to secession, the borders of a seceding territory, the post-secession relationship between a new state and a former central state, division of assets and so on (Norman 2001: 91). Furthermore, unlike a constitutional right to secession, some *ad hoc* political agreement between the government and secessionists would not necessarily legitimize the exit option at the level of the state as a whole and it might easily end up as a nontransparent bargaining between involved political elites. In conclusion, if this is the type of 'negotiated agreement' Sunstein has in mind, then, first, its content would hardly be any different from the one of a constitutional clause on secession (and yet, 'negotiated agreement' would contradict an unamended constitutional order), and, second, its form would certainly be less commendable than a constitutional clause, insofar as it would

---

16  I will not discuss 'a right of revolution', because it is *prima facie* clear that a peaceful solution to the secession crisis is, from the standpoint of liberal-democratic values, more preferable than the one involving violent means.

most likely violate certain fundamental liberal-democratic principles, such as accountability, transparency and legitimacy.[17]

If Sunstein argues in favour of the second type of 'negotiated agreement', then this potentially implies an excessive and critical involvement of international actors. Horowitz says: 'Whether and when a secessionist movement will emerge is determined mainly by domestic politics, by the relations of groups and regions within the state'. However, whether secessionists will be able to achieve their ultimate objective 'is determined largely by international politics, by the balance of interests and forces that extend beyond the state' (Horowitz 1985: 230). I proceed from the basic assumption that any state would prefer to take more rather than less control over its own internal affairs, and that states, after all, still assume the primary responsibility for the overall well-being of their citizens. In that respect, I argue that one of the prudential reasons to constitutionalize secession would consist in preventing the decisive interference of various international actors.

Why is an international involvement considered a menace? Simply put, even staunch propagators of international regulation of secession disputes, such as Buchanan, have to admit that '[e]xisting international law regarding secession is dangerously flawed' (Buchanan 2006: 139). According to Doering (2003: 4) the present practice of international law concerning recognition of secession resembles a 'game of lottery', because 'power, not rights decide the issue'. The story of the break-up of the former Yugoslavia, as well recent cases of Kosovo and South Ossetia and Abkhazia, clearly demonstrate this point.

By mentioning these cases, I do not imply that the same scenario would be repeated in the context of more stable liberal democracies. However, instead of a negotiated agreement, which might be a result of international power politics, a constitutionalized exit option might eventually influence a more principled stance of international actors toward recognition policy. The Canadian Supreme Court reminds all the relevant actors of a putative secession procedure that 'a failure of the duty to undertake negotiations and pursue them according to constitutional principles may undermine that government's claim to legitimacy', and that is 'generally a precondition for recognition by the international community' (*Reference*

---

17  Take the example of the so-called 'velvet divorce' of the Czech and Slovak Federation. Even though it was 'sustainable', 'mutually accepted' and maybe rational, as well, it clearly suffered from liberal-democratic 'deficits'. Namely, this state was dissolved in 1992 by mutual consent of the ruling political elites, but without the direct participation of people in either of the two emerging republics. Liberal principles were violated, insofar as party representatives and officials acted outside of the given constitutional framework since no particular provision on dissolution of the country was embodied in the highest legal document of the federation. Therefore, even though the required constitutional majority of three-fifths was accomplished, the substance of the enacted law was unconstitutional. Furthermore, democratic principles were vitiated as well, insofar as the political agreement suffered from a lack of clear voting procedure, with the majority in favour of separation. Moreover, public polls, conducted at the time, clearly indicated that the percentage of those wanting a split had never exceeded 50 percent in either republic (Hartl 2003: 40) (See also Part VI, 'Peaceful Secessions').

*re Secession of Quebec* 1998: 217 para. 103). Consequently, by constitutionalizing secession, states, and liberal-democratic ones in particular, leave international actors with no other choice than to merely confer recognition to an entity, which gained independence through a legitimate constitutional procedure, because it would be absurd for any other state to act differently from the parent state which consented to secession of a part of its territory (Shaw 2003: 250). And *vice versa*, in the case of a failed secession attempt, a secessionist movement could no longer seek extra-recognitional grounds beyond the accepted constitutional rules of the game.

## Constitutionalization of Secession and Liberal-Democratic Values

When Squires's schematic presentation of constitutionalism is taken into account, a constitutional right to secession would be a tool of *hybrid* nature, insofar as it has the potential of influencing the structural elements of a state's organization, while at the same time defining, as precisely as possible, the conditions under which the exit option might be exercised by a qualified collective right-holder. The separate issue, however, is which values of liberal-democratic constitutionalism, if any, might be protected in the case of the constitutionalization of secession. I would like to argue that there are at least three such values: The Rule of Law Value, The Extension of Democratic Rights Value, and The Peace Among Communities Value. I will briefly discuss each one of them.

### The Rule of Law Value

The history of secession crises is a history of turbulence, insecurity and violence (Jovanović 2007: 49–64). That is why even today secession conflicts are commonly associated with the use of violent means. As Tomuschat (1993: 18) puts it: 'Secession is an explosive issue. It should not be dealt with only in an ad hoc manner, when an actual need arises, but some forward-planning should take place'. Constitutionalization of secession can prove to be that institutional measure that would successfully prevent a potentially volatile situation from turning into open bloodshed. Mancini (2008: 580), in that respect, notices that there is 'one strong argument – perhaps the only argument – in favor of constitutionalizing the right to secede: the choice to subject an extremely delicate process, typified by a very high level of emotionality – and often irrationality – to rules of democratic logic.' I would go a step further and subscribe to Norman's (2001: 91) argument that such a move 'would ensure that there was never a break with the rule of law'.

More precisely, a constitutionalized secession procedure would promote *legal certainty*, as the vital part of the rule of law concept. Zippelius argues that legal certainty implies two interconnected, and yet distinctive elements: (a) predictability of rights and duties determined by legal norms (*certitudo*) and (b) certainty that these legal norms will be enforced (*securitas*).[18] As for the first element, a well-crafted constitutional clause on secession 'would regulate a form of politics by specifying clear criteria for success and failure'. In that respect, it would have a similar purpose as constitutional rules on elections and the amending procedures (Norman 1998: 48). As for the second element, once the central state (majority) expressed its willingness to incorporate an exit option into the highest legal document, there is every reason to expect that this clause would eventually be enforced. And, *vice versa*, once secessionists consented to legitimize its cause at the level of the state as a whole, there is every reason to expect that they will follow the established constitutional procedure. Consequently, constitutionalization of secession may not only 'minimise the risk of violence, but beyond that it can be thought of as an almost intrinsically worthy aim in a constitutional democracy' (Norman 2001: 91).

## The Extension of Democratic Rights Value

Is advocating secession as a legitimate political platform recognized as such in liberal democracies? From all we know from contemporary comparative politics, the answer to this question has to be positive.[19] In the Flemish part of Belgium, for instance, political parties, such as Vlaams Belang or the New Flemish Alliance openly agitate for an independent Flanders. A similar situation can be found in the Canadian Francophone province of Quebec, where Parti Québécois or Bloc Québécois call for the independent statehood of this federal unit (see Chapter 7). The provincial government of the Basque country has recently enacted legislation (Law 9/2008) which mandates 'convening and regulating a popular consultation for the purpose of ascertaining public opinion in Autonomous Community of the Basque Country on commencing negotiations for achieving peace and political normalisation'. This move was widely identified as the preparation of a quasi-referendum on the possible secession from Spain, and the Constitutional Court eventually struck down this document as unconstitutional (for the Basque country see Part VI). Finally, the Scottish Nationalist Party (SNP) is the largest party in the Scottish Parliament, and it is running a minority administration in the Scottish Government. The SNP is to propose a Scottish referendum on secession in the future (for Scotland see Part VI).

Taking all this into account, one may find 'the difficulty of fixing an arbitrary stopping point for the legality of secessionist politics'. In other words, 'if it is permissible to advocate secession, to form parties with secessionist platforms, to have those parties form provincial governments', why should the right to secession itself not be legalized as well (Norman 2003: 207)? Liberal-democratic

---

18  Zippelius (2007: 123–4) uses terms *Orientirungssicherheit* and *Realisirungsgewißheit*.
19  The list of active secessionist movements around the globe can be found at http://en.wikipedia.org/wiki/List_of_active_autonomist_and_secessionist_movements.

constitutionalism codifies the democratic 'rules of the game', inasmuch as it defines who can vote and on which issues (Bellamy and Castiglione 1997: 595). Consequently, if secessionists already exercise some fundamental democratic rights, such as the rights to organize, politically compete and freely use secessionist rhetoric, then putting the exit option on the menu of the voting agenda would represent nothing more than the extension of already recognized democratic liberties.

## The Peace among Communities Value

Unlike in the era of the classical liberal state, the underlying 'constitutional identity' of the contemporary state has to be understood as a complex 'interplay between identity and diversity' (Rosenfeld 1994: 7), between individuals and collectives, and between a majority and minority/minorities. Ethno-cultural collectives have gradually become recognized as legitimate constitutional subjects. Hence, 'if states with multicultural societies want to hold themselves together they cannot … restrict themselves to the pursuit of freedom as the highest political goal'. In addition, 'peace between ethnic communities must be an equally important state goal' (Fleiner and Basta Fleiner 2009: 526).

Does this constitutional goal necessitate the adoption of a constitutional right to secession? The straightforward answer is no. As already indicated, a constitutional exit option can hardly be justified as directly stemming from ethno-cultural justice. As Norman observes: 'I am not arguing that a just multinational federal constitution *must* contain a secession clause but only that such a clause is potentially beneficial in a number of ways that matter in multinational democracies' (Norman 2003: 227). That is, its introduction into the constitutional order of a state remains not more than *one possible strategy* for the realization of the discussed constitutional value.

One context in which the institutionalization of secession might help in inducing peaceful relations between major communities concerns the substantial constitutional refounding of a state (Norman 2006: 210). Buchanan points out that, when, for instance, 'a new political entity is being created out of two or more independent or semi-independent entities, including a right to exit in the constitution may be necessary as an inducement to join the new union'. In the situation when it is not certain 'as to how a new union will work, constitutional recognition of a "bail out" option may be necessary to get the new union going'. This was exactly the case in Ethiopia, where, in April 1993, Buchanan personally advised the Transitional Government to reconsider the introduction of a right to secession in the new constitution, but 'to hedge' it, if they chose to do that (Buchanan 2007: n. 6). A similar example can also be found in more stable liberal democracies. For instance, the clause on the possible secession of Northern Ireland from the United Kingdom and its unification with the Republic of Ireland was introduced precisely as a part of the comprehensive peace settlement (*The Good Friday Agreement*) between the two major communities – Catholics and Protestants (Thompson 1998/99). Finally, after a three-decade-long procedure of internal secession of the canton of Jura, which instigated some serious conflicts rooted in membership in different linguistic and religious communities, the Swiss constitutional drafters decided to introduce Article 53, which 'could arguably be used in the event of a major crisis also for external secession' (Fleiner and Basta Fleiner 2009: 555).

## A Concluding Note

President Abraham Lincoln's (1955: 252) saying that '[p]erpetuity is implied, if not expressed, in the fundamental law of all national governments' might be taken as a credo of the traditional constitutionalist doctrine. It seems that the era dominated by this slogan is behind us. In fact, one may reasonably argue that the era of 'perpetual' states never actually existed.[20] In the contemporary political philosophy it is widely acknowledged that '[i]n liberal democracies the right of a people to political self-governance, including the right to secession, is so deeply embedded that it cannot be easily overridden' (Nielsen 1998: 253).

Those opposing the constitutionalization of secession, hence, believe that the debate should focus on the real question, that is, 'whether a constitutional right to secede would significantly increase the level of secession activity, or whether a constitutional ban on secession would significantly decrease the level of such activity' (Sunstein 2001b: 353–4). Constitutions do rarely resort to the explicit prohibition of secession, relying instead on the well-known clauses on 'territorial integrity', 'indivisibility of state' or 'state unity'. It is obvious that these implicit prohibition clauses have never been capable of decreasing secessionist activities in certain states, including the liberal-democratic ones. Does this, then, imply that the constitutionalization of secession might produce the opposite effect or, quite the contrary, that it would even decrease secessionist activities? Neither of these conclusions can be drawn with certainty. In fact, 'whether secessionist politics would be more likely to be *fuelled* or *choked* by "legalising" secession ... is a question for political psychology and sociology' (Norman 2001: 87). In polities that are not seriously exposed to secessionist pressures, the constitutionalization of secession might prove to be a fuelling mechanism, whereas in those states that face the credible possibility of secession, such a rule might function as a choking mechanism.

It seems, thus, that once it is demonstrated that the entrenchment of a secession clause in the constitutional order of the state is, in principle, compatible with liberal-democratic constitutionalism, the discussion turns to the problem of the right timing for drafting such a clause. On the one hand, the longer a constitutional right to secession exists within the legal system, the more it would appear to be one of the legitimate rules of democratic politics in that state (Norman 1998: 58). On the other

---

20  Problematizing this saying of Lincoln's, Lindsay and Wellman (2003: 114) ask '[w]ould he really want to suggest that the American Colonies were unjustified in seceding from the British, for instance?'

hand, one's capacity for explaining the right timing for drafting constitutional rules on secession is in inverse proportion to one's capacity for explaining the timing of secession. Although the lack of knowledge about prospective secession crises may affect the timely decision on the constitutionalization of secession, one should certainly follow the general rule – 'the time to entrench a secessionist provision is probably when secession seems at most a distant possibility, rather than an imminent threat (Weinstock 2001: 198). Only then would the constitutionalization of secession not only be a prudential step, but it would even serve the aforementioned values of the contemporary concept of constitutionalism.

# References

Ackerman, B. (1997), 'The Rise of World Constitutionalism', *Virginia Law Review* 83:4.
Bellamy, R. and D. Castiglione (1997), 'Constitutionalism and Democracy: Political Theory and the American Constitution', *British Journal of Political Science* 27:4.
Beran, H. (1977), 'In Defense of Consent Theory of Political Obligation and Authority', *Ethics* 87, 260–71.
Bitzer, J. and H.-J. Koch (eds) (1997), *Sicherheit, Vielfalt und Solidarität. Ein neues Paradigma des Verfassungsrechts? Symposium zum 65. Geburtstags Erhard Denningers am 20. Juni 1997* (Baden-Baden: Nomos).
Buchanan, A. (1991), *Secession: The Morality of Political Divorce from Fort Sumter to Lithuania and Quebec* (Boulder, CO: Westview Press).
Buchanan, A. (2006), 'A Principled International Legal Response to Demands for Self-Determination', in I. Primoratz and A. Pavković (eds), *Identity, Self-Determination, and Secession* (Aldershot: Ashgate), 139–54.
Buchanan, A. (2007), 'Secession', in E.N. Zalta (ed.), *The Stanford Encyclopaedia of Philosophy*. [Online] At http://plato.stanford.edu/archives/spr2007/entries/secession/ [accessed 22 July 2011].
Denninger, E. (2000), '"Security, Diversity, Solidarity" Instead of "Freedom, Equality, Fraternity"', *Constellations* 7:4.
Dion, S. (2003), 'Democratic Governance and the Principle of Territorial Integrity', Government of Canada Privy Council Office, Intergovernmental Affairs. [Online] At http://www.pco-cp.gc.ca/aia/index.asp?lang=eng&Page=archive&Sub=Articles&Doc=20030716-eng.htm [accessed 22 July 2011].
Doering, D. (2003), 'Secession Rights in a Liberal Perspective', Paper presented at the Liberal Think Tank in Dakar, Senegal, 23 October 2003.
*Economist* (1996), 'Liberalism Defined: The Perils of Complacency', *The Economist*, 21 December.
Fleiner, T. and L.R. Basta Fleiner (2009), *Constitutional Democracy in a Multicultural and Globalised World* (Berlin, Heidelberg: Springer).
Habermas, J. (2000), 'Remarks on Erhard Denninger's Triad of Diversity, Security and Solidarity', *Constellations* 7:4.

Hartl, J. (2003), 'Ten Years after the Czechoslovak Split: What Really Happened', *New Presence: The Prague Journal of Central European Affairs* 5:1.

Henkin, L. (1994), 'A New Birth of Constitutionalism: Genetic Influences and Genetic Defects', in M. Rosenfeld (ed.), *Constitutionalism, Identity, Difference, and Legitimacy (Theoretical Perspectives)* (Durham, NC and London: Duke University Press), 39–54.

Horowitz, D.L. (1985), *Ethnic Groups in Conflict* (Berkley, CA: University of California Press).

Jovanović, M.A. (2007), *Constitutionalizing Secession in Federalized States: A Procedural Approach* (Utrecht: Eleven).

Jovanović, M.A. (2008), 'Consensual Secession of Montenegro: Towards Good Practice?', in A. Pavković and P. Radan (eds), *On the Way to Statehood: Secession and Globalisation* (Aldershot: Ashgate), 133–48.

Keating, M. (2001), *Plurinational Democracy: Stateless Nations in a Post-Sovereignty Era* (Oxford: Oxford University Press).

Kymlicka, W. (1995), *Multicultural Citizenship: A Liberal Theory of Minority Rights* (Oxford: Clarendon Press).

Lincoln, A. (1955), *The Collected Works*, Vol. 4 (New Brunswick, NJ: Rutgers University Press).

Lindsay, P. and C.H. Wellman (January 2003), 'Lincoln on Secession', *Social Theory and Practice* 29:1.

Mancini, S. (2008), 'Rethinking the Boundaries of Democratic Secession: Liberalism, Nationalism and the Right of Minorities to Self-Determination', *International Journal of Constitutional Law* 3 and 4, 553–84.

Marmor, A. (2007), 'Are Constitutions Legitimate?', *Canadian Journal of Law and Jurisprudence* 20:1.

Modood, T. (2007), *Multiculturalism: A Civic Idea* (Cambridge: Polity Press).

Monahan, P.J. and M.J. Bryant (1996), 'Coming to Terms with Plan B: Ten Principles Governing Secession', *C.D. Howe Institute Commentary* no. 83.

Nielsen, K. (1998), 'Liberal Nationalism, Liberal Democracies, and Secession', *University of Toronto Law Journal* 48:2.

Norman, W. (1998), 'The Ethics of Secession as the Regulation of Secessionist Politics', in M. Moore (ed.), *National Self-Determination and Secession* (Oxford: Oxford University Press), 34–61.

Norman, W. (2001), 'Secession and (Constitutional) Democracy', in F. Requejo (ed.), *Democracy and National Pluralism* (London and New York: Routledge), 84–102.

Norman, W. (2003), 'Domesticating Secession', in S. Macedo and A. Buchanan (eds), *Secession and Self-Determination* (New York and London: New York University Press), 193–237.

Norman, W. (2006), *Negotiating Nationalism: Nation-Building, Secession and Federalism in the Multinational State* (Oxford: Oxford University Press).

*The Northern Ireland Act (1998)*. [Online] At http://www.legislation.gov.uk/ukpga/1998/47/contents [accessed 22 July 2011].

Preuss, U.K. (1996), 'The Political Meaning of Constitutionalism', in R. Bellamy (ed.), *Constitutionalism and Democracy: American and European Perspectives* (Aldershot: Avebury), 11–30.

*Reference re Secession of Quebec* (1998), 2 S.C.R.

Requejo, F. (2001), 'Democratic Legitimacy and National Pluralism', in F. Requejo (ed.), *Democracy and National Pluralism* (London and New York: Routledge), 157–77.

Rosenfeld, M. (1994), 'Modern Constitutionalism as Interplay Between Identity and Diversity' in M. Rosenfeld (ed.), *Constitutionalism, Identity, Difference, and Legitimacy (Theoretical Perspectives)* (Durham, NC and London: Duke University Press), 3–36.

Sartori, G. (1962), 'Constitutionalism: A Preliminary Discussion', *The American Political Science Review* 56:4, 860.

Shaw, M. (2003), 'The Role of Recognition and Non-Recognition with Respect to Secession: Notes on Some Relevant Issues', in J. Dahlitz (ed.), *Secession and International Law: Conflict Avoidance – Regional Appraisals* (The Hague: T.M.C. Asser Press), 243–58.

Squires, J. (1996), 'Liberal Constitutionalism, Identity and Difference', *Political Studies* 44:3, 621.

Sunstein, C.R. (1991), 'Constitutionalism and Secession', *University of Chicago Law Review* 58:2.

Sunstein, C.R. (2001a), *Designing Democracy: What Constitutions Do* (New York: Oxford University Press).

Sunstein, C.R. (2001b), 'Should Constitutions Protect the Right to Secede: A Reply to Weinstock', *The Journal of Political Philosophy* 9:3.

Thompson, B. (1998/99), 'Transcending Territory: Towards an Agreed Northern Ireland?', *International Journal on Minority and Group Rights* 6:1–2, 235–66.

Thompson, S. (2006), *The Political Theory of Recognition: A Critical Introduction* (Cambridge: Polity Press).

Tierney, S. (2004), *Constitutional Law and National Pluralism* (Oxford: Oxford University Press).

Tomuschat, C. (1993), 'Self-Determination in a Post-Colonial World', in C. Tomuschat (ed.), *Modern Law of Self-Determination* (Dordrecht: Martinus Nijhoff), 1–20.

Tully, J. (1995), *Strange Multiplicity: Constitutionalism in an Age of Diversity* (Cambridge: Cambridge University Press).

Walker, G. (1997), 'The Idea of Nonliberal Constitutionalism', in I. Shapiro and W. Kymlicka (eds), *Ethnicity and Group Rights* (New York: New York University Press), 154–84.

Weinstock, D. (2000), 'Toward a Proceduralist Theory of Secession', *Canadian Journal of Law and Jurisprudence* 13:2.

Weinstock, D. (2001), 'Constitutionalizing the Right to Secede', *The Journal of Political Philosophy* 9:2.

Young, R. (1998), 'Quebec Secession and the 1995 Referendum', in M. Westmacott and H. Mellon (eds), *Challenges to Canadian Federalism* (Scarborough, ON: Prentice-Hall).

Zippelius, R. (2007), *Rechtsphilosophie*, 5th edn (München: C.H. Beck).

# Secession and State Succession

Tom Grant

## Introduction: Situations Giving Rise to State Succession[1]

At a given time during its existence, a state holds certain rights and obligations. The rights and obligations of a state change over time, as the state enters into new agreements, as new customary rules emerge, and as decisions are reached as to the reparation due for injuries caused by internationally wrongful acts.[2] The rights and obligations of a state also change upon a succession of states. State succession is the situation in which one state has replaced another in the responsibility for the international relations of territory.[3]

A succession of states may occur in a number of ways. It may be that an international boundary has moved, so that a state gives up responsibility over certain territory to its neighbour state. State succession also occurs when a territory breaks away from an existing state, so as to create a new state. Though this situation, too, involves the establishment of a new boundary – i.e. an international boundary

---

1   The topic of state succession has been addressed extensively. For academic works, see Craven (2007), Koskenniemi and Eisemann (2000), Stern (1996), Mullerson (1993), Verzijl (1974), Keith (1967), O'Connell (1967), Jenks (1952) and Klabbers (1999). See also the ILC Commentaries to the three main drafting projects relating to succession: Draft Articles on Succession of States in Respect of Treaties with Commentaries, Sir Francis Vallat, Special Rapporteur, ILC Ybk 1974, Vol. II Pt. One pp. 174ff; Draft Articles on Succession of States in Respect of State Property, Archives and Debts with Commentaries, Mohammed Bedjaoui, Special Rapporteur, ILC Ybk 1981, Vol. II Pt. One pp. 20ff; Draft Articles on Nationality in Relation to the Succession of States with Commentaries, Vaclav Mikulka, Special Rapporteur, ILC Ybk 1999, Vol. II Pt. One pp. 23ff.
2   *Case Concerning the Factory at Chorzów (Claim for Indemnity) (Jurisdiction)*, Judgment, 26 June 1927, PCIJ, Ser. B., No. 3, 1925 p. 21.
3   See Art. 2(1)(b), Vienna Convention on Succession of States in Respect of Treaties, adopted 23 August 1978, entered into force 6 November 1996 ('1978 Vienna Convention'): 1946 UNTS 3; Art. 2(1)(a), Vienna Convention on Succession of States in Respect of State Property, Archives and Debts, 8 April 1983, not yet in force, A/CONF.117/14; ILC Draft Articles on Nationality of Natural Persons in Relation to the Succession of States, ILC Ybk 1999 Vol. II Pt. Two p. 25.

has been introduced on what had previously been the territory of one state – it also involves considerations distinct from those arising from a shift of boundaries between two existing states. In particular, where the separation of territory results in the establishment of a new state, a new international legal person has emerged. State succession concerns the change of rights and obligations, as between the time before the boundary change or territorial separation – and the time after.

Any succession of states – whether by boundary shift, secession or other process (e.g. decolonization) – has implications for third states: the replacement of one state by another in the responsibility for the international relations of a territory means that a third state having an interest in the territory thus affected will have to deal, if it wishes its dealings to have effect, not with the predecessor but with the newly responsible state. And where a new state has been created, the third state will consider what the scope and content of its relations with the new state will be. At the threshold, the third state will consider whether to enter into diplomatic relations with the new state. It may consider whether to enter into new treaties with it. It also will consider which, if any, of the treaty relations it had with the predecessor state continue as between itself and the new state. The separateness and independence of the new state notwithstanding, the new state will hold certain rights and obligations, including, potentially, some which, before succession, had pertained to the predecessor state.

Not all new states which have been created by separation of territory from existing states are the result of secession. States have sometimes voluntarily ceded or devolved part of their territory in order to create new states. States have accepted the independence of colonial territories under Chapter XI and the Trusteeship system of the UN Charter. Voluntary transitions, in the United Nations era, have been more common than unilateral separations. Insofar as general rules and principles of state succession can be identified – and, as will be seen, this is a field in which *ad hoc* approaches fashioned to particular cases are more influential than a general legal position – they have not, with certain salient exceptions, concerned themselves with the distinction between voluntary and unilateral separation of territory. Yet doctrinal writers and those entrusted with progressive development and codification of the law recognize that a material difference exists between a process in which the predecessor assents to the independence of the new state from an early stage; and a process in which it contests independence. As a practical matter, the two paths to state creation present clearly distinct situations of state succession: the implementation of new inter-state relations following a succession have differed considerably, as between an agreed and a contentious separation.

A further variable is the survival – or otherwise – of the predecessor. Dissolution of states has been treated as a distinct process, distinguishable from separation in that it results only in new legal persons, leaving none of the old state behind. A state created through the action of a secessionist movement, where that action has escalated into the whole unravelling of the predecessor state, presents particular questions of state succession as well.

The classic secessionist movement seeks separation from the predecessor state and creation of a new state. There are also instances in which secessionists, instead, seek to remove territory from one state and attach it to another, existing state. This situation often is associated with an irredentist movement in the other state: one state's secessionists are the object of the other state's irredentist aims. The result there is the change of boundaries without change of legal personality and thus, at least in principle, is treated under general rules of state succession.

So more than one factual situation may entail state succession. Though a secessionist movement may result in succession as between two existing states, and state succession arises, too, from agreed changes of frontier, decolonization, state dissolution, etc., the present chapter is concerned chiefly with the act of secession which results in a new state.

Regardless of how the change in international responsibility for territory has come about, state succession involves the entire scope of activity of the state. The present chapter considers some of the main fields of state activity giving rise to issues of succession, including treaty-making, participation in international organizations, conferral of nationality and monetary policy. The prevalence of *ad hoc* approaches in this field (as distinct from application of general rules) is considered in view of the arrangements adopted in the case of the Socialist Federal Republic of Yugoslavia (SFRY). The chapter begins by considering how a secessionist movement may affect state responsibility; and how dissolution of a predecessor state may present questions of succession distinct from the situation where the predecessor state remains.

## Secession and the Transition of Responsibility

The International Law Commission (ILC), considering in 1972 the draft text which evolved into Article 34 of the Vienna Convention on Succession of States in respect of Treaties,[4] observed that, in the UN era, there had been comparatively few instances of secession.[5] The Commission noted as modern examples the separation of Pakistan from India (1947), the dismemberment of the Federation of Rhodesia and Nyasaland (1963), the separation of Singapore from Malaysia (1965), and the separation of Bangladesh from Pakistan (1972)[6] – though, in view of the agreement which regulated the separation, it is doubtful whether Singapore belongs to the category (for Singapore see Part VI).

The rules of international responsibility have special application when an insurrectional or other movement has fought to establish a new state on the territory of an existing state and accomplishes its aim. The ILC Articles on Responsibility of States for Internationally Wrongful Acts (ARSIWA) provide for the situation as follows:

---

4   See footnote 3.
5   Draft Art. 21 – Other Dismemberments of a State into Two or More States: Comment (10), ILC Ybk 1972 Vol. II Pt. Two p. 42.
6   Ibid., Comments (10), (11), (12), pp. 42–3.

*Article 10*

*Conduct of an insurrectional or other movement [...]*

*2. The conduct of a movement, insurrectional or other, which succeeds in establishing a new State in part of the territory of a pre-existing State or in a territory under its administration shall be considered an act of the new State under international law.*

Article 10 'deals with the special case of attribution to a State of conduct of an insurrectional or other movement which *subsequently* becomes the new government of the State or succeeds in establishing a new State' (Crawford 2002: 116 [emphasis added]). The result is the back-dating of the responsibility of the new state: the conduct of the liberation movement, from the inception of its effective control over at least some of the territory it claims, is 'considered an act of the new State'.

This is not to say that every act of every secessionist movement necessarily is to be treated as an act of the new state: there must be 'continuity between the organization of [the secessionist movement] and the organization of the State to which it has given rise' (Crawford 2002: 117).[7] Though in some cases continuity may be clear, cases of dispute have arisen. For example, the New York Supreme Court, in an action in equity, considered the situation in which the independence movement in Ireland was not the same as the eventual independent government of the Irish Free State.[8] The court held that a trust fund of which the movement was beneficiary could not be settled in favour of the government.[9]

## Dissolution *versus* Continuity

Continuity (or its absence) concerns the predecessor state as well. The provisions of Article 34, paragraph 1 of the 1978 Vienna Convention apply 'whether or not the predecessor State continues to exist'. This assimilates the case of dissolution in which the predecessor ceases to exist with the case of separation in which the predecessor continues. The ILC set out the position as follows:

*[T]here does not seem to be any sufficient reason to differentiate between a part of a State which becomes an independent State by secession and one which does so by division. Indeed, a division of a State extinguishing altogether the predecessor State is an even more radical transformation of the situation than a secession, so that it seems to follow* a fortiori *that the parts resulting from the division, assuming their recognition as States, should be*

---

7   ARSIWA Art. 10, Comment (6).
8   *Irish Free State v Guaranty Safe Deposit Co.*, 222 N.Y.S. 182 (1927).
9   222 N.Y.S. at 202. For criticism, see Uren (1929).

> *considered as in the same position as a seceded State for the purposes of the law of succession of States.*[10]

This position has proved not to be a perfect reflection of practice. Cases of extinction and continuity have presented distinct issues. In the main modern case of extinction, that of the SFRY, various difficulties resisted solution for a considerable time. Generally, with the disappearance of the predecessor, the possibility would seem to diminish of an easy transition regulated by agreement between the states involved – though the SFRY's problems were compounded by disagreement whether the predecessor in truth had disappeared (see Chapter 8).

The importance of agreement is explicit in the terms of the 1978 Vienna Convention. Article 34(2)(b) contemplates the case in which 'the States concerned otherwise agree' – meaning that automatic succession, as set out in paragraph 1, is overridden when the states so choose. This voluntary principle runs through the practice and is reflected in the attempted codification of the field.

In several of the modern situations where there was only succession and no continuity, the parties involved elected to treat the results of territorial adjustment as creating new states. Thus the unification of Yemen was characterized by the parties as producing a new state (not the extinction and merger of one state into a surviving predecessor state).[11] The dissolution of the Czech and Slovak Federal Republic on 31 December 1992 entailed the disappearance of the old state and its replacement by two new states. This, too, was by agreement of the parties (Malenovsky 1993). (For more on Yemen and the Czech and Slovak republic see Part VI.) The positions adopted by the states involved thus have been a significant factor in characterizing the situation.

But claims by the state wishing to establish continuity have not been determinative in all cases. The main example of the failure of such a claim is that of the Federal Republic of Yugoslavia (consisting of Serbia and Montenegro), which asserted its continuity to the Socialist Federal Republic of Yugoslavia (SFRY) through the 1990s but did not secure acceptance of that position from third parties. The other states which emerged out of the dissolution of the SFRY in particular rejected Yugoslavia's continuity claim.[12]

It is presumed that changes of government and constitutional re-organization do not affect the continuity of a state: 'it is a recognized principle of law that a State cannot avoid its obligations by a change of government or "political conditions".

---

10  Comment (17), ILC Ybk 1972 Vol. II Pt. Two p. 44.
11  See Art. 1, Agreement on the Establishment of the Republic of Yemen, 22 April 1990: (1991) *International Legal Materials* 30, 820, 822.
12  See letter dated 28 October 1996 from the Permanent Representatives of Bosnia and Herzegovina, Croatia, the Former Yugoslav Republic of Macedonia and Slovenia to the United Nations addressed to the Secretary-General: A/51/564-S/1996/885.

Otherwise, in a democratic republic a country could simply vote to repudiate its contracts'.[13] Even radical changes of territory have not disrupted the continuity of states – e.g. the 19th-century expansion of the Kingdom of Sardinia through the whole of Italy and the absorption by the *Norddeutsche Bund* of the southern German states (Frowein 1992: 137).[14] The case of secession presents the opposite situation – loss, possibly radical loss, of state territory. But, there, too, the presumption is that the predecessor state continues. Turkey, for example, was treated as a legal continuation of the Ottoman state after 1923, notwithstanding the loss of a substantial empire.[15]

The main modern example of continuity is the Union of Soviet Socialist Republics (USSR). The continuity of the Russian Federation after 1991 to the USSR was supported by the facts: the largest part of USSR's territory, population and material wealth was located in the Russian Soviet Federated Socialist Republic, and, so, on the political breakdown of the USSR, it was logical for that unit of the former federation to continue Soviet rights and obligations (see Chapter 8). Continuity was also expressly espoused by Russia. According to the President of the Russian Federation

> [T]he membership of the Union of Soviet Socialist Republics in the United Nations, including the Security Council and all other organs and organizations of the United Nations system is being continued by the Russian Federation (RSFSR) ... In this connection, I request that the name 'Russian Federation' should be used in the United Nations in place of the name ['USSR']. The Russian Federation maintains full responsibility for all the rights and obligations of the USSR under the Charter of the United Nations, including the financial obligations.[16]

Moreover, unlike in the SFRY, the continuity of the former core state was supported by the several successor states. Constituting a new Commonwealth of Independent States, the former USSR republics affirmed that 'The States of the Commonwealth support Russia's continuance of membership of the Union of Soviet Socialist Republics in the United Nations, including permanent membership of the Security Council, and other international organizations'.[17] Third parties, including the European Communities, accepted and acted consistently with Russia's position as

---

13   *Questech v Ministry of National Defence of the Islamic Republic of Iran* (1985) 9 Iran-US CTR 107, 142 (Holtzman, sep op).
14   Respecting Italy, see *Costa v Military Service Commission of Genoa* (1939) 9 ILR 26; *Gastalid v Lepage Hemery* (1929) 5 ILR 69.
15   *Ottoman Debt Arbitration* (Arbitrator Borel, 1925) 3 ILR 42; *Roselius & Co v Karsten & Turkish Republic* (1926) 3 ILR 35.
16   24 December 1991, reprinted at 31 ILM 138.
17   CIS Decision of 21 December 1991, 1st operative paragraph: (1992) 31 ILM 147, 151, reprinted from A/47/ε-S/23329, 30 December 1991.

well.[18] It may be that Russia's position would have been accepted anyway. The affirmative stance of others nevertheless was a factor easing the transition.

## Succession in Respect of Treaties

The general position with respect to treaties is that a new state may commence as beneficiary of treaty rights as at the date of independence. A limitation *ratione temporis* operates, such that the new state cannot claim damages in its own right for harm resulting from conduct prior to its creation. However, the position has been taken that this limitation does not apply with respect to obligations *erga omnes*. The classic example is the Genocide Convention,[19] as pleaded by the Republic of Bosnia and Herzegovina against the Federal Republic of Yugoslavia (FRY).[20]

Stability is needed in respect of the use of territory, and so treaties establishing boundaries or otherwise governing the use of territory present special considerations. The general rule, which follows from the stability principle, is set out in Article 11 of the 1978 Vienna Convention:

A succession of states does not as such affect:

*(a) a boundary established by a treaty; or*

*(b) obligations and rights established by a treaty and relating to the regime of a boundary.*

Article 12, 'other territorial regimes', further specifies that a succession of states does not affect, *inter alia*, 'obligations relating to the use of any territory, or to restrictions upon its use, established by a treaty for the benefit of any territory of a foreign State and considered as attaching to the territories in question'. Regional practice, especially in Africa, lends considerable support to the principle contained in Articles 11 and 12.[21]

The issue of succession to watercourse agreements arose in the *Gabčíkovo-Nagymaros Project* case. The Court relied on Article 12 of the 1978 Convention as reflecting customary international law. According to the Court:

---

18   EC Declaration of 23 December 1991: *EC Bull* 12, 121 (1991).
19   Convention on the Prevention and Punishment of the Crime of Genocide, 78 UNTS 277: signed 9 December 1948, entered into force 12 January 1951.
20   *Application of the Convention on the Prevention and Punishment of the Crime of Genocide (Bosnia and Herzegovina v Yugoslavia)*, Preliminary Objections, ICJ Rep 1996 pp. 595, 671 (para. 34). But compare to the modified position in *Croatia/Serbia (Preliminary Objections)*, Judgment of 18 November 2008, para. 19.
21   *Frontier Dispute (Benin/Niger)*, Judgment of 12 July 2005, ICJ Rep 2005 pp. 90, 108 (para. 23); *Frontier Dispute (Burkina Faso/Republic of Mali)*, ICJ Rep 1986 pp. 554, 565 (para. 20). See also *Continental Shelf Case (Tunisia/Libyan Arab Jamahiriya)*, Judgment of 24 February 1982, Sep Op Judge Jimenez de Arechaga, ICJ Rep 1982 pp. 18, 131–2 (paras 101–2).

> [M]ajor elements [of the Hungary-Czechoslovakia Treaty of 1977] were the proposed construction and joint operation of a large, integrated and indivisible complex of structures and installations on specific parts of the respective territories of Hungary and Czechoslovakia along the Danube. The Treaty also established the navigational régime for an important sector of an international waterway, in particular the relocation of the main international shipping lane to the bypass canal. In so doing, it inescapably created a situation in which the interests of other users of the Danube were affected ...
>
> [T]he 1977 Treaty ... must be regarded as establishing a territorial régime within the meaning of Article 12 of the 1978 Vienna Convention. It created rights and obligations 'attaching to' the parts of the Danube to which it relates; thus the Treaty itself cannot be affected by a succession of States. The Court therefore concludes that the 1977 Treaty became binding upon Slovakia on 1 January 1993.[22]

The Danube regime created by the Treaty thus became a source of international obligation for Slovakia and remained so for Hungary.

## Admission of States to Regional and International Organizations

To solidify its position in international relations, a secessionist entity is likely to seek admission to the United Nations and other international organizations (see Chapters 13 and 15). The Sixth (Legal) Committee addressed the matter of continuity, in respect of the United Nations membership of India following Partition in 1947. The Committee said:

> 1. [A]s a general rule, it is in conformity with legal principles to presume that a State which is a Member of the Organization of the United Nations does not cease to be a Member simply because its Constitution or its frontier have been subjected to changes, and that the extinction of the State as a legal personality recognized in the international order must be shown before its rights and obligations can be considered thereby to have ceased to exist ...
>
> 2. [W]hen a new State is created, whatever may be the territory and the populations which it comprises and whether or not they formed part of a State Member of the United Nations, it cannot under the system of the Charter claim the status of a Member of the United Nations unless it has

---

22   Ibid., pp. 71–2 (para. 120).

been formally admitted as such in conformity with the provisions of the Charter.[23]

India continued as a member state of the Organization, while Pakistan had to apply for admission as a new state. In comparison to the political upheaval, this was with little legal incident.

The dissolution of the SFRY, in contrast, led to a situation fraught both legally and politically. For nearly ten years, the status of the Federal Republic of Yugoslavia (FRY) was ambiguous. The situation was only finally resolved in 2000 with the UN admission of the FRY (Serbia and Montenegro) as a successor to the SFRY.[24] Earlier, during the controversy over Yugoslavia's membership, it was suggested by a number of Permanent Representatives that the FRY, in light of its conduct in the territory of the former Yugoslavia (SFRY), might fail to meet the requirements for admission.[25] Kosovo (which may or may not be described as a case of secession) as of 2010 had not sought admission to the United Nations, as against the opposition of two Permanent Members of the Security Council (the Russian Federation and China), whose veto(s) would prevent the necessary recommendation.

## Nationality Questions

The ILC Special Rapporteur for the topic of nationality in 1952 considered the effects of transfer of territory where a successor state had conferred its nationality on persons residing in its territory:

> *Where the transfer of territory and the conferment of nationality is in accordance with international law, the predecessor State is obliged to recognize it. Its sovereignty has been replaced by that of the successor State, and the predecessor State is, therefore, under an obligation of international law to withdraw its nationality from the inhabitants of the transferred territory upon whom the nationality of the successor State has been conferred.*[26]

---

23  Letter of the Chairman of the Sixth (Legal) Committee addressed to the Chairman of the First Committee, dated 8 October 1947: A/C.1/212, GAOR 2nd sess., 1st Comm. pp. 582–3, annex 14g.
24  By GA res 55/12, 10 November 2000, following recommendation in SC res 1326, 31 October 2000.
25  See e.g. statements of Ms Albright (USA) S/PV.3204 p. 7, 28 April 1993; Sir David Hannay (United Kingdom), A/47/PV.7 pp. 142–3, 22 September 1992.
26  Report of the Special Rapporteur, Manley O. Hudson, on the topic of nationality, including statelessness, 21 February 1952: ILC Ybk 1952 Vol. II p. 11.

The general trend since the mid-20th century in favour of international protection of human rights has affected the rules concerning nationality upon a succession of states. Article 15 of the Universal Declaration of Human Rights, for example, provides as follows:

> *(1) Everyone has the right to a nationality.*
>
> *(2) No one shall be arbitrarily deprived of his nationality nor denied the right to change his nationality.*[27]

The Economic and Social Council, not long after the adoption of the Universal Declaration, recommended that 'States involved in changes of territorial sovereignty … include in the arrangements for such changes, provisions, if necessary, for the avoidance of statelessness'.[28] The United Nations Convention on the Reduction of Statelessness of 30 August 1961,[29] under Article 8, though providing a number of exceptions, puts the matter as an obligation. The exceptions in Article 8 largely concern individuals who have taken steps to separate themselves from the state. The predecessor state may deprive such individuals of its nationality, but only in accordance with its legislation and in a non-discriminatory fashion.

The Ethiopia-Eritrea Claims Commission affirmed the rule against arbitrary deprivation of nationality in the event of state succession: 'In principle, [deprivation of nationality] should follow procedures in which affected persons are adequately informed regarding the proceedings, can present their cases to an objective decision maker, and can seek objective outside review'.[30] The Commission 'recognize[d] that international law limits States' power to deprive persons of their nationality', *inter alia* with a view to avoiding statelessness.[31]

The issue of state succession with respect to nationality was further discussed by the ILC in the 1990s, leading to the ILC Articles appended to GA resolution 55/153 of 12 December 2000.

---

27   GA res 217 (III), 10 December 1948.
28   ECOSOC res 319B (XI), Section III, 11 August 1950.
29   989 UNTS 176, entered into force 13 December 1975.
30   Partial Award, Civilians Claims, Eritrea's Claims 15, 16, 23 and 27–32, para. 71, reprinted at (2005) 44 ILM 601, 613–14. See also ibid. para. 62, noting that Ethiopia had not at all times 'properly implemented [its nationality law] in accordance with its terms': 44 ILM at 612–13.
31   Partial Award, Civilians Claims, Eritrea's Claims 15, 16, 23 and 27–32, para. 60: 44 ILM at 612.

## National Currency

The ILC considered a draft article on 'currency and the privilege of issue', but this, in the event, was not adopted as part of the draft articles on succession of states in respect of matters other than treaties.[32] As a general matter, a new state has the right to adopt a new currency and to establish its own bank of issue, a right which colonial administering powers sometimes formally acknowledged at the time of succession.[33] There are no mandatory rules of international law, however, controlling the precise conduct of a state succession in respect of monetary institutions and the currency. Diverse arrangements have been adopted.[34]

In some cases arrangements have been adopted, whereby a predecessor state retains competence over the successor state's monetary system for a period following independence or separation. The International Monetary Fund (IMF), as a matter of policy, 'may welcome such arrangements ... because they are likely to safeguard orderly exchange arrangements, especially where the successor State intends to accept membership in the Fund' (Aufricht 1962: 167). These are not the result of a default rule of international law. They are a matter for the parties in each case, and may be adopted on such terms as the parties choose.

As to relations with international lending and monetary institutions, a new state would likely seek admission to the IMF. This is governed by Article II, section 2 of the IMF Articles of Agreement.[35] It would be open to the Board of Governors to propose modifying the predecessor state's quota in the Fund, modification being subject to consent.[36]

## The Prevalence of *ad hoc* Approaches

Though the drafters of the Vienna Convention on Succession of States in respect of Treaties structured its provisions to treat succession as a general rule, in practice states have more often adopted special agreements than they have applied the rule. The difficulty in codifying the topic has been observed,[37] and subscription to the international instruments relating to succession has remained limited.

---

32 Mohammed Bedjaoui, Fourth Report on succession in respect of matters other than treaties, draft article 7, Comment (1), ILC Ybk 1971 Vol. II Pt. One, pp. 179–80.
33 Bedjaoui, Sixth Report, draft article 16, Comment (2), ILC Ybk 1973 Vol. II, p. 45.
34 See examples at Bedjaoui, Fourth Report, draft article 7, Comment (6), ILC Ybk 1971 Vol. II Pt. One, p. 180; Bedjaoui, Sixth Report, draft article 28, Comment (3), ILC Ybk 1973 Vol. II, p. 57; ibid., Comments (9), (11), p. 181; ibid., Comment (10), p. 181.
35 Adopted 22 July 1944, entered into force 27 December 1945, and as amended: 2 UNTS 134, 136.
36 Articles of Agreement, Art. III, sec. 2.
37 See Anthony Aust, 'Vienna Convention on Succession of States in Respect of Treaties', UN Audiovisual Library of International Law: www.un.org/law/avl.

The prevalence of *ad hoc* approaches can be seen in particular with reference to the allocation of state property, archives and debts following a succession of states. The Vienna Convention on Succession of States in respect of State Property, Archives and Debts of 1983 was an attempt to set out rules concerning succession of states in matters other than treaties. The 1983 Convention has not yet entered into force. Adopted on 7 April 1983,[38] it is in many respects an exercise in progressive development rather than a codification of existing rules. The Convention is nevertheless the main attempt to systematize this aspect of succession.

It is noteworthy that most of the states which have acceded to the 1983 Convention have faced particular problems of succession in recent years. Seven states have acceded: Croatia (11 April 1994), Estonia (21 October 1991), Georgia (12 July 1993), Liberia (15 September 2005), Slovenia (15 August 2002), the former Yugoslav Republic of Macedonia (2 September 1997) and Ukraine (8 January 1993). The SFRY (former Yugoslavia) had signed the Convention on 24 October 1983 but never ratified it.

Yet acceding states, when they have addressed problems of succession in practice, have designed their own solutions. Succession among the Yugoslav states was addressed more or less comprehensively in the Agreement on Succession Issues,[39] which proceeds on the basis that the SFRY has ceased to exist and that there is no predecessor state. The Agreement refers in broad terms to equitable considerations and to international comity. Its preamble states that the parties are '[m]indful of the need, in the interests of all successor States and their citizens and in the interests of stability in the region and their mutual good relations, to resolve questions of State succession'.[40] In Article 2, each party 'acknowledges the principle that it must at all times take the necessary measures to prevent loss, damage or destruction to State archives, State property and assets of the SFRY in which ... one or more of the other successor States have an interest'. Whether a successor state has an interest is determined 'in accordance with the provisions' of the Agreement (Article 2). The actual allocation of state assets – the functional part of the Agreement – was set out in annexes extending to some 50 pages and incorporating by reference a number of arrangements previously reached (e.g. allocation of former SFRY assets held in the Bank of International Settlements).[41] The Agreement and its Annexes sought to be comprehensive, but did not resolve all questions.[42]

Articles 10 and 11 of the 1983 Convention envisage parties referring certain aspects of succession to an 'appropriate international body'. Perhaps reflecting these provisions, the arrangements for succession in the SFRY included an institutional apparatus. There was the office of the High Representative acting under a specific

---

38   A/CONF./117/15.
39   Bosnia and Herzegovina, Croatia, Macedonia, Slovenia and Yugoslavia. Adopted 29 June 2001, entered into force 29 June 2004: 2262 UNTS 251.
40   Ibid., 2nd preambular para.
41   Ibid., Appendix, BIS Assets, para. 1.
42   See *Republic of Croatia v Republic of Serbia* [2009] EWHC 1559 (Ch).

mandate on succession issues.[43] Article 4 of the Agreement on Succession Issues provided for a 'Standing Joint Committee' to be comprised of 'senior representatives of each successor State'. Under Article 5, differences 'over the interpretation and application' of the Agreement, if not resolved through consultation between the states concerned, were to be referred either to an independent person or the Standing Joint Committee. The President of the Court of Conciliation and Arbitration of the OSCE was designated appointing authority, in default of agreement as to the expert to be appointed under Article 5, paragraph 3. In fact negotiations were conducted under the auspices of Sir Arthur Watts acting as conciliator. The arrangements with respect to succession issues in the SFRY were carried through under the overall framework of a Security Council resolution.[44] The Security Council operates under a significant discretion and would by no means be bound to adopt a similar resolution in a future case of succession. So, while its practice in connection with Yugoslavia might suggest a model with potentially wider application, the law-making effect must be taken as limited to the case addressed.

## Conclusion

As seen in this chapter, situations arise from time to time, in which the succession of rights and obligations between states is put in issue. The principal drafting projects by which the ILC has attempted to systematize the field have been noted here. However, states in addressing succession have relied to a considerable degree on *ad hoc* arrangements, adopted through agreement, sometimes supervised by international institutions. It is as much, or more, through agreements that states have addressed succession, than through customary rules or law-making treaties of general application.

Yet (unilateral) secession is the process of non-consensual separation which gives rise to a new state. So long as a predecessor state continues to view a declaration of independence as an act of (unilateral) secession, a resolution of succession issues is unlikely. The matter of succession in a given case thus is effectively and comprehensively addressed when the parties no longer regard the transformative events in issue as secession – or, at any rate, when they have replaced a contentious approach to the situation globally with a commitment to joint resolution of the questions arising out of their separation.

---

43  Agreement on Succession Issues, 4th preambular para.
44  SC res 1022 (1995), 22 November 1995, para. 6. See also ibid., 9th preambular para.

# References

Aufricht, H. (1962), 'State Succession Under the Law and Practice of the International Monetary Fund', *International and Comparative Law Quarterly* 11, 154.

Craven, M.C.R. (2007), *The Decolonization of International Law: State Succession and the Law of Treaties* (Oxford: Oxford University Press).

Crawford, J. (ed.) (2002), *The International Law Commission's Articles on State Responsibility: Introduction, Text and Commentaries* (Cambridge: Cambridge University Press).

Frowein, J.A. (1992), 'The Reunification of Germany', *American Journal of International Law* 86, 152.

Jenks, C.W. (1952), 'State Succession in Respect of Law Making Treaties', *British Year Book of International Law* 29, 105.

Keith, K.J. (1967), 'Succession to Bilateral Treaties by Seceding States', *American Journal of International Law* 61, 521.

Klabbers, J. (ed.) (1999), *State Practice Regarding State Succession and Issues of Recognition: The Pilot Project of the Council of Europe* (The Hague: Kluwer Law International).

Koskenniemi, M. and P.M. Eisemann (eds) (2000), *State Succession: Codification Tested Against the Facts/La succession d'Etats: la codification à l'épreuve des faits* (The Hague: Martinus Nijhoff/Hague Academy).

Malenovsky, J. (1993), 'Problèmes Juridiques Liés à la Partition de la Tchécoslovaquie', *Annuaire Français de Droit International* 39, 305.

Mullerson, R. (1993), 'The Continuity and Succession of States, by Reference to the Former USSR and Yugoslavia', *International and Comparative Law Quarterly* 42, 473.

O'Connell, D.P. (1967), *State Succession in Municipal Law and International Law* (Cambridge: Cambridge University Press).

Stern, B. (1996), 'La succession d'Etats', *Hag Rec* 262, 15.

Uren, C.K. (1929), 'The Succession of the Irish Free State', *Michigan Law Review* 28, 149.

Verzijl, J.H.W. (1974), *International Law in Historical Perspective: Part 7, State Succession* (Leiden: A.W. Sijthoff).

# PART V
# SECESSION: NORMATIVE APPROACHES

# Introduction to Part V

In this part secession is explored as a subject of moral or political assessment based on moral or political norms or principles. Since it is based on norms or principles, such an assessment is regarded as normative and not explanatory.

Until 1984 political theorists and philosophers in the English-speaking world have not made an attempt to explore systematically the issue of secession from the point of view of political theory or ethics. The first such attempt, the 1984 article 'The Liberal Theory of Secession' by Harry Beran, provoked a lively debate which, as Chapter 22 attests, is still continuing.

As outlined in Chapters 4 and 22, current approaches to normative assessment of secession may be classified into three broad categories:

- choice or democratic theories;
- remedial theories (called 'justice' theories in Chapter 4);
- communitarian or national theories.

In Part V, there is no discussion of a communitarian or nationalist theory of secession. But in Chapter 21, dealing with internal self-determination, Michel Seymour has outlined a normative framework which ranks values and arguments in a way almost identical to nationalist theories of secession such as, for example, the theory Margaret Moore advanced in her *Ethics of Nationalism*. In this framework, the political aspirations of peoples (or national groups) to self-determination is ranked as high as (if not higher than) individual liberties. In particular, Seymour argues that peoples (which other theorists would call nations or national groups) are moral agents who are a source of moral claims and who need to be politically and/or morally recognized. Since, in Seymour's view, peoples are defined not only in terms of their culture but in terms of their shared institutions, he believes that our recognition of peoples necessarily involves our recognition of their moral right to *internal* self-determination. In Chapter 21 the right of self-determination is defined as 'the right for a people to develop itself socially, economically and culturally'. But in this chapter Seymour primarily explores right to *internal* self-determination, that is, the right to develop 'within an encompassing [host, A.P.] state and to determine its political status within that state'. According to him, a people can gain a right to 'own' a state of its own, that is, the right to secede, only if the right to internal self-determination is denied to them (or it) in the 'encompassing' (that is, host) state.

Although he does not discuss the justification of secession in any detail, in Chapter 21 Seymour in effect advocates a kind of remedial theory of secession – a secession for him as a remedy of a breach of a right, in this case, the right of internal self-determination of peoples. In Chapter 22, Reinold Schmücker argues, at some length, that a remedial theory of secession can incorporate our moral intuitions better than either choice or national theories and that it can also resolve conflicts between opposing moral claims better than these two rival types of theories. In contrast to Seymour, however, he does not define the holders of the right to secession in terms of their shared culture and institutions. Hence, his theory is not a communitarian or national theory but a 'pure' remedial theory. Further, according to him, the remedy that secession provides is not, necessarily, a remedy to the breach of the right to self-determination. In fact, for Schmücker the right to secede is not derived in any way from the right to political self-determination. In order to be justified, secession, according to him, must remedy a *grave* injustice or harm – such as a threat to physical security of citizens (e.g. mass killing) or forced occupation of the country. Although both Seymour and Schmücker argue that secession is morally justified *only* as a remedy, they differ in their conception of harm or injustice which secession *should* remedy and in their conception of the group that is entitled to the right to secede.

In Chapter 23, David D. Speetzen and Christopher Heath Wellman base their choice theory on the respect for political self-determination. In their view, 'any group able and willing to perform the functions necessary for political legitimacy has a primary right to secede'. A key function necessary for political legitimacy is that of political decision-making. In their view, individuals which have shared personal, cultural and social attachments and similar social positions have both the motivation and ability to promote their common welfare. Such individuals form 'self-determining groups' which are in virtue of these social and cultural commonalities in a better position to promote their members' welfare. These 'self-determining' groups have a right to secede because they may be in a better position to perform the functions necessary for political legitimacy than their existing state. In addition, Speetzen and Wellman argue that it is morally impermissible to deny such groups their right to self-determination and to secession because it implies disrespect for their ability to make political decisions.

Thus Speetzen and Wellman conceive self-determination in a much broader sense than Seymour does in Chapter 21: in Chapter 23 self-determination is defined in the terms of political decision-making concerning the welfare of the groups and its members, including a decision to establish a new state, that is, to secede. In contrast to Seymour, Speetzen and Wellman do not restrict the primary or initial right to self-determination to the confines of the 'encompassing' state in which the group resides.

Chapters 24 and 25 discuss some of the shortcomings of the above normative approaches to secession. In Chapter 24 John McGerry and Margaret Moore show how 'just cause' theories (which in this Part are called 'remedial theories of secession') fail to identify injustice or moral unacceptability of real-life cases in which one group dominates over another. They first outline two opposed approaches to justifiability of secession: the statist and the 'just cause' approach. The first, statist, approach regards the territorial integrity of states as overriding any claims of secession and thus is unable to offer any such remedies to the injustice committed by states to individuals or groups. This view, discussed in Chapters 13 and 15, appears to be the most prevalent view among the political decision-makers today. This approach views domination of one group over another as perhaps regrettable but not remediable by secession of that group. The second, 'just cause' approach – advocated in Chapters 21 and 22 – regards some grave injustices to individuals as a just cause for secession. In their view, *the choice theories*, which allow secession by choice and not on the basis of just cause – advocated in Chapter 23 – have no political proponent and are thus not discussed in Chapter 24. McGerry and Moore focus on two types of domination – those occurring in authoritarian or non-liberal states and those occurring in liberal democratic states. The second type is carried by ostensibly democratic means, including electoral gerrymander, to ensure that members of the majority population keep exclusive control over political decision-making. The exclusion of minorities in this way provides a popular grievance, alienates the minorities from the state from which they are excluded and provides a basis for secessionist mobilization. In short, liberal democratic states do not always avoid injustices which may lead to secessionist mobilization and demands for secession. And yet, McGerry and Moore point out, just cause theories fail to identify this type of domination as a 'just cause' for leaving the dominating state, that is, for secession.

In Chapter 25, Aleksandar Pavković attempts to identify the following three conceptual problems the right to secede faces when employed in moral or normative theories of secession: first, it is difficult to establish who is the right-holder of this right – how the group which holds the right is distinguished from those that do not hold it. Second, it is individuals who exercise the right – that is, create a new state – and not groups; groups only benefit from the exercise of the right. And, finally, it is not clear what obligations/permissions the right to secede generates in other states and individuals who are not members of the right-holding group. Pavković believes that secessions involve a transfer of power from one elite to another and a transformation of a minority in a previous state into a majority in a new state; these acts are, according to him, morally neutral and do not require moral assessment. In this way he rejects the view, advocated in Chapters 21 and 23, that self-determination is, necessarily, of moral value. In his view, only some attempts at secession require moral assessment (when they cause or remedy harm) and our moral assessment of those secessions does not require the concept of a right to secede. In short, he argues that moral assessment of secessions need not be rights-based.

# Internal Self-Determination and Secession

## Michel Seymour

It is generally agreed that peoples have a right to self-determination. The principle is present in UN and other legal documents as a moral[1] or as a legal right (see also Chapter 17). But we must immediately distinguish between the right to internal self-determination and the right to external self-determination. The right to external self-determination is the right to own a sovereign state. It can apply to a population that already owns a sovereign state, but also to peoples that do not yet have one. In the latter case, it involves the violation of the territorial integrity of the encompassing state. It can take the form of secession when the people creates its own state, or association if the people associates itself with a neighbouring state. Internal self-determination is in general defined as the right for a people to develop itself socially, economically and culturally within an encompassing state and to determine its political status within that state. This is how the notion is defined in the *UN Charter* (UN 1945) and in the *Declaration on Friendly Relations among States* (UN 1970). This is also how it is defined in the *Declaration on the Rights of Aboriginal Peoples* (UN 2007). In this chapter, I focus essentially on the right to internal self-determination and its connection with secession. It is relevant to issues of external self-determination, because one of the main reasons for allowing unilateral secession to take place is the violation of the right to internal self-determination. If the encompassing state is not willing to grant internal self-determination to its component nations, this for the UN can count as an injustice and seems to justify a unilateral remedial right to secede. So in general, UN documents assert that peoples have a primary right to internal self-determination and have a remedial right to secession or external self-determination. Unilateral secession can be justified in the case of colonies, oppressed peoples and when the state does not secure internal self-determination for its internal minorities (see Chapter 17).[2]

---

1   For a different view see Chapter 25.
2   See for instance the *Declaration on Friendly Relations among States* (UN 1970): 'Nothing in the foregoing paragraphs shall be construed as authorizing or encouraging any action which would dismember or impair, totally or in part, the territorial integrity or political

## Different Forms of Internal Self-determination

Internal self-determination can take different forms. It can first be formulated in a very weak sense as the right to participate in the election of representatives coming from one's own community and as the possibility for those elected individuals to take part in the government of the encompassing state. This, for instance, is the sense in which the Supreme Court of Canada defines internal self-determination in the *Reference Case on the Secession of Quebec* (Supreme Court of Canada 1998). According to the Supreme Court, the Quebec people is not 'denied meaningful access to government to pursue their political, economic, social and cultural development' (Supreme Court of Canada 1998: #138).[3] In a second sense of the expression that might be called the canonic interpretation, internal self-determination can also mean the right to self-government. This is perhaps the most obvious sense of internal self-determination because it implies that the people has political control over its own institutions within the encompassing state. It is the sense in which, for instance, Will Kymlicka (2007: 206–13) uses the expression. But thirdly, internal self-determination can also mean a right to an even more sophisticated form of self-government such as one implying a special constitutional status. Here the idea is that a special asymmetric constitutional arrangement could be designed to meet the specific demands of the people. The right to internal self-determination, thus understood, is the right of the people to have its own constitutional arrangement within the state. In this case, we have a robust interpretation that goes beyond the idea of self-government, because self-government is compatible with the principle of equality of status among federated states, while a special constitutional status reflects a politics of difference, not of equality. The demands for a special juridical status granted to the province of Quebec within Canada or for a constitutionalized form of asymmetric federalism implying a unique distribution of powers between the federal state of Canada and the province, or for a special right of opting out of a federal programme with financial compensation, are illustrations of this third form of internal self-determination (see also Chapter 7).

---

unity of sovereign and independent States conducting themselves in compliance with the principle of equal rights and self-determination of peoples as described above and thus possessed of a government representing the whole people belonging to the territory without distinction as to race, creed or colour' (see also Chapter 17).

3   See also #136 of section Supreme Court of Canada (1998): 'The population of Quebec cannot plausibly be said to be denied access to government. Quebecers occupy prominent positions within the government of Canada. Residents of the province freely make political choices and pursue economic, social and cultural development within Quebec, across Canada, and throughout the world. The population of Quebec is equitably represented in legislative, executive and judicial institutions. In short, to reflect the phraseology of the international documents that address the right to self-determination of peoples, Canada is a 'sovereign and independent state conducting itself in compliance with the principle of equal rights and self-determination of peoples and thus possessed of a government representing the whole people belonging to the territory without distinction'.

These three different interpretations are not necessarily competing with each other, since each may be the correct institutional measure to put in place in a given political context. For instance, in a country where there are peoples with populations of equal size, a unitary state governed by an equal number of representatives coming from these different peoples could under normal circumstances allow each of them to self-determine themselves. So in this case, we would perhaps require only a weak form of internal self-determination. But when the populations involved have different interests on different territories with very different natural resources, it is perhaps important in addition to allow for self-government for each of the peoples, thereby creating local governments that are closer to the populations. This can be done by territorial federalism or by a devolution of powers to the constituent peoples. But we may also have cases where the third measure must in addition be implemented. This happens when the people is in a minority position within the state.

## Defining Peoples

In the framework of a theory that seeks to clarify the right to internal self-determination, it is important to define the 'people' to whom the theory assigns this right (see also Chapter 25). Most authors today have difficulty in coming up with a simple, univocal definition of 'people'. But the problem perhaps springs from the fact that there are several kinds of peoples. This situation makes it difficult to identify a definitive list of shared features. I think there are at least seven different kinds of peoples. The different concepts correspond to different forms of national conciousness. In particular, one can see oneself as belonging to an ethnic, cultural, civic, socio-political, diasporic, multisocietal or multiterritorial people.

One sees oneself as a member of a given *ethnic* people when one identifies oneself as sharing the same ancestral origins as the other members of the group. A number of aboriginal peoples find themselves in this situation. One sees oneself as a member of a given *cultural* people when one identifies oneself as having different ancestral origins, but sharing the same mother tongue, institutions and history (e.g. the Acadian people). One sees oneself as belonging to a given civic people when one shares the same sovereign country and when the country is seen as a state involving a single people (e.g. Portugal, Iceland and Korea). One sees oneself as a member of a given socio-political people when one participates in a political community that is not sovereign but involves within it a majority of individuals that belongs to the world's largest sample of a group sharing the same language, institutions and history (e.g. Quebec, Scotland, Catalonia). One sees oneself as a member of the same diasporic people when one belongs to a group whose members have the same culture and history, but who are spread across different discontinuous territories (e.g. the former Jewish diaspora) and form minorities on each of those territories. One sees oneself as a member of a multisocietal people when one is part of a sovereign state and the state is seen as comprising several national societal cultures (e.g. Great Britain, Spain, Canada). Finally, the idea of a multiterritorial people supposes that the group is located on a continuous territory that does not correspond to legally-defined borders. For example, the Kurdish people occupies a non-fragmented area (Kurdistan) that crosses the official borders of existing states. This also applies to the Mohawk people.

Of course, being able to correctly identify the conception adopted by the majority of a population is one thing, and being able to determine the legitimacy of that conception is another thing. There are also very often conflicts among sub-groups in the population with respect to how to describe the people as a whole. What we call a 'people' is often only the result of ideological conflict among these various sub-groups. A people's specific type depends on the image accepted by the majority of the population at a given time. A national self-image is correctly attributed when a majority of individuals in the population have that self-image. But the legitimacy of the self-image is entirely something else. This last question is a normative issue, and it depends largely on the ability of the population as a whole to apply politics of recognition for the minorities living on the territory.

Despite the very wide variety of peoples, there are shared features. In order to understand all of them, we need to use the concept of societal culture. This notion makes it possible to introduce a general concept of the people understood in the institutional sense. Societal cultures are to peoples what citizens are to persons. Even though they may have many different ways of viewing themselves as persons, individuals are citizens in the public arena. Likewise, despite the very wide variety of peoples, they are all to be understood as involving societal cultures in the public arena. As a matter of fact, peoples are either single societal cultures or aggregates of societal cultures. This institutional conception of the people is what we end up with when we proceed by abstraction from the diverse sorts of peoples and retain only their shared features. It closely resembles the conception advanced by Rawls (1999: note 17) and it is partly influenced by the work of John Stuart Mill. It also closely resembles the conception described by Jürgen Habermas (2001: 17), which was inspired by the work of Julius Fröbel.

A 'societal culture' involves first a 'cultural structure'. In the simplest case, a structure of culture has three important features: a shared public language, shared public institutions (those in which the shared public language is mainly spoken) and a shared public history (i.e. a common historical heritage of shared public institutions). These three components are compatible with the existence of minority languages, institutions and histories that are formally recognized, institutionally respected and financially supported.

According to this view, language plays an important role in the development of a particular national consciousness. It shapes a common understanding among the people and it creates bonds between them. Of course, two distinct peoples may differ even if they share the same language because the two communities are on different territories with different institutions and different histories. But this is not a reason for denying the importance of language as a fundamental source of common national consciousness among the members.

There can also be multilingual peoples, but this can be possible only because this multilingualism has become a shared common feature in the national consciousness of the population. Language is thus also crucial even for multilingual states because multilingualism can precisely be a tie that binds the population together.

Apart from being embodied into a structure of culture, a societal culture also has a character. If the shared public language, institutions and history make up the culture's structure, the culture's character is constituted by the beliefs, values, ends, lifestyles, customs and traditions shared by a critical mass of the population at a given time. But it is important to distinguish between the structure of culture and the character of culture (Kymlicka 1989: 166–8; Kymlicka 1995: 104). The culture's character can change even if the population keeps essentially the same structure. The reason is that language is not necessarily the expression of a single lifestyle or of a single conception of the good life or common good. It is compatible with an irreducible, reasonable pluralism of points of view on such matters. Shared public institutions are also not necessarily the reflection of a set of specific customs and traditions. They can also be subject to an irreducible pluralism of values and points of view. Finally, the shared public history is defined essentially by its subject, and is in principle compatible with an irreducible variety of narratives and interpretations. A shared public history is thus not necessarily the reflection of a commonly shared narrative identity.

In many cultures, institutions are not clearly distinguished from the culture's character. For example, an ecclesiastic institution is both an institutional component and the expression of a set of religious beliefs. Indeed, in some societies, the institutions can almost all be described as having a religious dimension. And in many societies, the majority very often imposes its own character on minorities. In traditional societies, the culture's structure tends to merge with the culture's character. The whole population shares the same set of beliefs, values, lifestyles, customs and traditions. However, in modern societies, the structure of culture tends increasingly to be separated from its character, and to leave room for an irreducible diversity of lifestyles, conceptions of the good life and ideas about the common good.

The concepts of societal culture, cultural structure and cultural character are all borrowed from Will Kymlicka (1989, 1995). According to him, societal cultures do carry 'lifestyles', 'memory', 'shared values', 'shared practices', 'traditions' and 'conventions'. A societal culture conveys a 'shared vocabulary of traditions and conventions' (Kymlicka 1995: 76). But even if they are always in a way incarnated in specific characters, they can more or less keep the same structure even when their characters change.

Peoples have an institutional identity, but it does not necessarily mean that they own a sovereign state. The institutional identity of a people can be minimal, such as in the case of aboriginal peoples on reserves. It can be extensive, as in the case of sovereign peoples. Peoples can also have non-sovereign governments, such as federated states (e.g. Quebec), semi-federated states (e.g. Catalonia) or governments stemming from a devolution of powers (e.g. Scotland). But some peoples' institutional identity does not involve any governmental organization at all. By a political conception of peoples, we simply mean that they have a distinctive institutional personality in the political realm. This does not mean that they are organized into political governments. It means that peoples come in the political space equipped with one or many common public languages, a set of common public institutions in which the common public language(s) is (are) spoken and a common public history, which is the common public heritage of the common public institutions. They may sometimes also have governmental institutions, but it is not necessary to have such institutions in order to have an institutional identity. Some peoples like the Acadian people, for instance, have a common public language, a common public history and various institutions such as schools, universities, hospitals, museums and newspapers without having any governmental institutions. The Scottish people also had a non-governmental institutional identity before the devolution of powers.

## Recognition as an Argument for Internal Self-determination

Peoples understood in the institutional sense of the term are acting entities in the political realm. Just as persons present themselves equipped with the status of citizens, peoples have an institutional identity of societal cultures. The concepts involved are political not metaphysical. There is no need to consider issues of personal identity or social ontology. Now according to the Rawlsian version of political liberalism, we owe respect to the various agents present in the political realm as long as they also show respect toward the other agents that are also present in the political realm. Given that persons and peoples are such agents, it means that persons and peoples can become moral agents and can be equal sources of valid moral claims. So the least we can do is to recognize the existence of persons and peoples. But what does it mean to recognize peoples?

Jean-Marc Ferry (1996) argues in favour of recognition policies that are strictly symbolic, that apply to past relationships among peoples and that serve to repair crimes that have been committed by certain peoples. In this sense, politics of recognition need not have any constitutional, institutional or financial implications. Recognition politics are politics of atonement and we rely on the virtues of symbolic recognition for resolving past grievances. Galeotti (2002) develops a slightly different approach. She accepts that there must be institutional (constitutional and financial) consequences that follow from a symbolic recognition, but she believes that these institutional consequences should not themselves be entrenched in the constitution. Peoples should be granted only symbolic recognition in the constitution, so she refuses to entrench rights that would describe particular institutional consequences that follow from accepting these symbolic rights.

But consider once again the concept of people and let us wonder what it means to recognize the existence of a given people understood in the institutional sense. If we suppose in accordance with political liberalism a political conception of peoples,

peoples will have an institutional identity. Now as we saw in the previous section, peoples can be defined in the political realm as having an institutional identity conceived as a societal culture, i.e. as forming a society involving institutions whether these are governmental or not. But if this is how we conceive peoples, then their recognition as peoples amounts to a recognition of their institutional identity, and this means that we must recognize their right to preserve and develop their institutional identity. Peoples may have all sorts of collective interests, but among these, those that relate to the development of their institutional identity must occupy a special position, because they relate to their very existence as peoples. The interests that relate to the preservation and development of their institutional identity can for this reason perhaps rank as legal rights.

Now the right to maintain and develop its own institutions is precisely the right to self-determination. This follows from our initial definition according to which internal self-determination is the right to develop oneself economically, socially and culturally within the encompassing state. So when peoples are understood as having an institutional identity, their recognition as peoples naturally leads to a right to internal self-determination (see also Chapter 19). So when we conceive peoples as having an institutional identity, we can understand why the right to internal self-determination plays a central role for the recognition of peoples. Since peoples are individuated in the political realm as having an institutional identity, there does not seem to be a clear way to separate the symbolic recognition of peoples from the constitutional, institutional and financial consequences of such a recognition. Internal self-determination is the minimal way by which we recognize peoples that behave as moral agents in the political sphere. The right to internal self-determination is a primary right, as opposed to a remedial right, because peoples have the right to preserve and develop their institutional identity as peoples, regardless of the fact that they have been the subject of various forms of misrecognition in the past, or some other kind of injustice (see also Chapters 22 and 23).

## Deliberative Procedure as an Argument for Internal Self-determination

We discussed above various substantial versions of internal self-determination. What makes them substantial is that they all have important institutional, constitutional and financial consequences. The collective representation of the people into the government of the encompassing state, self-government and special constitutional status imply changes in the institutional, constitutional and financial arrangements of society. But there is perhaps a less substantial account of the right to internal self-determination. It may be understood as the right to initiate a constitutional debate whether or not it leads to a constitutional amendment. This account has been proposed by those who argue for the importance of deliberative democracy, acknowledgement or patriotic democracy.

Let me dwell a little more on this alternative approach because it has a growing influence among philosophers and political scientists. A first version is one according to which internal self-determination involves at its core a deliberative democratic process. Among the promoters of deliberative democracy, we can mention Joseph Bessette (1994), Simone Chambers (1996, 2000a), John Dryzek (2000), Jon Elster (1998), James Fishkin (1991, 2003), Amy Gutmann (2003), Anthony Simon Laden (2001) and Dennis Thompson (2004). It is an approach that insists on the virtues of *deliberation*. But there is also another trend, perhaps nowadays less influential but with profound historical roots, available to those who follow the path opened up by Patchen Markell (2004) and Jim Tully (2000). They are trying to find a way out of the classical conception of struggles for recognition and sovereignty in favour of an approach based on acknowledgement and disclosure, and this has important consequences for internal self-determination. Here the insistence is on the *negotiating* process. Finally, patriotic democracy is an even less influential approach but with stronger historical roots that go back to Aristotle and Machiavelli. It is a position that Charles Blattberg (2003) has advocated. It is an approach based on patriotism. Here the insistence is on the process of a *conversation* taking place within a political community.

In spite of their very diverse theoretical sources and the important foundational disagreements taking place between them, these authors all seem to agree on important political issues and they all favour a new account of internal self-determination. For instance, Simone Chambers thinks that 'engaging in a civilising politics does involve a commitment to fundamentals. But it represents acceptance of certain procedural rules regulating the practice rather than agreement about substantive political visions' (Chambers 2000b: 66). As long as peoples are equal participants in constitutional debates, they may be described as exercising self-determination even if this does not lead to a constitutional amendment. Charles Blattberg (2003) also argues that by engaging in a true conversation this process could eventually lead, although this is not sure, to the formal recognition of the minority. Even if the end result is not always happy, we should be happy because the conversation keeps on going.

Similarly, James Tully argues that 'the intersubjectivity of striving for and responding to forms of mutual recognition is an intrinsic public good of modern politics which contributes to legitimacy and stability whether or not the form of recognition demanded is achieved' (Tully 2000: 5). For him, 'struggles for recognition are struggles of disclosure and acknowledgement'. Even if the end result is not obtained, it does not necessarily matter because what's important is that the state acknowledges the demand of the people, as well as the people that makes this demand. In order to achieve self-determination, a people only has to be able to challenge, if necessary, the constitutional rules of recognition and association, and try to introduce a constitutional amendment, whether or not the amendment passes. So peoples belonging to a multinational democracy should have a right to internal self-determination, but this last notion is to be partly understood in a purely procedural fashion, as part of a negotiating ethics, and not necessarily in the more substantial sense of allowing for a provision concerning internal self-determination in the constitution. Substantial self-determination, for Tully, is perhaps not an essential right, in the crucial sense that conditions the legitimacy of the constitutional order. For him, the 'formal and definitive recognition is not a necessary condition of self-respect and self-esteem' (Tully 2000: 22 n. 4) The true form of internal self-determination happens to be first and foremost a procedural right: 'When this kind of disclosure is not recognized constitutionally by the other members, it is still acknowledged by others in the very act of accepting it with public displays of their own' (Tully 2000: 21–2).

## A Major Malfunction

The most important problem affecting all three versions of what could be called the procedural concept of self-determination is that it is not involving a symmetric form of recognition. These approaches presuppose the existence of a single community to which all citizens belong. They are asking both parties to engage in a dialogue within this community, and this presupposes that the unrecognized minority has to recognize an encompassing community of deliberation, negotiation or conversation, and must do so as an *a priori* of communication. But since this community of dialogue is an encompassing people, accepting the invitation to engage in a deliberation, negotiation or conversation for a minority people amounts to recognizing the existence of the encompassing people.[4] But we are at the same time told that the fundamental constitutional provisions are perhaps not as important as the deliberation, negotiation or conversation. Therefore, the formal recognition of the minority and its right to self-determination is relegated to an uncertain future, while the encompassing community is to be recognized at the outset. The minority people cannot ask to be recognized as an *a priori* of communication, but the encompassing community appears to be entitled to make this requirement. And so it appears that recognition is not reciprocal or mutual. The minority people must recognize the encompassing people by accepting to be part of it in a community of dialogue, and this amounts to accepting its right to external self-determination. But on the other hand, this last people, more powerful and encompassing, may decide at the end of the dialogue not to recognize the minority people. We do not know what is the end result of the dialogue and we are told that it does not really matter as long as the deliberation, negotiation or

---

4    Chambers makes this point in a candid way when she writes: 'In giving up a unitary vision, we should not give up the goal of unity. Constitutional negotiation and dialogue is still about speaking as "We the people". This can be achieved in a conversation in which participants simply try to understand each other before they try to negotiate with each other or conclude a contract with each other. The sincere attempt to understand what one's interlocutor is saying, and why, can initiate a process that builds the bonds necessary to live together as a "people" without requiring that we give up our differences and unique identities' (Chambers 2000b: 69).

conversation keeps on going. This asymmetry is an unjust arrangement for the minority people.

My own account of internal self-determination turns it into a primary right that must be accepted as an *a priori* of communication because, as we saw, it is closely tied to the recognition of the very existence of the people, and this recognition is prescribed by a principle of respect for all agents present in the political realm. Respect for the internal self-determination of their constitutive peoples is thus an inescapable requirement that must be met before deliberation even takes place. And so, in order to be acceptable, the norms of deliberation, negotiation and conversation should be subordinated to the norm of recognition. The idea is that recognition is a two-way street: it involves both the minority people and the encompassing people. If recognition is not mutual and reciprocal, it is just the expression of domination. And the ideal of an unrestricted and unconstrained deliberation, negotiation or conversation, presented as the solution to ethnic, cultural and national conflicts, is not acceptable if it serves to conceal and maintain relations of domination between majority and minority within society (see also Chapter 24). The only way to avoid this consequence is to treat internal self-determination as a primary right and as something that follows from recognition. We must also accept that peoples must recognize each other even before they begin to deliberate, negotiate or converse.

## Primary Right Theories and Remedial Right Only Theories

Following Allen Buchanan (1998, 2003, 2007), we could distinguish between primary right theories of secession and remedial right only theories to secession. A primary right to secede is a right that a people would have even in the absence of past injustice that they would have suffered. There are according to Buchanan *associative* and *ascriptive* versions of the theory. According to the associative version, a majority vote within the population would be sufficient to justify secession. According to the ascriptive version of the theory, there are features belonging to the people as such that justify for their protection the exercise of a full right to external self-determination. A remedial right to secede, on the other hand, is a right that could not be granted unless injustices would have been committed to the seceding people. More generally, external self-determination understood as a remedial right is conditioned by the satisfaction of certain norms. When external determination takes the form of the violation of the territorial integrity of a given state, it can become legitimate only if some kind of injustice has been perpetrated on the seceding people. In the case of peoples that already have a sovereign state, they will have the right to maintain that state and thus exercise external self-determination if they have been able to accommodate their internal minorities.

It is important to notice that we are here talking about *general rights* as opposed to *special rights*, and about *unilateral* secession as opposed to *negotiated* secession. Once again, we owe these distinctions to Buchanan. It is of course possible to grant special rights to a people if the population of the encompassing state wishes to do so in its constitution. Understood as a special right, the right to secede does not follow from an obligation to do so and it does not concern us here. Similarly, when the right is the result of negotiations with representatives of the encompassing state, we should also allow a people to secede even in the absence of past injustices. What's troublesome is when, in the absence of a special right, we are considering a people engaged in a seceding process in the absence of a negotiated process.

It is here that we may want to impose important remedial conditions. It could be argued that external self-determination is conditioned by the satisfaction of remedial conditions. But notice that this applies not only to seceding peoples but also to peoples that already have a sovereign state. The peoples who already own a state do not have a primary right to external self-determination. They must comply with various conditions just like peoples who do not own a state. Granting a primary right to secede may sound like a generous idea, but since it means that the right to own a state is a primary right, it will be true also of those peoples who already own a state. And so with the notion of a primary right to external self-determination, we have nothing to say against a people which refuses secession to a group that lives within its own frontiers, because this group happens to be violating the primary right of the population as a whole to external self-determination. So defending a remedial right only theory of secession should not be seen as the expression of a bias in favour of already existing states. For they too must behave in accordance with certain norms of conduct. If they don't comply with these conditions, then they lose the right to have a sovereign state. Remedial theories of secession, under this interpretation, do not necessarily reveal a prejudice against seceding groups, because peoples organized into sovereign states are also targeted by a remedial account of external self-determination. Indeed, external self-determination is not a primary right, not even for peoples that do already have a state.

## Conclusion

In this chapter, I have examined the concept of internal self-determination and noticed that it could be interpreted in many different ways. I have also defined the concept of people, since peoples are the entities that are entitled to exercise the right to internal self-determination. I came up with an institutional definition of peoples that is perfectly well adapted to a political and not a metaphysical version of liberalism. In the course of using this definition, it appeared that among all the interests of peoples, those that relate to the development of the institutions of peoples must have a special place among all their interests, because they relate to their identity as peoples. So it should not be surprising if the interest to develop oneself economically, socially and culturally and to determine one's own political status within the encompassing state appears to be the expression of a fundamental right. Indeed, the international community has been led to recognize that internal self-determination is a primary right and that the state has an obligation to comply with that right. The reason is that it concerns the very existence of peoples understood in the institutional sense. This also explains why the obligation to comply with internal self-determination is not just an obligation to recognize symbolically the existence of a people. It is at the same time an obligation to allow national minorities to flourish in their institutional identity. I finally looked at a fairly new account that defines internal self-determination as a right to initiate a process leading to a constitutional amendment, and I have explained that in many instances, it could violate the idea that recognition must be reciprocal.

Finally, I briefly examined external determination or the right to own a state. My position on this issue is that there is no primary right to own a state. This is not a bias against stateless peoples because the remark also applies to those who already own a state. No people can claim that the right to own a state is its god given right, not even those who already own a state. There must be good moral grounds for justifying the act of secession, and states must also behave in a correct manner toward their internal minorities if they want to justify a right to maintain their territorial integrity. We already accept that peoples have a remedial right to unilateral secession when they are colonies, when they suffer violent military oppression or when they are subject to an unjust annexation of their territories. But as I have argued elsewhere (Seymour 2007), the international community also accepts that the failure of the state to respect the right to internal self-determination of its constituent peoples also induces a right to unilateral secession (for a discussion of this question see Chapter 17). Therefore it should be clear why it is so important to define in precise terms the concept of internal self-determination. The fact of the matter is that the notion has enormous normative political implications for the issues of secession and for the preservation of territorial integrity.

# References

Bessette, J. (1994), *The Mild Voice of Reason: Deliberative Democracy and American National Government* (Chicago, IL: University of Chicago Press).
Blattberg, C. (2003), *Shall We Dance? A Patriotic Politics for Canada* (Montreal and Kingston, ON: McGill-Queen's University Press).
Buchanan, A. (1998), 'The International Institutional Dimension of Secession', in P.B. Lehning (ed.), *Theories of Secession* (London: Routledge), 227–56.
Buchanan, A. (2003), *Justice, Legitimacy, and Self-Determination: Moral Foundations for International Law* (Oxford: Oxford University Press).
Buchanan, A. (2007), 'Secession', *Stanford Encyclopedia of Philosophy*.
Chambers, S. (1996), *Reasonable Democracy: Jürgen Habermas and the Politics of Discourse* (Ithaca, NY: Cornell University Press).
Chambers, S. (with A. Costain) (2000a), *Deliberation, Democracy, and the Media* (Lanham, MD: Rowman & Littlefield).

Chambers, S. (2000b), 'Democracy, Habermas, and Canadian Exceptionalism', in Ronald Beiner and Wayne Norman (eds), *Canadian Political Philosophy* (Oxford: Oxford University Press), 63–77.

Dryzek, J. (2000), *Deliberative Democracy and Beyond: Liberals, Critics, Contestations* (Oxford: Oxford University Press).

Elster, J. (ed.) (1998), *Deliberative Democracy* (Cambridge: Cambridge University Press).

Ferry, J.-M. (1996), *L'éthique reconstructive* (Paris: Éditions du Cerf).

Fishkin, J. (1991), *Democracy and Deliberation: New Directions for Democratic Reform* (New Haven, CT: Yale University Press).

Fishkin, J. (with P. Laslett) (2003), *Debating Deliberative Democracy* (Oxford: Blackwell).

Galeotti, A.E. (2002), *Toleration as Recognition* (Cambridge: Cambridge University Press).

Gutmann, A. (2003), *Identity in Democracy* (Princeton, NJ: Princeton University Press).

Habermas, J. (2001), *Postnational Constellation: Political Essays* (Cambridge, MA: MIT Press).

Kymlicka, W. (1989), *Liberalism, Community and Culture* (Oxford: Clarendon Press).

Kymlicka, W. (1995), *Multicultural Citizenship* (Oxford: Oxford University Press).

Kymlicka, W. (2007), *Multicultural Odysseys* (Oxford: Oxford University Press).

Laden, A.S. (2001), *Reasonably Radical: Deliberative Liberalism and the Politics of Identity* (Ithaca, NY: Cornell University Press).

Markell, P. (2003), *Bound by Recognition* (Princeton, NJ: Princeton University Press).

Rawls, J. (1999), *The Law of Peoples* (Cambridge, MA: Harvard University Press).

Seymour, M. (2007), 'Secession as a Remedial Right', *Inquiry* 4, 395–423.

Supreme Court of Canada (1998), *Reference re Secession of Quebec*, 2 S.C.R. 217.

Thompson, D. (with Amy Gutmann) (2004), *Why Deliberative Democracy?* (Princeton, NJ: Princeton University Press).

Tully, J. (2000), 'Introduction', in J. Tully and A.G. Gagnon (eds), *Multinational Democracies* (Cambridge : Cambridge University Press), 1–34.

UN (1945), *Charter of the United Nations*, June 26, 59 Stat. 1031, T.S. 993, 3 Bevans 1153, entered into force 24 October 1945.

UN (1970), *Declaration on Principles of International Law concerning Friendly Relation and Co-operation among States in Accordance with the Charter of the United Nations*, Resolution 2625 (XXV), 1883rd plenary meeting, 24 October 1970.

UN (2007), *United Nations Declaration on the Rights of Indigenous Peoples*, Adopted by General Assembly Resolution 61/295 on 13 September 2007.

# Remedial Theories of Secession

## Reinold Schmücker

## Introduction

Political philosophy does not first of all deal with the causes of secession attempts which – apart from a rough categorization[1] – can only be described in detail by way of case studies, as they are found in Parts I and VI of this book. Rather, it focuses on normative questions connected to secession attempts: is secession legitimate – and if so: who has a right to secede under which circumstances? Should the right to secede be guaranteed by the constitutions of democratic states under the rule of law (as it was fixed e.g. in the constitution of the Soviet Union)? Or, on the contrary, are existing states entitled to suppress secession attempts, at least under certain circumstances? (For a discussion of these issues from a legal point of view see Chapters 17 and 19.)

The philosophical discussion of such questions does not aim at evaluating the *legality* of secessions; it does not ask if secession is according to international law. Rather, it is interested in developing normative, valid law-transcending criteria which allow for judging on the *legitimacy* of secession attempts and on the *moral* appropriateness of regulations of international law. In so far, normative political philosophy is moral philosophy referring to political orders.

The moral analysis of secession attempts is of particular significance because for the time being there is no international legal norm which explicitly addresses the legality of secession. Indeed, from Article 6 of the *Declaration on the Granting of Independence to Colonial Countries and Peoples* from 14 December 1960 (GA Res. 1514 [XV]), from the ban on aggression, which is expressively confirmed by Article 2 of the UN Charter, as well as from the *uti possidetis* principle, confirmed by the International Court of Justice in 1986 (ICJ Rep. 1986: 586–7), which bans the change of existing borders by referring to the right to self-determination, we might conclude that currently international law generally negates a right to secede. However, many international law experts nowadays believe that under special circumstances, particularly in case of extreme violations of international law and human rights, the peoples' right to self-determination may go as far as to giving

---

[1] See, for example, Bartkus (1999: 217–18).

reason to a right to secede, as in particular the 1970 *Friendly Relations Declaration* (Annex to GA Res. 2625 [XXV]) indirectly connects a state's right to territorial integrity to observing the norms of international law and human rights (Hobe and Kimminich 2004: 118; Ipsen et al. 2004: 422–3; Cassese 2005: 62 and 68; see also Oeter 1992: 756–8). (See also Chapters 17 and 21.)

Outside legal theory, one can identify three prominent strategies of normatively justifying secession: *choice theories, communitarian theories* and *remedial approaches*.[2] As secessions have also always a territorial component, one might assume that secession is justified also by property theory; for property theories definitely play a role in the debate on the legitimacy of territorial claims (see Chapter 4). But property theories are not used to justify secession primarily because a state's political authority over a certain territory is of a nature different from a property title referring to a part of the planet's surface.[3] *Ownership of land* and *authority over a territory* are neither based on each other[4] nor do they result from each other.

*Choice theories* refer exclusively to the will of the majority of the population of a territory. A theory of this kind is introduced in Chapter 4 and outlined in some detail in Chapter 23. They do not interpret a collective's right to self-determination as a collective right *sui generis* but as a right derived from the right to self-determination of individuals: If the majority of individuals living in a sub-territory of a state agree on not longer delegating their individual right to self-determination to this state but to another state, which maybe must still be founded, according to a choice theory majority will of a territory's population legitimates an intended secession.

---

2 There are also theorists who justify secession on grounds other than these three, for example, Hoppe (1996 and 2001), according to whom secession is legal because in principle the biggest-possible number of states is desirable, among others for economic reasons and for reasons of migration policy. Chapter 25 also suggests an alternative approach to normative assessment of secessions and points out some problems common to all of those approaches.

3 However, for centuries it was common to make territorial sovereignty the subject of sale contracts and testaments, to acquire it by heritage, donation or marriage – thus not different from what is done with private property. In the context of the possibility of acquiring territory by way of cession, which is still recognized by international law – for example, Russia selling Alaska to the USA in 1867, France selling Louisiana in 1803 or Spain selling the Philippines in 1898 – the property-theoretical interpretation of territorial sovereignty appears to be legally institutionalized, and the domiciliary right granted to the owner of real estate is easily recognized as a *reproduction en miniature* of the state's sovereignty. Still today, the conviction that no territorial claims can be grounded on the acquisition of land is not common enough to calm down anxieties in this respect – otherwise it could not be explained why many states restrict or even rule out the acquisition of land by foreigners. In so far, however, as the principle of the 'sovereign equality' of states, codified by Article 2, No. 1 of the UN Charter, includes any state's claim to recognition of its territorial integrity, according to the interpretation by the *Friendly Relations Declaration* (see e.g. Simma 2002: 79–80), nobody can achieve territorial sovereignty simply by acquiring land.

4 A necessary precondition for land ownership is only the existence of a state's territorial sovereignty as such, for without it land ownership would not be legally protected.

Choice theories are advocated by Harry Beran (1984, 1988, 1990, 1994, 1998), David Gauthier (1994), Daniel Philpott (1995, 1998), Christopher Wellman (1995, 2005), David Copp (1997), Gabriele Dördelmann (2001), Frank Dietrich (2007, 2010) and others. These theories may also be called majority theories.

*Communitarian theories*, on the other hand, interpret a collective's right to self-determination as a right a collective as such is entitled to. Communitarian theorists such as Avishai Margalit and Joseph Raz (1990), Kai Nielsen (1993, 1998), David Miller (1995: 194; 1996), Daniel K. Donnelly (1996) or Margaret Moore (1997), however, do not grant such a right to self-determination to every collective but restrict this right to collectives which, as they speak a common language, have a common religion or a common cultural tradition, may be called peoples or nations. Communitarian theories are sometimes offered in the theoretical framework of 'modern' or 'liberal' nationalism and thus are sometimes called *national theories*.[5]

*Remedial theories* refer neither to an individual nor to a collective right to self-determination. They rather ground the legitimacy of secession on the legitimacy of freedom from unjust rule – a freedom which under certain circumstances may achieved by secession. Accordingly secession is legitimate if it promises to relieve grave injustice. Remedial theories of this kind are advanced by Henry Sidgwick (1919: 226), Allen Buchanan (1991: 74; 1997a: 37; 1997b: 310; 1998), Christine Chwaszcza (1998), Wayne Norman (1998: 41) and Otfried Höffe (1999: 392).

Of course, this typology is an ideal-typical distinction. In many cases, however, arguments for or against secession combine different kinds of justifications of secession. But, if we want to know if a certain claim to secession is morally justified or not, we need to know what kind of reasons can morally justify secession; not every reason stated in support of morally justifying a claim to secession will actually legitimate it.[6]

As choice theory is discussed in Chapter 23, in this chapter I will focus on remedial theories of secession. While doing so, I will pay particular attention to the question if – and if, how far – a remedial theory may justify secession also as a means of correcting historic injustice.

## Choice Theories and Communitarian Theories: Some Problems

At first sight, choice theories and communitarian theories seem to be very attractive strategies of morally legitimating unilateral secession, since both do not connect the legitimacy of a claim to secede to previous injustice. In contrast to remedial

---

5   Chapter 21 outlines a conceptual framework for moral assessment similar to those of the communitarian or national theories.
6   An instructive compilation of case-related *normative* analyses is offered by Coppieters and Sakwa (2003).

theories, they thus discharge the secessionist party from giving evidence to having suffered from injustice. To give evidence to the legitimacy of its claim to secede it must only explain that as a collective it is provided with certain qualities. According to communitarian theories, these are usually a common language, history, religion or cultural tradition. Choice theories demand even less: they are satisfied with the secessionist party being the majority of the population of the secessionist territory. The significance of this 'relief' can hardly be overestimated: this makes it much easier to justify a claim to secede in order to create a democracy under the rule of law than any other strategy of morally justifying unilateral secession.

Furthermore, choice theories may refer to the following two basic convictions of political liberalism which are widely accepted, at least among political theorists: (1) the assumption that every human has a moral right to political self-determination, and (2) the conviction that for conflicts resulting from all sides claiming this right to self-determination there is only one just solution, the democratic one, i.e. majority decision. In contrast, the *prima facie* plausibility of communitarian theories is not at last due to the fact that basically they restrict the right to secede to those collectives to which the existing international law has already granted the right to self-determination.[7]

At a closer look, however, both choice theories and communitarian theories lose their *prima facie* attraction. At least as far as appearing as a specifically democratic reason for secession, choice theories involve a self-contradiction. For, if the sheer majority vote of a territorial population was sufficient to legitimate a secession, the populations of sub-territories would be able to enforce the correction of majority decisions by threatening with the instrument of secession. In so far, a choice theory implies the possibility to devalue the majority principle, whose unconditional validity it postulates on the other hand (Lincoln 1989: 220; Buchanan 1998: 21–2; Chwaszcza 1998: 483).

Furthermore, a choice theory is incompatible with the deeply rooted intuition of justice that it would be illegitimate if by way of secession an economically prospering community 'got rid' of its 'poor relatives' (Chwaszcza 1998: 481). Additionally, since choice theories refer solely to the will of the majority of a

---

7   For details see e.g. Ipsen et al. (2004: 405–10): 'The right to self-determination is a peoples' right. ... Peoples must be identified according to subjective and objective criteria. The *subjective* approach assumes that a people is a group of humans understanding themselves as a people with an identity of its own. Thus, self-identification is the crucial aspect. ... The self-identification of peoples is co-determined by *objective* factors. That these are necessary becomes obvious by the fact that otherwise a people could be founded in the same way as a club is founded. ... The components of group-quality such as territory, language, culture, religion, mentality or common historical heritage must be assumed objective factors'. See also the definition of a people suggested during the UNESCO expert meeting 1989 as 'a group of individual human beings who enjoy some or all of the following common features: (a) a common historical tradition, (b) racial or ethnic identity, (c) cultural homogeneity, (d) linguistic unity, (e) religious or ideological affinity, (f) territorial connection, (g) common economic life' (quoted after Hailbronner 2001: 206 n. 186). See also Chapter 21.

# REMEDIAL THEORIES OF SECESSION

territory's population, they do not offer any possibility to restrict the progress of secessions above the existence of simple one-person-states. For, by choosing a sufficiently small territory, any group (and in the extreme case even a single person) might present their will as the majority will of a territory's population (Miller 1995: 111). Thus, choice theories threaten to support an extreme, worldwide fragmentation into very small states, resulting in the creation of states being so small that they will not be able anymore to solve their main task of securing peace (for a counter-argument see Chapter 23).

Communitarian theories avoid this consequence by granting a right to secede only to a majority of a territory's population which can be addressed as a people, nation or community, due to common language, culture or religion (Margalit and Raz 1990; Nielsen 1993; Miller 1995: 194; Moore 1997). However, this restriction raises the question of *why* only the majority of the population of an ethnically, religiously or culturally homogeneous territory shall be granted the right to their own state as well as the question of why only communities forming a territory's majority population.

Choice theories face a similar fundamental question: *why* should the collectives with a right to secede be restricted to *territorial* populations, if the collective right to political self-determination is due to the accumulation of individual rights to self-determination? *Why* should only those individuals be allowed to accumulate their rights who are settling on an integrated territory? Here, choice theories are forced to introduce a pragmatically motivated territorial clause. However, the latter must take the possibility into account that a territory is illegitimately annexed or its population is driven out by force. Thus, Copp emphasizes that in principle a right to political self-determination can be granted only to those collectives as either settling on a certain territory or for historical reasons having a claim to such a territory (Copp 1997: 295). This means that from the point of view of choice theorists the population of a certain territory is entitled to secede *only if* their claim to a territory is not contradicted by the claims of others to that same territory, based on historic injustice. Thus, choice theories implicitly raise the question of historically grounded claims to a territory as a source of the right to secession.

Communitarian theories cannot evade this question either. This becomes obvious if these theories are confronted with the following question: which of two equally sized groups which are both settled on the same territory of a state and meet the criteria for being nations or peoples, is allowed to realize its claim to secede? In principle, a communitarian theory must grant this right to both groups (unless it intends to support a normative hierarchization of cultures, languages or ethnicities – the criteria for which can only be arbitrary). But this means that under certain conditions a communitarian theory as such is not able to decide on conflicting claims to secede. For, if claims are conflicting which, according to its criteria, are equally justified – and that such a case may happen is shown by the conflict between Israel and the Palestinians – it must ask about the legitimacy of the respective claim to the territory (see also Chapter 25).

## Remedial Theories: Some Advantages

In contrast to choice and communitarian theories, remedial theories grant a collective a unilateral right to secede only if otherwise there is no possibility to remedy the gravely unjust rule of a state. Insofar, remedial theories are 'Remedial Right Only Theories' (Buchanan 1997a: 35; 2004: 353). Any state rule may be considered unjust if this state's authorities tolerate, support or commit grave violations of human rights, particularly those threatening the physical integrity of the state's population or a part of it. According to a remedial theory, secession is justified particularly if in this way the secessionist territory is liberated from a government which tolerates, supports or commits grave violations of the human rights of the secessionist population, without any other possibility for the secessionist population to be separated or liberated from this state.

Most supporters of a remedial theory, however, do not conceive the moral right to secede as a pure right of self-defence. For they recognize a moral right to secede also in those cases when by way of secession the previous sovereignty of an annexed state shall be re-established or an act of colonization shall be reversed (Birch 1984; Buchanan 1991: 74; 1997a: 37; 1998; 2004: 355–7; Chwaszcza 1998; Höffe 1999: 392; Schmücker 2002, 2006). However, in this context it often remains unclear how long ago this territorial injustice must have happened to justify secession. Furthermore, some remedial theorists assume that also 'serious and persisting violations of intrastate autonomy agreements by a state' may be a basis for a moral right to secede (Buchanan 2004: 357).

Compared to choice theories and communitarian theories, remedial theories show several essential advantages.

1. By *allowing* secession as an *ultima ratio*, remedial theories take into account that there may be situations in which a party willing to secede cannot be expected to give up on secession.
2. On the other hand, remedial theories take into account that, as experience shows, any unilateral secession is linked to the risk of violent conflicts, for example civil war, threatening with severe suffering. Only by recognizing secession as an instrument of collective self-defence and a means to reverse grave territorial injustice which cannot be re-compensated otherwise, remedial theories address the question of the degree of suffering that attempts at secession are allowed to cause. Remedial theories, in general, imply that suffering usually arising from unilateral secession can be morally acceptable only if the party willing to secede cannot be expected to give up on secession.
3. By tying the legitimacy of secession to *grave* injustice, remedial theories argue that any claim to secede must be weighed against legitimate claims of the remaining population of the host state and of a minority on the secessionist territory which is possibly against secession. In contrast, choice theories and communitarian theories take into account other parties' claims opposing the claim to secede only by introducing additional conditions for legitimacy

which depart from their main model of justification (based on either choice or community or both).
4. Remedial theories take into account that historical territorial injustice may give reason to a moral right to secede.
5. But remedial theories also take into account that historical territorial injustice may possibly give reason to third party claims to the secessionist territory which contradict a claim to secede.
6. Remedial theories also take into account the purposeful nature of a state's territorial sovereignty. Territorial sovereignty is at present a means of guaranteeing the rule of civil law, of human rights and of opportunities to participate in political decision-making. In the future, instruments other than territorial sovereignty may be devised to perform these functions. But as long as it is doubtful that these functions can be taken over by any other institution, the institution of the state's territorial sovereignty may be considered legitimate because – no matter how incompletely in the single case – it fulfils precisely these functions.

It is the lack of alternatives to such a teleological understanding of the territorial sovereignty of states which, in my opinion, provides remedial theories with their persuasiveness. Such a teleological understanding of the state's territorial sovereignty implies the recognition of the *prima facie* legitimacy of the territorial *status quo*: it implies that there can be no absolute justification of the state's territorial sovereignty. On the contrary, a certain territorial *status quo* is legitimate as long as it serves the purpose of the state's territorial sovereignty and does not contradict it. The *prima facie* legitimacy of the territorial *status quo* does not rule out a moral right to secede: the purpose of the state's territorial sovereignty might be better fulfilled by secession. However, a moral right to secede will always have to be weighed against those rights which oppose or are contrary to a change of the territorial *status quo*. And in so far as the territorial *status quo* serves the purpose of a state's territorial sovereignty, this weighing will be in favour of secession only if the latter is possible without violating the rights of third parties or is carried out by agreement of concerned third parties. This explains why a secession carried out on the basis of an agreement between the host state and the secessionist party is always morally permissible.

A further right to secede may arise if the *status quo* is unjust. This will always be the case if a state exerts its sovereignty in a way which is not according to the purpose of a state's territorial sovereignty. A state which tolerates, supports or even commits grave violations of human rights on its territory does obviously act unjustly. However, in such a case a right to secede can only be justified as a right to self-defence, based on the exhaustion of all other, less drastic, options. Accordingly, less drastic options, which perhaps will achieve the desired result even more quickly – such as the removal of a despotic government – must be preferred to changing the territorial *status quo* by way of secession (see also Chapter 25). But if secession *is the only way* to guarantee the appropriate use of territorial sovereignty, it is legitimated even if it cannot be achieved without violating the rights of third parties.[8]

The demand for appropriate use of a state's territorial sovereignty includes the need to correct territorial injustice. For we cannot speak of an appropriate use of territorial sovereignty if the latter implies the non-expiated and continued violation of the inhabitants' fundamental rights. Therefore, in the case of a territorial injustice (e.g. annexation), the demand for the just use of territorial sovereignty may under certain conditions justify the reestablishment of the illegally changed territorial status by way of a restitutive secession.

Against the above argument for remedial secession, it has been objected that injustice can only give reason to a remedial right but not to the right to a territory (Brilmayer 1991: 188; Copp 1998: 230–31). However, this objection does not take into account that a remedial theory considers a claim to secede, based on the inappropriate use of territorial sovereignty, as legitimate only if a change of the territorial *status quo* promises to remedy that situation. A few remedial theorists have also suggested that a host state that has inappropriately used its territorial sovereignty has thereby forfeited its claim to territorial sovereignty (Tesón 1998: 147).

More importantly perhaps it has also been objected that the recognition of a moral right to correct territorial injustice by way of secession would, for all practical purposes, question any existing state (Hösle 1997: 989). Furthermore, it would not be 'just to force the occupants' children to leave their homes only because that country has been illegally occupied, for they are innocent' (Hösle 1997: 826). The simple fact that most current states are based on historic territorial injustice and that thus a variety of collectives could claim a right to restituting secession, however, is not an objection against such a right: we do not deny the victims of a particularly frequent kind of injustice their claims for re-compensation simply because that type of injustice leads to too many claimants demanding compensation.

Moreover, in most cases the 'children of a country's occupants' do benefit from the *illegal* deeds of their ancestors. And to a certain extent, which usually declines from generation to generation, this is true even of the children's children of the occupiers. This *connection of profit*, which connects the children and children's children of unjust perpetrators to the latter's deeds, makes the general rejection of restitutive secession look implausible. On the other hand, however, this connection of profit does not in any case give reason to a compelling claim to restitution. For, the children and children's children of the (unjust) occupiers of a country are responsible only for benefiting from the act but not for the act of annexation or occupation itself: there is, therefore, no claim of punishment against them. Thus, we may indeed assume that due to the injustice of annexation the occupiers have forfeited claims they would have otherwise legitimately acquired, e.g. by having invested their work in the cultivation or the economic-cultural development of a territory. But in respect of the occupiers' children and children's children, such an assumption would be untenable. In this context, the chronological distance between

---

[8] The principle of proportionality in respect of violating the right of third parties restricts the exercise of this right as well.

a claim to secede and the act of occupation is of moral significance: the more time passes from the unjust act of occupation, the more legitimate claims against the restitution by way of secession may accumulate. For, in the course of time, the legitimate claims opposing this kind of a restitution grow with the ongoing cultural and economic investment by the descendants of (unjust) occupiers, who have themselves committed no injustice. The more time has passed since the annexation, the more likely it is that weighing these opposing claims will result in the rejection of the claim to secession as a restitution.

If the state in which the descendants of those people who were unjustly occupied or annexed now live is constituted democratically and according to the rule of law, the descendants are thereby *granted* their moral right to political self-determination (for a different view see Chapter 21). In this case it is not possible to derive any right to secede from the sheer fact that the state in which they live does not include the same territories or boundaries as the state in which their ancestors lived. For, individuals have indeed a moral right to political self-determination, but *not* a right to exactly the same state context or boundaries as their ancestor had. Thus, a claim to secede grounded on historic injustice may be justified only in so far as the above sketched connection of profit is linked to the following *connection of disadvantagement*. Only if the children and children's children of the occupied are more disadvantaged materially or in respect of their access to public offices and lucrative professions than would be the case if their ancestors' state had not been occupied, then the former would have a justified claim to restitution by secession. Often such a connection of disadvantagement decreases over time – from the time of the act of unjust annexation. For this reason a claim to secede resulting from historic territorial injustice will lose its effectiveness the longer ago the annexation of the territory happened (Brilmayer 1992: 559; Sunstein 1994: 33; Buchanan 1997b: 311; Miller 1996: 270 n. 14; Schmücker 2002).

Of course, chronological distance is not the only factor which must be taken into account for the weighing of a claim to secede against any contradicting claims. A state which has annexed another state but has then provided it with an exemplary system of social security for aged and sick people, for example, will be granted better claims to the preservation of the *status quo* than a state which has recklessly exploited the mineral resources of the annexed territory and has brought the population close to starvation. Independently of the results of the weighing of secession-legitimating against secession-delegitimating claims in the actual case, while taking all other factors into account, the time which has passed since the act of annexation will always have a secession-delegitimating effect – except if the act of annexation has been (so to speak) repeated by violently suppressing an attempt to regain independent statehood.

# The Consequences of a Remedial Theory of Secession for Legal Policy

Which consequences for legal policy are suggested by a remedial theory? If shaking off an unjust rule and the reverse of historic injustice are the only reasons by which secession can be morally legitimated, grounding a right to secede in the constitutions of single states does not make sense. Such a right would not be able to prevent either unjust rule or annexation, and we may also suppose that it would not be particularly helpful for shaking off an unjust rule and re-establishing the state sovereignty of an annexed state. For, it is improbable that an unjust regime or even an aggressor state which has conquered foreign territory will respect a constitutional right to secede. In contrast to this, it seems to be advisable to establish a right to secede in the context of international law, for the purpose of shaking off unjust rule or correcting historic injustice (see also Chapters 17 and 19). A right to secede which has been established in the context of international law and is restricted to these two cases might serve as a guideline for the international community of states in deciding whether or not to support secession attempts and to recognize seceded territories. This may in the long run restrict the chances for the success of illegitimate secession attempts and increase the chances of success of legitimate secession attempts. However, in establishing guidelines of this kind, one needs to take into account that in the course of time (from the time of the act of injustice) the moral right to secession so to speak, runs out. Thus, a right to secede which is established in the context of international law should be restricted by a statutory limitation clause which takes the secession-delegitimating effect of the chronological distance between the act of annexation and the secession attempt into account. In my opinion, such a limitation period should not be shorter than the time of one generation, which is (roughly measured) 30 years, and which in the legal systems of most states under the rule of law marks the upper limit of legally fixed limitation periods.

However, the restitution of *unjust* rule by way of secession would be illegitimate even if it happens before a limitation period stipulated by international law runs out. Thus, it is not sufficient to restrict a right to secede which is grounded on historical injustice only by a statutory limitation clause. Rather, restitutive secession may be recognized by international law within a limitation period, only if it meets one more condition: it may not result in the restitution of states which again would give reason to legitimate secession.

# References

Bartkus, V.O. (1999), *The Dynamic of Secession* (Cambridge: Cambridge University Press).
Beran, H. (1984), 'A Liberal Theory of Secession', *Political Studies* 32, 21–31.
Beran, H. (1988), 'More Theory of Secession: A Response to Birch', *Political Studies* 36, 316–23.
Beran, H. (1990), 'Who Should be Entitled to Vote in Self-Determination Referenda?', in M. Warner and R. Crisp (eds), *Terrorism, Protest, and Power* (Aldershot: Elgar), 152–66.
Beran, H. (1994), 'The Place of Secession in Liberal Democratic Theory', in P. Gilbert and P. Gregory (eds), *Nations, Cultures and Markets* (Aldershot: Ashgate), 47–65.
Beran, H. (1998), 'A Democratic Theory of Political Self-determination for a New World-Order', in P.B. Lehning (ed.), *Theories of Secession* (London and New York: Routledge), 32–59.
Birch, A.H. (1984), 'Another Liberal Theory of Secession', *Political Studies* 32, 596–602.
Brilmayer, L. (1991), 'Secession and Self-Determination: A Territorial Interpretation', *The Yale Journal of International Law* 16, 177–202.
Brilmayer, L. (1992), 'Groups, Histories, and International Law', *Cornell International Law Journal* 25, 555–63.
Buchanan, A. (1991), *Secession: The Morality of Political Divorce from Fort Sumter to Lithuania and Quebec* (Boulder, CO: Westview Press).
Buchanan, A. (1997a), 'Theories of Secession', *Philosophy and Public Affairs* 26, 31–61.
Buchanan, A. (1997b), 'Self-Determination, Secession, and the Rule of Law', in R. McKim and J. McMahan (eds), *The Morality of Nationalism* (New York and Oxford: Oxford University Press), 301–23.
Buchanan, A. (1998), 'Democracy and Secession', in M. Moore (ed.), *National Self-Determination and Secession* (Oxford and New York: Oxford University Press), 14–33.
Buchanan, A. (2004), *Justice, Legitimacy, and Self-Determination: Moral Foundations for International Law* (New York and Oxford: Oxford University Press).
Cassese, A. (2005), *International Law*, 2nd edn (New York and Oxford: Oxford University Press).
Chwaszcza, C. (1998), 'Selbstbestimmung, Sezession und Souveränität', in C. Chwaszcza and W. Kersting (eds), *Politische Philosophie der internationalen Beziehungen* (Frankfurt am Main: Suhrkamp), 467–501.
Copp, D. (1997), 'Democracy and Communal Self-Determination', in R. McKim and J. McMahan (eds), *The Morality of Nationalism* (New York and Oxford: Oxford University Press), 277–300.
Copp, D. (1998), 'International Law and Morality in the Theory of Secession', *The Journal of Ethics* 2, 219–45.
Coppieters, B. and R. Sakwa (eds) (2003), *Contextualizing Secession: Normative Studies in a Comparative Perspective* (Oxford and New York: Oxford University Press).

Dietrich, F. (2007), 'Das Sezessionsrecht im demokratischen Verfassungsstaat', *Leviathan* 35, 62–85.
Dietrich, F. (2010), *Sezession und Demokratie. Eine philosophische Untersuchung* (Berlin, New York: de Gruyter).
Donnelly, D.K. (1996), 'States and Substates in a Free World: A Proposed General Theory of National Self-determination', *Nationalism and Ethnic Politics* 2, 286–311.
Dördelmann, G. (2001), 'Dürfen Völker sezedieren?', in M. Anderheiden et al. (eds), *Globalisierung als Problem von Gerechtigkeit und Steuerungsfähigkeit des Rechts* (Stuttgart: Franz Steiner Verlag), 145–56.
Gauthier, D. (1994), 'Breaking Up: An Essay on Secession', *Canadian Journal of Philosophy* 24, 357–72.
Hailbronner, K. (2001), 'Der Staat und der Einzelne als Völkerrechtssubjekte', in W. Graf Vitzthum (ed.), *Völkerrecht*, 2nd edn (Berlin and New York: de Gruyter), 161–265.
Hobe, S. and O. Kimminich (2004), *Einführung in das Völkerrecht*, 8th edn (Tübingen and Basel: Francke).
Höffe, O. (1999), *Demokratie im Zeitalter der Globalisierung* (München: C.H. Beck).
Hoppe, H.-H. (1996), 'Small Is Beautiful and Efficient: The Case for Secession', *Telos* 107, 95–101.
Hoppe, H.-H. (2001), *Democracy: The God That Failed. The Economics and Politics of Monarchy, Democracy, and Natural Order* (New Brunswick, NJ and London: Transaction).
Hösle, V. (1997), *Moral und Politik. Grundlagen einer Politischen Ethik für das 21. Jahrhundert* (München: C.H. Beck).
Ipsen, K. et al. (2004), *Völkerrecht*, 5th edn (München: C.H. Beck).
Lincoln, A. (1989), *Speeches and Writings, 1859–1865* (New York: Library of America).
Margalit, A. and J. Raz (1990), 'National Self-Determination', *The Journal of Philosophy* 87, 439–61.
Miller, D. (1995), *On Nationality* (Oxford: Oxford University Press).
Miller, D. (1996), 'Secession and the Principle of Nationality', in J. Couture, K. Nielsen and M. Seymour (eds), *Rethinking Nationalism* (Calgary: University of Calgary Press), 261–82.
Moore, M. (1997), 'On National Self-Determination', *Political Studies* 45, 900–913.
Nielsen, K. (1993), 'Secession: The Case of Quebec', *Journal of Applied Philosophy* 10, 29–43.
Nielsen, K. (1998), 'Liberal Nationalism and Secession', in M. Moore (ed.), *National Self-Determination and Secession* (Oxford and New York: Oxford University Press), 103–33.
Norman, W. (1998), 'The Ethics of Secession as the Regulation of Secessionist Politics', in M. Moore (ed.), *National Self-Determination and Secession* (Oxford and New York: Oxford University Press), 34–61.
Oeter, S. (1992), 'Selbstbestimmungsrecht im Wandel', *Zeitschrift für ausländisches öffentliches Recht und Völkerrecht* 52, 741–80.
Philpott, D. (1995), 'In Defense of Self-Determination', *Ethics* 105, 352–85.

Philpott, D. (1998), 'Self-Determination in Practice', in M. Moore (ed.), *National Self-Determination and Secession* (Oxford and New York: Oxford University Press), 79–102.

Schmücker, R. (2002), 'Wiedergutmachung und Sezession', in R. Schmücker and U. Steinvorth (eds), *Gerechtigkeit und Politik* (Berlin: Akademie Verlag), 233–52.

Schmücker, R. (2006), 'Gerechtigkeit und Territorialität', *Deutsche Zeitschrift für Philosophie* 54, 597–621.

Sidgwick, H. (1919), *The Elements of Politics*, 4th edn (London: Macmillan).

Simma, B. (ed.) (2002), *The Charter of the United Nations: A Commentary*, 2nd edn (München: C.H. Beck).

Sunstein, C.R. (1994), 'Approaching Democracy: A New Legal Order for Eastern Europe – Constitutionalism and Secession', in C. Brown (ed.), *Political Restructuring Europe: Ethical Perspectives* (London and New York: Routledge), 11–49.

Tesón, F.R. (1998), *A Philosophy of International Law* (Boulder, CO: Westview Press).

Wellman, C.H. (1995), 'A Defense of Secession and Political Self-Determination', *Philosophy and Public Affairs* 24, 142–71.

Wellman, C.H. (2005), *A Theory of Secession: The Case for Political Self-Determination* (Cambridge: Cambridge University Press).

# Choice Theories of Secession

David D. Speetzen and Christopher Heath Wellman

A choice theory of secession holds that some groups have a right to secede at their own discretion, independently of whether they are now or have ever been victims of injustice. Choice theories are therefore in conflict with remedial-right only theories, which hold that unjust treatment of the seceding group is necessary to justify secession. Choice theories are often distinguished from nationalist theories of secession. Nationalist theories also affirm a primary right to secede, but they claim that this right belongs to only (and for some theorists, *all*) culturally distinct and territorially localized 'nations'. Nationalist theories are therefore typically distinguished from choice theories, because choice theories are not necessarily wedded to the claim that seceding groups must share a common culture, language, history and so on.

On the choice theory presented here, any group has a moral right to secede if and only if (1) it is able and willing to adequately perform the requisite political functions, and (2) it will not undermine the parent state's ability to perform those same functions for its remaining constituents by seceding (Wellman 2005). Two points are worth noting at the outset. First, it is possible (though doubtful) that as a matter of fact only national groups are likely to be able to perform the requisite functions, or (more likely) that only national groups would be sufficiently motivated to exercise their right to secede; but to claim that that right belongs to all or only national groups because of their nationhood would be, on our view, a mistake. Second, our focus here is on whether there is a primary moral right to secede – whether that right ought to be embodied in international law is a further question. It may turn out that a moral right to secede cannot or should not be institutionalized for independent reasons.

In what follows, we first sketch a theory of political legitimacy that underwrites the subsequent arguments for a primary right to secede, claiming that what justifies a state's exercise of coercive power over its subjects is that it performs the range of political functions needed to ensure that those subjects' human rights are adequately secure. From there, we set out three basic strategies for justifying a primary right to secede: arguments that ground a primary right to secede on the individual right to freedom of association, arguments that ground that right on the instrumental value group self-determination has for individual group members, and arguments that ground it on deontological reasons to respect group self-determination. In the final section, we address a number of objections.

## Legitimacy and Secession

Legitimacy is a term used to describe the normative relationship between a coercive government, the individuals subject to its coercion, and other, external agents. A legitimate government is one that has a *right* to coerce its subjects. Like most rights, a government's right to coerce is complex, consisting of various liberties, claims, powers and immunities. At its most basic, legitimacy is (1) a *liberty* to coerce the inhabitants of a given territory, that is, the lack of duty to refrain from coercing them; (2) a *claim* against interference in its coercion, which it holds against both its own subjects and against external parties; (3) a *power* to waive or alter those other parties' duties, as for example when one government waives its right to territorial integrity in order to permit another government to assist it in disaster relief; and (4) an *immunity* against having these aspects of the right to coerce unilaterally altered at the discretion of another party. Recent work in political philosophy has shown how intricate and complicated the contours of these rights can become, but we will leave these complications aside in order to focus on a range of broader issues surrounding legitimacy and secession.

When a separatist group secedes from its parent state, it withdraws or escapes from that government's coercive control and places itself under the control of a new government. To say that an instance of secession is morally justified is just to say that the parent state has no right to continue its coercive control over the inhabitants of the relevant portion of its territory. By maintaining a coercive system of law, states (and *only* states) are able to guarantee (1) the stability needed for social cooperation, (2) the deterrence and punishment needed to prevent serious and pervasive violence, and (3) the institutions and procedures needed to resolve disagreement and conflict peacefully and impartially. At the very least, then, legitimate states adequately secure their subjects' human rights by performing these necessary political functions.

Note that this account of legitimacy remains neutral with regard to where political boundaries are located, and with regard to how those boundaries may change, so long as each state secures the human rights of its subjects. In other words, any given distribution of a territory and its inhabitants between two states is permissible so long as both states are able and willing to perform the requisite political functions; if one of those states (or both) fails to perform those functions – or, as we will say, if it is politically nonviable – then that state is illegitimate, and thus lacks the liberties, claims, powers and immunities that comprise the right to coerce. At a minimum, this implies that secessions which would undermine the parent state's viability, that is, secessions which would undermine its ability to protect the human rights of its remaining subjects, are for that reason impermissible. Moreover, aside from this necessary condition (of preserving the legitimacy of the parent state), at this point nothing has been said about the conditions under which transfers of legitimacy may, or should, take place. This means that the foregoing account of legitimacy cannot by itself settle the fundamental normative question of secession. To answer that question we need to look to other morally relevant factors.

Many factors may be relevant to whether or not a separatist group can acquire legitimate coercive control over some portion of a parent state's subjects and territory. Nationalists argue that all and/or only national groups (groups united by shared cultural characteristics like ethnicity, language, religion and so on) should have a right to secede. Remedial-right only theorists, on the other hand, argue that secession is justified only if necessary to rectify or compensate for past injustices perpetrated against a group by their parent state (Buchanan 2004: 331–400) (for a further discussion see also Chapters 4 and 22). Choice theorists advance the most permissive view of secession. Choice theories hold that neither a shared culture nor a history of victimization is directly relevant to whether a group has a right to secede. Instead, choice theorists maintain that the primary consideration is the value of group self-determination, and that any group able and willing to perform the functions necessary for political legitimacy has a primary right to secede. In what follows, we present three distinct lines of argument which aim to show that state boundaries should be arranged so as to maximize respect for political self-determination, insofar as this is consistent with ensuring adequate security for human rights (see also Chapter 4).

## Freedom of Association Arguments

One common line of argument for choice theories of secession explains the importance of group self-determination in terms of individual autonomy, and specifically, in terms of individual freedom of association (see Beran 1984 and Gauthier 1994). On this view, a group's right to secede is just the sum total of its members' individual rights to disassociate from their parent state and to form a new political community of their own. Alternately, the argument can be framed in terms of consent: if a government's right to coerce depends on the consent of those subject to its coercion, and if those subjects may withdraw their consent at their own discretion, then there is nothing to prevent individual subjects from jointly opting out of one state and opting in to another whenever they wish.

On the one hand, liberals defend individual autonomy on instrumental grounds by arguing that interference in another person's self-regarding behaviour is likely to undermine her welfare, since each person is likely to be the (1) most knowledgeable, (2) most interested, and (3) best positioned to promote her own welfare. Since other agents – the state included – are generally less informed about particular persons' desires and preferences and less motivated to make choices that would satisfy those preferences, there is a strong case for allowing individuals to make many choices on their own behalf. This emphasis on freedom of association prompts some liberals to conclude that individuals should be free to disassociate from any groups, up to and including membership in a state. Thus, the instrumental value of autonomy appears to support the view that individual subjects, and groups of subjects acting jointly, have a primary right to secede.

But some people find instrumental arguments for individual autonomy lacking, because in some cases it may turn out that we are not, in fact, the most knowledgeable, most interested or best positioned to promote our own welfare, and in such cases, a purely instrumental defence would have to admit that some paternalistic interference by other persons or organizations might be justified. For instance, suppose I decide that I would be better off removing myself from civilization entirely, and returning quite literally to a state of nature – perhaps by packing a rucksack and heading into the wild. Suppose further that were I to persist in pursuing my project I would likely die a swift and uncomfortable death of starvation or exposure. Instrumental accounts of the value of individual autonomy appear to be committed to holding that, at least in this case, I am better off having my freedom of association limited: the state should prevent me from setting out on this predictably ill-fated quest of self-reliance because it can promote my welfare better than I can.

But, against this paternalistic view, some liberals would argue that individual autonomy is a matter of entitlement: it is *my* life, and so it is *my* decision whether to adopt a given project and accept the risks that go with it, regardless of whether the state (or anyone else) is better informed, better motivated or better positioned to promote my welfare. On this view, paternalistic treatment is wrong because each of us occupies a privileged position of moral dominion over our own affairs, whether we use that dominion to better our lives or not. Proponents of such deontological arguments for the value of individual autonomy can adopt an even more permissive theory of secession, because on their view, the freedom of association, and therefore the freedom to disassociate, does not turn on whether having that freedom will promote human welfare.

However, both instrumental and deontological versions of the freedom of association argument for a primary right to secede suffer from a crucial defect: they conflict with the account of legitimacy set out above, because they would undermine the parent state's ability to secure the human rights of subjects who choose not to secede. A legitimate state, recall, is a political organization that uses its near-monopoly on the means of coercion within a given territory to secure the human rights of its subjects. But in order to do so, the state must enforce a coercive system of law, which, for practical reasons, requires a certain degree of contiguity and integrity throughout the territory in which that system is to be enforced. Freedom of association arguments for a choice theory of secession rashly extend an individual right to secede to everyone and thus are incompatible with state legitimacy, because as more individuals and small groups secede, the state's jurisdiction would become riddled with holes, and its ability to secure the human rights of its remaining constituents would gradually be undermined.

If there is to be a primary right to secede, we argue that is should be justified not by appealing to the value of individual autonomy, but rather to the value of *group* self-determination. For the purposes of this chapter, we will assume that group self-determination requires, at the very least, a capacity for independent collective action and decision-making. As with individual autonomy, there are both instrumental and deontological arguments that support the value of group self-determination, and we address these arguments and their support for a choice theory of secession in the next two sections. But before turning to them, it is important to see that our reasons for respecting group self-determination cannot be the same reasons we have for respecting individual autonomy.

As explained above, individual autonomy is thought to be valuable either because it promotes the welfare of the autonomous person, or because persons are entitled to respect and deference when it comes to their self-regarding affairs. Group self-determination cannot be valuable for these reasons, because, presumably only the welfare of individual persons – and not the welfare of groups as such – matters from a moral point of view. Of course, this is not to say that group welfare has no value; many of our individual interests are strongly linked to the fortunes of the families, firms and teams to which we belong. What is crucial here, though, is that a group's flourishing matters *only* insofar as it promotes the welfare of individual group members. This is because groups are not moral subjects – they lack the ability to experience changes to their welfare in the same way that individual persons experience changes to their own. As L.W. Sumner writes, 'our common notion of an individual subject is of a unique, enduring centre of consciousness', a 'point of view' from which the satisfaction of the entity's interests matter *to the entity itself* (Sumner 1996: 30).

What is more, while groups are capable of collective deliberation and action, and are sometimes understood – as in the law – as a kind of artificial 'person', they nevertheless lack the cognitive unity and coherence of individual human persons. Since they lack a 'centre of consciousness' from which these decisions are made, it is difficult to see why they should be entitled to the dignity and respect afforded to human beings. Thus, if group self-determination has moral value, it does so only as a consequence of its importance to individual persons. In the following sections, we present two different ways to explain why group self-determination might be morally important to individual persons.

## Instrumental Arguments

We turn first to the *instrumental* argument for respecting group self-determination, which holds that, in general, respecting group self-determination promotes human welfare. The argument runs parallel to, and builds on, the instrumental argument for respecting individual autonomy presented above. It begins by noting once again that individual human agents have epistemic and motivational advantages over others when it comes to promoting their own interests: we are almost always more familiar with our own needs, desires and preferences than other people are. When these individuals are enabled to make political decisions on their own behalf, it stands to reason that those decisions are more likely to promote their welfare successfully than if those decisions were made by others. This is supported by a few general observations regarding the social psychology of group behaviour.

First, we are usually more familiar with and more concerned to promote the interests of our families, friends and extended circle of associates. Second, relationships other than kinship and direct association based on shared culture also often yield similar epistemic and motivational advantages *vis-à-vis* others' interests. Third, as Kai Nielsen suggests, even when these connections do not already exist between members of a self-determining community because of a shared culture, they will tend to develop over time as a result of shared social, economic and political experiences (Nielsen 1993: 109).

This appeal to culturally-based attachment in the instrumental argument should not, however, be conflated with nationalism. Nationalists typically accept three theses: (1) there is nothing inappropriate about identifying with one's nation and conationals; (2) conationals have special obligations toward one another; and (3) each nation has a right to political self-determination. But the instrumental argument need make no claim that conational identification grounds special obligations, obligations that we have over and above those we have toward other human beings. The argument neither relies on nor implies that each nation has a right to self-determination.[1] The only claim is that large numbers of conationals are often members of the same self-determining groups, and that these individuals will tend to have epistemic and motivational advantages in promoting each others' interests: the culturally-laden premises in the instrumental argument are purely descriptive and not normative.

We have claimed that the members of self-determining groups, owing to their personal and cultural attachments, as well as to their similar positions within the social, economic and political units in which they find themselves, are generally more familiar with and more concerned to promote the interests of their fellow group members than outsiders are. And they are beyond doubt more familiar and more concerned to promote their *own* interests. But if this is so, then it seems reasonable to suppose that allowing those same people to make and implement the political decisions by which they are to live, they are more likely than outsiders to do so in ways that promote their welfare. The corollary to this is that external parties are *less* likely to make and implement political decisions that promote the welfare of group members. Thus, on the self-evident assumption that human welfare is something worth protecting and promoting, external parties have *prima facie* reasons to respect a group's political self-determination.

Now, clearly these reasons are defeasible. Some group members will remain ignorant of some of their compatriots' interests as a result of physical or social distance, lack of education or a lack of known, tangible mutual concerns. Religious resentment, ethnic hatred, regional jealousies, ideological polarization and class warfare can, at their worst, rend asunder the general communal beneficence the instrumental argument presupposes. The existence of these regrettable

---

1  For a different view according to which 'peoples' (similar in their definition to 'nations' here) have a right to self-determination see Chapter 21.

circumstances is not itself an objection to the instrumental argument and it seems reasonable that an account of the value of political self-determination should be sensitive to cases in which self-determination would or does have disastrous consequences for members of the group in question.

The most effective objection to the instrumental argument is that it provides too flimsy a set of reasons against interference. The intuition behind the objection is that grounding the value of political self-determination on instrumental reasons opens up the possibility that even if self-determination is beneficial to group members, interference by outsiders might be even *more* beneficial. Thus, the objection claims, the instrumental argument allows reasons to respect self-determination to be overridden too easily, both when there is sufficient internal division to render self-determination harmful, *and* when there are outside parties able to interfere in beneficial ways, regardless of the level of internal division.

Two counterpoints must be borne in mind to assess accurately the force of this objection. First, the mere presence of social conflict does not undermine the instrumental argument; conflict and cohesion exist in all political communities, and for the instrumental argument to fail to justify political self-determination in particular cases (as it surely does) the conflict must be severe enough to overcome the cohesive effects discussed above. Perhaps the most important cohesive force is a stable consensus about the political mechanisms through which such conflicts are to be resolved. So long as all parties to a conflict continue to place value on the institutions and procedures that enable their political self-determination, they will share at least some values with their compatriots, and some motivation to refrain from actively undermining their interests.

Second, the instrumental argument for political self-determination need not be taken as a case-by-case guide to the moral force of the reasons for non-interference. That these reasons are defeasible does not mean that outsiders should consider intervening every time they are in fact defeated. Instead, the instrumental argument can be taken to support a heuristic, a rule of thumb or a general presumption against non-interference. The familiar thought here is that even though a general presumption against non-interference may err on the side of caution, leading outsiders to refrain from interference when it could do a considerable amount of good, it might promote human welfare better than a policy of consistently interfering whenever it appears that interference would benefit members of the self-determining group, because this latter policy would lead outsiders to err on the side of temerity. There are good reasons to think that this is generally true, namely, the fact that external parties contemplating interference are highly likely to overestimate their abilities and commitment to benefiting the self-determining group, and to underestimate the risk and uncertainty involved in such attempts, as a result of ignorance, hubris, bias and self-interest.

However, given that the number of states in the world is vastly smaller than the number of individual subjects residing in a state, it may be argued that a general presumption in favour of respecting self-determination is uncalled for, and that particular secessions should be justified (or not) on a case-by-case basis. If true, this would undercut the claim that the instrumental argument supports anything like a general primary right to secede. Moreover, because the argument is instrumental, it is highly sensitive to the empirical vicissitudes of international politics. For example, while a particular instance of secession might promote human welfare, a general policy of allowing individually beneficial secessions might be self-defeating. The systematic consequences of such a policy could actually end up undermining human welfare, and in such a case it would appear that instrumental arguments would cut in the other direction, prohibiting secession in all but exceptional circumstances. We address this and similar objections below; but before that, we turn to deontological arguments for respecting self-determination, which hold out the promise of supporting a much stronger primary right to secede, one less contingent on calculations about human welfare.

## Deontological Arguments

The objections to instrumental arguments present a challenge, then, to find non-instrumental, that is, deontological reasons to respect group self-determination – reasons which do not rely on value-collectivism. A possible response to this challenge is that interfering with a group's self-determination is impermissible because it wrongly disrespects the individuals within the group. But why are they owed this respect, and how does interfering with their group's self-determination disrespect them?

In order to answer these questions, it is important to appreciate that, while violations of personal autonomy are a paradigmatic form of disrespect, there are other forms, as individuals can be entitled to respect in virtue of their special roles, standing, abilities or achievements. Consider, for instance, the respect owed to a conscientious parent. If a mother abused or neglected her child, then external parties would presumably have a right (if not a duty) to interfere. If a parent is satisfactorily fulfilling her parental responsibilities, however, then she enjoys a privileged position over her young children, a dominion which entails that others are prohibited from interfering. Imagine, for instance, that a mother packs whole milk in her son's lunch each day. Even if the child would be better-off drinking skimmed milk, this child's teacher has no right to replace this boy's whole milk with a carton of skimmed milk, because in these circumstances, the parent is entitled to determine what type of milk her child drinks. And if the teacher replaces the whole milk with the skimmed milk, the teacher wrongly fails to respect the parent's authority over her child, authority to which she is entitled in virtue of her satisfactory performance of her parental responsibilities.

In this example, the teacher wrongs the parent by disrespecting her dominion over the child without violating the parent's autonomy over her self-regarding affairs. The mother is not entitled to this parental dominion *qua* autonomous person; she is owed this respect in virtue of her standing as a conscientious parent. And if a parent can be wronged without her autonomy being violated, then perhaps members of groups can be wronged without their personal autonomy being violated.

In moving from parental dominion to political self-determination, the first thing to notice is that parenting is not always done by a solitary individual. It could be that a mother and a father decide together that their son should take whole milk to school, and in this case the teacher would wrongly disrespect both parents if he daily confiscated their son's carton of whole milk. And if respect can be owed to groups of parents in virtue of their collective ability and willingness to adequately perform their parental responsibilities, then why can it not be equally owed to groups of citizens in virtue of their collective ability and willingness to adequately perform their requisite political functions. That is to say, perhaps the reason Canada is morally entitled to political self-determination is because interfering with its group autonomy would wrongly fail to give Canadians the respect they are owed as a consequence of their collective achievement of maintaining a political institution which adequately protects the human rights of all Canadians. And it is important to bear in mind that outsiders are morally required to respect a group's self-determination even in those instances in which the outsider reasonably believes that she could perform some particular function better than the group on its own would. The fact that the parents/Canadians satisfactorily carry out their parental/ political functions entitles them to their parental/political dominion, even in those instances in which they carry out their responsibilities less than perfectly.

Finally, it should be emphasized that Canada is not entitled to autonomy merely because it is an existing country; rather, its claim to political self-determination hinges upon its ability and willingness to perform the requisite political functions. As a consequence, this view does not imply that all and only existing states are entitled to self-determination. If a group within an existing state (like the Quebecois or the residents of California, for instance) were able and willing to perform the requisite political functions, then they would be entitled to political self-determination. In other words, if Californians were able and willing to perform the requisite political functions, it would be just as wrong for the United States to forcibly deny their secession as it would be for the United States to forcibly annex Canada. In each case, the denial of California's/Canada's political self-determination would be impermissible because it would fail to accord the Californians/Canadians the respect to which they are entitled in virtue of their collective ability and willingness to perform the requisite political functions.

## Objections

One of the most common objections to choice theories of secession is that recognizing a primary right to secede would lead to a process known as 'Balkanization' – the rapid dissolution of states into smaller and smaller political units. This kind of dissolution, the objection maintains, is likely to result in militarily defenceless, economically decrepit, politically unstable states that are unable to perform the functions necessary for legitimacy. But the theory of secession defended here supports only a conditional right of secession: all and only those groups able and willing to perform the requisite political functions have a right to secede, and only when their secession will not disable the remainder state from its ability to secure the human rights of the constituents it retains. On the assumption that it is not impossible to determine whether these conditions will be met in particular cases, a choice theory of secession grounded on the theory of legitimacy set out above avoids the Balkinization objection by prohibiting secessions that would result in illegitimate states. In other words, since both the instrumental and deontological arguments presented above rule out dangerously incompetent and unstable groups as potential bearers of a primary right to secede, they would halt any process of dissolution before it began to threaten human rights security (see also Chapter 22).

Another objection to choice theories of secession is that recognizing a primary right to secede would enable groups to coerce or exploit their compatriots by threatening political divorce. Cass Sunstein, for instance, has argued that writing a right to secede into domestic constitutions would 'create dangers of blackmail, strategic behavior, and exploitation' (Sunstein 1991: 634). The worry here is that a minority group – especially one whose secession would give it control over important resources – could use the threat of secession to 'obtain benefits or to diminish burdens on matters formally unrelated to its comparative advantage' in resources and (given the right to secede) political power (Sunstein 1991: 650). In light of these outcomes, the objection runs, a primary right to secede should not be recognized under the law, regardless of whether it can be justified in moral terms (see also Chapter 19).

It is far from clear that the possibility of such outcomes is a sufficient reason to deny a group a right to self-determination. The objection rests on the assumption that the possibility of unjustified strategic threats of secession is serious enough that the harms of such occurrences could not be offset by equal or larger moral gains. If there is a primary moral right to secede, then presumably this right should not be overridden or ignored simply because respecting it will have bad consequences – rights are typically thought to be largely immune to such easy tradeoffs. Consider an analogy to the right of marital divorce, for instance. Even if we can reliably predict that allowing couples to divorce will give wives and husbands less incentive to work through their marital problems in constructive ways, few would deny that the right to divorce should be legally protected. On the contrary, we value freedom of association enough to insist that divorce be legally available even if allowing exit from marriages will lead some to have less happy unions.

What is more, it is not clear that a minority group's use of a primary right to secession for strategic purposes or bargaining would necessarily be impermissible. Suppose some group enjoys a primary right to secede, and then threatens to secede if the wider political community does not enact its preference on some policy question. By attaching additional costs to the community's choice to do otherwise, the would-be secessionist group attempts to coerce their fellow citizens. And coercion is only impermissible when the coercer *wrongly harms* or *wrongly fails to benefit* the coercee, and not all harms, and not all failures to benefit, are wrongful.

But if the would-be secessionists would not undermine the remainder state's ability to perform the requisite political functions by seceding, that is, if they could secede without undermining the security of human rights for the wider political community, it does not seem as if the possibility of secession threatens wrongful harm. Or, to put the point another way, the worry about coercion also cuts in the opposite direction: failure to allow a politically viable group the option to secede may cripple its ability to protect itself from coercion and exploitation by the larger community. A group's claim to self-determination may not only *not* prompt them to unjustly manipulate their original government, but may operate as a way for them to seek more just accommodations from it.

A third objection to choice theories of secession is that their institutionalization would create perverse incentives for existing states to repress, rather than to accommodate, internal cultural diversity and regional aspirations to political autonomy. Allen Buchanan, for instance, believes that a system of federalism is the best way to accommodate these forces. He argues that if international law were to recognize a primary right to secede for viable separatist movements, state governments would be unlikely to allow more federalized systems to develop, because doing so would increase the political viability of regional groups, and thereby increase the chance that they would pursue independence. By contrast, a less permissive legal stance on secession would prevent regional groups from achieving recognized statehood under international law even if they were able to become viable. Since states would no longer fear that federalization would risk political divorce, they would be more likely to employ it as a way to accommodate multiculturalism (Buchanan 2004: 377–9).

As with the previous objection, the objection from perverse incentives attempts to rule out recognition for a primary right to secede under international law on the grounds that doing so would have negative consequences, without taking seriously the possibility that those negative consequences (even if they do come to pass) could be outweighed by foreseeable moral benefits. In fact there may be instrumental benefits to recognizing such a right under international law that offset the potential negatives. David Copp has argued, first, that many of the incentives states have to undermine regional autonomy already exist, even in the absence of institutional recognition of a primary right to secede, so recognition of such a right is not likely to increase them substantially (Copp 1997). Second, and more importantly, he argues that the benefits of having a clearly defined and institutionally monitored right to secede embodied in international law would more than make up for whatever marginal increase in perverse incentives there may happen to be. Another benefit of an institutionally recognized primary right to secede is that, as the foregoing objection made clear, it could provide groups with leverage they could use to avoid exploitation and abuse by the state. Rather than attempting to quash secessionist movements, governments might instead begin trying to give them incentives to remain within the state.

Nevertheless, Buchanan is surely right to note that an adequate case for a legal primary right to secede requires more than does the case for a purely moral right. It may turn out that while viable separatist groups possess a valid moral claim to secede, it may be impossible, given present institutional constraints, to recognize this right under existing international law. Since legal institutions should take into account the prospective costs and benefits of any reform, the negative consequences of recognizing such a right at this time could be prohibitively high. Nevertheless, if the instrumental and deontological arguments are correct, we have reason to take a group's moral right to secede very seriously – we should not assume that the mere presence of countervailing factors is a sufficient reason to rule out a legal analogue (see also Chapter 22).

Our strategy thus far has been to argue that those groups which are both able and willing to perform the requisite political functions necessary for securing the human rights of their members, and can do so without impairing their parent state's ability to secure the human rights of its remaining constituents, have a moral right to secede, independently of whether that right ought to be recognized under international law. While we believe the negative consequences of institutionalizing a primary right to secede are not as severe as some have claimed, we are prepared to concede that those consequences could be prohibitively high, especially for those who are inclined to accept only the instrumental argument (since, presumably, a deontological defence of the primary right to secede would be less sensitive to consequences). In any case, we and others who adopt this strategy rely on what has been called 'dualism' with regard to moral and legal modes of justification. The last objection we will consider attempts to undermine this dualist strategy by claiming that the moral and legal questions of secession are inseparable because, as Allen Buchanan has argued, the right of secession is 'inherently institutional'. His argument, in brief, is as follows.

Theories which claim that some groups have a primary right to secede, as all choice theories do, must hold that external parties – the group's parent state, other states and so on – have an obligation to refrain from interfering with the exercise of that right (see also Chapter 25). 'But,' Buchanan writes, 'whether states should refrain from interfering … will depend, among other things, upon how states acting in that way will affect the international legal system and its effectiveness in helping to protect human rights and secure peace' (Buchanan 2004: 27). In other words, to determine whether a group has a *moral* right to secede, one must first determine whether that right is consistent with the duties other actors have with respect to maintaining an effective system of international law. If those duties entail preventing groups that meet the given conditions from seceding, those groups cannot (contrary to the theory) have a moral right to secede. Thus, on Buchanan's view, we cannot attribute a moral right to secede to any type of group without first considering whether institutionalizing that right would be justifiable, all things considered.

The simplest way to rebut this objection is to imagine a world in which there is only one state. If Buchanan's claim that the right of secession is inherently institutional, then the notion that some group within this solitary state might have a right to secede should be unintelligible, since, on his view, we must first determine whether secession is consistent with the solitary state's duties to maintain an effective system of international law. Certainly, there is a moral question about whether the state should intervene to prevent the group from seceding – but in the absence of any system of international law, it is difficult to see how this question is institutional in the sense required for Buchanan's argument. It seems perfectly reasonable to think that the group in question has a right to secede, and that this right is logically independent of whether some non-existent system of international law ought to recognize it. The same point can be made for scenarios in which there is an effective system of international law. There is no inconsistency in claiming that a group is morally justified in seceding, while at the same time maintaining that the best system of international law presently attainable should prohibit that secession. While we are not convinced that this latter claim is correct, it is at least compatible with a primary moral right to secede.

# Conclusion

Secessionist conflicts are fundamentally territorial disputes: the parent state and the separatist group assert rival claims to exercise exclusive territorial jurisdiction over the same piece of territory. As a consequence, one cannot hope to provide a clear, systematic and theoretically informed account of the conditions under which a separatist group has the right to secede in the absence of an adequate understanding of what grounds a state's claim to its territory. In light of this, we began by sketching a theory of political legitimacy. On our view, a state is justified in exercising coercive power over all those in its territory just in case it performs the range of political functions necessary to protect the human rights of all of its constituents. Building upon this functional account of political legitimacy, we then defended a choice theory of secession, according to which any group has a moral right to secede as long as it (1) is able and willing to perform the requisite political functions adequately and (2) will not undermine the parent state's ability to perform these same functions for those citizens who remain. And because a group can be politically viable even if it has never been treated unjustly, we conclude that groups can qualify for the right to secede even in the absence of injustice. This conclusion provides a stark contrast to remedial-right only theories, of course, since the latter regard unilateral state-breaking to be permissible solely as a last resort, to be invoked only in the face of persistent, grave and otherwise unavoidable injustices. Our approach is also importantly distinct from nationalist accounts, which focus on the rights of culturally or ethnically distinct separatist groups. In our view, a group's distinctive nationality may well explain a group's *interest* in having its own independent state, but it is not the key feature which qualifies a group for its *right* to secede. On the contrary, it seems to us that a group's right to political self-determination depends first and foremost upon its political capacities, not its cultural attributes. Finally, although we are convinced that this theory is not undermined by any of the standard objections, it does not necessarily follow that primary rights to secede should automatically be embodied in international law. Without shrinking from our conclusion that those groups able and willing to perform the requisite political functions have a moral right to secede even in the absence of injustice, we acknowledge that the case for an international legal right to secede which mirrors our permissive stance on the morality of unilateral state-breaking would require arguments that we do not attempt to supply here.

## References

Beran, H. (1984), 'A Liberal Theory of Secession', *Political Studies* 32, 21–31.
Buchanan, A. (2004), *Justice Legitimacy, and Self-Determination* (Oxford: Oxford University Press).
Copp, D. (1997), 'International Law and Morality in the Theory of Secession', *The Journal of Ethics* 2, 219–45.
Gauthier, D. (1994), 'Breaking Up: An Essay on Secession', *Canadian Journal of Philosophy* 24, 357–72.
Nielsen, K. (1993), 'Liberal Nationalism and Secession', in M. Moore (ed.), *National Self-Determination and Secession* (New York: Oxford University Press), 103–33.
Sumner, L. (1996), *Welfare, Happiness, and Ethics* (New York: Oxford University Press).
Sunstein, C. (1991), 'Constitutionalism and Secession', *University of Chicago Law Review* 58:2, 633–70.
Wellman, C. (2005), *A Theory of Secession* (New York: Cambridge University Press).

# Secession and Domination

John McGarry and Margaret Moore

## Introduction

This chapter offers a partly normative and partly empirical discussion of the interplay between theories of justified secession, which are largely drawn from individualist (liberal-democratic) conceptions of the legitimate state and/or the just state, and empirical evidence that domination of one (ethnic/national/religious/racial) group over another group can occur even when there is formal adherence to liberal principles of (individual) fairness and democratic government. This is so because individual justice concerns sometimes mask or render (partly) invisible the kinds and methods of domination in the society. Democracy, we assume, is a sub-set of justice theory in the sense that a just state should be democratic and an undemocratic state is, to the extent that it is undemocratic, also unjust. Majoritarian democratic institutions, we argue, can be consistent with domination, especially when there is group bloc voting and majoritarian decision rules (rather than, for example, power-sharing).

The chapter argues that individualist liberal-democratic theories of state legitimacy, on which the ethics of secession literature is based, fail to track (some of) the bases for group mobilization behind secession projects, and group methods of domination and subordination. The main assumption of 'just cause' theory (called in this volume 'remedial theory') is that injustice legitimates secession, and there is also a further implication that injustice *causes* secession. This chapter argues that this latter implication is only partly right. We argue that individualist justice theories (which form the underlying theory of state legitimacy) fail to address the problem of the domination of one ethnic/national group over another. Individual norms of justice (understood as respect for human rights and equal or fair treatment of *individuals*) mitigate but do not fully address the domination of groups that is fundamental to secessionist mobilizations, and that is at the heart of collective injustice claims.

# Ethics of Secession

There are two dominant positions in the ethics of secession, one of which views secession as unacceptable in all circumstances, and as fundamentally disruptive to the international order; and another, which views secession as justifiable in certain circumstances, namely, when the state has been engaged in egregious violations of human rights.[1] This chapter discusses these two positions, and argues that they are both vulnerable to the same problem: they fail to track the mobilization of secessionist projects, or address satisfactorily the problem of what to do in the face of such projects.

## Statist Views of Secession

The dominant position regarding secession (self-determination) in international law and international relations is that there is no right to it outside the colonial context (see also Chapters 1, 13 and 17). This position is typically held by 'unionists' who view the secession of any part of the state as unjustifiable, and by state actors who seek to ensure the territorial integrity of the state. The position might be grounded in a number of different reasons, but liberal individualist and statist/realist ones are typical.

One statist argument depends on a realist view of the international system, which sees the state system as crucial to order; secure borders as crucial to the maintenance of the system; and secessionist movements as fundamentally destructive and de-stabilizing. This realist account of secession, though, presupposes exactly what is at issue: that the group in question does not have a right to secede in the first place. To see that this is an assumption of the argument, rather than its conclusion, we need only reflect on the nature of rights: part of having a right is a right to do wrong (or the wrong thing) and we sometimes think that people have rights, e.g. the right to divorce their partners, even if this would be destructive and destabilizing for other people affected. If it is a right, then the question of how to think about third party obligations is brought in, but it's not the case that the mere fact that there are negatively affected third parties means that there is no right.

Nevertheless, this view has been held by almost all of the (state) actors in the international order, who point out that, despite the reference to 'self-determination of peoples' in Article 1 and Article 55 of the United Nations Charter, the UN Charter also affirms the sanctity of the principle of the territorial integrity of states and denies the right of the UN or its member states to intervene in the internal affairs of recognized states (Emerson 1971: 463). According to the 1970 UN Declaration regarding the right of secession, the UN condemns 'any action aimed at the partial or total disruption of the national unity and territorial integrity of any other state

---

1   There is a third position – the individual autonomy or choice theory of secession – which has a considerable body of theoretical support, but hardly any political proponents. See Chapters 4 and 23 and Beran (1984), Copp (1997, 1998), Philpott (1995).

or country' (quoted in Heraclides 1991: 21). In 1970, UN Secretary-General U Thant argued that the recognition of a state by the international community and its acceptance as a member of the UN implied acceptance of its territorial integrity and sovereignty. He added that 'the United Nations' attitude is unequivocal. As an international organization, the United Nations has never accepted and does not accept and I do not believe it will ever accept the principle of secession of a part of its Member States' (Emerson 1971: 46). This means that secessionist movements seek to violate a fundamental right of states (to territorial integrity), and are to be viewed with suspicion and vigorously resisted (see also Chapter 25).

This has been the practice in international politics. Between 1947 and 1991, only a single instance of successful secession occurred, that of Bangladesh (see Part VI). During this period, the superpowers were committed to upholding existing state boundaries, and they encouraged the development of international law and practice in which borders were viewed as permanent – not negotiable – features of the international state system. Since 1991, there have been numerous instances of secession, but many of these can be more precisely conceived of as the disintegration of states along national lines, such as in the former Soviet Union and Czechoslovakia, rather than the secession of a region from a functioning state.

The realist view is supported by a set of strong normative considerations, including arguments based on democracy. A democratic account of the statist position has a democratic story of the transformation, through a defining constitutional moment, of the state's various peoples into a *single people*, and the government (or federal government, in federal systems) as expressive of this common will of the whole people, conceived monistically. If we accept this account of the relationship between the state's territory and popular sovereignty, then we must view the federal government as an agent of the people as a whole, and we have a democratic justification for a statist view of political boundaries.

Relatedly, statists associate the state order with a number of moral goods which secure the state's legitimacy: the protection of individual rights, the rule of law, peace and justice, and argues that secession from such a legitimate political order is unjustified. This view shades into the just cause theory of secession, since it is possible that some states will fail to uphold the requisite moral goods. It can be a statist argument, though, when the moral goods that the state is supposed to achieve to be legitimate are so minimal that they would be hard *not* to be achieved by any functioning political order. So, depending on how high the threshold is for justifying the state (and so rendering it legitimate) this version of the statist argument shades into the just cause (or remedial) theory of secession.

## Just Cause Theories

According to just cause (remedial) theories of secession, secession is justified if the state has committed egregious and long-standing injustices against its citizens. This is essentially Allen Buchanan's (1991) view, but it is also continuous with a long-standing view of state legitimacy as rooted in deeper justice considerations.

On this view, egregious injustice renders the state both unjust and illegitimate and secession would be justified (see also Chapter 22).[2]

This is relevant to the theory of secession, because the dispensation of justice legitimates a state; and there is no barrier to secession if the state is illegitimate. Typically, just cause theories argue in favour of a general right to secede for people who have suffered certain kinds of injustices at the hands of the state (Buchanan 1991). Different just cause theories focus on different kinds of injustices: some on prior occupation and seizure of territory; some on serious violations of human rights, including genocide; others on discriminatory injustice (Norman 1998). One advantage of this type of theory is that it suggests a strong internal connection between the right to resist tyranny – exploitation, genocide, oppression, wrongful seizure of territory – and secession. By suggesting a strong link between secession and human rights, this kind of argument grounds the ethics of secession within the generally accepted framework of human rights, and a generally accepted theory of state legitimacy.

This theory, however, is more restrictive than it first appears. It is restrictive in the obvious sense that it restricts secession to states that have victimized or discriminated against (some of) their members; but it sets the bar even higher by requiring that the injustice be the result of deep state structures, rather than simply the actions of an illegitimate government. However, unlike the previous (statist) theory discussed above, just cause theory suggests an attractive alternative strategy in dealing with secessionist mobilization and secessionist claims. It suggests that the state should ensure that it acts justly; that it protect individual human rights; that political choices are made democratically (assuming that democratic governance is a component of the just state); and that it otherwise uphold substantive justice, such as individual human rights. It is implicit in the just cause account of secession that the upholding of justice is not only crucial to the legitimacy of the state, but that it is the primary function of government. Further, this account is superior to the statist account in so far as it suggests a clear strategy for dealing with states that face a secessionist movement: that they should strive to uphold justice. It is a short step from the claim that injustice legitimates secession to the further claim that injustice is an important factor in mobilizing support for secession. The reverse

---

2   Buchanan's theory, like most justice theories, assumes that the unjust state is illegitimate, and that the just state is legitimate. When justice and legitimacy are distinguished, it is mainly to argue that legitimacy is a lesser standard, as in the concept of 'recognitional legitimacy'. Rawls, in *Law of Peoples* (1999), also employs the concept of legitimacy as a threshold concept. He argues that 'decent hierarchical peoples' might not be perfectly just, but that their government is legitimate at least in the sense that their authority is recognized by those subject to it, and it meets the conditions of (peaceful) compliance (not to be confused with consent). 'Decent hierarchical peoples', unlike pariah states, can be brought within the scope of the law of peoples. It is arguable whether the decent consultative hierarchies are legitimate only in the international relations sense that they have control of their societies; or they are legitimate in the sense that the moral quality of the relationship between the people and the state is sufficiently good that it merits inclusion in the law of peoples. We will assume the latter is true.

seems to follow: that secession from a just state is illegitimate and that there is no reason to want to secede from a state that upholds justice.

In the next section, we suggest that although this strategy for dealing with secession – the strategy of pursuing individual justice within the state – is a considerable improvement over the previous statist view of secession, it is insufficient in so far as it fails to deal with many of the mechanisms by which one group can dominate (an)other in a formally just, democratic state.

## Justice and Domination

The standard theory of state legitimacy, upon which the just cause theory of secession relies, is rooted in a liberal individualist conception of human rights, individual liberty and democratic governance. Even if we can't agree on a fine-tuned theory of distributive justice, Buchanan suggests, we can agree on the basic outlines of a just regime, as one that upholds basic human (individual) rights (Buchanan 2004).

The idea of justice as specifying an appropriate basis of state action *vis-à-vis* citizens, is quite different from a relational idea of groups of people within the state vying for power with each other, and the state as an institutional mechanism, or space, in which one group potentially dominates other groups. In his important work *Republicanism, A Theory of Freedom as Non-domination*, Philip Pettit criticizes the standard liberal views of freedom, which either invoke personal autonomy as a substantive moral foundation, or adopt a negative view of freedom as non-interference. Pettit argues that central to the republican tradition is the idea of non-domination, which is a fundamentally relational conception, and identifies freedom as non-interference, but non-interference that requires the entrenchment of institutional rules aimed at guaranteeing it over time. This is contrasted with domination, which is arbitrary in a pernicious sense, because it occurs at the will or pleasure of the dominant party, and fails to track the interests of the dominated party. On this view, the key normative concept is that of non-domination, which brings into view the relations between individuals or groups and state power, and its converse, domination, which speaks to the relative power of one person or one group over other persons or groups. In the context of this chapter, it refers to hierarchies of privilege within a political system, where one group can exert power over another, stamping its culture and authority on the collective life of the state. In this way, relations between groups can be conceptualized as ones of domination and subordination, which are mediated and reinforced in the state's basic institutions. Domination can vary in its extent, ranging from a relatively benign privileging of one community in certain areas of public policy to the profoundly coercive repression of a subordinate community.

Several of the world's states are clearly dominated by particular ethnic or national communities, which operate as 'staatsvolks', 'herrenvolks', 'titular nations', 'ethnocrats', 'bumiputra' or 'charter peoples'. In many cases, as might be expected, these states are not democracies. Before 2003, Iraq was an authoritarian state dominated by its Sunni Arab minority, while Iraq's neighbour Syria remains an authoritarian state dominated by its Alawite minority. Between 1948 and 1994, South Africa was presided over by Afrikaners, and although it gave the franchise to all whites and held competitive elections among white parties, it was not a democracy, as it denied the franchise to the majority of its citizens. China and Myanmar are authoritarian regimes led by particular communities, the Han Chinese and Burmans, respectively. Both are currently engaged in the coercive repression of their minority communities (for further discussion see essays on Tibet and Myanmar in Part VI).

In many other cases, however, domination takes place in states that are formally or institutionally democratic, with a universal franchise, competitive elections, regular turnovers of government and a varying range of personal (individual) freedoms. Domination has political, symbolic, cultural and economic dimensions. McGarry (2010) offers a typology of types of domination, where political domination is the foundation for the others and is reflected in the core community's control of the state's central political institutions, including the executive, legislature, judiciary and bureaucracy, as well as whatever decentralized institutions exist. Minorities are excluded from government, or when included, as in the case of Malaysia's Chinese community, their participation is token in nature and falls short of a genuine partnership in decision-making. The core community's control of political institutions is a reflection of its greater numbers, but is often reinforced by a range of institutional rules and practices that discriminate against subordinated groups and their political representatives.

Symbolic ownership of the state is often formally asserted through constitutions or laws. According to Amal Jamal, all of Israel's 11 Basic Laws emphasize its Jewish character (Jamal 2005: 12 n. 20). Less formal claims to ownership are asserted in the speeches of dominant community elites who describe their people as 'sons of the soil' and others as outsiders and interlopers, irrespective of how long their ancestors have lived there. As Sri Lanka's development minister declared in 1983, 'Sri Lanka is inherently and rightfully a Sinhalese state. This must be accepted as a fact and not as a matter of opinion to be debated' (cited in Yiftachel 2006: 23). States, and often their cities and towns, including those in minority inhabited regions, are often named after the core people, which also stamps its ethnic impress on the state's anthems, flags, stamps, symbols and public holidays.

In the next section we discuss how some forms of domination can be consistent with individual justice and democratic norms.

## Democratic Domination

This chapter seeks to identify methods, including directly democratic devices which are part of the institutional repertoire of liberal-democratic governance, that maintain various forms of domination. Parties that represent demographically dominant communities can win elections straightforwardly, if ethnicity is the main political cleavage and if the dominant community remains politically united. Elections and electoral systems can also be designed to prevent dominant group fissures, and/or prevent non-ethnic or minority parties from becoming electorally pivotal. States may also seek to reduce the representation of particular sorts of minority parties to promote stability and state unity, or for reasons of ethnocentrism or racism. Tactics used towards these ends include reducing the minority's share of the vote; implementing electoral formulae which under-represent minorities; drawing electoral boundaries to under-represent minorities; adopting anti-competitive practices which make it difficult for minority parties and politicians to compete for office; and post-election measures that discriminate against elected minority politicians. Some of these methods are straight-forwardly anti-democratic – they are employed by ostensibly democratic states, but they are undemocratic measures, and to the extent that a democratic state uses them, they lower their democratic credentials. However, in many cases, there is no democratic rule against such practices, although it is clear that these are often used to ensure that the minority (national or ethnic) group cannot gain sufficient legislative influence through electoral means.

Minorities, particularly if they are geographically dispersed, have been easily deprived of fair representation by the pluralitarian and majoritarian electoral systems for legislative and executive elections that are used in former British and French colonies around the world and which thereby ensure their subordinate status. These electoral systems are often selected precisely for their 'integrationist' advantages, i.e. because the effective thresholds required to win make it difficult for politically dispersed minorities to elect their own political parties, or select their own candidates. Such electoral systems are justified on the grounds that they produce 'catch-all' or ethnically neutral parties that reach out to all voters, but their effect in bipolar and divided polities is often to give seat 'bonuses' to the party or parties of the dominant ethnic group, i.e. a larger share of seats than of votes.

Where minorities are territorially concentrated and therefore capable of winning seats under pluralitarian or majoritarian electoral systems, they can be deprived of a proportional share of seats in the legislature if a high state-wide quota (threshold) of votes is required before seats can be won. Such thresholds exist in many countries, including Germany and New Zealand, but the most obvious example occurs in Turkey, which has an unusually high electoral threshold of 10 percent, and which, unlike Germany and New Zealand, does not have provisions which set the threshold aside if a party wins local constituencies. In the 2002 election in Turkey, the main Kurdish party, the People's Democracy Party (Halkın Demokrasi Partisi – HADEP) obtained approximately 45.95 percent of the vote (47,449 votes) in Sirnak province, but failed to win one of its three seats in parliament, as it failed to win 10 percent of the total vote across Turkey. Two of the seats went to the Turkish Islamist AK (Justice and Development) party and the other to an independent, with the three winning candidates gaining 25 percent of the provincial vote among them.[3] In Slovakia, just before the 1998 elections, the Slovakian nationalist Prime Minister Meciar adopted a 5 percent threshold for state-wide elections as a tactic to reduce the representation of opposition parties, including Hungarian parties, in Slovakia's legislature.

The drawing of electoral boundaries is also frequently used to under-represent territorially concentrated minorities and thereby deprive them of political voice. Boundaries are drawn either to divide the minority community across several constituencies, so that it is a minority in each, or by packing it into one or a few overly populous constituencies where it constitutes an overwhelming local majority. Widespread gerrymandering of this sort was used to under-represent Southern blacks in the US Congress and in several state legislatures. While South Carolina had a black majority in the 1880s, only one of its seven Congressional districts had a secure black majority. Similar gerrymanders prevailed in congressional districts throughout North Carolina, Alabama and Mississippi (Kousser 1984: 32). At the municipal level, blacks were under-represented by the tactic of switching from local ward-based to at-large (city-wide) elections, a move that was justified on 'efficiency' grounds, as permitting elected officials to take a city-wide perspective. At-large elections not only made black candidates dependent on white urban majorities for winning seats, but made elections more expensive, making it less likely that African Americans would prevail or even run (Guinier 1993: 50). In Northern Ireland, the opportunity for reapportionment brought about in 1929 by the switch from nine multi-member (proportional) constituencies to 48 single-member constituencies allowed Unionists – the pro-British party – to divide the nationalist majority county of Fermanagh into three constituencies, two of which came to be won consistently by Unionists.

Just as there is no set, or clear, institutional design for democratic governance, beyond a very general sense that the fundamental norm is the political equality of citizens, and that this can be institutionalized in very different ways, by different forms of representation and different rules for converting votes into legislative seats, there is no general normative principle for drawing boundaries, which are so crucial for empowering or disempowering, representing or failing to represent (collectively) different communities or different groups within the state. So, too, many of the administrative (voting) regulations which are essential components of functioning democracy can be used to ensure domination of one group over another. These, however, are too fine-grained, too precise to be considered by the general theories of justice on offer.

Moreover, voting regulations, like the actual design of the electoral system and the division of powers, operate differently in different contexts, so that it's not clear that one is (always) associated with injustice and another is always associated with justice (or more just outcomes).

The measures described above may have the result of facilitating domination by indirectly reducing the participation of minorities in elections. If there is a

---

3   http://sim.law.uu.nl/SIM/CaseLaw/hof.nsf/233813e697620022c1256864005232b7/10c60 98b3315ccf5c125727400367fea?OpenDocument, accessed 8 January 2011.

reduced chance of electing one's preferred candidate, there is, presumably, a reduced incentive to vote. However, electoral regulations can also directly reduce the number of minority voters. In the United States, African Americans in the South (and new immigrants in the north) were deprived of the ballot by a bewildering litany of measures, including literacy tests, property qualifications, residency requirements, provisions which barred petty criminals from voting (although not, strangely, murderers) and poll taxes.[4] By 1904, the payment of poll taxes was a pre-requisite for voting in all 11 southern states that had made up the confederacy in 1861. Illiterate whites, by contrast, were protected from disfranchisement by 'grandfather' and 'fighting grandfather' clauses (Kousser 1984: 33; Guinier 1993: 11).

In addition, there are a range of administrative regulations that can reduce participation in voting and in running for office, e.g. who has the right to vote; regulations on electoral deposits; rules on the eligibility requirements and signatures required to register and stand for office; rules on absentee or diaspora ballots; rules on the independence or partisanship of electoral commissions; and rules governing campaigning, competition over fund raising; and regulations on advertising and access to public and private media, which are also important to the various goals here – including participation and autonomy goals (O'Leary 2010). Many states prevent minority parties from competing in elections by banning parties that advocate 'secession' or by requiring parties to have support throughout the state before they can compete in 'national' elections.[5]

All of these strategies are undemocratic in spirit at least – they are aimed at undercutting the fundamental principle of political equality – although they can also be, and invariably are, argued for on other, instrumental or administrative, grounds. To that extent, they may satisfy the requirement of procedural neutrality: they can be justified in terms that are neutral between individuals and groups (although one could argue that this reveals the flaws with justificatory neutrality – many things can be justified on neutral terms, even though the real motive and support is based on other, less impartial grounds, like racism, intolerance and so on).

---

4   In five states, the poll tax accumulated for more than one year. In Georgia after 1877 and Alabama after 1901, it accumulated indefinitely. Some states made the poll tax due several months before elections were to be held, on the assumption that this would *reduce* payments (Kousser 1984: 32–5).

5   In addition to fixing elections to benefit dominant communities, the state can also shape its legislative, executive, and judicial institutions in ways that facilitate the domination of one group over another. The most obvious way for this to happen is if decisions within the legislature are made on the basis of a simple majority, the executive is comprised exclusively of the party or coalition of parties that win a simple majority of seats in the legislature, and the judiciary is subordinate to the executive and legislature. This, for those who do not recognize it, is known as the 'Westminster' system of government, but it is not fundamentally different from many Western forms of democracy. For a comprehensive examination of institutions of domination and the ways in which these can be justified on (individual-based) liberal and democratic arguments, see McGarry (2010).

## Conclusion

What is interesting about all these practices, from the point of view of this chapter, is that they are not always visible in standard justice theory – which specifies a certain number of individual rights – rights to freedom of speech, freedom of association, freedom of religion, freedom of conscience – as well as political rights, particularly the right to vote and hold office – as well as democratic institutions of government, of which there are many different kinds of institutional forms. From the perspective of these abstract rights and democratic institutions, many of these countries discussed here (as practising forms of domination) are formally democratic and liberal: they respect basic rights, the rule of law, and the results of periodic competitive elections, which means that a peaceful change of government is possible. Obviously, democratic governance – whether some kind of proportional representation or Westminster first-past-the-post or other system – combined with the protection of individual rights is an improvement over blatantly authoritarian and tyrannical regimes. Nevertheless, within many of these systems, there is still a wide range of tools at the disposal of the state (or the majority group in the state) to ensure its domination over state institutions, and, through this, over the society as a whole. There is the design of electoral systems, which can have serious effects on minority representation and majority domination; and the drawing of boundaries. In addition to these features, which political scientists often think of as fundamental to institutional democratic design, there are electoral regulations that concern the exercise of the franchise. Various rules and laws and conventions can also be used to ensure legislative and executive dominance, and thereby the political domination of one group over another.

The problem with the standard theories of liberalism and democracy is that they explain the fundamental principles of democracy in terms of ensuring *individual* political equality and respecting fundamental human rights, and they can argue that different institutional designs more or less can be grounded in ensuring justice. But they are not sufficiently fine-grained to see the ways in which various institutional rules regarding the conversion of votes into seats, the drawing of boundaries and regulations internal to the system can result – and are employed precisely in order to have that result – in one group's domination over another. It is only by focusing on groups in society, and on the fundamental norm of non-domination, which is a relational norm, that these hierarchies can be seen in the first place. The society may appear ostensibly just, and indeed capable of justifying these rules, processes and practices on purely administrative convenience or efficiency grounds, but the real effect, and intention of these rules, is to ensure the domination of the majority over the minority ethnic/national/religious group in society.

Secessionist leaders, who are almost always nationalists, are, of course, acutely aware of these group-based dynamics, and group-based 'injustices'. Although we cannot argue the point here, they tend to notice the ways in which groups are empowered by the state and disempowered by it, included and excluded, and especially the ways in which ostensibly individualist and neutral rights and rules can have profoundly unequal and unfair consequences for the different groups in the society. For this reason, we think the relational idea of non-domination is a better concept to analyse fairness and justice in a society marked by group differences (that is: almost all societies) because it permits an assessment not only of the justifying norm behind a particular policy, procedure or institutional device, but in terms of the consequences for domination of one group or groups over (an) other. This may connect it to other sources of national or ethnic mobilization: if a group is being dominated through these various institutional mechanisms, we have an explanation for their alienation from the state, and we also have the possibility of changing these practices, and not just practices which affect 'individuals', to reduce demand for secession. If a problem is not theorized, is not even in the purview of the theory, it cannot be addressed.

The potentially capacious just cause theory of the ethics of secession has the conceptual resources to include this insight: it requires only conceiving of non-domination as essential to justice, and theorizing various rights and rules and institutions in these terms. However, this is not how most liberal-democratic theories of justice have worked and it belies the individualist focus of most current theories of justice and democracy. It requires us to shift the lens to theorize group-based dynamics. It would also make the just cause theory of secession much less restrictive than it currently is, since it would bring into focus many more injustices than the theory currently 'sees'.

# References

Beran, Harry (1984), 'A Liberal Theory of Secession', *Political Studies* 32, 21–31.

Buchanan, Allen (1991), *Secession: The Morality of Political Divorce from Fort Sumter to Lithuania and Quebec* (Boulder, CO: Westview Press).

Buchanan, Allen (2004), *Justice, Legitimacy and Self-Determination: Moral Foundations of International Law* (Oxford: Oxford University Press).

Copp, David (1997), 'Democracy and Communal Self-Determination', in J. McMahan and R. McKim (eds), *The Morality of Nationalism* (Oxford: Oxford University Press), 277–300.

Copp, David (1998), 'International Law and Morality in the Theory of Secession', *Journal of Ethics* 2:3, 219–45.

Emerson, Rupert (1971), 'Self-Determination', *American Journal of International Law* 65:3, 459–75.

Guinier, L. (1993), *The Tyranny of the Majority* (New York: The Free Press).

Heraclides, Alexis (1991), *Self-determination of Minorities in International Politics* (London: Frank Cass).

Jamal, A. (2005), 'On the Morality of Arab Collective Rights in Israel', *Adalah's Newsletter* 12 (April).

Kousser, J.M. (1984), 'The Undermining of the First Reconstruction: Lessons for the Second', in C. Davidson (ed.), *Minority Vote Dilution* (Washington, DC: Howard University Press), 27–46.

McGarry, John (2010), 'Ethnic Domination in Democracies', in Marc Weller (ed.), *The Political Participation of Minorities: 10 Years after the Lund Recommendations* (Oxford: Oxford University Press), 35–71.

Norman, Wayne (1998), 'The Ethics of Secession as the Regulation of Secessionist Politics', in Margaret Moore (ed.), *National Self-Determination and Secession* (Oxford: Oxford University Press), 34–61.

O'Leary, Brendan (2010), 'Electoral Systems and the Lund Recommendations', in M. Weller and Katherine Nobbs (eds), *Political Participation of Minorities: A Commentary on International Standards and Practice* (Oxford: Oxford University Press), 363–99.

Pettit, Philip (1997), *Republicanism: A Theory of Freedom and Government* (Oxford: Oxford University Press).

Philpott, Daniel (1995), 'In Defence of Self-Determination', *Ethics* 105:2, 357–72.

Rawls, John (1999), *Law of Peoples* (Cambridge, MA: Harvard University Press).

Yiftachel, O. (2006), *Ethnocracy: Land and Identity Politics in Israel/Palestine* (Philadelphia, PA: University of Pennsylvania Press).

# The Right to Secede: Do We Really Need It?

## Aleksandar Pavković

> *All peoples have the right of self-determination. By virtue of that right they freely determine their political status …*
> (Article 1, *International Covenant on Civil and Political Rights* [1966]
> [http://www2.ohchr.org/english/law/ccpr.htm])

On the face of it, this UN covenant – and many other UN documents containing the above phrase – grants to:

a. every discrete group called 'a people';
b. a universal and unrestricted right to establish a sovereign state of their own which the people, or its representatives, would control.

From (a) and (b) it seems to follow that every such 'people' has a right to secede from the host state in which it resides. As it has been noted in Chapters 1, 6, 13 and 15, this is *not* how the article has been interpreted in practice and in legal theory. The main reason for this was another legal principle, most emphatically enunciated in the 1960 *Declaration on the Granting of Independence to Colonial Countries and Peoples* (which also contains, in its Article 2, the above quoted statement):

> *Any attempt aimed at the partial or total disruption of the national unity and the territorial integrity of a country is incompatible with the purposes and principles of the Charter of the United Nations. (Article 6)*

This principle of territorial integrity – repeated in many other UN conventions and resolutions – apparently overrides and restricts any right to self-determination of peoples.[1] Hence the above right to self-determination is, in practice, held either not to encompass the right to secede or is not to be granted to any discrete group within

---

1   Chapter 17 discusses how this restriction may be waived in some cases of discrimination of 'peoples' within the existing member states of the UN.

an existing state. In international legal practice and theory, there is no *universal* right of secession of 'peoples' or any other discrete groups inhabiting the present member states of the UN (as opposed to their overseas colonies).

And yet, as we have seen in Chapters 4, 21, 22 and 23, many political and moral theorists argue that there is a right to secede which is held by discrete groups of individuals *within* the existing member states of the UN. In other words, they hold that some groups – not necessarily called 'peoples' – hold or acquire the right to secede and thus freely to determine their political status by *'disrupting' the territorial integrity* of existing states. In their view, this is not a universal right but a right for which a group needs to qualify either in virtue of its characteristics or its actions, or in virtue of the actions committed by third parties against the group. What are these groups?

## Rights and Groups

A right is usually granted or held in order to *enable* the right-holder to act in a particular way and to *protect* its (or his/her) acting from the interference of others. Further, the right may involve the claim *for assistance* from third parties; thus a right may create obligations or duties on others (a) not to interfere with the protected action and/or (b) to assist in carrying out the action. In that sense, the above right to self-determination should *enable* 'peoples' (groups) to 'determine' their political status, *protect* that 'determination' from the interference of others and *require* (or oblige) others to assist, in any way that is necessary, that 'determination'. The right-holders here are thus both *actors* and *beneficiaries* of obligations and actions of others.

This leads to the first conceptual problem: the indeterminacy of right-holders. No international legal document specifies who these 'peoples' are. As suggested in Chapter 21, there are many possible accounts of who these 'peoples' are, and how to distinguish them from others. Attempts to specify the characteristics necessary for a people may lead to circularity and tautology. If one specifies the characteristics required for a group to control or establish a state – for example, its cohesiveness and sense of political purpose (as suggested in Chapters 21 and 23) – one would be in effect stating the characteristics which make the group worthy of the right of self-determination; and 'peoples' would thus become 'groups worthy of the right of self-determination'. This procedure, Makinson (1988: 75) noted, faces the danger of circularity: the groups that are said to hold the right are defined in terms of the right. In this chapter we shall only briefly discuss this issue.

The second conceptual problem concerns the right-holders' capacity for action: in general, when it comes to the creation of states, it is individuals and not groups that act and it is unclear what would constitute an act of state-creation by a group. One way of resolving this issue is to conceive of the right-holder as a corporate body which is a beneficiary of the right and those acting as its representatives, e.g. political leaders, who are acting on behalf of the corporate body as a unit.[2] But since both the actors and primary beneficiaries of this right are secessionist leaders and their secessionist movements, there arises the question: Are, in such cases, the right-holders in fact secessionist movements – and *can* such movements be holders of any such moral rights (Ewin 1995)? Another way of resolving the issue is to disregard the capacity of the right-holder for action and identify it only as the beneficiary of the exercise of the right to secede. But this raises the following question: does a non-acting *beneficiary* of the right need to be a *holder* of the right to secede? Perhaps the duties of others to assist (and thus to benefit) the alleged right-holder do not need to arise from its right to secede. This issue is discussed in the concluding part of the chapter.

The third conceptual problem is the scope and the target of the claims generated by the right to secession. A right to secede is usually regarded as generating two kinds of obligations: first, an obligation on the part of the host state not to interfere with the efforts of the right-holder to create a separate sovereign state on a selected territory and, second, the obligation on the part of the host state and other states and international organizations to recognize the independence of the new state. But does the right to secede also generate obligations of other states to assist, by military means, the right holder or its secessionist movement? Does it also generate the liberty to use lethal force or coercion against those who refuse to recognize this right? In other words, does it justify the use of force against those who deny the right to selected right-holders? As we shall see, very few contemporary theorists offer explicit answers to these questions.

The above conceptual problems need not arise in cases of *legal* rights to secede. As argued in Chapter 19, legal rights to secede are (or should be) introduced in states' constitutions for prudential and not moral reasons. The principal purpose of introducing a legal right in a state's constitution is to define the procedures by which a territory and its population may be detached from a state. Hence its holder is defined in terms of a territory to be detached and its exercise and scope are defined in terms of the procedures and legal obligations of the host state and secessionist authorities (but not of international actors). A legal right to secede can easily avoid most of the above problems.

The right to secede under discussion here is a non-legal right, most often conceived as a moral right which provides a basis for (or results from) a moral assessment of secessionist demands for an independent state. This chapter examines the usefulness of such a concept of right in the moral assessment of demands of this kind.

---

2   As Van Dyke (1977: 359), an advocate of this view and of the group right of self-determination, puts it 'Whatever the procedure, the "self" that is "determined" is always a group as a unit'.

## The Function of the Right to Secede

The right to self-determination was introduced in the above 1960 UN Declaration with a relatively narrow aim of granting independence to overseas colonies of European states. For this purpose, the 1960 Declaration, in its Article 5, requested that:

> [i]mmediate steps shall be taken, in Trust and Non-Self-Governing Territories or all other territories which have not yet attained independence, to transfer all powers to the peoples of those territories without any conditions or reservations ...

How this transfer is to take place and who are the 'peoples' to whom the transfer is to be made was left unspecified.[3] In practice, the transfer of power was made to native officials who claimed to be representing the population of whole colonies. Once the transfer of power was achieved – and in some cases before – the new state was formally recognized as an independent state by the former colonial power and by gaining membership of the UN (see Chapters 2 and 13). In other words, the right of self-determination supplied a general justification for the transfer of sovereign powers to the native officials of former European colonies and for international recognition of the new states as independent and sovereign states.

For most secessionists, the right to secede from the host state should perform the very same function: it should justify both the *transfer* of (all) sovereign powers to the secessionist political leaders and officials native to the seceded territory, and international *recognition* of the newly seceded state. In contrast to the secessionists, most[4] contemporary theorists of secession do not mention this dual function of the right to secede. In contemporary theories of secession, the right to secede follows from and exemplifies a variety of general norms of political theory and applied ethics; it is thus a part of a norm-based assessment of political, in this case, secessionist, demands. In short, in morally assessing secessionist demands or attempts at secession, theorists argue that some groups have and some do not have a right to secede. Some normative theorists of secession also argue that legal regulation of individual and group relations and of attempts at secession within the present state-based system should be based on such a norm-based moral assessment (Buchanan 2004; Copp 1998).

In contrast to the normative theorists of secession, the secessionists have no interest in the universally applicable norms and principled regulation of

---

3   Only in the case that independence was to be achieved by association with or integration into another independent state, the UN Resolution 1541 required 'an informed and democratic process' without specifying what this process should be (UN Resolution 1541, Annex Principles VII–IX). See also Chapter 6.

4   Some theorists, in particular Allen Buchanan, indicate that the right to secede does entitle the right-holder to international assistance and international recognition of 'its' state but do not mention the transfer of any (let alone 'all') powers.

relations among groups and individuals. For many of them, their political goal, the independent statehood of their selected territory, overrides many (if not all) political and moral principles and allows or justifies the use of violence for its achievement. In contrast, political theorists and philosophers, in general, show no interest in transfers of sovereign (or any other kind of) power or the regulation thereof or in moral assessment of the use of violence by the secessionists; some of them show interest in justifying, by appeal to general principles, the international recognition of new states. This divergence of views creates significant difficulties in the application of contemporary theories to real-life attempts at secession. In order to assess a particular case, theorists would need to apply general political or ethical norms to political goals, strategies and acts of secessionists and anti-secessionists – the principles which the actors themselves ignore or only pay lip service to. In many cases, the secessionists and anti-secessionists' political goals have no place in the evaluative framework of any theory of secession. For example, the principal secessionist goal, the secessionist group's exclusive control of the political institutions and political power, is not, as an overriding goal, subject to assessment by any of the principles/norms advanced in theories of secession. Secession theorists would be inclined to view this kind of control only as an instrument towards other morally more acceptable goals such as prosperity of a chosen group or its protection from domination. In consequence, they would not be in a position to assess this particular goal as a free-standing political goal, independent of the presumed moral and political ends that it is supposed to serve.

## The Right-Holders: Who Are They?

The UN-proclaimed right of self-determination appears to assume that 'peoples' are as easily identifiable as 'humans' or 'individuals' who are the right-holders of human rights. This assumption, to say the least, is highly misleading. All right-based theories of secession assign the right to secede to those groups whose members are concentrated and settled on a bounded territory. Groups made of members who are dispersed or not settled on a specific territory do not have any right to secede. But not all concentrated and settled groups within existing states have the right to secede. How does a secession theory decide which ones do have the right?

The most explicit are some *choice theories*: the groups whose members, *choose* to secede, usually by a majority vote, 'earn' or 'get' the right to secede (Beran 1984; see also Chapters 4 and 23). Although these groups – or rather their representatives – have to fulfil other conditions so as not to cause undue harm to others, it is via a majority vote (either of the representatives or of the members directly) that they get the right to secede. The majority group has the right to secede the territory on which it is a majority; but a minority group on the same territory can, by majority vote, secede from the initially seceding territory. The majority vote procedure allows for recursive secessions – secessions from secessions. This makes the boundaries of the right-holding groups (and territories) quite changeable and fluid.

The procedure of gaining the right to secede appears to be arbitrary because it assigns the right to secede on the basis of contingent and changeable features of groups – their majority vote or their desire to have a separate state. If the majority changes its mind, does it lose its right to secede? Dispersed groups who cannot form a majority on a territory are denied the right to secede and are forced to live in whatever state the concentrated group chooses to live.

According to the *remedial theories*, if the host state systematically acts (or condones the acts) against the interests or rights (as selected by a specific theory) of a group of individuals, that group gains the right to secede from the host state (see Chapter 22). Therefore, the right-holder is identified by being the target or subject of the actions of the host state or other agents associated with it. But the host state usually acts against *individuals* whom its agents identify as hostile or treasonous to the host state. Remedial theories of secession appear to assume that the systematic acts of the host state will reveal the target group – the right-holder – which will be easily distinguishable from other territorially concentrated groups in the host state.[5] But sometimes this does not happen – in fact, many governments kill or persecute individuals who are territorially dispersed over the whole territory; this happened in Cambodia in the 1970s, in Uganda and Iraq in the 1980s. Following Locke, one could argue that these dispersed groups have the remedial right of removing the tyrannical and murderous government, by force if necessary. If so, it seems different remedial rights are assigned on the basis of the size and concentration of group to which the right is being assigned – in spite of the injustice (which the right is supposed to remedy) being the same. This procedure of assigning rights on the basis of size and concentrations of groups alone appears to be quite arbitrary.

Remedial theories of secession assign a remedial right only to the non-political (usually national) groups whose members are *indiscriminately* subject to the injustice by the host state; that is, any of its members can be subject to the same grave injustice in virtue of their membership in the (national) group. If the host state targets only members or supporters of a *political* party or movement, this, according to remedial theories, would not generate the right of the whole national group to secede, nor would it generate the right to secede a territory. How does one decide which group is being subject to injustice and whether the group qualifies for this right? (And who is qualified to make such a decision?) In many politically divided societies many individuals who are *not* subject to indiscriminate injustice by the host state (because they do not support the secessionist movement) live intermixed with individuals who are subject to such injustice. Yet these individuals or groups, according to the remedial theorists, would be forced to live in a new state which is created to protect those individuals who had been subject to injustice by their old state. In pursuit of justice for some individuals, remedial theorists appear ready to subject other individuals to injustice of another kind.

---

5   Ewin (1995) explores a variety of conceptual problems arising from this task.

## The Right to Secede: Do We Really Need It?

*Nationalist theories* or ideologies appear to resolve the issue of the identity of the right-holder smoothly and practically: the right-holder is a group which has gained a (national) identity *prior* to any action that generates the right.[6] Thus a 'nation' is defined as a group with a shared history and culture, including language and customs. Similarly 'a people' or 'a society' is defined in terms of its shared history and its social and political relationships and shared social goals (Chapter 21; Copp 1998: 227–8). The first problem these theories face is the fluid nature of national and social boundaries: individuals can not only change their membership but also be members of several such groups, be those 'nations' or 'societies'. If so, it may be difficult – prior to mass mobilization in support of a state-building project – to determine who the members of a particular national or social group are and, therefore, how the right-holding group differs from others which have no right to secede.

Apart from this problem, this type of 'ascriptive' theory of secession faces the following dilemma: the right-holder is defined either by non-political (and seemingly) 'natural' features (e.g. language and customs) or by openly political features (e.g. political/social cooperation and institutions, shared political life). If the former, the question arises as to why non-political features of a group require the establishment of separate coercive and legal institutions (armed forces, police, judiciary and executive government) which this non-political group should exclusively control. How does one infer from a group's common cultural characteristics to its right to exclusive control of coercive governmental institutions? The maintenance of a culture, even if it is threatened by state policies, does not, necessarily, require armed forces and police controlled exclusively by the group sharing that culture.

If, on the other hand, the group is defined by its common political life and institutions, resembling that of the state-controlling group ('people' or 'society'), the following question seems to arise: does the group possess the right to secede *because* it has been organized for the purpose of a state-building project which, ultimately, provides support for a demand to secede? Many societies or national groups have in fact become so organized as a part of a state-building or overtly secessionist project. For example, many societies and national groups in the Balkans, Eastern Europe and Russia have been constructed in the 19th and 20th centuries for the purpose of state-building and secessionist projects. To argue that these political features give rise to or are necessary conditions for the right to secede is in effect to argue that if a group is politically organized so as to facilitate a state-building project or secession, it thereby gains a (potential) right to secede.

---

6 Most theorists who advocate distribution of the right to secede only to national groups or organized societies introduce further norms that need to be satisfied if their chosen group or society is to gain the right to secede. Some require a secession plebiscite (Margalit and Raz 1990; Moore 2001: 237; Copp 1998: 230); others assign the right as a general remedy for the disadvantages that national minorities face everywhere (Tamir 1995: 149) or for the lack of 'well-being' that the latter face in some states (Caney 1998: 169).

This appears to be question-begging inference of 'ought' from 'is'. Moreover, this type of theory denies the right to secede to those groups that had been denied any opportunity to organize in a suitable way (by oppressive governments, perhaps?) as well as to dispersed groups (whether or not they are suitably organized). Once again this distribution of the right to secede appears to be arbitrary if not unjust.

Some theorists hold that the nations (peoples) who are in the majority in a state 'own' or control those states. In their view, it is unfair to leave 'stateless' minorities, living in these 'alien' states, without a state (or at least self-government) in particular in the cases in which these minorities ('peoples') are clearly capable of 'owning' a state of their own as much as the majority nations are; it is unfair (or disrespectful) to treat differently nations or peoples who show the same capacities (see Chapters 21 and 23). In their view, a right to secede is a form of moral recognition of the capacity of a group for a politically organized life: once a group has shown itself capable of 'owning' a state, it should gain a right to a state, that is, a right to secede as a sign of respect or recognition. But why is a particularly high level of political and/or cultural organization of a group to be an object of moral reward or recognition? And who is to be morally rewarded or recognized – apart from the (secessionist) political leaders and their supporters? Finally, why do political leaders and supporters of secessionist movements need any moral reward or recognition for their work? Having or gaining a state of one's own is not a self-evident moral good – however good it may prove to be to some individuals or groups. Why should striving to gain a state of one's own be morally rewarded with a right to have that state, that is, to secede? No theorist of secession has, to my knowledge, offered a reasoned answer to this question.

In spite of their pursuit of fairness and justice, many secession theorists appear ready to treat individuals and groups unequally, depending on their demographic or geographic position: for example, groups dispersed over a territory are not granted the right to a state of their own (only because they are not concentrated) and are thus not worthy of the recognition and respect that concentrated groups get. In view of this, the right to secede appears to be privilege based on a geographic or demographic position and not a right based on moral considerations.

## The Capacity of the Right-Holder to Act and to Benefit

Right-holders are, in general, supposed to be capable of exercising the right they hold: for example, individuals who have the right of free speech are supposed to be capable of exercising the right by expressing their views in public. How are the right-holding groups to exercise the right to secede?

Secession is a creation of a new state on a territory detached from an existing state. The groups who are alleged right-holders do not in fact detach a territory or create new states: it is individuals, claiming to represent these groups, who create new institutions, office-titles and state symbols and appoint the office holders. While the right is supposed to be granted to a group, its exercise seems to be restricted to representatives of the group who almost invariably happen to be the leaders and activists of a secession movement.[7]

In contrast to the capacity to exercise the right, many members of the right-holding group are capable of *benefiting* from the right or its exercise. Once a new state is created by secession, those who remain in the former host state lose all political power or capacity for decision-making within the new state. As a result, the former minority is now a 'master of its own house', no longer sharing political decision-making with or being dominated by its former co-citizens. The right to secede thus creates *a new set of relations* between the right-holding group and the other groups in the (former) host state: a minority, by exercising its right to secede, severs all political ties with other groups and becomes a majority in its own state. By transforming a minority into a majority, the seceded state removes the previous constraints on the political power of the former minority by *excluding* the former majority (or other dominant group) from the political decision-making. Precisely because the aim of secession is to *exclude* groups and their members from a political process, the beneficiaries of the act of secession and of the right to secede are sharply distinguished from those that do not hold that right. For this purpose it does not much matter which criteria one uses to distinguish those who are to be excluded from those who are to benefit from the right, as long as the exclusion of the former majority is achieved.

Excluding former majorities from political decision-making or transforming former minorities into majorities in a new state are, in situations in which these acts cause no moral harm, morally neutral: there is nothing about these acts that calls for moral assessment. If political self-determination – the value of which has been promoted in Chapters 21 and 23 – amounts to the exclusion of former majorities and transforming minorities into majorities, then, in my view, self-determination has no particular moral (as opposed to political) value. If so, there is no reason to claim that any group has a moral right to become a majority in a new state and to exclude a former majority from decision-making. At least this is what I shall argue in the section following the next one.

## The Obligations Arising from the Right

All contemporary theories of secession assume or argue that the right to secede generates an obligation on the host states and other states to respect the *liberty* of the right-holder to secede and to establish a state of its own and to obtain recognition

---

7   Many members of the secessionist group express support for the secession, by engaging in various political activities – such as demonstrations – or by engaging in and/or supporting warfare against the host state. None of those are acts exercising the right to secede; at most they are exercises of the right to express support for secession or a secessionist movement. For a different view, according to which 'peoples' are 'moral agents', see Chapter 21.

of its independence: the correlate of the right is thus the obligation to respect this liberty. Some theories – in particular the remedial theory of Allen Buchanan – introduce additional obligations: other states are, according to him, obliged to recognize the independence of the seceded state and in this and other ways to assist the establishment of the state (Buchanan 2004: 44, 436–9). This includes military ('humanitarian') intervention to assist those groups which have the right to secede to establish their own state (Buchanan 2004: 438–9). Some remedial theories regard the secessionist attempts to establish a state as a last-resort remedy for grave injustices – and hence the obligation on other states to intervene, on humanitarian grounds, to help them in implementing these remedies (see also Chapter 22). But other theories – in particular, choice theories – generate no such obligations on other states.

But does the right to secede also generate the right to use violence in efforts to secure its exercise? For example, if the host state does not recognize the right to secede and uses its sovereign coercive powers to suppress the secessionist efforts (for example, by lawfully imprisoning secessionist leaders and their followers) does the right to secede give the right to *any* members of the right-holding group to use violence against the host state agents? In other words, does the liberty to establish a new state include the liberty to use violence against those who attempt to restrict or deny this liberty? In particular, does the right to secede generate a right or permission to kill those who attempt to impede its exercise? And who is the holder of the right or liberty to kill? This point of indeterminacy of the right-holders may present serious moral problems: if the right-holder is defined in terms of its cultural and social characteristics, the right to kill can be granted to those who display those characteristics. In the absence of any other procedure, displaying the essential group characteristics (e.g. displaying the requisite cultural markers) would give a person the liberty to kill or otherwise coerce *others* who oppose the establishment of a state to which her or his group, as a corporate body, has a right. These *others* may be neighbours or co-citizens living on the same territory who do not 'belong' to the group and/or who oppose the creation of a new state (for example, because the seceding state is 'foreign' to them).

No contemporary normative theory of secession addresses the question of the right to use violence or lethal force in pursuit of its secessionist claims. Only Buchanan's remedial theory appears to imply that the group which has gained the right to secede also has gained the right to use violence in defence of this right (Pavković 2008). But it is not clear whether the right to use lethal force is generated by the right to secede itself or by a general right to self-defence.[8]

---

8   In many cases, secessionist mobilization and secessionist movements arise *before* any of the grave injustices are committed which, according to various remedial theories, give rise to the right to secede. But once secessionist mobilization starts and secessionists resist the suppression of their secessionist movement by public protest or by force, the host state in response often starts to commit the grave injustices that, in turn, give rise to the right to secede to the group exposed to them. In this way, prior to gaining the right to secede, secessionists can and do engage in acts of violence or public protest which, in

## What Does the Right to Secede Do?

As Michel Seymour points out in Chapter 21, contemporary normative theorists are concerned with the recognition of discrete groups within a state and with the normative implications of such a recognition. Accordingly, the right to secede is to provide a moral basis for the recognition of a specific group's *political equality* as well as its (alleged) *political aspiration* – the aspiration to form a state over which its members have an exclusive control. If so, this right should provide a moral ground for the exclusion of the members of another – usually the majority – group from the political process and thus to prevent them from sharing or dominating the political decision-making relating to the right-holder. But as we have seen, there is no consensus as to who the right-holders here are, how they are to be distinguished from non-right-holders and what claims, obligations and permissions the right in fact generates. This indeterminacy of the right-holders and of the claims and obligations that the right generates is possibly related to the above mentioned functions/purposes of the right to secede. Its purpose is to provide for recognition not of a particular kind of group but of groups of different kinds and size that have (allegedly) aspired and/or are likely to aspire to such recognition. Its purpose, further, is to provide protection to the secessionist activists who are endeavouring to establish state institutions and take control over the territory regardless of the means that they are using: hence there is no need to determine, in advance, the permissible instruments or the obligations of outsiders who may provide such protection.

The right to secede thus appears to be an instrument with a rather indeterminate scope and function which serves secessionists in furthering their claims. Disregarding its particular service to secessionists, one can surely ask: are there any other instruments in the normative repertoire of contemporary secular ethics – other than the right to secede – that can be used to provide a normative assessment of secessions?

In attempting to answer this question, one needs to ask what is it, in the cases of secession, that requires normative evaluation and, possibly, regulation. The transfer of sovereign political power from one elite to another and from one set of political institutions/offices to another may indeed be subject to the evaluation of political legitimacy; it is unclear whether, in addition, such transfers can or need to be regulated/assessed by another set of norms, whether moral or legal. In view of this, it is not self-evident that the *political* aspiration to create a new state by effecting such a transfer of sovereign political powers from one elite to another is, necessarily, subject to moral evaluation. Aspiring to create a new state, by itself, may be a morally neutral aspiration. Of course, political domination over a group based on systematic political discrimination against its members – as outlined in

---

turn, are causally necessary for gaining the right to secede. Remedial theorists, such as Buchanan, appear to regard this way of gaining the right to secede morally permissible. From this it appears that secessionists have the right to use violence in their attempts to gain the right to secede. For a further discussion see Pavković 2010.

Chapter 24 – is indeed subject to moral evaluation: it is arguably morally wrong to discriminate and to dominate in the way described in this chapter. Thus a situation in which one group discriminates against and dominates over another is arguably morally impermissible or unacceptable. Creating a new state for the discriminated group is then a morally justifiable way of remedying this morally impermissible situation (although perhaps this is not the only morally justifiable remedy).

But if one is morally to justify secession in this way, one is justifying it only as one *possible* instrument for the remedy of a specific type of morally impermissible actions, not as an action or instrument that is morally justifiable in all cases of state-creation. In some situations – such as that of mutually agreed secession – secession is morally neutral and requires no moral evaluation. In these situations, secession is not an instrument for the remedy of harm or injustice but a result of a political agreement among the elites who are to effect the required transfer of power; an example would be that of the secession of Slovakia in 1993 or of Norway in 1905 (see Part VI). Further, an attempt at secession that only aims to put in effect the political choice of a majority of a population (e.g. expressed through a referendum/plebiscite) may be morally permissible without, necessarily, being morally commendable or praiseworthy. It is permissible in situations in which the harm that secession causes may be minimized or compensated in various ways or in situations in which secession leads to the loss primarily of privileges (political or economic) that a limited number of people enjoyed in the (former) host state (Pavković 2004). A secession may thus be morally permissible because its harm is limited and can be redressed. If a secession is morally neutral or morally permissible, there is no need to introduce the concept of moral right in the evaluation of such secessions: these can be morally evaluated (or not) without having recourse to this concept.

As we have seen above, if a unilateral (not mutually-agreed) attempt at secession aims to remedy a particular harm (e.g. systematic discrimination) it may be morally justified simply as a remedy of that harm. One can argue that the harm it remedies – for example, the systematic discrimination – outweighs any harm that such a unilateral secession may cause the host state and those who have not been discriminated against. The abuse that it remedies is, in a moral hierarchy of values, ranked as a greater harm than the harms that this secession may cause. In this way an attempt at a unilateral secession may be given a moral justification which again need not refer to a right to secede.

But what about the obligations of the host and other states? If a secession is morally permissible, it is morally wrong of the host state to attempt to suppress it. One could further argue that other states and individuals may be, in some situations, obliged to assist those who are wronged by their host state. And other states may also have an obligation to recognize a new state arising from a morally permissible secession. Whether or not such an obligation would be of a moral kind is an open question which is beyond the scope of the present chapter. But in cases of morally permissible secessions, other states may also be morally obliged to assist the secession authorities on general humanitarian grounds: they may be thus obliged to assist in protecting non-combatants from systematic violence, even if the latter are not their citizens. Therefore, a variety of moral norms which are not based on group rights can generate moral constraints and obligations which the right to secede is supposed to generate; if so, the right to secede is not needed for this purpose.

The right to secede, in many theories of secession, imposes moral constraints on host states but not on secessionists. Yet the actions of secessionists as well as the host states, are subject to moral evaluation and both types of actors are subject to moral constraints to avoid causing harm (Laoutides 2008). The following general principle, originally called 'the no irreparable harm principle', can be used to assess actions of both types of actors:

> *Thou shalt not kill non-threatening non-combatants or evict them in pursuit of any claim, secessionist or anti-secessionist. (Pavković with Radan 2007: 214)*

Both the host state and secessionists are bound by the principle: violent suppression of a secessionist movement is equally impermissible as the use of violence and lethal force in pursuit of secessionist aims. The principle does not prohibit the use of violence in self-defence against violence, nor does it rule out the possibility that the creation of state institutions – in particular military forces – may be an instrument of self-defence. But the principle rules out any moral justification of the use of violence to protect or to pursue a secession that is not itself an attempt to protect the secessionist population from unprovoked violence. A few attempts at secessions – such as that of Biafra from Nigeria in 1967 – were attempts to protect populations who had been exposed to violence prior to the declaration of secession or independence (see Chapter 6). But many attempts at secession are not aimed at protection from unprovoked violence for the simple reason that host states, *prior* to declaration of secession or intention to secede, usually are not threatening to use indiscriminate violence against their own citizens (Pavković with Radan 2007: 209–10).

The harm arising from the use of politically organized violence is, in my opinion, morally the most apprehensible harm arising in secession. Moreover, this kind of harm is avoidable. Hence I believe that normative assessment of attempts at secession should aim at violence-minimization; the no-irreparable harm principle proposed above has this aim. This, of course, does not rule out other forms of normative/moral assessment of secession. But when embarking on the project of moral assessment of political processes such as secession, it would be also useful to ask: do such processes, by themselves, require moral assessment and, if so, what is moral assessment supposed to achieve in that particular realm?

# References

Beran, H. (1984), 'A Liberal Theory of Secession', *Political Studies* 32, 20–31.
Buchanan, A. (2004), *Justice, Legitimacy and Self-Determination: Moral Foundations for International Law* (Oxford: Oxford University Press).
Caney, S. (1998), 'National Self-determination and National Secession: Individualist and Communitarian Approaches', in P.B. Lehning (ed.), *Theories of Secession* (London: Routledge), 152–81.
Copp, D. (1998), 'International Law and Morality in the Theory of Secession', *Journal of Ethics* 2:3, 219–45.
Ewin, R.E. (1995), 'Can There Be a Right to Secede?', *Philosophy* 70, 341–62.
Laoutides, C. (2008), 'The Collective Moral Agency of Secessionist Groups', in A. Pavković and P. Radan (eds), *On the Way to Statehood: Secession and Globalization* (Aldershot: Ashgate), 146–62.
Makinson, D. (1988), 'Rights of Peoples: The Point of View of a Logician', in J. Crawford, *The Rights of Peoples* (Oxford: Clarendon Press), 69–92.
Margalit, A. and J. Raz (1990), 'National Self-Determination', *Journal of Philosophy* 87, 439–61.
Moore, M. (2001), *The Ethics of Nationalism* (Oxford: Oxford University Press).
Pavković, A. (2004), 'Secession as a Defence of a Liberty: A Liberal Answer to a Nationalist Demand', *Canadian Journal of Political Science* 37:3, 695–713.
Pavković, A. (2008), 'Liberalism, Secession and Violence', in M. Jovanović and K. Henrard (eds), *Sovereignty and Diversity* (Amsterdam: Eleven International), 15–32.
Pavković, A. (2010), 'By the Force of Arms: Violence and Morality in Secessionist Conflict', in D.H. Doyle (ed.), *Secession as an International Phenomenon* (Athens, GA: University of Georgia Press), 259–76.
Pavković, A. with P. Radan (2007), *Creating New States: Theory and Practice of Secession* (Aldershot: Ashgate).
Tamir, Y. (1995), *Liberal Nationalism* (Princeton, NJ: Princeton University Press).
UN Resolution 1541 (1960), UN General Assembly Resolution 1541 (XV) *Principles which should guide Members in determining whether or not an obligation exists to transmit the information called for under Article 73 of the Charter*.
Van Dyke, V. (1977), 'The Individual, the State and Ethnic Communities in Political Theory', *World Politics* 29:3, 343–69.

# PART VI
# SECESSIONS AND SECESSIONIST MOVEMENTS IN THE WORLD

# Introduction to Part VI

The short chapters in this Part are case studies of attempts at secessions and secessionist movements around the world. A great variety of cases outlined have one common feature: the principal political goal of the movements or parties is the creation of a new state independent of the host state. The methods employed to attain this goal, the responses of the host state and the geopolitical and social context in which these movements or parties operated, differed considerably from one case to another. But perhaps the most striking differences concern the sources and type of grievance that led to the formation of a secessionist movement or secessionist demands.

Another obvious difference is found in the outcome of the secessionist demands. In a few cases, these demands led to the creation of an independent state that gained international recognition and became a UN member. This was the outcome of secessionist demands that resulted in the creation of Bangladesh, Singapore, Eritrea, Norway, Iceland and Slovakia. In some cases, the *de facto* state created by secession did not gain international recognition: Abhkazia, South Ossetia, Transdniestria, Chechnya, Somaliland and Serb Krajina belong to this category. As noted in Chapters 13 and 15, seceded states lacking international recognition are not afforded the protection of the UN or regional security alliances and are thus exposed to military conquest by their host state. The *de facto* states of Chechnya and Serb Krajina were re-incorporated into their previous host state by military conquest. Others depend on regional or neighbouring states for protection from their former host states: this is the case with Abhkazia, South Ossetia and Transdniestria. Taiwan, a *de facto* state with only limited international recognition, belongs to this category too, as it depends on the protection of the USA. In the case of Somaliland, it is the weakness or, rather, systemic failure of its host state, Somalia, that prevents its re-incorporation.

In all the other cases, the secessionist movements did not succeed in establishing control over the territory they claimed and thus did not succeed in establishing a *de facto* state.[1] In the cases of West Papua, Mindanao and possibly South Yemen, the secessionists' movements are disunited and relatively weak and thus organizationally incapable of establishing control over the territory they claim. Secessionist movements in Aceh, Kurdistan and Myanmar/Burma lacked support

---

1   For a discussion of the conditions necessary for the establishment of a *de facto* state, see Chapter 15.

from outside states for their secessionist projects and, in the case of Aceh and Myanmar/Burma, faced regimes which have military capacities superior to theirs. Although the secessionist movement of Tibet has some support from outside states, its host state is a global power which has repeatedly used its superior military force to suppress secessionist uprisings. In Scotland and the Basque region the secessionist movements have not, as yet, attempted to secede but may do so in the future through a framework negotiated with the host state.

In view of the above, the cases in this Part could have been classified into three basic categories: successful secessions, attempted secessions and potential secessions/secessionist movements. Yet we cannot offer any systematic explanation as to why some secessions are successful, some are not and some are not even attempted. And in view of this, we did not think that a classification along the lines of *success/attempt/absence of attempt* would be of much use here. Nonetheless, the cases discussed in this Part raise two important questions, namely:

1. Under what conditions are secessions attempted?
2. What factors lead to a successful secession?

These questions are discussed in Chapters 3, 10 and 15; and as indicated in these chapters, we have (perhaps as yet) no definitive answers to these – and many other – questions about secessions.

The present geographical classification of our case studies, we thought, may be of help to those who are seeking information about secessions and secessionist movements. And of course our treatment of secessions and secessionist movement is, as already suggested in the Preface, far from exhaustive. Secessionist movements such as those of the Tamils in Sri Lanka, the Flemish in Belgium, Albanians in Macedonia, Kurds in Turkey and the Uyghur in Xinjiang province of China have not been discussed. Likewise the attempts at secession of the Serb Republic from Bosnia and Herzegovina, the Turkish Republic of Northern Cyprus, Western Australia from Australia and Bougainville from Papua New Guinea, to name a few, have not been given the analysis they deserve.

ASHGATE
**RESEARCH**
COMPANION

# ASIA

# Case Study 1:
# Aceh: The Secession That Never Was

## Edward Aspinall

In the late 1990s and early 2000s, after the 1998 downfall of the authoritarian regime of Indonesia's President Suharto, many informed observers thought that the Indonesian province of Aceh was on the cusp of independence. Inspired by a recent UN-supervised vote in East Timor, in 1999 a pro-independence movement organized massive demonstrations in favour of an independence referendum throughout the territory. Insurgents of the Free Aceh Movement (Gerakan Aceh Merdeka, GAM) controlled most of Aceh's countryside, and a bitter armed conflict was underway. Everywhere in Aceh, people spoke of independence as both imminent and desirable. Yet Aceh was a case of secession that did not happen. Though nationalist sentiment ran deep, the independence movement lacked both the international allies and the military muscle it needed to break free of Indonesia. In the end, Aceh's secessionist crisis was resolved by a solution that is common in such circumstances: an autonomy deal.

The independence movement in Aceh had deep roots in the territory's history. Indonesia is a supremely multi-ethnic yet surprisingly cohesive country, within which Aceh was always rather distinctive. From the 16th century, the Acehnese sultanate had been significant in Southeast Asia as a military force, a trading power and a centre of Islamic learning and culture. When the Dutch invaded in 1873 with the aim of incorporating Aceh into their Netherlands East Indies, resistance lasted for several decades. During the 1945–49 Indonesian independence struggle against the Dutch, the Acehnese were ardent supporters of Indonesia, but also maintained considerable control over their own affairs; they also aimed at an Islamic rather than a secular state. Thus, in the 1950s, many Acehnese participated in a *Darul Islam* (Abode of Islam) revolt against the new Indonesian government. Their goals were more regionalist and Islamic than secessionist: they wanted Aceh to be part of an Islamic Indonesian state, not for it to become an independent country. This revolt was resolved by granting Aceh 'special territory' status, which entailed greater autonomy. However, an increasingly authoritarian and centralizing Indonesian government did little to honour this deal.

It was not until the mid-1970s that the compounding disillusionment in Aceh gained expression in an out-and-out independence movement. The founder of GAM was Hasan Tiro, an intellectual who, inspired by his reading of Aceh's glorious history and his years of study and political engagement in the United States, returned to Aceh to declare independence in December 1976. He tried to mould his demands in terms of international discourse on self-determination by arguing that Indonesia was exercising a form of colonial control over Aceh, that Aceh's struggle was an anti-colonial one, and that Acehnese independence would not be an instance of secession but merely reinstatement of Aceh's pre-colonial sovereignty.

Early on, Tiro failed to gain much support either internationally or within Aceh. His new movement was effectively suppressed by Indonesian security forces, and Tiro himself fled abroad, eventually settling in Sweden. In the late 1980s and early 1990s, GAM revived its struggle, after some fighters received training in Libya. Indonesian security forces responded harshly, with many Acehnese villagers killed, tortured or otherwise abused. This military violence effectively stopped the rebellion, but at the price of deepening popular disillusionment with Indonesian rule.

GAM's rebellion revived once more and peaked in the immediate post-Suharto years after 1998. Taking advantage of a moment of weakness in Jakarta, the guerrillas recruited massively and fought the security forces more boldly than in the past. Many Acehnese who had previously been indifferent to the independence cause, or fearful of expressing support for it, now flocked to the GAM banner. The movement's leaders also believed that international actors were becoming more open to intervening in internal conflicts in places like Aceh, so they campaigned for the international community to either support independence, pressure Indonesia to reduce its use of military force or, at least, participate in the search for a peaceful resolution to the conflict. For the first time, there was substantial international involvement, with a European-based NGO facilitating negotiations between GAM and the Jakarta government. However, the government made it clear that the most it would cede was expanded autonomy for Aceh, a solution that GAM leaders strongly rejected.

This situation changed after two events: another Indonesian military offensive in 2003–04 which again greatly weakened the rebel movement's military capacity, and the devastating Indian Ocean tsunami of 26 December 2004. The tsunami killed approximately 160,000 people in Aceh alone, increasing moral pressure on the parties to resolve the conflict and opening a window of opportunity for renewed international involvement. A series of peace talks were held in Helsinki. At this point, the ironic outcome of GAM's search for international support became apparent. GAM leaders had always believed that internationalization of the conflict would constrain Indonesia's freedom to take military action and facilitate Aceh's independence; in fact, international actors now made clear that the price of their involvement was GAM's agreement to a peace deal that kept Aceh within the Indonesian state.

GAM leaders relented, and the 'Helsinki Memorandum of Understanding' was signed in August 2005. GAM gave up its arms and its independence goal. In exchange, Aceh was promised 'self-government' as part of Indonesia. In 2006, the national parliament in Jakarta passed a Law on the Government of Aceh, which GAM leaders say fails to deliver fully on the promise of self-government. Yet former rebel leaders have also swept to power in local executive government and legislative elections in Aceh. Many of them still talk about Aceh's history of struggle, the distinctiveness of its culture and the injustices of rule by Jakarta. But they do not now campaign for independence. Instead, their main focus is on delivering greater economic growth and welfare to the local population, a population that has been deeply wounded by years of armed conflict and is suspicious of official politics of all types. Secession may be dead in Aceh, at least for now, but many of the grievances that gave birth to the secessionist movement live on.

## Further Reading

Aspinall, Edward (2009), *Islam and Nation: Separatist Rebellion in Aceh, Indonesia* (Stanford, CA: Stanford University Press).
Drexler, Elizabeth F. (2008), *Aceh, Indonesia: Securing the Insecure State* (Philadelphia, PA: University of Pennsylvania Press).
Kell, Tim (1995), *The Roots of Acehnese Rebellion, 1989–1992* (Ithaca, NY: Cornell Modern Indonesia Project).

***

*Edward Aspinall is a Senior Fellow in the Department of Political and Social Change, College of Asia and the Pacific, Australian National University, Canberra.*

# Case Study 2:
# Bangladesh: Secession Aided by Military Intervention

## Peter Radan

From its creation in 1946 through independence from the British Empire, Pakistan was a geographical anomaly, divided into two non-contiguous regions, East and West Pakistan, with serious imbalances in relation to land, resources and people. These imbalances were compounded by linguistic, cultural and social differences, which in effect made the Urdu-speaking West and the Bengali-speaking East two distinct peoples.

As the Pakistani polity developed, East Pakistan experienced oppression and discrimination at the hands of the ruling elite in West Pakistan. Bengalis were not only economically deprived of development funds and an equitable portion of the Pakistani budget, but were also politically disenfranchised and prevented from obtaining important and influential administrative positions throughout the whole of Pakistan. Bengali political leaders were jailed, and the armed forces remained the almost exclusive domain of West Pakistanis.

Bengali separatism gathered serious momentum in 1966, when the leading political party in East Pakistan, the Awami League, issued a call for political and economic autonomy. In Pakistan's national election of December 1970, the Awami League secured 75 percent of the votes in East Pakistan, thereby gaining an absolute majority in the Pakistani national assembly. Although President and Martial Law Administrator General Yakya Khan initially attempted to honour the election outcome, mass demonstrations by West Pakistanis against the election results led him to postpone the convening of the duly elected national assembly. West Pakistani authorities meanwhile instigated a massive military build-up in East Pakistan which, in March 1971, led to a campaign of killing and destruction resulting in the death of several hundred thousand Bengalis.

On 26 March 1971 Bangladesh political leaders, invoking the right to self-determination of the Bengali people of East Pakistan, declared independence from Pakistan. Bangladeshi militia forces, although unable to repel the West Pakistani onslaught, nonetheless prevented a quick and decisive victory by the latter. Central to this resistance was the assistance of India, which allowed the Bangladeshi forces to use Indian territory as a base, and provided them with arms, advice, training and supplies. On 6 December, India recognized Bangladesh, invaded the country and by mid-December had defeated Pakistani forces and presented the world with a *fait accompli*.

On the broader international scene, the UN resisted lending any support to Bangladesh, despite the bloodshed and carnage perpetrated by West Pakistani forces. Preoccupied with the politics associated with the conflict, it was even unable to tackle the humanitarian problems generated by the crisis, namely, the nine million Bengali refugees which fled over the Indian border.

The Indo-Pakistani war generated by the Bangladesh crisis did, however, come before the UN Security Council. However, a draft pro-Pakistan resolution was vetoed by the USSR which had recently signed an alliance treaty with India. The conflict was then referred to the General Assembly, where a pro-Pakistani resolution calling for an immediate ceasefire and the withdrawal of Indian and Pakistani troops to their respective territories was supported by 104 member states, with ten abstentions and 11 against. In effect, this resolution, notwithstanding its obvious humanitarian implications, left the Bengalis largely defenceless to face the wrath of Pakistan's army.

However, the attitude of individual states gave a somewhat different interpretation of events. Pakistan's main 'allies' throughout the crisis, the USA and China, refrained from offering significant support to Pakistan's central government, refusing to send military advisers and curtailing arms shipments. The US government chiefly sought to garner some support for Pakistan, as a direct counter to the burgeoning friendship between India and the USSR. Similarly, the Chinese government, as a result of the Sino-Soviet split, principally supported Pakistan in order to oppose the USSR, a strategy which had the added benefit of achieving a degree of alignment with the USA.

Other states offered forms of support to Bangladesh. The UK and France, abstained from the various pro-Pakistan draft resolutions in the UN, and called for Pakistan's government to honour the 1970 election results. More tangibly, the UK government cancelled its development aid to Pakistan and contributed relief aid to the refugees along the Indian border. It also provided military supplies to the Indian army, much of which was used against Pakistani forces in Bangladesh.

The most important factor that enabled the secession of Bangladesh was the support it received from India, a powerful and pro-active patron state in the region. Initially, India did not support the Bangladeshi's independence. Indeed, during the first months of the 1971 crisis, India urged the settlement of the conflict on the basis of the 1970 election results. It was only later that India offered support by giving refuge to Bangladesh's government-in-exile and eventually embarking on a full-scale military operation against Pakistani forces. Without such support Bangladesh would not have achieved independence, notwithstanding the years of oppression and discrimination inflicted upon the Bengali population of what had been West Pakistan. Moreover, India's support led to eventual widespread recognition of Bangladesh and its eventual admission to the UN in September 1974.

## Further Reading

Heraclides, A. (1991), *The Self-Determination of Minorities in International Politics* (London: Frank Cass), 147–64.

Nanda, V.P. (1980), 'Self-Determination Outside the Colonial Context: The Birth of Bangladesh in Retrospect', in Y. Alexander and R.A. Friedlander (eds), *Self-Determination: National, Regional, and Global Dimensions* (Boulder, CO: Westview Press), 193–220.

Sisson, R. and L.E. Rose (1990), *War and Secession: Pakistan, India, and the Creation of Bangladesh* (Berkeley, CA: University of California Press).

\*\*\*

*Peter Radan is Professor of Law at Macquarie Law School, Macquarie University, Sydney.*

# Case Study 3:
# Kashmir: Separatism as Possible Trigger for Inter-State Conflict?

## Matthew J. Webb

The inception in 1989 of a bloody separatist insurgency aimed at separating Kashmir from Indian rule brought yet another violent secessionist conflict to many others that have been taking place in India, Pakistan and Mynamar. Geographically located at the confluence of the three great powers of the region – India, China and Pakistan – while also proximate to the former states of the USSR, Kashmir's geo-strategic and ideological significance has placed it at the centre of regional rivalries for more than half a century. The term 'Kashmir' typically refers to the 'Vale of Kashmir'; a valley 84 miles in length and 24 miles in width located at a height of approximately 2,000 metres. The Indian-administered state of Jammu and Kashmir (J&K) comprises the Sunni Muslim–dominated Kashmir valley together with the Hindu-majority region of Jammu and the Buddhist area of Ladakh.

Although the contemporary separatist conflict in Kashmir can be traced to independence from the British in 1947, its roots lie in the colonial period when Kashmir was part of a Muslim-majority princely state ruled by a Hindu Maharaja, Hari Singh, who in 1947 was forced to choose between joining India or Pakistan. While the Maharaja vacillated the state was invaded by tribesmen from the North West Frontier Province of what is now Pakistan, forcing the Maharaja to accede to India in return for promises of military assistance. The Pakistani regular army was involved from May 1948 in what was the first Indo-Pakistan war that ended in January 1949 with the former princely state divided between the two countries and the creation of the Indian state, or federal unit, of J&K. Since this time there has existed an irredentist movement seeking to unite the two populations divided by the arbitrary ceasefire line that ended the war and has remained largely unchanged since. The enduring nature of the conflict is due in no small measure to the ideological significance of this Muslim-majority state: its incorporation is regarded as an essential demonstration of India's founding ideology of secularism (India as a homeland of peoples of various religions) and of Pakistan's founding ideology as a sanctuary for Muslims in South Asia.

Post-independence politics in the state were dominated by Sheikh Abdullah and his National Conference party. Abdullah at times publicly repudiated the ruling Indian National Congress (INC) party's views on Kashmir's final status. This uneasy relationship was further complicated by the 1948 Indian offer of a plebiscite to resolve the state's final status – a plebiscite that has never been held. Abdullah was removed from office in 1953 but later returned to govern the state in 1975 and following his death in 1982 was succeeded by his son, Farooq Abdullah, as head of the National Conference and Chief Minister of the state. The dynastic politics of the state coupled with interference by New Delhi, corruption, vote rigging, the lack of economic opportunities for Kashmiri youth (who were increasingly well educated and politically mobilized), institutional decay and Pakistani interventions are usually cited as the main reasons for the violent rebellion against Indian authority that began in 1989. These factors are, of course, far from mutually exclusive and the most plausible explanatory account of the violent separatism that continues to wrack the state is premised upon a changing combination of all these factors. For example, many commentators attribute the outburst of separatist violence in 1989 to the public perception that the 1987 legislative assembly election had been rigged by the National Conference-INC coalition, and widespread anger at the subsequent removal of Farooq Abdullah as Chief Minister by New Delhi. While this might have been the main factor triggering the insurgency at the time, later other factors came into play in motivating and sustaining opposition to Indian rule. Whereas the initial wave of so-called 'militancy' was very much an urban, middle-class affair conducted by former university students, unemployed youths and opposition activists that was dominated by the pro-independence Jammu and Kashmir Liberation Front, by 1991 Islamist groups that favoured the state's accession to Pakistan such as the Hizbul Mujahideen began to dominate. They were in turn followed by even more hard-line groups, many of which included non-Kashmiris in their ranks, such as the Harkut-ul-Ansar and Jaish-e-Mohammed. These groups sought the creation of a pan-Islamic state in South Asia and enjoyed considerable Pakistani support, but their indiscriminately violent and often brutal tactics alienated many ordinary Kashmiris. The initial Indian reliance upon the Border Security Force (BSF) and Central Reserve Police (CRP), whose members were untrained in counter-insurgency operations, resulted in atrocities against the civilian population that played into the separatists' hands. By the mid-1990s, however, greater use was made of the local J&K police and former militants who had been turned to the government side, and the conflict entered a new phase extending outside the Valley of Kashmir to southern areas of the state including Doda, Jammu, Rajouri and Poonch.

That the number of incidences of political violence in Kashmir has decreased markedly in comparison to the 1990s may be regarded as something of a tactical military victory for the Indian security forces. However, the mass protests against Indian rule by a new generation of Kashmiri youth in 2010 and the violent response of the security forces to them indicate that Kashmiris remain as alienated from Indian rule as ever before, while India appears both unwilling and unable to address the core concerns that underpin the secessionist/irredentist aspirations of many Kashmiris. Moreover, the risks and dangers of the conflict continuing are not confined to Kashmiris and the occupying Indian forces alone; nuclear-armed India and Pakistan have come dangerously close to military conflict over Kashmir, threatening to spread violence and an unprecedented level of destruction over the entire sub-continent.

## Further Reading

Ganguly, S. (1997), *The Crisis in Kashmir: Portents of War, Hopes of Peace* (Cambridge: Cambridge University Press).
Hewitt, V. (1995), *Reclaiming the Past?* (London: Portland Books).
Schofield, V. (1996), *Kashmir in the Crossfire* (London: I.B. Tauris).
Swami, P. (2007), *India, Pakistan and the Secret Jihad: The Covert War in Kashmir, 1947–2004* (New York: Routledge).
Zutshi, C. (2004), *Languages of Belonging: Islam, Regional Identity and the Making of Kashmir* (New York: Oxford University Press).

***

*Matthew J. Webb is Assistant Professor of Politics and Department Head of Humanities and Social Sciences at the Petroleum Institute, Abu Dhabi, United Arab Emirates.*

# Case Study 4:
# Separatism in Mindanao

## Damien Kingsbury

When the Spanish first arrived in the southern Philippines in the late 16th century, having just expelled Islamic 'Moors' from Spain, they were dismayed to find that Islam had already taken root there. Islam was more shallow in the centre and north of the archipelago and was eventually replaced by Spanish Catholicism. But Islam was more firmly established in the south. Spanish colonization of the Philippines faced a number of revolts, in particular on Mindanao where Islam flourished in a number of inter-linked sultanates.

The 'Moros' of Mindanao – named after the Spanish Moors – came under Spanish rule only in 1878, when the Sultan of Sulu signed a peace agreement. In its Spanish iteration, Mindanao and the Sulu Archipelago ceded full sovereignty to Spain but the local Tausug language version described the region as a 'protectorate' retaining meaningful independence. Despite disagreement about the status of the peace agreement, when Spain ceded the Philippines to the United States in 1898, it included Mindanao and the Sulu archipelago as part of the sovereign colony.

In 1899, when the United States attempted to occupy the region, the Moros launched a war for independence, being defeated only in 1913. The Moros never accepted the defeat, however, or the incorporation into the Philippine state that implied.

Following the Philippines' independence in 1946, its governments attempted to resolve problems of landless peasants that had been fuelling a communist rebellion by resettling some of them in Mindanao. The Philippines government refused to recognize the Moro's traditional ownership, leading to disputes over land ownership; this entrenched Moros's distrust of the government. In 1968 on the island of Corregidor, Moro army trainees (as few as 28 by government accounts and as many as 200 by MNLF estimates) rebelled over their mission and pay and were then murdered by their Christian colleagues. Already feeling that the Catholic Philippines government discriminated against them in areas of housing and education and deeply angered by this event, Mindanao Muslims at that point associated with the revolutionary Kabataang Makabayan (KM – Patriotic Youth) organization and decided to separate from the Philippines. The KM was founded in 1964 by academics and trade union leaders in response to the then Philippines economic crisis. Its goals were to overthrow comprador elites and landlords and to remove US military bases from the Philippines.

The first Islamic independence group, under the leadership of academic Nur Misuari (who had left the KM earlier), was the Mindanao Independence Movement, which in the early 1970s transformed itself into the Moro National Liberation Front (MNLF). The goal of the MNLF was to create a separate Islamic state in Mindanao. At its height, the MNLF had around 30,000 armed combatants. In 1976 a peace agreement was signed establishing a ceasefire and an autonomous Muslim region including 13 provinces in the south of the island. Despite the ceasefire, the Philippines government failed to establish an autonomous Muslim region, leading to internal disagreements within the MNLF and the establishment, in 1981, of the more hard-line Moro Islamic Liberation Front (MILF) led by Salamat Hashim.

In the new 1996 peace agreement with the MNLF, the government finally agreed to create the more limited Autonomous Region of Muslim Mindanao with Nur Misuari as governor. While the MNLF accepted the agreement, the MILF did not. Following a failure of the Arroyo government to fully implement the 1996 agreement (citing Misuari's administrative incompetence), in 2001 Misuari led an unsuccessful rebellion then fled the country. He was captured in Malaysia the following year and sent back to the Philippines where he was placed under house arrest. He was allowed bail in 2008. The MNLF has, however, fallen into disrepair, with most of its members since joining the MILF.

The MILF signed a ceasefire agreement in 1997, which was abandoned by President Joseph Estrada in 2000. Peace talks resumed in 2007 but a Memorandum of Agreement on the definition of Ancestral Domain (MOA-AD) that had been initialled by both the government and the MILF was rejected by the Philippines Supreme Court in 2008, leading to renewed fighting. The MOA-AD was to be the foundation agreement upon which a comprehensive peace agreement on a high degree of regional autonomy was to be based.

Apart from the remnants of the MNLF and the still fully active MILF, the Abu Sayyef Group (ASG) in the Sulu Archipelago also continues to engage in a more regionally specific separatist campaign. The ASG was established in 1991, also as an MNLF break-away, and formally seeks to establish an independent Islamic province in the Sulu area (islands of Jolo and Basilan and Zamboanga on Mindanao). While this area approximates the pre-colonial Sulu sultanate, Basilan in particular is also one of the most impoverished parts of the Philippines. The ASG has since appeared to develop a wider Islamist orientation. The Philippines government considers the ASG to be a local branch of the regional Jemaah Islamiyah organization, which in turn has links to Al Qaeda. Some of ASG's senior members had previous experience fighting with the *mujahedeen* in Afghanistan, from which it developed its extremist ideology.

The ASG was estimated to have had a maximum strength of about 1,000 fighters, by 2010 reduced to 200 to 400 including the loss of senior leaders, but it still has a large, active support base. While the ASG is regarded as an Islamist separatist organization, in a number of ways it replicates the practices of previous inhabitants of the archipelago who engaged in piracy, kidnapping/ransom and extortion. Some observers believe the ASG has functionally moved away from its original political aims and now functions largely as a criminal rather than political organization.

## Further Reading

Anthony, T. (2008), *Rebels of Mindanao* (New York: Beaufort Books).
George, T. (1980), *Revolt in Mindanao: Rise of Islam in Philippine Politics* (Kuala Lumpur: Oxford University Press).
Rood, S. (2005), *Forging Sustainable Peace in Mindanao: The Role of Civil Society* (Washington, DC: East-West Center).
Santos, S. (2001), *The Moro Islamic Challenge: Constitutional Rethinking for the Mindanao Peace Process* (Quezon City: University of the Philippines Press).

***

*Damien Kingsbury is Professor in the School of International and Political Studies at Deakin University, Melbourne.*

# Case Study 5: Myanmar/Burma: Secession and the Ethnic Conundrum

## Renaud Egreteau

Since achieving independence from British rule in 1948, Burma (renamed Myanmar in 1989) has experienced neither national unity nor a peaceful state building. For the past six decades, political and cultural tensions between a two-thirds majority of ethnic Burman (*Bamar*) (historically dominant in Burma's central plains and Irrawaddy delta) and one-third of ethnic and tribal minorities (dwelling a horse-shoe shape range of peripheral hills) have fuelled a protracted civil war. Neither the parliamentarian and democratically-elected central governments (1948–58 and 1960–62) nor the successive military rulers (1958–60 and post-1962) have been in position to unify the country, whether through federalist political initiatives or the use of state-sponsored violence aimed at curbing centrifugal ethnic secessionist forces.

Colonial legacies have deeply shaped the Burmese ethnic conundrum. After the complete annexation of Burma in 1885, the British have divided the province into two separate administrative entities: 'Ministerial Burma' (the Burman heartland articulated around Rangoon and Mandalay) and the 'Frontiers Areas' mainly dominated by Karen, Karenni, Kachin, Naga, Chin and Shan ethnic groups. The latter ethnic groups – especially the Christianized Karens, Chins and Kachins – were favoured by the colonial power and were awarded dominant positions in Burma's security, administrative and education system (and this to the detriment of the Burman majority). After World War Two, reconciliation between Burma's alienated ethnicities within the territory inherited from the British era was attempted under the aegis of the independence hero General Aung San. The February 1947 Panglong inter-ethnic agreement on a federal union was one of the results. However, only the Kachins, Chins and Shans accepted the political compromise with the Burman majority, while the other ethnic groups opted for a secessionist struggle. By far the most powerful insurgent force, the Karens (Karen National Union) went underground as early as 1947 to fight for their independent 'Kawthoolei' state. During the 1950s, despite the federal union created by the 1947 Constitution and the 'right of secession after 10 years of independence' guaranteed in its Chapter X, ethnic armed movements expanded throughout the territory of Burma as the Mon and Karenni separatists joined the Karen insurgents. In 1958, Prime Minister U Nu's central government denied the constitutional right to secede to the Shans; this sparked the Shan secessionist movement. The Christian Kachins and Chins also rose to armed insurgency in the early 1960s in response to the tentative imposition of Buddhism as state religion by the central government.

After a two year interlude of military caretaker administration in 1958–60, the coup orchestrated by the Burmese Armed Forces (*Tatmadaw*) in 1962 was then justified by the military leadership as the only way to prevent the full disintegration of the Union, a rationalization still put forward by the Burmese junta five decades afterward. General Ne Win's autarkical and xenophobic regime (1962–88) indeed promoted a Jacobinist and Burman-centred view of the country illustrated by the centralizing 1974 Constitution. Conducting extensive counter-insurgency operations throughout the ethnic border areas, the one-party militarized system created by Ne Win made no compromise with peripheral insurgencies. But by the 1970s and 1980s, while maintaining their separatist agendas, various ethnic rebellions had created 'liberated' zones in which they could effectively organize their own autonomous administrations, run lucrative trans-border economies and pursue distinct (non-Burman) cultural policies, without posing an actual security threat to central government in Rangoon. In the late 1980s, the KNU, the Kachin Independence Organization (KIO), the New Mon State Party (NMSP), the Shan State Army (SSA), the Karenni National Progressive Party (KNPP) and other minor Arakanese (Rakhine), Chin, Palaung, Lahu and Pa'O ethnic rebellions as well as the Mong Tai Army (MTA) of the drug lord Khun Sa constituted an anti-Rangoon rebel force of about 60–70,000 armed insurgents which nonetheless had a rather defensive and marginal position.

After 1988, with the advent of a new military junta, inter-ethnic political dynamics significantly evolved. The new regime was more open to its rising neighbours (India, China, Thailand) and opted for a skilful policy of ceasefire 'gentlemen's agreements' with 17-odd ethnic insurgent groups dwelling in the border areas. Between 1989 and 1995, various Kachin, Wa, Kokaung, Shan, Pa'O, Palaung and even Karen armed outfits chose to normalize their relations with the still Burman-dominated central military authorities through fragile but peaceful autonomous deals that enabled them to control economic flows and local administration on their territories while effectively abandoning armed secessionist struggle against the Burmese central government. With around 40–50,000 rebels pacified in this way, the Burmese military could then focus its counter-insurgency campaigns against the remaining Karen, Karenni, Shan or Naga insurgents driven back to the edges of the Thai and Indian borders.

After years of direct military rule, the junta eventually started a strictly controlled transitional political process through a 'Road Map to a Disciplined

## Case Study 5

Democracy' unveiled in 2003. A key element of it, the 2008-adopted Constitution (the third since independence), established a new praetorian parliamentary system. Although federalist in its spirit (as it makes provision for 14 federal parliaments and local governments, one for each of Burma's seven Burman-dominated regions and seven ethnic minorities-dominated states), the newly imposed Constitution has not settled all the inter-ethnic contentious issues. On the ground, the era of the 1989-born ceasefire agreements (incompatible with the unifying state-building process based on the junta-inspired Constitution), has come to an end. With some ethnic minorities willing to play the electoral/parliamentarian game offered by the dominating Burmese military forces (Kachins, Palaungs, Mons, Pa'O and others), others forced to do so (Kokaung) and others ready either to continue or to resume the secessionist armed struggle (Was, other Kachins, Karens, Shans, Rakhine, Karennis and others), Burma's ethnic question is far from being settled and will remain at the core of the country's (in)stability in coming years.

## Further Reading

Lintner, Bertil (1999), *Burma in Revolt: Opium and Insurgency since 1948* (Chiang Mai: Silkworm Books).

Smith, Martin (1999), *Burma: Insurgency and the Politics of Ethnicity* (London: Zed Books).

South, Ashley (2008), *Ethnic Politics in Burma: States of Conflict* (London: Routledge).

\*\*\*

*Renaud Egreteau is Research Assistant Professor at the University of Hong Kong, Hong Kong, China.*

# Case Study 6: Singapore: Expulsion or Negotiated Secession?

## Bill K.P. Chou

There are two versions of the history of Singapore's secession from Malaysia. According to the Singaporean official version, the political leaders of Singapore did not pursue independence but Singapore was expelled from the Federation of Malaysia in 1965. Another unofficial version, to be considered below, is that the Singaporean Prime Minister at the time negotiated secession with the Malaysian leaders but did not want that to be known publicly. After the Merger Referendum in Singapore in 1962, Singapore joined the Federation of Malaysia in 1963 along with Malaya, Sabah and Sarawak. Singapore had neither natural resources nor an adequate supply of fresh water. Staying in the Federation enabled Singapore to access the Malaysian market and hinterland for its export trade, a very important pillar of Singaporean economy before industrialization took place. At that time its survival depended heavily on the newly-formed Malaysia.

There were, however, several issues on which the Singaporean and Malaysian political leaders disagreed. The Malaysian Federal Government under the leadership of the United Malays National Organization (UMNO) was worried that inclusion of Singapore would increase the proportion of Chinese people in the population of the Federation so substantially that the privileged position of Malay people would be challenged. The Prime Minister of Singapore, Lee Kuan Yew, publicly opposed UMNO's *bumiputera* policy – an affirmative action towards Malays who were the original settlers of Malaya but failed to adapt to the capitalist economy during the colonial rule. Lee believed that the policy discriminated against Chinese and wanted it repealed. In addition, Lee's People's Action Party (PAP) from Singapore campaigned for seats in Malaysia's federal parliament. Though PAP could win only one seat in the general election, the Malayan Chinese Association (MCA) in Malaysia feared that PAP would grow in power and replace it in the future ruling coalition of Malaysia. MCA urged UMNO to prevent the PAP from gaining influence in the federal government.

In regard to the economic development of the Federation, UMNO leaders were worried that Singapore's vibrant economy may replace the capital Kuala Lumpur to become the most important city in Malaysia. Singapore continued to face trade barriers in other states (federal units) of Malaysia despite an agreement to set up a common market, and Sabah and Sarawak were dissatisfied by Singapore's refusal to provide them with developmental aid as promised.

The 'trigger' for Singapore's secession was a series of race riots in Singapore. Fighting between Malays and Chinese led to bloodshed and property damage. The price of food skyrocketed during this period, due to the disruption in transport. Unable to resolve the crisis, Malaysian Prime Minister Tunku Abdul Rahman decided to expel Singapore from Malaysia. On 9 August 1965, the Prime Minister of Singapore Lee announced with teary eyes the independence of Singapore in a televised press conference. The images of his emotional announcement on television continue to appear from time to time on Singaporean media, reminding Singaporeans of the expulsion from Malaysia and the hardship that followed.

The second, unofficial version of Singapore's secession from Malaysia is that the secession was planned by Prime Minister Lee Kuan Yew. According to Goh Keng Swee, the Deputy Prime Minister of Singapore between 1973 and 1984, Singapore negotiated to secede from Malaysia before its independence. Tunku Abdul Rahman, then Prime Minister of Malaysia, was reported to be surprised when he saw Lee crying on television saying that Lee should be pleased with the result. Dr Toh Chin Chye, Deputy Prime Minister in Singapore at the time of independence, was also puzzled by Lee's tears. According to a de-classified memo from a UK official in Singapore in 1965, Lee Kuan Yew was reported to have 'threatened "punitive" measures against any newspaper which printed pictures of him smiling' ('Do Not Print Pictures of Me Smiling' 2010).

No Singaporean or Malaysian leaders who were involved in the series of negotiations before the independence admit that the secession was planned by both sides in advance. It is not clear which of the two above versions is true. But joining the Federation in 1963 certainly helped Singapore to achieve full independence from the UK and benefited Singapore's economy.

# Reference

'Do Not Print Pictures of Me Smiling: Lee Kuan Yew' (2010), *The Online Citizen: A Community of Singaporeans*. [Online] At http://theonlinecitizen.com/2010/07/do-not-print-pictures-of-me-smiling-lee-kuan-yew/ [accessed 22 August 2010].

## Further Reading

Lee, K.Y. (2000), *From Third World to First: The Singapore Story, 1965–2000* (New York: HarperCollins).

Pham, P.L. (2010), *Ending 'East of Suez': The British Decision to Withdraw from Malaysia and Singapore, 1964–1968* (Oxford and New York: Oxford University Press).

Pillai, M.G.G. (2005), 'Did Lee Kuan Yew Want Singapore Ejected from Malaysia?', *Malaysia Today*, 1 November. [Online] At http://web.archive.org/web/20071013161748/http://www.malaysia-today.net/columns/pillai/2005/11/did-lee-kuan-yew-want-singapore.htm.

***

*Bill K.P. Chou is Associate Professor in the Department of Government and Public Administration, University of Macau, Macau, China.*

# Case Study 7:
# Taiwan–China: A Case of Secession or a Divided Nation?

## Jean-Pierre Cabestan

Taiwan, under the official name of Republic of China (ROC), is a *de facto*, but ill-recognized, nation-state also claimed by the People's Republic of China (PRC) (see also Chapter 15). This politico-legal complexity underscores the ambiguity of Taiwan's status. Since Taiwan has never been part of the PRC, is it really a case of secession? At the same time, because most Taiwanese do not wish to reunify with the PRC and some still want to move to permanent and *de jure* independence, contrary to Beijing's hope and in spite of its threat, this case does not totally fit with the divided nation model either.

Taiwan was integrated in the Manchu Empire at the end of the 17th century but taken away by Japan in 1895 at the end of the first Sino-Japanese War. It was returned to China in 1945 after the Japanese defeat in World War Two. In 1949, because of the civil war between the Nationalists and the Communists and the latter's military victory on the Chinese mainland, the ROC government 'provisionally' moved its capital from Nanking to Taipei in Taiwan. Controlled by the Kuomintang (KMT or Nationalist Party) and in particular Chiang Kai-shek's family, which imposed their dictatorship and for a long time their dream of military re-conquest with the mainland too, the island was able to survive as a separate entity because of the Cold War (more specifically the Korean War) and the United States' military protection. Although the PRC replaced the ROC in the United Nations in 1971 and later, in 1979, normalized its relations with the USA, the USA has since continued to offer security protection to Taiwan.

For its part, in 1949 the PRC declared the demise of the ROC and since then has claimed Taiwan as part of its territory. Although Deng Xiaoping in 1979 replaced Mao Zedong's policy of Taiwan's armed liberation with a peaceful reunification policy, Beijing has refused so far to compromise on its 'one China principle' and consider the possibility of recognizing the ROC as a state with international status. True, since 2007, PRC president Hu Jintao has given priority to 'the peaceful development of cross-strait relations' over 'peaceful reunification'. Nevertheless, the PRC has simultaneously continued both to multiply cross-strait business links which make Taiwan more and more dependent on the PRC and to build up a large military force made of short-range missiles, modern aircraft and ships able to be projected over the Strait.

A crucial change in the equation has been Taiwan's gradual democratization: in 1986, Chiang Ching-kuo, Chiang Kai-shek's son, legalized opposition parties and a year later lifted martial law; in the following years, free elections could rapidly take place. As a result, since 1990, under Lee Teng-hui's presidency, the KMT has moved to a policy of long-term peaceful coexistence and non-official dialogue with the 'Chinese Communists' – and possibly a gradual reintegration of the ROC in the international community, relegating unification to a distant future. But in 1996, China lobbed missiles over the island when Lee Teng-hui tried too actively to enhance Taiwan's international status. Today, the KMT still does not formally recognize the PRC and legally considers mainland China as part of the ROC. However, Taiwan's specific history, the dominant influence of its largest and oldest community, the Minnan (the Han people who migrated from Southern Fujian mostly before 1895 and who form 70 percent of the population), the imprint of Japanese colonization, and the island's renewed separation from the Chinese mainland since 1949 have contributed to crafting a particular sense of Taiwanese identity and a strong nativist political movement. This movement is mainly organized in the Democratic Progressive Party (DPP), whose aim until the late 1990s was Taiwan's *de jure* independence from mainland China. Since then the DPP has moderated its view, in particular after the 2000 election of its candidate Chen Shui-Bian as the President of Taiwan; at the moment, the DPP accepts the ROC framework as Taiwan's name by default, but contrary to the KMT, it excludes mainland China from the ROC and identifies it solely with the PRC.

In 2008, after eight years of President Chen Shui-bian's independence-leaning policies, the KMT came back to power in Taiwan, promoting accommodation and *détente* with the PRC. However, the island's new president Ma Ying-jeou is having difficulties convincing the Taiwanese voters that such a rapprochement would help the ROC to eventually reintegrate into the international community. The PRC's lack of flexibility, its military threat and its authoritarian polity have become both the main obstacles to any further reconciliation and the principal feeders of Taiwan's nation-building process.

As a result of these political developments in Taiwan and of the PRC's rapidly growing power, Taiwan's *de jure* independence appears less and less feasible. But, spurred by a dynamic local cultural and political identity and a rapid democratization process, Taiwan's nation-building process cannot be ignored either, putting the three actors involved, the governments of Taiwan, PRC and USA into an unsolvable quandary.

Although Taiwan has always legally remained part of the Chinese nation under the official name of ROC, most of the Taiwanese refuse to identify with the PRC. According to recent opinion polls, while preferring the *status quo*, they are open to any solution that would respect their dignity and *de facto* independent democratic polity. Beijing, on its side, while excluding *de jure* independence, arguing that most

Chinese on the mainland oppose such an option, is aware that there is no solution to the Taiwan problem without the support of not only the KMT but also the DPP, in other words, without the support of a large majority of the island's voters.

The US government has always claimed to be 'agnostic' about Taiwan's future as long as both sides find an agreement. Nevertheless, China's more assertive foreign policy as well as stronger military will probably force Taiwan's unique protector to assume a more active protective stance in this *sui generis* case of *de facto* coexistence of two states that do not recognize each other. Under the US protection, and unless the PRC democratizes, the anti-unification forces in Taiwan will continue to dominate the political developments on the island even if the growing integration of both economies, and the increasing contacts between both societies push both sides of the Strait towards moderation rather than confrontation.

## Further Reading

Cabestan, Jean-Pierre (2002), 'Integration without Reunification', *Cambridge Review of International Affairs* 15:1, 95–103.

Cabestan, Jean-Pierre (2006), 'The Taiwan Conundrum', in Jae Ho Chung (ed.), *Charting China's Future: Political, Social and International Dimensions* (Lanham, MD: Rowman & Littlefield), 165–90.

'Cross-Strait Integration: A New Research Focus in the Taiwan Studies Field', special issue of *Journal of Current Chinese Affairs*, 1 (2010) (Hamburg).

Tucker, Nancy Bernkopf (2009), *Strait Talk: United States–Taiwan Relations and the Crisis with China* (Cambridge, MA: Harvard University Press).

\*\*\*

*Jean-Pierre Cabestan is Professor and Head, Department of Government and International Studies, Hong Kong Baptist University.*

# Case Study 8:
# Tibet: Secession Based on the Collapse of an Imperial Overlord

## Robert Barnett

The Tibetan question is a century-long dispute over whether a secondary country or nation within an imperial system should be allowed to become an independent state once that empire has collapsed. Tibet had been in some sense within the Qing empire from at least the 18th century, but was a separate and distinct entity, ruled by its own government under the Dalai Lamas. Some Qing Emperors played an occasional role in choosing and ennobling Tibetan leaders, and even passed a law to that effect in 1792, but for much of the time their relationship with Tibet was loose and undefined, and seems to have become increasingly ceremonial.

The Qing empire disintegrated in 1911. Two years later Tibet and Mongolia jointly declared themselves independent states, and in 1914 Tibet signed an agreement with the British defining the borders between it and British India. But while Mongolia cultivated Russian and, later, Soviet support and so was able to force China to recognize its statehood in 1946, the Tibetans received little from the British. Officials in London, even then reluctant to antagonize Beijing, agreed to recognize Tibet only as an 'autonomous' entity under China suzerainty, an arangement which the British later referred to even more evasively as China's 'special role' in Tibet.

For 36 years after 1913 Tibet was able to function as a totally independent state in practice. But, facing intense pressure from conservative monasteries and minimal support from Britain or, later, India, Tibet's leaders made only token efforts to obtain international recognition, acquire modern arms or carry out social change. Instead, they relied on geographic isolation to maintain their status. This only served to delay invasion and the imposition of a brutal form of socialism once China had recovered from civil war and Japanese invasion.

When the Chinese Communist Party finally took over China in 1949, it reneged on a 1931 commitment that allowed the right of secession for Tibetans, Uighurs and other nationalities and claimed all Qing-administered territories except Mongolia as integral parts of the new Chinese state. It thus asserted in effect that all parts of the previous empire were automatically the sovereign territory of the successor states.

In 1950 the Chinese army invaded Tibet, defeating the lightly-armed Tibetans within days. The Tibetan government appealed to the UN, but the British, then engaged in the Korean War, destroyed the Tibetans' efforts by claiming that Tibet's status was 'extremely obscure' and blocking debate, despite their earlier treaties with Tibet. India already regarded China as a socialist ally and avoided involvement. In 1951, after hearing that the Americans would not give a written guarantee of military support, the Tibetans signed a surrender document in Beijing known as the 17 Point Agreement. It was the first time that Tibet had declared itself to be a part of China.

The Dalai Lama was no longer the sole religious and political leader of Tibet, but was allowed to remain as head of the 'local government' while becoming at the same time a nominal leader in China's National People Congress. At the time he was clearly entranced by Mao's promise in 1956 that Tibet would be allowed to retain 'autonomy' and would not have to undergo immediate social reform. But Mao's promise of gradualism had not applied to the eastern Tibetan areas, now parts of Sichuan, Qinghai and other provinces, much of which had long been claimed by the government in Lhasa, the capital of Tibet. Land reforms were imposed in those areas from 1955, leading eastern Tibetans to form an army of resistance. The widespread conflict that ensued led thousands of refugees to flee to Lhasa from the violence and the destruction of monasteries in the East, in turn triggering a mass revolt against Chinese rule in the Tibetan capital in 1959. It was put down quickly by the PLA, but by then the Dalai Lama and his government, followed by some 80,000 others, had fled into exile in India, where they still remain.

Once in India, the Dalai Lama declared that the 17 Point Agreement had been signed under duress and re-asserted Tibet's historical claim to have been an independent state, citing Tibetan documents that for centuries had described Tibet's connection to the Qing as a personal relationship between the Dalai Lamas and their Manchu patrons. His shift coincided with a dramatic cooling of China's relations with India, which led to a border war between the two in 1962, decisively won by the Chinese. A force of some 3,000 Tibetan guerrillas in Nepal, initially supported by the CIA, continued to stage raids into Tibet until 1974, but had little impact on the wider situation.

Inside Tibet, the Chinese began a 20-year process that they called 'democratic reform', 'elimination of rebellion' and later 'cultural revolution'. This relieved farmers of their debts to former landlords and briefly gave them land before organizing them into communes. These movements were described by many Tibetans at the time and since as an orgy of mass imprisonment, executions, cultural destruction and economic disaster. In 1979, three years after the death of Mao, even China publicly acknowledged that its policies for at least the previous ten years had been 'an error' that had led to thousands of cases of abuse, wrongful imprisonment and death.

Under its new, reformist leader, Deng Xiaoping, the Chinese Communist government and the exile Tibetans began a 30-year process of intermittent talks. In these the Dalai Lama retained his view that Tibet was independent in the past but renounced violence and agreed not to seek independence in the future. Instead he made a series of increasingly mild proposals: that Tibet should be an internationally-supervised 'zone of peace' (1987), an entity 'in association with China' (1988), possibly 'staying with China' (1992), 'self-rule' (1997), 'ensuring the unity and stability of the People's Republic of China' (1998), an entity with 'genuine autonomy' (2002) and finally 'genuine national regional autonomy' within 'the constitutional framework' of the PRC (2005). In effect, these proposals were successive attempts to re-establish first something like the suzerainty arrangement of the 19th century, then the Hong Kong 'special autonomous region' arrangement and then the autonomy promised in the 17 Point Agreement of 1951.

Waves of major protests opposing Chinese rule took place inside Tibet in the late 1980s and in 2008, and the Dalai Lama's offers of compromise gained him widespread support in the democratic countries. These led China to continue the talks process, but it nonetheless rejected all the Tibetan proposals as no more than 'veiled attempts' to regain independence. In the meantime, China has become a major world power. In 2008 the British, for no apparent reason, abruptly abandoned their 94-year recognition of Tibet's historic right to autonomy as a separate entity and accepted China's claims to sovereignty. Although Mongolia had established the principle that a nation with a minor role in a 19th-century empire can proceed to independence once that empire dissolves, Tibetans' belated efforts to argue the same case seem increasingly unlikely to succeed.

***

*Robert Barnett is Director of Modern Tibetan Studies at Columbia University, New York.*

# Case Study 9:
# West Papua: Secessionism and/or Failed Decolonization?

## Damien Kingsbury

Since 1998, Indonesia has been reforming its political system with the introduction of free speech and democratic elections (held in 1999, 2004 and 2009). In this continuing process, Indonesia's politically involved armed forces (Tentara Nasional Indonesia, or TNI), too, have been increasingly brought under control of the elected officials. The tendency for Indonesia to fragment that was prevalent in the first years of the 21st century has thus disappeared, with the exception of West Papua.

In 2001 the central government in Jakarta decided to establish provincial autonomy in West Papua, as a means of buying off disaffection with the state of Indonesia. But this strategy has been largely undermined because West Papua itself has been divided into two, with a plan for a further division. In West Papua, freedom of speech is curtailed, human rights violations continue largely unabated and the political process is characterized by corruption, vote buying and violence. As a consequence, despite Indonesia's reforms elsewhere, West Papua's independence movement is continuing to gain support.

The West Papua independence movement grew out of Dutch plans to grant West Papua (then Dutch New Guinea) independence. Having been expelled from Indonesia upon its independence in 1948, during the 1950s the colonial Dutch groomed West Papuan leaders for separate independence, establishing a New Guinea Council in 1961. However, the Indonesian government under Sukarno argued that Indonesia should be the successor to the Dutch East Indies in its entirety, including West Papua.

In 1962, Indonesia launched an unsuccessful military campaign to wrest the colony from the Dutch, but as a result of American pressure, the Dutch handed over West Papua to the UN in 1962, which in turn handed it to Indonesia in 1963. In 1969, Indonesia marginally complied with the UN's requirement for a ballot on self-determination, known as the 'Act of Free Choice', in which a little more than 1,000 selected tribal leaders 'voted' under Indonesian guard in favour of formal incorporation into Indonesia.

West Papuans who had been working for independence protested at each stage of this process, in 1965 established the Free Papua Organisation (Organisasi Papua Merdeka, OPM) and declared 'independence' in 1971. The OPM and its military wing, the Papua National Army (Tentara Papua Nasional, or TPN) began a low-level campaign of insurrection, leading to massive TNI responses. Particularly from the late 1960s, there were mass human rights violations including murder, torture, rape and disappearances of West Papuans. There are no accurate assessments of the loss of life as a result of various TNI campaigns, but the death toll is estimated to be at least several tens of thousands.

Along with Indonesian occupation came economic exploitation, including huge mining projects on tribal lands, deforestation and intra-state migration from other parts of Indonesia. West Papuans expelled from their homes for mining and other projects rarely received compensation and, where they have, it has been inadequate. More than 40 percent of West Papua's population is now non-Melanesian, while indigenous West Papuans are second-class citizens in their own land. Despite being Indonesia's richest province in terms of economic output, human development indicators for West Papuans, including infant mortality and average life expectancy, nutrition, literacy and income, are among the lowest in Indonesia. All of this has continued to add fuel to the secessionist fire.

While the grounds for secessionist sentiment are strong, West Papuans are ethnically diverse, with 16 major language groups and more than 200 minor groups. Ethnic differences and disagreements over strategy led to a split in the OPM, formalized in 1982. One wing preferred a military approach to achieving independence while the other sought independence primarily through diplomacy. This split greatly weakened the already small and poorly armed TPN and decreased the OPM's claim to internationally recognized legitimacy.

Despite this split, the TPN conducted a number of small military actions, including kidnappings, to highlight the continuing claim for independence. 'Flag raising' ceremonies and street protests have been used by the OPM to encourage a sense of unity around the independence struggle. Both, however, have resulted in attacks by the TNI and Indonesian police, leading to numerous deaths, disappearances, torture and imprisonment.

In particular since the 1990s, there has been a plethora of church and NGO-based groups established with a view to seeking independence. In 2005, more than two dozen of these groups, including the OPM-TPN, formally came together to establish the West Papua National Coalition for Liberation (WPNCL), which has adopted diplomacy as its primary method of achieving independence. There has, however, remained a division in the pro-independence movement as a result of the 1982 split, with the West Papua National Authority (WPNA) refusing to recognize the legitimacy of the WPNCL, even if it also follows the pro-diplomacy path.

Both organizations seek to overturn the 1969 'Act of Free Choice' and to hold a full referendum on self-determination, with the WPNA demanding a unilateral referendum and the WPNCL seeking external, independently monitored negotiations ahead of holding a referendum. Both groups see a referendum as leading to independence.

# Further Reading

Bertrand, J. (2004), *Nationalism and Ethnic Conflict in Indonesia* (Cambridge: Cambridge University Press).
Chuavel, R. (2005), *Constructing Papuan Nationalism: History, Ethnicity, and Adaptation* (Washington, DC: East-West Center).
Fernandes, C. (2006), *Reluctant Indonesians: Australia, Indonesia and the Future of West Papua* (Melbourne: Scribe Press).
Singh, B. (2008), *Papua: Geopolitics and the Quest for Nationhood* (New Brunswick, NJ: Transaction).

***

*Damien Kingsbury is Professor in the School of International and Political Studies at Deakin University, Melbourne.*

ASHGATE
RESEARCH
COMPANION

# AFRICA

# Case Study 10:
# Eritrea:
# A Belated Post-Colonial Secession

## Kathryn Sturman

Eritrea gained recognition as a sovereign state in 1993 following a UN-monitored independence referendum. The Eritrean People's Liberation Front (EPLF) rejected the term 'secession' for what they considered to be a liberation war of independence from Italian colonial rule and then from Ethiopian imperialism. Yet Eritrea stands as an exceptional case as the only successful secession to change African post-colonial borders in the late 20th century. Recognition by the Organisation of African Unity (OAU) – the Pan-African body founded and based in the Ethiopian capital, Addis Ababa – was a remarkable feature of the immediate post-Cold War window of opportunity for new nation-states.

An Italian colony from 1890 until World War Two, Eritrea chose to return to these colonial boundaries as the basis of a nation-state separate from Ethiopia. Eritreans' distinct identity was forged in the decades of Italian colonialism, but the liberation movement mobilized on the basis of a much longer 'invented tradition' of cultural and historical differences from Ethiopia. The region has both Christian and Muslim roots in the Coptic kingdom of Aksum in the Tigre highlands (overlapping with modern Ethiopia) and in three centuries of Ottoman rule from the Red Sea coast.

The treaty of Uccialli was signed between Emperor Menelik of Ethiopia and the Italians in 1889, which ceded northern Ethiopian territories to Italy's new colony of Eritrea. Italian ambitions to conquer Ethiopia were crushed by Menelik's forces in the Battle of Aduwa in 1896. Massawa in Eritrea was the port of entry for the Italian invasion of Ethiopia (then Abyssinia) in 1935, following which Eritrea and Ethiopia were united under fascist rule into Italian East Africa. A British and Ethiopian alliance during World War Two defeated Italy in Africa, granted independence to Ethiopia and placed Eritrea under temporary British trusteeship. In 1953, the UN made Eritrea part of a loose federation with Ethiopia, with an autonomous constitution and elected government.

Ethiopian Emperor Haile Selassie soon interfered with this autonomy, removing Muslims from government posts and abolishing the federal status of Eritrea altogether in 1962. His heavy-handed, centralized rule from Addis Ababa inadvertently swayed many Tigrayan Christians to the independence cause and a guerrilla war began between Ethiopia and the Eritrean Liberation Front (ELF). The ELF split in 1970 and a leftist military faction, the EPLF, united the fight for independence with a secular Marxist ideology. When the Mengistu regime (known as the Dergue) overthrew Emperor Selassie in 1974, the USSR replaced the USA supporting Ethiopia's war against the Eritrean secessionists. It was not until the superpower USSR itself collapsed that the EPLF, in alliance with the Tigre Peoples' Liberation Front, finally defeated Mengistu in 1991.

The April 1993 referendum results were 99 percent in favour of independence for Eritrea. The EPLF formed a transitional government a month later, under President Isaias Afwerki and the political party named the Peoples' Front for Democracy and Justice (PFDJ). International recognition followed, most significantly with Eritrea's membership of the OAU in 1993. It was the second last country (before South Africa in 1994) to join the regional organization, which now comprises all independent states of Africa and its surrounding islands (except for Morocco, which withdrew over the OAU's recognition, in 1985, of Western Sahara as an independent state from Morocco).

The independence which followed has not brought peace or democracy to Eritrea. The failure of the EPLF to make a successful transition from liberation movement to political party is typical of post-independence one-party states in Africa. Rather than compete openly with opposition parties to win over a younger generation of Eritreans, its party cracked down on civil liberties and signs of 'disunity'. Eritrean society remains highly militarized and caught up in 'the traditions ... of violent domination rather than plurality in the state-formation process' (Reid 2005: 472).

From 1998 to 2000, war with Ethiopia resumed over a border dispute around the town of Badme. The dispute was referred to the Permanent Court of Arbitration, which found in favour of Eritrea's claim in 2002. Ethiopia at first refused to accept the decision, but has backed down considerably on the issue since November 2004. Relations between the two countries, as well as Eritrea's relations with the international donor community, remain tense. The diversion of public funds to military spending and the damage to infrastructure during this renewed conflict has seriously undermined the economic development of this fragile new state.

International relations with the West have been strained by the country's poor human rights record. However, Eritrea won temporary favour with the US Bush administration in 2003 when it became one of the few African countries to support the 'coalition of the willing' in the Iraq War. As a secular, authoritarian state, Eritrea is vulnerable to radical Islamic movements. This has seen the emergence of the Eritrean Islamic Jihad group, allegedly sponsored by Sudan's Khartoum government.

Ultimately, the successful consolidation of this state depends on a more open government, which is able to look forward rather than backwards when rebuilding the economy and political relations with its bigger neighbours, the region and the international community.

## Reference

Reid, R. (2005), 'Caught in the Headlights of History: Eritrea, the EPLF and the Post-war Nation-state', *Journal of Modern African Studies* 43:3, 467–88.

## Further Reading

Jacquin-Berdal, Dominique and Martin Plaut (eds) (2005), *Unfinished Business: Ethiopia and Eritrea at War* (Lawrenceville, NJ and Asmara: Red Sea Press).

Kibreab, Gaim (2008), *Critical Reflections on the Eritrean War of Independence: Social Capital, Associational Life, Religion, Ethnicity and Sowing the Seeds of Dictatorship* (Lawrenceville, NJ and Asmara: Red Sea Press).

Wrong, Michaela (2005), *'I Didn't Do It for You': How the World Betrayed a Small African Nation* (London: HarperCollins).

\*\*\*

*Dr Kathryn Sturman is Head of the Governance of Africa's Resources Programme at the South African Institute of International Affairs, South Africa.*

# Case Study 11: Somaliland: An Escape from Endemic Violence

## Kathryn Sturman

Somaliland is an atypical case of secession in two respects. First, the people of Somaliland are not an ethnic or religious minority within the greater state of Somalia. To the contrary, Somalia is one of the most homogeneous nation-states in Africa, in terms of both Somali ethnic identity and near universal adherence to Islam. The Somali nation also reaches well beyond the borders of Somalia to include people living in the Ogaden region of Ethiopia and in Northern Kenya. Under European colonial rule in the 19th and 20th centuries, the Somalis were divided into five territories: British Somaliland (which included the Somaliland claiming independence and Puntland), Italian Somaliland (southern Somalia with the capital, Mogadishu), French Somaliland (Djibouti), Kenya and Ethiopia. The struggle for decolonization in the Horn of Africa included a nationalist project to unite these territories into a single, centralized state of greater Somalia, leading to war with Ethiopia and lingering inter-state tensions throughout the region.

Second, Somaliland's claim to statehood rests on the former colonial borders created by the British. The basis of this claim does not hark back to an original, 'natural' boundary based on group coherence and common history, with origins lost in the distant past. Rather, the argument for recognition of Somaliland is a rational one: this state works, whereas Somalia quite clearly does not. This has become increasingly apparent in the 20 years since the end of the Cold War exposed Somalia's dictatorial regime of Siad Barre to collapse and civil war. Barre seized power on 21 October 1969 in a *coup d'état,* which saw the suspension of the Constitution and National Assembly, arrests and persecution of members of the former government and banning of political parties.

The motivation for secession developed from a sense of marginalization among northern clans within Somalia ruled from Mogadishu in the south. Leaders of the Isaaqs and other clans formed the Somali National Movement (SNM) with the original aim of overthrowing General Barre. This evolved into a northern independence movement in reaction to Barre's bombing of Somalia's second largest city, Hargeisa, and displacement of around 300,000 Somalilanders to Ethiopia in the late 1980s. The SNM was able to mobilize support through the traditional leadership structure of the clan elders, while uniting the urban centres of Hargeisa, Burco and Berbera around a modern nationalist claim for Somaliland's independence based on a transitional constitution leading to elections. Thus, the movement could present itself to Somalilanders as a 'home-grown' solution to the political vacuum left by the implosion of Somalia, and a recognizably democratic, constitutional order to the international community.

Following General Barre's defeat in January 1991, the SNM initiated a reconciliation process between Isaaq and non-Isaaq clans of the northwest, holding a series of meetings with all clan elders, which became known as the Guurti Congress of the Elders. This grouping put pressure on the SNM to declare Somaliland's independence, which it did on 18 May 1991.

Short of achieving international recognition, Somaliland has built the foundations for statehood since unilaterally declaring independence from Somalia in 1991 (see also Chapter 15). Three elections have been held in 2002 (local), 2003 (presidential) and 2005 (legislative), establishing internal legitimacy for self-determination. Widespread representation, including a high level of women's representation unusual for the region, has balanced modern and traditional forms of authority. This has contributed to relative stability and order, which is in stark contrast to the anarchy and violence besetting the southern parts of Somalia. More recently, Somaliland has seen its democratic image somewhat tarnished by the postponement of presidential elections scheduled for April 2008 until June 2010; the elections were eventually won by the opposition candidate Ahmed M. Mahamoud Silanyo.

The deciding factor for successful secession – international recognition by the community of nation-states – has eluded Somaliland (see also Chapters 13 and 15). Reasons for this lie in African states' reluctance to allow changes to existing boundaries and in the international project of imposing order on the collapsed state of Somalia. Although Somalia's anarchy is a dire threat to the region, to international shipping along the East African coast and to international security from terrorism, these common interests have been subordinated to strategic differences between neighbouring states. For example, Kenya has invested much time and effort into engineering and hosting the Transitional Government of Somalia (TNG), which has been unable to occupy its own capital city of Mogadishu. Egypt has vehemently opposed recognition of Somaliland, in an effort to block Ethiopia's trade access to the coast, and any increase in its economic and political power, which could reduce Egypt's downstream share of the Nile. The Egyptian former Secretary-General of the United Nations, Boutros Boutros-Ghali was influential in preventing UN recognition of Somaliland's bid for sovereignty in the early 1990s. Saudi Arabia has backed Egypt and led the Arab League's opposition to Somaliland.

Ethiopia has cultivated good relations with Somaliland, with a view to securing access to the coast through Berbera. Eritrea's secessionist war since 1961 and independence in 1993 left the Horn's most populous country, Ethiopia, landlocked and dependent on the overused port of Djibouti. Thus, Ethiopia has economic interests in recognizing Somaliland but, at present, it is unlikely to initiate calls for recognition. Further afield, South Africa has taken a pragmatic stance in support of Somaliland as a workable solution to governance of at least part of Somalia. The UK has led international support for recognition of Somaliland, while the USA afforded *de facto* recognition in March 2010 by inviting an official delegation from Somaliland to talks in Washington.

While Somaliland awaits a change in this complex interplay of international relations, its leaders have every incentive to maintain their democratic credentials by maintaining the present multi-party political system and thus to prove a successful case of state reconstruction where the wider state of Somalia has so clearly failed.

## Further Reading

Drysdale, John (2000), *Stoics without Pillows: A Way Forward for the Somalilanders* (London: HAAN).
International Crisis Group (2009), *Somaliland: A Way Out of the Electoral Crisis*, Africa Briefing No. 67, 7 December.
Jhazbhay, Iqbal (2009), *Somaliland: An African Struggle for Nationhood and International Recognition* (Johannesburg: Institute for Global Dialogue and South African Institute of International Affairs).
Sturman, Kathryn (2008), 'New Norms, Old Boundaries: The African Union's Approach to Secession and State Sovereignty', in Aleksandar Pavković and Peter Radan (eds), *On the Way to Statehood: Secession and Globalization* (Aldershot: Ashgate), 67–83.

\*\*\*

*Dr Kathryn Sturman is Head of the Governance of Africa's Resources Programme at the South African Institute of International Affairs, South Africa.*

# Case Study 12: Southern Sudan's Secession from the North

## Petrus de Kock

The case of Southern Sudan's secession from the North should be understood within the context of Sudan's post-colonial history. During January 2011 Southern Sudan conducted a referendum wherein nearly 100 percent of eligible voters decided to secede from North Sudan in order to create Africa's newest independent state. Southern Sudan officially gained independence in July 2011; this was a result of the Comprehensive Peace Agreement (CPA) that brought the north–south civil war to an end in 2005.

The Sudan is Africa's largest state with a territory encompassing more than 2 million square kilometres. Animosity between forces from Southern and Northern Sudan started in the year preceding Sudan's independence from Egypt and the UK (1 January 1956). Some Sudanese commentators believe that animosity between the North and South stems from colonial maladministration, and the neglect the peoples of Darfur and the South suffered during colonial times. The post-colonial governments, based in the capital Khartoum in the North, continued these policies. In the run up to decolonization, Egypt and the UK placed more of the executive powers and civil administration functions in the hands of Khartoum. This created internal conditions for the development of resentment at what was seen as Khartoum's domination of the South.

Yet, regardless of its colonial experience, Sudan went through two civil wars. The first, beginning in 1955 and lasting to 1972, was brought about by political frustrations in the South regarding governance, policy making and a perception that the South did not have sufficient input into issues of national concern. At a cultural level issues of identity, religious differentiation (Islam dominates in the North but not in the South), ethnic divisions within the country and a weak post-colonial state incapable of acting as unifying institution, created conditions for civil war. During the first civil war the Southern rebel groups appeared to have aimed at the secession of the South from the North by forcing the military forces from the North to withdraw from the South. On 27 March 1972 the Khartoum government signed a peace agreement with the Southern Sudan Liberation Movement (SSLM). This agreement came to be known as the Addis Ababa Accords which brought Sudan's first civil war to an end.

The issue of the distribution of natural resources, especially oil, did not play a role in the first civil war: the US oil giant, Chevron, made the first discovery in Sudan only in 1979. At the time of the discovery Sudan was ruled by Col. Gaofar Muhammad Nimeiri, who, due to alienating himself from his power base in Sudan's Islamic constituency, as well as the Socialist constituency of his own party, presided over a minimalistic state with little popular legitimacy. Due to the political weakness of the Sudanese state, and attempts by Nimeiri to impose the policies and will of Khartoum on the South, a mutiny by Southern soldiers against Khartoum in September 1983 ignited the second round of Sudan's civil war. It is only during the late 1980s, and especially the 1990s that possession of and/or control over oil reserves became a major issue that furthered the cause of war in both the Southern capital Juba and Khartoum.

In spite of the coup in Khartoum by Omer Hassan Al Bashir in 1989, the civil war continued. During the 1980s and 1990s, the Sudan People's Liberation Movement (SPLM) and other rebels fighting the Khartoum government kept the issue of Southern independence on their agenda. During the 1990s, regional powers led several attempts at bringing the warring factions to the negotiating table. The Intergovernmental Authority on Development (IGAD), an East African regional organization, led several peace-talk initiatives which paved the way for new rounds of peace talks in the early 2000s. In July 2001 the SPLM and the government of Khartoum signed the Machakos Protocol whereby all parties to the negotiations accepted two basic principles: self-determination for Southern Sudan, and the role of – or relationship – between state and religion. The Machakos Protocol is a landmark event which put in place the basic building blocks of a larger comprehensive peace agreement, called the Comprehensive Peace Agreement (CPA) which was signed into effect on 9 January 2005. From then on, all claims to Southern self-determination were based on this agreement.

The case for secession of Southern Sudan from the rest of the country is informed by the following two sets of overlapping issues: firstly, historical grievance and an entrenched history of confrontation between the North and South; secondly, the legal basis for secession, as articulated in the CPA, which entrenches the right of Southern Sudanese to choose their political fate through a referendum eventually carried out in 2011. The CPA also entrenches the principle of power sharing in a government of national unity and of wealth sharing through the establishment of a Land and Petroleum commission that will address issues of sharing income and revenue from Sudan's oil reserves.

## Case Study 12

The story of the South's secession has been long in the making. It is estimated that more than 2 million people died during the second civil war, and Southern Sudan is still battling to deal with displacement, economic underdevelopment and a lack of infrastructure. Southern Sudan's independence is the most significant case of secession ever on the African continent, which stands to have a lasting impact on not only Sudan, but the continent as a whole.

***

*Petrus de Kock is Senior Researcher in the Governance of Africa's Resources Programme, South African Institute of International Affairs.*

# EUROPE

ASHGATE
**RESEARCH**
COMPANION

# Case Study 13:
# Basque Secessionism:
# From Bullets to Ballots?

## Marc Sanjaume i Calvet

The Basque Country is situated on the Atlantic coast and covers an area divided between France and Spain. Basque nationalism has been mainly a political issue within the Spanish borders despite the presence of Basques within French territory. Rooted in the 19th-century European Romantic Movement and strongly suppressed by the Francoist dictatorship, Basque nationalism has expressed secessionist demands since the 1960s. Since 1978, when democracy re-emerged in Spain, secessionism has been expressed in parliamentary form mainly through the party Herri Batasuna (HB) but also through the Basque Nationalist Party (BNP), in office from 1980 to 2009.

One section of the Basque nationalist movement chose in 1959 the use of violence as its strategy and organized itself as the armed group Euskadi Ta Askatasuna (ETA). This organization describes itself as secessionist, Basque nationalist and Marxist-Leninist. During the Francoist dictatorship it gained prominence and popularity. Following the Transition (to democracy), ETA continued its violent acts and is still active today. Up to now 828 people (including civilians, military personnel and politicians) have become victims of ETA and there are currently nearly 800 ETA-affiliated people detained in Spanish and French prisons.

Three main characteristics are usually considered as distinguishing factors of Basque nationalism. Firstly, secessionism and general support for nationalism have been comparatively strong in the Basque Country. Secondly, rejection of Spanish identity and social support for independence have been much stronger than, for example, in the other two minority nations in the Spanish State, in Catalonia and Galicia. Thirdly, the characteristic that has most differentiated the Basque case has been the support, albeit partial, for violent tactics.

The Spanish central government's fight against ETA has included negotiations and clandestine war. From 1976 to 1982 autonomous paramilitary groups supported by security forces and secret services killed 48 people. Between 1983 and 1989 the central government, using the so-called GAL (Autonomous Liberation Groups), carried out a dirty war. This paramilitary group committed 27 assassinations, kidnappings and tortures. In 1997 high-level civil servants, including the former Homeland Minister José Barrionuevo, were declared responsible for these activities and imprisoned. In 2009 Amnesty International reported a high number of torture allegations and denounced the detention regime permitted under Spanish law as abusive.

Spanish governments have attempted to negotiate with ETA on a number of occasions, but without success. We can distinguish three negotiation periods. The first attempt was in 1988 with the so-called Algiers talks which led to a ceasefire that lasted for over 60 days. The second attempt, during the conservative government in 1998, resulted in the declaration of an 'indefinite truce and ceasefire'. In December 2000, after ETA had broken the ceasefire, the two largest Spanish parties, the PSOE and the PP, signed an agreement to unite against ETA and agreed a repressive anti-terrorist strategy. As a result the secessionist party Herri Batasuna was declared illegal and it was gradually expelled from participating in the democratic institutions. This strategy also included the banning of many secessionist organizations (mainly youth organizations and propaganda groups) and media, such as the newspaper *Egunkaria*. Finally, the third attempt, in 2006, resulted in an indefinite ceasefire that was ended once again by ETA. In September 2010, after some years of severe counterterrorist policies, ETA announced a ceasefire but the Spanish central government has not considered it sufficient: the violent conflict is thus yet to be resolved.

The secessionist party Batasuna (formerly Herri Batasuna), considered to be the political arm of ETA, is still illegal; when it was made illegal, its electoral support was around 15 percent in the Basque Autonomous Community. In 2001 it split into two groups. The first group refused to condemn ETA's violence and remained illegal (Batasuna), and the second publicly condemned ETA violence (and state violence) and was accepted by Spanish authorities as a legal party (Aralar). The largest party in the Basque Autonomous Community, the centre-right Basque Nationalist Party (BNP), despite its orientation to non-secessionist demands, has promoted initiatives to obtain more sovereignty. Leading a three-party coalition, the former Basque president Juan José Ibarretxe (BNP), presented two concrete plans with two different objectives: the end of the violent conflict and the achievement of more political power for the Basque government through democratic means. In 2001 he presented a proposal to the Basque Parliament for a New Political Statute. His proposal entailed a referendum in the Basque Country to decide a new political status for itself based on 'free association' with the Spanish state. This new status envisages a quasi-independent Basque state sharing a few competences with the Spanish authorities such as the merchant navy and foreign policy. The proposal was passed by the Basque Parliament but rejected in the Spanish lower chamber with the votes of both main Spanish parties, PSOE and PP. The Basque president presented a second pro-sovereignty plan laying down a sort of 'road map' aimed at finding a long-term solution to the existing violent and political conflict between Basque and Spanish authorities. It proposed two parallel negotiation processes. The first on the political future of the Basque country with the participation of all the political parties and the second aimed at solving the armed conflict. This plan envisaged two referendums: one to mandate the Basque government to negotiate; and a second one to vote on the final result of the negotiations. The Spanish government responded by referring the proposals to the Constitutional Court which declared them unconstitutional. Presently, the new Basque government has put an end to institutional pro-sovereignty and secessionist demands. The new Basque president, the socialist Patxi López, governing with the support of the PP, has expressed a wish to avoid pro-sovereignty activities and maintain the *status quo*. Batasuna has recently rejected, through its imprisoned leader Arnaldo Otegui, the use of violence as a strategy to achieve its political objectives. This new position of Basque secessionists challenges ETA's approach; however, the central government's response has been to strengthen its repressive strategy.

Basque secessionism today faces enormous obstacles. The violent conflict, despite ETA's current weakness, divides Basques, Basque nationalists and even secessionists. The historical secessionist party Batasuna remains illegal. The traditional Basque nationalist majority in the Basque Autonomous Community has been defeated due to divisions and the illegalization of Batasuna. Finally, as the rejection of Ibarretxe's plans has shown, current Spanish law does not allow for a referendum on the political future of the Basque Country.

## Further Reading

Requejo, F. (2010), 'Federalism and Democracy: The Case of Minority Nations: A Federalist Deficit', in M. Burgess and A. Gagnon (eds), *Federal Democracies* (London: Routledge), 275–98.

Requejo, F. and M. Sanjaume (2010), 'Secession and Liberal Democracy: The Case of the Basque Country', Working Paper: GRTP.

***

*Marc Sanjaume i Calvet is a teaching assistant at Universitat Pompeu Fabra in Barcelona, Spain.*

# Case Study 14:
# Peaceful Secessions:
# Norway, Iceland and Slovakia

## Aleksandar Pavković

Attempts at secession are usually accompanied by politically organized violence: in the 20th century – until 1990 – there were only two secessions which were peaceful: those of Norway in 1905 and Iceland in 1944. As we have seen in Chapter 8, the dissolution of the USSR in 1990–91 was mainly peaceful; in contrast, the dissolution of SFR Yugoslavia was accompanied by violence, with the exception of the secession of Macedonia and, in 2006, Montenegro (see Chapter 7). In 1993 the Czech and Slovak Republic (formerly Czechoslovakia) also dissolved peacefully.

What, if anything, do peaceful secessions have in common? There are two obvious features which distinguish the above three peaceful secessions from the great majority of violent secessions. First, the host states from which these states seceded were, at the time, functioning multi-party parliamentary regimes in which the seceding territories had already established separate parliamentary government. This enabled the secessionist parties to gain majorities in their territories' parliaments and to negotiate the terms of secession with the representatives of the host state, who were in turn accountable to their parliaments. Second, the host state (or non-secessionist) political leaders did not see the territorial integrity of their host state as something sacred that needs to be defended against the secessionists and were therefore not considering the use of military force for the purposes of its defence.

## Norway: From a Unilateral to a Mutually Agreed Secession

Norway was transferred from the Danish to the Swedish crown in 1814 and by 1882 had an independent parliament and government, including its own armed forces. Only a few governmental functions, including foreign affairs and consular services, were shared with or performed by the Swedish government. In 1892 the Norwegian government, dominated by the secessionist Party of the Left, demanded from the Swedish government a separate consular service for Norway. This request was refused, but in 1903 when repeating the same request the Norwegian government planned, in the case of its expected rejection, to withdraw its representatives from the central government and thus make it impossible for the Swedish king to appoint the central government's cabinet. This plan was put in effect in May 1905 and, as a result, the Norwegian parliament proclaimed, on 7 June 1905, that '… the union with Sweden under one king is dissolved in consequence of the king's ceasing to function as King of Norway'.

The Swedish government and king refused to recognize this act of unilateral secession but were ready to negotiate the terms of a mutually agreed secession, provided that the Norwegian population, through a plebiscite, show support for Norwegian independence. Faced with the refusal of major powers to recognize their independence, the Norwegian government agreed and hastily organized a plebiscite in which only 186 out of over 300,000 votes were against independence. Following lengthy negotiations, both parties agreed to dissolve the United Kingdoms of Sweden and Norway by repealing the acts of union or unification. But before and during the negotiations, both sides mobilized their armed forces as a pre-emptive defence measure. As a result of the negotiated settlement, Norway's initial unilateral secession became a mutually agreed one.

## Iceland: A Peaceful Secession of a US-Occupied Island from Its Nazi Occupied Host State

Like the Norwegian, Icelandic secessionism grew out of the national awakening movement of the mid-19th century. The nationalist parties in the early 20th century split between those which demanded devolution of powers to Iceland's parliament and executive and those which demanded outright independence from Denmark. In 1917 the revived Icelandic parliament Althing (which dated back to the 10th century) demanded from the Danish government the recognition of the Icelandic flag as equal to the Danish flag on all Icelandic vessels. In response the Danish government formed a Danish-Iceland Committee and in 1918 enacted a new Union treaty which established Iceland as an independent state with the Danish monarch as its head. Foreign affairs were to be handled by the Danish ministry and Denmark was to notify all countries that Iceland is a neutral country without a defence force. The treaty was due for revision in 1940 and if no agreement on revision could be found, either side could unilaterally terminate the agreement. After the Nazi occupation of Denmark in 1940, the Althing temporarily suspended the Union and in 1941 the British, later replaced by the US, occupied Iceland. The secessionist pressure for independence grew during the war and, following a plebiscite on independence in 1944 (in which only 0.5 percent of voters voted against the dissolution) the Althing proclaimed Iceland an independent republic.

CASE STUDY 14

The Danish King sent a telegram to the Althing and the people of Iceland from the still-occupied Denmark, congratulating them on their independence.

## Slovakia: A Mutually Agreed Secession without a Referendum

Slovakia's secessionism developed in the wake of the collapse of the mono-party communist system in 1990 and transfer of power from the Czechoslovak Communist party to former dissident groups, which operated separately in the Czech and Slovak units. Under the communist constitution, enacted in the wake of the Soviet invasion in 1969, the two federal units had nominal equality as well as separate parliaments and governments, and no federal legislation could be passed without the support of a majority of deputies from each unit in the upper house of the federal parliament. In 1990 Slovak political parties and cultural organizations started mobilizing the population in support of full political, cultural and symbolic equalization of the Slovak with the Czech unit; once this was achieved, their demands shifted to the assertion of Slovak sovereignty through a confederal association with the Czech unit. Since a confederal arrangement was not acceptable to any of the major Czech parties, in July 1992 the new Czech Prime Minster, Venceslav Klaus, negotiated with the Prime Minister of Slovakia, Vladislav Mečiar, the dissolution of the Czech and Slovak federation. Following mass demonstrations in Slovakia, in September 1992 the Slovak parliament issued a Declaration of Sovereignty and a new constitution for Slovakia as an independent state. Public opinion polls, however, indicated that at the time there was no majority in either unit in support of the dissolution; the federal parliament proved reluctant to pass the set of legislative acts which the two prime ministers and their officials had agreed on. Nevertheless, after a few failed attempts, on November 25 the federal parliament finally passed the key law on the termination of the federation, dissolving the state on 1 January 1993.

Unlike the two secessions outlined above and the 2006 peaceful secession of Montenegro from Serbia (see Chapter 7), the secession of Slovakia was not preceded by a referendum. The political leaders and their political parties in both units were committed to the dissolution, in spite of the apparent lack of popular support for this as evidenced in the opinion polls. The Czech Prime Minister, the neoliberal economist Klaus, regarded Slovakia, with its economy heavily dependent on unprofitable state enterprises, as an economic burden to the Czech Republic. Hence he regarded its secession as 'good riddance' (see also Chapter 19, note 17).

## Mutual Agreement and Legality of Peaceful Secessions

These three peaceful secessions, as well as the Montenegrin one, were all mutually agreed secessions: the host state agreed to the secession or the dissolution of the state. Further, all three were either legal or were legalized within the domestic law of the host state or the former unified state. Not all peaceful secessions are legal or legalized: the peaceful (but mutually agreed) secession of Macedonia from the SFRY in 1991 was not legalized in the way that these four secessions were. Mutual agreement thus appears to be a necessary condition for a peaceful secession (see also Chapter 18).

## Further Reading

Elster, J. (1995), 'Transition, Constitution-making and Separation in Czechoslovakia', *European Journal of Sociology/Archives Europennes de Sociologie* 36:1, 105–34.
Karlsson, G. (2000), *The History of Iceland* (Minneapolis, MN: University of Minnesota Press).
Kirschbaum, S.J. (1995), *A History of Slovakia: The Struggle for Survival* (London: Macmillan).
Lindgren, R.E. (1959), *Norway-Sweden: Union, Disunion and Scandinavian Integration* (Princeton, NJ: Princeton University Press).
Pavković, A. with P. Radan (2007), *Creating New States: Theory and Practice of Secession* (Aldershot: Ashgate).
Young, R. (1994), *The Breakup of Czechoslovakia* (Kingston, ON: Institute of Intergovernmental relations, Queen's University).

\*\*\*

*Aleksandar Pavković is Associate Professor of Politics at Macquarie University, Sydney and University of Macau, China.*

# Case Study 15: Scotland's Independence

## Michael Keating

Scotland was united with England to form Great Britain in the Acts of Union of 1707. While this formally abolished the parliaments of both countries in a permanent union, Scotland has retained its own sense of nationality, its law, a distinct civil society and an extensive system of administrative devolution. From 1999, it has possessed a devolved power in a more-or-less federal relationship with the United Kingdom.

There have historically been three stands of opinion about the Union. Unionists are, of course, for it, but do not deny Scottish nationality or even the right of Scotland to secede should they want to do so. Even former Conservative Prime Ministers Margaret Thatcher and John Major conceded this right, while at the same time refusing any move towards limited self-government within the Union. Nationalists favour an independent Scottish state. Home Rulers, who have always comprised a plurality of Scottish opinion, favour limited self-government called, since the 1960s, 'devolution'.

The dividing line between nationalists and home rulers has always been blurred. When Scottish nationalism emerged in the late 19th century as part of the wider European 'awakening of the nations', it aimed at home rule in imitation of Irish movements. Some wanted a federal United Kingdom while others saw Scotland as a self-governing Dominion within the Empire, like Canada or Australia. After World War One and the Statute of Westminster (1935) it became apparent that the Dominions were independent states, so that this middle road was closed off. It was at this time that the Scottish National Party (SNP) was formed, largely from people disillusioned with the failure of the British parties to deliver on home rule. Many people, nonetheless, wavered between a rupture with the United Kingdom (the fundamentalists) and a gradual extension of self-government (the gradualists).

Scottish nationalism was contained by the UK parties through a series of economic concessions including financial measures and regional industrial policies, and an ever-extending field of administrative devolution centred on the Secretary of State for Scotland, a minister in the UK Cabinet chosen from among the Scottish MPs of the ruling party. Both Conservative and Labour Governments set their faces against political devolution, fearing that this would provide a 'slippery slope' to secession. This system started to break down from the 1960s, with a notable SNP breakthrough in 1974 prompting the Labour Government to propose a devolution bill, which gained a narrow majority in a referendum but came to grief on internal Labour opposition and procedural obstacles.

From the 1980s Scottish nationalism revived again. The Thatcher and Major Governments (1979–97) never enjoyed even a plurality of Scottish support and by 1997 the Conservatives had lost all their Scottish parliamentary seats, producing a crisis of legitimacy. Support for home rule grew again and for the first time polls suggested that independence, rather than the *status quo*, was the second preference of the majority of electors. Another factor was the SNP's acceptance of European integration, which provided an external support system for an independent Scotland and answered all manner of questions about access to markets, viability and the management of externalities.

Support for independence, according to opinion polls, climbed from 20 percent, where it had been since at least the 1960s, to the low 30s. Yet home rule remained the plurality option and support for independence could range from the low 20s up to 50 percent, depending on the wording of the question. Using the words 'separate' or 'separation' always reduces support in questionnaires. There are no significant ethnic divisions within Scotland on the issue, the Irish Catholic minority (the only one of historic importance) having been assimilated. English-born people comprise 8 percent of the population but are not politically mobilized.

In 1997 the Labour Party returned to power and enacted devolution with the support of some three-quarters of the voters in a referendum. In 1999 the Scottish Parliament came into being and in 2007, the third election, the SNP formed a minority government committed to a referendum on independence preceded by a National Conversation. They lacked the votes to get the referendum bill through the Scottish Parliament and in 2010, after a series of white papers and draft bills, they withdrew the proposal, promising to put it to the people at the election of 2011. All the opinion polls suggested that a referendum would not pass in any case.

Probing deeper into the polls, it appears that Scots, like their counterparts in many other stateless nations, do not make a sharp distinction between independence and strong forms of devolution. The SNP itself recognized this in the successive documents it published during the National Conversation, proposing the possibility of keeping joint institutions and what was vaguely described as a 'social union'. They even propose keeping the Pound Sterling unless a decision is taken in the future to join the Euro. The concept of 'devolution max' was floated, with many commentators noting that this could equally be labelled 'independence lite'.

It is likely that Scots will stay within the Union as long as it is flexible enough to accommodate their aspirations, which according to the polls are more devolution, managing the bulk of their internal affairs but remaining part of a wider political unit. The future thus depends less on them than on developments in England. A strand in English political opinion resents Scots having their own Parliament but also sending representatives to Westminster to vote on English matters (the

CASE STUDY 15

West Lothian question),[1] as well as their supposed advantages in spending (the Barnett question).[2] If this increases, they may halt further movement towards devolution and provoke Scotland into secession. If England moves increasingly in a Eurosceptic direction or should withdraw from the European Union altogether, Scottish political opinion[3] may want to keep the European Union at the expense of the British one.

## Further Reading

Keating, Michael (2009), *The Independence of Scotland: Self-Government and the Shifting Politics of Union* (Oxford: Oxford University Press).
Kidd, Colin (2008), *Union and Unionisms: Political Thought in Scotland, 1500–2000* (Cambridge: Cambridge University Press).
MacLean, Iain and Alistair McMillan (2005), *State of the Union: Unionism and the Alternatives in the United Kingdom since 1707* (Oxford: Oxford University Press).

\*\*\*

*Michael Keating is Professor of Politics and ESRC Professorial Fellow at the University of Aberdeen, UK.*

---

1 Named after anti-devolution Scottish Labour MP Tam Dalyell, who asked why he should be able to vote on matters affecting various places in England but not in his own constituency of West Lothian.
2 The Barnett Formula allocates spending for devolved matters in Scotland, Wales and Northern Ireland. Properly applied, it would reduce Scotland's spending advantage but English opinion seems unaware of this, blaming the formula, rather than the way it has regularly been by-passed, for Scotland's spending advantage. The existence of such an advantage is, of course, denied by the nationalists.
3 Scottish public opinion is almost as Eurosceptic as that in England, but elites in Scotland are much more pro-European and Euroscepticism is almost absent in the public domain or the Scottish Parliament.

# Case Study 16:
# The Serb Krajina:
# An Unsuccessful Secession from Croatia

## Peter Radan

In the late 1980s, against a background of difficult economic circumstances and the collapse of the Berlin Wall, the continued viability of Yugoslavia's multi-national federal political system came under serious pressure. Attempts by the increasingly nationalist leaders of Yugoslavia's six republics (federal units) to resolve the political crisis by a reconfiguration of the federation proved fruitless. On 25 June 1991, Croatia and Slovenia, Yugoslavia's two most economically developed republics, invoking the right of peoples to self-determination, declared their independence (see Chapter 8).

Prior to Croatia's declaration of independence, leaders of Croatia's Serb minority population had threatened secession from Croatia if Croatia sought its own independence. Almost half of the Serb population (which formed 12 percent of the population of Croatia) lived in the areas adjoining the federal units of Bosnia and Herzegovina and Serbia. Serb fears of a future independent Croatia were ignited by memories of the genocide against them that took place in the Axis-sponsored Independent State of Croatia during World War Two. These fears were further fuelled by amendments to Croatia's constitution in December 1990 which declared Croatia to be the 'national state of the Croat nation' and repealed provisions that had until then treated Croats and Serbs as constituent nations and constitutional equals in Croatia.

In the war that erupted following Croatia's independence declaration, local Serb militia forces, backed by the federal Yugoslav People's Army and paramilitary forces from Serbia, gained control of territories on Croatia's borders with Bosnia and Herzegovina and Serbia. These territories formed the basis of the Republic of Serb Krajina (Krajina) which, invoking the right of peoples of self-determination, declared its independence on 19 December 1991.

During the latter part of 1991 the international response to the crisis in Yugoslavia was led by the European Community (EC) which attempted to broker a resolution to the conflict, albeit unsuccessfully. On 16 December 1991 the EC invited Yugoslavia's republics seeking independence to apply for recognition by the EC. Both Croatia and Krajina made applications.

Croatia was recognized by the EC on 15 January 1992, on the basis of a hurried assurance, obtained from Croatia's President Tudjman on 13 January 1992, that Croatia's minority Serb population would be granted special autonomous status. On 18 May 1992 the United Nations (UN) Security Council recommended Croatia's admission to the UN. The UN General Assembly formally admitted Croatia to the UN on 22 May 1992. Krajina's application was not eligible for consideration as it did not have the status of a republic in Yugoslavia's constitutional framework. Furthermore, the EC took the view that independence for Krajina was not possible on the basis of the inter-related principles of the inviolability of Croatia's borders and the absence of the right to external self-determination of its minority Serb population.

Running parallel to the process of obtaining recognition of Croatia were efforts by the UN to broker a lasting ceasefire in Croatia. This was achieved on 2 January 1992. This was soon after followed by an agreement, approved by the UN Security Council on 21 February 1992, which provided for UN peacekeeping forces in Croatia to patrol the three United Nations Protected Areas (UNPAs) of Krajina, Western Slavonia and Eastern Slavonia. The UNPAs corresponded closely to the territory under the control of Croatia's Serbs, who in turn were dependent for survival on economic and military support from Serbia and Montenegro.

From early 1992 to May 1995 the UN presence in Croatia, in general terms, preserved the *status quo* established by the February 1992 UN-brokered agreement. Serbs remained largely in control of the territories within the UNPAs. However, Croatia was determined to reclaim full control of these territories from the Serbs at any cost. By early 1995 Croatia, despite a UN arms embargo imposed on all Yugoslavia territories in September 1991, had considerably improved its military position *vis-à-vis* the Serbs in Croatia, especially through covert aid from private military organizations in the United States. Serbia's hitherto support for Krajina dwindled in the wake of the economic sanctions which had been imposed against Serbia, Montenegro and the Serbs of Croatia by the UN Security Council in May 1992. In two short offensives, first in the Western Slavonia UNPA in May 1995, and then in the Krajina UNPA in August 1995, Croat forces easily regained the territories from Serb forces which had no support from Serbia and Montenegro. The Croatian military campaigns resulted in a mass exodus of over 150,000 Serbs from the areas captured by Croatian forces to Serbia and Bosnia and Herzegovina. As for the Eastern Slavonia UNPA, it was to be progressively handed over to Croatia pursuant to the Basic Agreement of the Region of Eastern Slavonia, Baranja and Western Srem negotiated on 12 November 1995 as a prelude to the Dayton Accords relating to Bosnia and Herzegovina. With these Croatian victories the attempted secession of the Republic of Serb Krajina was effectively suppressed.

## Further Reading

Ahrens, G-H. (2007), *Diplomacy on the Edge: Containment of Ethnic Conflict and Minorities Working Group of the Conferences on Yugoslavia* (Baltimore, MD: Johns Hopkins University Press), 101–94.

Barić, N. (2005), *Srpska pobuna u Hrvatskoj 1990–1995* (Zagreb: Golden Marketing).

Casperson, N. (2010), *Contested Nationalism: Serb Elite Rivalry in Croatia and Bosnia in the 1990s* (New York: Berghahn Books).

\*\*\*

*Peter Radan is Professor of Law at Macquarie Law School, Macquarie University, Sydney.*

# REST OF THE WORLD

ASHGATE
RESEARCH
COMPANION

# Case Study 17:
# Abkhazia, South Ossetia and Transdniestria: Secessions in the Post-Soviet Space

## Mikhail Ilyin

On 3 April 1990 the USSR adopted a Law on Secession. At the time, a debate on the sovereignty of union republics (the highest level units of the Soviet Federation) was underway. A few lower level autonomous republics had also made claims to statehood. Partly as a result of these conflicting claims over territory and sovereignty, political tensions and violent conflicts erupted in various parts of the USSR including Chechnya and Tatarstan in Russia, Abkhazia, South Ossetia and Adjara in Georgia, Nagorni Karabach and Talysh areas in Azerbaijan, Crimea and Transcarpatia in Ukraine, and Transdniestria and Gagauzia in Moldova. The outcomes of these conflicting claims over territory and statehood were influenced by various factors including ethno-cultural traditions, historical identity patterns, independent political accomplishments, the actual practice of state-building and the formal status within the USSR. Three cases of secession – Abkhazia (an autonomous republic), South Ossetia (and autonomous region) and Transdniestria (peoples having no territorial administrative unit) – highlight the various attempts to achieve statehood in the area of the former USSR. To date, all have fallen short of fully recognized *de jure* independence (see also Chapter 15).

## Abkhazia: From an Autonomous Republic to a State

Abkhazian ethno-cultural traditions date back to the times of the Kingdom of Colchis in the period between the 9th and 6th centuries BC. Its population was most likely a mixed one with a predominance of Kartvelian tribes (distantly related to Georgians) and a significant number of North Caucasian ones (related to the

Abkhaz). In the 8th century BC the Kingdom of Abkhazia was established. This important political accomplishment strengthened Abkhazian historical identity. At the beginning of the 11th century Abkhazia became part of an extended Georgia state under the rule of King Bagrat III. From the 13th to the 16th century the area was dominated by the Mongol empire and its successors. In the 16th century an independent Principality of Abkhazia emerged. However, it was soon absorbed into the Ottoman Empire and became one of its dependencies. By the early 19th century Abkhazia became a protectorate of the expanding Russian empire and was formally incorporated into it in 1864. With this development, the door was opened to the settlement of Armenians, Georgians, Russians and other groups within the area in which the Abhkaz people formed the majority population.

The October Revolution of 1917 in Russia and the ensuing Civil War witnessed the creation of an independent Georgian state in 1918 which included Abkhazia within its borders. However, in March 1921 the Soviet Union's army took control of Abkhazia's capital Sukhumi and the Socialist Soviet Republic (SSR) of Abkhazia was formally established. This was the beginning of a new tradition of Abkhaz republican statehood. In December 1921 Abkhazia signed a special treaty of alliance delegating some of its sovereign powers to the Georgian SSR. In 1931, the USSR, under the rule of Joseph Stalin, downgraded Abkhazia's status to that of an autonomous republic within the Georgian SSR.

With the crisis of the USSR in the 1980s and rising secessionist sentiment in Georgia, tensions between the Abkhaz and Georgians increased significantly. Many Abkhaz feared a loss of their autonomy if Georgia became an independent state. Following Georgia's independence, its ruling Military Council announced, on 21 February 1992, that Georgia's Constitution of 1921 was to be restored. This meant and increase in Georgian control over Abhkazia, and a restriction on the latter's autonomy. In response, the Abkhaz Supreme Council declared Abkhazia's independence from Georgia in July 1992. In August 1992 Georgia's military forces invaded and overran most of Abkhazia, including its capital, Sukhumi. However, by the end of 1992 Abkhazian forces had pushed back the Georgian forces and, following a short ceasefire arranged by the Russian government, recaptured the capital in September 1993. As a result of Russian mediation, the Agreement on a Ceasefire and Separation of Forces was signed by the warring parties in May 1994. This agreement allowed for the deployment into Abkhazia of the peacekeepers of the Commonwealth of the Independent States, led by Russia. Relations between the parties to the conflict gradually improved and in the late 1990s Georgia's economic blockade of Abkhazia was lifted.

Although it did not recognize Abkhazia's independence at the time, from 1994 Russia provided vital support to Abkhazia enabling it to maintain its *de facto* independence from Georgia. When the war in South Ossetia erupted in 2008 (see below), Russia sent reinforcements to its peacekeepers in Abkhazia and on 26 August 2008 recognized its independence. The only other states to have recognized South Ossetia are Nicaragua, Venezuela and Nauru (see also Chapter 15).

CASE STUDY 17

# South Ossetia: From an Autonomous Region to a State

The ethno-cultural traditions of Ossetians date back to the first centuries AD. Their ancestors, called Alans or Alani, were nomadic pastoral peoples who spoke East Iranian dialects. Invasion by the Huns in the late 4th century led to the dispersal of the Alans into several groups one of which moved into the Caucasus region. The historical identity of the Caucasian Alans and present-day Ossetians dates back to the late 8th century when the Kingdom of Alania was established in the area of Circassia and Ossetia with the Darial Pass forming the nucleus of its territory. The kingdom flourished until the Mongol invasion of the 1220s. Thereafter, the Ossetians continued to live in tribal groups which moved within the territory of the Caucasus. With the southern expansion of the Russian empire Ossetia came under Russian control in 1806. Russia's first, and most important, stronghold in Caucasus, called Vladikavkas (literally, 'the rule the Caucasus'), became the capital of Ossetia. By the early 1920s, with the region under Bolshevik rule, the area in which the Ossetians lived was split into two autonomous regions – Northern Ossetia within the Russian Federal Soviet Republic and South Ossetia within the Georgian SSR. In 1936 Northern Ossetia was upgraded to an autonomous republic. However, South Ossetia retained its lower status of an autonomous region.

Following the dissolution of the USSR in 1991, Northern Ossetia transitioned relatively easily to the status of the Republic of North Ossetia-Alania within the Russian Federation. However, South Ossetia's demand in 1989 to upgrade its status to an autonomous republic within Georgia was rejected by the Georgian Supreme Council. In the summer of 1990 the Georgian Supreme Council adopted a law barring regional political parties. Ossetians saw this as an attempt to restrict, and eventually remove, the national autonomy of Georgia's minorities. In September 1990, the South Ossetian Council responded by proclaiming the South Ossetian Democratic Republic to be a sovereign entity within the USSR. Georgia's parliamentary election of December 1990 was boycotted by the Ossetians who organized their own election. The Georgian government declared the Ossetian election illegitimate and terminated South Ossetia's autonomous status.

In January 1991 war broke out between Georgia and South Ossetia. Following a bitter conflict, Russian mediation led to a ceasefire agreement being reached in 1992. The agreement established a joint peacekeeping force of Ossetian, Russian and Georgian soldiers along the frontline dividing the rival armed forces. On 6 August 2008 violent clashes erupted along this frontline. Each side blame the other for starting hostilities. A ceasefire was agreed to on the following day. However, in the early hours of the 8 August 2008 Georgia launched a major military offensive. Georgian ground forces, with air support, entered South Ossetian-controlled territory with the aim of capturing its capital Tskhinval and caused large-scale destruction in the city. Twelve Russian peacekeepers were killed and nearly 150 injured as a result of the attack. This led Russian deploying its forces into in South Ossetia who, together with the South Ossetian forces, pushed the Georgian army out of South Ossetia and moved into Georgia itself. A ceasefire between Georgia and Russia, brokered by the EU, led to Russian forces withdrawing from Georgia.

In August 2008 South Ossetia was officially recognized as an independent state by the Russia. The only other states to have recognized South Ossetia are Nicaragua, Venezuela and Nauru.

## Transdniestria: A River Bank into a State

In their everyday parlance the people of Transdniestria call their country 'Pridnestrovie' – literally 'on the Dniester' or on the banks of the Dniester. Over the centuries various peoples, languages and cultures passed across these river banks. In addition, the territory also changed its rulers: at various times, Kievan Rus, the Moldovan Principality, Crimean Khanate, the Grand Duchy of Lithuania and Rzeczpospolita all claimed authority over the Dniester basin. In 1792–93 the riverside of the Dniester came under the control of the Russian Empire. The collapse of the Russian Empire in 1917 and the occupation of Moldova (Bessarabia) by Romania made the Dniester a border dividing the Kingdom of Romania and the USSR. In 1924 the Moldovan Autonomous Soviet Socialist Republic, based on Transdniestria and within the Ukrainian Soviet Socialist Republic was proclaimed. However, when Moldova was transferred from Romania to the USSR in 1940, Transdniestria became part of the newly created federal unit within the USSR – the Moldavian Soviet Socialist Republic. While Moldova (with the exception of its capital Chişinău and a few other towns) was predominantly rural, under the Soviet regime the more urbanized Transdniestria became the locus of Moldovan industrial production, cultural development and elite recruitment.

The nationalist movement that swept Moldova during the Perestroika period during the late 1980s was predominantly a revolt of authenticity and was thus based on rural attitudes. Nationalist leaders of the Popular Font of Moldova, who came to power in the early 1990s, not only played with the idea of re-uniting with Romania but also insisted on eliminating the 'Soviet legacy'. As the centre of Soviet modernization, and thus its legacy, was located in Pridnestrovie, its population – Moldovan, Ukrainian and Russian – felt threatened by the policies of the emergent Moldovan political elites.

On 2 September 1990 the Congress of the Peoples' Representatives of Transdniestria, an ad hoc assembly, proclaimed the formation of the Transdniestrian Moldovan Soviet Socialist Republic within the USSR. In November 1990 Moldovan volunteers attacked the town Dubasari, trying to capture bridges across the Dniester. The attack was repelled. However, further clashes escalated into warfare which, following the dissolution of the USSR, reached its peak between March and July 1992. During the war, former Soviet army forces stationed in the area intervened on the side of the Transdniestrian authorities. The ceasefire agreement, mediated by the Russian government and concluded in July 1992, created a demilitarized zone along the border with Moldova. A joint Moldovan, Transdniestrian and Russian commission to supervise the ceasefire was also created.

# Case Study 17

Since then, although Transdniestria has enjoyed *de facto* independence, it has not been formally recognized by any other state, although Russia continues to be its major sponsor. In spite of the efforts of the OSCE and other international organizations to mediate between the two parties, to date no progress has been made in re-integrating Transdniestria within Moldova.

## Further Reading

Kolstø, P. (2008), 'Living with Non-recognition: State- and Nation-building in South Caucasian Quasi-states,' *Europe-Asia Studies* 60:3, 483–509.

Lynch, D. (2004), *Engaging Eurasia's Separatist States: Unresolved Conflicts and de facto States* (Washington, DC: United States Institute of Peace Press).

Pavković, A. (2011) 'Recursive Secession of Trapped Minorities: A Comparative Study of Serb Krajina and Abkhazia', *Nationalism and Ethnic Politics* 17:3, 297–318.

Roeder, P. (2007), *Where Nation-states Come From: Institutional Change in the Age of Nationalism* (Princeton, NJ: Princeton University Press).

\*\*\*

*Mikhail Ilyin is Professor at the Moscow State Institute for International Relations (MGIMO University) in Moscow, Russia.*

# Case Study 18:
# Chechnya:
# A Military Suppression of a Secession at a Cost

## Kristin M. Bakke

In the early-1990s, many of the autonomous regions in Russia issued declarations of sovereignty, requesting greater autonomy, even independence, from Moscow (see also Chapter 8). While most demands in this 'parade of sovereignties' were resolved peacefully through power-sharing agreements with the federal government, the Chechen nationalists' demand for independence resulted in two wars. The first war lasted from late-1994 to 1996, and the second war began in the autumn of 1999. In 2007, the federal government declared that it had succeeded in its latest war in Chechnya, but reports about violent clashes continued, and in 2009, violence in and around Chechnya, including the neighbouring republics Dagestan and Ingushetia, picked up.

Like other ethnic minorities in the North Caucasus, the Chechens have a long history of resisting central rule – perhaps most famously in the Caucasian War (1817–64) against the Russian imperial army – and accompanying memories of hardship at the hands of central rulers – perhaps most infamously, Joseph Stalin's deportation of nearly the entire Chechen population in February 1944. The immediate backdrop to the first Chechen war in 1994 was the Chechen Revolution of 1990–91, which brought the nationalists to power. Initially, the nationalist movement, which originated in 1989–90, sought to revive Chechen culture and traditions, but its demands quickly came to encompass political sovereignty. After ousting the republic's communist-led Supreme Soviet, in October 1991 the nationalist leader Dzohkhar Dudayev, a former Soviet Air Force general of Chechen origin, was elected president of the Chechen Republic of Ichkeria. On November 1, 1991, he declared the republic independent.

The Chechen leadership's insistence on independence increasingly soured the republic's relationship to the Russian government in Moscow. After nearly three years of failed negotiations – and several attempts by Moscow and pro-Moscow groups in Chechnya to forcibly remove Dudayev from power – in December 1994, Russian President Boris Yeltsin opted for the use of military force, citing the lack of 'constitutional order' in Chechnya.

In early December 1994, Russian troops were deployed along the Chechen border, and all-out war broke out in the final days of 1994 when the troops stormed Grozny, the Chechen capital. They were met with fierce resistance from Chechen fighters, but air strikes gave the Russians the upper hand. By March 1995, the Russian forces controlled Grozny. The Russian human rights organization Memorial estimated that by then, as many as 27,000 civilians had lost their lives, and Grozny was in ruins. The Chechen fighters retreated to the mountains in the south, from where they continued guerrilla campaigns. In August 1996, the Russian troops withdrew, and the Chechens emerged as the victors – albeit in the presence of a massive death toll, including the killing of President Dudayev in April 1996, and material destruction. Indeed, while Chechnya had faced severe economic difficulties prior to 1994, these problems were only intensified by the war.

The Chechens' battlefield victory was partial and short-lived. The Khasavyurt accord brokered by the Russian general Alexander Lebed and the Chechen field commander Aslan Maskhadov left Chechnya's status (i.e. formal independence) – the key issue at stake – undecided until 2001. Following his battlefield success and widely supported by the Chechen population, Maskhadov was elected president of the Chechen republic in January 1997. His presidency was, however, challenged by power struggles within Chechnya, including voices who expressed dissatisfaction with the Khasavyurt accord, the lack of economic recovery and Maskhadov's secular leanings. The powerful Chechen field commander Shamil Basayev, while initially part of Maskhadov's government, increasingly worked against him. Unsanctioned by Maskhadov, in August 1999 Basayev staged an attack into neighbouring Dagestan with Emir Khattab, a fighter of Saudi Arabian origin, with the aim of creating an Islamic Republic of Chechnya and Dagestan. In the Kremlin it was rumoured that Basayev was also responsible for a series of apartment bombings in Moscow in September 1999. The incursion into Dagestan and the Moscow apartment bombings were central to Moscow's justification for the second invasion of Chechnya in September 1999. The attack was strongly encouraged by Prime Minister Vladimir Putin, who in 2000 was elected president on an agenda that emphasized the re-establishment of control over Chechnya. Over the next few years, the conflict continued and spread to other regions of the North Caucasus.

The second Chechen war was infamous for brutal insurgency and counter-insurgency campaigns, with human rights violations on both the Russian and Chechen side. The Russian forces employed indiscriminate violence in the form of 'mop-up' operations in villages – detaining, torturing, disappearing and killing civilians suspected of being or supporting Chechen separatist fighters. On the separatists' side, the second war was characterized by a growing kidnapping and extortion industry, and the increasing use of large-scale terrorist attacks outside the republic's borders, such as the Nord-Ost theatre siege in Moscow in 2002, the

Beslan school siege in neighbouring North Ossetia in 2004 and the Moscow subway attack in 2010.

In 2000, the Putin administration began to implement a policy of 'Chechenization', transferring responsibility for the counter-insurgency campaign to pro-Moscow Chechens, initially under the appointed leadership of Akhmad Kadyrov, a former Chechen secessionist commander. Central to Akhmad Kadyrov's reign was the paramilitary group under the leadership of his son, Ramzan Kadyrov, known – and widely feared – as the *Kadyrovtsy*. When Akhmad Kadyrov was assassinated in 2004, his son quickly rose to prominence, and in 2007, President Putin nominated Kadyrov president of the Chechen republic.

From Moscow's perspective, the 'Chechenization' strategy has worked to the degree that key militant leaders, such as Maskhadov and Basayev, have been killed by Russian forces, and Ramzan Kadyrov rules Chechnya with an iron fist. By showing his allegiance to Moscow, Kadyrov has managed to attract reconstruction funds and a high degree of autonomy for Chechnya and his government. However, the brutal reign of Kadyrov has helped keep the Chechen separatist movement alive. Indeed, violence still continues, but the conflict today looks more like an internal Chechen struggle, between and among Kadyrov's pro-Moscow forces and different militant factions opposed to Moscow, Kadyrov, but also one another.

While the first Chechen war began as a nationalist struggle for Chechen independence, in the second war references to the establishment of an Islamic state became increasingly prevalent. In recent years, some Chechen militants have framed the struggle in terms of Chechen independence, but others have argued that it is a broader *jihadist* struggle. At the time of writing the dominant voice appears to be Doku Umarov, who calls for the establishment of an Islamic Caucasian Emirate that goes beyond Chechnya. Tens of thousands have lost their lives in this struggle.

## Further Reading

Dunlop, John B. (1998), *Russia Confronts Chechnya: Roots of a Separatist Conflict* (New York: Cambridge University Press).
Gall, Carlotta and Thomas de Waal (1998), *Chechnya: Calamity in the Caucasus* (New York: New York University Press).
Russell, John (2007), *Chechnya: Russia's 'War on Terror'* (London: Routledge).
Sakwa, Richard (ed.) (2005), *Chechnya: From Past to Future* (London: Anthem Press).
Tishkov, Valery (2004), *Chechnya: Life in a War-Torn Society* (Berkeley, CA: University of California Press).

\*\*\*

*Kirstin M. Bakke is Lecturer in Political Science at the University College, London.*

# Case Study 19:
# Kurdistan:
# A Suspended Secession from Iraq

## Peter Sluglett

Few Kurds today aspire to a 'Grand Kurdistan' extending over eastern Turkey, western Iran and northern and north-eastern Iraq. Instead, most aspire to some form of self-government or local autonomy within the borders of the states in which they live. However, recent events in Iraq have revived the possibility of secession in the minds of some Iraqi Kurds.

The notion that the Kurds of the Ottoman Empire might identify themselves as 'Kurds' (rather than simply as 'Muslims') surfaced at the end of the 19th century. Kurdish intellectuals in exile began to promote the cause of some form of decentralized administration of the Kurdish provinces, or (much more rarely) of Kurdish independence, although neither sentiment had much resonance at the local level. After the end of World War One, the Kurds of what would become Turkey fought alongside Atatürk's forces to expel foreign troops, and succeeded in preventing the division of Anatolia envisaged in the unratified Treaty of Sèvres (1920).

In November 1918, British troops occupied Mosul, and for a while, the British considered the possibility of an autonomous Kurdistan within Iraq. Eventually, broader political considerations led to Britain becoming committed to the establishment of an Arab state in Iraq, and to the inclusion of Mosul within that state. In 1924–25 the League of Nations Boundary Commissioners decided that Mosul should be part of Iraq. This recommendation found general favour, partly because the Kurdish leaders assumed that the status of the area and its people would be underwritten by a continuing British presence. Hence Britain's announcement that its Mandate would end in 1932 caused serious misgivings, especially when it became known that the Anglo-Iraqi treaty contained no minority guarantees, and a Kurdish revolt broke out in the spring of 1931. It was decisively defeated, but almost simultaneously, a new and generally more effective nucleus of Kurdish opposition was developing in the Barzani tribal lands, where Mulla Mustafa Barzani emerged as the principal figure in Iraqi Kurdish politics.

The only instance of a Kurdish secessionist movement was the Republic of Mahabad, based in a small town in north-western Iran, which lasted for a few months in 1946. It came into existence largely with the assistance of Barzani and his 3,000 fighters, who had fled from Iraq into Iran late in 1945, at the same time as a number of prominent citizens in Mahabad were considering a declaration of independence. But on 16 December 1946 the Iranian army entered Mahabad, the republic came to an end, and its leaders were executed. Barzani was forced out of Iran into Iraq, and fled to the USSR, where he remained until 1958.

Although Iraqi Kurdish politics remained in limbo until the Revolution of July 1958, the Iraqi Kurds enjoyed certain basic freedoms denied to their fellows in Iran and Turkey, perhaps most significantly the recognition, tacit and grudging though it may often have been, of their separate ethnic status. In the end, the Iraqi republic proved as uninterested in advancing Kurdish autonomy as its predecessors, and Kurdish militias and the Iraq Army became involved in constant fighting between 1961 and 1975. In 1969–70 the newly installed Ba'th government offered Barzani a form of Kurdish self-government (*hukm dhati*), but its 'March Manifesto' was merely a temporizing device. Thus large numbers of Kurdish families were forcibly removed from their homes to change the ethnic balance of particular areas, especially in and around Kirkuk, which the leadership insisted should form part of the Kurdish area.

By 1975 the regime's concern to get the better of the Kurds coincided with the Shah of Iran's desire to end a series of frontier disputes that had inflamed relations over the previous decade. In March, Saddam Hussein and the Shah came to an agreement in Algiers, which gave Iran rights of navigation in the Shatt al-'Arab, and closed the frontier in the north, thus preventing military supplies reaching the Kurds and preventing the Kurds from regrouping in Iran. Barzani left for the USA, where he died in 1979. By that time some 200,000 Kurds had been deported from the frontier area and some 700 villages destroyed.

These developments were followed by major splits in the Kurdish movement; it was also the case that some armed Kurdish groups would switch sides during the fighting, sometimes going with the government and sometimes with the rest of the Kurdish forces. However, by 1987 the main groups had formed an alliance against Baghdad, and agreed to press together for autonomy within Iraq. This took place against a background of the most terrible brutality on the part of the Iraqi regime: 8,000 members of the Barzani clan were arrested in 1983 and have not been seen since. A further 2,000 hamlets were stripped of their population, and half a million Kurds were deported to lowland Kurdistan or southern Iraq. In March 1988, Halabja, which had been briefly occupied by Iranian troops, was attacked with chemical weapons, and over 6,000 civilians were killed. Fearing further chemical attacks some 60,000 Kurdish civilians fled to Turkey and about 150,000 to Iran. As part of the Iraqi regime's policy of depopulation and destruction known as *al-Anfal*, about 100,000 Kurds were taken to southern Iraq in 1988 and 1989, where they were executed and buried in mass graves.

After the defeat of the Iraqi ground forces at the end of the Gulf War in February 1991, two spontaneous risings broke out, one in the south and the other in the

Kurdish area. Eventually, Kurdish forces were driven out of the northern cities, and by the beginning of April some 1.5 million Kurdish refugees were stranded on the Iranian and Turkish borders. A major consequence was the declaration by the US-led coalition forces of a no-fly zone over northern Iraq. This led to the *de facto* separation of the Kurdish parts of northern Iraq from Baghdad, which had been in existence for some 11 years by the time of the US invasion in 2003.

In consequence, the possible secession of the Kurdish provinces (Dohuk, Arbil, Sulaymaniyya, and perhaps Ta'mim, which includes Kirkuk) to form an independent 'Iraqi Kurdistan' became and (in 2010) remains very much on the political agenda. In January 2005, unofficial referendum booths were set up alongside the regular polling stations for the Iraqi elections. Of the two million Kurds who voted in the unofficial referendum, 98 percent chose independence. Of course, the circumstances of Iraqi Kurdistan are very different from those of the small states of *Mitteleuropa*, surrounded by friendly neighbours who have every interest in the free movement of goods and individuals (or at least individuals holding the appropriate passports). Given the Iraqi Kurds' recent history, secession is a morally defensible objective. Nevertheless it is difficult to see how independence, or secession from Iraq, will benefit them in the long run, and even more difficult to imagine how such a fragile state might survive in the contemporary regional environment.

## Further Reading

McDowall, David (1996), *A Modern History of the Kurds* (London: I.B. Tauris).

Romano, David (2006), *The Kurdish Nationalist Movement: Opportunity, Mobilisation and Identity* (Cambridge: Cambridge University Press).

Sluglett, Peter (2010), 'Common Sense, or a Step Pregnant with Enormous Consequences: Some Thoughts on the Possible Secession of Iraqi Kurdistan', in Don H. Doyle (ed.), *Secession as an International Phenomenon: From America's Civil War to Contemporary Separatist Movements* (Athens, GA: University of Georgia Press), 319–37.

Stansfield, Gareth (2003), *Iraqi Kurdistan: Political Development and Emergent Democracy* (London: Routledge Curzon).

\*\*\*

*Peter Sluglett is Professor of Middle Eastern History in the History Department, University of Utah, Salt Lake City.*

# Case Study 20:
# Yemen:
# The Resurgent Secessionism in the South

## Iain Walker

The origins of the contemporary secessionist movement in Yemen lie in the colonial period. Following the post-World War One Ottoman withdrawal from southwest Arabia, Yahya Muhammad, Imam of the Zaydis of northern Yemen, began to consolidate his authority and extend the area under his control; but faced with conflicts with both an increasingly expansionist Saudi kingdom to the north and the British, who had held Aden since 1839, to the south, and unable to sustain fighting on two fronts, he ceded much of his claim in southern Yemen to the British. This effectively divided the Yemeni cultural area in two. The two regions remained divided until 1990: following the 1962 revolution the northern Yemeni Imamate became the Yemen Arab Republic while in the south the Federation of South Arabia gained independence from Britain in 1967 as the People's Republic of South Yemen; the Protectorate of South Arabia – the contemporary governorates of Hadramawt and al Mahra – was incorporated into the latter, which in 1970 became the Marxist People's Democratic Republic of Yemen.

Despite political separation, culturally and socially the people of the western areas of southern Yemen had much in common with their neighbours across the border; and since many politicians in Aden had northern connections, unification was never far from the agenda. It came to fruition in 1990: following the end of the Cold War, and in the context of domestic conflict in the south and economic crises in both states, the two were unified as the Republic of Yemen. Unification was poorly managed however: the two armies were never effectively merged, and the political parties retained their regional powerbases: in the south the former ruling party (the Yemeni Socialist Party) remained strong while President Ali Abdullah Saleh's General People's Congress remained dominant in the north. A third party, Islah, also draws most of its support from the north. In the 1993 elections the YSP only gained 18 percent of the vote, and a similar share of seats, all in the south; unhappy with the result, the party pressed for 50:50 participation in the government, which President Saleh denied them. In April 1994 dissatisfaction within the southern military and among southern politicians boiled over and civil war broke out; three weeks later the southern leader, Ali Salem al-Beidh, declared independence from his base in Aden.

The numerically superior northern army won the war easily; as part of the reconciliation process President Saleh promised decentralization and appointed a number of southerners to his government. However, the promised decentralization never materialized and the nominations proved to be largely symbolic. Indeed, Saleh has since begun appropriating southern economic resources (largely oil revenues) to finance his relationships with his supporters in the north; he has handed positions of power in the south to members of his own tribe; and a growing influx of northerners into the south – the former southern Yemen was almost twice the size of the north but at unification had barely a third of the population – are taking both jobs and, more significantly, land that southerners see as rightfully theirs. The land issue is particularly acute, as northerners are granted land nationalized under the Marxist southern regime – and viewed as being southern lands – but now claimed to belong to the unified state and thus within Saleh's purview.

Political processes in the north are significantly different from the south. Tribal affiliations remain strong. Saleh's powerbase lies within the Hashid tribal group, the country's largest: Saleh himself is a Hashidi, while the former speaker of parliament and leader of the opposition Islah party until his death in 2007, Sheikh Abdullah al-Ahmar, was the head of the Hashidis. In the south, however, tribal affiliations – never as strong nor as politicized as in the north – were largely suppressed during the 20 years of Communist rule, and Saleh's attempts to play the tribal card in the south not only failed but turned many tribal leaders against him. In the 15 years since the end of the civil war, therefore, resentment against the north has continued to grow and in 2007 a recrudescence of dissatisfaction in the south coalesced as the Southern Movement. Worryingly perhaps for Saleh, the Southern Movement has emerged from the reconciliation of several different and formerly opposing factions in the south. Most notably, the staunchly pro-Saleh and anti-Marxist southern politician Tareq al-Fadhli, formerly an implacable opponent of the southern leader al-Beidh, defected to the Southern Movement in 2009 and has declared his support for an independent southern state.

In an effort to fight the Southern Movement, Saleh invokes Al-Qaeda's expression of support for the Southern Movement; any such alliance is strongly disavowed by the southerners, however, and attempts by Saleh to tar the Southern Movement with the Al Qaeda brush may well backfire on him (and on his Western backers) as he refuses to address the real issues. The continued centralization of power in San'a', the perceived (and undoubtedly real) exploitation of southern economic resources for and by northerners, and interference in southern affairs are compounded by very real social and cultural problems; for while analysis largely focuses on the political and economic aspects of the failure of unification, there are very real differences within the south, particularly between the western areas and the eastern governorates of Hadramawt and Al Mahra. Many Hadramis and Mahras do not consider themselves to be Yemeni; there are significant cultural and linguistic differences. There is also much resentment at the northern introduction of arms and qat to southern areas where, prior to unification, arms were largely absent and qat – produced in the north and 'imported' by the south, thus adding to the south's economic woes – was rarely chewed.

## Further Reading

al-Suwaidi, Jamal (1995), *The Yemeni War of 1994: Causes and Consequences* (London: Saqi Books).

Clark, Victoria (2010), *Yemen: Dancing on the Heads of Snakes* (New Haven, CT: Yale University Press).

Day, Stephen (2010), *The Political Challenge of Yemen's Southern Movement*, Carnegie Papers Middle East Program, Number 108, March (Washington, DC: Carnegie Endowment for International Peace).

***

*Iain Walker is Research Fellow at the Institute of Social and Cultural Anthropology at the University of Oxford.*

# Index

Page numbers in *italic* refer to a table. Page numbers followed by 'n' refer to a note at the bottom of the page.

17 Point Agreement  488, 489

Abdullah, Farooq  468
Abdullah, Sheikh  468
Abkhazia  36, 40, 46, 147, 294, 529–30
    and foreign intervention  60, 355
    and Georgia  14, 19, 55, 149, 156, 220, 290, 530
    recognition of statehood  221, 261, 292, 455, 530
    and Russia  39, 62, 64, 154, 155, 221, 264, 290, 530
Abu Sayyef Group (ASG)  472–3
Acadian people  390
Aceh  455–6, 459–61
Act of Free Choice  491, 492
Acts of Union  519
Addis Ababa Accords  506
Aden  543
Adjara  529
Adoula, President  123
Aduwa, Battle of  497
Adzharia  149
affirmation model  153
Afghanistan  289
Africa
    and borders, national  61–2, 268, 308, 315–16, 371
    colonization/decolonization  15–16, 32, 122–3, 308, 315, 317, 501, 505
African Bantustan  33n
Afwerki, Isaias  498
*Agenda for Peace*  17

aggression, and international law  291, 399
agreement, mutual  518
Agreement on Succession Issues, Yugoslavia  376–7
Ahtisaari, Martti  181–2, 263
Al Qaeda  472, 544
Alabama  111, 434
al-Ahmar, Sheikh Abdullah  544
Alaska  12, 336, 400n
Albania  54, 285, 289
    Albanians in Kosovo  18, 54, 100, 157, 159–61, 164, 171–83, 215, 217, 289
    Albanians in Macedonia  54, 168, 215
Albanian language  174, 175, 176
al-Fadhli, Tareq  544
Algeria  2, 35, 38
Algerian National Liberation Front (FLN)  38
Algiers talks  512
Althusius, Johannes  82n
Alto Adige/South Tyrol  30
American Civil War  103–4, 111–16, 211, 238, 255
American Constitution  105, 109, 111, 333–5, 336, 341, 342
American Declaration of Independence  11, 25, 26, 103, 105, 126
American Pledge of Allegiance  104
Amnesty International  512
Anatolia  539
Anglo-Iraqi treaty  539
Anglo-Irish treaty  240
Angola  2, 30, 35, 36, 38, 258n

Anjouan 31, 293
annexation, unjust 24, 85, 104, 396, 406–7, 408, 475
apartheid 288
Appomattox, Virginia 115
April Accords 134
Arab League 502
Arbitration Commission (Badinter Commission) *see* Badinter Commission
archives 376
Argentina 27
Arkansas 112
Armenia 64, 148, 149, 150, 156
Articles of Confederation 104–5
Atatürk 539
Aung San, General 475
Australia 211
Austria 29, 37n, 161, 165, 285, 333
Austro-Hungarian Empire 58, 161, 234, 235n, 285
authoritarianism 151, 178, 218, 230, 231, 233, 383, 432, 460, 498
autonomy 58, 85n, 459, 472, 476, 489, 497–8, 529, 531, 537
Awame League 463
Azerbaijan 19, 64, 148, 149, 151, 217
and Nagorno-Karabakh 156, 290, 529

Badinter Commission 142, 166, 262n, 322, 335
Bagrat III 530
Balkanization 15, 421–2
Baltic republics 149, 150, 152, 257
Baluba people 55
Bangladesh 3, 32, 48, 55, 199, 293, 312, 429, 463–4
 and foreign intervention 17, 39, 216, 260, 271, 277, 287, 464
 and India 4, 17, 39, 216, 217, 260, 271, 277, 287, 464
 and international law 324–5, 367
 recognition of statehood 4, 5, 217, 287, 323, 455, 464
 and United Nations 5, 260, 287, 323, 455, 464
Bantustans of Transkei 287, 288, 292
Barnett question 521
Barre, Siad 501, 502
Barzani, Mulla Mustafa 539, 540

Basayev, Shamil 536, 537
Basic Agreement of the Region of Eastern Slavonia, Baranja and Western Srem 524
Basque Autonomous Community 512, 513
Basque Country 30, 37, 87, 89, 243, 357, 456, 511–13
Basque Nationalist Part (BNP) 511, 512
Batasuna party (formerly Herri Batasuna) 38, 511, 512
Ba'th government 540
'Battle Hymn of the Republic' 114
Belarus 149, 150, 153–4
Belfast (Good Friday) Agreement 30n
Belgian Thesis 117, 118, 122
Belgium 38, 46, 122–3, 267, 357
Belorussia 148
Beran, Harry 90–92, 93, 377
Berlin Conference 15–16, 315
Berlin, Congress of 132
Bertrand, Guy 135
Biafra 4, 50, 259–60, 293
 and conflict, violent 104, 124, 215, 451
 and decolonization 99, 117, 124
 and ethnicity 100, 124, 215, 218
 and foreign intervention 101, 124, 129, 259
 human rights 100, 124, 209, 259
 recognition of statehood 16, 259–60, 287, 292, 294
*Bill 1, An Act respecting the Future of Quebec* 135, 142, 144
*Bill 99 – An Act Respecting the Exercise and Fundamental Rights and Prerogatives of the Quebec People and the Quebec State* 139, 143, 144
Black Hand/Unification or Death 235
blood sacrifice 229
BNA Act 137
Bolivia 27
Bophuthatswana 287
Border Security Force (BSF) 468
borders 25–6, 81–93, 303–18, 429
 and Africa 61–2, 268, 308, 315–16, 371
 and Britain 312, 487, 501
 and China 20–21, 309
 and colonization 19, 25, 119, 122, 156, 194, 301, 307–8, 497, 501
 and conflict, violent 52, 308
 and democracy 311, 434

and European Community/European
    Union 309, 311–12
and India 20–21, 312, 487
and international law 304–5, 314–17,
    399
and Ireland 241, 242, 245, 312, 434
and minority communities 309–10,
    312–13, 315, 318
post-secession 66, 301, 303–18
and Quebec 86, 144–5, 311, 340
and Soviet Union 19, 156, 159, 310, 313,
    316
and stability 311–14, 371
and territorial rights 86, 91–2, 93,
    144–5, 221, 268, 308–9, 365–6, 407
and Yugoslavia 19, 309, 310, 311–12,
    316
Bosnia and Herzegovina 1, 40, 233–7
  and conflict, violent 165, 188, 218,
      235–7, 243, 244
  and Croatia 220, 236, 237
  and democracy 235, 236–7, 245, 339
  ethnicity 2, 162–3, 168, 211, 313, 339
    and Serbs 26n, 55, 162, 167, 215,
        233–7, 289–90, 292, 313
  foreign intervention
    and European Community/
        European Union 101, 166, 168,
        237
    NATO (North Atlantic Treaty
        Organization) 165, 166, 167, 189,
        262, 263
    United Nations 165, 166, 167
    United States 101, 165, 166, 168
  recognition of statehood 166
  religion 162, 234
  and territorial rights 221, 236, 262
  and Yugoslavia 158, 159, 162–3, 164–5,
      339, 371
Bougainville 17, 18, 31, 50, 259, 293
Boutros-Ghali, Boutros 17, 502
Brazil 106
Brezhnev, Leonid 154
Britain 12, 46
  and borders 312, 487, 501
  and colonization 2, 195, 255, 287, 433,
      475–6, 501, 505
  and Confederation of American States
      112, 114, 115
  and devolution 141, 195, 519–21

and foreign intervention 464, 497, 503,
    516, 539, 543
  and Biafra 124, 259
  and Kosovo 171, 182
  non-intervention 252–3, 255–6
  and Tibet 15, 487, 488, 489
and Ireland 30, 202, 237–42, 312, 352,
    358–9
and United States 4, 103, 255
Brown, John 109
Buchanan, Allen 85–7, 424–5, 448
Buddhism 467, 476
Buganda, Kingdom of 25
Bush administration 498

Cairo Resolution 128n
California 107, 108
Cambodia 444
Canada 38, 267, 309, 353
  constitution 37n, 132–4, 335, 337
  and Quebec 17, 100, 131–45, 215, 311,
      326–7, 353, 357
    and constitutional law 322, 333,
        337–9, 340, 341, 342, 351–2, 355,
        386
Cancado-Trindade, Judge 329, 330
Cape Verde 258n
capitalism, and minority communities 154,
    191–2, 194–9, 203–4, 228
Caribbean 106, 113
Carment, D. 62
Cartier, George-Etienne 134
Cassese, Antonio 324, 325, 326
Catalans 227
Catholicism 161, 238–9, 471
Caucasian War 535
Caucasus 36, 64, 147, 149, 152, 154–5
causal accounts 193, 199–203
Central America 113
Central Reserve Police (CRP) 468
centralization 155, 192, 196, 231, 544
  decentralization 57, 58, 210, 309, 544
  recentralization 158, 159, 160, 162
Charlottetown Accord 134–5
Chechen Revolution 535
Chechen Wars 57, 536
Chechnya 50, 293
  and conflict, violent 209, 218
  recognition of statehood 261, 289, 292,
      455

and Russia 19, 30, 57, 64, 151, 154–5,
    288–9, 529, 535–7
Chen Shui-Bian 484
Chiang Ching-kuo 484
Chiang Kaishek 483
Chile 27
China 20, 51
    and borders 20–21, 309
    foreign intervention 63, 182, 281, 464
    and right of secession 37n, 334
    and Taiwan 286–7, 294, 483–5
    territorial rights 11, 20–21, 286
    and Tibet 15, 20, 51, 93, 456, 487–9
Chinese people 432
choice theories 90–92, 93, 400–3, 404,
    413–26, 443–4
Christianity 161, 238–9, 273, 471, 497
circularity 440
Ciskei 287
citizenship 13, 25, 140–41, 311, 336–7
civil rights 13, 23, 34, 240, 241
civil wars 34–5, 46, 57, 65–6, 210–11, 215,
    228
clan politics 154, 179
Clarity Act 139, 140, 143, 144, 338, 339
Cold War 15, 17, 132, 238, 244, 260, 464, 483
Collier, Paul 201–2, 203
Colombia (New Mexico) 27
colonial secession *see* colonization/
    decolonization
colonization/decolonization 2, 4, 27, 30–32,
    40, 261, 396
    Africa 15–16, 32, 122–3, 308, 315, 317,
        501, 505
        Biafra 99, 117, 124
        Eritrea 18–19, 315, 497
    and borders 19, 25, 119, 122, 156, 194,
        301, 307–8, 497, 501
    and conflict, violent 35, 396
    European 2, 15–16, 28, 30, 195, 285, 491
        Britain 2, 195, 255, 287, 433, 475–6,
            501, 505
        France 433, 501
        Italy 497, 501
        Portugal 30, 32, 119–20, 127n, 255
        Spain 26–7, 255
    India 2, 118, 122
    and international law 253–4, 428
        and United Nations 28, 30, 125, 128,
            189, 257–8, 366, 442
    'salt-water' colonialism 118, 126, 127
    Soviet Union 148, 152
    Spain 12, 26–7, 255
        and Latin America 189, 252, 315–16
        and Philippines 400n, 471–3
        and Western Sahara 127n, 288
    unilateral decolonization 27
commercial exchange 11, 12
Commonwealth of Independent States
    (CIS) 150, 530
Communism 100, 148–9, 174, 233
Communist Party of the Soviet Union
    (CPSU) 148
communitarian theories *see* national
    theories
community, sense of 86, 88, 93, 294, 311,
    358–9
compact theory 134, 137
compliance 253, 305–6, 316, 324, 430
Comprehensive Peace Agreement (CPA)
    40, 505, 506
Compromise of 1850 108
Confederate States of America (CSA) 27,
    99, 100, 101, 103–16, 189, 211, 257
conflict, frozen 217
conflict, violent 1, 32–7, 40, 45, 163–5, 188,
    227–46, 404, 448
    Biafra 104, 124, 215, 451
    and borders 52, 308
    Bosnia and Herzegovina 165, 188, 218,
        235–7, 243, 244
    Chechnya 209, 218
    and colonization/decolonization 35,
        396
    Croatia 164, 218, 235, 523
    and culture 228, 229
        and ethnicity 52, 188, 207–21,
            229–30, 235–7
    deaths 32, 35, 36, 45, 164, 165, 536
        American Civil War 104, 115
        Kosovo 175, 178
        Sudan 32, 506
    and democracy 59, 230, 235, 237–42,
        245, 356–7
    and economic resources 50, 228
    and foreign intervention 221, 251–64,
        273, 274, 276, 277, 305
    and international law 291, 305, 306, 399
    and nationalism 210, 229–30
    post-secession 65–6, 68

states free of conflict 46, 163, 177, 214, 215, 227
and territorial rights 210, 221, 306
Congo/Zaire 2, 4, 55, 122–3, 258, 259, 287
connection of disadvantagement 407
connection of profit 406–7
conquest 11, 107, 455
consent 3, 4, 21, 255, 261, 293, 302, 327, 355, 357
   and borders 314, 315
   and colonization 258, 259
   constitutional 126, 134, 333–4, 341–2, 350, 356
   and individual rights 90, 125, 256, 301–2, 415
   and territorial rights 13, 82, 83, 84, 258–9
   and Yugoslavia 311, 312, 316
constitutional arrangements 100, 137, 143, 291, 349, 386
Constitutional Framework for Provisional Self-Government, Kosovo 181
constitutional law 13, 37, 121, 302, 333–42, 345, 441, 477, 523, 530
   Austria 37n, 333
   Canada 37n, 132–3, 134, 135–9, 333–4, 335, 337
   Ethiopia 37n, 333, 335, 337, 339, 358, 497
   Kosovo 175, 176
   Liechtenstein 333, 335, 336, 338–9
   Quebec 142, 322, 333, 337–42, 351–2, 355, 386
   Russia 155, 334
   Saint Kitts and Nevis 37n, 333, 335, 338, 339, 341
   Serbia and Montenegro 37n, 47n, 140, 143
   Soviet Union 37n, 148, 150, 529
   United States 105, 109, 111, 333–5, 336, 341, 342
   Yugoslavia 131, 132, 143, 157, 333–4, 335, 339–40
*Constitutional Recomposition of the Federal Republic of Yugoslavia*, Ronald Watts 139
constitutionalism 145, 347–8, 350, 351–2, 355–9
constitutionalization 142–4, 345–60

Contact Group initiative 166, 180, 181
contagion 269
continuity 368–71
contractual theory 82, 90
Convention on the Reduction of Statelessness 374
conversation 392, 393–4
Copenhagen Document 261
Correlates of War Project 26, 34, 190, 271, 272
corruption 154, 491
Corsica 31, 255
cotton industry 106, 112
Council of Citizens of the Federal Assembly 132
Crawford, James 3
Crimea 51, 62, 156, 261, 529
Crittenden, Senator 111
Croat Democratic Union (CDU) 161–2
Croatia 1, 2, 30, 267, 376, 523–4
   and Bosnia and Herzegovina 220, 236, 237
   and conflict, violent 164, 218, 219, 235, 523
   ethnicity, Serbs 55, 161–2, 168, 215, 289–90, 292, 313, 523–4
   and foreign intervention 218–19
   and European Community/European Union 5, 101, 166, 262
   and United Nations 164, 166, 167, 262, 524
   and United States 39, 101, 165, 168, 524
   human rights 161, 523
   and recognition of statehood 166, 286, 335, 524
   and Serb Krajina 289–90, 523–4
   and Serbia 277, 524
   and Yugoslavia 132, 134, 157, 159, 161, 163, 164, 523
Croats 132, 162, 164, 313, 339
cronyism 154
cultural diversity 389
culture *see also* ethnicity
   and communitarian theory 401, 402
   and conflict, violent 52, 188, 207–21, 228, 229–30, 235–7
   cultural diversity 348–9, 358–9, 387–8, 423, 492

cultural rights 23, 211
and ethnicity 52, 152, 188, 207–21,
  229–30, 387, 475–7
  Serbs 233, 235–7
and geopolitics 232, 242
and homogenization 196, 198
and language 153, 388–9, 401, 402, 403,
  463
and nationalism 34, 194–5, 204, 240,
  242–3, 348–9, 358–9, 388, 403, 445
and territorial rights 84, 86, 88, 89, 93
culture, shared 418
culture, societal 388–90, 391
currency 375, 520
Cyprus 4, 30, 58, 60, 147, 288, 291, 292, 294
Czech Republic 19, 68, 355n, 517
Czechoslovakia 37, 67, 285
  dissolution 46, 147, 261, 294, 316, 355n,
    369, 515, 517

Dalai Lama 487, 488, 489
Danube, river 372
*Daral Islam* 459
Davis, Jefferson 111, 114
Dayton agreement 165, 167, 177, 222, 236,
  290, 524
de Vattel, Emmerich 254
debts 376
decision-making 382, 449
Declaration of Sovereignty 517
*Declaration on Principles of International Law
  Concerning Friendly Relations* 125,
  126–8, 291, 323, 324, 326, 329–30,
  385, 400
*Declaration on the Granting of Independence
  to Colonial Countries and Peoples see
  also* United Nations – UN General
  Assembly Resolution 1541 118–19,
  189, 399, 439, 442
*Declaration on the Occasion of the Fiftieth
  Anniversary of the United Nations*
  325–6
*Declaration on the Rights of Aboriginal Peoples*
  385
defence 152, 157–8
  self-defence 34, 306, 404, 448, 451
deliberation 391–4
democracy 14, 20, 231, 391–3, 402, 502, 511
  *see also* majority rule; referendums;
  voting rights

and borders 311, 434
and conflict, violent 59, 230, 235,
  237–42, 245, 356–7
and constitutionalism 347–8, 350,
  351–2, 355–9
democratization 17, 151, 215, 231, 233,
  484
  Bosnia and Herzegovina 235,
    236–7, 245, 339
and domination 427, 429, 430, 431–5,
  436
and human rights 121, 125–6, 402–3
and Ireland 238, 245, 352
liberal 90–92, 99, 347, 350, 351–2, 355–9
and minority communities 230, 245,
  383, 432–5
Montenegro 99, 131, 140–41
and nationalism 114, 351n
Quebec 131, 134, 135, 335–40, 342–3,
  351–2
and United States 113–14, 336, 434–5
Democratic Party 109
Democratic Progressive Party (DPP) 484,
  485
demography 48, 50–3
demonstrations, peaceful 218
DEMOS 161, 162
Deng Xiaoping 483
Denmark 68, 293, 515, 516–17
devolution 4, 141, 387, 389, 516 *see also*
  Iceland; Scotland
diasporas 216, 387
diplomatic support 39, 62, 165–6, 189
discrimination 301, 449–50, 463
  discriminatory legislation 48, 50, 121,
    330
  racial 56, 63, 291, 479
disillusionment 177, 182, 197, 460
dissolution 27, 147–68, 368–71, 429 *see
  also* Czechoslovakia; Soviet Union;
  Yugoslavia
diversionary war theory 55–6
divorce 351, 352, 422–3
Dniester, river 532
domination 194, 427–37, 449–50, 484, 498
Douglas, Stephen 108–9
Downes, Alexander 56
*Draft Bill – An Act Respecting the Sovereignty
  of Quebec* 135
Dudaev, Johar 151

Dudayev, Dzohkhar 535, 536
Đukanović, President 141, 144
Durkhemians 229

East Timor 1, 15, 18–19, 40, 46, 199, 258n, 287
Economic and Social Council (ECOSOC) 374
economic development 48–50, 152, 191–204, 232, 294, 480
   and inequality 48–50, 58, 187, 191–204, 228, 233, 243
   and Ireland 240, 243
   and nationalism 49–50, 191–2, 194–5, 199–202
   and Yugoslavia 158, 160, 161, 243
education 34, 48, 153, 175, 176, 215, 234
Egypt 122, 502, 505
Eide, Kai 181
electoral boundaries 433, 434
Electoral College 109
electoral systems 432–7
Emancipation Proclamation 113
Emmett, Robert 239
enclaves 92, 220, 315, 317
Enlightenment 20, 103, 106
Eritrea 35, 46, 199, 293, 374, 497–9
   colonization/decolonization 18–19, 315, 497
   and foreign intervention 63, 497
   and recognition of statehood 259, 455, 497, 498
Eritrean Islamic Jihad group 498
Eritrean Liberation Front (ELF) 498
Eritrean People's Liberation Front (EPLF) 497, 498
Estonia 2, 148, 150, 152, 157, 258n, 376
Estrada, Joseph 472
Ethiopia 31, 36, 38, 497, 501, 503
   constitution 37n, 333, 335, 337, 339, 358
   and Eritrea 18–19, 35, 46, 199, 259n, 315, 374, 497, 503
Ethiopia-Eritrea Claims Commission 374
ethnic cleansing 100, 157, 161, 175, 180
ethnicity 45–69, 212–13, 269–81, 387–90, 492, 501, 505, 544 *see also* culture; minority communities
   Biafra 100, 124, 215, 218
   Chinese people 432, 479
   and conflict, violent 52, 187–8, 207–21, 229–30, 235–7
   and culture 52, 152, 188, 207–21, 229–30, 387, 403, 475–7
      Serbs 233, 235–7
   and domination 431, 432, 433
   and economics 49–50, 192, 193, 196–7, 199–202
   and ethnic demography 48, 50–54, 56, 446
   and foreign intervention 62–3, 64, 190, 216–17, 218–19, 267–8, 269–81
   minority rights 258, 358–9
   and nationalism 25, 46, 47, 99, 197–8, 210, 213, 229–30, 233–5, 311
      and economics 49–50, 199–202
   and politics 48, 54, 190, 197, 215, 269–70
   Russia 154–7, 278, 531
   Soviet Union 2, 152, 529–30, 531
   and territorial rights 210, 221, 234, 245
   and Yugoslavia 2, 313, 322–3 *see also* Bosnia and Herzegovina
      Croatia 55, 161–2, 168, 215, 289–90, 292, 313, 523–4
      Kosovo 18, 54, 100, 157, 159–61, 164, 171–83, 215, 216, 289
      Macedonia 54, 168, 215
      Montenegro 54, 144, 168, 213, 215
      Serbia 213, 313
ethno-linguistic fractionalization (ELF) 52
Europe 15–16, 28, 36, 39
European Community/European Union 288
   and borders, national 309, 311–12
   and Ireland 241, 242
   and Russia 264, 370–71
   and Scotland 520, 521
   and Slovenia 5, 164, 166
   and Soviet Union 25n, 312
   and Yugoslavia 25n, 101, 165, 166, 168, 262, 311–12, 524
      and Bosnia and Herzegovina 101, 166, 168, 237
      and Croatia 5, 101, 166, 262
      and Kosovo 39, 101, 166, 168, 221, 262
      and Montenegro 101, 131, 140–41, 143–4
      and Slovenia 5, 164, 166

Euskadi Ta Askatasuna (ETA) 511–12, 513
exploitation 50, 119, 492
Extension of Democratic Rights Value 357–8

FARK (Armed Forces of the Republic of Kosovo) 179
federalism 57–8, 132, 151, 154–7, 387, 389, 423, 477, 519
    Quebec 99, 134, 137, 386
    United States 104–5, 107–8, 112, 113, 154–5
Fenian Brotherhood 239
Ferdinand, Franz 233
Fiji 58
Finland 258n
Fire-Eaters 108, 109, 112
First Nations 144, 311
Flanders 30, 357
Flemish Interest party (VB) 38
Florida 12, 111, 113
force, use of 85, 90, 155, 305, 306, 313, 441
foreign intervention 38–9, 47, 60–65, 100–101, 188–90, 251–64, 419 *see also* Britain; European Community/European Union; NATO (North Atlantic Treaty Organization); recognition of statehood; United Nations; United States
    Abkhazia 60, 355
    Biafra 101, 124, 129, 259
    Bosnia and Herzegovina
        and European Community/European Union 101, 166, 168, 237
        and NATO (North Atlantic Treaty Organization) 165, 166, 167, 189, 262, 263
        and United Nations 165, 166, 167
        and United States 101, 165, 166, 168
    China 63, 182, 281, 464
    and conflict, violent 221, 251–64, 273, 274, 276, 277, 305
    Croatia 218–19
        and European Community/European Union 5, 101, 166, 262
        and United Nations 164, 166, 167, 262, 524
        and United States 39, 101, 165, 168, 524
    Eritrea 63, 497
    and ethnicity 62–3, 64, 190, 216–17, 218–19, 267–8, 269–81
    humanitarian intervention 167, 180, 253, 254, 257, 260n, 262–3, 273, 448, 464
    India 218, 488
        and Bangladesh 17, 39, 216, 260, 271, 277, 287, 464
    and international law 355–6, 376–7
    Ireland 239, 242, 245, 368
    Kosovo 19, 253, 355
        and European Community/European Union 101, 168, 262
        and NATO (North Atlantic Treaty Organization) 100, 101, 163–8, 180, 189, 219, 262, 263, 281
        and United Nations 18, 166, 179–81, 262, 289, 327–30, 373
        and United States 101, 165, 168, 179, 181, 182, 216, 217, 281
    military intervention 101, 167, 255–6, 257, 262, 441, 524
        arms supply 124, 127, 165–6, 239, 245, 259, 460, 464
        Kosovo 167, 180, 253
    Montenegro 101, 131, 140–41, 143–4, 166, 285
    and non-governmental organizations (NGOs) 217, 460, 492
    non-intervention 189, 252–4, 255–6, 464
    Serbia 166, 262
    Slovenia 5, 164, 166
    Sri Lanka 218, 260n
    Tibet 15, 487, 488, 489
    Yugoslavia
        and European Community/European Union 25n, 101, 165, 166, 168, 262, 311–12, 524
        and NATO (North Atlantic Treaty Organization) 100, 101, 163–8, 180, 189, 219, 262, 263, 281
        and United Nations 373, 377
        and United States 101, 168
foreign policy 54, 190, 267–81
Fort Sumter 112

fragmentation 17, 194, 291, 294, 403
France 12, 35, 37, 255, 464
    and colonization 433, 501
    and Confederation of American States 112–13, 114, 115, 189
    and Kosovo 171, 267
    and Lousiana 12, 400n
Franco, General 511
'Free Soil' movement 107, 108, 109
freedom of individuals 20, 90–92, 125, 431
freedom of movement 181, 308
French Revolution 11, 14, 238, 255, 349
Fretilin movement 287
Fröbel, Julius 388
Front for the Liberation of the Enclave of Cabinda (FLEC) 38

*Gabcikovo-Nagymaros Project* case 371–2
Gabon 260
Gagauzia 261, 529
GAL (Autonomous Liberation Groups) 511
Galicia 149, 152
Gellner, Ernest 192, 198, 203
General People's Congress 543
Genoa 255
genocide 124, 153, 167, 211, 221, 444, 523
Genocide Convention 371
geography 35, 48, 50–54, 56, 119–22, 155, 446, 467, 487
geopolitics 188, 231–2, 234–7, 238, 239, 242–6
Georgia 46, 151, 217, 267, 376, 530
    and Abkhazia 14, 19, 55, 149, 156, 220, 290, 529, 530
    and Armenia 51, 64
    and Russia 147, 152, 156, 157, 216, 219, 221, 264
    and South Ossetia 14, 19, 55, 149, 156, 219, 220, 290, 529, 531
    and Soviet Union 55, 148, 150
Georgia (US state) 111
Gerjakan Aceh Merdeka (GAM) 459, 460
Germany 26n, 67, 239, 433
    German Empire 3n, 132, 285, 370
    and Kosovo 171, 182, 258n
    and Yugoslavia 165, 286
Ghandi, Mrs 17
globalization 13, 201, 311
Goa 15
Goh Keng Swee 480

gold rush 108
Gorbachev, Mikhail 101, 148–9, 150–51, 153, 154
governance 55, 58
government control 211, 216, 218, 291, 421
Greece 23, 54, 213, 334
greed 50, 215
Greeks 67
grievance 48, 53, 100, 142–4, 197, 215, 455, 468
Groteus, Hugo 254
group leaders/representatives 446–7, 461
Group of 8 (G8) 264
group rights 413, 416–21, 440–41
guerrilla warfare 35, 109, 239, 240
Guinea Bissau 258n
Gulf War 540
Guurti Congress of the Elders 502

Haiti (Saint Domingue) 106, 260, 287
Hamas 264
Haradinaj, Ramush 179
Hari Singh 467
Hausa-Fulani people 124
Hechter, Michael 201–2, 203
Helsinki Final Act 261
Helsinki Memorandum of Understanding 461
heroism 229
heterogeneity 16, 53, 58, 60, 65, 66, 88, 124, 305
historical injustice 405, 406, 407, 408
history, shared 388, 389, 402
Hizbul Mujahideen 468
Hobbes, Thomas, *Leviathan* 21
Hoeffler, Anke 201–2, 203
Holbrooke, Richard 180
Holy Alliance 255, 256
Home Rule movement 239
homelands 87–8, 92, 93
homogenization 196, 198
Horowitz, D.L. 49, 156, 182
host states 302, 333, 341, 441, 450–51
Hroch, Miroslav 197–8, 204
human rights *see also* territorial rights
    civil rights 240, 241
    and cultural rights 23, 211
    and democracy 121, 125–6, 402–3
    and domination 427, 431, 436
    equal rights 324–5, 329–30

individual rights 90–3, 415–23, 429, 431, 436, 444
   and consent 90, 125, 256, 301–2, 415
   and property rights 82–3, 84, 89, 400
   and international law 125–6, 221, 301–2, 306, 321–30, 374, 399–400, 404
   minority rights 17, 20, 91, 118, 258, 261n, 358–9, 413, 416–21, 440–51
   moral rights 81, 92, 106, 381, 385, 402, 404–8, 413, 422–6, 447–50
   political rights 34, 126, 447–50
   and religion 325, 326, 329–30
   and right of secession 385, 413–23, 428, 429–31, 447–8
   and territorial rights 82–3, 84, 85, 86, 89, 400, 403–7, 414
   violation of 100, 218, 288, 498, 512, 536, 540
     Biafra 100, 124, 209, 259
     Croatia 161, 523
     West Papua 491, 492
   voting rights 309, 310, 336–7, 357–8, 386, 433, 434–5, 443
humanitarian intervention 167, 180, 253, 254, 257, 260n, 262–3, 273, 448, 464
Hungarians 157
Hungary 29, 161, 256–7n, 372
Hungary-Czechoslovakia Treaty 372
Hyderabad 15

Ibo people 100, 124
Iceland 68, 293, 455, 515, 516–17
ideology 232, 234–7, 238, 241, 242–6
imperialism 11, 20
income distribution 49, 58, 199
independence 1–2, 23, 26, 32, 106, 134, 197–8, 442
independence parties 38
India 12, 15, 20–21, 31, 117, 129, 267, 334
   and borders 20–21, 312, 487
   and China 20–21, 488
   and colonization 2, 118, 122
   foreign intervention 218, 488
     and Bangladesh 4, 17, 39, 217, 260, 271, 277, 287, 464
   and Kashmir 20, 39, 209, 467–9
   and Pakistan 39, 46, 121, 220, 271, 277, 312, 367, 469
   and United Nations 260, 372–3

Indian National Congress (INC) 468
Indians (American) 67
indigenous people 67, 305, 339, 340, 387, 389
individual rights 90–93, 415–23, 429, 431, 436, 444
   and consent 90, 125, 256, 301–2, 415
   and property rights 82–3, 84, 89, 400
indivisibility 334, 359
Indonesia 2, 15, 31, 46, 459–61, 491–2
   and East Timor 15, 18–19, 199, 287
Indo-Pakistan war 464, 467
industrialization 196, 198–9, 203
inequality 53, 121
   economic 48–50, 58, 187, 191–204, 228, 233, 243
   equal rights 324–5, 329–30
   political 233, 436, 448
   racial equality 113–14, 291, 325, 326, 329–30
institutional identity 67–8, 93, 388, 389–91, 396
institutionalization 245, 350, 358, 423
insurgency 38, 54, 113, 215, 357–8, 468, 536
   counter-insurgency 56, 57, 66, 179, 218, 468, 476, 537
Intergovernmental Authority on Development (IGAD) 506
International Bill of Rights 126
International Commission of Jurists 324–5
International Court of Justice (ICJ) 120, 189, 257, 264, 289, 301, 304, 316, 327–30, 399
*International Covenant on Civil and Political Rights* 125–6, 321–2, 439
*International Covenant on Economic, Social and Cultural Rights* 125–6, 321–2
International Criminal Tribunal for Yugoslavia 167–8, 237, 262
international law *see also* constitutional law; United Nations
   and Bangladesh 324–5, 367
   and borders 304–5, 314–17, 399
   and colonization/decolonization 253–4, 428
   and United Nations 28, 30, 125, 189, 257–8, 366, 442
   and conflict, violent 291, 305–6, 399
   and human rights 125–6, 221, 301–2, 306, 321–30, 374, 399–400, 404

and recognition of statehood 4–5, 114,
    253, 290–92, 294, 355
and right of secession 39, 136–7, 301–2,
    321–30, 354–5, 391, 399, 402, 408,
    423–5
  and secession, unilateral 136, 138,
      139–40, 142–3, 258, 321–30, 333
  and territorial rights 122, 144–5, 304–5,
      321
International Law Commission (ILC)
    367–8, 373, 375, 376–7
International Monetary Fund (IMF) 39,
    171, 291, 375
international relations 267–81
international standing 34
internationalization 242, 244, 313, 460
Ionians 23
Iran 277
Iran, Shah of 540
Iraq 277, 285, 432, 444, 498, 539–41
Ireland 23n, 37, 38, 58, 218, 238–42, 258n
  and borders 241, 242, 245, 312, 434
  and Britain 30, 202, 237–42, 312, 352,
      358–9
  civil rights 240, 241
  and democracy 238, 245, 352
  and economic development 240, 243
  and European Community/European
      Union 241, 242
  and foreign intervention 239, 242, 245,
      368
  and geopolitics 188, 238, 239, 244
Irish Free State 368
Irish Republican Army (IRA) 240, 241, 242
Irish Republican Brotherhood 239
irredentism 23n, 62, 63, 64, 188, 240, 244,
    352, 367, 467
Isaaq clans 502
Islah party 543, 544
Islamic Caucasian Emirate 537
Israel 88, 92, 403, 432
Italy 3n, 25, 38, 49, 132, 286, 370, 497–9, 501
Ivory Coast 260

James Bay Crees 144, 340
Jammu and Kashmir Liberation Front 468
Japan 11, 286, 483, 484
Jashari, Adem 178–9
Jashari, Kaqusha 175
Javakheti 51, 64

Jefferson, Thomas 256
Jemaah Islamiyah organization 472
Jordan 285
Juarez, Benito 112
Judaism 387, 432
Jura 359
justice, international 167–8
justice theories (remedial theories, just
    cause theories) 6n, 85–7, 156–7,
    382–3, 394–6, 400, 401, 404–8, 415,
    425
  and domination 383, 427, 429–32, 437
  and human rights 86, 385, 405, 444, 448
  and sense of community 87, 92–3

Kabataang Makabayan (KM) 471–2
Kachin Independence Organizatin (KIO)
    476
Kadyrov, Ramzan 155, 537
Kansas-Nebraska Act 109
Kant, Immanuel 255
Karakalpak republic 151
Karen National Union 476
Karenni National Progressive Party
    (KNPP) 476
Kashmir 20, 39, 209, 293, 467–9
Katanga 55, 99, 122–3, 293, 315
  and natural resources 16, 50, 100, 119,
      122
  and recognition of statehood 4, 287,
      292, 294
  and United Nations 101, 117, 118,
      122–3, 129, 258–9
Kaufmann, Chaim 219–21
Kazakhstan 149
Kenya 16, 501, 502
Khasavyurt accord 536
kinship 62, 208, 272, 279, 418
kin-states 56, 215, 216
*Kitona Agreement* 123
Klaus, Venceslav 517
Korea 35, 36, 309
Koroma, Judge 329–30
Kosovo 30, 40, 46, 147, 155, 157, 171–83
  and conflict, violent 175, 178, 218
  ethnicity
    Albanians 18, 54, 100, 157, 159–61,
        164, 171–83, 215, 217, 289
    ethnic cleansing 175, 180
    Serbs 160, 172, 173

foreign intervention 19, 253, 355
   and European Community/
      European Union 101, 168, 262
   and NATO (North Atlantic Treaty
      Organization) 100, 101, 163–8,
      180, 189, 219, 262, 263, 281
   and United Nations 18, 166, 179–81,
      262, 289, 327–30, 373
   and United States 101, 165, 168,
      179, 181, 182, 216, 217, 281
natural resources 50, 173
recognition of statehood 171, 182, 258n,
   262–4, 267, 292, 295, 301, 355
   and China 182, 281
   and European Community/
      European Union 39, 101, 166,
      221
   and Russia 18, 39, 182, 258n, 263,
      267, 281
   and United States 18, 39, 101, 171,
      217, 221, 263–4, 267
   and Serbia 89, 159–61, 171–83, 262–4,
      316
   and Yugoslavia 100, 157, 163
*Kosovo Declaration of Independence* 189,
   328–9
Kosovo Liberation Army (KLA) 163, 167,
   177–80, 262
Kuala Lumpur 480
Kuomintang (KMT) 483, 484, 485
Kurdistan 37, 245, 388, 455–6, 539–41
Kurds 209, 277, 540
Kuwait 63
Kyrgyszstan 149, 154

labour 82, 84
Labour Party 520
Lajcák, Miroslav 141
land use and ownership 84, 238, 400
language 192
   and culture 153, 388–9, 401, 402, 403,
      463
   and ethnicity 161, 272, 273, 274, 276,
      278–9, 387, 403, 492
      Albanian 174, 175, 176
      Ukrainian 153, 156
Lansing, Robert 29
Latin America 189, 252, 255–6, 315
Latvia 2, 148, 150, 152

law *see* constitutional law; international
   law
leadership 34, 436, 440–1, 446–7, 515
League for Democratic Kosovo (LDK) 161,
   163, 176–7, 178
League of Nations 258, 285, 539
League of Prizren 172
Lebanon 58, 285
Lee Kuan Yew 479, 480
Lee Teng-hui 484
legitimacy *see* right of secession
Leon I, Prince of Abasgia 530
liberalism 159, 233, 347, 350, 351–2, 355–9,
   383, 427
   neo-liberalism 280, 302
Liberia 376
Libya 63, 245, 460
Liechtenstein 333, 335, 336, 338–9
Liga Nord party 38
limitation periods 408
Lincoln, Abraham 107, 109–10, 111, 112,
   113, 114, 115, 333, 359
literacy levels 172
Lithuania 1, 2, 148, 150, 151
Locke, John 82–3, 92
López, Patxi 513
Louisiana 12, 111, 400n
loyalties, divided 13
LTTE 218
Lukashenko, Alexander 153
Lyall, J. 57

Ma Ying-jeou 484
Maakhir state 55
Macedonia 2, 166, 267, 335, 376
   and Albanians 54, 168, 215
   recognition of statehood 166
   and Yugoslavia 157, 163, 515, 517
Machakos Protocol 506
Mahabad, Republic of 540
majority rule 90–92, 131, 139–41, 338–9,
   357, 394, 402–3, 433, 443
majority theories *see* choice theories
Malayan Chinese Association (MCA) 479
Malaysia 151, 259n, 294, 367, 432, 479–80
Maldives 12
Mali 294
Manchukuo 286
Manchuria 286, 291, 292

Mao Zedong 483, 488
marriage 11, 235–6
martyrdom 229
Marxism 240, 241, 243, 498
  neo-Marxism 159, 191–2, 228
Maskhadov, Aslan 536, 537
Mauritania 288
Mboya, Tom 16
Meciar, Vladislav 434, 517
media 1, 99, 219, 240, 273, 279
mediation 18, 179–82, 251, 255, 530
Meech Lake Accord 134–5
Memorandum of Agreement on the definition of Ancestral Domain (MOA-AD) 472
*Memorandum of the Serbian Academy of Sciences* 160
Memorial, human rights organization 536
Menelik, Emperor 497
Mengistu regime 498
Metropolitan Colonial State 118
Mexico 26–7, 107–8, 112, 309
microstates 92
migration 18, 51, 82–3, 152, 492
  forced 67, 220–21, 540
Military Council of Georgia 530
military intervention 101, 167, 255–6, 257, 262, 441, 524
  arms supply 124, 127, 165–6, 239, 245, 259, 460, 464
  Kosovo 167, 180, 253
Mill, John Stuart 255, 388
Milošević, Slobodan 132, 160, 162, 163, 174–5, 180, 182
Mindanao 455, 471–3
Minnan people 484
Minorities and Potential Supporters Dataset (MAPS) 190, 271–80
Minorities at Risk Dataset (MAR) 190, 271
minority communities 13, 14, 23, 65–8, 89
  *see also* Albania; ethnicity; Serbs
  and borders 309–10, 312–13, 315, 318
  and capitalism 154, 191–2, 194–9, 203–4, 228
  and constitutional law 137, 139, 339
  and democracy 230, 245, 339, 383, 432–5
  and domination 432, 433, 449–50

human rights 17, 20, 91, 118, 258, 261n, 358–9, 413, 416–21, 440–7
  and identity 322–3, 387–91, 440
  and population numbers 51–2, 215, 322–3, 387–91, 440
  slaves 105, 108
  state behaviour 25n, 47, 54–60, 64, 69, 100
Mississippi 111, 434
Missouri 107
Misuari, Nur 472
modernism 14
modernization 21, 194, 235
Mohawk people 388
Moldavia 148, 156, 532
Moldova 36, 46, 149, 150, 151, 152, 217
  and Transdniestria 55, 147, 149, 156, 290, 529, 532–3
Mong Tai Army (MTA) 476
Mongol empire 530
Mongolia 487, 489
Monroe Doctrine 256
Montenegro 100, 131–45, 524
  constitutional law 37n, 47n, 140, 143
  democracy 99, 131, 139–41, 336–7, 338, 339
  and ethnicity 54, 144, 168, 213, 215
  and foreign intervention 101, 131, 140–41, 143–4, 166, 285
  and international law 139–40, 294
  and Serbia 19, 37n, 131–45, 261
  and Yugoslavia 132–3, 157, 158, 159, 163, 515
    and European Community/European Union 101, 131, 140–41, 143–4
Montenegro *Declaration of Independence* 143–4
Montevideo Convention on Rights and Duties of States 290, 292
moral rights 81, 92, 106, 381, 385, 402, 404–8, 413, 422–6, 447–50
moral theory 383, 439–51
Moro Islamic Liberation Front (MILF) 472
Moro National Liberation Front (MNLF) 472
Morocco 11, 288, 294, 315, 498
Mozambique 30, 258n

Muhajir 55
Muhammad, Yahya 543
Muslims 161, 162, 273, 459, 471, 497, 498, 501, 505
   Sunni Muslims 432, 467
Myanmar/Burma 31, 286, 293, 432, 455–6, 475–7
myth 208, 233–4

NAFTA (North American Free Trade Agreement) 100
Nagorno-Karabakh 36, 64, 147, 149, 156, 261, 290, 294, 529
Nairn, Tom 194–6, 203–4
Namibia 35, 36, 258n
Napoleon III 112–13
Nasheed, Mohammed 12
National Conference party (Kashmir) 468
National Conversation 520
National People Congress 488
national theories 87–9, 92, 93, 400–403, 404, 413, 415, 418, 425, 445
nationalism 14, 21, 24–6, 30, 87, 305–6, 373–4
   and conflict, violent 210, 229–30
   and culture 34, 194–5, 204, 240, 242–3, 348–9, 358–9, 388, 403, 445
   and democracy 114, 351n
   and economics 49–50, 191–2, 194–5, 199–202
   and ethnicity 25, 46, 47, 99, 197–8, 210, 213, 229–30, 233–5, 311
      and economics 49–50, 199–202
   nationalist ideology xxiii, 20, 26, 238–42
   Soviet Union 152, 153, 154–5
   stateless nations 84, 87, 374, 396, 446
   United States 111, 113–14, 115–16
   Yugoslavia 159, 160, 233–5
nationalist parties 38
NATO (North Atlantic Treaty Organization) 217, 264
   and Yugoslavia 100, 101, 163–8, 180, 189, 219, 262, 263, 281
natural resources 34, 84, 119, 125, 200, 215, 407, 492, 506, 544
   Katanga 16, 50, 100, 119, 122
   Kosovo 50, 173
Nauru 264, 290, 530, 532

Navarre 89
Ne Win, General 476
negotiation 354–6, 392, 393–4
neo-decolonization 261
Netherlands 254, 258n, 459, 491
New Brunswick 134
New Guinea Council 491
New Mon State Party (NMSP) 476
New York City 114
New York Supreme Court 368
New Zealand 433
New-Caledonia 92
Nicaragua 264, 290, 530, 532
*Nicaragua* decision 257
Nigeria 2, 31, 46, 58, 151 *see also* Biafra
Nimeiri, Colonel Gaofar Muhammad 506
Nine, Cara 84–5, 92
'no irreparable harm principle' 451
non-governmental organizations (NGOs) 217, 460, 492
*Norddeutsche Bund* 370
Normans 12
North Carolina 112, 434
North Sea oil 200
Northern Ireland *see* Ireland
*Northern Ireland Act 1998* 352
Norway 68, 214, 293, 309, 450, 455, 515–16
Nyasaland 367

occupation 292, 325, 326, 383, 406–7
Ogaden National Liberation Front (ONLF) 38
oil industry 18, 50, 200, 506, 544
Okinawa 11
Ontario 134
Operation Storm 39
opportunism 11, 48, 280
oppression 21, 92, 100, 241, 254, 396
Organisasi Papua Merdeka (OPM) 492
Organization of African Unity (OAU, later African Union) 16, 124, 259, 280, 288, 315, 497, 498
Organization for Security and Cooperation in Europe (OSCE) 166, 180, 217, 261n, 262, 264, 377, 533
Orthodox Church 161, 171–2
Ottoman Empire 58, 132, 234, 235n, 285, 370, 497, 530, 539
   Kosovo 161, 172

Pakistan 165, 267, 373, 463–4 *see also* Bangladesh
   and India 39, 46, 121, 220, 271, 277, 312, 367, 469
   and Kashmir 39, 469
Palestine 92, 93, 209, 288, 292, 294, 403
Palestine Declaration of Independence 288
Palestine Liberation Organization (PLO) 288
Pan African movement 25
Papua New Guinea 17, 18, 58
Paraguay 27
parallel systems of government 176
Paris, Charter of (1990) 261
Paris Peace Conference (1919–20) 309
Paris, Treaty of (1763) 12
Parti Quebecois (PQ) 38, 134, 135, 357
partition 220–21, 240, 293
patriation 134, 144
*Patriation Reference* 134
patriotism 192, 391, 392
*Pax Africana* 16
Peace among Communities Value 358–9
peacekeeping 101, 166–7, 251, 259, 290, 524, 531
Peasant-Democratic Coalition 233n
peasants 234, 235n, 238
People's Action Party (PAP) 479
People's Defence 235
Peoples' Front for Democracy and Justice (PDFJ) 498
*perestroika* 148–9
Permanent Court of Arbitration 498
Persia 23
Peru 27
Philippines 35, 400n, 471–3
Pius IX, Pope 114
Poland 29, 149, 258n, 285
police, Serbian 178–9
Polignac Memorandum 256
Polisario independence movement 288
political power 34, 447, 449
   balance of 61, 63, 100, 106, 108, 137, 215, 244–5
   and ethnicity 48, 51, 54, 190, 197, 215, 269–70
   relative 270–71, 278, 280
   and territorial rights 84, 85, 90, 92, 231–2
political recognition 390–91, 394

political rights 34, 126, 447–50
political violence 227–46
Polk, James K. 107
poll tax 435
population numbers 290–91
   Kosovo 172, *173*
   and minority communities 51–2, 215, 322–3, 387–91, 440
   United States 105–6, 108
Portugal 117, 119–20, 254
   decolonization 30, 32, 119–20, 127n, 255
   and East Timor 19n, 287
   and Latin America 189, 252
Portuguese Guinea 30
post-secession 65–8
poverty 48, 53, 173, 215
power-sharing 58, 220, 310
PP party 511, 512
predation 271, 278
prestige 34, 51
primary right theories 394–5, 396
primordialism 14, 208, 212, 229, 242–3
privilege 20, 50, 84, 187n, 431, 446, 450
property rights 82–5, 92, 112, 376, 400
protection, state 25n, 83, 89, 137, 354
protest marches 240
Protestants 238–9, 312
Provisional Institutions of Self-Government (PISG) 181, 329
Provisional Irish Republican Army (PIRA) 30n, 238, 241
proximity, geographic 52, 270–71, 279–80
   contiguity 272, 274, 275, 278
PSOE party 512
Puerto Rico 31
Punjab 20
Puntland 55
purchase, of territory 12, 83
Putin, Vladimir 155, 536, 537

Qing empire 487
Quebec 12, 38, 86
   and borders 86, 144–5, 311, 340
   and Canada 17, 100, 101, 131–45, 215, 311, 326–7, 353, 357
   and constitutional law 322, 333, 337–9, 340, 341, 342, 351–2, 355, 386
   democracy 131, 134, 135, 335–40, 342–3, 351–2

federalism 99, 134, 137, 386
  sovereignty 100, 134, 135, 137–8, 389
Quebec National Assembly 139
Quebec Superior Court 135
*Quebec Veto Reference* 134

race 208, 272, 274, 276, 278–9 *see also* ethnicity
racial equality 113–14, 291, 325, 326, 329–30
radicalization 214–16, 217–18, 219, 235, 236, 241
Ranković, Aleksandar 174
rational choice theory 193, 200–201, 227–8, 242–3
realism 270–71, 277, 278, 280
reciprocity 190, 268, 277, 280
recognition of statehood 4–5, 189, 190, 257–64, 285–95, 441, 455, 487
  Abkhazia 221, 261, 292, 455, 530
  Bangladesh 4, 5, 217, 287, 323, 455, 464
  Biafra 16, 259–60, 287, 292, 294
  Bosnia and Herzegovina 166, 335
  Chechnya 261, 289, 292, 455
  Confederate States of America (CSA) 101, 114, 115
  Croatia 166, 286, 335, 524
  Eritrea 259, 455, 497, 498
  Katanga 4, 287, 292, 294
  Kosovo 171, 182, 221, 258n, 262–4, 267, 292, 295, 301, 355
    and China 182, 281
    and European Community/European Union 39, 101, 166, 221
    and Russia 18, 39, 182, 258n, 263, 267, 281
    and United States 18, 39, 101, 171, 217, 221, 263–4, 267
  Macedonia 166, 335
  Slovenia 166, 335
  Somaliland 455, 502
  South Ossetia 221, 261, 292, 294, 455, 532
  and territorial rights 258–9, 262, 291
  Transdniestria 261, 455, 533
*Reference re Secession of Quebec* 131, 134–42, 136, 322, 326, 327, 333–42, 345, 352–3, 355, 386

*Referendum Act* 139
referendums 335–40, 342, 492, 505, 513, 520, 541
  Eritrea 497, 498
  Montenegro 131, 139–41, 336–7, 338, 339
  Quebec 131, 134, 135, 351–2
  Soviet Union 150, 151
refugees 90n, 93, 164, 167, 179, 464, 524, 541
relative deprivation 56, 187
religion 161–2, 197, 467–8, 471–3, 476, 501, 505
  Bosnia and Herzegovina 162, 234
  and communitarian theory 401, 402
  Eritrea 497, 498
  and human rights 325, 326, 329–30
  Ireland 238–9, 240
  religious ties 272–3, 274, 278–9, 389
religious movements, transnational 217
ReLogit 275
remedial theories *see* justice theories (remedial theories, just cause theories)
repression, state 56–7, 58, 59, 295
  and Ireland 239, 240, 241
  Kosovo 174–5, 180, 182
  and radicalization 215, 216, 218
Republican Party 108–10
republicanism, Ireland 238
Republika Srpska 55, 233, 237, 290, 293
resource mobilization theory 56
respect 394, 420–21, 446
responsibility 355, 365, 366, 367–8
Responsibility of States for Internationally Wrongful Acts (ARSIWA) 367–8
return, right to 93
revolutions 255, 354
Rhodesia 258n, 287, 291, 292, 367
right of secession 131–45, 350–59, 399–408, 413–26, 439–51 *see also* constitutional law; territorial rights
  and China 37n, 334
  and human rights 385, 413–23, 428, 429–31, 447–8
  and international law 39, 136–7, 301–2, 321–30, 354–5, 391, 399, 408, 423–5
  and secession, unilateral 136, 138, 139–40, 142–3, 258, 321–30, 333

political 84, 341, 354–5, 382, 391–3, 401–2
and United Nations 39, 439
right-holders 440–41, 442n, 443–9
Rights and Freedoms, Charter of 134, 135
*Rights of Passage* Case 120
'Road Map to a Disciplined Democracy' 476–7
Romania 149, 532
Roth, Brad 330
Ruanda 315
Rugova, Dr Ibrahim 161, 176–7, 178, 179, 182, 215
Rule of Law value 356–7
Russia 46, 64, 154–7, 165, 216, 256–7n, 370
  and Abkhazia 39, 62, 64, 154, 155, 221, 264, 290, 530
  and Alaska 12, 400n
  and Chechnya 19, 30, 57, 64, 151, 154–5, 288–9, 529, 535–7
  constitutional law 155, 334
  and Crimea 62, 156
  and ethnicity 154–7, 278, 531
  and European Community/European Union 264, 370–71
  and Georgia 147, 152, 156, 157, 216, 219, 221, 264
  and Kosovo 18, 39, 182, 258n, 263, 267, 281
  and nationalism 153, 154–5
  and South Ossetia 39, 62, 64, 154–7, 219, 221, 264, 290, 530–32
  and Soviet Union 150, 151, 153, 370
  and Tatarstan 64, 151, 154–5, 337, 529
  and Transdniestria 62, 533
Russian Federation 19, 148, 370
Russianization 152, 153
Russians 313

sacralization, of national territory 13
Saddam Hussein 540
Sahrawi Arab Democratic Republic (SADR) 288, 294
Saint Kitts and Nevis 37n, 333, 335, 338, 339, 341
Saleh, Ali Abdullah 543, 544
Samtskhe 51
Sarajevo 164
Sardinia 370
Saudi Arabia 63, 165, 502, 543

Scandinavian countries 309
Scotland 30, 38, 86, 200, 357, 390, 456, 519–21
Scottish National Party (SNP) 38, 200, 357, 519, 520
Scottish Parliament 520
secession, by default 153–4
secession, colonial 4, 19, 26n, 30, 40 *see also* colonization/decolonization
secession, consensual 4, 189, 293 *see also* Soviet Union; Yugoslavia
secession, devolutionary *see* devolution
secession, dissolving 4 *see also* Soviet Union; Yugoslavia
secession, failed *see* Biafra; Katanga; Quebec; West Papua
secession, non-consensual *see* secession, unilateral
secession, peaceful *see* Iceland; Norway; Slovakia
secession, recursive 66, 68, 91, 93, 143, 220, 345, 444 *see also* Abkhazia; Bosnia and Herzegovina; Croatia; South Ossetia
secession, right of *see* right of secession
secession, unconstitutional 136, 333, 336, 341–2, 355n, 357, 513 *see also* secession, unilateral
secession, unilateral 4, 17–18, 251, 293, 294, 377 *see also* Bosnia and Herzegovina; Bougainville; Kosovo; Montenegro; Quebec; Sudan
  and right of secession 189, 190, 253, 258, 261, 394–5, 396, 401–2, 404
  and international law 136, 138, 139–40, 142–3, 258, 321–30, 333
  and moral justification 385, 450
secession, voluntary 366, 369
*Secession Reference see Reference re Secession of Quebec*
security 270–71
Selassie, Haile 498
self-determination, internal 385–96
self-interest 199, 200–201, 228
Senegal 294
separatism 30, 64, 151, 233–7
Serb Krajina 55, 164, 289, 290, 293, 455, 523–4
Serbia 234, 237, 316
  constitutional law 37n, 47n, 140, 143

and Croatia 277, 289–90, 524
ethnicity 168, 213, 313
and foreign intervention 166, 262
and Kosovo 89, 159–61, 171–83, 262–4, 316
and Montenegro 19, 37n, 131–45, 261
and Yugoslavia 100, 132–3, 157, 158, 159
Serbian Academy of Arts and Science 174
Serbs
  in Bosnia and Herzegovina 26n, 55, 162, 167, 215, 233–7, 289–90, 292, 313
  in Croatia 55, 161–2, 168, 215, 289–90, 292, 313, 523–4
  in Kosovo 160, 172, 173
  in Montenegro 144, 168
settlement schemes 51
Sèvres, Treaty of 539
Seward, William 111–12, 115
Shan State Army (SSA) 476
Sherman, William T. 114
Siberia 50, 153
Sikkim 20
Sindh 55
Singapore 37n, 259n, 294, 333, 367, 455, 479–80
Sinn Fein 38, 240
slavery 101, 105, 106–16
Slavonia 524
Slovakia 201–2, 286, 372, 434, 455
  peaceful secession 2, 68, 214, 355n, 450, 517
Slovenia 1, 160, 376
  economic development 49, 172
  and ethnicity 49, 55, 168, 235
  and European Community/European Union 5, 164, 166
  recognition of statehood 166, 335
  and Yugoslavia 132, 134, 157, 158, 159, 161, 162, 163, 164, 523
social class 201, 228, 238, 239, 241, 243
social mobility 48, 192, 197
Socialist Federal Republic of Yugoslavia (SFRY) *see* Yugoslavia
Solidarity 161, 176
Solzhenitsyn, Alexander 153
Somali National Movement (SNM) 502
Somalia 16, 55, 289, 501–3
Somaliland 46, 55, 289, 294, 315, 501–3

recognition of statehood 40, 259, 289, 292, 455, 502
South Africa 35, 287–8, 432, 503
South Carolina 110, 111, 434
South Ossetia 36, 40, 147, 294, 355, 531–2
  and Georgia 14, 19, 55, 149, 156, 219, 220, 290, 529, 531
  recognition of statehood 221, 261, 292, 294, 455, 532
  and Russia 39, 62, 64, 154–5, 219, 221, 264, 290, 530–32
South Papua 455
South Yemen 63, 455
Southern Sudan 17, 18, 48, 259, 456, 505–7
Southern Sudan Liberation Movement (SSLM) 506
sovereignty 90, 103, 148, 244, 254, 291
  dynastic 12, 13, 24, 189, 255, 256
  popular 13, 24, 137–8, 389
  and Quebec 100, 134, 135, 137–8, 389
  territorial 89, 374, 400n, 405–7
Soviet Union 32, 55, 100, 101, 147–57, 261, 285, 515
  and Abkhazia, Georgia, South Ossetia 55, 148, 150, 530, 531
  and borders 19, 156, 159, 310, 313, 316
  and Cold War 17, 36
  constitutional law 37, 148, 150, 529
  ethnicity 2, 152, 529–30, 531
  and European Community/European Union 25n, 312
  foreign intervention 63, 124, 240, 259, 464, 498
  and minority communities 25n, 48, 313
  and Russia 150, 151, 153, 370
Spain 38, 46, 84, 254–5, 286, 511
  and Basque Country 357, 511–13
  colonization/decolonization 12, 26–7, 255
    and Latin America 189, 252, 315–16
    and Philippines 400n, 471–3
    and Western Sahara 127n, 288
'special territory status' 459
Squires, J. 347
Sri Lanka 12, 35, 432
  and Tamils xxiii, 209, 216, 218, 219, 259, 260n, 264
Srinivasan, Krishnan 20–21
stability 20, 119, 310–11, 317–18, 352–4, 371

Stalin, Joseph  156, 530, 535
Stambolić, Ivan  174, 175
'Standards for Kosovo'  181
state behaviour, towards ethnic minority groups  47, 54–60, 64, 69, 100
state consolidation  27
state extinction  33, 369, 372
state failure  54
state institutional arrangements  204, 230–31, 232, 243, 376–7, 445–6, 515, 529
stateless nations  84, 87, 374, 396, 446
states, weak  35, 54–5, 58, 190, 271, 278, 280, 281, 455, 505–6
states within a state  55, 134, 316
statist theory  383, 428–9
Statute of Westminster  519
Steiner, Hillel  83
Stockholm International Peace Research Institute (SIPRI)  46
strategic ties  63, 64
Sudan  63
    Southern Sudan  17, 18, 31, 32, 35, 40, 48, 259, 456, 505–7
Sudan People's Liberation Movement (SPLM)  506
suicide bomb attacks  209
Sulu Archipelago  472
Sunstein, Cass  350, 351–6
superpowers  20–21, 30, 36, 216, 221, 429
Supreme Court of Canada  see Secession Reference
Sweden  149, 293, 309, 515–16
Switzerland  46, 141, 258n, 285, 286, 359
Syria  63, 285, 432

Taiwan  286–7, 292, 294, 455, 483–5
Tajikistan  149
Tamils  xxiii, 209, 216, 218, 259, 260n, 264
Tanzania  260
Tatars  51
Tatarstan  49, 50, 64, 151, 154–5, 337, 529
tax evasion  50
taxation  176, 199, 309
Tennessee  112
Tentara Nasional Indonesia (TNI)  491, 492
Tentara Papua Nasional (TPN)  492

territorial rights  81–93, 394, 396, 400, 403–7, 440
    and borders  86, 91–2, 93, 144–5, 221, 268, 308–9, 365–6, 407
    and Bosnia and Herzegovina  221, 236, 262
    and China  11, 20–21, 286
    and choice theories  403, 425
    and conflict, violent  210, 221, 306
    and consent  13, 82, 83, 84, 258–9
    and constitutional law  334, 359
    and culture  84, 86, 88, 89, 93
    and ethnicity  210, 221, 234, 245
    and geography  119–22, 155
    and human rights  82–3, 84, 85, 86, 89, 400, 403–7, 414
    and international law  122, 144–5, 304–5, 321
    and political power  84, 85, 90, 92, 231–2
    and recognition of statehood  258–9, 262, 291
    and state secession  365–6, 367
    and United Nations  128, 190, 245, 291, 305, 321, 399, 428–9, 439
    and use of force  85, 90, 155, 305
    and Yugoslavia  158, 159, 262
territorialism, multiterritorialism  388
territory  12–16, 63, 290–91
terrorism  13, 36, 217, 498, 502, 536–7
Texas  107, 111, 257
*Texas v White*  336
Thailand  48
Thant, U  259, 429
Tibet  15, 20, 38, 51, 93, 293, 456, 487–9
Tibetan Youth Congress  38
Tierney, Stephen  337
Tigre People's Liberation Front  498
timing  49, 239, 243, 359–60, 408
Timor-Leste  285, 287
Tiro, Hasan  460
Tito, President (Josip Broz)  157, 158, 174, 175
trade  34, 64, 199, 305, 308, 480, 502, 503
Transcarpatiea  529
Transcaucasian Ferderation of Armenia, Azerbaijan and Georgia  148
Transdniestria  36, 294, 529, 532–3

and Moldova 55, 147, 149, 156, 290, 529, 532–3
recognition of statehood 261, 455, 533
and Russia 62, 533
and Ukraine 156, 532
transition 151, 197, 366, 367–8, 371, 476, 498
Transitional Government of Somalia (TNG) 502
triadic nexus model 216, 217
Trudeau, Pierre Elliott 134
trusteeship 119, 294, 366, 497
Tshombe, Moise 123
tsunami 2004 460
Tudjman, Franjo 159n, 162, 524
Tunku Abdul Rahman 480
Turkey 147, 165, 173, 218, 267, 288, 370, 433
Turkish Republic of Northern Cyprus (TRNC) *see* Cyprus
Turkmenistan 149, 150
Turks 67
tyranny 21, 430, 444, 468

Uccialli, treaty 497
UÇK *see* Kosovo Liberation Army (KLA)
Uganda 31, 444
Ukraine 30, 148, 149, 150, 153, 156, 376, 529, 532
Umarov, Doku 537
UN General Assembly Resolution 1541 120–2, 257, 258, 323, 442
UN General Assembly Resolution 2625 258
UN Security Council Resolution 1244 181, 182, 263, 327, 328–9
UN Security Council Resolution 169 258–9
UN Security Council Resolution 836 262
unemployment 172
unification 2–3n, 50
Union Treaties 150
United Irishmen 238
United Malays National Organization (UMNO) 479
United Nations 39, 117–29, 217, 287, 488, 491, 502
and Bangladesh 5, 260, 287, 323, 455, 464
and Bosnia and Herzegovina 165, 166, 167
and colonization/decolonization 15, 28, 30, 125, 128, 189, 257–8, 366, 442
and Croatia 164, 166, 167, 262, 524
and decolonization 28–9, 30, 125–6, 442
and Eritrea 455, 497
and India 260, 372–3
and international law 257, 258, 321–2, 323, 325–6, 366, 385
colonization/decolonization 28, 30, 125, 189, 257–8, 366, 442
*Declaration on Principles of International Law Concerning Friendly Relations* 125, 126–8, 291, 323, 324, 326, 329–30, 385, 400
*Declaration on the Granting of Independence to Colonial Countries and Peoples* 118–19, 189, 399, 439, 442 *see also* United Nations – UN General Assembly Resolution 1541
UN General Assembly Resolution 1541 120–2, 257, 258, 323, 442 *see also*- Declaration on the Granting of Independence to Colonial Countries and Peoples
UN Security Council Resolution 1244 181, 182, 263, 327, 328–9
and Katanga 101, 117, 118, 122–3, 129, 258–9
and Kosovo 18, 166, 179–81, 262, 289, 327–30, 373
membership 5, 285, 288, 291, 370, 372–3, 455
and Montenegro 141, 166, 285
peacekeeping 101, 242, 251, 259, 290, 524
and Serbia 166, 262
and territorial rights 128, 190, 245, 291, 305, 321, 399, 428–9, 439
and trusteeship 119, 366
and Yugoslavia 373, 377
United Nations Protected Areas (UNPAs) 524

# INDEX

United Nations Special Committee on Decolonization 30
United Nations Trusteeship Council 119, 366
United States 12, 67, 104–5, 108, 309 *see also* Confederate States of America (CSA)
   American Declaration of Independence 11, 25, 26, 103, 105, 126
   and Britain 4, 103, 255
   and Cold War 15, 17, 36, 464
   constitutional law 105, 109, 111, 333–5, 336, 341, 342
   and democracy 113–14, 336, 434–5
   federalism 104–5, 107–8, 112, 113, 154–5
   and foreign intervention 141, 252–3, 464, 471–2, 498, 503, 516 *see also* Kosovo
      and Bosnia and Herzegovina 101, 165, 166, 168
      and Croatia 39, 101, 165, 168, 524
      and Iraq 498, 541
      and Ireland 242, 368
      and Taiwan 455, 483, 485
   and nationalism 111, 113–14, 115–16
   population numbers 105–6, 108
United States Congress 434
unity, national 334, 359, 393n
Universal Declaration of Human Rights 374
universalism 21
Uruguay 27
Ustasha 161, 236
*uti possidetis juris* 16, 17, 19, 301, 314, 315, 316, 322, 399
Uzbekistan 149, 151

Vanuatu 31
Venda 287
Venezuela 27, 255, 264, 290, 530, 532
Venice Commission 140, 141
Versailles, Treaty of 25n
victimization 56, 57, 415, 430
Vienna Convention 367, 368–9, 371, 372, 375–6
Vienna Declaration 258n
Vietnam 35, 36
Virginia 112
Vllasi, Azem 175

Vojvodina 157, 172, 175, 235
voting rights 309, 310, 336–7, 357–8, 386, 433, 434–5, 443
vulnerability 63, 268–9, 272, 274, 275, 277–8, 280

Wallerstein, Immanuel 194, 195
water resources 18, 479
watercourses 371–2
Watts, Sir Arthur 377
wealth 34, 49, 50, 53, 125, 506
welfare 89, 309, 407, 415–23
West Lothian question 521
West Papua 491–2
Western Bosnia 165n, 211
Western Sahara 30n, 127n, 258n, 288, 292, 498
'Westminster' system 435n
Westphalia, Treaty of 15, 23n, 255
Whig Party (American) 109
*Williams v Bruffy* 342
Wilson, Woodrow 15, 28, 30n, 125
Wolff, Christian 254
women, in authority 502
World Bank 39, 171, 291
World War I 26, 29
World War II 13, 15, 30, 148, 497, 523

Xingjian province, China xxiii, 51

Yakya Khan, General 463
Yeltsin, Boris 153, 536
Yemen 63, 369, 455, 543–5
Yemeni Socialist Party 543–4
Yoruba people 124
Young Bosnia (Mlada Bosna) 234–5
Young Ireland 239
Yugoslav Communist Party 157, 159
Yugoslav People's Army (YPA) 158, 162, 163, 164, 166, 236
Yugoslavia 157–68, 280, 285, 355, 376 *see also* Bosnia and Herzegovina; Croatia; Kosovo; Macedonia; Montenegro; Serbia; Slovenia
   and borders 19, 309, 310, 311–12, 316
   and consent 311, 312, 316
   constitutional law 131, 132, 143, 157, 333–4, 335, 339–40
   dissolution 32, 33, 46, 100, 147, 157–68, 261–2, 369

and economic development 158, 160,
   161, 243
and ethnicity 2, 313, 322–3
Federal Republic of Yugoslavia (FRY)
   133, 262, 263, 371, 373
and foreign intervention
   and European Community/
      European Union 25n, 101, 165,
      166, 168, 262, 311–12, 524
   and NATO (North Atlantic Treaty
      Organization) 100, 101, 163–8,
      180, 189, 219, 262, 263, 281
   and United Nations 373, 377
   and United States 101, 168
nationalism 159, 160, 233–5
Socialist Federal Republic of Yugoslavia
   (SFRY) 157–68, 261–3, 309, 311–16,
   367, 369–71, 373, 376–7
territorial rights 158, 159, 262
Yusuf, Judge 329, 330

Zambia 260
Zimbabwe 287
Zionism 88